Kant

'*Kant* is an absolutely first-rate general introduction to Kant's Critical Philosophy. Paul Guyer's interpretations are extremely well-supported, carefully and crisply argued, and highly insightful.'

Robert Hanna, University of Colorado

'An impressive overview of the various strands of Kant's philosophy. With great skill Guyer manages to compress Kant's critical thought into a few hundred pages. This book will provide an excellent introduction to Kant's thought.'

Philip Stratton-Lake, University of Reading

'The book is impressive in very many ways. It demonstrates a mastery of the Kantian corpus and an ability to explain exceedingly complex arguments in a clear and accessible fashion. I think it will become essential reading for students wanting to grasp the broad sweep of Kant's thought without losing much by way of depth.'

Andrew Chignell, Cornell University

'That Guyer is able to cover this much material, clearly and without over-simplification, in a single, reasonably sized volume represents a unique accomplishment, which should prove to be extremely useful to a broad audience.'

Eric Watkins, University of California, San Diego

Routledge Philosophers

Edited by Brian Leiter
University of Texas, Austin

Routledge Philosophers is a major series of introductions to the great Western philosophers. Each book places a major philosopher or thinker in historical context, explains and assesses their key arguments, and considers their legacy. Additional features include a chronology of major dates and events, chapter summaries, annotated suggestions for further reading, and a glossary of technical terms.

An ideal starting point for those new to philosophy, they are also essential reading for those interested in the subject at any level.

Hobbes	A P Martinich
Leibniz	Nicholas Jolley
Locke	E J Lowe
Hegel	Frederick Beiser
Rousseau	Nicholas Dent
Schopenhauer	Julian Young
Freud	Jonathan Lear
Kant	Paul Guyer

Forthcoming

Husserl	David Woodruff Smith
Aristotle	Christopher Shields
Spinoza	Michael Della Rocca
Hume	Don Garrett
Fichte and Schelling	Sebastian Gardner
Rawls	Samuel Freeman
Merleau-Ponty	Taylor Carman
Darwin	Tim Lewens
Heidegger	John Richardson

Paul Guyer

Kant

Routledge
Taylor & Francis Group

LONDON AND NEW YORK

First published 2006
by Routledge
2 Park Square, Milton Park, Abingdon, Oxon OX14 4RN

Simultaneously published in the USA and Canada
by Routledge
270 Madison Ave, New York, NY 10016

Reprinted 2007

Routledge is an imprint of the Taylor & Francis Group, an informa business

Typeset in Joanna MT and Din by Taylor & Francis Books
Printed and bound in Great Britain by TJ International Ltd, Padstow, Cornwall

British Library Cataloguing in Publication Data
A catalogue record for this book is available from the British Library

Library of Congress Cataloging in Publication Data
Guyer, Paul, 1948-
  Kant / Paul Guyer.
    p. cm. -- (Routledge philosophers)
  Includes bibliographical references and index.
  ISBN 0–415–28335–3 (hardback : alk. paper) – ISBN 0–415–28336–1
  (pbk. : alk. paper) I. Kant, Immanuel, 1724–1804. I. Title. II. Series.
    B2798.G89 2006   2005033078

ISBN10: 0–415–28335–3   ISBN13: 978–0–415–28335–9 (hbk)
ISBN10: 0–415–28336–1   ISBN13: 978–0–415–28336–6 (pbk)

Acknowledgements viii
Abbreviations ix
Chronology xi

Introduction I

Nature and Freedom 1
Skepticism and Critique 8

A Life in Work One 15

Childhood and Student Years 16
Return to the University 18
Toward the Critical Philosophy 21
The Critical Philosophy 32
Final Works 37
Further Reading 41

Part One
Nature 43

Kant's Copernican Revolution Two 45

Introduction 45
Space and Time: The Pure Forms of Sensible Intuition 51
The Contributions of the Understanding 70
The Metaphysical Deduction 72
The Transcendental Deduction 80
The Principles of Empirical Judgment 95
The Refutation of Idealism 116
Further Reading 123

The Critique of Metaphysics Three 126

The Ideas of Pure Reason 129
The Metaphysics of the Self 134
The Metaphysics of the World 138
The Metaphysics of God 145
Further Reading 153

Building upon the Foundations of Knowledge Four   155

The Systematic Science of Body	157
The Systematicity of Cognition in General	165
Further Reading	173

Part Two
Freedom   **175**

Laws of Freedom: The Foundations of Kant's Moral Philosophy Five   177

The Derivation of the Categorical Imperative	179
Universal Law and Humanity as an End in Itself	191
Confirmation of the Categorical Imperative from Commonly Recognized Duties	196
Autonomy and the Realm of Ends	203
Further Reading	207

Freedom, Immortality, and God: The Presuppositions of Morality Six   **210**

The Moral Law and Freedom of the Will	213
Immortality and the Existence of God	230
Further Reading	238

Kant's System of Duties I: The Duties of Virtue Seven   **239**

Kant's Division of Duties	239
The General Obligation of Virtue	247
The Specific Duties of Virtue	249
Further Reading	261

Kant's System of Duties II: Duties of Right Eight   **262**

The Universal Principle of Right, Coercion, and Innate Right	262
The Right to Property	268
Political Rights and Obligations	279
Rebellion and Reform	284
Toward Perpetual Peace	294
Further Reading	302

Part Three
Nature and Freedom   **305**

The Beautiful, the Sublime, and the Morally Good
Nine   **307**

Bridging the Gulf   307
Varieties of Aesthetic Judgment   312
Aesthetics and Morality   324
Further Reading   332

Freedom and Nature: Kant's Revision of
Traditional Teleology Ten   **335**

The Rejection of Traditional Teleology   335
From Organisms to Nature as a Whole   339
Freedom, Happiness, and the End of Nature   349
Further Reading   358

A History of Freedom? Eleven   **360**
Further Reading   371

Glossary   **373**
Notes   **380**
Select Bibliography   **413**
Index   **426**

Acknowledgements

This book is the distillation of a lifetime's study of Kant, and it would be impossible to thank every teacher and colleague from whom I have gained insight into Kant over four decades. I would like to thank Stanley Cavell, who not only supervised my early work on Kant but has also urged me to write a book like the present one for many years. I would like to thank the members of my family – my wife, Pamela Foa, my daughter, Nora, my father, Irving, and my siblings Mark, Daniel, and Léonie – who have likewise urged me to write a book like this for some time. I would especially like to thank Frederick Rauscher, who read the entire manuscript carefully and made innumerable helpful suggestions, for which the final product is much better than it would otherwise have been. Michael Rohlf and Steven Jauss also read much of the manuscript and made useful suggestions. My colleague Gary Hatfield suggested several important improvements in my treatment of Kant's philosophy of science in Chapter 4. And several of the anonymous readers of the manuscript for Routledge made helpful suggestions. I thank Brian Leiter for the invitation to write the book, and my editor at Routledge, Tony Bruce, for his enthusiasm and helpful suggestions. I am especially grateful to Julian Wuerth, who took valuable time away from his own work to help me with proofreading.

Excerpts from Critique of the Power of Judgment by Immanuel Kant, edited and translated by Paul Guyer and Eric Matthews, 2000 © Cambridge University Press. Reprinted with kind permission of the publisher and editors.

Excerpts from Critique of Pure Reason by Immanuel Kant, edited and translated by Paul Guyer and Allen W Wood, 1998 © Cambridge University Press. Reprinted with kind permission of the publisher and editors.

Excerpts from Practical Philosophy by Immanuel Kant, edited by Mary J Gregor, 1996 © Cambridge University Press. Reprinted with kind permission of the publisher.

Citations to Kant's texts are given parenthetically. Citations from the *Critique of Pure Reason* are located by reference to the pagination of Kant's first ("A") and/or second ("B") editions. All other passages from Kant's works are cited by the volume and page number, given by arabic numerals separated by a colon, in the standard edition of Kant's works, *Kant's gesammelte Schriften*, edited by the Royal Prussian, later German, then Berlin-Brandenburg Academy of Sciences, 29 volumes (volume 26 not yet published) (Berlin: Georg Reimer, later Walter de Gruyter & Co., 1900–). Where Kant divided a work into numbered sections, his section number typically precedes the volume and page number. These references are preceded by abbreviations from the following list, except where the context makes that unnecessary. Unless otherwise indicated in the individual essays, all translations are from the *Cambridge Edition of the Works of Immanuel Kant*, edited by Paul Guyer and Allen W. Wood (Cambridge: Cambridge University Press, 1992–).

CB	"On the Conjectural Beginning of Human History" (1786)
CF	*Conflict of the Faculties* (1798)
Corr	Kant's correspondence, in volumes 10-13 of the Academy edition or in Zweig (see Bibliography)
CPJ	*Critique of the Power of Judgment* (1790)
CPracR	*Critique of Practical Reason* (1788)
CPuR	*Critique of Pure Reason* (1781 and 1787)
DDS	"Concerning the Ultimate Ground of the Differentiation of Directions in Space" (1768)
DSS	*Dreams of a Spirit-Seer, Elucidated by Dreams of Metaphysics* (1766)
FI	First Introduction to the *Critique of the Power of Judgment* (posthumous)

G	Groundwork for the Metaphysics of Morals (1785)
ID	Inaugural dissertation, On the Forms and Principles of the Sensible and Intellectual Worlds (1770)
LEC	Lectures on Ethics, Moral Philosophy Collins (dated 1784-85, but based on lectures from several years earlier)
LF	On the True Estimation of Living Forces (1747)
Logic	Immanuel Kant's Logic: A Handbook for Lectures, edited by G.B. Jäsche (1800)
MFNS	Metaphysical Foundations of Natural Science (1786)
MM	Metaphysics of Morals (1797)
MMV	Lectures on Ethics, Metaphysics of Morals Vigilantius (1793-94)
NE	A New Elucidation of the First Principles of Metaphysical Cognition (1755)
NF	Notes and Fragments
NFey	Naturrecht Feyerabend (1784-85)
NQ	"Attempt to Introduce the Concept of Negative Quantities into Philosophy" (1763)
OFBS	Observations on the Feeling of the Beautiful and Sublime (1764)
OP	Opus postumum (1797-1803)
OPB	The Only Possible Basis for a Demonstration of the Existence of God (1763)
OT	"What Does it Mean to Orient Oneself in Thought?" (1786)
PFM	Prolegomena to Any Future Metaphysics that will be able to come forth as a Science (1783)
PM	The Employment in Natural Philosophy of Metaphysics combined with Geometry, of which Sample I Contains the Physical Monadology (1756)
PNTM	Inquiry concerning the Distinctness of the Principles of Natural Theology and Morals (1764)
PP	Toward Perpetual Peace (1795)
RP	What is the Real Progress that Metaphysics has made in Germany since the Time of Leibniz and Wolff, edited by F.T. Rink (1804)
R	Reflexionen (Kant's notes and marginalia in volumes 14-20 and 23 of the Academy edition)
RBMR	Religion within the Boundaries of Mere Reason (1793)
TP	"On the old saying: That may be correct in theory but is of no use in practice" (1793)
UH	"Idea towards a Universal History from a Cosmopolitan Point of View" (1784)
UNH	Universal Natural History and Theory of the Heavens (1755)
WE?	"Answer to the Question: What is Enlightenment?" (1784)

1724	Kant born on April 22 in Königsberg, Prussia
1730-32	Attends elementary school at *Vorstädter Hospitalschule*
1732-40	Attends the Pietist *Collegium Fredericianum*
1740-46	Attends the *Albertina*, the university at Königsberg; left without degree
1748-54	Employed as private tutor by families in Judtschen, Arnsdorf, and Rautenberg
1749	Publishes *True Estimation of Living Forces*
1754	Return to Königsberg; publishes "Whether the Earth Has Changed in its Revolutions" and "Whether the Earth is Aging from a Physical Point of View"
1755	Receives M.A. for "On Fire"; earns right to lecture as *Privatdozent* with *A New Exposition of the First Principles of Metaphysical Cognition* and begins lecturing; publishes *General Natural History and Theory of the Heavens*
1756	Publishes doctoral dissertation on *Physical Monadology*; three essays on Lisbon earthquake and essay on the theory of winds
1757	Announces lectures on physical geography
1758	Publishes "New Doctrine of Motion and Rest"
1759	Publishes "Essay on Optimism"
1762	Publishes "The False Subtlety of the Four Syllogistic Figure"
1763	Publishes *Only Possible Basis for a Demonstration of the Existence of God* and "Attempt to Introduce the Concept of Negative Magnitudes into Philosophy"
1764	Declines professorship of poetry; publishes *Observations on the Feeling of the Beautiful and Sublime* and *Inquiry concerning the istinness*

of the Principles of Natural Theology and Morality, second-prize essay in Berlin Academy competition

1766   Adds position as sublibrarian at the castle and university library; publishes Dreams of a Spirit-Seer Elucidated by Dreams of Metaphysics

1768   Publishes "On Ultimate Ground of the Differentiation of Directions in Space"

1769   Declines offer of professorship at Erlangen

1770   Declines offer from Jena; appointed Professor of Logic and Metaphysics at Königsberg; defends and publishes inaugural dissertation On the Form and Principles of the Sensible and Intelligible World

1772   February letter to Marcus Herz outlines project of a critique of pure reason; begins anthropology lectures; gives up position as sublibrarian

1775   Essay "On the Different Human Races" as announcement for anthropology lectures

1776   Essay on the educational philosophy of the Dessau Philanthropinum

1778   Declines professorship in Halle

1781   Critique of Pure Reason published in May

1782   First, negative review of Critique appears

1783   Responds in Prolegomena to any Future Metaphysics

1784   Essays on "The Idea for a Universal History from a Cosmopolitan Point of View?" and "What is Enlightenment?"

1785   Publishes Groundwork for the Metaphysics of Morals, review of Herder's Ideas for the Philosophy of the History of Mankind and essays on "Volcanoes on the Moon," "The Wrongful Publication of Books," and "The Definition of the Concept of a Human Race"

1786   Publishes Metaphysical Foundations of Natural Science, essays on "Conjectural Beginnings of the Human Race" and "What Does Orientation in Thinking Mean?"; serves for the first time as rector of the university and becomes external member of the Berlin Academy of the Sciences

1787   Second edition of Critique of Pure Reason

1788   Publishes Critique of Practical Reason and "On the Use of Teleological Principles in Philosophy," which continues debate on race

1790   Publishes Critique of the Power of Judgment and defense of his philosophy from polemic by J.A. Eberhard, "On a discovery that is to make all new critique of pure reason dispensable because on an older one"

1791   Publishes "On the Failure of All Attempts at a Theodicy"

1792   Publishes essay that will become Part I of Religion within the Boundaries of mere Reason

1793   Publishes whole Religion within the Boundaries of mere Reason, essay "On the Old Saying: That may be correct in theory but it is of no use in practice"

1794   Prohibited from publishing further on religion; elected to Academy of Sciences in St. Petersburg

1795   Publisher Toward Perpetual Peace

1796   Publishes "On a newly elevated tone in philosophy"; gives final lecture on July 23

1797   Publishes Metaphysics of Morals and "On a presumed right to lie from philanthropic motives"

1798   Publishes The Conflict of the Faculties and Anthropology from a Practical Point of View

1800   Publication of Kant's Logic, edited by B.G. Jäsche

1802   Publication of Kant's Physical Geography, edited by F.T. Rink.

1803   Publication of Kant's Pedagogy, edited by Rink.

1804   Dies on February 12; publication of What Real Progress has Metaphysics made in Germany since the Time of Leibniz and Wolff?, edited by Rink

NATURE AND FREEDOM

Perhaps the most famous words that Immanuel Kant wrote during a publishing career of more than fifty years are these from the conclusion to his 1788 work on the foundation and possibility of morality, the Critique of Practical Reason:

> Two things fill the mind with ever new and increasing admiration and rever-ence, the more often and more steadily one reflects on them: **the starry heavens above me and the moral law within me**. I do not need to search for them and merely conjecture them as though they were veiled in obscurity or in the transcendent region beyond my horizon; I see them before me and connect them immediately with the consciousness of my existence. The first begins from the place I occupy in the external world of sense and extends the connection in which I stand into an unbounded magnitude with worlds upon worlds and systems of systems, and moreover into the unbounded times of their periodic motion, their beginning and their duration. The second begins from my invisible self, my personality, and presents me in a world which has true infinity but which can be discovered only by the understanding, and I cognize that my connection with that world (and thereby with all those visible worlds as well) is not merely contingent, as in the first case, but universal and necessary. The first view of a countless multitude of worlds annihilates, as it were, my importance as an **animal creature**, which after it has been for a short time provided with vital force (one knows not how) must give back to the planet (a mere speck in the universe) the matter from which it came. The second, on the contrary, raises my worth as an **intelligence** infinitely through my personality,

in which the moral law reveals to me a life independent of animality and even of the whole sensible world, at least so far as this may be inferred from the purposive determination of my existence by this law...

(CPracR, 5:161–2)

With these dramatic words, Kant alludes to the two great problems and accomplishments of his philosophical career. On the one hand, he wants to know how we who as creatures are a mere part of nature can discover how all of nature, even those parts of it that are well beyond our physical reach, does and even must work: how is it that we can become certain of the fundamental principles of everyday experience and natural science and by their means gain ever increasing knowledge of the natural order? On the other hand, he wants to display the unconditional value that we have as rational rather than merely natural beings, to show that the fundamental principle of morality is nothing but the necessary and sufficient condition of realizing this unconditional value, and that we are always free to act in accordance with and indeed for the sake of this principle, thus free to realize the unconditional value for which we unlike anything else in nature have the potential.

However, Kant's confidence in our complete freedom to live up to the demands of morality seems to be irreconcilable with his conception of the fundamental laws of nature: Kant understands our freedom to choose to act in accordance with the moral law as an ability to act in any set of circumstances as that law requires, no matter what our past behavior or even present inclinations might suggest we will do in such circumstances; but at the same time he understands the laws of nature as fully deterministic, so that the condition of nature at any one time entails its condition at any subsequent time, including our own behavior as objects within nature, with as much rigor as the premises of a syllogism logically entail its conclusion. But for Kant, this conflict, which would undermine not only our confidence in our ability to understand nature but also our motivation to attempt to live up to the demands of morality, can be avoided, for the only philosophical theory that can explain how we can know the deterministic laws of nature also allows, contrary to all appearances, that at its deepest level our own conduct is not dictated by those laws, but can be governed by pure practical reason and the moral law that is its only adequate expression. This theory is Kant's equally famous and controversial doctrine of "transcendental idealism." According to transcendental idealism, we can know the fundamental laws of nature with complete certitude because they are not descriptions of how things are in themselves independently of our perception and conception of them, but are rather the structure that the laws of our own minds impose upon the way things appear to us[1] – and the laws of the mind themselves are not hidden mysteries that can be discovered only by the empirical researches of psychologists or neuroscientists, but can readily be discovered by every normal human being competent at elementary arithmetic, geometry, and logic. But precisely because the most fundamental laws of nature are in fact only our own impositions on the appearance of reality, we can also believe that our own choices, contrary to their appearance, are not governed by the deterministic laws of nature, but can be freely made in accordance with and for the sake of the moral law. At the same time, Kant will argue, the very "fact of reason" (as he calls it) that we are free to act for the sake of and in accordance with the moral law also implies that we are free to flout it, and thus that the possibility of doing evil is equally fundamental to the human will as the possibility of doing right, thus that all human beings are at risk of doing evil not because of the original sin of some distant ancestors but because of the radical nature of freedom itself.

Kant thus argues that the only possible explanation of our certitude about the theoretical laws of nature also leaves room for the efficacy of practical reason, that is, the freedom to act in accordance with the moral law, although not for any certitude that we will so act, for such a certitude would conflict with the most fundamental fact about freedom itself. But now it looks as if Kant has avoided a conflict between nature and freedom, between science and morality, only by making them irrelevant to each other, or by dividing our own characters and placing us in two parallel universes: in one realm where our actions are as fully determined by antecedent events and deterministic laws as anything else in nature is, but in another, in some sense underlying realm where our choices are completely free even though they somehow manifest themselves in appearance as if they had been seamlessly caused by antecedent events.

It may seem as if Kant was content with such a radically dualistic view of human action, but ultimately he was not. For after he had argued in his first great work, the *Critique of Pure Reason* of 1781 (substantially revised in 1787), that our own imposition of the fundamental laws of nature upon appearance leaves open at least the possibility of freedom at a deeper level of reality, and then added in the *Critique of Practical Reason* (CPracR) (1788) that our awareness of our obligation to live up to the demands of the moral law implies not merely the possibility but the actuality of our radical freedom at this deeper level, Kant wrote a third great work, the *Critique of the Power of Judgment* (CPJ) (1790), precisely in order to bridge:

[the] incalculable gulf fixed between the domain of the concept of nature, as the sensible, and the domain of the concept of the freedom, as the supersensible, so that from the former to the latter (thus by means of the theoretical use of reason), no transition is possible, just as if there were so many different worlds, the first of which can have no influence on the second.

Such a gulf, the idea that the realms of nature and of morality are basically two different worlds that do not really influence each other, is unacceptable, for what morality itself requires is that the "second" world of morality "**should** have an influence on the former," that is, on the world of nature:

namely the concept of freedom should make the end that is imposed by its laws real in the sensible world; and nature must consequently also be able to be conceived in such a way that the lawfulness of its form is at least in agreement with the possibility of the ends that are to be realized in it in accordance with the laws of freedom. – Thus there must still be a ground of the **unity** of the supersensible that grounds nature with that which the concept of freedom contains practically, the concept of which . . . makes possible the transition from the manner of thinking in accordance with the principles of the one to that in accordance with the principles of the other.

(CPJ, Introduction, section II, 5:175–6)

What Kant is assuming here is that morality is not just a matter of making rightful or virtuous choices, but also requires us to put those choices into practice by attempting to realize the goals or ends that they entail in the arena of action, that is, nothing less than the realm of spatial, temporal, and causal nature in which we live and act. Kant then embarks upon an extended argument that we can experience the existence of natural beauty, of works of artistic genius that are themselves products of a creative spirit that is as much natural as rational, and of the marvelous organization that we find in organisms within nature and then project onto the whole of nature, as palpable confirmation of our theoretical assumption that nature must be a realm in which the ends that we choose in the name of morality can be realized.

In the third *Critique* Kant also suggests that his two apparently opposite conceptions of human action can be bridged by recognizing that there are not just two but three forms of human autonomy, the third of which unifies the first two. Autonomy is the central conception of Kant's moral philosophy, where he defines it as "the property of the will by which it is a law to itself (independently of any property of the objects of volition)" (G, 4:440). The central argument of Kant's moral philosophy is that such autonomy, as the ability to choose the principles and ends of our actions freely rather than having them imposed upon us by the inclinations and desires that we may merely happen to have, is our most basic value, but that the only way to free ourselves from domination by such inclinations is by adopting a purely formal law of action, which can be nothing other than the law that our maxims of action must be universally acceptable – Kant's famous principle of universalizability. But in the third *Critique*, Kant goes further and suggests that the fundamental principle of *each* of our three main cognitive powers – theoretical understanding, practical reason, and the power of judgment – can be understood as a form of autonomy. He writes:

> In regard to the faculties of the soul in general, insofar as they are considered as higher faculties, i.e., as ones that contain an autonomy, the understanding is the one that contains the **constitutive** principles *a priori* for the **faculty of cognition** (the theoretical cognition of nature); for the **feeling of pleasure and displeasure** it is the power of judgment, independent of concepts and sensations that are related to the determination of the faculty of desire and could thereby be immediately practical; for the **faculty of desire** it is reason, which is practical without the mediation of any sort of pleasure, wherever it might come from, and determines for this faculty, as a higher faculty, the final end, which at the same time brings with it the pure intellectual satisfaction in the object.
>
> (CPJ, Introduction, Section IX, 5:196–7)

The full meaning of this passage can hardly be apparent yet, but a preliminary interpretation suggests this much: The solution to the central problem of theoretical philosophy is to recognize our fundamental *cognitive* autonomy, that is, that we ourselves are the authors of the most basic laws of nature, and for that reason can know them with certainty. The key to moral philosophy, as already suggested, is the recognition that our *practical* autonomy can only be achieved and sustained by our free adoption of the moral law, a law that stems from our own practical reason and is not imposed upon us by some external agency any more than the fundamental laws of nature are. But the moral law, as it turns out, is not merely negative, imposing upon us only the restriction of not acting on principles that are not universally acceptable; it also imposes upon us the positive objective of promoting the particular ends that people freely choose in the exercise of their autonomy, the collective realization of which would be the "final end" or "highest good" consisting of the maximal distribution of human happiness consistent with and indeed resulting from the maximal realization of human virtue. And our experience of natural beauty and organization, a form of experience in which we take pleasure independently of any immediate cognitive or practical concern, gives us emotionally powerful confirmation of the realizability of this final end in nature. But such an experience of pleasure can itself be understood as a form of *affective* or we might even say *emotional* autonomy: a pleasure that does not arise from the satisfaction of any immediate cognitive or practical concern, although at the same time it also suggests to us that nature is hospitable to our most general cognitive and practical objectives. In other words, the autonomous pleasure that we take in the experience of natural beauty and organization supports our otherwise purely rational conviction of the realizability of our theoretical and practical autonomy.[2]

Indeed, Kant did not wait until the third *Critique* to signal that the transcendental idealist resolution of the apparent tension between the determinism of nature and the freedom of human action, which seems to assign determinism and freedom to two parallel universes, is not his last word on the subject. Late in the *Critique of Pure Reason*, he wrote that:

All interest of my reason (the speculative as well as the practical) is united in the following three questions:

1 What can I know?
2 What should I do?
3 What may I hope?

(CPuR, A 804–5 / B 833)

Transcendental idealism is supposed to have provided the answer to the first two of these questions: What I can *know* with certitude is the fundamental laws of nature (although never all of its concrete detail) because these laws are nothing but the laws of human thought itself, accessible to me as a normal human being. What I should *do* is what the moral law that is given to me by my own reason and not by any external authority commands, and I am assured of the possibility of my freedom to act as that law demands by transcendental idealism but also assured of the actuality of my freedom by my sense of obligation to so act. But what I may *hope* is nothing less than that I can realize the ends enjoined upon me by the moral law in the world of nature, or that I may transform the natural world into a "moral world," "the world as it would be if it were in conformity with all moral laws (as it **can** be in accordance with the **freedom** of rational beings and **should** be in accordance with the necessary laws of **morality**)" (CPuR, A 808/B 836). From the start of his mature thought, in other words, Kant insisted that the free choice to do what morality requires of us is not unrelated to the natural world, but imposes objectives on us that can only be realized in the natural world, and which we must be able to hope can be realized in that world if we are coherently to act as morality commands us at all. What the third *Critique* adds to this is only the argument that we may use our experience of natural beauty and organization as a certain kind of emotional support for the plausibility of this hope.

Kant clearly liked his reduction of the problems of philosophy to these three questions, for he repeated them in the very last work to be published in his name in which he still had a hand, the textbook on logic edited under his supervision by his student Gottlob Benjamin Jäsche in 1800. But here Kant added a fourth question to the three listed in the first *Critique*. "The field of philosophy in this cosmopolitan sense," he wrote, that is, the sense in which philosophy "is in fact the science of the relation of all cognition and of all use of reason to the ultimate end of human reason, in which, as the highest, all other ends are subordinated, and in which they must all unite to form a unity," "can be brought down to the following questions":

1 What can I know?
2 What should I do?
3 What may I hope?
4 What is the human being?

(*Logic*, 9:25)

By adding the question "What is the human being?" to his list, Kant hints at the underlying theme of his answer to the first three questions: what I can know is the framework of nature that is dictated by the laws of human thought, and then an indefinite extent of the infinitely many particular facts of nature that can be discovered within that framework; what I should do is act in accordance with the principle of autonomy that is dictated by no other authority than human practical reason itself, and work at the open-ended project of realizing human happiness within the framework of mutual freedom demanded by this principle; and what I may hope is that this project can be realized in nature as we encounter it, a hope about which the distinctively human experiences of natural beauty and organization give us some vital confirmation. The human being, in other words, is nothing less than the source of natural and moral law as well as of the experience that assures us that these two forms of legislation are mutually consistent.

In his waning years, Kant worked ceaselessly, although ultimately in vain, to complete a final book that would give full expression to this vision of the human being as the source of the laws of nature, the moral law, and of an experience of nature that exhibits the ultimate unity of these two forms of legislation. He died leaving only a mass of notes toward this book, the so-called *Opus postumum*. But among these notes we find drafts of title pages such as these:

> The Highest Standpoint of Transcendental Philosophy in the System of Two Ideas,
>> By
>
> God, the World, and the Subject which connects both Objects,
> the Thinking Being in the World.
> God, the World, and what unites both into a System:
> The Thinking, Innate Principle of the Human Being (*mens*) in the World.
> The Human Being as a Being in the World, Self-limited through Nature and Duty.
>
> (OP, 21:34)

In these notes, Kant makes it clear that by "God" he ultimately means nothing more than an idea that is the projection of the dignity of our own power to legislate the moral law – "There is a God," he writes, "not as a world-soul in nature, but as a personal principle of human reason" (OP, 21:19) – and that by "Nature" he means the ordering of our experience in accord with fundamental laws that are the projection of our own laws of thought. So it is the "thinking, innate principle of the human being" that is the source of both the laws of nature and the laws of morality, and in the end we cannot but experience ourselves as living in a world in which nature and morality are not only compatible but also mutually reinforcing. Or so at least Kant fervently hoped until his dying day.

SKEPTICISM AND CRITIQUE

This vision of the human being as the source of the laws of nature, the moral law, and of an experience of nature in which these are both compatible and cooperative is the substance of Kant's philosophy, which we shall pursue here through an exposition of his three great critiques and their companion texts, the *Metaphysical Foundations of Natural Science* (1786) in the case of the first *Critique* and the *Groundwork for the Metaphysics of Morals* (1785) and the *Metaphysics of Morals* (1797) in the case of the second, as well the series of essays on human history and religion, especially the *Religion within the Boundaries of Mere Reason* (1793), in which Kant attempted to bring these apparently refractory domains of human experience into his own unifying vision of the efficacy of practical reason in nature. But there is also a methodological theme that runs throughout Kant's philosophy, namely the defense of his "critical" vision from the Scylla and Charybdis of "dogmatism" and "skepticism" as well as from the yawning abyss of "indifferentism" (see CPuR, A ix–x), and our exposition of Kant's philosophy will have to attend to his methodological as well as to his substantive concerns.

We already have a sense of what Kant's "critical" approach to philosophy involves, namely an examination of the human powers of cognition and reason as the basis for all claims about the laws of nature and morality. And it is not too difficult to say what Kant means by "dogmatism" and "indifferentism." The former is an uncritical assertion of laws for nature and morality, that is, a confident assertion of the truth of such laws that is not grounded in an antecedent critique of human intellectual powers, which inevitably results in the assertion of conflicting dogmas about many of the most important matters of human concern; and indifferentism is simply the indifference to philosophical questions that the spectacle of unending dogmatic conflicts can all too readily produce. But to say what Kant means by skepticism and how he proposes to combat it is a more complicated matter.

In the Preface to the second edition of the *Critique of Pure Reason*, Kant writes:

> [I]t always remains a scandal to philosophy and universal human reason that the existence of things outside us (from which we after all get the whole matter of our cognitions) should have to be assumed merely on **faith**, and that if it occurs to anyone to doubt it, we should be unable to answer him with a satisfactory proof.
>
> (B xxxix)

Doubt about the provability of the existence of objects distinct from but related to our own representations is what we think of as Cartesian skepticism, and even though Kant does not mention the name of Descartes here, his suggestion that thus far philosophy has delivered only an unsatisfactory proof of the existence of external objects through "faith" is a barely veiled allusion to Descartes' argument that skepticism about this can be avoided only by first proving the existence of an infinitely benevolent as well as omnipotent God. And later in the second edition of the *Critique*, in the new "Refutation of Idealism" to which the footnote in the Preface refers, Kant makes it explicit that his target is "the **problematic** idealism of Descartes, who declares only one empirical assertion, namely **I am**, to be indubitable," and who then attempts, although in Kant's eyes fruitlessly, to infer the existence of external objects from his own indubitable existence (B 274–5). Many readers have taken the refutation of Cartesian skepticism to be central to Kant's philosophical enterprise. Since Kant does call it a "scandal to philosophy," there can be little doubt that he is concerned to refute or undermine it. But it would be seriously misleading to think of the refutation of Cartesian skepticism as exhausting Kant's concern with skepticism, or even as the most important part of it. Two other forms of skepticism are of far more concern to Kant and play a larger role in determining the structure not only of his theoretical philosophy but of his practical philosophy as well.[3]

As Kant makes plain in the opening paragraphs of the Preface to the first edition, his first concern is with the form of skepticism that is the inevitable response to the seemingly endless and intractable conflicts between metaphysical dogmas that seem to be well grounded but cannot all be true:

> Human reason has the peculiar fate in one species of its cognitions that it is burdened with questions which it cannot dismiss, since they are given to it as problems by the nature of reason itself, but which it also cannot answer, since they transcend every capacity of human reason.
>
> Reason falls into this perplexity through no fault of its own. It begins from principles whose use is unavoidable in the course of experience and at the same time sufficiently warranted by it. With these principles it rises (as its nature also requires) ever higher, to more remote conditions. But since it becomes aware in this way that its business must always remain incomplete because the questions never cease, reason sees itself necessitated to take refuge in principles that overstep all possible use in experience, and yet seem so unsuspicious that even ordinary common sense agrees with them. But it thereby falls into obscurity and contradictions . . . The battlefield of these endless controversies is called

> **metaphysics** . . . In the beginning, under the administration of the
> **dogmatists**, her rule was **despotic**. Yet because her legislation still
> retained traces of ancient barbarism, this rule gradually degenerated
> through internal wars into complete **anarchy**; and the skeptics, a kind of
> nomads who abhor all permanent cultivation of the soil, shattered civil unity
> from time to time.
>
> (A vii–ix)

Once human reason attempts to reach beyond the immediate limits of our
ordinary experience and to determine the truth about such matters as the
nature of the soul, the boundaries of the universe, or the nature and
the existence of God – which, Kant stresses, it is entirely natural for reason
to do – it inevitably falls into contradictions "from which it can indeed
surmise that it must somewhere be proceeding on the grounds of hidden
errors" (A viii) but which, without a thorough scrutiny of its own powers,
"it cannot discover." Skepticism about the power of human reason to arrive
at any well-founded belief about matters of the most fundamental human
concern is the equally inevitable result. In the present passage, Kant stresses
the inevitability of this sequence of dogmatic controversy leading to
despairing skepticism by saying that "ordinary common sense" is impli-
cated in this process. In the introduction to his moral philosophy he makes
the same point by saying that there is a "**natural dialectic**," in this case
about the possibility or impossibility of the freedom of the will that Kant
takes to be the necessary condition of morality itself, on account of which

> **common human reason** is impelled . . . to take a step into the field of
> practical philosophy . . . so that it may escape from its predicament about
> claims from both sides and not run the risk of being deprived of all genuine
> moral principles through the ambiguity into which it easily falls.
>
> (G, 4:405)

We might call the skepticism that is induced by contradictory but apparently equally well-grounded propositions about matters of the most
fundamental human concern "Pyrrhonian" skepticism, after Pyrrho of Elis
(c. 365–c. 275 BC), the founder of the ancient school of skepticism that
purported to be able to induce doubt by producing equally good arguments on either side of any philosophical question. Kant does not mention
the name of Pyrrho in the Critique of Pure Reason, but he does name him as
the paradigmatic skeptic in the brief history of philosophy included in the
introduction to his logic textbook:

If we begin the epoch of skepticism with Pyrrho, then we get a whole school of skepticism, who are essentially different from the **dogmatists** in their mode of thought and method of philosophizing, in that they made it the first maxim for all philosophizing use of reason **to withhold one's judgment even when the semblance of truth is greatest**; and they advanced the principle that **philosophy consists in the equilibrium of judgment and teaches us to uncover false semblance**.

(*Logic*, 9:31)

It will become clear that undermining Pyrrhonian skepticism, not about all forms of judgment whatever but about the most fundamental principles of theoretical and practical reason, by determining the proper use and limits of human reason through a critical scrutiny of its powers is the methodological project that structures the whole of Kant's presentation and defense of his substantive theory of the theoretical and practical autonomy of human beings.

There is yet one more form of skepticism that is central to Kant's concerns. This is the form of skepticism that Kant explicitly associates with the name of David Hume: "I freely admit that the reminder[4] of *David Hume* was the very thing that many years ago first interrupted my dogmatic slumber and gave a completely different direction to my researches in the field of speculative philosophy" (PFM, 4:260). As Kant interprets him:

Hume started mainly from a single but important concept in metaphysics, namely, that of the **connection of cause and effect** . . . and called upon reason, which pretends to have generated this concept in her womb, to give him an account of by what right she thinks that something could be so constituted that, if it is posited, something else necessarily must thereby be posited as well . . . He indisputably proved that it is wholly impossible for reason to think such a connection *a priori* and from concepts.

(PFM, 4:257)

As Kant quite rightly stresses, Hume "never put in doubt" "whether the concept of cause is right, useful, and, with respect to all cognition of nature, indispensable"; what he questioned was only "whether it is thought through reason *a priori*, and in this way has an inner truth independent of all experience, and therefore also a much more widely extended use which is not limited merely to objects of experience" (PFM, 4:258). That is, Hume's problem – which Kant quickly generalizes from the concept of causation to all the fundamental concepts of metaphysics (PFM, 4:260) – is not that the concept of causation lands us in some sort of Pyrrhonian contradiction; it is rather the challenge to demonstrate that a principle like the principle that every event has some cause is truly universal and necessary, not known only from some finite range of prior cases and thus valid only for those cases, but necessarily valid for all cases, whether already experienced or not, and therefore known "*a priori*," that is known independently from any particular experience in some way that obviously needs to be explained.

Indeed, once Kant had discovered the Humean problem of skepticism about the universality and necessity of first principles, he generalized it not only to the first principles of "speculative philosophy," that is, theoretical cognition, but also to the first principle of practical philosophy, the fundamental principle of morality. Thus, from a methodological point of view, Kant's project in philosophy became that of undermining both Humean and Pyrrhonian skepticism in both theoretical and practical philosophy, and, much more incidentally, along the way refuting Cartesian skepticism about external objects as a nagging but by no means central problem in theoretical philosophy. How would Kant accomplish this set of objectives? By what he came to call a "critique" of both theoretical and practical reason and ultimately of our power of judgment as well. Such a scrutiny of the most fundamental powers or "faculties" of human intellect – sensibility, judgment, understanding, and reason – would reveal that we do indeed find the bases of natural and moral law within ourselves, thus that we are capable of theoretical and practical autonomy, thereby refuting Humean skepticism. But it would also show that if we properly modulate the claims we make on behalf of our own reason – limiting its claims to knowledge to those that are consistent with the limits of our sensibility or perceptual abilities while recognizing that we can and indeed must have reasonable "belief" or "faith" about matters beyond the reach of sensibility when, but only when, the very possibility of morality demands that – then we can avoid the "obscurities and contradictions" that inevitably lead to Pyrrhonian skepticism. How – and how well – Kant accomplishes these complex objectives will be our focus in what follows.

FURTHER READING

Valuable overviews of Kant's philosophy by single authors include the following. Cassirer, although originally published in 1918, presents a neo-Kantian perspective on Kant by the greatest of all modern historians of philosophy, while de Vleeschauwer, originally published in 1939, is a condensation of a massive work on the argument structure of Kant's philosophy. Körner is an approach to Kant from the heyday of analytical philosophy, and Shell and Wood stress the relation between the natural and the rational in Kant's conception of human nature.

Ernst Cassirer, *Kant's Life and Thought*, trans. James Haden (New Haven, CT: Yale University Press, 1981).

Herman-Jean de Vleeschauwer, *The Development of Kantian Thought: The History of a Doctrine*, trans. A. R. C. Duncan (London and Edinburgh: Thomas Nelson, 1969).

Stefan Körner, *Kant* (Harmondsworth: Penguin, 1955).

Susan Meld Shell, *The Embodiment of Reason: Kant on Spirit, Generation, and Community* (Chicago: University of Chicago Press, 1996),

Allen W. Wood, *Kant* (Oxford: Blackwell Publishing, 2005).

Two multiple-author overviews of Kant's philosophy are:

Paul Guyer (ed.), *The Cambridge Companion to Kant* (Cambridge: Cambridge University Press, 1992) (with an extensive bibliography).

——(ed.), *The Cambridge Companion to Kant and Modern Philosophy* (Cambridge: Cambridge University Press, 2006) (all new material, stressing Kant's place in the history of modern philosophy, and with a greatly expanded bibliography).

One

A Life in Work

Many of the great philosophers of the seventeenth and eighteenth centuries had dramatic lives. Descartes started his career as a soldier of fortune during the Thirty Years War, and spent much of his life in seclusion in the Netherlands out of fear that he could not work freely in France. Spinoza suffered excommunication and exile from the Jewish community of Amsterdam because of his unconventional views. Hobbes was an intimate of the noble house of Cavendish, and spent the years of the English Civil War in fearful exile in France. Locke trained as a physician, and it was as a physician that he first came to the attention of the powerful first Earl of Shaftesbury, with whom he became a close political associate, with the result that he was forced to spend the years of conflict over the succession to the restored Stuart kings Charles II and James II living in hiding and under an assumed name in Amsterdam, before becoming an important civil servant during the reign of William and Mary. Leibniz spent his life as a courtier, with a range of duties including diplomacy, engineering, and historiography. Hume took part in a number of British diplomatic and military missions before enjoying public fame and fortune as the author of his controversial but popular *History of England*. Rousseau wrote music and novels as well as philosophy while never holding a steady job and leading a disorderly personal life that got him banished from his native city as well as into many other scrapes. Kant, however, was the first truly important modern philosopher to spend his career almost exclusively as a university teacher, indeed as a teacher in a single university in the town of his birth. The drama in Kant's life was intellectual, so the story of his life must be told through his works.

CHILDHOOD AND STUDENT YEARS

Kant was born in the city of Königsberg on April 22, 1724, the same city where he would die almost eighty years later, on February 12, 1804.[1] Königsberg, at the eastern end of the Baltic Sea, fell into Russian hands at the end of World War II, becoming the naval base of Kaliningrad and remaining off-limits to non-Soviets for fifty years. But it was originally the capital of East Prussia, the base of Prussian power before the acquisition of Brandenburg and the growth of Berlin, and in Kant's time it remained the administrative center of East Prussia and a leading Hanseatic mercantile city, the most important outlet east of Danzig for the vast Polish and Lithuanian hinterlands. While it was never a capital of art and culture, in Kant's time, Königsberg was a business, legal, military, and educational center with many connections to the rest of Europe. And though it was not a publishing center like Leipzig, Frankfurt, or Stuttgart, through its book-sellers and its local as well as imported literary journals it was firmly plugged into the intellectual life of the rest of Europe.

Kant's father, Johann Georg Kant (1683–1746) was a harness maker, and his mother, Anna Regina née Reuter (1697–1737), herself the daughter of a harness maker from Nürnburg, was an educated and pious Christian. The Kants were adherents of Pietism, a reform movement within Lutheranism, which placed great stress on personal faith and conscience, like other eighteenth-century Protestant movements such as Methodism in England and the Great Awakening in New England.[2] Immanuel, the second oldest and the first son among the four of the nine children of his parents to survive childhood, was obviously bright, and with the help of the leading Pietist pastor of Königsberg, Franz Albert Schulz, he was able to attend the leading school in the city, the Pietist *Collegium Fredericianum*, from the ages of 8 to 16. Of course, Pietist theology was taught at the school, but it also offered a rigorous training in the Latin language and a thorough grounding in Latin literature, both of which would stand Kant well throughout his life, as well as Greek, Hebrew, and French, logic and the history of philosophy, history and geography, and arithmetic, geometry, and trigonometry, the latter taught from the textbooks of Christian Wolff, who was already becoming the dominant philosopher of Germany. The school even offered vocal and instrumental music, although this aspect of its curriculum seems to have had little positive effect on Kant.[3]

Kant's mother died when he was 13, after nursing a friend through an illness, and while her selflessness left a profound impression on Kant, her death also left his family in reduced circumstances. But Kant was nevertheless able to enroll at the university in Königsberg, the *Albertina*, in September, 1738, at the age of 16 – an average rather than precocious age for starting university in those days. Although enrolling only 300 to 500 students per year through most of the eighteenth century, the *Albertina* enrolled a wide range of students from Prussia but also from the Baltic regions. Schulz and the Pietists had clearly intended Kant for the ministry, but at university Kant did not matriculate in theology (or law or medicine), instead pursuing as unrestricted course of study in classical literature, philosophy, and natural science. His main teacher, Martin Knutzen (1713–51), was an eclectic thinker, influenced by both Pietism and John Locke's empiricism as well as by Wolff – he was actually very critical of the Leibnizo-Wolffian rejection of real interaction among bodies as well as between minds and bodies in favor of the theory of pre-established harmony – and was also an enthusiast for Newtonian physics and contemporary astronomy.[4] Kant was also exposed to other philosophical and scientific influences – one professor defended Aristotelian ethics, another Aristotelian logic, one defended the pre-established harmony while Knutzen attacked it, another taught English literature and philosophy, and yet another studied the newly important phenomenon of electricity.[5] Thus Kant's university teachers offered a broad introduction to contemporary European philosophy and science. Kant's own intellectual life would always be marked by the breadth of his interests and information as well as by the depth of his thought.

Kant left university in 1746 without receiving the usual degree of *Magister*, although he had completed what would become his first book, the *True Estimation of Living Forces*, which would eventually be published in 1749. It had traditionally been thought that Kant left the university because of financial necessity resulting from the death of his father in March, 1746, but recent research suggests that the award of his degree and the possibility of continuing on as a lecturer were actually blocked by his own teacher Martin Knutzen and other Pietists because Kant was too sympathetic toward Leibniz's vision of a harmonious world[6] – an ideal that Kant would always try to preserve in his philosophy in spite of many specific disagreements with Leibniz. The *True Estimation* was primarily a scientific work, attempting to mediate between Cartesian and Leibnizian conceptions of force by assigning Descartes's measure of force, mv, to "dead" or inertial force and Leibniz's measure, mv^2, to "living" or "active" force. (There were limits to information in Königsberg: Kant did not know that the Frenchman J.L. D'Alembert, later famous as the co-editor of the great *Encylopédie*, had already shown that the correct measure of all force was

$\frac{1}{2}mv^2$.) Although Kant's work was not a scientific success, it was an early demonstration of his philosophical penchant for undercutting continuing controversies by drawing distinctions where others had not and thus opening up alternatives that had not been considered. Another place in the work where he attempted to resolve a debate by drawing a new distinction was in his discussion of the philosophical debate over the Leibnizian idea of pre-established harmony: Kant accepted "physical influx," that is, real causation, the opposite of pre-established harmony, which postulates that all changes in objects are self-generated and only appear to be caused by changes in other objects, for some interactions between matter, but not for all relations between mind and matter. Thus, he departed from Knutzen's complete rejection of the pre-established harmony, and Knutzen may not have liked this.[7]

RETURN TO THE UNIVERSITY

Whatever the reason, after two more years in Königsberg, much of the time apparently devoted to straightening out the affairs of his deceased father, Kant was forced to resort to the livelihood of many other impecunious intellectuals in his time, namely, work as a household tutor for a wealthy upper-middle-class or noble family. He spent the years 1748 to 1754 in such employment with several families in the vicinity of Königsberg. Evidently Kant's duties as a tutor did not demand all of his time, for in 1755 after he returned to the city, he was able to publish in rapid succession three Latin treatises that earned him his delayed master's degree, his doctoral degree, and the right to teach at the university as an unsalaried *Privatdozent* (earning only fees directly paid to him by students at his lectures); a number of articles on the rotation of the earth and earthquakes (a popular topic after the epochal Lisbon earthquake of 1755); and a lengthy treatise on cosmology, the *Universal Natural History and Theory of Heavens*, in which Kant, anticipating the French astronomer Pierre Simon de Laplace by forty years although with less mathematics, argued for a completely physical explanation of the origin of the solar system from a cloud of dust – the so-called Kant–Laplace nebular hypothesis. Unfortunately for Kant, the publisher of this book went bankrupt, his stock was impounded, and Kant's anticipation of Laplace remained unknown until the nineteenth century.[8]

Of the three Latin treatises, the first, *Meditationum quarundam de igne succincta delineatio* ("Some succinctly delineated meditations on fire") (1755) is a scientific work of little continuing interest. A second scientific treatise,

Metaphysicae cum geomtria iunctae usus in philosophia naturali, cuius specimen I. continent monadologiam physicam ("The joint use of metaphysics and geometry in natural philosophy, the first example of which contains a physical monadology") (1756), is of much greater interest, for here Kant attempts to reconcile the mathematical infinite divisibility of space with the Leibnizian insistence that substance must ultimately consist of simple parts by arguing that these simple parts are not non-spatial indivisible minds or "monads" but spatially extended yet indivisible fields of force, "physical monads." For reasons we will consider later, Kant would eventually and notoriously deny the reality of space and extension assumed in this work, in part because of the infinite divisibility of space and time and anything in them, but he would retain the dynamical model of substance as composed of attractive and repulsive forces introduced in this early work in his physical theory.[9]

The most revealing of the three Latin treatises, however, is Kant's first entirely philosophical work, the *Principiorum primorum cognitionis metaphysicae nova delucidatio* ("A new elucidation of the first principles of metaphysical cognition") of 1755. In this work, while by no means entirely breaking from the rationalist framework that had been imposed on continental philosophy first by René Descartes and then in Germany by Gottfried Wilhelm Leibniz and Christian Wolff, Kant explicitly attacks some of the most central doctrines of rationalism. First, Kant attacks the "ontological" argument for the existence of God, which Descartes, Leibniz, and Wolff had made the foundation not only of philosophical theology but of all of ontology and, even in the case of Descartes, epistemology, and indeed attacks it in a way that would ultimately lead to one of the most central ideas of Kant's eventual masterwork, the *Critique of Pure Reason* of 1781. The ontological argument begins with the definition of God as the most perfect being or the being who possesses all perfections, assumes that existence is a perfection – for surely it is more perfect for something (which is otherwise good) to exist than for it not to – and then concludes that God necessarily exists, for it would be a contradiction and thus necessarily false to deny him the perfection of existence when he is the most perfect of all beings.[10] Kant argues that this proof is fallacious, because no matter what realities are "conceived as existing together . . . the existence of that being is . . . only an existence in ideas" (NE, Proposition VI, 1:395). In other words, you can include whatever you want in a concept, but that by itself can never prove that any object corresponding to that concept actually exists. Kant would subsequently express this criticism by saying that existence is not a real predicate of an object, but rather something *presupposed* by

the truth of any assertion of a predicate of an object. This would lead to
the rejection of Leibniz's extreme form of rationalism, which was
committed to the view that all true propositions are true because their
predicates are contained in their subject-concepts and that they may therefore at least in principle be known entirely on the basis of logical
analysis,[11] and would lead instead to Kant's own view that assertions of
existence are "synthetic" rather than "analytic," that is, they add information (the fact of existence) to the concept of the object rather than merely
unpacking it. This would in turn lead Kant to the recognition that even the
most fundamental propositions of metaphysics are synthetic rather than
analytic, and that metaphysics would have to find an entirely new method
distinct from the method of merely logical analysis it had attempted to use
thus far – but it would take Kant another twenty-five years to discover that
new method. In the New Elucidation, Kant is by no means ready to reject
rationalism altogether, and in fact he presents what he takes to be a new
proof of the existence of God based on the premise that nothing can be
possible unless something is actual (Proposition VII, 1:395–6) to which
he remains attached for some years. Thus, after criticizing the particular
proofs of the "principle of sufficient reason" – the principle that everything that exists has a cause or other adequate ground or explanation –
that had been offered by Christian Wolff and his disciple Alexander
Gottlieb Baumgarten (1714–62), who was the author of the textbooks in
metaphysics and ethics from which Kant would teach for his entire career,
as well as a pioneer in the new field of aesthetics and coiner of its name,[12]
Kant offers a new proof of the logical necessity of this principle.
However – and this is the second main clue in the New Elucidation pointing
toward Kant's future views – on the basis of the principle of sufficient
reason Kant now also rejects the doctrine of pre-established harmony,
which Leibniz had insisted characterizes all relations between substances
and Wolff had allowed in the case of mind and body. Kant argues that if
every change requires an explanation, then a substance can change its
state, including its representational state – what it perceives or conceives –
only if acted upon by another substance; for if the cause of its state were
entirely internal to it, then it would have been in that state all along, and
not undergone any change (Proposition XII, 1:410). Although in the
Critique of Pure Reason Kant would ultimately give a radically different account
and proof of the principle of sufficient reason, as a principle of the "possibility of experience," this account of the "Principle of Succession" in the
New Elucidation points the way toward Kant's subsequent insistence on
the reality of causality generally and on the particular thesis that the deter-

minate succession of representations or experiences in the mind can only be known if the mind interacts with physical bodies, the thesis of his eventual "Refutation of Idealism."[13]

Finally, the *New Elucidation* takes up an issue that would be central to Kant's moral as well as his theoretical philosophy. Having committed himself to the principle of sufficient reason, or as he calls it the "principle of determining reason" – even though he has not yet found what he would later consider a satisfactory proof of it – Kant is inevitably forced to address the conflict between determinism and free will. Leibnizian philosophers regarded themselves as committed to determinism by the principle of sufficient reason – Wolff had even been banished from Prussia in 1723 because the king had been persuaded that Wolff's determinism implied that his soldiers were not responsible for their actions, even for desertion – but had tried to salvage our belief in our own freedom of the will by representing our actions as free when they are caused by an internal rather than external cause, specifically by a representation of a course of action as the best available to us. The Pietist philosopher and critic of Wolff Christian August Crusius had objected that this is not enough, and that a choice is free only if at the moment of action the agent is not irremediably inclined one way rather than its opposite, and can spontaneously choose either.[14] Kant took the part of the Leibnizians here, rejecting Crusius's version of what is usually called the "liberty of indifference" because it meant that even an agent who has previously "decided to follow the path of virtue" cannot count on doing so when a moment of choice arrives (NE, Proposition IX, 1:402).[15] Later, however, Kant would come to consider the conception of freedom of the will advocated by Leibniz as nothing but the "freedom of a turnspit" (CPracR, 5:97), and move in the direction of Crusius. In fact, Kant would ultimately seek to reconcile the Leibnizian and Crusian conceptions of freedom through his transcendental idealism, which would allow for thoroughgoing determinism at the level of appearance while postulating the complete spontaneity of action at the level of reality. This raises one of the most vexed issues of Kant's mature philosophy – Kant himself would say that on his own theory the reality of freedom remains inexplicable or inscrutable – so for the moment let us stay with our narrative of Kant's development.

TOWARD THE CRITICAL PHILOSOPHY

After his burst of publications in 1755–56 established Kant as a lecturer at the university, the demands of actually offering enough courses in logic, metaphysics, and ethics and, beyond those philosophical subjects, lectures on mathematics, physics, geography, and even fortification to eke out a modest living prevented Kant from publishing anything other than a few brief papers, including one on optimism (1759), for another half-dozen years. (Subsequently, Kant would have to add the position of university and castle under-librarian to supplement his lecture fees!) But then in the years from 1762 to 1766 Kant published another torrent of papers and books that, without yet reaching his mature philosophical views, made significant strides in that direction. In 1762, Kant published an essay on "The False Subtlety of the Four Syllogistic Figures"; in 1763, an essay on the "Attempt to Introduce the Concept of Negative Magnitudes into Philosophy" and a substantial book confidently entitled *The Only Possible Basis for a Demonstration of the Existence of God*; and in 1764 both a popular little book *Observations on the Feeling of the Beautiful and Sublime* and an essay on philosophical methodology called the "Inquiry Concerning the Distinctness of the Principles of Natural Theology and Morality." The latter was Kant's entry in a Berlin Academy of Sciences competition on the question of whether philosophy could use the mathematical method, which had taken place in 1762;[16] the first prize was awarded by the Wolffian-dominated Academy to the Wolffian Moses Mendelssohn, but Kant's essay was thought sufficiently worthy of note to be published alongside of Mendelssohn's (although Kant did not receive any share of the fifty golden ducats that Mendelssohn received).

The essay on syllogisms foretold little of Kant's future philosophy, but the three other philosophical essays are all significant. In *The Only Possible Basis*, Kant reiterated his charge that "Existence is not a predicate or a determination of a thing" (OPB, 2:72), and further developed his own argument that the existence of God can be proven as the necessary condition of any *possibility* whatever (2:79–80).[17] The argument moves from the premise that if anything is possible, then something actual must exist to the conclusion that something necessary must exist, and this may seem to depend on a slide from the conclusion that something actual necessarily exists to the claim that something necessary necessarily exists (2:83). The argument might be defended, but Kant would not attempt to do so in his later critique of metaphysical arguments for the existence of God. At the same time, the work also defended at length a view of "purified" (2:113) teleology according to which any divine purposes for the world would have to be achieved not through any direct interventions in the course of nature but entirely through the operation of the laws of nature divinely established for the world – in other words, a reconciliation of efficient and final causation (see OPB, Fourth Reflection, 2:108–15). While the mature Kant would make it one of his most fundamental tenets that the existence of God can be asserted not as a "logical" but only as a "moral certainty" (CPuR, A 829/B 857), as a "postulate of pure practical reason" that we must believe in order to make our attempts to fulfill the demands of morality rational, he would also argue in the *Critique of the Power of Judgment* that this practical belief in God can be reconciled with natural science only through such a "purified" teleology.[18]

More immediate stepping-stones toward Kant's mature theoretical philosophy are found in the essays on "Negative Quantities" and the "Distinctness of the Principles of Natural Theology and Morality." The former starts with the observation that the opposition between a positive and a negative quantity is not a logical opposition, but a real opposition: while to assert p and not-p is always just a meaningless contradiction, by contrast to say, for example, that the wind acting on the sails of a ship has an eastward velocity of 5 knots per hour while the current has a westward velocity of the same speed, would not be to utter a contradiction, but to offer a meaningful and informative explanation of why the ship is not moving (OPB, 2:177). This might not be of much interest by itself, but it led Kant to the important insight that there are other differences between "logical" and "real" relations, and in particular to the insight that *causal* relations are real relations between states of objects and not logical relations of implication from concepts to predicates contained in them. This meant that the question why "because something is, something else is?" (2:202) could not be answered by mere logic or analysis at all, and that "something completely different" would have to be found on which to base our belief in causation. This was the end of Kant's flirtation with rationalist derivations of the principle of sufficient reason, and would ultimately lead to the entirely different approach to the principle of sufficient reason and metaphysical principles generally that he developed in the *Critique of Pure Reason*.

In the essay for the Berlin Academy's 1762 competition on philosophical method, Kant firmly rejected the idea that philosophy could reach certainty by the same method as mathematics, which the Academy obviously hoped would be defended – as it indeed was in the prize-winning essay by Mendelssohn. Mendelssohn argued that both mathematics and philosophy contain two elements: on the one hand a conceptual structure in which conclusions follow from premises with complete certainty and necessity, and on the other hand an indubitable experience through which the key premises of that structure are anchored in reality. Thus, he held, our sensory experience indubitably confirms the axioms of geometry, while the experience of our own thought (Descartes' famous *cogito*) and the ontological argument for the existence of God are the indubitable foundations for all of metaphysics.[19] Kant had already rejected the ontological argument, but now – without advance knowledge of Mendelssohn's essay – he rejected Mendelssohn's way of combining rationalism and empiricism more generally. For Kant (at this stage of his career), mathematics did not apply an analytical structure to empirical experience, but attained certainty because it could literally construct its objects from its own definitions, and then determine the further properties of those objects. Philosophy, on the contrary, could not construct its objects out of its own definitions, but could only reach definitions gradually through the analysis of common concepts, such as the concepts of substance or obligation. The use of the mathematical method would be a mere pretense in philosophy.

The Academy was quite right to give the prize to Mendelssohn's polished essay, for Kant's less well-written submission only dimly adumbrated the revolutionary views he would expound almost two decades later. Kant's view that mathematics can construct its own objects while philosophy cannot would remain a centerpiece of his philosophy, but at this time he gave no account of the relationship between the constructed objects of mathematics and the actual objects that we measure with mathematics in everyday life and science; supplying such an account would be the role of the controversial doctrine of transcendental idealism in the *Critique of Pure Reason*. And while Kant's discussion of metaphysics and morality in his essay had some interesting insights – the essay contains Kant's first published exposition of the distinction between hypothetical and categorical imperatives that would be the foundation of his mature moral philosophy (2:298–9) – it was really quite unclear what the method of philosophical analysis that Kant had in mind actually was. In fact, Kant would ultimately argue for a different account of the contrast between mathematical and philosophical method than the one he presents here: in his mature view, philosophy could not construct its own objects but nor could it be mere analysis; philosophy would turn out to contain not the construction of objects but the rules for the construction of our experience of objects, and these rules would come from a process of synthesis rather than analysis. But all of that remained to be explained.[20]

Kant's other publication of 1764, the little book of *Observations on the Feeling of the Beautiful and Sublime*, was not a theoretical work in aesthetics, as its title might have suggested,[21] but an essay in what we might call the anthropology of gender, culture, and race: Kant was primarily concerned with supposed differences among the aesthetic and more importantly the moral sensibilities – differences in the taste for the beautiful and the sublime, but also for learning, for duty and honor, and so on – between men and women, different nations, and, alas, different races.[22] But the work was popular, enjoying a second edition in 1771, and serving then as an advertisement for the lectures on anthropology that Kant would begin giving the next year and continue until his retirement in 1797. In the months after the book was first published, Kant used his own copy to write down a series of notes, some of which reveal significant progress at this time toward his mature moral philosophy.[23]

Two years after these publications, Kant published a very strange book called *Dreams of a Spirit-Seer Elucidated by Dreams of Metaphysics* (1766).[24] The book began as a critique of the Swedish mystic Emanuel Swedenborg (1688–1776), a once respectable scientist who (after what we would now call a mid-life crisis) claimed to have direct spiritual communication with the spirits of the departed and with God himself. Kant had little trouble debunking Swedenborg, but used the book as an occasion to criticize the claims of traditional metaphysics as well, especially the competing claims to understand the mind–body relationship: from a theoretical point of view, these were of no more merit than Swedenborg's spiritualist fantasies. However, Kant did not deny that the fantastical idea of direct communication among spirits could provide an image of the "universal reciprocal interaction" between *wills* or the "dependency of the private will on the general will" (DSS, 2: 335) that is the goal of morality – an image, in other words, of what Kant would later come to call the "realm of ends." Yet Kant also insisted that the possibility of morality is not dependent upon any knowledge of metaphysics, for "the human heart contain[s] within itself immediate moral prescriptions," and "it is more consonant with human nature and moral purity to base the expectation of a future world on the sentiments of a nobly constituted soul than, conversely, to base its noble conduct on the hope of another world" (DSS, 2: 273). The *Dreams of a Spirit-Seer* is sometimes held to be evidence of an "empiricist" phase in Kant's development. It is no such thing, because while it insists that sensory experience is *necessary* for genuine knowledge, it never suggests that sensory experience is *sufficient* for knowledge without additional rational principles. However, the book is clear evidence of Kant's lifelong belief that the fundamental principle of morality is readily accessible to every human being without any special learning, and that while morality might *ground* belief in God and even immortality, it does not *presuppose* such beliefs. This is the doctrine that Kant would later call the "postulates of pure practical reason," and with which he would conclude each of his three critiques.

We can gain a glimpse of Kant as a teacher during this productive period in his life from a fascinating document, his "Announcement of the program for his lectures for the winter semester 1765–66."[25] Still an unsalaried *Privatdozent*, Kant offered four lecture courses that semester: logic, metaphysics, ethics, and physical geography. Kant made his overriding aim as a teacher clear at the beginning of his advertisement for students:

> The teacher is . . . expected to develop in his pupil first the man of **understanding**, then the man of **reason**, and finally the man of **learning**. Such a procedure has this advantage: even if, as usually happens, the pupil should never reach the final phase, he will still have benefitted from his instruction. He will have grown more experienced and become more prudent, if not for school then at least for life.
>
> (2:306)[26]

Just as Kant's ultimate concern as a philosopher would become the preservation of the fundamental principle of morality from the metaphysical obstacles to it that we can create for ourselves, so his ultimate concern in teaching even the most abstract and abstruse subjects was the moral development of his students.[27] This is no surprise in the case of ethics, where Kant's aim was to "establish which perfection is appropriate to" human beings in the state of their "**primitive** innocence and which perfection is appropriate to" them "in the state of **wise** innocence." Nor is it surprising that in geography Kant's concern was more with "**moral** and **political** geography" than with the "physical features of the earth," and that "the second part of this subject," which several years later would become a separate course on anthropology, "considers the **human being**, throughout the world, from the point of view of the variety of his natural properties and the differences in that moral aspect in him" (2:312). But in logic Kant was also more concerned to develop "a critique and canon of **sound understanding**" than one of "**learnedness proper**" (2:310), and even in metaphysics Kant stressed that he would begin with "**empirical psychology**, which is really the metaphysical science of the **human being** based on experience," before discussing "**corporeal nature** in general" and theology, so that even if during the course of the semester the "lecture theater gradually grows empty" – as "everyone knows" it will! – the student will nonetheless have benefitted this much: he will have heard something which he can understand, on account of its easiness; he will have heard something which he can enjoy, in virtue of its interest; and he will have heard something which he can use, because of the many cases for its application in life.

(2:309–10)

But while the broad range as well as the underlying moral impetus of Kant's philosophizing had been illustrated by his burst of publications between 1762 and 1766, his two remaining publications in the decade would be specialized and academic. Returning to his early but long-standing interest in natural philosophy, in 1768, Kant published a little paper on "The differentiation of directions in space."[28] This paper returns to the great debate between the Newtonian conception of absolute space and the Leibnizian conception of space as a system of apparent relations between monads that are not intrinsically spatial, published in 1717 as the *Leibniz–Clarke Correspondence*.[29] Breaking with his countrymen, who took the side of Leibniz, Kant argued on behalf of absolute space, as **independent of the existence of all matter and itself . . . the first ground of the possibility of its composition**" (DDS, 2:378), by pointing to certain differences among otherwise qualitatively identical objects – the difference between right- and left-handed spirals in screw threads, hop vines, or snail shells (2:380), the difference between the right and left hand themselves (2:382–3) – which, according to Kant, do "not depend simply on the relation and position of [their] parts to each other," but also "on the reference of that physical form to universal absolute space" (2:381).[30]

In this short paper, Kant asked neither the metaphysical question "What is absolute space?" nor the epistemological question "What is the difference between the ways in which we know the relation of an object to absolute space and other relations among its properties?" Both of these questions would become central to his next work. In 1770, after he had declined the chair of poetry at Königsberg (he did not want to waste his time composing Latin poems for university and state ceremonies) and offers from the non-Prussian universities in Erlangen and Jena, Kant's long wait for a salaried professorship in philosophy finally came to an end when Frederick the Great named him to the chair of logic and metaphysics (paying 160 thalers per annum). The circumstances of the appointment do not reflect altogether well on Kant: it was actually the chair in mathematics that had become vacant, and at Kant's instigation the authorities freed the chair in logic and metaphysics for Kant by transferring its current occupant, who was apparently never consulted, to the chair in mathematics.[31] The rights and privileges of tenure were obviously neither well defined nor respected in absolutist Prussia. Be that as it may, his elevation to the chair required Kant to present and defend an inaugural dissertation, and this was the occasion for Kant's fourth and last Latin treatise, *De mundi sensibilis atque intelligibilis forma et principiis* ("On the form and principles of the sensible and intelligible worlds"), which was defended on August 21, 1770.[32] The inaugural dissertation took up precisely the metaphysical and epistemological questions that had been left hanging in the paper on space from two years before.[33]

Several years later, Kant remarked that "the year '69 gave me great light,"[34] and it was apparently at this time that he discovered that certain ancient and endless metaphysical controversies – is the world finite or infinite in extent and age, does it consist of indivisible simple parts or is it infinitely divisible? – are "antinomies" that can be solved or set aside only by radically reconceiving the nature of space and time and their relation to the abstract concepts of reality that we form by pure reason alone.[35] The inaugural dissertation begins with an analysis of the concept of a "world" as a "whole which is not a part" (ID, §1, 2:387). It then argues that space and time, although they do possess the formal properties of Newtonian absolute space and time that Kant ascribed to them in 1768, are in fact nothing but our own ways of "representing" or perceiving the world, and should not be thought to give us insight into the ultimate nature of reality (§§3–5, 13–15, 2:392–4, 398–406). The pure intellect alone, Kant now held, could give us such insight, through its conception of the world as a universe of substances connected to each other through their common dependence on their underlying cause, that is, God (§§6– 9, 16–44, 2:394–6, 406–10). The endless disputes of metaphysics could then be avoided by recognizing that the limits of our "sensibility" or sense-perception – not contingent limits in its range or acuity, but its necessary restriction to a spatio-temporal representation of reality – are not the limits of reality itself (§§23–30, 2:410–19).

Kant thought that the first part of this argument, the reduction of space and time, was a complete revolution in philosophical thought, although it would ultimately cost him considerable effort to distinguish his new view from apparently similar doctrines previously offered by Leibniz and the Irish philosopher George Berkeley. As for the second part of his argument, that the pure intellect gives us the insight into the nature of reality that our spatio-temporal sensibility does not, Kant himself would reject this after a further decade of arduous work: when the *Critique of Pure Reason*, after many promises, finally appeared in 1781, it would argue that although sensibility and intellect are fundamentally different cognitive capacities, sensibility producing "intuitions" or representations of particular objects and the intellect "concepts" or representations only of general types of objects, the latter could not yield genuine knowledge without the data provided by the former, and thus that *all* of our knowledge is restricted to the way in which the world necessarily appears to creatures like us – although we also remain free to *think* of the world in other ways, and even *must* do so for the purposes of morality. This would be Kant's full-blown doctrine of "transcendental idealism."

The inaugural dissertation was thus a way-station on the way to the first *Critique*. But since its conception of space and time would be largely taken over in the subsequent work, it is worth spending a moment with that now. Kant begins the book with a distinction that is crucial to all his subsequent work: building upon the distinction between spatial properties of objects that can be captured by concepts and those that cannot, which was the basis for his argument in the 1768 essay on regions in space, he now introduces a general distinction between "sensibility," as the "receptivity" of a cognitive "subject in virtue of which it is possible for the subject's own representative state to be affected . . . by the presence of some object," and "intelligence" as the "power of a subject in virtue of which it has the power to represent things that cannot by their own quality come before the senses of that subject" (ID, §3, 2:392). Kant then introduces a general premise, which he in fact will not mention in the *Critique of Pure Reason*, that "whatever in cognition is sensitive" – that is, comes to us through sensibility – "is dependent upon the special character of the subject in so far as the subject is capable of this or that modification by the presence of objects," from which it immediately follows "that things which are thought sensitively are representations of things *as they appear*" (§4, 2:392). Thus, he will here take any feature of objects that can be shown to be essentially connected to the sensible representation of them to be a feature only of the appearances of those objects to creatures constituted like ourselves. Conversely, he premises that "things which are intellectual are representations of things *as they are*," so that whatever turns out to be essential to any thought of things but is independent of their appearance to our sensibility will be taken to be knowledge of those things as they are in themselves. Borrowing ancient terminology, Kant calls the objects of sensibility, which are merely the way things appear to us, "*phenomena*" (from the Greek verb *phainō* "to appear"), while the things as they are in themselves and as they are known to be through pure intellect (*nous*) are called "*noumena*" (§3, 2:392).

Kant then argues that there are two "absolutely primary and universal formal principles of the *phenomenal universe*": forms that are indispensable to all sensible representation of objects, but, given Kant's premise, for that very reason properties only of the appearances of things, not properties of those things as they are in themselves. These are time and space. For each of these, Kant argues first that the ideas of them are singular and not general: that we do not conceive of space and time as general kinds of things each of which may have multiple instances, but always represent particular times and spaces as limited regions of a single larger time and space (*ID*, §§14.2–3, 2:399, 15.B–C, 402–4). Second, Kant argues that time and space are not anything "objective and real," neither "a substance, nor an accident, nor a relation," but rather "the subjective conditions" which are "necessary, in virtue of the nature of the human mind, for the co-ordinating of all sensible things in accordance with a fixed law" (§§14.5, 2:400, 15.D, 2:403). Kant offers several considerations in behalf of this position. First, he argues that we can distinguish substances and accidents from each other and relate them to each other only in time and space, so space and time cannot be identical to either of the former. Second, he argues that to think of time and space as none of those but as some other form of external reality – like Newton's absolute space and time – is absurd. And, finally, he argues, particularly in the case of space, that it is only if the forms of sensible intuition are *nothing but* subjective conditions or the forms of our own representations of things that we can have knowledge of the absolute rather than merely comparative universality and necessity of the most fundamental propositions about them, which he takes it we surely do, as is witnessed by our absolute certainty with regard to geometry as a description of the structure of space (§15.D, 2:404). Kant does not use these terms here, but his argument is the same as what he would later express by saying that we can have synthetic *a priori* cognition of the structure of space and time only if we have *a priori* representations of space and time and indeed only if space and time are nothing but those *a priori* representations, or the *a priori* forms of all of our sensible representations of particular objects. We can save questions about the necessity or even plausibility of this conclusion until later, but even now we should note that this argument from synthetic *a priori* cognition to the subjectivity of what is cognized is independent of the general premise that whatever is characteristic of sensibility is merely a matter of how things appear to us.

For better or worse, Kant's view of space and time will not undergo substantial revision in his subsequent works. However, his view of the intellect and its role in knowledge will undergo a complete reversal. In the inaugural dissertation, Kant first describes a "logical use" of the intellect, which is basically just a matter of properly sorting out and organizing appearances we have experienced (ID, §5, 2:394), in contrast to its "real use," in which it gives us knowledge of the nature of things as they are in themselves. Kant states that metaphysics is the part of philosophy that "contains the first principles of the [real] use of the pure understanding," and thus that such typical metaphysical concepts as "possibility, existence, necessity, substance, cause, etc.," give us insight into the nature of things in themselves (§8, 2:395). On this basis, he then constructs an argument that multiple substances can comprise a single world only if they are all effects of a common cause, which must itself be a necessary being – in other words, God (§§16–22, 2:406–10). Finally, he argues that metaphysical confusions such as the "antinomies," that is, the endless and apparently undecidable arguments about whether the world is finite or infinite and the like – arise only because "principles which are native to sensitive cognition" are allowed to "transgress their limits, and affect what belongs to the understanding" (§24, 2:411). The way to avoid metaphysical confusion, in other words, is to recognize that the intellect gives us knowledge of things as they are in themselves, and that concepts that are essential to our sensible representation of things should not be allowed to get in the way of that knowledge. In particular, Kant argues, we should not think of the limits of our senses and their formal principles as if they were limits on the nature of reality itself or of our knowledge of reality (§26, 2:413).

When Kant's student and respondent Marcus Herz took copies of his teacher's inaugural dissertations to the leading philosophers in Berlin – Johann Heinrich Lambert, Johann Georg Sulzer, and Moses Mendelssohn – they did not object at all to Kant's confidence that we can have metaphysical insight into the nature of reality. They were, however, astonished at Kant's claim that time is only a feature of how things – more precisely, our own representations of things – appear to us, not a feature of how things are in themselves. If our representations themselves change, they asked, how can time not be a real property of our representations, thus of our minds and of reality itself? As Lambert succinctly put it, "If changes are real, then time is real, whatever it may be . . . even an idealist must grant at least that changes really exist and occur in his representations."[36] Kant was not much worried by this objection; in the Critique of Pure Reason, a decade later, he would raise it only to reject it out of hand (A 36–7 / B 53–4). Instead, he began to worry about the theory of the intellect that he had offered. As he wrote in a now-famous letter to Herz in February, 1772, "in my dissertation I was content to explain the nature of intellectual representations in a merely negative way," but "had failed to consider . . . the key to the whole secret of metaphysics," namely how the "intellectual representations" or "pure concepts of the understanding," that is, precisely such concepts as "possibility, existence, necessity, substance, cause, etc.", can "depend on our inner activity" and yet also be supposed to be in agreement with objects (Corr, 10:130–1). Kant thought he could answer this question shortly – indeed, in three months' time – in a work that he would entitle The Bounds of Sensibility and Reason.[37] In fact, it would take Kant nearly ten years to write the work that would explain how such purely intellectual concepts, which must originate in the mind because we have a priori knowledge of them, must nevertheless apply to all of our experience, but also that they can yield genuine knowledge only when we apply them to experience. We may use them to think of objects that would be beyond the reach of all experience, Kant would eventually argue, such as God or an immortal soul, but since the pure concepts of the understanding cannot yield any knowledge except by being applied to our sensible representations, they cannot provide us any knowledge of things beyond the reach of our senses. This would be the gist of what Kant had taken to calling by 1776 a "critique of pure reason."[38]

THE CRITICAL PHILOSOPHY

For the rest of the 1770s, Kant published virtually nothing. Perhaps it had been a mistake to grant him a salaried and tenured professorship after all his years as a lowly lecturer.[39] But at the Easter book fair in April, 1781, the book finally appeared that would not only secure Kant's personal reputation but change the face of all subsequent philosophy, the book entitled, as Kant had hinted to Herz five years earlier, the Critique of Pure Reason. Two years after the book was published, Kant would write to Moses Mendelssohn – who had protested, perhaps disingenuously, that much as he wanted to, the Critique was so difficult that his "weak nerves" prevented him from finishing it[40] – that "although the book is the product of nearly twelve years of reflection, I completed it hastily, in perhaps four or five months, with the greatest attentiveness to its content but less care about its style and ease of comprehension."[41] It is hard to credit Kant's statement that he wrote a book of 883 pages in four or five months,[42] but it is certainly true that Kant had not made the book easy for its initial readers. This became clear when, after what seemed to Kant like an interminable wait, the first review of the Critique appeared in January, 1782: the review in the important Göttingen Scholarly News dismissed the part of the work that had cost Kant the most trouble, the "transcendental deduction of the pure concepts of the understanding" that would explain why such concepts must be applied to appearances and only to appearances, as unintelligible, and dismissed Kant's new "transcendental idealism" as nothing but the "subjective idealism" of Bishop Berkeley with a new name.[43] Kant was already at work on what he hoped would be a more accessible introduction to the *Critique*, but then used the occasion both to simplify his argument for the universal and necessary application – or "objective validity" – of the pure concepts of the understanding, and to defend his "transcendental idealism" from the charge of subjectivism. This summary and defense of the *Critique of Pure Reason* appeared in 1783, under the mouthful of a title *Prolegomena to Any Future Metaphysics that will be able to come forth as a Science*. But Kant's first attempt to defend the *Critique* was far from completely successful, and Kant would make substantial revisions at least in the presentation if not in the substance of his argument in a second edition of the *Critique* published in 1787. There would be occasion for further polemics over the meaning after that year as well.[44]

The *Critique of Pure Reason* argues that all knowledge requires both input from the senses and organization by concepts, and that both sensory inputs and organizing concepts have pure forms that we can know *a priori*, thus know to be universally and necessarily valid. The pure forms of ordinary sensory inputs, or what Kant calls empirical intuition, are the structures of space and time studied by mathematics, and the pure forms of ordinary empirical concepts are the pure concepts of the understanding, or the categories, which make it possible to apply the various aspects and forms of judgment studied by logic to objects of experience. Mathematics itself contains synthetic *a priori* judgments that are universally and necessarily true of all appearances, and must be derived from the construction of mathematical objects in pure intuition rather than from the analysis of concepts; and the categories yield synthetic *a priori* principles – such as the principles of the conservation of substance and of the universality of causation – when they are applied to experience with its necessarily spatio-temporal structure. This is the constructive theory of the *Critique of Pure Reason*. But the *Critique* also contains a critical argument: that although through our power of inferential reason we can use the pure concepts of the understanding to conceive of objects that lie beyond the limits of our sensible intuition – we can imagine a spatio-temporal universe that has a kind of completeness that our indefinitely extendable actual intuitions never have, or objects such as God or an immaterial soul that cannot be represented in sensory experience at all – such conceptions do not amount to knowledge, and to think that they do only leads to the fallacies and contradictions of traditional metaphysics. However, Kant also held a teleological conception of human powers, according to which none of our powers fails to have a proper use if only we understand it correctly (see G, 4:395), and argued that the ideas of pure reason – a name he adopted in homage to Plato (see CPuR, A 312–20/B 369–77) – do have a legitimate use, or yield a "canon" (A 795–831/B 823–59), but in morality rather than scientific theory. Although knowledge of the existence of God and our own freedom and immortality cannot be theoretically demonstrated, Kant argues, neither can they be disproven, and they are necessary presuppositions of moral conduct – objects of moral belief or faith although not knowledge. This is what Kant meant by his famous statement in the Preface to the second edition of the Critique that he found it necessary "to deny **knowledge** in order to make room for **faith**" (B xx).

At the time that he wrote the Critique, Kant clearly thought that this combination of constructive and critical argumentation would provide adequate foundations for all of philosophy, and after his initial defense of the Critique in the Prolegomena he was prepared to proceed directly from "transcendental philosophy" to his revised form of "metaphysics," the application of the synthetic a priori principles of experience won in the former to the most elementary concepts of natural science and morality. And he did indeed quickly produce a work entitled Metaphysical Foundations of Natural Science, published in 1786, in which he attempted to derive the fundamental principles of Newtonian physics by applying his synthetic a priori principles of experience to the concept of matter as that which is moveable in space. But before he could proceed directly to an analogous "Metaphysics of Morals" (which he had been promising since the 1760s), Kant realized that more foundational work for moral philosophy needed to be done. The first fruit of this effort was the Groundwork for the Metaphysics of Morals (1785), in which Kant first showed that the fundamental principle of morality can be derived from both the common-sense notion of a good will as the only thing of unconditional value (Section I) and the philosophical conception of a categorical imperative (Section II), and then attempted to argue that we must have free will and that any being with free will can act only in accordance with this fundamental principle of morality (Section III). The heart of this work, today the most widely read of Kant's works and indeed, along with several of Plato's dialogues and John Stuart Mill's On Liberty, probably the most widely read of all works in the Western philosophical tradition, is Kant's analysis of the "categorical imperative" in Section II. The categorical imperative is the form that the fundamental principle of morality takes when applied to imperfectly rational creatures like ourselves: even though this principle can originate only in our own reason, and is not externally imposed upon us by any other divine or human ruler, it can still appear like a constraint because we also have inclinations that would if unchecked lead us to act contrary to it (G, 4:412–14). On Kant's analysis, the categorical imperative requires us to act only on "maxims" or principles of action that can be "universalized," that is, that could be accepted and acted on by everyone who would be affected by our own actions. We must act only on universalizable principles, in turn, because that is the way to treat every person, ourselves as well as all others, always as ends and never merely as means (4:429). And, finally, what would result if indeed we all acted on the categorical imperative is a "realm of ends," a "whole of all ends in systematic connection (a whole both of rational beings as ends in themselves and of the ends of his own that each may set himself") (4:433) – that is, a situation in which each person is treated as intrinsically valuable, not as a mere means to the ends of anyone else, and in which for that very reason the particular ends set by each person are promoted by all to the extent that this can consistently be done. When he finally came to publish the long-promised *Metaphysics of Morals* itself a dozen years later (1797), what Kant would offer would be an analysis of private property, contract, and family as the forms of justice necessary to ground the implementation of the abstract ideal of a realm of ends, and then a derivation of the public institutions and the private virtues necessary to maintain these forms of justice and the individual ends – and thus happiness – that they ultimately make possible.

By 1786, the long-silent Kant had thus suddenly published four books of immense accomplishment. During the same years, Kant also published a number of briefer essays of enduring interest, including his famous "Reply to the Question: What is Enlightenment?" and "Idea for a Universal History from a Cosmopolitan Point of View," both in 1784; a critical review of Johann Herder's *Ideas for the Philosophy of the History of Mankind* and an essay on "The Determination of the Concept of a Human Race" in 1785, and "The Conjectural Beginning of Human History" and "What Does it Mean to Orient Oneself in Thought?", an intervention on the debate then raging between Moses Mendelssohn and Friedrich Heinrich Jacobi on the relation between faith and reason, both in 1786. He must have thought that with the *Critique of Pure Reason* and then the *Groundwork* his work on the foundations of philosophy was largely done, and that he could finally turn to the long-awaited and cherished project of the *Metaphysics of Morals*. But this was not how things turned out. In 1786, the publisher's stock of the first edition of the Critique of Pure Reason was dwindling, and Kant took the opportunity of a request for a second edition to make some substantial revisions that he thought would facilitate comprehension of his position, notably a completely rewritten "Transcendental Deduction of the Pure Concepts of the Understanding," that is, the deduction of the categories, and an entirely new "Refutation of Idealism," which he clearly hoped would distinguish his own "transcendental" or, as he now called it, "critical idealism" from the merely "subjective idealism" of George Berkeley. This revised edition was published in 1787. At some point in working on it, Kant also decided that he needed to clarify the relation between treatments of the freedom of the will in the Critique of Pure Reason and the Groundwork as well as to expand upon the doctrine of the presuppositions of morality or "postulates of pure practical reason" offered in the Critique; this work soon grew beyond what he could fit into the revision of the first Critique and led to the publication of a previously unplanned Critique of Practical Reason in 1788. This work does not initially appear to add much to Kant's normative moral philosophy, that is, the analysis of the categorical imperative already published in the Groundwork, and instead seems to be aimed at providing a more cogent treatment of freedom of the will and a fuller exposition of the postulates of God and immortality, which had not been mentioned in the Groundwork at all. But in order to provide the latter, Kant expands upon a concept merely touched upon in the first Critique, namely that of the "highest" or "complete good," and argues that the conjunction of maximal virtue and maximal happiness which constitutes this highest good is what requires the presupposition of God and immortality. The last step in this argument is controversial, but the concept of the highest good is itself of the highest importance for Kant's moral philosophy, for it casts doubt on the total separation between the formal principle of obligation and the concern for the ends of our actions that has often been thought to be the essence of Kant's view. Needless to say, we shall return to these issues.

Even after the Critique of Practical Reason, Kant still could not turn directly to the concrete metaphysics of morals, that is, his theory of political justice and individual virtue. This is because he suddenly saw the need to write a third Critique. Kant had long been interested in the subject of aesthetics that had emerged in eighteenth-century philosophy, and even his first plan for the Critique of Pure Reason had suggested it would include a "Doctrine of Taste."[45] That plan had apparently been long forgotten, but suddenly re-emerged in 1787, and by the end of that year had become connected with the plan to write a critique of teleological thinking, a subject Kant had not really touched since his 1763 book on the only possible basis for a proof of the existence of God. Kant announced this plan in a letter to his then disciple Karl Leonhard Reinhold, sent on December 31, 1787, but by no means made clear what connection between aesthetics and teleology he had in mind. The first fruit of this new work was an essay on "The Use of Teleological Principles in Philosophy" that he published in 1788, but this was primarily a contribution to the debate about race that he had already engaged with in 1775, and says nothing about the connection between aesthetics and teleology. However, the work on the third Critique went quickly, and it was published at Easter in 1790, just nine years after the first Critique, under the title Critique of the Power of Judgment. Kant begins this work with the claim that there is "an incalculable gulf" between the "domain of the concept of nature . . . and the domain of the concept of freedom" which is now to be bridged (CPJ, 5:175–6). It is not immediately clear what this gap is, for had not the Critique of Practical Reason already shown how freedom of the human will can subsist alongside of the thoroughgoing determinism of nature argued for in the Critique of Pure Reason? But as the book progresses, it becomes clear that what Kant thinks is that as creatures who are sensible as well as rational, we need sensory representation and confirmation of the idea of the consistency of morality and nature, and that we find this in the experience of natural beauty, natural sublimity, artistic genius, the quasi-purposiveness of the internal organization of living beings, and even in the view of nature as a systematic whole to which we are psychologically even if not logically compelled by our experience of individual organisms within nature. When he was attempting to expound the fundamental principle of morality in its purest form, Kant often made it look as if there could be nothing but conflict between our sensory inclinations and our moral principles, but the point of the third Critique is to show nothing less than that human beings are rational beings who can nevertheless be at home in nature, indeed the nature within their own skins as well as outside them.

FINAL WORKS

With the Critique of the Power of Judgment, Kant's work on the foundations of philosophy was surely done; but now external events intervened to delay the Metaphysics of Morals yet again. While Kant had been writing the second and third critiques, the world of the Enlightenment had been falling apart around him, in Prussia with the death of Frederick the Great in 1786, and the succession of his religiously conservative nephew Frederick William II, and in France, of course, with the encouraging start of the French revolution in 1789, and then its degeneration into the Terror by 1793; and these events called for responses from Kant. In 1793, Kant published an essay "On the Old Saying: That May Be Correct in Theory but Is of No Use in Practice," which offers what may be his clearest exposition of his conception of the highest good, and then goes on to provide his first statement of his political philosophy, uneasily combining an insistence on republican government with a rejection of forcible rebellion as the means to its achievement. This would be followed in 1795 with his famous pamphlet *Toward Perpetual Peace*, which argues that republican government for all states is the only possible basis for enduring peace (while skirting the question of how such widespread republicanism is to be achieved). Meanwhile, in 1792, Kant published another essay, "Concerning Radical Evil in Human Nature," which would become the first of the four parts of *Religion within the Boundaries of Mere Reason*, published with the imprimatur of the Königsberg philosophy faculty – but not its faculty of theology – in 1793. This book continues the project of the third *Critique* by arguing that the central ideas of Christianity can also be taken as sensory images of the fundamental concepts of morality, but is far more radical than the preceding book in its argument that this is the best way to comprehend the central ideas of Christianity: religion within the boundaries of mere reason is nothing but a religion grounded in pure morality. This book so incensed Frederick William II and his equally conservative minister Wöllner that in October, 1794, Kant was issued a royal rescript prohibiting him from publishing further criticisms of religion, to which Kant was forced to accede.[46]

Prohibited from further publication on religion, Kant finally followed the essay on peace with the long-awaited *Metaphysics of Morals*, the first part of which, "The Metaphysical Foundations of the Doctrine of Right," appeared early in 1797, with the second part, on the "The Metaphysical Doctrine of Virtue," following some months later, and an amplified book containing both following in 1798. In the first part of this work, Kant argues that because of the inescapable fact of our common habitation of an undivided earth, our rights to property and contract can be secure only within a republic, and that our innate freedom to acquire property entails that we have not merely a right but also a duty to establish republican government – although again only by reform, not by rebellion. In the second part of the book, he argues that because we are not pure but are also embodied reasoners, morality does not just require an abstract decision to conform our maxims to the moral law, but an enduring effort to cultivate the virtues of both mind and body that will allow us to strive successfully for our own perfection and the happiness of others. The recognition that we are embodied creatures with material needs living on an undivided earth is the basic empirical fact to which the *Metaphysics of Morals* applies the entirely rational moral law, just as the idea of matter as the moveable is the basic empirical fact to which the *Metaphysical Foundations of Natural Science* applies the synthetic *a priori* principles of the possibility of experience.

Also in 1797, Frederick William II died, and Kant believed himself to be free from what he understood to be his personal promise to that king only not to publish further on religion. The result was Kant's last major work, the *Conflict of the Faculties*, published in 1798. This work addresses not the conflict among the faculties of mind such as sensibility and reason which had been the subject of Kant's critiques, but the conflict among the university faculties of theology, law, medicine, and philosophy. The gist of Kant's argument is that while the faculties of theology, law, and medicine prepare their students to execute governmentally defined functions in civil society, and therefore must train them to obey well-established regulations, the role of the philosophy faculty is to search for truth regardless of current prejudices and regimes – and even that since the philosophy faculty is itself an organ of the state in the Germany of Kant's day (all universities were public rather than private) the state has the duty to support the organ of its own critique! A stronger argument for academic freedom has rarely been offered.

At the age of 72, Kant gave up lecturing in 1796, although only then, too late to benefit from it financially, did he turn to the common practice of publishing handbooks for one's own courses, issuing an *Anthropology from a Pragmatic Point of View* under his own name in 1798 and permitting Benjamin Gottlob Jäsche to compile a logic textbook from his lecture notes in 1800. This was the last published work in which Kant had a hand, although textbooks on pedagogy and physical geography were issued in 1802 and unfinished drafts of an essay on the progress of metaphysics in Germany since the time of Leibniz and Wolff were published shortly after his death.

But Kant had been far from idle in his final years. From 1796 or 1797 to 1800 or even 1801, he worked constantly on a manuscript that was first to be a "transition from the metaphysical principles of natural science to physics," and was ultimately to be a final statement of the transcendental philosophy itself. Kant's first conception of the project was to take *a priori* physics even further than he had in the *Metaphysical Foundations* of 1786 by giving an *a priori* derivation of all possible inorganic and organic forces, and even of an all-pervasive ether as the medium for the transmission of energy throughout the universe, including the transmitted energy that is the basis of our own perception of the physical world.[47] In the later stages of his work, Kant was attempting to show that the concepts of nature and of God are both projections of our own thought, the former an expression of the conditions of our experience and the latter an expression of the power of our own reason to give ourselves moral legislation. This last point represents a final step in Kant's critique of traditional religion, for while he had previously considered the existence of God to be the subject of a theoretical proposition that can be asserted only on practical grounds, he now denied that God is a substance outside of our own minds at all – he is nothing but our own idea of our moral power. But this thought went unknown in Kant's time: with his powers failing, Kant was not able to complete the projected work before his death on February 12, 1804, and the many pages of manuscript that he had accumulated but not finished were only published in the twentieth century.[48]

SUMMARY

Kant was brought up on both the German version of rationalism and the new science of Newtonianism, and from the beginning of his career he tried to reconcile both of these. In his first philosophical works of 1755–56 and 1762–64, his characteristic project of trying to establish both the foundations of natural science and the possibility of freedom of the will emerged. Kant developed transcendental idealism as the solution to the problem of our synthetic *a priori* knowledge of the structure of space and time by 1770, but it took him until the *Critique of Pure Reason* in 1781 to develop his complete theory of knowledge, his critique of traditional metaphysics, and the idea of a new form of metaphysics grounded in the necessities of practical rather than theoretical reason. During the remainder of the 1780s, Kant defended his new philosophy, worked out its application to natural science, and developed the foundations of his moral philosophy. The *Critique of the Power of Judgment* of 1790 inaugurated Kant's final project of applying his *a priori* principles of theoretical and practical reason to the natural condition of humankind, which led to his aesthetics, the final statement of his teleology, his philosophy of religion, his political philosophy, and his conception of specifically human virtue. In his last years, Kant attempted a restatement of the entire critical philosophy, but his powers waned before he could complete it.

With this outline of Kant's life and career before us, we can now turn to a more detailed discussion of Kant's mature philosophy, beginning with the *Critique of Pure Reason*.

FURTHER READING

The standard biography of Kant is now:
Manfred Kuehn, *Kant* (Cambridge: Cambridge University Press, 2001).

Two indispensable works on the background of Kant's philosophy are:
Lewis White Beck, *Early German Philosophy: Kant and his Predecessors* (Cambridge, MA: Harvard University Press, 1969).
J.B. Schneewind, *The Invention of Autonomy: A History of Modern Moral Philosophy* (Cambridge: Cambridge University Press, 1998).

An earlier but still valuable work on the development of Kant's ethics is:
Josef Schmucker, *Die Ursprünge der Ethik Kants* (Meinsenheim am Glan: Verlag Anton Hain, 1961).

Two valuable works on Kant's development prior to the *Critique of Pure Reason* already mentioned are:
Alison Laywine, *Kant's Early Metaphysics and the Origins of the Critical Philosophy* (Atascadero, CA: Ridgeview Publishing Company, 1993).
Martin Schönfeld, *The Philosophy of the Young Kant: The Precritical Project* (Oxford: Oxford University Press, 2000).

A work that places Kant's work throughout his career in the context of the major philosophical debates of his own time is:
Frederick C. Beiser, *The Fate of Reason: German Philosophy from Kant to Fichte* (Cambridge, MA: Harvard University Press, 1987).

Books on the major works from 1781 to 1790 will be suggested in later chapters. Two works that do offer synoptic views of the less-studied works of the 1790s are shown below. The Fenves book views Kant's final works as constituting a major departure from rather than consolidation of the work of the 1780s, the view to be taken here:
Heiner Bielefeldt, *Symbolic Representation in Kant's Practical Philosophy* (Cambridge: Cambridge University Press, 2003).
Peter Fenves, *Late Kant: Towards Another Law of the Earth* (London and New York: Routledge, 2003).

Important works on Kant's *Opus postumum*, which will not be further discussed in this volume, include:
Eckart Förster, *Kant's Final Synthesis: An Essay on the Opus postumum* (Cambridge, MA: Harvard University Press, 2000).
Forum für Philosophie Bad Homburg (eds), *Übergang: Untersuchungen zum Spätwerk Immanuel Kants* (Frankfurt am Main: Vittorio Klostermann, 1991).
Michael Friedman, *Kant and the Exact Sciences* (Cambridge, MA: Harvard University Press, 1992), Part Two.

Part One

Nature

Two

Kant's Copernican Revolution

This chapter and the next will consider the central themes of Kant's theoretical philosophy as presented in the *Critique of Pure Reason*: this long chapter will discuss Kant's positive view of the elements and limits of human knowledge, and the next, shorter chapter will discuss the criticism of the pretensions of traditional metaphysics that Kant makes on the basis of his own positive view. After first explaining how Kant conceives of the basic problem for theoretical philosophy as a problem about the possibility of "synthetic *a priori* judgment," I will then review the series of steps he takes in the *Critique* in order to demonstrate that such cognition is indeed possible.

INTRODUCTION

In the Preface to the second edition of the *Critique of Pure Reason*, Kant writes that the "general" and "real problem of pure reason is . . . contained in the question: **How are synthetic judgments *a priori* possible**?" (B 19). Kant would henceforth formulate the deepest questions of philosophy, such as the questions about the unconditional authority of the moral law and even about the universal validity of judgments of taste, as questions about the possibility of synthetic *a priori* judgments (see G, 4:444–5, and CPJ, §36, 5:288). So the first question about Kant's mature philosophy is: what is a synthetic *a priori* judgment?

Kant arrives at his conception of synthetic *a priori* judgment by giving new names to two old distinctions, and then combining them. First, he distinguishes "**cognitions** *a priori*...from **empirical** ones, which have their sources *a posteriori*, namely in experience" (B 2). Earlier philosophers had used the terms *a priori* and *a posteriori* to designate different kinds of inferences or arguments: those from causes to effects and those from effects back to causes, respectively;[1] but Kant uses these two terms to characterize different kinds of knowledge.[2] Empirical, *a posteriori* cognitions are simply those that are based on the experience of particular objects – for example, my knowledge that the copy of the *Critique of Pure Reason* from which I have just quoted is bound in blue cloth is empirical and *a posteriori* because it is based on my visual perception of the book today and many previous times. *A priori* cognitions, conversely, are those that are not based on any experience of particular objects, even though they may – indeed, as Kant ultimately argues, must – *apply* only to such objects. *A posteriori* knowledge is always knowledge of something contingent for Kant,[3] who accepts the position earlier argued by Hume that "Experience teaches us, to be sure, that something is constituted thus and so, but not that it could not be otherwise" (B 3). Experience tells us only that those objects that have actually been observed are a certain way, not that all objects, even of some particular kind, must be that way. By contrast, if we are ever in a position to claim that all objects of some kind must be some particular way, that is, to make judgments that claim "**necessity**" and "true or strict . . . **universality**," then our knowledge cannot be *a posteriori*, but must be *a priori* – we must somehow make our judgment independently of appeal to any particular experiences.[4] "Necessity and strict universality are therefore secure indications of an *a priori* cognition" (B 4).

Next, "analytic" and "synthetic" are Kant's terms for two kinds of judgments, or in more contemporary terms, propositions that are the contents of acts of judgment, thus of belief or knowledge. An analytic judgment is one in which "the predicate B belongs to the subject A as something that is (covertly) contained in this concept A," and which is therefore thought to be true "through identity" (A 6–7 / B 10). In other words, where the meaning of a concept A is actually constituted by a conjunction of predicates including B, for example BC, the proposition "A is B" is true because it is really equivalent to "BC is B," and this is true because "B is B" is always true; for example, the proposition "All bachelors are unmarried" is true just because "bachelor" means "unmarried male," and the proposition "All unmarried males are unmarried" is true "through identity."[5] In our terms, then, analytic propositions are those that are true simply in virtue of the meanings of their terms and the laws of logic.[6] Synthetic propositions, conversely, are those in which the predicate "B lies entirely outside the concept A, although to be sure it stands in connection with it" (A 6 / B 10); thus, true synthetic propositions are those that are true in spite of the fact that the predicate is *not* contained in the concept of the subject, and must therefore be made true by something other than the meanings of the terms involved and the laws of logic. Kant states that analytic judgments can also be called "**judgments of clarification**," for they simply clarify what is already implicit in our concepts, while synthetic judgments can be called "**judgments of amplification**," because − when they are true, of course − they genuinely add information to what is already contained in our concept of their subjects (A 7/B 11).

What happens when we combine these two distinctions? Well, analytic judgments clearly can and must be known *a priori*: once we understand the meaning of the terms "bachelor," "male," and "unmarried" and know the laws of logic (although learning the meaning of concepts, to be sure, may itself be a matter of experience, for Kant, learning the laws of logic cannot be), we can know that all bachelors are unmarried by applying the laws of logic to the meaning of "bachelor" without making empirical observations of any bachelors. Indeed, we can only know that *all* bachelors are unmarried by such an inference from the meaning of the terms, since any amount of observation could only teach us that *some* bachelors − namely, those we have observed − are unmarried. In fact, we can only classify an observed male *as* a bachelor in the first place if we already know him to be unmarried − that's what it means for "unmarried" to be part of the meaning of "bachelor." Equally clear, many synthetic propositions can only be known *a posteriori*, that is, from observation or experience: I can only know that my copy of the *Critique of Pure Reason* is blue by observing it, because the predicate "blue" is certainly not contained in the concept *book*, or the concept of the *Critique of Pure Reason*, or of an English translation of the *Critique* − different editions and translations of the *Critique* have come in many different colors. So there are analytic *a priori* cognitions − that is, analytic propositions known *a priori* − and synthetic *a posteriori* cognitions. Is that all? An earlier philosopher such as Hume had thought so: in his terms, "All the objects of human reason or enquiry may naturally be divided into two kinds, to wit, *Relations of Ideas*" − that is, analytic and therefore *a priori* cognition − "and *Matters of Fact*" − that is, particular synthetic propositions known *a posteriori*.[7] But in Kant's view, while there cannot be such a thing as an analytic proposition known *a posteriori* (even though some of the concepts in such propositions may be empirical), there not only can be but are synthetic *a priori* cognitions. Indeed, for Kant, all the fundamental propositions of philosophy as well as the contents of pure mathematics and even the basic principles of natural science are nothing less than synthetic *a priori* cognitions,[8] and the project of the *Critique of Pure Reason* is precisely to convince us that Hume was wrong to disallow synthetic *a priori* principles in philosophy – although of course Hume had not expressed his doubts about philosophical principles in these terms – and thus to refute Humean skepticism about first principles, the position that even the most fundamental principles of our knowledge, such as that every event has a cause, are based on experience, and therefore never have real necessity and true or strict universality, but are contingent propositions with at best "assumed and comparative" universality (B 3).[9]

Now it must be noted at the outset that Kant creates some confusion about just what questions about synthetic *a priori* cognition his philosophy is intended to answer. In the *Prolegomena* and in some passages carried over from that work into the revised introduction of the second edition of the *Critique of Pure Reason*, Kant makes it seem as if everyone already knows that there is such a thing as synthetic *a priori* cognition – in pure mathematics and pure physical science – and that the task of philosophy is just, first, to explain *how* such actual cognition is possible, and then, second, to demonstrate *from* that explanation that there are some *further* synthetic *a priori* cognitions in metaphysics itself (*Prolegomena*, §§2–4, 4:268–75; *Pure Reason*, B 14–22). This is why Kant says that the *method* of the *Prolegomena* is analytic – here now using the term in its traditional sense of a regress from effects back to their causes rather than in his own new sense – for it relies "on something already known to be dependable, from which we can go forward with confidence and ascend to the sources, which are not yet known, and whose discovery not only will explain what is known already" – that is, pure mathematics and physics – "but will also exhibit an area with many cognitions that all arise from these same sources" (4:275) – that is, whatever is legitimately known in metaphysics.

Of course, if one doubts that mathematics and physics do contain synthetic *a priori* cognition, then the use of this analytic or regressive method to arrive at further metaphysical truths is in trouble from the outset. But in the *Prolegomena*, Kant says that "In the *Critique of Pure Reason* I worked on this question *synthetically*, namely by inquiring within pure reason itself, and seeking to determine within this source both the elements and the laws of its pure use, according to principles" (4:274). This statement is gnomic, but seems to suggest that at least in the first edition of the *Critique*, thus in his original conception of it, Kant did *not* intend to *presuppose* that we have any synthetic *a priori* cognition, in mathematics or in metaphysics, but instead meant somehow to identify some indisputably basic elements of *any* cognition and then to show from those results that we in fact have synthetic *a priori* cognition not only in metaphysics but in pure mathematics and physical science as well. As he put it in the Preface to the first edition of the *Critique*, talking about his central "Deduction of the

Pure Concepts of the Understanding," his objective is both "to demonstrate and make comprehensible the objective validity of its concepts *a priori*" (A xvi), that is, to both prove *that* we have synthetic *a priori* cognition in mathematics, science, and metaphysics and then explain *how* such knowledge is possible. Throughout what follows, I will understand Kant to have this twofold aim in the central arguments of the *Critique of Pure Reason*.[10]

So how can Kant show that the first principles of mathematics, science, and philosophy itself are synthetic propositions known *a priori*, not merely *a posteriori* – that is, how can he refute Humean skepticism that what may seem to us to be universal and necessary principles are in fact nothing but contingent and incomplete generalizations – without flying off into ungrounded metaphysics? Kant's proposal is to try a procedure analogous to the "first thoughts of Copernicus" (B xvi) – what has come to be known as his "Copernican revolution" in philosophy. Just as Copernicus,

> when he did not make good progress in the explanation of the celestial motions if he assumed that the entire celestial host revolves around the observer, tried to see if he might not have greater success if he made the observer revolve and left the stars at rest,

so

> in metaphysics we can try in a similar way regarding the **intuition** of objects. If intuition has to conform to the constitution of the objects, then I do not see how we can know anything of them *a priori*; but if the object (as an object of the senses) has to conform to the constitution of our faculty of intuition, then I can very well represent this possibility to myself. Yet because I cannot stop with these intuitions, if they are to become cognitions, but must refer them as representations to something as their object and determine this object through them, I can assume that the concepts through which I bring about this determination also conform to the objects, and then I am once again in the same difficulty about how I could know anything about them *a priori*, or else I assume that the objects, or what is the same thing, the **experience** in which alone they can be cognized (as given objects) conforms to those concepts, in which case I immediately see an easier way out of the difficulty.
>
> (B xvii)

In other words, Kant argues, if we assume that the basic forms of our intuitions and concepts of objects, that is, of their sensory representations and conceptual organization, are derived from our experience of given objects, then our knowledge of them will never be more than *a posteriori*, thus contingent and limited, but if we can discover fundamental forms for the sensory representation and conceptual organization of objects within the structure of our own minds, then we can also know that nothing can ever become an object of knowledge for us except by means of these forms, and thus that these forms necessarily and universally apply to the objects of our knowledge – that is, that they are synthetic *a priori*.

Now, at first glance, Kant's proposal seems to be the exact opposite of Copernicus's procedure. Copernicus thought that Ptolemaic astronomy was a mathematical mess because it assumed that everything revolves around us here on earth, and introduced its mathematical simplification by demoting the significance of our own position as observers, positioning us on what is merely one more body rotating around the sun.[11] Kant, however, glorifies our significance as observers, holding that all objects must conform to the conditions of our experience rather than the conditions of our experience conforming to the independent character of the objects. The analogy seems to be only that in philosophy, as in astronomy, progress sometimes requires a radical reversal of traditional assumptions. Of course, should Kant's revolution in philosophy prove as enduring as Copernicus's revolution in astronomy, we wouldn't mind this confusion![12]

The Copernican revolution in philosophy, that is, the assumption that we can find fundamental conditions of the possibility of our own experience to which the objects of our experience must conform, is the basis for Kant's first claim of autonomy, the claim that sensibility and understanding, as two main faculties of the mind, contain "the **constitutive** principles *a priori* for the **faculty of cognition** (the theoretical cognition of nature" (CPJ, 5:196). But just how strongly does Kant mean this claim of autonomy to be taken? Very strongly, it turns out: what Kant will argue throughout the *Critique of Pure Reason* is not just that objects must conform to the conditions of our cognition of them if we are to have success in coming to know them, but that we can actually *impose* such conformity to the conditions of our cognition upon them – that "as exaggerated and contradictory as it may sound to say that the understanding is itself the *source* of the laws of nature . . . such an assertion is nevertheless correct and appropriate to the object, namely experience" (A 127; emphasis added). But, as Kant had made clear since his famous letter to Marcus Herz, he does not suppose that we are actually gods or demiurges who literally create the objects of our experience. Instead, what he will argue is that we can and must impose conformity to the conditions of the possibility of our own experience on the way that objects *appear* to us, but *precisely for that reason* how objects may be in themselves is bound to remain unknown to us. In other words, Kant's refutation of *Humean* skepticism, that is, his proof and explanation of the existence of synthetic *a priori* cognitions by appeal to the very conditions of the possibility of our own experience, seems to drive him into something like *Cartesian skepticism*, the denial that our way of representing things has any necessary resemblance to the way things are in themselves.

Here Kant seems to go well beyond his analogy with Copernicus. It is true that on the Copernican model of the solar system, our observations of the motions of the planets are downgraded to merely apparent motions: the apparent progressions and retrogressions that were earlier thought to be genuine epicycles on the planetary orbits are now explained away as nothing more than the way the motions of other planets revolving around the sun appear to an observer whose own planet is also revolving around that body. But this explanation convinces precisely because it can derive the apparent motions of the planets from a substantive and ultimately well-grounded hypothesis about the real motions of the planets around the sun. On Kant's theory, however, we are supposed to downgrade our experience of objects to mere appearance without knowing anything about the real character of those objects at all. What leads Kant to such a radical position, and do we have any reason to follow him there?[13]

We now have two great questions to ask about Kant's theory of knowledge. First, how does he identify the basic elements of knowledge which, in the "synthetic" method of the *Critique of Pure Reason*, are supposed to lead to the foundational synthetic *a priori* cognitions of mathematics, natural science, and philosophy itself? Second, why does Kant suppose that we can have synthetic *a priori* cognition only of the appearance of objects, not of their real nature? Why does the autonomy of human knowledge seem to come at such a high cost? Throughout the exposition that follows, both of these questions must be kept in mind.

SPACE AND TIME: THE PURE FORMS OF SENSIBLE INTUITION

Following the model of the logic textbooks of his time,[14] the *Critique of Pure Reason* is divided into a very long "Doctrine of Elements" and a comparatively short "Doctrine of Method." The "Doctrine of Elements" is in turn divided into two further parts. The longer of these, which Kant calls the

"Transcendental Logic," is divided into an "Analytic of Concepts" and an "Analytic of Principles" in which Kant presents his own account of the synthetic *a priori* conditions of knowledge, and a "Dialectic" in which he diagnoses the fallacious inferences of pure reason in traditional metaphysics. This division mirrors the traditional division of logic texts into three parts on concepts, judgments, and inferences, although in traditional texts the last of these parts concerns the forms of valid inference in general rather than the specific *invalid* metaphysical inferences that Kant discusses. But Kant precedes the "Transcendental Logic" with a much briefer section that has no parallel in traditional logic texts, namely the "Transcendental Aesthetic." (The organization of the whole book is shown in Box 2.1.)

Box 2.1 The organization of the *Critique of Pure Reason*

Transcendental Doctrine of Elements
  First Part: Transcendental Aesthetic
  Second Part: Transcendental Logic
    Division One: Transcendental Analytic
      Book I: Analytic of Concepts
        1. The Clue
        2. The Transcendental Deduction
      Book II: Analytic of Principles
        1. The Schematism
        2. The System of all Principles
        3. The Distinction between *Phenomena* and *Noumena*
    Division Two: Transcendental Dialectic
      Book I: The Concepts of Pure Reason
      Book II: The Dialectical Inferences of Pure Reason
        1. The Paralogisms of Pure Reason
        2. The Antinomy of Pure Reason
        3. The Ideal of Pure Reason
    Appendix: The Regulative Use of the Ideas of Pure Reason
      The Final Aim of the Dialectic of Human Reason
Transcendental Doctrine of Method
        1. The Discipline of Pure Reason
        2. The Canon of Pure Reason
        3. The Architectonic of Pure Reason
        4. The History of Pure Reason

The "Transcendental Aesthetic" concerns the *a priori* elements of sensible perceptions rather than the *a priori* forms of concepts and judgments, and is unparalleled in traditional logic texts because, at least as Kant saw things, the rationalist tradition to which these texts belonged did not recognize that sensibility makes an indispensable contribution to knowledge at all. Kant explains that he is rescuing the term "aesthetics" from its very recent use as the name for the philosophical investigation of taste and art,[15] because he does not think there can be any science of those subjects, but there can and must be a fully scientific investigation of the contribution of the senses to knowledge in general and the *a priori* forms of that contribution, for which he can appropriate the name (A 21/B 35–6).

The thesis of the "Transcendental Aesthetic" is that space and time are the pure forms of all our sensible representation of objects, and as such are sources of synthetic *a priori* cognition in both pure and applied mathematics; but also that they are *nothing but* the pure forms of our own representations of objects, or forms of the appearances of things rather than forms of things as they are in themselves, and that only as such subjective forms of representation can they yield synthetic *a priori* cognition. The claim that space and time are nothing but the essential forms of our own representations of things is Kant's doctrine of "transcendental idealism." The "Transcendental Aesthetic" thus not only lays the first stone in Kant's constructive theory of knowledge; it also lays the foundation for both his critique and his reconstruction of traditional metaphysics. It argues that all genuine knowledge requires a sensory component, and thus that metaphysical claims that transcend the possibility of sensory confirmation can never amount to knowledge. But it also prepares the way for Kant's view that since the forms of sensory representation and any limits inherent in those forms apply only to the appearances of things, not to things as they are in themselves, we are at least free to *think* or *conceive of* things as they are in themselves independently of those forms – a possibility that Kant will require for his eventual reconstruction of metaphysics as a matter of practical rather than theoretical knowledge.

Before we can examine Kant's arguments for these momentous claims, we must get a grip on his terminology. Kant puts his general point that all genuine knowledge requires both sensory input and intellectual organization by saying that all knowledge requires both "intuitions" and "concepts" (e.g., A 50/B 74). Intuitions and concepts are two different species of the genus "representation" (*Vorstellung*), Kant's most general term for any cognitive state (see A 320/B 376–7). At the outset of the "Transcendental Aesthetic," Kant states that an "intuition" is our most direct or "immediate" kind of representation of objects, in contrast to a "concept," which always represents an object "through a detour (*indirecte*)," that is, merely by some "mark" or property that the object has (A 19/B 33). In his logic textbook, Kant defines an intuition as a "*singular* representation," that is, one that represents a particular object, while a concept is always a "*universal* (*repraesentation per notas communes*)," which represents properties common to many objects (*Logic*, §1, 9:91). But there is no difference between Kant's two definitions of intuitions and concepts, for if one is a nominalist – that is, if one believes that the only objects that there are are particulars, not universals – then an immediate representation of an object is necessarily a singular representation, and anything that represents universally cannot represent any object directly, but represents only a feature that is common to many particular objects. Kant recognizes these equivalences later in the *Critique* when he writes that an intuition is "immediately related to the object and is singular," while a concept "is mediate, by means of a mark, which can be common to several things" (A 320/B 377).[16]

Kant quickly inserts a substantive claim among his initial definitions, namely that "at least for us humans" intuition is possible "only insofar as the object is given to us" or "only if it affects the mind in a certain way," that is, only insofar as we have a "capacity (receptivity) to acquire representations through the way in which we are affected by objects," in other words, "sensibility" (A 19/B 33). This is obvious in the case of what Kant calls "empirical intuitions," that is, immediate representations of particular objects involving sensation: when I have a sensory perception, or empirical intuition, of my copy of the *Critique*, it is because the particular object on my desk *acts on* me – by reflecting light waves that pass through the lenses of my glasses and eyes, and then stimulate my retinas, optic nerves, and so on – to put me into a certain mental state, namely, one in which it (at least) seems to me that there is a blue, rectangular object before me. Kant calls the "undetermined object of an empirical intuition" an "appearance" (A 20/B 34), but by this term he does not – thus far – mean that we have any reason to think that empirical intuitions do *not* represent things to us as they are in themselves. He means only – what is surely not controversial – that no single observation of an object gives us fully determinate knowledge of that object, and further – what should also not be controversial, although Kant thinks that empiricist philosophers failed to recognize this – that even multiple observations of an object do not yield determinate knowledge of it until such observations are organized by means of and subsumed under concepts.

The last point will be the subject of the "Transcendental Logic," but now we must turn to the main claims of the "Transcendental Aesthetic." How does Kant argue that space and time are the pure forms of intuition, and why does he conclude that they are nothing but the pure forms of our representations of objects? Kant reaches this last conclusion by what we may think of as three main steps. First, he argues that all of our representations of particular objects must be given to us in space and/or time, so that space and time are the forms of all intuitions, but also that space and time must themselves be represented like particular objects rather than general kinds of objects, so they are themselves intuitions. Second, he argues that we know both of these things about space and time a priori, so that space and time must be pure forms of intuition and themselves pure intuitions. Finally, he argues that we can only have this a priori knowledge about space and time if they are nothing but the pure forms of our own representations, due "to the subjective constitution of our mind," not, as he puts it, "actual entities" nor "determinations or relations of things . . . that would pertain to them even if they were not intuited" (A 23/B 37). Let's look at these steps in some detail.

In the second edition of the Critique, Kant separates into the "metaphysical" and "transcendental expositions" of the "concepts of" space and time arguments that he had lumped together in the first edition. The new distinction reflects the difference between the "synthetic" method supposed to be used in the Critique and the "analytic" method allowed for the Prolegomena. What Kant now calls the "transcendental exposition of the concept of space" presupposes that the propositions of geometry are synthetic a priori, and argues only that such synthetic a priori cognition must rest on a pure intuition of space. The analogous transcendental exposition of time presupposes that some analogous axioms about time, such as that it has only one dimension, are synthetic a priori, so we must likewise have a pure intuition of time. The arguments now called "metaphysical expositions," however, are not intended to presuppose the existence of any synthetic a priori cognitions, but are rather supposed to show that some completely elementary and obvious facts about the representation of objects in space and time imply that we must have pure intuitions of space and time – from which the possibility of synthetic a priori cognition about the structure of space and time, expressed in the propositions of geometry and the analogous generalities about time, would follow. Let us consider the arguments of the metaphysical expositions first, not only because Kant begins with them but also because they are at least apparently less vulnerable to the charge that Kant is simply begging a fundamental question about the nature of mathematical knowledge.

There are four claims in Kant's reorganized metaphysical exposition of space.[17] The first two try to show that an antecedent, pure representation of space is the condition of the possibility of our empirical intuitions of particular objects, while the latter two (the fourth and fifth arguments in the original version of the "Transcendental Aesthetic," before its third argument, from geometry, had been removed to the transcendental exposition) aim to show that space is itself necessarily represented as a singular object, thus is not just the pure form of empirical intuition but is itself a pure intuition. Kant makes analogous claims about time in the first and second and fourth and fifth arguments of its metaphysical exposition, not bothering to remove the third argument although he also adds a separate transcendental exposition of time.

In the first argument about space, Kant claims that "Space is not an empirical concept that has been drawn from outer experiences," because "in order for certain sensations to be related to something outside me . . . the representation of space must already be their ground" (A 23 / B 38). His idea seems to be that I could not acquire my conception of space by induction from any number of experiences that I recognize as representations of external objects, because in order to recognize one object as external to others, in the first place, I must already represent it as in a different position in space from those others, *a fortiori* in order to represent any object as external to myself I must already represent it as in a different position in space from my own – all of which means that the representation of objects external to one another in space presupposes a representation of space itself that cannot be empirically derived from representations of particular things in space. In that sense, the representation of space must be the *a priori* form for the representation of particular objects in space.[18] Similarly, Kant claims, we cannot derive our representation of the temporal properties of simultaneity and succession from an experience of objects already represented as distinct from one another (A 30 / B 46), because the only way to represent objects in time as distinct from each other is already to have the framework in which they can be represented as either simultaneous or successive.

Next, Kant claims that we must have *a priori* representations of space and time that do not depend upon empirical intuitions of objects, because although we cannot represent particular objects without representing space and time, we could represent space and time themselves without also representing any particular objects in them (A 24 / B 38–9, A 31 / B 46). This claim that we can represent empty space and time may seem incompatible with some claims Kant will later make, especially that "time itself cannot be perceived" (B 219), the premise for his eventual argument that we can make determinate judgments about the relations of states of affairs in time only by appealing to enduring and law-governed objects in space (the central thesis of the "Analogies of Experience"). Perhaps Kant can be saved from inconsistency here by a distinction between representing the structure of space and time as such and representing determinate relations between objects or states of affairs in space and time, but this is a problem we shall defer for now.

In the third and fourth arguments of the revised metaphysical exposition of space (that is, the fourth and fifth arguments of the original version) and the corresponding fourth and fifth arguments about time, Kant tries to show that we necessarily represent space and time as singular, so that we must have a pure intuition of each, since singular representations are intuitions. First, he argues that we always represent particular spaces and times only as regions of a larger, surrounding space or time, and that we do so by delimiting such regions in the larger realm (A 25/B 39, A 31–2/B 47). This also means that we do not conceive of particular spaces and times as *instances* of the general *concepts* "space" and "time," but rather as *parts* of the larger *individuals*, space and time.[19] This is enough to establish that our representations of space and time are themselves pure intuitions, not just pure forms of intuition; but in the final argument in each section, Kant goes on to add that space and time – that is, the wholes of which any particular regions are parts – must both be represented as infinite or unlimited magnitudes (A 39/B 40, A 32/B 47–8). Kant does not spell out his reasoning here, but presumably his thought is that if *any* space or time can be represented only as part of a larger, surrounding space or time, then no matter how large a space or time we represent, we must always represent it as part of a yet larger one, thus we must ultimately represent space and time as infinite. Kant does suggest this interpretation in one of his notes for his uncompleted final work when he writes "Space is a quantum, which must always be represented as part of a greater quantum – hence, as infinite, and *given* as such."[20]

This argument that space (or time) must be represented as infinite seems undeniable, although one might worry about whether every determinate region of space must be represented as part of the *same* larger space, thus whether it is possible to represent *more than one* infinite space – a possibility that would have to be excluded to guarantee that our pure representation of space is, in fact, a pure intuition.[21] But even if we choose not to worry about such an arcane possibility, we must be careful about Kant's claim that space and time are *given* as infinite (see also A 25/B 39,

A 32/B 48), for it will later be central to Kant's argument in the
"Transcendental Dialectic" that we *cannot* represent the universe as infinite
in spatial or temporal extent, but only as *indefinitely* extended and extendable; this is because we can never *complete* an enumeration of an infinite
number of parts, or, in Kant's terms, an infinite "synthesis." How can his
two claims be reconciled? Again, presumably the answer will depend on a
distinction between space and time as such and the world in space and
time, that is, what fills space and time: on the one hand, we cannot represent any limit to space and time as such, so we cannot but represent them
as infinite; on the other, we cannot complete the enumeration of an infinite number of objects in space or time, so we cannot represent the world
as more than indefinitely extendable.

How good are these arguments? Science fiction aside, it seems hard to
argue with Kant's view that we represent particular regions of space and time
as parts of larger particulars, space and time as such. It is less clear that we
must have an *a priori* representation of space independently of our representation of particular objects in space in order for this to be so. It is not obvious
that we can exclude that in the course of our early cognitive development we
gradually acquire the representation of space as a whole along with our
ability to represent distinct objects in space – say, during the first six or twelve
or eighteen months of development. It might seem plausible that the baby
who first formulates the idea of the space of her crib or her room does not
conceive of it as part of a larger space. However, the transition from recognizing smaller spaces to recognizing them as parts of larger spaces around
them might also seem so natural that it might be plausible to argue that we
do inherently represent any space as part of a larger one even though as small
children we are not explicitly conscious of this feature of our cognitive structure. Kant's argument that we can perceive space without perceiving objects
in it seems more problematic, however. If this is supposed to be established
by some sort of introspection or thought-experiment, how exactly would we
tell the difference between representing empty space and simply not representing space at all?[22] But even if we let Kant's arguments pass, there still
seems to be a bigger problem. This is that even if sound, these arguments tell
us how we must *represent* space and time, thus that we must have *a priori representations* of them; but it is not clear that anything in these arguments yet suggests
or even supplies a premise for the conclusion that space and time are *nothing
but* our *a priori* representations of them.[23] Do Kant's "transcendental expositions" of space and time do so?

The transcendental expositions of the concepts of space and time are very
brief, but in view of the weight that they carry in Kant's entire philosophy,

we must examine them carefully. We can focus on the transcendental exposition of space. First, Kant defines what he means by a transcendental exposition:

> I understand by a **transcendental exposition** the explanation of a concept as a principle from which insight into the possibility of other synthetic *a priori* cognition can be gained. For this aim it is required 1) that such cognitions actually flow from the given concept, and 2) that these cognitions are only possible under the presupposition of a given way of explaining this concept.
>
> (B 40)

Clause (1) says that the "explanation of a concept" profferred by a transcendental exposition must be a *sufficient* condition for the synthetic *a priori* cognition that it explains, and clause (2) says that it must be a *necessary* condition, that is, the *only* sufficient explanation. These conditions seem like straightforward constraints on any conclusive argument from an effect to a cause – that it be not merely an inference to an adequate explanation, but to the only explanation. What the first sentence of the quotation means is a little less clear: while it could just mean that a transcendental exposition demonstrates that some concept or representation is the basis for *some* relevant synthetic *a priori* cognition, Kant's statement that such an exposition yields insight into the possibility of *other* synthetic *a priori* cognition might be taken to mean that the *premise* of such an argument *assumes* the existence of *some* synthetic *a priori* cognition from which the existence of *further* such cognition can be inferred. If this is indeed the form of a transcendental exposition, then such an argument may be vulnerable to rejection if the synthetic *a priori* status of the knowledge from which it begins is questioned, or it may even be question-begging if the synthetic *a priori* cognition that it assumes is really the same as the other synthetic *a priori* cognition, the existence of which it is supposed to prove. Kant's subsequent argument may indeed be dubious or question-begging in just this way.[24]

The heart of Kant's argument comes next:

> Geometry is a science that determines the properties of space synthetically and yet *a priori*. What then must the representation of space be for such a cognition of it to be possible? It must originally be intuition; for from a mere concept no propositions can be drawn that go beyond the concept (Introduction V). But this intuition must be encountered in us *a priori*, i.e., prior to all perception of an object, thus it must be pure, not empirical

intuition. For geometric propositions are all apodictic, i.e., combined with consciousness of their necessity.

(B 40–1)

Kant's argument makes two claims. First, it claims that geometry must rest on an intuition of space or objects in space, because any analysis of geometrical concepts can yield only analytic propositions, but the propositions of geometry are synthetic. Second, it claims that the intuition on which geometry rests must be an *a priori* intuition because the synthetic propositions of geometry are necessarily true, and therefore could never be confirmed by merely empirical or *a posteriori* intuitions. So, Kant concludes, we must have *a priori* intuition of the form of space and of all possible objects in space.

To support the first claim, Kant refers us back to Section V of the (second-edition) Introduction. But Kant actually makes two distinct claims about mathematical propositions there. First, although he makes this point by appeal to an arithmetical rather than geometrical example, he claims that mathematical propositions are synthetic because we must go beyond the mere analysis of concepts and appeal to intuition in the course of their proof. To show this, he uses his famous example that we cannot show that $7 + 5 = 12$ by analyzing our concepts of *seven*, *five*, and *sum*, but that we actually have to go through some sort of process of *counting* first seven units, then perform the act of *adding* five more, and then in some sense *see* that the result is twelve units. Much later in the book, he makes a similar argument about geometrical proof. This comes in the "Doctrine of Method," where Kant is arguing that the methods of mathematics and philosophy are not the same. There he writes that "**Philosophical** cognition is **rational cognition** from **concepts**, mathematical cognition that from the **construction** of concepts," where "to **construct** a concept means to exhibit *a priori* the intuition corresponding to it" (A 713 / B 741). In other words, philosophical cognition is analytic, while mathematical cognition is synthetic. Kant then gives this example:

> Give a philosopher the concept of a triangle, and let him try to find out in his way how the sum of its angles might be related to a right angle. He has nothing but the concept of a figure enclosed by three straight lines, and in it the concept of equally many angles. Now he may . . . analyze and make distinct the concept of a straight line, or of an angle, or of the number three, but he will not come upon any other properties that do not already lie in these concepts. But now let the geometer take up this question. He

begins at once to construct a triangle. Since he knows that two right angles together are exactly equal to all of the adjacent angles that can be drawn at one point on a straight line, he extends one side of his triangle, and obtains two adjacent angles that together are equal to two right ones. Now he divides the external one of these angles by drawing a line parallel to the opposite side of the triangle, and sees that here there arises an external adjacent angle which is equal to an internal one, etc. In such a way, through a chain of inferences that is always guided by intuition, he arrives at a fully illuminating and at the same time general solution of the question.

(A 716–17 / B 744–5)

In other words, starting with knowledge that the angles on one side of a straight line equal 180°, the geometer constructs the lines necessary to show that the interior angles of any randomly chosen triangle are equivalent to the angles on one side of a straight line, and can then infer that they equal two right angles, i.e., 180°. In both the mathematical and the geometrical case, Kant's point is that solving a mathematical problem is never a matter of merely logical inference from concepts alone, but always requires a *process*, whether of counting or constructing, that can only be understood as an appeal to intuition rather than an analysis of concepts.

Now this claim seems to be open to the objection that Kant was simply working with inadequate axiomatizations of arithmetic and geometry, so that once Gustav Peano had shown how to axiomatize arithmetic and David Hilbert geometry, there was no longer any basis for his claim that mathematical proof always requires an appeal to intuition.[25] But here is where the second point that Kant makes in Section V of the second edition comes in. For what Kant actually says there about geometry is that no *principle* of geometry is analytic, rather that, for example, "That the straight line between two points is the shortest is a synthetic proposition. For my concept of **the straight** contains nothing of quantity, but only a quality" (B 16). In other words, it is not just the *theorems*, that is, the conclusions, of geometrical proofs that are synthetic, but also the *axioms*, that is, the premises. The appeal to intuition is necessary to confirm the *truth* of the axioms of mathematics, whether or not any further appeal to intuition is necessary in the course of carrying out mathematical *proofs* from those axioms. Kant explains this point by saying that it would be a mistake to think that mathematical conclusions are analytic just because they can be proved by "inferences . . . in accordance with the principle of contradiction," that is, as we would say, in the strictly logical way that an adequate axiomatization permits, "for a synthetic proposition can of course be comprehended in accordance with the principle of contradiction, but only insofar as another synthetic proposition is presupposed from which it can be deduced" (B 14). In other words, for Kant, regardless of how logically rigorous it is, the result of any mathematical proof is synthetic if the axioms on which the proof depends are synthetic.

So Kant's argument that mathematics, particularly geometry, depends on an appeal to intuition itself depends on his claim that its axioms are true yet synthetic propositions. How plausible is this claim? From one point of view, that of formalism in the modern philosophy of mathematics, it is not plausible: mathematical axioms define formalisms in which certain inferences are valid, just like the rules of a game define certain moves that are allowed, but as definitions the axioms are not themselves either true or false, *a fortiori* neither analytic nor synthetic – it does not make any more sense to talk of the truth of the axioms themselves than it does to talk of the truth of the rules of a game like chess or bridge. On another view, it might be held that something like this is the case in *pure* mathematics, but that it makes perfectly good sense to talk about the truth of axioms (and the consequent truth of theorems) in *applied* mathematics, that is, when the axioms are taken to describe real rather than merely formal objects. Of course, the standard contemporary version of this view would then continue that it is an *empirical* question whether a particular mathematical formalism does truly describe physical reality, as it is now thought to be an empirical question (answered in the negative) whether Euclidean geometry truly describes physical space (over large distances).[26]

But this is precisely the possibility that Kant rejects in the second claim of the central paragraph of the transcendental exposition: the intuition of space on which our cognition of the axioms of geometry rests must be *a priori*, "pure, not empirical intuition," because "geometrical propositions are all apodictic, i.e., combined with consciousness of their necessity, e.g., space has only three dimensions" (B 41). Kant insists that the conclusions of geometry are synthetic because the axioms are, but rejects any thought that those axioms could be synthetic *a posteriori*. They must be synthetic *a priori* and rest on an *a priori* intuition of space and its structure because all geometrical propositions, like other mathematical propositions, are universally and necessarily true. But does Kant have any *argument* that this is so, even as much of an argument as the appeal to examples that he used to establish that the axioms and therefore the theorems of geometry are synthetic? The answer to this can only be "no": this seems to be an assumption that Kant cannot imagine questioning, and that he cannot imagine anyone else questioning.[27]

So while Kant may have gone some distance toward proving that mathematics consists of synthetic propositions and therefore depends on intuition, he merely assumed that it consists of apodictic propositions and therefore depends upon *a priori* intuition. This is of vital importance in what comes next. In discussing the metaphysical expositions of space and time earlier, we saw that even if we allowed Kant's claim that we have *a priori* intuitions of space and time, that does not itself imply that space and time are *nothing* but our intuitions of them. Following the transcendental expositions, Kant does attempt to prove that space and time are nothing but our intuitions of them. But what we will now see is that his proof depends precisely upon his assumption that propositions about space and time – whether the specific ones expressed in geometry and mathematics, or even only the more general ones adduced in the metaphysical expositions – are *necessarily* true, and on his interpretation of that assumption. If that assumption is unsupported, then so is Kant's central argument for transcendental idealism itself.

In the "Transcendental Aesthetic," Kant first explicitly argues for transcendental idealism following the metaphysical and transcendental expositions of space and time. Here he argues that space and time cannot be properties of things in themselves nor relations of them to each other because "neither absolute nor relative determinations can be intuited prior to the existence of the things to which they pertain, thus be intuited *a priori*." He then infers from the fact that space and time cannot be properties of things in themselves that they can only be "subjective condition[s] of sensibility" – space "merely the form of all appearances of outer sense" (A 26/B 42) and time "nothing other than the form of inner sense, i.e., of the intuition of our self and our inner state" (A 33/B 49). In other words, Kant does *not* infer directly from the alleged fact that we must have pure intuitions of space and time that space and time are nothing but our own representations, nor does he simply fail to consider the possibility that space and time might be *both* the necessary forms of our representations and properties or relations of things in themselves;[28] rather, he infers the transcendental ideality of space and time only from an intermediate premise about the possibility of *a priori* knowledge.

But why exactly can't we have *a priori* knowledge of something that is a genuine property or relation of anything other than our own representations? It would seem as if in many cases we do have *a priori* knowledge of things that exist independently of ourselves. For example, we have come to know, through empirical science, the generalization that human beings can only hear sounds in the range of 20 to 20,000 herz (while dogs, for example, can hear sounds pitched higher than 20,000 herz, while hump-backed whales can hear those lower than 20 herz). So why can't we say that we know *a priori* of any *particular* sound that we do hear that it cannot have a pitch higher than 20,000 herz, and yet say at the same time that any partic-ular sound we do hear really does, in itself and quite apart from the fact that we hear it, have a pitch no higher than 20,000 herz? In other words, given that there are certain constraints on our perception, why isn't the best expla-nation that we succeed in perceiving an object that it really does satisfy those constraints? To go back to Kant's case, if we somehow know *a priori* that we can only perceive objects distinct from ourselves in space, indeed in three-dimensional Euclidean space, why isn't the explanation of our success in perceiving some particular outer object precisely that it really is spatial, indeed three-dimensional, quite apart from our representing it as such?[29]

The reason why Kant does not allow this possibility, the "missing alter-native" to transcendental idealism, is that in his view only our own representations *necessarily* conform to our pure forms of intuition, while if any objects other than our own representations did conform to the condi-tions of these pure forms they would only do so *contingently* – and that, he takes it, is incompatible with our *a priori* cognition of space and time, because he interprets that to mean that anything we know to be spatial or temporal is *necessarily* so. He makes the nature of his assumption particularly clear in a passage in the *Prolegomena*, which is explicitly about the synthetic *a priori* cognition we supposedly have in pure mathematics but would apply to any allegedly synthetic *a priori* knowledge about space and time at all:

> Pure mathematics, and especially pure geometry, can have objective reality only under the single condition that it refers merely to objects of the senses, with regard to which objects the principle remains fixed, that our sensory representation is by no means a representation of things in them-selves, but only of the way in which they appear to us. . . . It would be completely different if the senses had to represent objects as they are in themselves. For then it absolutely would not follow from the representation of space, a representation that serves *a priori*, with all the various proper-ties of space, as foundation for the geometer, that all of this, together with what is deduced from it, must be exactly so in nature. The space of the geometer would be taken for mere fabrication and would be credited with no objective validity, because it is simply not to be seen how things would have to agree necessarily with the image that we form of them by ourselves in advance.
>
> (PFM, §13, Note I, 4:287)

What Kant assumes is that objects in space *do* agree necessarily with our *a priori* image of them, and so, paradoxical as it may seem, they cannot be things in themselves, but only our own representations of things. Kant makes the same assumption in the *Critique of Pure Reason* when he asks:

> If there did not lie in you a faculty for intuiting *a priori*; if this subjective condition regarding form were not at the same time the universal *a priori* condition under which alone the object of this (outer) intuition is itself possible; if the object ([e.g.,] the triangle) were something in itself without relation to your subject: then how could you say that what necessarily lies in your subjective conditions for constructing a triangle must also necessarily pertain to the triangle in itself?
>
> (A 48 / B 65−6)

Kant's assumption is precisely that we can say that everything we premise and everything that we prove about triangles is *necessarily* true of triangles, and therefore triangles (and every other object in space) can be nothing but a species of our own representations, for those are the only things that *necessarily* conform to the pure forms of our intuition.[30]

It is crucial to note that Kant is making two distinct assumptions in all of this. First, he takes himself to have shown in both the metaphysical and transcendental expositions that we necessarily have certain forms of intuition, or necessarily represent space and time in certain ways. Second, he is assuming that we can say of any particular object that we perceive in space and time that it necessarily has the spatial and / or temporal properties that we perceive it to have. Without the second assumption, the argument for transcendental idealism cannot be completed, for it would then show only that we have *a priori* intuitions of space and time but not that space and time and all objects in them are nothing more than those intuitions. But it is not clear that Kant's second premise is anything more than a bare assertion: he does not seem to have an argument that particular objects necessarily rather than merely contingently conform to the subjective conditions of our intuition of them, nor does he have any direct argument that things in themselves could not be spatial but only contingently so. Kant's argument for transcendental idealism is thus incomplete.

Even if Kant fails to prove transcendental idealism, he might still prove a great deal if he proves that we have *a priori* knowledge of the conditions to which those external objects that we do perceive contingently conform, and thus have *a priori* knowledge of the structure of space and time, and through that synthetic *a priori* cognition of a great deal of mathematics. Does Kant prove even that much? The transcendental expositions are certainly not conclusive. Even if we accept Kant's claim that geometrical theorems, for example, are synthetic because geometrical axioms are, there are simply too many alternative models for the relation between mathematics and reality for Kant's claim that we know that the particular objects described by mathematics *necessarily* satisfy their descriptions to be the last word on the subject. Kant has no argument sufficient to exclude the standard position, represented in his own time by Moses Mendelssohn, that our moves within the formal systems of mathematics may be *a priori* but the application of any particular mathematical formalism to real objects is a matter for empirical judgment.

What about the metaphysical expositions, that is, the arguments that, quite apart from mathematics, we must have pure intuitions of space and time to explain our ability to experience particular objects in space and time and our knowledge of the unitary and infinite character of space? I have already suggested that in the first instance these arguments prove only that we have *a priori representations* of space and time, and that we would need some further argument to prove that space and time are *nothing but* these representations of them. For Kant to assume that space and time and all objects in them *necessarily* conform to our representations of them and therefore can be nothing other than our representations once again seems like an unsupported assumption on his part. What about the initial claim that we have *a priori representations* of space and time? Here things are less clear. It seems hard to deny that at least as adults we must be able to represent space and time as some sort of wholes in order to represent the position and duration of objects and events in them, that we can represent the structure of space and time without representing any particular objects in them, and that we represent all particular spaces and times as parts of a larger space and time, and therefore represent space and time as infinite. But is there no other explanation of why this is so than that we have *a priori* representations of space and time? What if all of these are just such obvious features of space and time that we learn them in our first months of perception, long before memory kicks in, and therefore simply can never remember having learned these things even though they are, strictly speaking, empirical? It is not clear that there are philosophical methods to resolve such a question, which might seem more like a matter for cognitive psychologists – but then again it is not clear whether there is any way for cognitive psychologists to place an unequivocal interpretation on their observations of the responses of infants without already using the categories of adult perceivers. Maybe there is no way to settle whether our most fundamental representations of space and time themselves are necessary or contingent. Kant does not quite admit this, although he does eventually admit that no "further ground . . . can be offered . . . for why space and time are the sole forms of our possible intuition" (B 146). Thus, even if we were to grant that all human beings do have an *a priori* representation of space and time, or, what might be more plausible, an inherent capacity to represent space and time in certain ways, it might still not be clear that we are entitled to assert that this is a *necessary* truth about human beings. But if Kant really cannot prove beyond any doubt that even our representations of space and time or our capacity to represent them are necessary, then there may be no basis for his argument that these representations are *a priori* and for the foundation of transcendental idealism upon that stone.

An inconclusive proof of transcendental idealism would not, it must immediately be said, doom Kant's entire enterprise in the *Critique of Pure Reason*. For he also wants to argue that the logic of judgment is a source of synthetic *a priori* cognition, and this might be true even if there is an ineluctably empirical element in the spatial and temporal representations to which the *a priori* forms of judgment are applied. That will be our next major question. But before turning from Kant's theory of sensibility to his theory of the understanding, I should certainly say that the interpretation of Kant's argument for transcendental idealism that I have offered here, and thus the critique of it that I have suggested, are by no means the only view that can be taken of this fundamental Kantian idea. The interpretation that I have suggested is one on which Kant moves from an epistemological claim to an ontological claim: that is, on which he infers from our alleged synthetic *a priori* cognition of space and time that only our representations and not things independent of our representations can have spatial and/or temporal properties. There is another view on which transcendental idealism is only an epistemological or methodological position and not an ontological or metaphysical theory at all. According to this interpretation, which has been most prominently defended by Henry Allison, Kant's arguments are only supposed to show that space and time are indispensable features of our knowledge of anything else, or what Allison calls "epistemic conditions," and that once he has shown this, Kant introduces two *conceptions* or *standpoints* about things: one in which we include these epistemic conditions, which is nothing other than our ordinary, common-sense view of objects, and another conception *of these very same objects* from which we exclude these epistemic conditions, which is the transcendental view of objects or the conception of them as things in themselves. In other words, things in themselves are not some peculiar objects which lack spatial and / or temporal properties; rather, spatial and temporal properties are simply omitted from one version of our *conception* of things.[31] Such an interpretation of transcendental idealism has been called a "two-aspect view," in contrast to the kind of account that has been given here, which is called a "two-object" or "two-world" view because a domain of objects that are not spatial and temporal has to be numerically distinct from a domain of objects that are.[32]

This "two-aspect" interpretation of transcendental idealism makes sense of many of Kant's statements, notably his claim in the Preface to the second edition of the *Critique* that the book teaches "that the object should be taken in a **twofold meaning**, namely as appearance or as thing in itself" (B xxvii). And it may seem more sensible to claim that we have two kinds of conceptions of objects than that there are objects that really do not have spatial or temporal properties at all – indeed, given Kant's own claims that knowledge always requires intuitions as well as concepts and that space and time are the necessary forms of intuitions, his readers have from the very beginning asked how he could allege to know that there are objects that do not have spatial and temporal properties. Nevertheless, there are several grounds for not ascribing the "two-aspect" view to Kant. First, one might ask why Kant would have chosen to emphasize that space and time are the indispensable "epistemic conditions" of all of our knowledge of objects precisely by formulating a conception of objects that *omits* or abstracts from those conditions. Second, it is not clear how the "two-aspect" view can address Kant's explicit and repeated argument that if things other than our own representations have spatial and temporal properties, they could have them only contingently, which would undermine the alleged necessity of mathematics and indeed all our claims about the spatial and temporal properties of objects. This is not the only argument for transcendental idealism that Kant ever offers, but it is so prominent in both the *Critique* and the *Prolegomena* that Kant obviously sets great store by it – and it clearly implies that no *things* other than our representations can have spatial or temporal properties, not merely that we have a *concept* of things that omits reference to those properties. Third, the "two-aspect" view will create difficulties for Kant's subsequent treatment of the freedom of the will, for it will imply that we can have a *conception* of ourselves in which we abstract from the causal determination of our actions in space and time, but not that we *are not in fact* causally determined in space and time; and again, while this suggestion is certainly consistent with some of the things Kant says about freedom, it is not evidently consistent with all of them. This is an issue to which we shall have to return much later.[33] Finally, it should also be noted that there is something misleading in calling the ontological rather than merely methodological interpretation of transcendental idealism a "two-object" or "two-world" view. This makes it sound as if Kant is being supposed to have entirely made up a mysterious world behind the world of ordinary objects, to have needlessly duplicated the objects of our experience while at the same time stripping them of their most important properties.[34] But, for Kant, as for virtually every philosopher in the seventeenth and eighteenth centuries, there already were two sorts of objects to hand, namely, ordinary objects and our mental representations of them, and all that Kant was doing, as he saw it, was relocating spatial and temporal properties from one kind of object that everybody recognized – non-representations – to the other kind of object that everybody recognized – representations. So of course he held a "two-object" view: everyone (except Berkeley) did, though few would have agreed with Kant's reassignment of spatio-temporal properties from ordinary objects to representations. Any interpretation of Kant's transcendental idealism needs to take account of the fact that, like the vast majority of his contemporaries, he was in fact committed to a "two-object" view independently of transcendental idealism.

Another recent approach to transcendental idealism argues that by things in themselves Kant meant things understood in light of their intrinsic or non-relational properties, so that from the fact that spatial and temporal properties are inherently relational it immediately follows that they are not properties of things as things in themselves.[35] Again, this sort of interpretation makes good sense of at least some things Kant says, notably an argument that he adds to the second edition of the "Transcendental Aesthetic," where he says that:

> through mere relations no thing in itself is cognized; it is therefore right to judge that since nothing is given to us through outer sense except mere representations of relation, outer sense can also contain in its representation only the relation of an object to the subject, and not that which is internal to the object in itself.
>
> (B 67)

However, Kant does not seem to have been well advised in adding this argument to his basic argument for transcendental idealism. For while the equation of only non-relational properties with properties of things in itself may make it tautologically true that spatio-temporal properties are not properties of things when described as things in themselves, it does not entail that there are any things that actually lack spatio-temporal properties, for it does not deny that any particular things actually lack relational properties. But if things really have relational as well as intrinsic properties, then they can really have spatial and temporal properties, and indeed there is no reason why we cannot know them to have such properties, let alone know them not to have such properties. But the premise that Kant takes himself to need to save the alleged necessity of both non-mathematical and mathematical synthetic *a priori* propositions about things in space and time is that nothing other than our own representations really has spatio-temporal properties at all – and there is no way to get that from the interpretation under consideration.

So the position to be taken in the remainder of this book is that Kant's transcendental idealism asserts that things other than our own representations – indeed, even our own selves as contrasted to our representations of ourselves – really do lack spatial and temporal properties, although this thesis rests primarily on claims about necessity that Kant does not successfully justify. We must now move on to Kant's theory of concepts, judgments, and inference, that is, his theory of understanding and reason as contrasted to sensibility. We will consider both whether Kant introduces any independent arguments for transcendental idealism in these further parts of his theory and also whether Kant's views on these matters can be accepted independently of transcendental idealism.

THE CONTRIBUTIONS OF THE UNDERSTANDING

As earlier mentioned, the largest part of the "Doctrine of the Elements" of the *Critique of Pure Reason* is the "Transcendental Logic," which in turn consists of the "Transcendental Analytic" and the "Transcendental Dialectic." The "Analytic" expounds all of Kant's constructive theory of knowledge that has not already been presented in the "Transcendental Aesthetic," while the "Dialectic" contains the critique of all traditional metaphysics that he erects on the basis of his theory of knowledge. The "Analytic" is itself divided into an "Analytic of Concepts," which is in turn subdivided into two chapters, what Kant came to call the "metaphysical" and the "transcendental" deductions of the pure concepts of the understanding, and an "Analytic of Principles," containing three main chapters, the "Schematism of pure concepts of the understanding," the "System of all principles of pure understanding," and the "Distinction of all objects in general into *phenomena* and *noumena*." The last of these is really the transition from the constructive theory of the "Analytic" to the critical theory of the "Dialectic." The remainder of this chapter will be concerned with the constructive theory, and Chapter 3 will be concerned with Kant's critique of traditional metaphysics.

There are three main stages in Kant's constructive theory of knowledge. In the first, which he calls the "clue" or "guiding-thread"[36] to the "discovery of all pure concepts of the understanding," and in the second edition names the "metaphysical deduction" of the categories (B 159), Kant argues, first, that all knowledge of objects is expressed in judgments, and thus is never constituted by intuitions alone – simply having an observation of an object, for example, does not amount to knowledge of it, for knowledge requires thinking or asserting about what is observed, thus applying a concept to it. Second, Kant argues that judgments about objects necessarily have certain characteristic forms, determined by what he calls the "functions" of judgment. Finally, he concludes that all our concepts of objects must correspondingly have certain forms, which allow us to apply the forms of judgment to them. These forms are what Kant calls the "pure concepts of the understanding" or "categories." In the second stage of his argument, the "transcendental deduction," Kant argues that the categories possess "objective validity," or *necessarily* apply to *all* of our representations: we can have no experience of any kind that is not subject to the categories, thus the categories are the "conditions of the possibility of experience." In the third stage of the argument, beginning in the text of the "Transcendental Deduction" and extending through the first two chapters of the "Analytic of Principles," Kant reintroduces his claim that we need intuitions as well as concepts in order to have knowledge, so that the categories must be applied to our experience of empirical intuitions with its spatio-temporal form, through what he calls their "schematism"; and he then argues that the necessary application of the categories to our spatio-temporal experience yields a number of synthetic *a priori* principles, above all, the three principles that in all change the quantum of substance is always conserved, that every change occurs in accordance with a causal law, and that all objects existing simultaneously in space are in mutual interaction. Kant's demonstration of these synthetic *a priori* principles is the centerpiece of his response to Humean skepticism about first principles of theoretical cognition, that is, the kind of doubt that Hume raised with his famous argument that we have no rational basis for our belief in causation (though Hume never denied that such belief is entirely natural). In a "Refutation of Idealism" added to the "System of All Principles" in the second edition of the *Critique*, Kant also responds to Cartesian skepticism, that is, doubt about the inference to external objects from our internal representations.[37] But it is clearly Humean skepticism that is his original and primary target in the "Transcendental Analytic."

Kant's answer to Humean skepticism will depend upon his "Copernican revolution" and his assertion of our cognitive autonomy, that is, on the claim that we carry the fundamental principles of theoretical cognition of nature within ourselves – that, "as exaggerated and contradictory as it may sound . . . the understanding is itself the source of the laws of nature" (A 127). As in the case of his argument for transcendental idealism in the "Transcendental Aesthetic," however, we may conclude that Kant overstates the force of our cognitive autonomy, indeed by once again assuming a claim to necessity to which he may not be entitled.

The next three sections will thus spell out the "contributions of the understanding" to Kant's refutation of Humean skepticism, while the final section of this chapter will consider Kant's refutation of Cartesian skepticism.

THE METAPHYSICAL DEDUCTION

The argument of the "metaphysical deduction" is compact, and in part more compact than it should be. The premise of Kant's argument is that all cognition involves the combination of concepts into judgments, which in the first instance subsume more particular concepts under more general ones. For example, the judgment "All bodies are divisible" subsumes the more particular concept "body" under the more general concept "divisible" (that is, more things than bodies are divisible) (A 68/B 93). Now since all (synthetic) knowledge also involves intuition, which presents the objects to which concepts can refer, in all judgments the concepts must ultimately, whether directly or indirectly, refer to intuitions; in a typical judgment of the form "The F is G" the concept of the subject ("F") will refer to a particular object of intuition, while the concept of the predicate ("G") will refer to some sensible property that is being ascribed to the particular object of intuition introduced by the subject-concept. Kant insists, however, that there are no singular concepts, but only singular *uses* of concepts (*Logic*, §1, 9:91). That is, in a judgment about a particular object, the subject-concept, which is general and therefore could refer to any object in a certain class, refers to that particular object because in the actual context in which the judgment is asserted, it is understood to refer to a particular intuition, which is always singular. When I say "This body is divisible," the term "body," which is entirely general, refers to a particular object because in the relevant context the "this" links it to an intuition, a unique presentation of an object at a definite location in space and time. (The singular use of general concepts may not always involve an explicit indexical like "this," but something must do the job of linking the general concept to something particular. A definite description like "the current president of the United States," for example, does this with the help of the background knowledge that the Constitution of the U.S. specifies that at any given time there will be one and only one president.)

Kant's next claim is that there are certain features or "functions" of the ways in which concepts may be linked to form judgments, and thus in turn a certain number of "forms" of judgment, those arising from the permissible permutations of the "functions" of judgment. Specifically, he claims that every judgment has a "quantity," that is, it refers to all, some, or merely one of the objects in a certain class; that every judgment has a "quality," that is, it affirms a predicate of its subject, or denies it, or denies it while still implying that the object does have other predicates (this is the difference between what Kant calls "negative" and "infinite" judgments);[38] that every judgment expresses a "relation," either between a predicate and a subject-concept, or between two or more elementary judgments of which it is composed (if a judgment maintains that if one of its component judgments is true, then the other must also be true, it is a "hypothetical" judgment, while if it maintains that if one of its member judgments is true the other or others must be false, then it is a "disjunctive" judgment); and finally, that every judgment has a "modality," that is, it asserts that something may (or may not) be the case, that something is (or is not) the case, or that something must (or must not) be the case. Thus Kant maintains that there are four "titles" of the functions of judgment, each of which contains three particular functions beneath it: the quantity of judgments is either universal, particular, or singular; the quality is either affirmative, negative, or infinite; the relation is either categorical, hypothetical, or disjunctive; and the modality is either problematic, assertoric, or apodictic (A 70 / B 95).

It is easy enough to see what Kant means. A judgment like "All humans must die" is a universal, affirmative, categorical, and apodictic judgment, for it asserts that a certain predicate necessarily applies to all the individuals in a certain class; a judgment like "Some humans are learned" is particular, affirmative, categorical, but merely assertoric, for it maintains that a certain predicate does apply to some members of a certain class as a matter of fact, but not necessarily; a judgment like "If all humans must die, then none can be immortal" is a hypothetical judgment linking two categorical judgments which are themselves in one case universal, affirmative, and apodictic and in the other universal, negative, and apodictic; and so on. Every judgment does indeed seem to have some quantity, quality, relation, and modality, although as we see from these examples the modality of a judgment is not always explicitly expressed by a special term in its linguistic expression – in the judgment that "Some humans are learned" there is no specific word that reveals that it is assertoric as well as categorical. Kant's explanation of this is that modality does not add anything to the content of the judgment, but only concerns the "value of the copula in relation to thinking in general," that is, our attitude toward the content of the judgment.[39]

Intuitive as it may seem, is Kant's table of the functions of judgment *necessary*, thus a proper starting-point for a theory of *a priori* knowledge and a rejection of skepticism about first principles? Kant has often been accused of just cobbling it together from traditional logic textbooks, taking what he would need to derive the categories that he wants to prove next. There can be no doubt that Kant does not do much to explain the derivation of the functions of judgment, but in fact much if not all of Kant's table follows from a few simple thoughts. If you think of judgments as making connections between some domain of objects and some domain of properties, then you will quickly see that there are in fact only a few ways the connections can be made: a particular property can be asserted of one, some, or all of the objects in the domain; or it can be denied of one, some, or all of them; if you think that all judgments are either true or false, then in any conjunction of two of them either both will be true, both false, or one true and one false; if some judgment may be false, then its negation may not be false, i.e., is necessarily true; and so on. With the possible exception of Kant's "infinite" judgment, it looks as if the table of functions may easily be derived from the simple ideas that judgments link domains of predicates to domains of objects, and that they can only do so either truly or falsely.[40] But what about the underlying assumptions here, for example, that predicates must always be linked to some determinate number of objects, or that any proposition must be either true or false: are *they* strictly speaking necessary? It is not easy to see how we would prove that they are, but neither is it easy to see how they could not be, that is, to imagine alternatives to them.[41] I propose that we not worry about the necessity of Kant's table of functions of judgments: in asking whether the categories that he associates with the functions are really necessary and whether those really apply necessarily to all of our experience, we will have more than enough to worry about as we continue.

The next main step in Kant's "metaphysical deduction" is the claim that "The same function that gives unity to the different representations **in a judgment** also gives unity to the mere synthesis of different representations **in an intuition**, which, expressed generally, is called the pure concept of the understanding" (A 79 / B 104). I take this to be a highly compressed statement that if our *judgments* necessarily have certain forms, as has just been shown, then our *concepts of the objects* of those judgments must be structured in such a way that we can use those concepts in such judgments, and then that if this is the case then our *intuitions*, which are presentations of those objects, must also be structured in certain ways in order to allow such concepts and through them such judgments to apply to them. To take a simple example, if categorical judgments assert that particular predicates apply to particular subjects, then in order to make categorical judgments about objects we must conceive of those objects as substances that have properties, and further we must be able to recognize and distinguish substances and their properties in our intuitions, the ultimate target of our judgments. The ways in which we must structure our concepts of objects in order to make judgments about them are the pure concepts of the understanding, or the categories. Kant also puts this point by defining the categories as "concepts of an object in general, by means of which its intuition is **determined** with regard to one of the **logical functions** for judgments" (B 128); for example, the concept of substance determines that we should regard the object to which it is applied as the subject of a judgment, while the concept of a property (in Kant's language, an "accident"), determines that we should regard the aspect of intuition to which it is applied as a predicate. One thing that should be noted immediately is that the categories are not by themselves concepts of objects: the concept of a substance is not a concept of any particular substance, such as lead or gold, and the concept of a property is not a concept of any particular property, such as white or yellow. Rather, the categories are forms for particular concepts of objects, and those particular concepts must always have some empirical content – like whiteness or yellowness – in addition to their categorical form. In this regard, the categories are like space and time as the pure forms for the empirical intuition of particular objects, although in the case of space and time we also have pure intuitions of them as singular objects, while we have no such thing as a pure concept of substance or accident as such.[42]

It seems hard to deny that if there are certain ways in which we must form our judgments about objects, then there must also be certain ways in which we must form our concepts of objects in order to be able to make these but only these forms of judgment about them. But some questions do need to be raised about the table of categories that Kant correlates with the table of the logical functions of judgment (A 80/B 106). To the logical functions of quantity, namely universal, particular, and singular, Kant correlates the categories of quantity, namely unity, plurality, and totality; and it seems clear that if we are to be able to make universal, particular, and singular judgments, then we must be able to conceive of the objects of our judgments as units or individual members of some relevant class, as forming subgroups of such a class, or as exhausting the class. To the logical categories of quality, that is, the recognition that judgments may be affirmative, negative, or infinite, Kant coordinates the categories of quality, namely reality, negation, and limitation. At least the first two of these correlations seem unproblematic: if we are to make affirmative judgments, then we must be able to conceive of something in our experience of an object as a reality that is a basis for affirmative judgment, while something else can be conceived of as a "negation" and thus as a basis for a negative judgment, although in fact such a "negation" will not be a sheer absence (for that could be the negation of *any* predicate), but the presence of a particular property incompatible with the particular one being negated. In fact, the presence of the same property might count as a reality for one judgment but as a negation for another: for example, the presence of observable squareness might count as reality with regard to the affirmative judgment "My room is square" but as a negation with regard to the negative judgment "My room is circular," because being square verifies the predicate "is square" but negates the property "is circular." The case of the "infinite" judgment and the category of "limitation" is more problematic, however. Kant typically represents the infinite judgment as a judgment with the form "*x* is non-A," in contrast to an ordinary negative judgment, which has the form "*x* is not A," and seems to think that while the latter, because it merely denies a predicate of the concept of an object, does not imply that any object for that concept exists at all, the former, because it actually *asserts* "non-A" of its subject, *does* imply that an object for that concept exists and therefore has some property other than A, e.g., B or C or . . . – it leaves open an infinite range of predicates for *x*, but implies that *some* predicate applies to it (see the explanation of infinite judgments at *Logic*, §22, 9:104). But even if all this makes sense, it is not clear that in order to use both the negative and infinite forms of judgment we need to assume anything more than that properties may sometimes count as the basis for affirming a predicate of an object (a "reality"), and sometimes as a reason for denying a predicate of an object (a "negation"), although in some cases to deny a predicate of an object is to deny that the object exists at all, while in other cases it may leave open that the object exists and has other predicates. But then two categories – reality and negation – seem sufficient for making three kinds of judgment – affirmative, negative, and infinite – and it is not clear that a third category of "limitation" is required.

Further problems arise with regard to the three categories of relation that Kant correlates with the three forms of relation in judgments. To the categorical form of judgment, Kant correlates the category of "inherence and subsistence (*substantia et accidens*)"; to the hypothetical form of judgment, Kant correlates the category of "causality and dependence (cause and effect)"; and to the disjunctive form of judgment, Kant correlates the category of "community (reciprocity between agent and patient)." Each of these correlations is problematic. First, while it seems clear that if we are to use the categorical form of judgment, e.g., "All S's are P" (in modern symbolism, "$(x)(Sx \longrightarrow Px)$"), then we must be able to conceive of some aspects of our experience as subjects or bearers of properties and others as properties that can inhere in such subjects, it is not clear how much of the traditional concept of a *substance* needs to be packed into the concept of a *subject* that this requires – do we need to conceive of something that can *only* be the subject of a judgment and never a predicate in order to make categorical judgments? Second, while it is clear that we must be able to recognize relations of ground and consequence or dependency among the objects of our experience if we are to use the hypothetical form of judgment, that is, the "If – then. . . . " form of judgment, it is not clear that such relations need always or even ever be *causal*,[43] nor in fact is it clear that *only* the hypothetical judgment gives expression to relations of ground and consequence. Thus, as our modern symbolization of the categorical form of judgment already suggested, categorical judgments can also express relations of ground and consequence: a categorical judgment like "All bachelors are unmarried" can give expression to the fact that by definition if someone is a bachelor *then* he must be (male and) unmarried. More importantly, given Kant's own theory of mathematics there must also be non-definitional, *synthetic* implications that are still not causal but are expressed by the hypothetical form of judgment, e.g., "If a figure is a triangle, then its interior angles must equal two right angles." So the availability or even the necessity of using the hypothetical form of judgment does not by itself imply that we must apply the category of causality to the objects of our experience. Finally, what Kant has in mind by the disjunctive form of judgment, that is, "Either p or not-p," e.g., "Either the world is just or the world is unjust" (cf. A 74/B 99) seems to be the exact opposite of what he has in mind with the category of "community" or "reciprocity": in the case of a disjunctive judgment, the truth of one disjunct is supposed to entail the *falsehood* of all the others, while in the case of community, the condition of one object is supposed to entail that of another and *vice versa*, that is, we might say, the truth about one object is supposed to entail and be entailed by the truth of the other. So the category of community seems very different from the logical relation of disjunction.

Finally, in order to make use of the modal functions of judgment, that is, the problematic ("There might be . . . "), assertoric ("There are . . . "), and apodictic ("There must be . . . ") forms of judgment, Kant claims that we must be able to apply the modal categories of possibility and impossibility, existence and non-existence, and necessity and contingency to the objects of our experience. Here the problem seems to be one of defining the differences between these categories and between them and some of the categories earlier introduced. What is the difference between the modal categories of "existence" and "non-existence" and the categories of "reality" and "negation" earlier introduced as categories of "quality"? Isn't what exists just what has reality, and consequently that which does not exist that which is the subject of negation? And what is the difference between "possibility" and "impossibility" on the one hand, and "necessity" and "contingency" on the other? Can't the second pair of concepts be completely defined in terms of the first two pairs, that is, isn't the contingent just that which is something actual, which is therefore of course possible, but the negation of which is not impossible, and isn't the necessary just something actual the negation of which is impossible? Do we need three pairs of modal categories rather than just two?

These are serious questions. The problems about the relational categories in particular might seem to raise fundamental problems for Kant's project of answering Humean skepticism by showing that we can know *a priori* that we must apply categories such as substance and causality to our experience. Just how serious these problems are, however, depends on the precise structure of Kant's argument in the rest of the "Analytic." If he assumes that the metaphysical deduction has already shown that we must in fact make judgments using *all* of the available logical functions of judgment and also that the categories he has listed are necessary conditions for using those logical functions, that is, the only way those functions of judgment can ever be applied to objects, then indeed his entire argument will indeed be in deep trouble – for he has not even shown that we must use all of the logical functions of judgment at all, let alone that his categories are the only means by which these functions can be applied to objects. But remember, Kant calls the "metaphysical deduction" a mere "clue to the discovery of all pure concepts of the understanding," not anything like a conclusive argument for their necessity. In fact, what Kant will do in what follows is to provide entirely *independent* arguments from premises about the nature of our experience that have not yet been introduced that we must use all of the *categories*, from which it will then in turn follow that we not only can but also must use all the *logical functions of judgment* – the exact opposite of simply inferring that we may or must use the categories because we are entitled to use the logical functions of judgment. For example, in the "Analogies of Experience" Kant will provide arguments from a key fact about the temporal structure of our experience – which was established in the "Transcendental Aesthetic," not in the present "metaphysical deduction" – for why we must use the *categories* of substance and accident, cause and effect, and interaction, from which it would then *follow*, not be *presupposed*, that we must also use the categorical, hypothetical, and disjunctive *forms of judgment* (well, the last of these may still be problematic). And if this strategy works, then it would not matter if there are other ways in which the logical functions of judgment can be applied to object than through the categories Kant has singled out: if, for example, Kant proves that we must apply the category of causality to our experience and therefore use the hypothetical form of judgment to express judgments of causality, it is simply irrelevant that this same form of judgment can also be used to express analytic or definitional entailments and synthetic but mathematical rather than causal implications. Kant's aim is to prove that we must use the category of causality and therefore the logical form of disjunctive judgment, not to prove that we must use the latter and therefore the former.[44]

To see if this strategy is going to work, we should now turn from the "metaphysical deduction" to the main arguments of the "Analytic," those of the "Transcendental Deduction" and the "System of Principles." Before we do so, however, a quick comment about the modal categories is in order. As we saw, some of the modal categories seem to be definable in terms of other modal categories and the categories of quality, which raises questions about whether all of these categories are really necessary. We might also ask if by introducing the modal pairs possibility / impossibility, existence / non-existence, and necessity / contingency, Kant means to

suggest that there is such a variety of modal properties manifest in our experience of the world in the same way that, for example, substance, causality, and
interaction will be argued to be manifest in that experience. That might be
strange, too. However, Kant will not in fact be committed to the primacy
of all the modal categories or to any sort of modal realism. In fact, what he
will subsequently argue (in the section of the "System of all Principles"
called "The Postulates of Empirical Thinking") is precisely that all of
the modal categories are applied on the basis of other forms of experience: the possible is simply that the concept of which is free of internal
contradiction and is consistent with the spatio-temporal form of our experience; the actual is that which satisfies the conditions of possibility and is
also attested to by sensation, i.e., real; and that which is necessary is
simply the real regarded as subject to causal laws of nature, i.e., it is coex-
tensive with the actual but regarded in light of its thoroughgoing
subjection to causality (see A 218/B 264–5). In other words, the defin-
ability of the modal categories in terms of the categories of quality and
relation and the fact that the modal categories do not introduce any properties into our experience other than the spatio-temporal structure of our
empirical intuition and the subjection of the latter to the categories of
relation such as causality is precisely what Kant will insist upon, and what
he is preparing the way for in his initial discussion of these categories.

THE TRANSCENDENTAL DEDUCTION

In the Preface to the first edition of the Critique of Pure Reason, Kant wrote:

> [there were] no investigations more important for getting to the bottom of
> that faculty we call the understanding, and at the same time for the deter-
> mination of the rules and boundaries of its use, than . . . [the] **Deduction
> of the Pure Concepts of the Understanding**.

He went on to add that "they are also the investigations that have cost me
the most, but I hope not unrewarded, effort" (A xvi). Unfortunately, his
efforts were unrewarded; nobody understood the argument of the transcendental deduction. In response, Kant tried to minimize the role of the
argument in his next two works in theoretical philosophy, the Prolegomena to
Any Future Metaphysics of 1783 and the Metaphysical Foundations of Natural Science of
1786. But there was clearly something that Kant was trying to say in the
transcendental deduction that he said in no other part of his work, and so
he was forced to come back to it, and in the end he completely rewrote

the heart of the argument for the second edition of the *Critique* in 1787. The new version certainly clarifies some questions about Kant's argument, but some puzzles remain.

Part of the problem in understanding the transcendental deduction is that in its introductory sections, which Kant left unchanged in the second edition, he suggests at least three different accounts of what the argument is meant to accomplish. He begins with a famous image, saying that the deduction is like a legal argument about what is "lawful (*quid juris*)" rather than about what is mere "fact (*quid facti*)" (A 84/B 116) – it concerns our right to use the categories that have been identified in the metaphysical deduction, not the mere fact that we do. But just what question about our right to use the categories has been left open by the previous argument is by no means immediately clear. The first thing that Kant says is that the "**transcendental deduction**" is to be an "explanation of the way in which concepts can relate to objects *a priori*" rather than a mere "**empirical**" deduction, which shows how a concept is acquired through experience and reflection on it, and therefore concerns not the lawfulness but the fact from which the possession has arisen" (A 85/B 117) – the kind of explanation of our possession of concepts that Kant took John Locke to have offered (A 86/B 119). This is reminiscent of Kant's account of his (analytic or regressive) method of argument in the transcendental expositions of space and time, namely, an inference from some unquestioned synthetic *a priori* cognition to its *a priori* ground or basis. But in the preceding paragraph Kant had suggested that the *a priori* categories are like the concepts of "**fortune** and **fate**" in that we have to show whether we are entitled to use them, or to assume them to be *a priori*, at all; so the model of simply revealing the *a priori* conditions for the use of concepts already known to be *a priori* does not seem to be very promising. Moreover, in the first-edition Preface Kant had said:

> This inquiry, which goes rather deep, has two sides. One refers to the objects of the pure understanding, and is supposed to demonstrate and make comprehensible the objective validity of its concepts *a priori*; thus it belongs essentially to my ends. The other side deals with the pure understanding itself, concerning its possibility and the powers of cognition on which it itself rests; thus it considers it in a subjective relation, and although this exposition is of great importance in respect of my chief end, it does not belong essentially to it; because the chief question always remains, "What and how much can understanding and reason cognize free of all experience?" and not: "How is the **faculty of thinking** itself

possible?" . . . even in case my subjective deduction does not produce the
complete conviction that I expect, the objective deduction that is my
primary concern would come in its full strength.

(A xvi–xvii)

But the explanation of how the categories can relate to objects a priori that
Kant says at A 85/B 117 will constitute the transcendental deduction
sounds very much like this merely "subjective" deduction, and thus would
not seem to be at the heart of what Kant is after, the "objective" deduction.

In the passage just cited, however, Kant says that the essential, "objective" deduction is supposed "to demonstrate and make comprehensible
the objective validity" of the a priori concepts of the understanding. Does
that tell us what the transcendental deduction is really supposed to accomplish? Well, Kant shortly says that if "**subjective conditions of thinking**"
have "**objective validity**" then they are "conditions of the possibility of
all cognition of objects," that is, necessarily and universally apply to
objects of cognition (A 89–90/B 122). And he says that while it has been
easy to show, "with little effort," that space and time "necessarily relate to
objects," since the categories are not conditions of the intuition of objects
their objective validity remains to be demonstrated. So this makes it look
as if what is essential for the transcendental deduction is for it to show that
the categories universally and necessarily apply to all objects of our cognition, and for that reason, of course, must be known a priori. Demonstrating
that would be the "objective" deduction, and then filling in the details of
how a priori concepts relate to objects given in intuition would be the
"subjective deduction."

The problem with this suggestion, however, is that the metaphysical deduction has already shown that the categories must apply to any and all objects
of our cognition, and thus have "objective validity" as just defined: the
metaphysical deduction claimed that all cognition of objects is expressed
through judgments about those objects, and then argued that since our
judgments must have certain forms, so must our concepts, thus that there
are a priori categories that are the conditions of any possible judgments and
therefore any possible cognition of objects. Unless the transcendental
deduction is completely redundant, therefore, it must prove something
more than this. But what more could Kant want to prove at this point?

He gives us a clue about what more might be at stake a few pages
further on when he says that what must be proven in the transcendental
deduction is that "all experience contains in addition to the intuition of
the senses, through which something is given, a **concept** of an object that

is given in intuition, or appears; hence concepts of objects in general lie at the ground of all experiential cognition as *a priori* conditions," and that

> The transcendental deduction of all *a priori* concepts therefore has a prin-
> ciple toward which the entire investigation must be directed, namely this:
> that they must be recognized as *a priori* conditions of the possibility of
> experiences (whether of the intuition that is encountered in them, or of the
> thinking).
>
> (A 93–4/B 126)

If "experience" here means something like *consciousness as such*, as opposed to empirical knowledge of objects, which is how Kant sometimes uses the term but which would make the deduction question-begging, then these statements suggest that the transcendental deduction will not *presuppose* that we have cognition of objects but must somehow *prove* that we have knowledge of objects from some more general claim about the nature of consciousness.[45] If the transcendental deduction does this, then it will not repeat what the metaphysical deduction has done, but will provide an even more fundamental premise to which the results of the metaphysical deduction can be applied. That is, if the transcendental deduction can prove that all of our experience must be cognition of objects, then it will follow from the metaphysical deduction's proof that all cognition of objects involves the categories that the categories must apply to all of our experience, bar none. The proof of the objective validity of the categories at which the transcendental deduction aims would then be the proof that the categories universally and necessarily apply to all our experience, to whatever might be presented to us in space and/or time.

If this is what the transcendental deduction is supposed to prove, however, then some of the arguments that Kant sketches under that rubric are not going to work. The first edition version of the deduction begins with a "preliminary reminder" or provisional presentation of the argument, in which Kant includes a famous theory of "threefold synthesis." He argues here that there are three elements involved in all experience of objects: first, we must sequentially "apprehend" several intuitions of an object (a "manifold of intuition"); second, we must be able to "repro-duce" earlier items in such a manifold as we apprehend the later ones, so that we can even raise the question of whether the earlier ones represent the *same* object as the later ones do; and finally we must "recognize" the unity of the manifold under a concept, that is, recognize that our several intuitions constitute knowledge of a single object because it follows from some concept of the object that it must have just the sorts of properties that those successive intuitions represent it as having (A 99–104). To borrow an example from later in the book (A 141/B 180), our concept of a dog can allow us to recognize that our several representations of a four-legged shape, a barking sound, and a, well, doggy smell comprise the representation of a dog, because the concept tells us that those sorts of properties go together in dogs (but not, say, cats). However, there are two problems with this line of thought. First, as our example makes clear, this argument demonstrates the need for *empirical* concepts in the cognition of objects; unless empirical concepts can themselves be shown to depend in some way on the *a priori* categories of the understanding, the argument tells us nothing about the objective validity of the latter. Of course, if the metaphysical deduction has already shown that cognition of objects requires the categories, we might not need any further proof of this point. The more important problem with the argument, however, is that while it is an insightful *analysis* of what is involved in our cognition *of an object*, it is not a *proof* from some more general feature of our experience *that all our experiences must also be experiences of objects*, and thus that the categories have "objective validity" in the sense of necessarily applying to all our experiences. So the argument does not seem to realize the aim that will distinguish the transcendental from the metaphysical deduction.[46]

Kant himself seems to think that the analysis of the threefold synthesis does by itself show at least that our cognition of objects must involve *a priori* concepts, although his conclusion seems to be based on a fallacious inference from the necessity of a concept to unify our experience of an object to the necessity of a *necessary* and therefore *a priori* concept (A 104–6). (That is a fallacy because, as we saw from the case of the concept *dog*, an ordinary empirical concept can do this job.) But in then attempting to explain where such *a priori* concepts could come from, Kant introduces a new concept that may be precisely the more general feature of experience that is needed. This is the concept of "transcendental apperception," a "unity of consciousness that precedes all data of the intuitions" or a "pure, original, unchanging consciousness" of the "numerical identity" of oneself in all of one's various experiences (A 107, A 113). Although Kant uses the terms "apperception" and "unity of consciousness" in a variety of ways,[47] the basic idea of "transcendental apperception" seems to be that any time I have any experience I can also know that I have that experience, and that knowing *that* is equivalent to knowing that that experience belongs to the *same* self that has all my other experiences – the self that is numerically identical throughout all my experiences.

This premise seems able to stand on its own, independent of the previous argument about the threefold synthesis. The question now is whether the fact of transcendental apperception somehow entails the necessary application of the categories to all of the experiences to which it itself applies, that is to say, to all of our experiences without exception. If so, the fact of transcendental apperception could be the basis for the desired proof of the objective validity of the categories. But how does Kant propose to get from transcendental apperception to the categories?

Kant tries out a number of different tactics in the hope of solving this strategic problem. His main tactic in the first edition of the "Deduction" is to begin with the premise that the unity of consciousness in transcendental apperception is both synthetic and *a priori*, so it must rest on a synthesis that is itself *a priori*:

> Now the unity of the manifold in a subject is synthetic; pure apperception therefore yields a principle of the synthetic unity of the manifold in all possible intuition.
>
> This synthetic unity, however, presupposes a synthesis, or includes it, and if the former is to be necessary *a priori* then the latter must also be a synthesis *a priori*.
>
> (A 117–18)

In saying that apperception is synthetic and therefore presupposes a synthesis, Kant means that in ascribing a manifold of representations – a multiplicity of particular observations or empirical intuitions – to ourselves, we assert that there is a connection among them – each of them belongs to the same self as all the others belong to – that is not a logical part of the content of any one of them considered by itself; thus the connection between the different representations that belong to a single self cannot be known by any mere analysis. This seems perfectly plausible. It does not follow from the fact that I am now looking at a red book that a moment ago I was looking at a blue one, or vice versa. But in fact I have just had both of these experiences. Thus they both belong to the unity of my consciousness or to my numerically identical self, and it therefore seems reasonable to suppose that the connection between them must in some way be synthetic rather than analytic. However, what does Kant mean by calling this connection in consciousness not just synthetic but synthetic *a priori*? In fact, he says two different things about this, one of which seems true but trivial, the other of which, however, seems substantive but problematic. In the second edition of the "Deduction," Kant says that "the principle of the necessary unity of apperception is . . . itself identical, thus an analytical proposition" (B 135), and this could be taken to say simply that what it *means* to ascribe one representation to oneself is that it is ascribed to the same self as any and all other representations that are ascribed to oneself. This could be regarded as merely a definition of the idea of a self, from which nothing follows about whether any particular representation must be ascribed to such a self, let alone on what basis this would happen. In the first edition, however, Kant seems to have in mind that we have not a merely definitional but a substantive certainty that any representation we can have will in fact be ascribed to a numerically identical self. He writes:

> All intuitions are nothing for us and do not in the least concern us if they cannot be taken up into consciousness . . . and through this alone is cognition possible. We are conscious *a priori* of the thoroughgoing identity of ourselves with regard to all representations that can ever belong to our consciousness, as a necessary condition of the possibility of all represen-tations. . . . This principle holds *a priori*.

> (A 116)

Kant then makes a number of very striking inferences from this principle. First, he argues that if we know that there is a unity among all of our representations even before we know anything about the particular content of those representations, yet this unity is synthetic, then there must be an *a priori* synthesis of all of our representations prior to any particular empir-ical syntheses of them (the sort of syntheses by which we determine whether some particular representations represent a dog or a cat, for example), which he calls the "**productive synthesis of the imagination**" (A 118); and if this synthesis is *a priori*, he assumes, then it must have its own *a priori* rules. Next, he assumes that all synthesis is ultimately a product of the faculty of *understanding*, and, "in relation to the **transcen-dental synthesis** of the imagination," by which he means the *a priori* synthesis that he has just postulated, "the **pure understanding**" (A 119); and since, as he takes the metaphysical deduction to have shown, the cate-gories are the "pure *a priori* conditions that contain the necessary unity" of all syntheses of the pure understanding, he then infers that the categories must be the conditions of the pure synthesis which results in the unity of apperception. Finally, since this means that we not only can but must apply the categories to any of our representations, and yet the categories are also the pure forms for all concepts of objects, Kant takes this to mean that through the categories we can always supply concepts for any experiences that we have, or that there is a necessary "affinity" among all our representations: "the necessity of a law extending through all appearances, a law, namely, for regarding them throughout as data of sense that are associable in themselves and subject to universal laws of a thoroughgoing connection" (A 122). Given the assumptions he has made, the existence of this affinity does indeed follow from the premise that it is "only because I ascribe all perceptions to one consciousness (of original apperception) [that] I can say of all perceptions that I am conscious of them." And since the transcendental unity of apperception implies this affinity, Kant feels entitled to assert that "the understanding is itself the source of the laws of nature, and thus of the formal unity of nature" (A 127).

This is an extraordinary argument,[48] starting from what we might think of as a sort of Cartesian assumption of certainty about the unity of the self and concluding with the profoundly anti-Humean conclusion that the understanding is necessarily the source of unity in nature. By this argument, Kant's initial, Copernican idea that the fundamental principles of knowledge must be autonomous, must lie within ourselves, is revealed as the assumption that the understanding forms nature and thus can always impose its principles upon nature. But the argument is vulnerable to several objections. First, it could be argued that although Kant is entitled to the *analytic* principle that we must be conscious of a synthetic connection among whatever representations we can as a matter of fact call our own, this does not imply the *synthetic* principle that we can *have* no representations that we cannot call our own: the analytic principle leaves open whether any particular representation that we have must also be one that we are aware of having and therefore can associate with others. Kant's assertion of the stronger, synthetic principle in saying that any intuition of which we are not aware is "nothing for us" and does "not in the least concern us" does not, the objection would continue, prove that his assumption is synthetic *a priori*: it might well be true that a representation that we are not aware of having does not concern us (or this might sometimes be true, although if it were always true, it would be hard to understand why some people spend so much money on psychoanalysis), but this does not imply that we cannot have any such representations.

Second, the argument seems to identify the transcendental synthesis that allegedly underlies the unity of apperception with a synthesis of the understanding conducted in accordance with the categories arbitrarily; that is, it just asserts that the understanding is the source of all synthesis and therefore that the categories are involved in all synthesis.[49] Another way of putting this point would be to say that Kant's argument is at the very least too abstract: it assures us that the understanding is the source of the unity of apperception, but does not tell us what sorts of particular judgments about the unity of the self are made possible by the application of the categories to our representations, and therefore cannot convince us that the categories are really the necessary conditions of the unity of apperception. Moreover, the idea that the categories are involved in an *a priori* synthesis that somehow precedes or underlies empirical syntheses does not seem to sit very well with the conception of the categories as the forms of our empirical concepts that was suggested by the metaphysical deduction: that way of thinking about the categories suggests that they must guide us in the formation of empirical concepts, but that in turn means that the only syntheses of our data that there will be (apart from those in pure mathematics) will be *empirical* syntheses, of empirical data and using empirical concepts, although empirical concepts formed in accordance with the *a priori* categories.

Finally, Kant's idea of the necessary *affinity* of all appearances might be an excessively strong notion of cognitive *autonomy*: it is one thing to claim that by turning into ourselves we can *discover* the necessary conditions of any possible knowledge of objects, which are conditions that must be satisfied by any particular objects that we do in fact succeed in comprehending; but it is quite another thing to say that we can always *impose* the principles of our own understanding on any objects of nature, whatever they might be like in themselves. To say the latter would be to say that there can be nothing in nature that we cannot succeed in comprehending, and it is not clear that we could prove such a strong claim by reflection on the conditions of the possibility of what is after all a certain kind of *self*-knowledge.

As mentioned earlier, Kant completely rewrote the transcendental deduction for the second edition of the *Critique*. Did he do so because he recognized any of the problems just mentioned and now knew how to resolve them? He must have realized that the connection between apperception and the use of the categories to form concepts of objects was at least inadequately supported in the first-edition deduction, because in the new version he tries to make that connection more persuasive.

The new version of the argument begins with an explicit assertion of the premise that "all combination . . . is an action of the understanding" (§15, B 130). The next section of the argument begins with Kant's famous assertion that "The **I think** must be able to accompany all my representations . . . Thus all manifold of representation has a necessary relation to the **I think** in the same subject in which this manifold is to be encountered" (§16, B 131–2). In other words, to ascribe any one representation to oneself is to ascribe it to the "same subject" that also possesses the "manifold" of the rest of one's representation, and for that reason entails an act of combination on the part of the understanding. Kant reiterates this point when he says that:

> It is only because I can combine a manifold of given representations **in one consciousness** that it is possible for me to represent the **identity of the consciousness in these representations** itself, i.e., the **analytical** unity of apperception is only possible under the presupposition of some **synthetic** one.
>
> (B 133–4)

The analytical unity of apperception is what I assert when I call a single representation mine, as if I were simply ascribing to it a property like that of being red; the synthetic unity of apperception is what I assert when I call all of my representations together mine, and what Kant is claiming is that the former depends on the latter – so to call a representation mine is not like calling one apple red at all, since that does not depend upon what I call any other apples. In all of this, it looks as if Kant is simply emphasizing the synthetic character of apperception, and then preparing us, by appeal to the premise introduced in §15, for the same sort of direct argument from the understanding as the source of combination or synthesis to the categories as a necessary condition of this synthesis that he attempted in the first edition (B 134–5).

But Kant slows down, and tries to establish an independent connection between apperception and the objective validity of the categories by showing that apperception is itself intrinsically connected to judgments *about objects*[50] and thus, given the argument of the metaphysical deduction, necessarily involves the categories. His first attempt to do this, however, looks like it runs in the wrong direction: in §17, Kant writes that "An **object** . . . is that in the concept of which the manifold of a given intuition is **united**," and that "the unity of consciousness is that which alone constitutes the relation of representations to an object" (B 137). This makes it look as if it is being suggested that the unity of apperception is a sufficient condition for cognition of objects, so that whatever is necessary for unity of apperception also applies to objects (actually, this would only follow if unity of apperception were a necessary condition for cognition of objects; maybe Kant means to say it is both necessary and sufficient). This in turn would tell us that the categories must apply to all objects, or have universal validity in the sense originally defined at A 93/B 126, if they are involved in apperception itself.[51] But if what we are looking for is a reason to believe that the categories are necessary conditions of apperception itself, then this argument seems to be presupposing what is supposed to be proven.[52]

In the next two sections, however, Kant tries to argue that apperception is a form of judgment about objects and therefore intrinsically involves the categories. He does this by stating in §18 that the "**transcendental unity** of apperception" is an "**objective**" rather than "**subjective unity** of consciousness" (B 139) while arguing conversely in §19 that "a judgment is nothing other than the way to bring given cognitions to the **objective** unity of apperception" (B 141). This makes it sound as if apperception necessarily involves judgment as well as judgment necessarily involving apperception, so if judgment necessarily involves the categories then so will apperception itself. If this is so, then, since all of our experiences are part of our unity of apperception, all of them will involve the categories – in other words, the categories will have objective validity, which is what the whole transcendental deduction is supposed to prove. However, Kant may here make the crucial connection between apperception and judgment about objects too easily. When he defines the "subjective" unity of consciousness in contrast to the "objective," he is making a contrast between associations of ideas that are "entirely contingent" and perhaps valid only for a single subject and those that are valid for any and all subjects (B 140). But that is just to say that the "objective unity of consciousness" is consciousness of an objective relation of representations, or *of an object*, rather than non-objective. We can concede that the metaphysical deduction has already shown that the categories are necessary conditions for the cognition *of objects*; now Kant seems to be showing that they are also conditions for the unity of apperception itself simply by *equating* unity of apperception with cognition of objects. But that does not independently establish that apperception *as it was originally understood* – that is, as a connection among all of our representations *as such*, regardless of what they may or may not represent – involves judgments about objects, from which we could *infer* that we must make objective judgments using the categories about all of our experience. Further, if we were to accept Kant's present move without qualification, we would have a dilemma on our hands: either some of our experience is merely subjective, and does not involve the categories, which means that the categories do not after all have objective validity, that is, apply to all our experience; or else all of our apperception is objective and the categories do apply to all our experience, but only because we do not have any merely subjective experience at all. Neither horn of this dilemma seems attractive.[53] Kant presupposes that he has successfully shown that apperception always involves judgment when he concludes in §20 that it therefore involves the logical functions of judgment, and that "the **categories** are nothing other than these very functions of judging, insofar as the manifold of a given intuition is determined with regard to them" (B 143); but he has not, at least not for the general sense of apperception introduced in §16 rather than the question-begging sense smuggled into §18.

So is Kant's second version of the deduction as much of a failure as his first attempt? The sections we have considered thus far (§§15–20) have not done better than the first version in establishing a direct connection between the unity of apperception and the objective validity of the categories for all of our experiences, but Kant next makes a move that opens up another and altogether more promising line of argument. In §21, Kant says that in the previous sections only "the **beginning** of a deduction of the pure categories of the understanding has been made," which has abstracted "from the way in which the manifold for an empirical intuition is given," that is, from the necessary spatio-temporal form of all of our experience, demonstrated in the "Transcendental Aesthetic." The argument now has to be completed in a way that takes account of that sensible condition of the possibility of our experience.[54] To be sure, Kant assumes that he has already successfully shown that the categories necessarily apply to all of our experience, and in now reminding us that our experience is spatio-temporal so the categories necessarily apply to an experience that is spatio-temporal, his primary aim seems to be to make clear the limits on our use of the categories: since our spatio-temporal experience is experience only of how things appear, not how they are in themselves, and the categories necessarily apply to our spatio-temporal experience, they too yield knowledge only of how things appear, not how they are in themselves – although since the categories do not directly have spatio-temporal content, they may still be used to think about non-spatio-temporal objects, that is, things as they are in themselves (§22, B 146). This is consistent with Kant's original claim in the Preface to the first edition that what is essential to the transcendental deduction is to determine "What and how much can understanding and reason cognize free of all experience" (A xvii), that is, to both secure and to limit our a priori knowledge of and through the categories.[55] And the next several sections are indeed devoted to emphasizing that the categories do yield knowledge merely with respect to appearance, even, paradoxical as it may seem, in the case of ourselves: since "we must order the determinations of inner sense as appearances in time in just the same way as we order those of outer sense in space" (§24, B 156), through the categories "I therefore have **no cognition** of myself **as I am**, but only as I **appear** to myself" (§25, B 158). The thesis that through the categories we can only have cognition of things as they appear but that we can nevertheless use the categories to think how they might be in themselves will be crucial to Kant's eventual argument that we can have practical grounds for belief in metaphysical claims of which we can have no theoretical cognition, and in particular to his argument that the thoroughgoing causal determinism entailed by the necessary application of the category of causality to the appearance of our selves is compatible with freedom of the will in the self considered as it is in itself. These are clearly positions of the utmost importance to Kant, and of course we shall have to return to them later. But what is of interest now is the alternative strategy for demonstrating the objective validity of the categories that Kant suggests in the penultimate section of the second half of the second-edition deduction (§26).

Kant begins this section by reminding us that "space and time are repre-sented *a priori* not merely as **forms** of sensible intuition, but also as **intuitions** themselves (which contain a manifold" (B 160). He then adds that although in the "Transcendental Aesthetic" he "ascribed this unity merely to sensibility, . . . in order to note that it precedes all concepts," in fact "it presupposes a synthesis, which does not belong to the senses but through which all concepts of space and time first become possible" (B 160–1n.). From these premises he concludes that "this synthetic unity can be none other than that of the combination of the manifold of a given **intuition in general** in an original consciousness, in agreement with the categories" (B 161). In other words, Kant now argues that the unity of space and time themselves depend upon the categories, so of course the categories are objectively valid, or necessarily apply to every experience that we can have, since all of our experience is spatio-temporal. Now in making this argument, Kant cannot mean that our recognition of the purely formal fact that every space and every time can only be represented as a part of a larger space or time, which immediately implies the unity (and also infini-tude) of space and time, rests on the categories. For not only would that undermine a central and as we saw quite persuasive argument of the "Transcendental Aesthetic"; it is also hard to see how the categories are involved in that insight at all, or at least any categories beyond the categories of quantity, if we are willing to interpret the concepts of "part" and "whole" as a version of the categories of "unity" and "totality." So what could Kant mean here that would make sense and not undermine the "Transcendental Aesthetic"? Well, his remark that space and time "contain a manifold" could suggest that it is our cognition of the unity of what fills space and time, that is, our cognition of the unitary and determinate order of *objects* and their *states* in space and time, that depends upon the use of the categories. This is also what Kant suggests when he offers some examples to illustrate what he has in mind. He maintains that in making "the empirical intuition of a house into perception" I rely not merely on the formal intuition of space but also on the category of quantity, "the synthesis of the homogeneous in an intuition in general" (B 162), presumably meaning by this that in order to think of my several empirical intuitions, that is, my glimpses of windows, doors, walls, and so on, as perceptions of a single house, I have to think of them as representing parts of a single enduring whole; and he says that in order to "perceive the freezing of water" I have to "apprehend two states (of fluidity and solidity)" not merely as occurring in time but as occurring in a *determinate order* in time – fluidity first and solidity second, not the other way around, for that would be melting, not freezing – and that in order to do that I need to apply the category of causality to my observations (B 162–3). This suggests that determinate knowledge of objects and events in space and time depends upon the use of a wide range of the categories, specifically including the categories of substance and causality, which are the pure forms of such empirical concepts as those of houses and freezing. But what about apperception, that is, cognition of the numerical identity *of oneself*? Well, if Kant could successfully argue that it is necessary to employ the categories to have any determinate cognition of objects and their states in space and time, he could also argue that we must use those categories to have determinate cognition *of ourselves* as enduring objects with determinate sequences of experiences. That is, if Kant could argue that the use of the categories is a necessary condition for any determinate knowledge of objects in space and time, *and then show us that self-knowledge is also determinate knowledge of an object in space and time*, he could finally show us that the categories are necessarily involved in self-knowledge as well as in knowledge of objects other than the self.

Now so far this is only the outline of a strategy. But we shall shortly see that it is precisely the strategy that Kant executes in considerable detail in the "Analytic of Principles," particularly in the sections he calls the "Analogies of Experience" and the "Refutation of Idealism" (added in the second edition).[56] The latter title also suggests that Kant recognizes that his use of this strategy might leave him vulnerable to skepticism. If he is going to resolve Humean skepticism about first principles such as the universal validity of causation by demonstrating that such principles are necessary conditions for cognition of external objects and even of the numerically identical self, he will have to confront not only Cartesian skepticism about external knowledge but also the even more radical Humean doubt that we have any real knowledge of a continuing self at all. Kant will indeed attempt to do this, but we will have to wait until we have considered the more detailed arguments of the "Principles" section to see how successful this attempt is. For now, we may conclude our discussion of the second-edition deduction by noting that, as in the first edition, Kant ends it by asserting the very strong thesis that "Categories are concepts that prescribe laws *a priori* to appearances, thus to nature as the sum total of all appearances" (B 163). Thus, he does not just infer that our experience of nature had better turn out to be sufficiently orderly to allow us to apply the categories to it if we are to get knowledge of objects out of that experience; rather, as with the first edition doctrine of "affinity," he infers that we can always "prescribe" or impose the categories upon our experience of nature, in other words, that there is no way nature could prove resistant to our thought structured through the categories. This time, however, he recognizes that this strong conclusion needs support, and so he adds an argument that is reminiscent of his basic argument in support of transcendental idealism in the "Transcendental Aesthetic" and the *Prolegomena*: he says that if we were to entertain "a kind of **preformation-system** of pure reason" (§27, B 167),[57] that is, to presuppose that nature happens to have the kind of structure that the application of the categories to it would require independently of the fact that we ourselves must think in accordance with the categories simply because we think in judgments, we would not be able to say that nature *necessarily* satisfies the categories – for example, in the case of causation:

> I would not be able to say that the effect is combined with the cause in the object (i.e., necessarily), but only that I am so constituted that I cannot think of this representation otherwise than as so connected; which is precisely what the skeptic wishes most.
>
> (B 168)

Kant here makes the same move that he made about space in his central argument for transcendental idealism in the "Transcendental Aesthetic": if the categories apply to objects independently of our imposition of them, then they do so only contingently; and if our knowledge of objects and even our knowledge of ourselves depends upon the application of the categories to objects, then our knowledge of objects and even our self-knowledge would also, in the end, be contingent. He clearly assumes that it is not contingent that we have knowledge, and especially not contingent that we have knowledge of the numerical identity of our own selves. But just as it was in the "Transcendental Aesthetic," the real question now is whether Kant is ultimately entitled to such an assumption of necessity: Can we really say that it is necessary *that* we have knowledge of our own numerically identical selves, or are we entitled only to say what conditions our experience must satisfy if we are to have such knowledge?

Perhaps we should not worry too much about this question. After all, most of us clearly do have knowledge of the unity and coherence of our own experiences over considerable periods of time, and if Kant can show that the application of the categories to the objects of our experience is a necessary condition of such knowledge, that would be a considerable philosophical accomplishment and perhaps an adequate answer to all but the most excessive and implausible skepticism. So let's leave the question open for the time being and see how in the "Analytic of Principles" Kant executes in detail the strategy finally suggested in the second half of the second-edition "Transcendental Deduction." This strategy, recall, is that of showing that our determinate knowledge of objects in space and time and also our determinate knowledge of our own selves as objects in space and time depends not only on the *a priori* forms of space and time but also on the use of empirical concepts formed in accordance with such key categories of the understanding as substance and causality, and by that means showing that the categories have objective validity in the sense of necessarily applying to anything we can count as experience at all.

THE PRINCIPLES OF EMPIRICAL JUDGMENT

The "Analytic of Principles" is divided into three chapters: a brief first chapter "On the schematism of the principles of the pure concepts of the understanding," a lengthy second chapter on the "System of all principles of pure understanding," and a third chapter "On the ground of the distinction of all objects in general into *phenomena* and *noumena*" (which was heavily rewritten for the second edition of the *Critique*). The first two chapters continue Kant's exposition of his theory of the contribution of our own principles to theoretical knowledge of nature, and take steps toward the defense of his theory of our cognitive autonomy from Humean and (in the second-edition) Cartesian skepticism. The third chapter lays the foundation for Kant's critique of traditional metaphysics, which will be expounded in detail in the "Transcendental Dialectic" and which is also Kant's response to Pyrrhonian skepticism.

The "Schematism"

The chapter on the "schematism" can seem mysterious. Kant begins by stating that "In all subsumptions of an object under a concept the representations of the former must be **homogeneous** with the latter" (A 137/B 176), and suggests that a third thing, a "schema," is needed to intervene between concept and object (A 138/B 177). This must be produced by a "schematism of our understanding with regard to appearances and their more form," which is "a hidden art in the depths of the human soul, whose true operations we can divine from nature and lay unveiled before our eyes only with difficulty" (A 141/B 180). All this seems to suggest that we can never simply apply a concept directly to our experience, for example that we cannot simply apply the concept *gold* to a lump of metal because we find it to be heavy, yellow, malleable, etc., but that we need something intervening between our concept and our experience. What could that be, and isn't there a danger that once we have found that we might need yet another intermediary to apply it to our experience, and thus be off on an infinite regress? (Kant himself raises such a danger at A 133/B 172.)

Such worries as well as Kant's own melodramatic language are misplaced. What Kant is worrying about is that the *categories* are not self-evidently applicable to the objects of our experience, because the categories have merely *logical* content – the category of a substance, for example, is simply the category of something that is necessarily the subject of a predication – but our experience does not immediately present itself in logical terms; it presents itself in spatio-temporal terms, that is, as experience of objects that are near to or far from us, now present or merely remembered, short-lived or long-lasting, and so on.[58] Thus, in the case of the categories our concepts are not "homogeneous" with our objects, and some intermediary has to be found in order to make them so. But this is not the case with our other concepts, which are inherently homogeneous with their objects. A pure mathematical concept like *circle* is homogeneous with our experience, because it describes its object in terms of properties that can be directly presented in experience – that something is a curved, closed line every point of which is equidistant from its center is the kind of thing we can observe because the pure form of all our outer intuition is spatial. And an empirical concept like *plate* or *dog* is already homogeneous with its object because it includes predicates that correspond immediately to observable properties of objects, whether those properties are pure, like the circularity of a plate, or empirical, like its nonporousness or like the furriness or noisiness of a typical dog. Such concepts can be thought of as rules for the application of a name on the basis of observable properties: the concept *circle* is equivalent to the rule "Call a figure a circle if it is a curved, closed line every point of which is equidistant from its center" and the concept *dog* is equivalent to the rule "Call an animal a dog if it is a four-footed, barking mammal with a certain kind of teeth, and so on" (empirical concepts, of course, are not always well defined). Kant says that the schema of a geometrical figure such as a circle or triangle "can never exist anywhere except in thought, and signifies a rule of the synthesis of the imagination with regard to pure shapes in space," and likewise that an empirical concept "is always related immediately to the schema of the imagination, as a rule for the determination of our intuition in accordance with a certain general concept" (A 141/B 180). This makes it sound as if there is a numerical difference between the schema and the concept in these cases, but there really is not: the "immediate relation" is in fact identity, for the concept itself is nothing but the rule for constructing or recognizing instances of the concept. Only in the case of the categories do some rules not already contained in the content of those concepts themselves have to be found in order to apply those concepts to objects.

Kant's idea is then that the *a priori* but merely logical content of the categories can be applied to objects only if it can be associated with some equally *a priori* and universal properties that are immediately manifest in our experience – a "mediating representation" that, like the categories themselves, "must be pure (without anything empirical) and yet **intellectual** on the one hand and **sensible** on the other" (A 138/B 177). Since time is the "formal condition of the manifold of inner sense, thus of the connection of all representations," yet we can know its structure entirely *a priori* "in pure intuition," Kant proposes that the schemata must be various "transcendental time-determinations," features of the structure of time or of relations in time, that can be associated with the categories. Such transcendental time-determinations will be "homogeneous" with the categories because they are universal and *a priori*, but will also be homogeneous with "**appearance** insofar as **time** is contained in every empirical representation" (A 139/B 178). This may again sound mysterious, but Kant's examples quickly make clear that he means something quite straightforward: the category of substance, for example, which has the logical meaning of something that is a subject of predications, can be applied to experience through the temporal "schema" of something that endures through the change of its properties; the concepts of cause and effect, which thus far mean merely objects or states of affairs, whatever they might be, that are fit to be the subjects of antecedent and consequent clauses in a hypothetical judgment, can be applied to experience through the temporal "schema" of states of affairs that follow one another in time in accordance with a rule; and so on (A 144/B 183).

Although the general thrust of Kant's theory of the schematism is therefore quite clear, there are problems both with his assumption that only temporal and not spatial determinations can serve as transcendental schemata and with some of the particular temporal schemata that he describes. Kant's reason for holding that all the schemata must be time-determination is that as the form of inner sense time is the form of all representations, those of inner sense directly and those of outer sense indirectly, while as the form of outer sense space is the form only of some of our representations; thus if there were spatial schemata for the categories, they could apply only to some but not all of our representations. But to infer from this that there can be no spatial schemata for any of the categories would require the additional assumption that *each* of the categories must be able to be applied to *all* of our experiences, which Kant does not explicitly assert. There are also three more concrete problems with Kant's claim. First, he will claim that the "pure **schema** of magnitude . . . as a concept of the understanding" is "**number**, which is a representation that summarizes the successive addition of one (homogeneous) unity to another" (A 142/B 182). But it is indifferent to the concept of number whether the units that are added in any particular enumeration are themselves units of space, units of time, or units of something else altogether, and the fact that it might take us some time to perform the operation of addition seems irrelevant to the abstract concept of enumeration. Second, in at least some cases the conditions necessary for applying the pure categories to experience seem to involve spatial as well as temporal relations: if we accept Hume's analysis of the concept of causation, for example (although not his critique of its necessity), cause and effect are not only *successive* (a temporal relation) but also *contiguous* (a spatial relation), while on Kant's own account the condition for applying the pure category of community is interaction between objects existing *simultaneously* (a temporal relation) *at different locations* (a spatial relation). And, finally, Kant will explicitly argue that certain temporal relations themselves can only be represented through spatial relations – the passage of time, he asserts several times, can only be represented by a line drawn in space (B 156, B 290). For all of these reasons, it seems as if Kant should have stated that the transcendental schemata are certain spatial *and/or* temporal structures through which the pure categories can be applied to experience.

There are also problems with some of Kant's particular correlations between the categories and their schemata. As we have seen, there is only one schema for all three categories of quantity, namely number: that is, the logical concepts of one, some, and all can only be applied to domains of objects that can be counted. That is unproblematic, although as we saw it is dubious whether the idea of counting is intrinsically temporal. Kant provides two schemata for reality and negation as pure concepts of quality, namely "being (in time)" and "non-being (in time)" (A 143/B 182). This again seems unproblematic, although Kant's suggestion that the schema for the concept of limitation is to be found in the fact that "a transition from reality to negation ... makes every reality representable as a quantum" that has "a degree" seems to rest on an empirical assumption that all sensations come in a continuum of degrees, which does not seem to be derivable from the pure structure of time. Next, Kant claims that there are three schemata for the three pure categories of relation: "The schema of substance is the persistence of the real in time"; "The schema of cause and of the causality of a thing in general is the real upon which, whenever it is posited, something else always follows," or "the succession of the manifold insofar as it is subject to a rule"; and "The schema of community (reciprocity), or of the reciprocal causality of substances with regard to their accidents, is the simultaneity of the determinations of the one with those of the other, in accordance with a general rule" (A 144/B 183–4). As we observed earlier, there is a problem with the assumption that causality in time is a *necessary* condition for the use of the "if – then" form of judgment, as opposed to a *sufficient* condition for that, because there are clearly non-temporal relations of ground and consequence; and there is likewise a problem with the assumption that "reciprocal causation" is the only possible condition for the use of the disjunctive form of judgment, when in fact we often use a disjunction to express the fact that two states of affairs are completely incompatible and therefore *cannot* coexist with each other, e.g., "The world is either just or unjust." However, if Kant does not simply infer that we are entitled to believe in causation or interaction because they are supposed to be the schemata of certain categories, but instead provides *independent* arguments for the necessity of making judgments about causation and interaction, which *entail* that we must therefore use the relevant forms of judgment and categories to express them, no harm will be done – and that is exactly what Kant will go on to do in the second chapter of the "Analytic of the Principles."

Finally, Kant writes that "The schema of possibility is the agreement of the synthesis of various representations with the conditions of time in general . . . thus the determination of the representation of a thing to some time" or other; "The schema of actuality is existence at a determinate time"; and "The schema of necessity is the existence of an object at all times" (A 145/B 184). These definitions are also misleading: the first, because at least some possible objects must surely satisfy the conditions of space in general and not just those of time (a square circle is no more possible than someone who is married and unmarried at the same time); and the third for the more complex reason that Kant will ultimately and importantly argue that the only sense of necessity that we are entitled to use in empirical knowledge is necessity in accordance with causal laws, and causal laws do not entail the existence of any objects at all times but rather the existence of particular states of affairs (effects) at particular times (following the existence of their causes). Further, Kant will subsequently argue that there is something we can know to exist at all times, namely, the total quantum of substance in the universe, but he does not maintain that we can know this to be a *necessary* being (as God was traditionally thought to be). So there is not a perfect match between Kant's initial definitions of the schemata for the categories of modality and the claims about the conditions for the actual use of the concepts of possibility, actuality, and necessity that he will subsequently make.

But in this case too, Kant's overall argument does not really suffer, because his subsequent arguments about our use of the modal categories stand on their own rather than depending on the present associations. Throughout the chapter on the "System of all principles," Kant will essentially provide arguments from fundamental features of our experience that require us to apply the categories to our experience in particular ways; we can thus take the argument of that second chapter to entail a certain schematism of the categories rather than vice versa. So let us now turn to the "System of all principles."

The System of all principles

The "System" begins by reminding us that while analytic judgments can be known to be true on the basis of the contents of their subject- and predicate-concepts and the principle of non-contradiction alone (A 151–2/B 190–1), the "supreme principle of all synthetic judgments" is that "a third

thing is necessary in which alone the synthesis of two concepts can originate," and that, given the argument of the "Schematism," this third thing
must be the temporal structure of our experience, because "There is only
one totality in which all of our representations are contained, namely inner
sense, and its *a priori* form, time" (A 155/B 194). Thus reminded, we
would expect that each of the following sections, the "Axioms of
Intuition," the "Anticipations of Perception," "the Analogies of Experience,"
and the "Postulates of Empirical Thinking," would appeal to one or another
aspect of the temporal structure of experience in order to demonstrate the
necessity of one or another synthetic *a priori* principle, employing one or
another of the categories. What Kant actually does, however, is a little more
complicated than this suggests, although the strategy of demonstrating that
the temporal structure of our experience requires the use of certain
synthetic *a priori* principles employing the categories of substance, causation, and interaction is certainly essential to the heart of the "System of all
principles," namely the "Analogies of Experience."

The axioms of intuition and the anticipations of perception

The actual contents of these first two sections come as something of a
surprise, because instead of inferring their conclusions from the temporal
reinterpretation of the categories of quantity and quality, as the
"Schematism" would suggest, or explicitly arguing that the temporal
structure of our experience entails the necessary application and therefore
the objective validity of those categories, as the account of Kant's strategy
just given would suggest, what Kant actually does in these sections is to
argue that the spatial as well as the temporal structure of our experience
justifies the application of certain parts of mathematics to its objects, namely,
the mathematics of "extensive" and "intensive" quantities. By an "extensive" quantity or magnitude Kant means one that can be conceived of as
consisting of separable parts, while by an "intensive" magnitude he means
a measure of a quantity that cannot be conceived of as consisting of separate parts even though it can be expressed as a multiple of some unit. It is
easy to see what he means by an extensive quantity: a mile, for example, is
an extensive quantity consisting of 5,280 parts, each a foot long (although
of course it can also be divided up in other ways, e.g., into 1,760 yards,
63,360 inches, and so on), and you can actually separate these parts from
each other, for example, by walking half a mile but not a whole mile or
cutting up a mile of filament into 5,280 equally long pieces. An intensive
magnitude, however, or a degree (A 166/B 207), does not consist of parts

even though we measure it as a multiple of units: today's temperature of 72° F does not consist of seventy-two (or any other number of) parts, although we may measure it through something that does have separable parts, namely the height of a column of mercury in a thermometer.

Kant's argument, then, is that the mathematics of extensive and intensive magnitudes necessarily apply to our experience. His argument in the "Axioms of Intuition" about extensive magnitude is straightforward, indeed one may think it hardly needs to be made by this point in the book. The argument is simply that because our experiences of objects necessarily have spatial and temporal form, and space and time can always be represented as extensive magnitudes – any extension in space or duration in time can be represented as consisting of some number of smaller extensions or durations – the objects that we experience *in* space and time also can and must be representable as extensive magnitudes. "Every appearance as intuition is an extensive magnitude, as it can only be cognized through successive synthesis (from part to part) in apprehension" (A 163/B 204). Kant may think this argument has something special to do with time because he thinks of the synthesis of part to part as taking time to perform, but that seems to be a contingent fact about us that does not bear on the essential point that since space and time themselves are extensive magnitudes, "pure mathematics in its complete precision [is] applicable to objects of experience" (A 165/B 206). However, having established this, Kant does not go on to draw the conclusion that we might have expected him to draw, namely that since objects in space and/or time are always represented as extensive magnitudes, we must apply the *logical* concepts of quantity – one, some, all – by carving up our experience into representations of objects with determinate extensive magnitudes, or that carving up our experience in this way is only possible if we also use the logical categories of quantity. That is, in order to use the logical concept of a unit, we must chose some spatial or temporal unit, and to use the logical concepts *some* and *all* we must represent multiples of the spatial or temporal unit that we have selected, while conversely in order to form conceptions of extensive magnitudes, we must use the logical concepts: an extensive magnitude is a *totality* of some *units*, it has subparts that consist of *some* but not *all* of those units, and so on. Had he argued thus, Kant could have made explicit that the intuitional (spatial as well as temporal) structure of our experience necessitates the objective validity of the logical categories of quantity.

The argument of the "Anticipations of Perception" is trickier. Here Kant argues that the mathematics of intensive quantities – degrees – is necessarily applicable to the objects of our experience because sensation, which is that in perception or empirical intuition which represents the "real," itself necessarily comes in different degrees of intensity: his claim is that "In all appearances the sensation, and the **real**, which corresponds to it in the object (*realitatis phaenomenon*), has an **intensive magnitude**, i.e., a degree" (A 207) (by the parenthetical Latin Kant means to remind us that he is only talking about the appearance of the real, not anything as it ultimately is in itself). Kant's claim is problematic for two reasons: first, because it is not clear that he has a sound argument that sensations can always come in a range of degrees; and second because even if that is true it does not necessarily follow that we must think of the external (although still phenomenal) reality that *causes* our sensations in terms of intensive rather than extensive magnitudes. The second point is easy to see: the measured or felt temperature of 72° in my study today, although it does not itself *consist* of seventy-two or any other number of parts, is certainly *caused* by some finite number of molecules of matter moving at some finite velocities in the finite volume of my room, all of which are (in principle) measurable extensive magnitudes.[59] Thus, the *intensive* magnitude of a sensation may correspond to an *extensive* magnitude in the real object that causes it. (In chapter four, we will see that in his philosophy of science Kant explains matter in terms of attractive and repulsive forces which may themselves be intensive rather than extensive magnitudes. But he certainly does not attempt to prove this physical theory by beginning from the character of our *sensations* of matter, as he is trying to do here.)

The first problem is different. Kant argues that any sensation can be assigned a degree on a scale of intensity because although "Apprehension, by means of sensation, fills only an instant," nevertheless "every sensation is capable of a diminution, so that it can decrease and thus gradually disappear," hence "between reality in appearance and negation there is a continuous nexus of many possible intermediate sensations," thus any sensation has some degree on a continuous scale (A 167–8/B 209–10). There are a number of questions that might be raised about this argument, but the most fundamental is simply that the claim that any sensation can gradually or continuously diminish to nothing, or more generally that any kind of sensation can come in a range of intensities, would seem to be empirical rather than *a priori*, and thus not the basis for any synthetic *a priori* principle of judgment. Even if it is true, it is simply not clear how one could argue on *a priori* grounds that our sensory receptors are like rheostats with a continuous range between "off" and "high" rather than simple on–off switches with no gradations between "on" and "off." At one point

Kant suggests that sensation must be continuous because "from . . . empirical consciousness to . . . pure consciousness a gradual alteration is
possible" (B 208), but this makes it sound as if the difference between
pure intuition and empirical intuition is a matter of degree, which it
surely is not: although we may be able to have pure intuitions of geometrical figures such as lines and triangles in the mind's eye as well as
empirical intuitions of linear and triangular physical objects, when it
comes to the latter the difference between pure and empirical is a difference between form and matter, not a difference of degree. Kant's deeper
thought seems to be that both space and time are themselves continuous
and "flowing" magnitudes (A 169–70/B 211), from which he infers that
changes in time must be continuous rather than sudden, so if any particular
sensation represents a change from a previous sensory state (as it surely
does), then that change is continuous, so could have been stopped a bit
sooner or later, therefore the sensation could have occurred in some lesser
or greater degree of intensity. But this still seems like an empirical rather
than *a priori* claim, or at least to depend very heavily on the "Transcendental
Aesthetic": one might well think that our *mathematical representation* of time is
continuous without assuming that all real, physical changes in time are
continuous – unless one has already bought into transcendental idealism.
And even if one buys all this, how is it to be reconciled with Kant's initial
claim that apprehension by means of sensation fills only an instant?

Kant obviously wanted to prove that any sensation has an intensity that
is only a point on a continuous scale so that he could argue that we must
have a pure concept of "limitation" in addition to the categories of
"reality" and "negation" – if all our experience were of a simple on – off
variety, the latter two categories might seem enough. But he really did not
have to go down this road to explain why we can use three rather than just
two *logical functions* of "quality." If we assume that all of our empirical assertions and denials about the objects of our experience are based on
sensation, as Kant does, we can say that affirmative judgments are straightforwardly based on the occurrence of certain sensations, negative
judgments on an absence of certain expected sensations, and infinite judgments on the absence of some expected sensation but the presence of
some *other*, perhaps un- or underdescribed sensation. That is, my assertion
"There's a cat here" (pointing to some particular place in my environment) would be based on the occurrence of certain characteristic and
expected sensations (the sound of meowing, the feeling of itching if one
is allergic to cats, and so on); my assertion "There is not a cat here" could
be based on the simple absence of any of those expected sensations from

my experience of a certain region; and my assertion "There's a non-cat here" would be based on the occurrence of some sensations different from the ones I expect in the case of a cat but not (yet?) sufficient for me to classify what is here in any more determinate way (I know from the absence of itching that it's not a cat, but I don't have enough information to tell whether it's a raccoon or an opossum or a Yorkshire terrier – or perhaps I have plenty of sensations of the beast before me, but I don't know how to classify it, I just know it's not a cat, or is a non-cat). The point is just that Kant could well establish that we apply the categories of reality, negation, and limitation to our experience on the basis of our sensations, and that because sensations can be present, absent, or appear in unexpected combinations we can make affirmative, negative, and infinite judgments, thus using the relevant associated categories – all without insisting upon the specialized and perhaps controvertible empirical thesis that all sensations come in a range of intensities rather than the simple, empirical but incontrovertible assumption that our assertions and denials about reality are based on *some sort* of sensations.

The analogies of experience

The heart of Kant's argument in the "System of all principles," however, is surely the "Analogies of Experience." Here Kant clearly uses the strategy we have found in the second stage of the second-edition transcendental deduction, that is, the strategy of arguing that certain fundamental assumptions about the structure of our experience, particularly its temporal structure, necessitate our assumption of certain synthetic *a priori* principles that in turn use *a priori* concepts of the greatest concern to both traditional metaphysicians and skeptics – the concepts of substance, causation, and interaction.

Kant bases the "Analogies" on a crucial assumption, namely, that although time is the *a priori* form of all of our experience, "time itself cannot be perceived" and must instead be represented through certain "*a priori* connecting concepts" of objects (B 219) – none other than the *a priori* concepts of substance, causation, and interaction. In fact, it turns out that Kant means two distinct things by his claim that "time itself cannot be perceived." One thing he means is that the *formal structure* of time – for example, its one-dimensionality, that moments of time are not themselves ever simultaneous with each other, but are only antecedent or successive to each other – cannot be directly perceived, and must somehow be perceived through features of objects in time. The other thing he means is that the *objective temporal relations of objects in time* cannot be immediately perceived in our empirical intuitions, because the temporal relations of our representations may not match the objective temporal relations – for example, our perceptions of an external object may change while the object itself is not changing. His claim will then be that in order to make judgments about *objective* temporal relations that we cannot make on the basis of our empirical intuitions alone we must apply certain principles about substance, causation, and interaction to the objects of our experience, and thus assume the objective validity of the categories of substance, causation, and interaction. As we will see, the second kind of argument is more compelling than the first.

In the course of the three "Analogies," Kant uses both interpretations of the premise that time itself cannot be perceived and both of the styles of argument that these two interpretations suggest. Kant's dual lines of argument are particularly clear in the first "Analogy." Here Kant aims to prove that "All appearances contain that which persists (**substance**) as the object itself, and that which can change as its mere determination" (A 182), that is, that all experiences of change are experiences of change in the states of something that endures through that change, and even that "In all change of appearances substance persists, and its quantum is neither increased nor diminished in nature" (B 224). His idea, in other words, is to prove that there is something that persists through any and indeed all change in nature, and then to show that we must use the category of substance to express this fact. He first attempts to show this by assuming that both succession or change as well as simultaneity are features of appearances in time, but that the "time . . . in which all change of appearances is to be thought lasts and does not change," and then inferring that since time itself cannot be perceived, neither can its permanence. Yet, he argues, there must be something *in appearance* that represents the permanence of time and thus allows it to be perceived, and this, he claims, can be nothing but substance, "the substratum of everything real" (B 224–5). From the assumption of the permanence of time and the need for all features of time to be represented by something in appearance, that is, Kant infers that there must be something permanent in appearance, and that changes can only be changes from one state to another of this permanent thing. The category of substance is then necessary in order to express this assumption of permanence.

Even if we grant that it makes sense to speak of time itself as permanent, the epistemological assumptions that Kant makes at the second stage of this argument are problematic. He is now assuming that we cannot know that time itself is permanent from the pure intuition of time, although that change takes place in time and therefore time does not change would seem to be the chief thing that we know about the pure intuition of time. He is also assuming that a representation must have the same property as what it represents, although this is certainly not true in general. To take Kant's own example, why cannot a drawn line represent the permanence of time (B 156) even if the drawing of the line is not itself permanent? (After all, the next time we need to represent the permanence of time, we could just draw another line.) This line of thought just does not seem promising.[60]

Toward the end of the section, however, Kant writes that "the representation of the transition from one state into another, and from non-being into being . . . can be empirically cognized only as changing determinations of that which lasts" (what he calls "alterations") (A 188/B 231). This is not a claim about what is needed in order to have empirical knowledge of the permanence of time itself, but a claim about under what conditions we can have knowledge of the occurrence of changes of objects in time. Kant's basis for this claim is that in order to know that the existence of some state of affairs represents a change, we have to know that it began at some point in time, and that in turn requires that we be acquainted with some preceding time in which it did not exist. But we cannot know the latter simply by perceiving an empty moment of time, "for an empty time that would precede is not an object of perception" (A 188/B 231). Instead, we can only perceive some thing in some state of affairs at the previous time, so Kant infers that we can only perceive or have empirical cognition of change by perceiving one substance that is changing from one state to another. This might seem like a *non sequitur*: why couldn't we perceive one (impermanent) object in one state being followed by a different (impermanent) object in a different state at the next moment of time? Wouldn't that be a perception of a change not involving any perception of empty time? But further reflection can suggest that Kant's conclusion is right, because unless we perceive the *same* object as being first in one state and then in another, we will have no way of knowing whether we have perceived any change in *an object* at all, or just a change in *which* object we are perceiving (a change due, perhaps, to an unwitting and unperceived movement in our own body or perceptual organ). In other words, the endurance of a persisting object through a change of its states is a condition of the possibility of empirical knowledge of an *objective* change, a change in the object and not just in our own perceptions of it.[61]

Now even if this argument is accepted, it could still seem as if Kant is guilty of another *non sequitur* when he apparently infers from the endurance of some particular substance through any particular change to the endurance of substance through *all* changes, thus that the quantum of substance in nature is never increased or diminished.[62] Could we not just assume that some substance or other must endure through any particular changes or finite series of changes, but not that any single substance nor a single quantum of substance endures through *all* changes? However, although Kant has no basis to reject this as a *logical* possibility, his argument is an *epistemological* argument. His claim is that we have no basis for *empirical cognition* (or as we might now say *confirmation*) of the occurrence of an objective change except as an alteration in some persisting substance, and thus we have no way of knowing that a substance as opposed to its state simply comes into or goes out of existence. So as far as our empirical knowledge goes, we in fact have no choice but to assume the conservation of substance.

The principle that a substance cannot (be known to) come into or go out of existence is certainly not compatible with all of our ordinary usage of the term "substance": we might well call a human or a pig or a porcelain pig[63] a substance, but also think that such things are precisely the sort of things that can come into or go out of existence by being born or manufactured and then by being killed, butchered, or smashed. But there is also a more scientific usage of "substance" in which such everyday objects are not genuine substances, but only whatever is thought to persist through the creation and destruction of such everyday objects is a genuine substance: the elements and minerals of which everyday objects are made, or, if those can be created or broken down as well, then the atoms of which they consist, or, if atoms can be created or broken down, then the protons, neutrons, and electrons of which they consist, or, if they can be broken down, then the quarks of which they consist, and so on, until we get down to miniscule strings – or *whatever* science will eventually discover to be the ultimate survivors and therefore substrata of all change. Kant's point is not that anything that we casually call substance is permanent, but that in both everyday life and scientific inquiry we must assume that there is *some* sort of thing that endures through all changes, although maybe only science can tell us what that is, and maybe even science will never reach a final theory of what that is.[64]

If we think of Kant as arguing along this second line, then he is not inferring that substance exists, let alone that it is permanent, from the mere availability of the categorical form of judgment and the pure concepts of substance and accident. On the contrary, he is starting from what he takes to be a fundamental feature of our experience – that we can have empirical knowledge of objective changes – and showing that the application of the category of substance to all such changes is a necessary condition of such knowledge. In this way, he can be seen as finally proving the objective validity of the category of substance from his proof of the conservation of substance, rather than vice versa. While the metaphysical deduction may have shown that we *can* use the category of substance in judgments about objects of experience, this argument shows that we *must* use it for all objects of experience.

In the second "Analogy of Experience," Kant attempts to prove the universal principle that "All alterations occur in accordance with the law of the connection of cause and effect" (B 232). Since it was Hume's skepticism whether we have any rational basis for accepting this principle that Kant then generalized into the general doubt about metaphysics to be resolved by the *Critique of Pure Reason*, the second Analogy is obviously central to Kant's entire project.

There is one point in it where it looks as if Kant is offering an argument analogous to the first Analogy's "substratum" argument directly from the permanence of time to the permanence of substance in it; halfway through the section, he writes:

> Now if it is a necessary law of our sensibility, thus **a formal condition** of all perceptions, that the preceding time necessarily determines the following time . . . then it is also an indispensable **law of the empirical representation** of the temporal series that the appearances of the past time determine every existence in the following time . . . in accordance with a rule. For **only in the appearances can we empirically cognize this continuity in the connection** of times.
>
> (A 199/B 244)

If this were meant as an independent argument rather than just a summary of what has been proven on other grounds,[65] it would be a poor argument: it would transform the merely formal fact that every moment of time follows another one into the substantive claim that whatever *state of affairs* exists at one moment of time was caused by *what existed* at the previous moment of time. This would beg any reasonable question about the justifiability of belief in causation, and it would also be far too general a thesis to accept (the only way to make any sense of it in light of the untold numbers of states of affairs that exist at any one time would be to hold that the entire state of the universe at one moment is caused by its entire state at the previous moment, which renders the concept of causation pretty useless).

But Kant may have intended this paragraph as a summary of what he takes himself to have proved prior to it rather than as an independent argument, and indeed everything that precedes it in the exposition of the second Analogy is in the same vein as the second argument of the first Analogy, which held that the existence of enduring substance is a necessary condition for empirical knowledge of the occurrence of objective change. In fact, the main argument of the second Analogy is more than itself an analogy to that argument in the first Analogy; it actually completes that argument by maintaining that the validity of the universal law of causation is a further necessary condition for the empirical knowledge of objective change, in addition to the existence of enduring substance: the principles proven in the two Analogies have to be used together in order to yield empirical knowledge of such change. Kant states and restates the argument numerous times, but it is basically simple.[66] He begins by pointing out that our experience of parts or states of objects is always successive, whether or not (we think) the object is undergoing any change (A 189/B 234, A 198/B 243). For example, we perceive the different parts of a house in succession, just as we perceive in succession the several positions of a ship as it sails down a river, even though we think there is an objective change – change in the object of perception – in the second case but not in the first (A 191–2/B 236–7). However, we believe that in the case of perception of an objective change, the order of our several perceptions is irreversible, while it is not so in the case of a succession of perceptions of something that is not itself changing – that is, we take it that in the case of a ship that is sailing downstream, we could (other things being equal) only have perceived it downstream after we perceived it upstream, not vice versa, while in the case of a house (which is not currently being built or demolished), while we may have perceived its ground floor before we perceived its roof, we could just as easily have perceived its parts in the opposite order (for example, by altering the movements of our own body). But, Kant maintains, the irreversibility of our perceptions in the one case and their reversibility in the other is not something that we are in any way immediately given. We are not immediately given these modal facts by the objects of our perception, for we are only given objects through our representations of them (A 190/B 235). And we are not immediately given these facts by our representations themselves, for the representations do not carry any internal sign of their objective temporal significance within themselves. As Kant puts it, in imagination we can always "combine the two states in question in two different ways, so that one or the other precedes in time" (B 233, A 201/B 246). So even though we could in principle infer the occurrence of an objective change from the irreversibility of our representations of its several states, we cannot in fact do so, because we are not directly given this irreversibility. Instead, Kant argues, our only basis for determining that an objective change has taken place in any substance is our use (whether explicit or tacit) of a rule that entails that in the conditions that obtain one state of it *could only* have followed the other – from which it will then also follow that one of our *representations* had to follow the other, i.e., that they were irreversible. In Kant's words

> If my perception is to contain the cognition of an occurrence, namely that something actually happens, then it must be an empirical judgment in which one thinks that the sequence is determined, i.e., that it presupposes another appearance in time which it follows necessarily or in accordance with a rule.
>
> (A 201 / B 246; see also A 193 / B 238, A 198 / B 243)
>
> Therefore I always make my subjective synthesis (of apprehension) objective with respect to a rule in accordance with which the appearances in their sequence . . . are determined through the preceding state, and only under this presupposition alone is the experience of something that happens even possible.
>
> (A 195 / B 240)

But a causal law is nothing less and nothing more than a rule in accordance with which, under relevant conditions, one particular state of affairs must be followed by another state of affairs, so the experience of objective change is only possible through knowledge of causal laws, and wherever we have experience of objective change we must know that some causal law applies.[67]

Now this is the start of an answer to Hume's worries: it shows that our knowledge of something so basic that even Hume never thought to doubt it, namely that we can recognize objective change, presupposes the very thing he thought he could doubt, namely knowledge of causal laws. It does not show that the universal principle that every event has some cause is *logically* necessary, that is, that it would be *self*-contradictory to deny it, which was one test Hume used, nor does it actually show that there is any sort of absolute necessity that we be able to recognize objective change itself – maybe some truly radical skeptic could doubt this, although Hume did not. What it does show is that the validity of the universal principle of causation is a presupposition of a form of experience that any reasonable person takes himself to have, namely experience of objective change; in Kant's words, "Thus the principle of sufficient reason is the ground of possible experience, namely the objective cognition of appearances with regard to their relation in the successive series of time" (A 201 / B 246).[68] If this is conceded, then from the necessity of using the *principle* of causation (along with the principle of the conservation of substance) as a necessary condition for this fundamental epistemic capacity, we can also infer the necessity of using the *category* of causation, or its objective validity, for any knowledge of change in objects, and from that in turn we can infer the necessity of using the hypothetical form of judgment to express our causal judgments, even though that form of judgment can be used for other purposes as well, for example to express non-causal mathematical implications. Once Kant has proved that the principle of causality is a condition of the possibility of experience, he does not have to infer this from a prior metaphysical or transcendental deduction of the category of causation, but can instead use his proof of the principle to prove the objective validity of the category itself.

In recent decades, there has been extensive debate about the probative value of a "transcendental argument" such as Kant's argument in the second Analogy.[69] The bottom line in this debate is ultimately that no argument can ever prove more than that if we believe one thing (the premise) then we must believe another (the conclusion) – there is no way a conclusion can ever be proven unconditionally, because there is no way a premise can be proven unconditionally (although of course it may be proven conditionally on the basis of some other premise, which itself can at best be proven conditionally). As far as premises go, Kant's premise that we are capable of distinguishing between mere change in our own perceptions and change in the objective, external world seems difficult to doubt seriously, and unless someone can explain how we could make this distinction without appeal to causal laws applying to the objects of our experience, which no one has, his conclusion seems sound. But it must also be noted that Kant's conclusion is entirely general: that is, he explains why we must presuppose the universal law that every event has some cause, but this does not entail the truth or *a priori* cognition of any particular causal laws, nor does Kant think that it does (see B 165). But in the *Treatise of Human Nature* (of which, however, Kant had only limited knowledge), Hume had asked how we know *particular* causal laws,[70] and it is clear that Kant's explanation of the role of the *general* principle of causality *presupposes* that we can and do have knowledge of such particular laws: we cannot determine that a series of our representations represents the objective event of a ship sailing downstream, as opposed to standing still or sailing upstream, on the basis of the general law that every event has some cause, but only on the basis of particular causal laws concerning winds, tides, sails, and so on – that is, particular laws that would entail that in the particular circumstances obtaining the particular ship we are observing must be sailing downstream. So it looks as if the biggest question about Kant's treatment of causation is whether he has an account of our knowledge of particular causal laws to go along with his account of the presupposition of the general principle of causality.[71] Does Kant have such an account? He clearly does not suggest one in his exposition of the second Analogy. He may suggest one in the Introduction to the *Critique of the Power of Judgment*, where he takes up the question of how we get from the most universal laws of nature demonstrated in the *Critique of Pure Reason*, indeed in the very "System of all principles" we are now considering. So we will have to defer further consideration of the completeness of Kant's answer to all of Hume's problems about causation.

In the third Analogy, Kant argues that we can only determine states of different substances to be simultaneous insofar as those substances are in "thoroughgoing community" or "interaction," that is, where the state of one is the cause of the state of the other and vice versa (A 211).[72] If it seemed implausible that we cannot determine that one state of affairs follows another without relying upon a causal law linking them, it may seem even more implausible that we cannot tell that two states of two substances are simultaneous simply by observing them both simultaneously. But Kant has in mind substances separated in space, and indeed sufficiently separated so that we *cannot* simply observe both simultaneously – he refers to the earth and moon, for example, assuming that we can only observe them sequentially, not simultaneously. But still, couldn't I know that the earth and moon are simultaneously in certain states because even though I must first observe one and then the other, I *could have* observed them in the opposite order, something possible only if each was in the relevant state throughout the period of my observation? Kant's argument is precisely that although this is true, that is, if two objects are in certain simultaneous states then we *could* perceive first one and then the other or vice versa (A 211/B 258), we have no way of knowing this modal fact from our representations alone – because, again, our representations themselves are always successive, and we have no other direct perception of things and their states, thus no direct perception of their reversibility in time: "one cannot perceive time itself and thereby derive from the fact that things are positioned at the same time that their perceptions can follow each other reciprocally" (B 257). Rather, Kant argues, we can only *infer* that two states of substances that cannot be observed simultaneously are nevertheless simultaneous from laws of interaction which tell us that one object cannot be in a certain state at a certain time or during a certain period without the other also being in a certain state at that same time – a complex relationship that Kant models by conceiving of the state of one object as the cause of the simultaneous state of the other, but the latter as at the same time the cause of the former (A 212–13/B 259). Such laws will entail the simultaneity of the states of the two objects, and of course from the simultaneity of the two states we can also infer the reversibility of our successive perceptions of them, something that we could not as it were simply read off from the perceptions themselves.

It should be noted that Kant's argument does not apply to all cases of simultaneity; for example, we could infer that two states of affairs are simultaneous from the fact that they are both effects of the same cause. Still, the third Analogy does reveal the character of Kant's underlying strategy, because here Kant offers the kind of epistemological argument about the necessary conditions for judgments about relations among *objects in time* that we found in the first and second Analogies, but this time without the other kind of argument about supposed conditions for representing the structure of time itself that disfigured those passages. Perhaps this is because it is simply self-evident that simultaneity is a relation between states of affairs *in* time, and not a property *of* time itself. It should also be evident that the third Analogy presupposes the availability of particular laws of interaction in the same way that the second Analogy presupposes the availability of particular causal laws, and so just as in the case of causation, Kant's explanation of our ability to use the category of interaction – something that he wanted to defend against Leibniz, whose monadology allows only the appearance but not the reality of interaction among objects, just as he wanted to defend our use of the category of causality against Hume – ultimately depends upon an account of our knowledge of particular laws which he does not provide in the "Analogies of Experience." But we should also note that there is one disanalogy between the third Analogy and the first two. In those cases, we could see how Kant could have demonstrated the objective validity of the categories of substance and causation without presupposing his prior metaphysical and transcendental deductions, and how he could then have inferred back from the necessity of using these categories to the necessity of using the categorical and hypothetical forms of judgment to give expression to the judgments that we make with these categories. In the third Analogy, however, the relation between the category of interaction and the disjunctive form of judgment remains elusive. This is because while Kant understands a disjunctive judgment as a compound judgment in which the truth of one of its component judgments entails the *falsehood* of all the others (that is, he understands disjunction as the exclusive "either . . . or . . . " form of judgment), in cases of genuine interaction between objects the truth of our judgment about the state of one object entails the *truth* of a judgment about the state of the other. Of course, perhaps we should not worry about this very much, since as we have just seen the actual content of the third Analogy does not assume that the availability of the disjunctive form of judgment entails the objective validity of the category of interaction, but offers an entirely independent proof of the latter, and in any case the disjunctive form of judgment has plenty of other uses: it is employed in every argument by elimination.

The postulates of empirical thinking in general

Just as the logical functions of modality did not, according to Kant, add anything to the possible contents of judgments, so the "Postulates of empirical thinking" are not intended to add any additional principles to the foundations of empirical knowledge that Kant has now attempted to defend from Humean skepticism. Instead, they show us how the modal categories of possibility, actuality, and necessity should be used given both the foundations and limits of empirical knowledge that Kant has thus far demonstrated. His view is that the category of possibility should be used to express that the idea of an object "agrees with the formal conditions of experience (in accordance with intuition and concepts)," that is, is consistent with the basic structure of space, time, and logic; the category of actuality should be used to express not only that the idea of an object is in agreement with these formal structures of our intuitions and concepts but also shown to be applicable to our experience by the occurrence of some sensation that can be taken as evidence for its reality (Kant illustrates this with the example of a magnetic field, which cannot be directly observed, but which is inferred to be actual because it is connected by well-confirmed causal law to a pattern of iron filings on a paper that can be directly observed; A 226/B 273); and the concept of necessity should be used to express that an object's "connection with the actual is determined in accordance with general conditions of experience" (A 218/B 265). By the latter, Kant means that what we assert when we call an object or more precisely its state "necessary" is just that it is entailed by causal laws – "Now there is no existence that could be cognized as necessary under the condition of other given appearances except the existence of effects from given causes in accordance with laws of causality" (A 227/B 279) – and (he should have added) laws about the conservation and interaction of substances as well.

Since Kant has just shown that empirical knowledge of the actual depends upon the assumption of the three "Analogies of Experience," what he is now saying is that we cannot make judgments about the actual without also making judgments about the necessary: the actual is not only given by sensation, but must also be subsumed under the "general conditions of experience." So the use of the concept of the actual is not any wider than the use of the concept of the necessary. But Kant is also telling us, at least tacitly, that the concept of necessity has no legitimate – or at least theoretically legitimate – use *beyond* the sphere of the empirically actual: leaving aside purely analytical implications (like "Any bachelor must be unmarried"), we can only use the concept of necessity to express that something is entailed by the laws of pure intuition (in the case of mathematics) or by the laws of conservation, causation, and interaction that apply to empirical intuition. This will turn out to be the central thesis of Kant's critique of traditional metaphysics: we simply have no (theoretical) basis for asserting the necessity of anything beyond the limits of our pure and empirical intuition.

THE REFUTATION OF IDEALISM

The section on the "Postulates of empirical thinking" thus really begin the transition from Kant's constructive theory of knowledge – and thus his refutation of Humean skepticism – to his diagnosis of the errors of traditional metaphysics – and thus to his resolution of Pyrrhonian skepticism. But before we can turn to the latter, we must consider the "Refutation of Idealism" that Kant inserted into the discussion of the postulate of actuality in the second edition of the *Critique* (B 274–9). This is Kant's response to Cartesian skepticism, or as he calls it "problematic idealism" – uncertainty about the existence of external objects on the basis of internal representations of them. Given the obsession with refuting Cartesian skepticism that has been characteristic of so much twentieth-century philosophy, it may seem surprising that Kant takes it up only so late in his argument (in fact, in the first edition he took it up only even later, in the fourth "Paralogism of Pure Reason," A 366–80). But clearly Kant thought that the refutation of Humean and Pyrrhonian skepticism were far more urgent and far-reaching projects: he thought that Cartesian skepticism was a "scandal of philosophy" (B xxxix) but really only of and for philosophy: a brain-teaser for academics, perhaps, but not anything that can threaten the real conduct of scientific inquiry and moral practice, and thus the good sense and well-being of every human, which Humean and Pyrrhonian skepticism, in his view, certainly could.

Although it is thus not central to Kant's philosophical concerns, indeed, it is something of an afterthought, Kant's response to Cartesian skepticism is nevertheless as interesting as it is intricate. He diagnoses "problematic idealism," that is, uncertainty about whether our internal representations imply the existence of external objects that both cause and resemble them,[73] as arising from the assumption that we must infer the existence of external objects from our own representations but cannot conclusively do so because we can never exclude alternative explanations of our representations – for example, Descartes' famous "evil demon" (A 368, B 274–5). In the first edition, Kant thought he could get around this problem of inconclusive inference by arguing that in claiming to know that there are outer objects, we are merely claiming to know that there are spatial objects, that is, objects that appear in space (A 372), and since of course many of our representations are immediately given as spatial, we do not have to go beyond the sphere of our own representations – we do not need any inference at all – in order to be sure of the existence of spatial objects (A 373–5). This immediately produced the outcry that Kant's "transcendental" or "higher" idealism was nothing but a restatement of Berkeley's idealism, which did indeed reduce all objects to representations (esse est percipi), a criticism that stung Kant to the quick.[74]

Kant was clearly impelled to add the new "Refutation of Idealism" to the second edition of the Critique by the charge of Berkeleianism, but he did not actually think he had to say very much about Berkeley himself. Kant interpreted Berkeley as having challenged the coherence and necessity of space (B 274), and always thought that the "Transcendental Aesthetic" contained an adequate response to that challenge. What he did think he needed to do was to explain more clearly both why we must believe in the existence of objects beyond but grounding our own representations of them, and also how we can believe this while still maintaining transcendental idealism, which asserts that spatiality is only a feature of our own representations. This is what Kant attempts to do in the new "Refutation," although his argument there is excessively compact and incomplete – something Kant quickly recognized, because he immediately amplified it in the Preface to the new edition of the Critique (B xxxix–xli) and then wrote close to a dozen additional versions of it after the new edition was published.[75]

The thesis that the "Refutation" is to prove is that "The mere, but empirically determined consciousness of my own existence proves the existence of objects in space outside me" (B 275). This statement immediately raises questions about both the starting-point and the conclusion of the argument. First, what does Kant mean by "the empirically determined consciousness of my own existence"? Second, what does he mean by the "existence of objects in space outside me"? Is this just redundant, that is, does "outside me" mean nothing more than "in space," where that in turn could merely mean "represented as spatial"; or is it non-redundant, implying that objects in space are also something other than my own representations? That is what one would expect in an answer to Cartesian skepticism, of course, but that is not what Kant tried to prove in the first-edition reply to such skepticism, so it is not immediately clear what he has in mind here.

These questions can only be answered through an examination of Kant's argument. The statement of the key premises in the published version is very compact:

> [1] I am conscious of my existence as determined in time. [2] All time-determination presupposes something **persistent** in perception. [3] This persistent thing, however, cannot be something in me, since my own existence in time can first be determined only through this persistent thing. [4] Thus the perception of this persistent thing is possible only through a **thing** outside me and not through the mere **representation** of a thing outside me. [Conclusion] Consequently, the determination of my existence in time is possible only by means of the existence of actual things that I perceive outside myself.
>
> (B 275)

Kant's emphatic contrast between "a **thing** outside me" and "the mere **representation** of a thing outside me" in (4) makes it pretty clear that he does not mean to settle here for what seemed such an easy answer to skepticism in the first edition of the *Critique*, namely, that we are immediately aware that we have spatial representations, as does his remark in a long footnote in the Preface of the second edition, which expands upon the "Refutation," that the thing that persists must "be a thing distinct from all my representations and external" (B xli). But these remarks do not yet explain *how* Kant thinks he can both prove that we have knowledge of things that really exist independently of our representations and yet also maintain that space and everything in it are nothing but our own representations.

Let's leave that question hanging, however, while we consider the previous steps in the argument. (1) What does Kant mean by consciousness of my existence as determined in time? (2) Why does time-determination require something permanent in time? And (3), why must the permanent that is required for consciousness of my existence in time be something other than my enduring self itself? That is, if the answer to (2) is just what Kant proved in the first "Analogy of Experience," to which he seems to be alluding here, that the only kind of change of which we can have empirical cognition is an alteration of the changing states of an enduring substance, why would we need anything more than an enduring *self* to satisfy this condition?

An emendation that Kant makes to the proof in the second-edition "Preface" might point to some answers to these questions. There Kant says that what I have labeled step (3) of the argument should be replaced with the following: "But this persisting element cannot be an intuition in me. For all the determining grounds of my existence that can be encountered in me are representations, and as such they need something persisting distinct from them, in relation to which their change, and thus my existence in the time in which they change, can be determined" (B xxxix). This emendation suggests several things. First, an answer to (1): what Kant means by "empirical consciousness of the self" or "consciousness of my existence as determined in time" is consciousness of the *change* in my representations, or perhaps even more precisely consciousness of the *order* of the change of my representations. Second, an answer to (2): I cannot just appeal to my enduring self, because my empirical self is in some sense a *consequence* of my changing representations; it is in fact nothing other than the order of those changing representations. And (3): the order of my changing representations, and thus the content of my empirical self, needs to be determined "in relation to" some persisting thing that is not itself a representation, thus my empirical consciousness of myself as determined in time depends upon knowledge of the existence of something other than my own representations.

Kant's reasons for step (3) are still obscure, but he suggests what he has in mind in a pregnant paragraph in one of the notes he later wrote attempting to clarify the published "Refutation":

> Since the imagination and its product is itself only an object of inner sense, the empirical consciousness (*apprehensio*) of this state can contain only succession [*crossed out*: of temporal conditions]. But this itself cannot be [*crossed out*: determined] represented except through that which persists, with which that which is successive is simultaneous.
>
> (R 6313, 18:613)

Kant's telegraphic note was meant only for himself, but if we think about some of the terms he uses here we may be able to see at last what he has in mind. We might think that nothing is better known to each of us than the order of our own representations or mental states, regardless of what they might represent in the external world. But remember Kant's claim in the second "Analogy of Experience" that in imagination we can always alter the succession of our own representations: this implies that at any given moment we can imagine the order of our prior representations having been different from what we now think it is, and thus, in the absence of some further basis for attributing a particular order to our representations, we do not automatically know their order, thus the empirical self which that order constitutes. Moreover, a moment's reflection will suggest that this further basis cannot be something within our mental, representational capacity as such, because if that is ever even to be able to represent something outside itself, the order of our representations will have to be able to be responsive to changes going on in the outside world; if that is not the case, then the actual sequences of our own representations will be worth no more than dreams. Putting all this together, Kant's idea seems to be that the way that we assign a determinate order to our own representations is by correlating them with the determinate order of the changing states of something in the external world that is not itself a mere representation, something the states of which do have a determinate order, and which imply a determinate order for our representations of them. In other words, the only way to lend determinate order to our own representations and thereby attain empirical self-consciousness or constitute an empirical self is by interpreting them as representations of an objective, law-governed external world. (Thus Kant's "Refutation" relies at least as much on the second "Analogy of Experience" as on the first.)

But now how does *space* come into the argument? Sometimes Kant writes as if space is itself the only permanent thing – for example, he continues the passage from his notes that was quoted above by saying that "this persisting thing, with which that which is successive is simultaneous, i.e. space" – but that does not seem like a very promising tack: after all, the first "Analogy" was clearly intended to prove that substances are enduring things in space. All we need for the purposes of the "Refutation" are enduring substances in space, not space as itself permanent. Kant's better idea, however, is that space, or the spatial form of our intuitions, is that *by means of which we represent what is other than our own representation* – the form of outer rather than inner sense, after all. Representations are by their very nature "variable and changing," something permanent must therefore be something other than mere representation, and spatiality, by means of which we can picture the separation of our own bodies from other bodies, is just how we represent something other than mere representation. As Kant writes in another one of his afterthoughts on the "Refutation," space "is a special kind of representation in us, which cannot represent that which is in us," but "really signifies . . . a relation to a real thing outside us" (R 6317, 18:627–8).

This, in turn, finally suggests how Kant's refutation of Cartesian skepticism is to be reconciled with his own transcendental idealism. To be sure, the argument does not really *need* to be reconciled with transcendental idealism, for unlike Kant's simple response to Descartes in the first edition, the

"Refutation" does not actually *presuppose* that we have immediate knowledge of spatiality because it is nothing but a form of our own representation. Still, Kant obviously believed his own doctrine of transcendental idealism, so it is natural to ask how *he* thought it could be reconciled with the "Refutation." Kant suggests an answer to this question in another of his notes: "In order that something can appear to be outside us, there must really be something outside us, though not constituted in the way we have the representation of it, since other kinds of sense could afford other ways of representing the same thing" (R 6312, 18:613). In other words, as transcendental idealism maintains, space may be just *our* way of representing things other than our own representations; but it *is* our way of doing that, and since we need to represent things other than our own representations in order even to assign a determinate order to those representations, we need to use our representation of space for that purpose. Just as the arguments of the "Analogies" proved against Hume that we must employ the categories of substance, causation, and interaction which the "metaphysical deduction" of the categories had merely made available, so the "Refutation" proves against Descartes that we must use what the "Transcendental Aesthetic" had as it were merely made available to us, namely space as the form of outer sense and thus our way of representing things other than our own representations.

There are many questions we could ask about this argument, but one is certainly pressed upon us by Kant's general project of defending the autonomy of human knowledge against the threats of skepticism. Descartes' own response to "Cartesian skepticism" was the model of a non-autonomous conception of human knowledge: he thought we could be sure of anything beyond our own representations only because of the benevolence of God.[76] But what kind of alternative to Descartes' answer does Kant supply? Remember that he thought that Descartes' problem arose because Descartes tried to *infer* from his own representations to something beyond them, but could not do so conclusively. Doesn't the very fact that Kant needed to construct a "Refutation of Idealism" – indeed, one that he had to write and rewrite numerous times before he got it right – really show that for him too our knowledge of the external world is inferential and therefore still vulnerable to skepticism? Kant denies that his argument shows the need for an inference (B 276; R 5654, 18:312–13); his view is rather that the existence of external objects is and must be *presupposed* in the project of assigning a determinate temporal order to our own experiences: "The consciousness of other things as outside me, . . . as intellectual, must also be presupposed" (R 5653, 18:306). We cannot pretend that we would have determinate knowledge of the order of our own experiences without any presuppositions, and *only then* infer from those representations that there are external objects. Rather, unless we assume that there are external objects, we will not have any determinate knowledge of the order of our own experiences to begin with – we will have only imagined orders for them, which we can just as easily imagine being otherwise.

What sort of answer to skepticism is this? It is not an answer to a no-holds-barred skeptic willing to doubt even whether he can know the order of his own experiences, even whether he had experiences five minutes or five seconds ago. But of course, you would have to be crazy to doubt *that*, and as even Descartes recognized, we cannot expect to prove anything to a lunatic[77] – lunacy can be defined at least in part as the inability to be persuaded by a sound argument. But that suggests the more general point about arguments that we touched upon earlier: no argument can ever do more than show us that if we believe one thing *then* we must also believe something else. If the "Refutation of Idealism" truly shows us that if we believe we are justified in assigning a determinate temporal order to our experience *then* we must also presuppose that our representations are representations of an orderly and rule-governed world of objects other than our own representations but causing us to have those representations in a determinate order, then it has proven all that we can reasonably ask of it.

Of course, as Kant himself points out, the necessity of the general assumption that there are outside objects does not imply that we are always certain about our *particular* judgments about external objects: "From the fact that the existence of outer objects is required for the possibility of a determinate consciousness of our self it does not follow that every intuitive representation of outer things includes at the same their existence" – we do, after all, suffer from dreams and delusions (B 278). Can we ever become certain of our particular judgments about external objects? Unlike the parallel question about how we can come to know particular causal laws when they are not implied by the general principle of causation, Kant does not return to this further question; and he may well be right not to do so, for to expect that philosophy could ever give us a failsafe method of guaranteeing our particular empirical judgments may itself be a form of lunacy. What about the more reasonable question left hanging by this chapter, namely, can philosophy give us *any* method for making particular judgments using the category of causation, as well as the categories of substance and interaction, even if not a method for making those particular judgments with complete certitude? Kant leaves that question hanging while he uses the results he has obtained thus far to conduct his critique of traditional metaphysics. We shall now follow his example.

SUMMARY

Kant formulates the problem of theoretical philosophy as that of whether the fundamental propositions of mathematics, natural science, and metaphysics itself can be shown to be synthetic *a priori* cognitions. He argues that our experience of objects in space and time is possible only if we have *a priori* intuitions of the form of space and time, and that we can ground synthetic *a priori* cognition in geometry and arithmetic in such intuitions. But he also infers that we can know that the forms of our intuition *necessarily* apply only to our representations of objects, not independently existing objects themselves: his doctrine of transcendental idealism. He next argues that cognitions are always expressed by judgments, which have their own distinctive forms and which require our concepts of objects to be structured in certain ways: the categories. In the "Transcendental Deduction," he tries a variety of means to show that we must be able to make judgments about and therefore apply the categories to any and everything that we can experience. His most promising method for showing this is to show that the use of the categories and the synthetic *a priori* principles of judgment that employ them is necessary both to distinguish an objective order of states of affairs from our mere perceptions of them (the "Analogies of Experience") and even to have determinate knowledge of the order of our mere perceptions (the "Refutation of Idealism"). These arguments do not for the most part themselves entail transcendental idealism, although of course Kant believes that he has proven transcendental idealism and therefore attempts to reconcile the idea of an objective realm that is established in the "Analogies" and the "Refutation" with the non-spatiality of things in themselves by holding that spatiality itself represents the properties of things existing independently of us without actually being a property of those things. (He tries to reconcile the essential temporality of our representation of ourselves with the non-temporality of our real selves in passages of the second-edition deduction to which we only briefly alluded.) In the "Transcendental Dialectic," he will use both his view that knowledge (as opposed to faith) always requires both intuitions and concepts and his doctrine of transcendental idealism to dissolve the problems of traditional metaphysics.

FURTHER READING

The literature on the *Critique of Pure Reason*, even just in English, is vast, and many worthy books will have to be omitted here. However, the two classical commentaries below continue to have their merits, Kemp Smith providing a rich historical context for the Critique, and Paton a section-by-section commentary through the "Transcendental Analytic" that was the first, and for many years the only, work in English to make use of Kant's own notes and fragments.

Norman Kemp Smith, *A Commentary to Kant's 'Critique of Pure Reason'*, rev. edn (London: Macmillan, 1923).

H.J. Paton, *Kant's Metaphysic of Experience*, 2 vols (London: George Allen and Unwin, 1923).

The two commentaries below from the 1960s which did so much to stimulate renewed interest in Kant, remain insightful and challenging, although they reflect assumptions of the "analytical" philosophy of that period, Strawson especially interpreting Kant as analyzing the *concept* of experience rather than the confirmation conditions of *judgments* of experience, as he has been interpreted here.

Jonathan Bennett, *Kant's Analytic* (Cambridge: Cambridge University Press, 1966).

P.F. Strawson, *The Bounds of Sense: An Essay on Kant's Critique of Pure Reason* (London: Methuen, 1966).

The two main commentaries of the 1980s, which defined the poles in the continuing debate about the meaning of transcendental idealism, are:

Henry E. Allison, *Kant's Transcendental Idealism: An Interpretation and Defense* (New Haven, CT: Yale University Press, 1983, rev. edn, 2004).

Paul Guyer, *Kant and the Claims of Knowledge* (Cambridge: Cambridge University Press, 1987).

Allison's "two-aspect" interpretation of transcendental idealism was anticipated by:

Graham Bird, *Kant's Theory of Knowledge: An Outline of One Central Argument in the Critique of Pure Reason* (London: Routledge and Kegan Paul, 1962).

Gerold Prauss, *Kant und das Problem der Dinge an Sich* (Bonn: Bouvier Verlag, 1974).

Two recent introductions to the constructive epistemology of the Critique are:

Georges Dicker, *Kant's Theory of Knowledge: An Analytical Introduction* (Oxford and New York: Oxford University Press, 2005).

Anthony Savile, *Kant's Critique of Pure Reason: An Orientation to the Central Theme* (Oxford: Blackwell, 2005).

On Kant's views on space, time, and mathematics, as presented in the "Transcendental Aesthetic," the following are particularly valuable. Hatfield traces the influence of Kant's theory of space on subsequent German psychology and Shabel examines Kant's theory of proof in algebra as well as geometry:

Lorne Falkenstein, *Kant's Intuitionism: A Commentary on the Transcendental Aesthetic* (Toronto: University of Toronto Press, 1995) (provides a section-by-section commentary).

Michael Friedman, *Kant and the Exact Sciences* (Cambridge, MA: Harvard University Press, 1992) (Part I of which includes crucial essays on Kant's philosophy of mathematics).

Gary Hatfield, The Natural and the Normative: Theories of Spatial Perception from Kant to Helmholtz (Cambridge, MA: MIT Press, 1990).

Lisa A. Shabel, Mathematics in Kant's Critical Philosophy: Reflections on Mathematical Practice (New York and London: Routledge, 2003).

On the "Transcendental Deduction," see in addition to Part II of my Kant and the Claims of Knowledge:

Dieter Henrich, "Identity and Objectivity: An Inquiry into Kant's Transcendental Deduction" (1976), translated in his The Unity of Reason: Essays on Kant's Philosophy, ed. Richard L. Velkley (Cambridge, MA: Harvard University Press, 1994), pp. 123–208.

Robert Paul Wolff, Kant's Theory of Mental Activity: A Commentary on the Transcendental Analytic of the Critique of Pure Reason (Cambridge, MA: Harvard University Press, 1963).

On the "Analogies of Experience," see the following. Edwards gives special attention to the third "Analogy of Experience" and its influence on Kant's later philosophy of science. Melnick (1973) is a source for the approach taken here, while his (1989) work is a challenging but innovative study of Kant's conception of the role of rules of construction in both mathematical and empirical knowledge. Van Cleve offers a rigorous analysis of the first and second analogies in Chapters 8 and 9. Watkins offers a detailed study of the historical context of Kant's thought about causality as well as a metaphysical rather than epistemological analysis of it.

Jeffrey Edwards, Substance, Force, and the Possibility of Knowledge: On Kant's Philosophy of Material Nature (Berkeley and Los Angeles: University of California Press, 2000).

A.C. Ewing, Kant's Treatment of Causality (London: Routledge & Kegan Paul, 1924).

Arthur Melnick, Kant's Analogies of Experience (Chicago: University of Chicago Press, 1973).

——, Space, Time, and Thought in Kant (Dordrecht: Kluwer, 1989).

James van Cleve, Problems from Kant (New York: Oxford University Press, 1999).

Eric Watkins, Kant and the Metaphysics of Causality (Cambridge: Cambridge University Press, 2005).

On the "Refutation of Idealism," in addition to Chapter 14 of Bennett, Kant's Analytic, and Part IV of Kant and the Claims of Knowledge, see:

A.H. Smith, Kantian Studies (Oxford: Clarendon Press, 1947).

Three

The Critique of Metaphysics

In the second part of the "Transcendental Logic," its "Transcendental Dialectic," Kant turns to the critique of traditional metaphysics that he will carry out on the basis of the analysis of the necessary conditions of knowledge that he has offered in the "Transcendental Aesthetic" and "Transcendental Analytic." Plato had used the term "dialectic" in an entirely positive sense, to designate the highest sort of philosophical reasoning about the Forms or Ideas that he thought lie behind the objects of ordinary experience, such as the perfect geometrical Forms that lie behind the inevitably imperfect copies of them that we find in physical reality or the perfect Forms of justice or goodness that lie behind the inevitably imperfect copies of them that we find in actual human conduct.[1] But Kant uses "dialectic" in a negative sense, because he thinks that Plato's Forms are only the illusion of knowledge, "a dream of perfection that can have its place only in the idle thinker's brain" (CPuR, A 316/B 372). They are the product of an attempt to acquire knowledge by the use of pure reason without regard to the necessity of sensibility for any actual knowledge, and thus without regard to the limits of sensibility. His aim in the "Transcendental Dialectic" is thus a critique of the pretensions of pure reason in the hands of Plato and all subsequent metaphysicians, especially his recent predecessors such as Leibniz, Wolff, and Baumgarten, to provide knowledge of objects beyond the limits of sensibility, such as God or our own souls. This diagnosis of the errors of traditional metaphysics is of immense importance to Kant – the critique of the pretensions of pure reason in the "Transcendental Dialectic" and its continuation in much of the "Doctrine of Method" takes up more than half of the Critique of Pure Reason, and is indeed the source of the title of the book.

Kant's purpose in his critique of metaphysics, however, is by no means entirely destructive. He believes that the illusions of metaphysics are natural: they arise from an ambition of pure reason that is natural, an ambition that leads to illusion when not constrained by a proper under- standing of the conditions necessary for knowledge but which, precisely because it is natural, must also have some proper function. "Everything that nature itself arranges," Kant writes, "is good for some aim" (A 743/B 771). Kant's grand argument is that pure reason leads to illusion when we attempt to use it independently of sensibility and its inherent limitations in order to gain *theoretical* knowledge of objects lying beyond the limits of our senses (thus "supersensible" objects) such as God and our soul, but that only pure reason can provide what is necessary in the *practical* sphere of moral conduct: only pure reason, not the inclinations of sensibility – that is, our merely natural wishes and passions – can provide the fundamental principle of morality, the "practical law" of right and wrong, and, as postulates of pure *practical* reason that are *necessary* for our moral conduct, the ideas of the freedom of our own wills and even of the immortality of our souls and the existence of God are objects of justified belief. When Kant writes that he has "to deny **knowledge** in order to make room for **faith**" (B xxx), at least part of what he means is that he has to curb the pretensions of pure reason to deliver *theoretical cognition* precisely in order to make room for the recognition that pure reason is the sole and proper source of the *moral law* and the *practical* postulates on which the possibility of our acting in conformity with that law depends.

However, the positive function of pure practical reason is not yet our concern; this chapter will concern Kant's critique of pure theoretical reason. Kant makes it clear at the outset of the *Critique of Pure Reason* that this critique is also part of his response to skepticism. He writes that the "despotic" dogmatism of metaphysics inevitably calls forth a skeptical response (A vii–ix), and although there are never enough skeptical "nomads" to prevent the dogmatists from rebuilding their meta- physical castles in the air altogether, there are always enough around to poke holes in the rebuilt castles, thus creating a never-ending cycle of dogmatism and skepticism. The battle between dogmatism and skepticism is like two opponents "fencing in the air and wrestling with their shadows": "Fight as they may, the shadows that they cleave apart grow back together in an instant, like the heroes of Valhalla, to amuse themselves anew in bloodless battles" (A 756/B 785). This endless and inconclusive spectacle might seem like a proper object for a further response of utter "indifference" to the non-provable but apparently also irrefutable claims of metaphysics (A x), but, Kant argues, the stance of indifference cannot be maintained, precisely because of the ultimately moral importance of the ideas and beliefs at issue. That is why a critique of pure reason is indispensable.

What does Kant have in mind when he claims that metaphysics induces skepticism? Here he has in mind not the Humean skepticism about first principles of ordinary knowledge that he aims to refute in the "Transcendental Analytic" but rather something more akin to the ancient, Pyrrhonian skepticism, according to which equally plausible arguments can be made on either side of every issue. He is thinking in particular of topics in metaphysics that engender what he calls "antinomies," that is, arguments for incompatible theses that appear to be equally sound on both sides, which inevitably lead us to question the reliability of the very faculty of reason that produces such contradictory arguments. In the middle section of the "Transcendental Dialectic," called the "Antinomy of Pure Reason," Kant will discuss and attempt to resolve four such conflicts: incompatible but apparently equally sound theses and antitheses about the extent of the world in space and time and about the divisibility of objects in space and time; the incompatible theses that every event in the world is determined by something else and that some events must be uncaused causes of further chains of events; and the incompatible claims that everything is contingent and that somewhere, either within the world or outside it, there must be some necessary being. These conflicts are central to Kant's critique of pure reason, because they are the kinds of conflicts that call forth a skeptical attitude about the possibility of metaphysics altogether, but they also suggest to someone with faith in reason that beneath such disputes there must somewhere be a false assumption that can be discovered. This false assumption is in fact the idea that knowledge of objects can be gained by pure reason *alone*, without the assistance of intuitions from sensibility, and thus without restriction to the limits of sensibility. Kant will also argue that there are other metaphysical inferences, especially about the self and God, that do not lead to such obvious conflicts and therefore have not so loudly cried out for a critique of pure reason, but which can nevertheless be revealed to be illusions by the same critique of pure reason that will finally resolve the age-old antinomies of pure reason. Kant's ambition is to show that all of the theoretical claims of traditional metaphysics are illusions ultimately produced in the same way, namely, by failing to recognize the necessity of intuitions as well as concepts for any cognition, and the ensuing restriction of all possible cognition within the limits that are inherent in the forms of our sensible intuition.

Kant's critique of metaphysics is thus another central battleground for his response to skepticism. It is also a key to his conception of the nature and limits of human autonomy. In the previous chapter, we have seen what Kant's conception of our autonomy as knowers comprises: in order to understand the possibility of synthetic *a priori* knowledge, he has argued, we must realize that the fundamental forms of both sensibility and understanding have their origin within our own minds, and that we impose these forms upon our experience of objects rather than depending upon objects for them. This is a very strong conception of cognitive autonomy. But in the "Transcendental Dialectic" he will argue that what might seem to be an even stronger form of cognitive autonomy, namely the autonomy of pure *reason* to acquire metaphysical insight on its own, without the assistance but at the same time without the restrictions of sensibility, is misguided. But this will not mean that our faculty of reason has nothing genuine to contribute to human autonomy. On the contrary, autonomy in the *practical* sphere – "the property of the will by which it is a law to itself" (G, 4:440) – is possible only through pure reason, because only pure reason can give our will a genuine law to act upon. In other words, Kant's grand argument, as I called it a moment ago, is that theoretical autonomy of pure reason alone is an illusion, but practical autonomy, self-government in our moral choices and actions, can be achieved only through pure reason.

THE IDEAS OF PURE REASON

Kant sets up his critique of pure reason in several steps. He actually announces his rejection of the idea that pure reason alone can give us real knowledge of objects beyond the limits of our senses in the final chapter of the "Transcendental Analytic," on the "distinction of all objects in general into *phenomena* and *noumena*," for in arguing as he does there that we can have no knowledge of objects as "noumena in the positive sense" what he means is precisely that we can have no knowledge of objects through pure reason alone, for "noumena in the positive sense" would be nothing other than objects known by intellect (in Greek, *nous*) alone. Kant begins this chapter by concluding from the preceding chapters "That the understanding can therefore make only empirical use of all its *a priori* principles, indeed of all its concepts, but never transcendental use" (A 238/B 297, see also A 246/B 303). His use of the term "transcendental" here is confusing, because elsewhere this term connotes the conditions of the possibility of synthetic *a priori* cognition (e.g., B 40–1), whereas here it refers precisely to that which lies *beyond* the possibility of any knowledge at all; in other words, Kant should have said "transcendent." But his meaning is clear enough: our concepts can only yield knowledge through "being related merely to **appearances**, i.e., objects of a possible **experience**," and any attempt to obtain knowledge by applying them "to things **in general** and **in themselves**" (A 238–9/B 298) will be at best incomplete and at worst lead to confusion and illusion. Nevertheless, Kant continues, we do need the thought of an "**object in itself**" even merely to express the contrast that is inherent in the limitation of our actual knowledge to mere appearances; we need some way to refer to the way objects are in themselves independently of our sensible representation of them. And because any representation of such an object that does not involves our senses would have to be purely intellectual, Kant calls it a "noumenon," that is, an object of *nous*. But our idea of a noumenon is entirely negative, simply the idea of something that is *not* known as it is in itself by means of sensibility, and it would be a mistake to think that we can use the idea of a noumenon "in a **positive** sense," that is, as something actually *known* by intellect alone. To think that we are entitled to use the concept of a noumenon in a positive rather than merely negative sense, or to be "misled into taking the entirely **undetermined** concept of a being of understanding, as a something in general outside of our sensibility, for a **determinate** concept of a being that we could cognize through the understanding in some way," is the general form of all metaphysical illusion (B 306–7). Of course, it will subsequently turn out to be Kant's considered view that we *can* and indeed *must* use the idea of a noumenon in a positive sense for practical purposes – we must use reason alone to conceive of our own free wills and immortal souls and of the existence of God as conditions of the possibility of morality – but that use will fall under the rubric of practical belief or faith, not theoretical cognition.[2]

Kant does not think that we stumble into using the negative idea of an object undetermined by sense as if it were a positive idea of an object fully determined by reason alone from mere ignorance or inadvertence. Rather, he thinks that there is a natural and inevitable pressure coming from within our faculty of reason itself that leads us to think we can have theoretical cognition of objects transcending the limits of our senses. This is because it is characteristic of the faculty of reason to "assume that when the conditioned is given, then so is the whole series of conditions . . . which is itself unconditioned, also given (i.e., contained in the object and its connection)" (A 307–8/B 365). By the "unconditioned," Kant means something that is a condition for other things but not itself dependent on any other condition, for example a primary subject that has properties but is not itself the property of anything else or a first cause that has effects but is not the effect of anything else. Kant's view is that reason inevitably leads us to form ideas of such "unconditioned" realities, that we cannot think of such things as if they were given by sensibility because everything given by sensibility is inherently "conditioned" (remember that any space we can represent can only be represented as part of some larger space and any time only as part of a larger time), and so we inevitably think of anything "unconditioned" as if it were an object that lies beyond and transcends the limits of sensibility – in other words, as a noumenon in the positive sense. Thus the faculty of reason hijacks the harmless concept of a noumenon in the negative sense to express its own positive conception of the "unconditioned."[3]

But why does Kant think that reason inevitably leads to the idea of the "unconditioned"? This sounds like it comes out of thin air, but Kant at least starts down the road to this idea simply enough. On his account, the faculty of understanding is our ability to form concepts and to link concepts into judgments (although he sometimes ascribes this capacity to a separate faculty of judgment), but the faculty of reason is in the first instance the ability to perform inferences by linking judgments. His paradigm here is the syllogism, that is, an inference such as "All As are B, All Bs are C, therefore all As are C." But both the premises and conclusions of inferences can typically themselves be connected to other judgments in further inferences: for example the premise of our syllogism, "All As are B," might itself be the conclusion of some logically prior syllogism, e.g., "All As are Z, All Zs are B, therefore all As are B," and the conclusion of our syllogism, "All As are C," may in turn be the premise of some further syllogism, e.g., "All As are C, all Cs are D, therefore all As are D," and so on. Now, we might think that this "and so on" is just that – that is, that it is an open matter whether any given syllogism can be seamlessly linked to others, and if so, how long the chain that thus arises is. Such matters, we might well think, are determined by the subject-matter of our inferences and the state of our knowledge about them, not by the faculty of reason itself. Here, however, Kant departs from what might seem like an innocuous conception of our ability to reason or perform inferences, and assumes that the faculty of reason inevitably posits completeness in its chains of inferences, in two senses: it posits that there are no insurmountable gaps in our chains of inferences, but also that every chain of inferences can ultimately be carried back to some first premise that is not itself the conclusion of yet another chain of inferences. Such a first premise would be something "unconditioned." Reason thus gets its principle that for everything conditioned there is also an unconditioned by combining our ordinary conception of reason as the ability to perform inferences with its own assumption that every chain of inference must have an ultimate starting-point.

Kant then generates three fundamental "ideas of pure reason" or "transcendental ideas" (A 321 / B 378) by supposing that reason applies its goal of inference to the unconditioned to those "species of relation represented by the understanding by means of the categories." His idea is that since inferences depend upon relations among judgments, and there are three categories of relation, there will be three sorts of chains of inference for which reason seeks an unconditioned starting-point: reason "must seek an **unconditioned, first**, for the **categorical** synthesis in a **subject, second** for the **hypothetical** synthesis of the members of a **series**, and **third** for the **disjunctive** synthesis of the parts in a **system**" (A 323 / B 379). With what might seem like a further wave of the hand, Kant then equates the unconditioned that reason seeks for each of these three relations and kinds of inference with the *soul* as the absolute *subject* of all *categorical* judgments, with the *world-whole* or the *whole of all appearances* as the completion of all *series*, and finally with *God* as the unconditional ground of all *possibilities* whatsoever:

> Consequently, all transcendental ideas will be brought under **three classes**, of which the **first** contains the absolute (unconditioned) **unity** of the **thinking subject**, the **second** the absolute **unity** of the **series** of **conditions of appearance**, the **third** the absolute **unity** of the **condition of all objects of thought** in general.
>
> (A 334 / B 391)

In other words, the traditional metaphysical concepts of the soul, of the world-whole, and of God are not supposed to be the arbitrary inventions of philosophers, but the natural products of the human faculty of reason assuming that it can posit an unconditioned object for each of its three categories of relation and the corresponding forms of inference.

As if all this were not complicated enough, Kant captures even more of the concepts and arguments of traditional metaphysics by distinguishing a number of different kinds of "series of conditions of appearance," that is, aspects of the world of appearance, for which unconditioned stopping-points are supposedly sought by reason. Thus, while his initial list of transcendental ideas is formed by transforming each of the three relational categories into the idea of something unconditioned, the idea of a series of appearances is itself divided into four further series under the rubrics of the four classes of categories, that is, quantity, quality, relation, and modality. Reason seeks the unconditioned in the series of objects in space and events in time (quantity), in the division of objects and events in space and time (quality), in the series of causes and effects (relation), and in the dependence of contingent things or states upon something necessary (modality). And in each of these series, moreover, reason finds two *incompatible* ways of conceiving of the unconditioned, thus generating the insoluble conflicts that have always called forth the response of Pyrrhonian skepticism. These conflicts are what Kant calls the "antinomies" of pure reason.

From his conception of reason as positing the unconditioned for everything that is unconditioned, Kant thus generates an elaborate reconstruction of the contents of traditional metaphysics, including its hitherto irresolvable internal disputes. For reasons that we shall shortly see, he calls the inference to the absolute unity of the thinking subject and some additional inferences based on that the "Paralogisms of Pure Reason"; the inferences to the unconditioned in the series of appearances, as we have just seen, the "Antinomies of Pure Reason"; and the inference to God as the absolute ground of the system of all possibilities the "Ideal of Pure Reason."

But even if reason is tempted by some natural path to formulate or posit these transcendental ideas of absolutely unconditioned entities, can it acquire any *knowledge* by so doing? Don't claims to knowledge have to answer the *quid juris*, or give an account of the "objective reality" of their ideas to show that they are not merely "usurpatory" ideas like the ideas of fate and fortune, witches and goblins (A 84 / B 117)? Of course they do, and Kant's argument against traditional metaphysics is precisely that although it has formed its transcendental ideas by a natural mechanism, it has ignored the chief result of Kant's own critical philosophy, namely that concepts yield knowledge only when applied to intuitions, and as a result has failed to recognize that all ideas of the unconditioned are *fundamentally incompatible* with the structure of our sensible intuition, *which is always conditioned* – remember, *every* region of space can *only* be represented as *part* of a larger space, and *every* region of time *only* as *part* of a larger time. In other words, it is the most fundamental characteristic of our intuitions that they are always *conditioned* by further intuitions, and so nothing *unconditioned* can ever be "given" or represented in our sensible intuition; no representation of space or time is ever complete. Therefore nothing unconditioned can ever be an object of knowledge for us. So if metaphysics interprets its transcendental ideas as concepts of *unconditioned objects of experience*, that is, sensible intuition, its claims must therefore be false. Where its claims can be interpreted as claims about objects beyond our senses, then they are not necessarily false, but neither can they ever be demonstrated to be true on any theoretical grounds. Still, as long as metaphysical concepts do not pretend to have any sensible content, they are at least *conceivable*. Ultimately, Kant will argue that we have practical reasons for believing in the existence of three sorts of objects that never pretend to be sensible objects of experience, namely our own free wills, our immortal souls, and God. So these can be objects of practical *faith*, but never of *knowledge*.

Kant's discussion of the "Paralogisms," "Antinomies," and "Ideals of Pure Reason" is immensely lengthy and detailed – he was fighting an opponent that was very much alive in many quarters. But we do not need to go into all of the detail that Kant provides in order to see the basic points in each of Kant's arguments: that reason forms its transcendental concepts in a way that is incompatible with the limits of sensible intuition and therefore with the possibility of knowledge, but in at least some cases can still formulate concepts of possible objects for practical faith.

THE METAPHYSICS OF THE SELF

In the "Paralogisms of Pure Reason," Kant criticizes metaphysical claims about the soul made by "rationalist psychologists" from Descartes to Wolff and Baumgarten, supposedly on the basis "of the single proposition **I think**" (A 342/B 400). Kant's explanation of why he calls the arguments of the rational psychologists "paralogisms" is obscure: a "logical paralogism," he says, "consists in the falsity of a syllogism due to its form" (A 341/B 399) or "an inference which is false in its form (although its matter (the premises) are correct)" (R 5552, 18:218), while a "transcendental paralogism" has "a transcendental ground for inferring falsely due to its form" (A 341/B 399). His diagnosis of the paralogisms about the soul suggests that what he actually means is that the paralogisms look like valid arguments but are not, because the major and minor premises use the same term in two different senses (B 411–12), but that this is not mere carelessness – there is a "transcendental ground" that compels us all to make this mistake as long as we are not enlightened by the critical philosophy. But the source of this "transcendental ground" is not entirely clear in Kant's account.[4]

Kant attributes four linked assertions to the "rational psychologists." In the first three "Paralogisms," he argues that the rational psychologists invalidly infer (1) that the soul is a substance which is (2) simple and therefore incorruptible and immortal as well as (3) aware of its numerical identity throughout its existence, and then in the fourth "Paralogism" he argues (4) that "problematic idealism" arises from thinking of both the soul and external objects as distinct substances, so that the soul can only know the latter by means of some sort of inference from its own states (its own accidents), which however can never be conclusive. Kant is not as clear in the first-edition fourth "Paralogism" about the role of thinking of the soul as a substance in the genesis of "problematic idealism" as he might be, but is a little clearer in the second-edition version: here he says that from the distinction of

> my own existence, [as] that of a thinking being, from other things outside me . . . I do not thereby know at all whether this consciousness of myself would even be possible without things outside me through which representations are given to me, and thus whether I could exist merely as a thinking being.
>
> (B 409)

What Kant is saying here is that from the distinction between the *representations* of my thinking self and of outer objects (including my own body) it does not follow that my thinking self and other things are distinct kinds of *substances* at all – for things being able to exist independently of each other is a criterion of their being separate substances, but that is precisely what cannot be inferred from the mere distinction between kinds of *representations*.

In any case, Kant's second-edition version of the fourth "Paralogism" demonstrates the character of his criticism of all the doctrines of the rationalist psychologists: they mistake merely formal features of the *representation* of the self for metaphysical characteristics of the self as a substance. This is easy to see in each of the first three "Paralogisms." Kant represents the first "Paralogism" as the following syllogism:

> That the representation of which is the **absolute subject** of our judgments, and hence cannot be used as the determination of another thing, is **substance**.
>
> I, as a thinking being, am the **absolute subject** of all my possible judgments, and this representation of myself cannot be used as the predicate of any other thing.
>
> Thus I, as thinking being (soul), am **substance**.
>
> (A 348)

Kant's charge is that this inference is invalid because the term "absolute subject" is being used in different senses in the major and minor premises. In the major premise, an "absolute subject" is that which can have properties but cannot be the property of anything else, and that is just the traditional definition of "substance" (so the first premise is analytically true). But in Kant's view, the second premise is talking about something entirely different: I am the "absolute subject" of all my judgments in the sense that I attribute them to myself, or can make myself the subject of any of my judgments – instead of just saying "p" I can always say "I think that p" – but this just means that I can include a *representation* of myself in all of my judgments, or *represent* myself as the subject of all my judgments. It does not tell me anything about what the actual physical or psychological basis of my capacity to think is, so even though the *representation* of myself may be the subject of all my judgments, I have no basis for inferring that the *self* itself is a substance.

It is even easier to see what the fallacy is supposed to be in the remaining "Paralogisms." In the second "Paralogism," Kant states that the simplicity of the soul – from which, according to traditional metaphysics, its incorruptibility (indissolubility) and therefore its immortality would follow – is supposed to be inferred from the definition of that "whose action can never be regarded as the concurrence of many acting things" as "simple" (A 351). But all that we are actually entitled to claim, Kant responds, is that the *concept* of the self is simple, that "this representation I encompasses not the least manifoldness within itself, and that it is an absolute (though merely logical) unity" (A 355) – and this tells us nothing about whether the *thing* that thinks this thought is itself simple or complex. Likewise, in the third "Paralogism" Kant represents the rational psychologist as inferring the "personality" of the self or its necessary consciousness "of the numerical identity of its self in different times" from the fact that "the identical-sounding 'I' is assigned to it" (A 353), but in fact this only means that each and all of us always *represents* ourselves, whenever and for as long as we happen to be conscious, by means of the same *sign* "I," but not that we are in any sense always conscious of ourselves as a continuing substance throughout our entire – and according to the second "Paralogism" immortal – existence. Once again the property of a sign has been confused with an alleged property of the thing signified. (Kant does not make the following argument, but it is easy to see that the rational psychologist's inference must be invalid because it would prove way too much: since we all use the same sign "I" or its equivalent in other languages to represent ourselves, if sameness of sign were enough to prove sameness of substance *then we would all be a single substance* – which no one in the Western philosophical tradition except perhaps Spinoza has ever believed.) Finally, we have already seen how the fourth "Paralogism" trades on the fallacy of equivocating between sign and thing: it treats minds and bodies as separate and independent substances just because our *representations* of them are distinct.

This is the gist of Kant's critique of the traditional metaphysics of the soul: it all depends upon an equivocation about the representation of the self, or "the taking of a **subjective** condition for thinking for the cognition of an **object**" (A 396). What is not clear in Kant's account is what role the conception of the faculty of reason as seeking cognition of the unconditioned regardless of the limits of sensibility is supposed to have to do with this diagnosis. In the conclusion of the first-edition exposition of the "Paralogisms," Kant states that they arise from seeking the unconditioned in "The synthesis of the conditions of a thought in general" (just as the "Antinomies" will arise from seeking the unconditioned in "The synthesis of the conditions of empirical thinking" and unsound theoretical arguments for the existence of God will arise from seeking the unconditioned in "The synthesis of the conditions of pure thinking") (A 397). What Kant seems to mean is then that since the only content that is common to all thoughts in general is "the universal proposition 'I think'," reason applies its concept of the unconditioned to the idea of the self that is expressed by this proposition and comes up with the idea of a subject of thought that is unconditioned in the sense of not being dependent on anything else, and thus a substance in the traditional sense. But the fundamentality, simplicity, and identity of the mere thought "I think" does not imply that thought is produced by an object that has those properties, nor does the difference between the *representations* of self and other objects imply that they are different substances that can only be related by a dubious inference.

Whatever we might think of this explanation of the inevitability of the invalid inferences of rational psychology, Kant's chief point is just that they arise from trying to derive theoretical knowledge about the real nature of the self from the *concept* of the self alone, and thus without any empirical *intuitions* of the self – which are always necessary for any knowledge, but which of course will also never reveal that the self is unconditioned in any sense, because empirical intuitions, by their very form, never reveal that *anything* is unconditioned. And this means that when it comes to the traditional alternatives in the philosophy of mind, Kant's position can only be "a pox on both your houses." Kant does not think that materialism, the reduction of thought to properties or products of extended matter, can be demonstrated, because there is something simple about the contents of thought, namely the representation of the self, and it is not clear how matter, which is always divisible and never simple, can explain that. But neither does he think that spiritualism, that is, the doctrine that the self is something completely distinct from matter, can be demonstrated, for from the simplicity of the representation of the self we can "in no way whatsoever . . . cognize anything about the constitution of our soul that in any way at all concerns the possibility of its separate existence" (B 420). A basis for deciding between materialism and spiritualism is simply beyond the limits of our knowledge. And this in turn means that the traditional alternatives for providing a metaphysical explanation of the relation *between* mind and body – the theories "of **physical influence**, of **preestablished harmony**, and of **supernatural assistance**" or occasionalism (A 390) – are all entirely idle, because we have no way of even determining whether they are responses to a genuine problem or not. Both the third "Analogy of Experience" and the "Refutation of Idealism" show that Kant is committed to genuine interaction or "physical influence" in *empirical* knowledge and science, but the point of the "Paralogisms" is to sweep all *metaphysical* theories about the relation between mind and body off the table.

THE METAPHYSICS OF THE WORLD

Kant's view is that we have such a strong interest in believing in our own immortality – and ultimately, he will argue, sound *moral* reasons for such a belief – that we would never have noticed the fallacies in the traditional metaphysics of the soul unless led to do so by the critical philosophy. When it comes to metaphysical thinking about the world as a whole (the cosmos), however, he argues that reason itself necessarily produces contradictions, a problem that either calls forth the unsustainable attitudes of skepticism or indifference about reason itself or else requires a solution. These contradictions are the "Antinomies of Pure Reason."

Kant often claims that the "Antinomies" are contradictions produced by pure reason itself. This is somewhat misleading: as his initial account that the "Antinomies" arise from attempting to apply the principle that if anything conditioned is given then the unconditioned is also given *to the series of appearances* (A 334 / B 391, A 397) implies, the "Antinomies" actually arise from attempting to apply the idea of the unconditioned to the *intuition* of the world, but in two different ways that turn out to be contradictory. More precisely, each side of each antinomy – its "thesis" and "antithesis" –

seeks to find reason's goal, the unconditioned, *in sensible experience*, but the very form of sensibility precludes ever finding anything unconditioned in experience. In the cases in which the unconditioned that reason is seeking is something that could only be found in sensible experience if it could be found at all, that will mean that both ways of conceiving of something that is sensible yet unconditioned are incoherent, and both thesis and antithesis are false. In the cases in which the unconditioned can be conceived as something that lies beyond the limits of sensibility, then reason's idea of the unconditioned is not necessarily false, but precisely because it lies beyond the limits of sensibility it can be at most an object of belief, not knowledge. Either way, the assumption that reason's idea of the unconditioned whether within or beyond the limits of sensibility can give knowledge of any object turns out to be groundless, and with that a large chunk of traditional metaphysics collapses.

The first "Antinomy" concerns the extent of space and time. The thesis argues that the world – that is, the connected series of all objects in space and time – must have a beginning in time and boundaries in space (A 426/B 454), because if it does not then any point in time or space must be preceded or bounded by another, and so might have to be reached by an infinite synthesis of other spaces or times. But this is impossible, reason supposes; any such series must begin with a condition that is not itself conditioned by something else, that is, something that is unconditioned. Conversely, the antithesis argues that "The world has no beginning and no bounds in space, but is infinite with regard to both time and space" (A 427/B 455) because a beginning in time would be a time preceded by an empty time and a boundary in space would be a space not bounded by any other space, both of which defy the form of sensibility itself.

But although each of these arguments initially seems plausible, obviously their conclusions cannot both be true. Kant argues that each is actually false, because in each case the idea of the unconditioned conflicts with the forms of sensibility themselves. Thus, while it might seem true that every series must have an unconditioned beginning or a boundary, we simply cannot perceive unconditioned beginnings or boundaries in time or space; but that does not in turn mean that we can perceive an infinite world in time or space either, because we cannot in fact ever complete an infinite synthesis of moments in time or places or objects in space. Reason's idea of the unconditioned is simply inapplicable to our perception of the extent of time and space and the series of things in them, so reason's attempt to gain cognition of anything unconditioned in the extent of time and space is doomed.

The second "Antinomy" presents the dispute over whether there must be something simple and indivisible in space and time or whether everything in space or time is infinitely divisible – historically, the dispute about atomism. The thesis asserts that "Every composite substance in the world consists of simple parts," because if "composite substances do not consist of simple parts, then if all composition is removed in thought, no composite part, and (since there are no simple parts), no simple part, thus nothing at all, would be left over; consequently, no substance would be given" (A 434/B 462). This is Kant's version of Leibniz's oft-stated argument that "There must be simple substances everywhere, because, without simples, there would be no composites."[5] The antithesis argues that "No composite thing in the world consists of simple parts, and nowhere in it does there exist anything simple" (A 435/B 463), because everything in the world must exist in some region of time or space, yet every time or space always consists of more times or spaces. Again, each argument seems plausible, but both conclusions cannot be true; and again, Kant argues, both sides are mistaken in their attempt to apply reason's idea of the unconditioned to objects in space and time. The inference that if composite things exist there must ultimately be simple and therefore unconditioned things, things that are unconditioned in the sense that they are not composed out of any other things, is, as it were, perfectly rational; however, we simply can never be given anything simple and indivisible through our forms of sensibility, in which any region of space and time is always further divisible.[6] Yet it would also be a mistake to assume that objects in space and time are actually *infinitely* divisible, because we cannot complete an infinite synthesis of division any more than we could complete an infinite synthesis of extension. However finely we have divided things, we can always divide them more finely, but that is not the same as having completed an infinite division of them. Again, Kant's point is that reason's idea of the unconditioned, whether it takes the form of a part that is not itself comprised of any further parts or of a synthesis that is actually completed, is simply inapplicable to the form of our sensibility, and thus we can never have knowledge of anything unconditionally simple or unconditionally divisible in space and time.

In the remaining two antinomies, Kant deals with objects that do not have to be conceived of as parts of the series of appearances in space and time and therefore as subject to the limits of their form, and so the possibility arises that both thesis and antithesis at least *may* be true if properly understood. The third "Antinomy" is Kant's first mature consideration of the problem of freedom of the will. The thesis argues that "Causality in accordance with the laws of nature is not the only one from which the appearances of the world can be derived," and that "It is also necessary to assume another causality through freedom in order to explain them" (A 444/B 472). The argument is that if every event in nature were always the result of another event which is in turn the effect of yet another event, then there could never be a complete series of causes or a complete explanation of any event, but that this would violate the principle of sufficient reason understood as the principle that every event does have a complete explanation, which in order to be complete must terminate in a cause that is not itself an effect of something else – a free act that is an uncaused cause. This is an application of the idea of the unconditioned to causal explanation. The antithesis, however, argues that "There is no freedom, but everything in the world happens solely in accordance with laws of nature," because a free act or uncaused cause would have to be an event that "will begin absolutely, so that nothing precedes it through which this occurring action is determined in accordance with constant laws" (A 445/B 473) – but this violates the condition for assigning any state of affairs or event a determinate position in time, which as was seen in the second "Analogy of Experience" cannot be done through the direct perception of the position of any such thing in absolute time, but only through the subsumption of states of affairs under causal laws. Here the idea of the unconditioned is expressed in the idea that every state of affairs which is a cause is indeed also the effect of another state that is also caused, and so on *ad infinitum*.

In this case, however, Kant argues not that both thesis and antithesis are false, but rather that each can at least be conceived of as being true by conceiving of the act of freedom which is the uncaused cause posited by reason in the argument for the thesis as lying *outside* of or *beyond* the series of temporally successive, always determined appearances that constitutes nature and is described in the antithesis. Such a cause would be an "intelligible" rather than a "sensible" cause, that is, a cause conceived of through reason alone rather than through sensibility. Kant says that:

> Such an intelligible cause, however, will not be determined in its causality by appearances, even though its effects appear and so can be determined through other appearances. Thus the intelligible cause, with its causality, is outside the series; its effects, on the contrary, are encountered in the series of empirical conditions. The effect can therefore be regarded as free in regard to its intelligible cause, and yet simultaneously, in regard to appearances, as their result according to the necessity of nature.
>
> (A 537/B 565)

While within the series of events in time, any event must, because of the nature of both our sensibility and our understanding, be conceived of as the effect of an antecedent cause, we can also conceive of such an event as the effect of an event that is not itself part of the temporal series, which is therefore not subject to the causality in accordance with laws of nature that membership in the temporal series of events entails.

Several points should be noted about this argument. First, if the problem on which the indirect argument for the thesis turns is the need to stop an infinite regress of events, then a single act of uncaused causation outside of the temporal series would suffice for this purpose – for example, a single act of divine creation that could leave individual human actions just as fully entrenched in the chain of natural causality as they are for any full-fledged determinist. In other words, the thesis might be true without that being of any help to the cause of human freedom. Second, as regards the antithesis, while in the preceding antinomies Kant was insistent that the form of space and time does not allow the completion of any actually infinite synthesis in space and time, here, in countenancing the possibility that the antithesis might be just as true of events in the temporal series of appearances as the thesis is true of some event of causation outside of that series, he seems to overlook that scruple. He should say only that any causal explanation of an action can always be extended indefinitely further back, not that it actually extends back infinitely. That is, Kant should have argued that the idea of unconditioned completeness in the explanation of events cannot yield knowledge of an actually infinite series of causes.

This scruple, however, should not worry any determinist about human action: the damage to a libertarian conception of freedom is always done as soon as the determinist can argue that the first cause of any action lies further back in time than the birth of the particular agent, or even just back in time before the first apparently voluntary act of the agent – it need not lie infinitely far back in time. But the first problem seems more troublesome: what relevance could the freedom of a single divine act of creation have for the freedom of the apparently innumerable voluntary actions of human beings?[7] However, all Kant wants to prove at this point is the possibility of human freedom, not its actuality – that, he will eventually argue, can be inferred only from our awareness of our obligation under the moral law. All he wants to do now is open up conceptual space for the idea of the freedom of action from determination by causal laws of nature, and his reasoning seems to be that if one case of such freedom is conceivable then other cases are also at least conceivable. But again, even if we think of an act of creation or choice as an unconditioned cause, a cause that is not itself an effect, Kant is insistent that such a conception of reason does not amount to any *knowledge* and can never amount to knowledge, given the limits of our sensibility.

Finally, the fourth "Antinomy" concerns necessity and contingency. The thesis argues that "To the world there belongs something that, either as a part of it or as its cause, is an absolutely necessary being," while the antithesis argues that "There is no absolutely necessary being anywhere, either in the world or outside the world as its cause" (A 452–3/B 480–1). The arguments essentially equate the idea of something contingent with something that is conditioned or caused by something else and the idea of something necessary with something that is not conditioned or caused by anything else, and then basically repeat the moves of the previous "Antinomy": the series of conditions must terminate in something unconditioned, or the series of contingents must terminate in something necessary; but nothing necessary can ever be given as the cause of anything contingent in time, because the existence of an uncaused cause in time would conflict "with the dynamic law of the determination of all appearances in time" (A 453/B 481). Here again Kant is slightly misleading when he suggests that both thesis and antithesis can be true if each is properly *understood*; what he needs to say is that each can be true if properly *restricted*. That is, if we can conceive of a necessary cause of contingent things as outside of time then we can conceive of an absolutely necessary being as the *cause* of the world but not as *part* of it; and conversely, if we conceive of the causes of contingents in time, then we cannot conceive of any absolutely necessary being as existing anywhere in the world but cannot deny the possibility of such a being as existing *outside* of the world, that is, the series of appearances in time. And again, of course, Kant's conclusion is that we do not have any *knowledge* of unconditional necessity or unconditional necessity: we cannot have knowledge of an absolutely necessary cause of the world lying outside of the world, because we do not have knowledge of anything outside the world at all; at the same time, we do not actually have knowledge of the unconditional *contingency* of *everything* inside the world, for the simple reason that we cannot actually complete an infinite synthesis and therefore never have *knowledge* of everything even inside the world.

In a crucial appendix to the "Transcendental Dialectic," Kant will argue that the use of our power of reason in the *pursuit* of knowledge of objects and events in the world is hardly entirely misguided, rather that it is absolutely necessary, but that the assumption that we can ever have *complete knowledge* of the natural world is fundamentally misguided. We shall return to this theme in the following chapter, but first we must make a concluding comment on the "Antinomy of Pure Reason" and then consider the final main section of the "Dialectic," Kant's critique of metaphysical arguments for the existence of God.

In the Preface to the *Critique of Pure Reason* (e.g., B xviii–xix n.) and throughout his lengthy commentary on the "Antinomy" (e.g., A 490–7/B 518–25), Kant claims that the "Antinomy" provides an indirect proof of transcendental idealism, that is, of the distinction between appearances and things in themselves. That is, he argues that only the distinction between appearances and things in themselves allows us to resolve the disputes between the theses and antitheses of the antinomies. But that claim seems too strong. To be sure, transcendental idealism is one way to avoid these disputes, but it is not the only way. In the case of the first two antinomies, while we can argue that both the theses and the antitheses are false because space and time are merely indefinitely extendible forms of appearance that are neither finite nor truly infinite, we could also resolve the conflicts by supposing that objects really are in space and time and that the series of objects and events in time must therefore really be either finite or infinite, but that because of the always indefinitely extendible but never actually infinite character of our *perception* of space and time we can never *perceive* the series of objects and events in space and time to be either finite or actually infinite, and thus simply cannot *know* whether it is finite or infinite. In the case of the second set of antinomies, where Kant argues that transcendental idealism allows us merely to conceive of both thesis and antithesis as true, we could again suppose that either but not both of them are true yet that the always indefinitely extendible character of our perception of objects and events in space and time simply does not allow us to determine *which* of them is true. The only way that Kant could reject these alternative resolutions of the antinomies would be by maintaining that whatever is actually true or false of objects in space and time must also be something that we can *know* to be true or false – but the only way to guarantee *that* epistemic assumption would be if we were to assume that space and time are nothing but the forms of our own intuition and therefore necessarily transparent to us. If Kant were to make that assumption, however, then he would simply be *presupposing* transcendental idealism on the basis of his prior arguments for it, not providing an *independent* proof of it. And if Kant's prior arguments for transcendental idealism are inconclusive, then it is no more conclusively proven by the fact that it offers *one* way to resolve the antinomies of pure reason than it was before.[8]

THE METAPHYSICS OF GOD

Kant calls his critique of theoretical or "speculative" arguments for the existence of God, that is, arguments that are supposed to deliver knowledge of the existence of God rather than rational faith in it, the "Ideal of Pure Reason." This is because in Kant's usage an "ideal" is a conception of a single being that satisfies all the requirements of an idea of reason, that is indeed "determined through the idea alone" (A 568/B 596). Since Kant is certainly concerned with a monotheistic conception of God – both the speculative metaphysics he rejects and the moral theology or practical faith with which he will replace it concern only such a conception of God – for him the rational idea of God must be an ideal.

The third chapter of the "Transcendental Dialectic" is divided into two main parts: the first (sections one and two) expounds and then criticizes a way of conceiving of God that is not part of the historical tradition of philosophical theology, but is really an allusion to an argument Kant had himself earlier constructed, and the second (sections three through seven) criticizes the chief arguments of traditional "rational" theology and of eighteenth-century "natural" theology, namely the "ontological" argument of St Anselm and Descartes, the "cosmological" argument found in Aquinas and favored by Wolff, and finally the "physico-theological" argument, or argument from design, especially popular among British divines influenced by John Locke and already mercilessly lampooned by David Hume in his *Dialogues concerning Natural Religion*.[9]

In early works such as the *New Elucidation of the First Principles of Metaphysical Cognition* (1755) and the *Only Possible Basis for a Proof of the Existence of God* (1763), Kant had already rejected Descartes' ontological argument, and had replaced it with one of his own. According to this new argument, anything can be possible only if at least something is actual, and since that something cannot itself be merely possible, it must be necessary; Kant then derived the traditional predicates of God – that He is an intelligence, omniscient, omnipotent, and so on – from the idea of a necessary being. This argument is patently fallacious, because it infers from "Necessarily, something exists" to "Something necessary exists." In the *Critique*, Kant provides a less obviously fallacious alternative to the opening steps of this argument. He argues that in conceiving of any particular object, we conceive of it "under the principle of **thoroughgoing determination**, according to which, among **all possible** predicates of **things**, insofar as they are compared with their opposites, one must apply to it" (A 571–2/B 599–600). What he means is that we can conceive of any particular thing as if it were determined by the choice of one possibility rather than the other from among all possible pairs of opposed predicates: while any object might be an animal or not, this one is an animal; while any animal might be a mammal or not, this one is a mammal; while any mammal might be a human or not, this one is a human; while any human might be a male or a female, this one is a female; and so on, until we have a complete specification of a particular person, e.g., Kant's oldest sister. In order to think of particular things in this way, we have to conceive of the "**the whole of possibility**, as the sum total of all predicates of things in general," as if it were a pool of possibilities by selecting from which actual things are constituted. But, according to Kant, guided again by reason's idea of the unconditioned, we conceive of this pool of possibilities as if it were not just actual, but a *single thing*, "an individual object that is thoroughly determined merely through the idea, and then must be called an **ideal** of pure reason" (A 674/B 602). Further, Kant argues, since negation is always introduced by a thing's limitation by something else, our concept of the ideal of pure reason will include only *positive* predicates, or will be the idea of a maximally real and perfect being (an *ens realissimum*), or "nothing other than the idea of an All of reality (*omnitudo realitatis*)" (A 575/B 603) – in other words, the ideal of pure reason will be nothing other than God as conceived by traditional theologians and metaphysicians. So, just as pure reason attempted to arrive at its concept of the simple and immortal soul by conceiving of an unconditioned subject of thought that is not itself a property of anything else, and at its idea of the cosmos by attempting to conceive of the series of all appearances as unconditioned in its several dimensions, now pure reason attempts to prove the existence of God through the idea of an unconditioned ground of all possibilities (or of any thought of all objects in general; see A 331/B 394).

But as before, pure reason's attempt to prove the existence of something unconditioned is doomed. Although we can form an abstract conception of the determination of any thing from a pool of possibilities, in fact it is sense-perception to which we must turn to determine the concept of any particular object (only sense-perception actually tells us whether something is an animal or not, a human or not, a male or a female, and so on) – and since sense-perception, by its very spatial and temporal form, is never complete but is always indefinitely extendible, the determination of any particular object is also never complete but is always indefinitely extendible, and in turn our conception of the possible predicates for things is also never complete. We therefore can never have a complete conception of the pool of possibilities for particular things, *a fortiori* a complete conception of a single thing possessing all those possibilities. Once again, reason's idea of the unconditioned, this time the idea of a being that is unconditioned in the sense of including all positive possibilities in itself and is not conditioned by anything outside itself, shatters on the fact that sense-perception can never give us cognition of anything unconditioned (A 580–2 / B 608–10).

Having exploded his own earlier argument, Kant next turns to the three main more traditional arguments. His section titles suggest that he will simply discuss the ontological, cosmological, and physico-theological arguments in turn, but his discussion is in fact more intricate than that. While Descartes had introduced a causal argument for the existence of God in his third *Meditation* (only a being that really has all of the perfection of God could cause us to have an idea of all that perfection), he had introduced the ontological argument in his fifth *Meditation* as if it stands entirely on its own. And the latter argument was quite simple: Descartes assumed that the idea of God is that of a being that possesses all perfections, then assumed that existence is itself a perfection, and so inferred that God must possess the perfection of existence, so he exists, indeed, he necessarily exists, because his existence follows directly from his concept. According to Kant, however, the human mind does not naturally come up with the idea of most perfect being out of thin air. Rather, it is natural for us to begin with the *cosmological* argument, that is, with the argument that if anything exists at all, even anything contingent (that is, if there is any kind of world at all, or any cosmos – hence the name; see A 605 / B 633), then something necessary must also exist (A 584 / B 612). We then seek to specify the concept of this necessary existent (A 585 / B 613), and conclude that the only thing that could exist necessarily is something that "contains all reality," which is not conditioned by anything else, and whose existence therefore flows from its own concept (A 587 / B 615). Rather than being a straightforward inference from the mere idea of a perfect being to its actual and indeed necessary existence, as it was for Descartes, for Kant the ontological argument is a more involuted line of thought, leading from the existence of anything contingent to something necessary (the cosmological argument as the first step of the ontological argument), to the idea of a being comprehending all reality, and then as it were back down to the idea of the existence of this being as a necessary existence – following from its own concept and not being dependent upon and therefore possibly precluded by the existence of anything else.

But this whole involuted line of thought is, according to Kant, subject to two fatal objections. First, as he makes clear in his subsequent separate criticism of the cosmological argument, we never have any justification for assuming that the series of contingently existing things terminates in something absolutely necessary – that, as has already been shown in the fourth "Paralogism," is just an illegitimate application of pure reason's idea of the unconditioned to the world of our experience, whose form does not permit this application (A 609–10/B 637–8). Second, even if we could legitimately form the idea of something absolutely necessary by some route, we can never prove the actual let alone necessary existence of such a thing from its concept, because, according to Kant, "**Being** is obviously not a real predicate, i.e., a concept of something that could add to the concept of a thing. It is merely the positing of a thing or of certain determinations in themselves" (A 598/B 626). That is, being or existence is not something that we can properly include in a concept, but is rather something we add to a concept when we say that the concept has an object. But what do we add to a concept when we assert that an object satisfying it exists? For Kant, what is added to the concept can only be intuition, whether pure or empirical – and again, intuition will never give us anything unconditioned, thus it will never give us anything absolutely necessary.

Does Kant have an argument for his claim that being or existence is not a "real predicate" that can be contained in a concept, but rather is always something additional to the concept – what we posit when we posit that a concept has an object? He attempts to motivate this claim with a demonstration that there is no difference between the concept of something as merely possible and the concept of that thing as actual, indeed that there cannot be any difference between the concept of what is merely possible and what is actual if when the object actually exists it is to be the same thing that was previously conceived of as merely possible. In Kant's famous example, there can be no difference in the contents of the concepts of one hundred merely possible dollars and one hundred actual dollars if the actual dollars are supposed to be just the same as the possible dollars – no more or less, merely actual rather than possible (A 599/B 627). To think that the difference between the actual dollars and the merely possible dollars can be contained within the concept of the actual dollars would be to think of the actual dollars as containing something more than the possible dollars, as if they were, for example, a hundred and one dollars. But then of course the actual dollars would not be the same dollars that were merely possible.

Is this argument compelling? It has certainly been accepted by the mainstream of modern logic: the representation of a sentence asserting the existence of an object with a particular predicate in the form "There is some x which is F" rather than the form "The thing which is A (exists) is also F" reflects the assumption that existence is not a predicate but rather the condition for the assertion of a predicate of an object. But just because the denial that existence is a predicate is assumed by the very set-up of contemporary logic, it is not something that could be proved within that logic. What about Kant's example of the hundred possible and actual dollars? Well, one could quibble with that: one could argue that existence is a predicate, but not a predicate like the amount of dollars; there are plenty of differences between possible and actual dollars, like the fact that you can pay a bill with actual but not possible dollars, so actual but not possible dollars are entitled to the predicate "bill-payers" – and maybe the predicate of existence is like that one. Of course, one could then come back with the rejoinder that you can pay bills with actual but not possible dollars *because* the former but not the latter exist – in other words, existence is not *another* predicate like "bill-payer" but rather the *presupposition* of such a predicate, which is Kant's view.

It is not clear how this argument would be resolved. One could say that Kant's insistence that existence is not a predicate is just a brief statement of the distinction between what can be derived from the analysis of a concept and what requires a synthesis going beyond the contents of a concept on which his whole philosophy depends, and that his premise does not stand alone but acquires its force from his whole philosophical framework. But then again, one might also argue that the whole philosophical framework depends upon the premise that existence is not a predicate, and that unless that can be independently proved the whole framework may collapse. I find the difference between analysis and synthesis, between unpacking a concept and demonstrating that the concept has an object, so convincing in all cases of empirical knowledge and even in mathematical knowledge (see B 146) that I don't see why we should make an exception to this difference for just one concept, even the concept of God; so I am convinced by Kant's argument that we could never prove the existence of God from his concept alone, as well as by his even more general suggestion that all that arguments can ever really do is to take us from one concept to another. But perhaps others will think there is a good reason to treat the concept of God differently from all other concepts.[10]

The final attempt at a theoretical proof of the existence of God that Kant considers is what he calls the "physico-theological proof," or the argument from design that was so popular in the eighteenth century.[11] This argument was considered to be part of "natural theology" – in Kant's view, in contrast to "transcendental theology" (see A 632/B 660) – because it begins from our experience of nature, arguing that the design and organization that we encounter in nature can only be explained by a divine intelligence as the author of nature. Kant writes that "This proof always deserves to be named with respect," as the "oldest, clearest, and the most appropriate" of the proofs of the existence of God for "common human reason" (A 623/B 651), and he presents a sympathetic account of it:

> [1] Everywhere in the world there are clear signs of an order according to a determinate aim, carried out with great wisdom . . . [2] This purposive order is quite foreign to things of the world, and pertains to them only contingently, i.e., the natures of different things could not by themselves agree in so many united means to determinate final aims, were they not quite properly chosen for and predisposed to it through a principle of rational order grounded on ideas. [3] Thus there exists a sublime and wise cause (or several), which must be the cause of the world . . . as an intelligence, through **freedom**. [4] The unity of this cause may be inferred from the unity of the reciprocal relation of the parts of the world as members of an artful structure, inferred with certainty wherever our observation reaches, but beyond that with probability in accordance with all principles of analogy.
>
> (A 625–6/B 653–4)

In the distinction between certainty within the reach of our observation and probability beyond its reach that Kant introduces into step (4), he recognizes the epistemic modesty that some advocates of the argument from design observed. Nevertheless, the argument is doomed for two reasons. First, although Kant does not lavish the detail upon this point that Hume does, he does not, at least here, think that we actually experience the kind of design and organization in nature that we could only explain by appeal to a perfect designer: "experience never offers us the greatest of all possible effects (such as would bear witness to this as its cause)" (A 637/B 665).[12] Second, we have no legitimate way to infer from anything we do experience to an unconditioned being, outside of the series of natural causes and effects, like the God of theology: "If the highest being were to stand in the chain of" conditioned experiences, "then it would be a member of their series, and, like the lower members, . . . a further investigation for a still higher ground would be presupposed for it"; but "if, on the contrary, one would separate" God "from this chain, and, as a merely intelligible being, not include [him] within the series of natural causes, then what bridge can reason build so as to reach it?" (A 621/B 649). In other words, the fact that every experience and every object in experience is conditioned blocks any hope of inferring the existence of God from anything in experience: as conditioned, nothing in experience is so great that we need to postulate an absolutely unconditioned cause to explain it; yet if, ignoring this fact, we attempt to infer the existence of God by including him within the chain of natural causes, then he too must be conditioned rather than unconditioned, limited rather than unlimited; and finally if, recognizing this (but still ignoring the initial fact that there is nothing in experience that requires an unconditioned cause in the first place), we attempt to place God outside of the chain of natural causes, then we have no basis for using causal reasoning to infer to his existence at all – "For all laws of transition from effects to causes, indeed, all synthesis and extension of our cognition in general, are directed to nothing other than possible experience" (A 621/B 649). Perhaps reason's drive to conceive of the unconditioned for every kind of condition leads it both to transform the kind of organization that we undeniably do find in nature into an idea of unconditionally complete and perfect organization, and then to posit an unconditioned cause of this, but neither of these moves is compatible with the conditioned character of every object that we encounter in nature and therefore every cause that we can posit in the chain of natural causes.

So all of the classical arguments for the existence of God, although they express reason's natural urge to conceive of the unconditioned, violate the basic rules for "synthesis and . . . cognition in general," at least as Kant sees them. The ontological argument ignores the fundamental difference between forming a concept of an object, in which we may be constrained only by general logic's requirement that we avoid any internal contradiction, and obtaining knowledge of the existence of an object answering to such a concept, which for us always requires an intuition. The cosmological argument ignores the fact that at least for us the only use we can make of the concept of necessity is to characterize objects or events within the chain of natural causes as necessary insofar as they are subject to causal laws as relatively necessary, that is, necessary relative to their antecedent conditions – but those antecedent conditions are themselves always at most only relatively necessary, that is, necessary relative to some yet other antecedent conditions, and we can make no use of the concept of absolute necessity. The physicotheological argument ignores the fact that we cannot find anything unconditioned within experience, and thus can find within experience neither the unconditioned design or organization that would need to be explained nor the unconditionally perfect and intelligent designer that would explain it, as well as ignoring the fact that we cannot transform our inferences from conditioned effects to conditioned causes within nature into an inference to an unconditioned cause beyond nature. And even Kant's own thought that we might need to posit an unconditioned pool of possibilities in order to explain the complete determination of any individual object falls afoul of the objection that the complete determination of a particular object is itself only an ideal that is never fully satisfied within experience: within actual experience we always have only incomplete concepts of objects, indeed rather small concepts that apply to objects in virtue of only a few of their most obvious properties, and we rely again on intuitions to attach our concepts to individual objects.[13] Now since Kant's criticisms of the metaphysical arguments for the existence of God depend on the central assumptions of his own epistemology, rather than on self-contradictions or other flaws internal to those arguments themselves, it is possible to maintain that they are not knock-down criticisms. By the same token, however, Kant's criticisms have the weight of his whole theory of knowledge behind them: you cannot accept his basic distinction between concepts and intuitions and his theory that our intuitions are empirical intuitions, with our *a priori* intuition of the structure of space and time providing only the *a priori* form of our empirical intuitions of objects in space and time, and continue to accept the traditional arguments for the existence of God.

Even so, Kant does not despair of the possibility of philosophical insight into the nature of God and of a philosophical basis for belief in the existence of God. He concludes his critique of rational theology by pointing toward an alternative *moral* theology, in which the existence of God is to be postulated not as a condition of "**what exists**" but rather of "**what ought to exist**." He will argue that:

> Since there are practical laws that are absolutely necessary (the moral laws), then if these necessarily presuppose any existence as the condition of the possibility of their **binding** force, this existence has to be postulated, because the conditioned from which the inference to this determinate condition proceeds is itself cognized *a priori* as absolutely necessary.
>
> (A 633−4 / B 661−2)

Of course, such a moral theology will presuppose a demonstration that there is an absolutely necessary moral law and that it does in some way presuppose the existence of God as a condition of its possibility. In a later section of the *Critique of Pure Reason*, the "Canon of Pure Reason" (A 795−831 / B 823−59), Kant gives an initial sketch of his emerging moral theory precisely in order to begin to redeem this pledge of a moral theology, but he saves the main defense of it for his central writings on moral philosophy themselves. We will follow Kant's example and return to his moral theology only once we have examined the foundations of his moral philosophy.

Kant seems to conclude the "Transcendental Dialectic," then, by arguing that apart from the mundane business of executing syllogisms, reason has no genuine contribution to make in the acquisition of knowledge, and has an indispensable role only in the moral guidance of our conduct. In an appendix to the "Dialectic," however, he suggests that the faculty of reason does have a constructive role to play in the acquisition and growth of empirical knowledge, even though it does not have a *constitutive* role, that is, it does not by itself yield *a priori* knowledge of objects as it attempted to do in rational psychology, rational cosmology, and rational theology. In the next chapter, we will briefly examine Kant's fuller theory of empirical, scientific knowledge and the role of reason within it before turning to Kant's moral philosophy.

SUMMARY

Kant holds that the chief doctrines of traditional metaphysics arise from the natural tendency of human reason to use the categories for knowledge of unconditioned objects beyond the limits of human sensibility, but even when that tendency does not give rise to outright contradiction, pure concepts can never yield knowledge apart from intuitions and their inherent limits. In Kant's analysis, the traditional metaphysics of the self arises from attempting to obtain knowledge of the soul as a substance from the mere representation of the self. The conflicting "Antinomies" of pure reason arise from either using the ideas of pure reason without respect to the limits of sensibility or taking the limits of sensibility to be the limits of all conceivable reality, neither of which is valid. The arguments for the existence of God as the pool of all possibilities, the sole necessary being, or the most real of all possible beings all illicitly assume existence of something that is a mere idea. Nevertheless, Kant will subsequently argue that reason has a proper regulative role in the conduct of theoretical inquiry as well as its indispensable role as the source of unconditionally valid practical principles.

FURTHER READING

In spite of its length, the "Transcendental Dialectic" has not drawn nearly as much commentary as the "Transcendental Aesthetic" and "Analytic." This is presumably because, in spite of minor flaws, most philosophers have found the main lines of argument in the "Dialectic" clear and convincing. The following two books provide the only analyses of the "Dialectic" as a whole in English:

Jonathan Bennett, *Kant's Dialectic* (Cambridge: Cambridge University Press, 1974).

Michelle Grier, *Kant's Doctrine of Transcendental Illusion* (Cambridge: Cambridge University Press, 2001).

The latter is more sympathetic to Kant's particular analyses than the former. On the "Paralogisms of Pure Reason," see Ameriks. Both Kitcher and Brook discuss the paralogisms in the context of contemporary philosophy of mind, and Powell emphasizes the foundation of the paralogisms in Kant's positive theory of the self:

Karl Ameriks, *Kant's Theory of Mind: An Analysis of the Paralogisms of Pure Reason* (Oxford: Clarendon Press, 1982, new edn, 2000) (argues that Kant endorses more of traditional metaphysics than has usually been thought).

Andrew Brook, *Kant and the Mind* (Cambridge: Cambridge University Press, 1994),

Patricia Kitcher, *Kant's Transcendental Psychology* (New York: Oxford University Press, 1990) (see Chapter 7).

C. Thomas Powell, *Kant's Theory of Self-Consciousness* (Oxford: Clarendon Press, 1990).

On the "Antinomies," see the following. Al-Azm sees the origin of the "Antinomies" in the conflict between Leibniz and Newton, recorded in the *Leibniz–Clarke Correspondence* (1717), a narrow view of Kant's historical sources. Falkenburg discusses the "Antinomies" in the context of Kant's philosophy of science throughout his career.

Sadik Al-Azm, *The Origin of Kant's Argument in the Antinomies* (Oxford: Clarendon Press, 1972).

Brigitte Falkenburg, *Kants Kosmologie: Die wissenschaftliche Revolution der Naturphilosophie im 18. Jahrhundert* (Frankfurt am Main: Vittorio Klostermann, 2000).

On the "Ideal of Pure Reason," see the following. Henrich places Kant's critique of the ontological argument in its historical context. Van Cleve's Chapter 12 is a compact analysis of Kant's critique of rational theology. Wood provides a rigorous analysis of Kant's criticisms of the arguments for the existence of God, drawing on Kant's *Lectures on Rational Theology* as well as the *Critique of Pure Reason*.

Dieter Henrich, *Der Ontologische Gottesbeweis*, rev. edn (Tübingen: J.C.B. Mohr, 1960).

James van Cleve, *Problems from Kant* (New York: Oxford University Press, 1999).

Allen W. Wood, *Kant's Rational Theology* (Ithaca, NY: Cornell University Press, 1978).

Four

Building upon the Foundations of Knowledge

Much of the critique of traditional metaphysics that we have just examined has been based directly on Kant's most fundamental claim about the foundations of knowledge, namely that knowledge always requires the application of concepts to the sensible intuitions that are our immediate contact with objects. Given this premise, traditional metaphysics can only be regarded as a baseless attempt to derive knowledge of real objects from the pure concepts of understanding alone, dressed up as "ideas of pure reason" by the supposedly natural but unjustified assumption that whenever anything conditioned is given so is something entirely unconditioned on which the conditioned rests. Of course, Kant's constructive labor in the "Transcendental Aesthetic" and "Transcendental Analytic" was not confined to establishing merely the general claim that all knowledge requires both intuitions and concepts; he also established that space and time are the pure forms of all sensible intuitions, that the categories are the pure forms for all concepts of objects, and that using the categories to make determinate judgments about objects in space and time also requires the principles that he demonstrated under the titles of the "Axioms of Intuition," the "Anticipations of Perception," and above all the "Analogies of Experience." The pure forms of intuition, the categories, and the principles are thus *necessary a priori* conditions for all determinate knowledge of objects, conditions that both can and must be confirmed independently of the particular claims to empirical knowledge that they frame and ground. We can now ask, however, whether they are the *only a priori* conditions for knowledge, or whether there are any further *a priori* conditions that we could discover before turning to the business of everyday life and everyday science, that of fleshing out the *a priori* framework of knowledge by empirical observation and theory-building.

As noted in the previous chapter, Kant's view of nature, including our own nature, is teleological in the sense that he believes that we should presuppose that everything in nature has some proper purpose and use this assumption to guide our investigations into nature, although this teleological assumption must always be provisional, because we cannot prove it and it could in principle be defeated by refractory evidence. This applies to the investigation of the human mind itself, and thus even though he had gone to great lengths to demonstrate that the attempt to derive metaphysical knowledge from the unaided use of the faculty of reason alone is misguided and hopeless, Kant assumes that we must be able to discover some important function for the faculty of reason, indeed a function that will in some way preserve its ambition to do something indispensable. As we saw, even before he concluded the "Transcendental Dialectic" he hinted that the ambitions of reason will be satisfied in its *practical* use, thus that while its ambitions at *cognitive* autonomy are illusory, it is in fact the source of our *practical* autonomy. But in an appendix that he adds to the "Transcendental Dialectic," which explicitly begins with the teleological premise that "Everything grounded in the nature of our powers must be purposive and consistent with their correct use" (A 642/B 670), Kant also suggests that pure reason does have a vital role to play in the cognitive as well as the practical sphere, although not a role in which it provides knowledge by acting entirely on its own. What "reason quite uniquely prescribes and seeks to bring about . . . is the **systematic** in cognition, i.e., its interconnection based on one principle" (A 645/B 673). Reason cannot provide cognition of objects independently of the understanding, which itself must always be applied to the fruits of sensibility, but it is indispensable for systematizing the results of applying the understanding to sensibility. And while through much of this appendix Kant seems content to suggest that the systematization of cognition is an *addition* to the knowledge that can be constructed, at least piece by piece, on the foundations provided by the pure forms of intuition, conceptualization, and judgment alone, in one or two places he goes further and suggests that the idea of systematic interconnection that only reason can prescribe is actually indispensable for any cognition at all, thus a further *necessary* condition for knowledge:

> For the law of reason to seek unity is necessary, since without it we would have no reason, and without that, no coherent use of the understanding, and, lacking that, no sufficient mark of empirical truth; thus in regard to the latter we simply have to presuppose the systematic unity of nature as objectively valid and necessary.

(A 651/B 679)

This is a dramatic claim; but while Kant goes to some length in the appendix to spell out what he means by the idea of systematic interconnection that only reason can prescribe, it is by no means immediately apparent in what way this idea of systematicity serves as a "sufficient mark" or further necessary condition for "empirical truth." Some interpretation is needed.

This interpretation must proceed in several steps, because Kant does not confine his discussion of the systematicity of empirical knowledge to the appendix to the "Dialectic." He also claims that "Systematic unity is that which first makes ordinary cognition into science" in the "Architectonic of Pure Reason," near the very end of the *Critique of Pure Reason* (A 832/B 860). He repeats that any science must be a "system, that is, a whole of cognition ordered according to principles," in the *Metaphysical Foundations of Natural Science* (4:467), which followed the *Critique of Pure Reason* by five years (1786). And he returns to the theme of systematicity again in the introduction to the *Critique of the Power of Judgment*, published another four years later (1790). Each of these later works adds something essential to Kant's picture of the systematicity of scientific empirical knowledge. The *Metaphysical Foundations* argues that more of the systematic structure of natural science is actually entailed by the pure forms of intuition, the categories, and the principles of empirical judgment than the *Critique of Pure Reason* has revealed, while the *Critique of the Power of Judgment* returns to the general idea of systematicity associated with the faculty of reason in the appendix to the "Transcendental Dialectic" and sheds some light on why systematicity may be not just an additional ideal to be applied to individual bits of cognition already established by the sensibility and understanding but also an additional and indispensable condition of the possibility of any empirical knowledge at all. This chapter will accordingly first look at the special model of systematic scientific knowledge developed in the *Metaphysical Foundations of Natural Science*, and then return to the more general conception of a system of nature proposed in the appendix to the "Transcendental Dialectic" and clarified in the *Critique of the Power of Judgment*.

THE SYSTEMATIC SCIENCE OF BODY

The *Metaphysical Foundations of Natural Science* begins with the claim that any genuine science must be systematic. It then adds to that the claim that "What can be called proper science is only that whose certainty is *apodictic*," not merely empirical (4:468). This means that "natural science must derive the legitimacy of this title only from its pure part – namely, that which contains the *a priori* principles of all other natural explanations" (4:469). However, Kant's previous account of the necessity of empirical intuition for any genuine cognition means that even the most systematic and apodictic natural science must begin from something empirical if it is to be more than the mere form of possible knowledge. Thus, Kant claims that natural science "*properly* so called" must begin with a "metaphysics of nature," which both has a "transcendental part" that makes "possible the concept of a nature in general, even without relation to any determinate object of experience," but must also "concern itself with a particular nature of this or that kind of things, for which an empirical concept is given, but still in such a manner that, outside of what lies in this concept, no other empirical principle is used for its cognition" (4:470). This statement is abstract, but what Kant means is that the metaphysical foundations of natural science must begin with a fundamental *empirical* concept of the object of such science but then determine what can be known *a priori* about that object solely on the basis of the pure principles of the transcendental part of the metaphysics of nature, which are nothing other than the fundamental principles for all knowledge already demonstrated in the *Critique of Pure Reason*. More concretely, Kant thinks that there are two fundamental empirical concepts that between them exhaust the domain of nature, namely the concepts of body and of mind, "corporeal or thinking nature" (4:470), and the project of providing metaphysical foundations for natural science is thus to determine what can be known about body and mind *a priori* solely on the basis of the pure principles of knowledge already established in the first *Critique*.

Kant further understands this task to be that of determining what can be known *a priori* about the objects of natural science through both of the *a priori* sources of knowledge established by the *Critique*, namely mathematics, which follows from the pure forms of intuition, and the categories and principles of judgment, which follow from the pure forms of understanding. Thus, he claims that "in any special doctrine of nature there can be only as much *proper* science as there is *mathematics* therein" (4:470) – a statement that would be misleading if it were taken to mean that mathematics is a *sufficient* condition for actual natural science, and so must mean that mathematics is a *necessary* condition for natural science, along with those principles that follow from the form of thought as further necessary conditions. Kant then argues that there can be no genuine science of thinking nature, that is, no science of psychology, because the empirical concept of mind does not allow enough purchase for mathematics: the unidirectional temporal structure of thought might allow for the application of a "'*law of continuity*' in the flux of inner changes," but that does not allow for an adequate application of mathematics to the mind, anymore than the "properties of the straight line" would be adequate to establish the contents of "the whole of geometry" (4:471). Later psychologists would of course have very different views about how much mathematics can apply to the mind, or whether the application of mathematics is the criterion for the possibility of a genuine science. Be that as it may, for Kant there can be a genuine natural science only of body, and the contents of such a science can be systematically determined by seeing what follows from the application of the mathematics that is grounded in the pure forms of intuition and the principles of judgment that are grounded in the pure forms of thought to the empirical concept of body.[1] (Indeed, Kant also doubted whether chemistry as he knew it permitted of adequate mathematics to count as a genuine science; for him the science of body was only physics.)[2]

For such a project, the empirical concept of body must be precisely determined, and in order to make the results of such a metaphysics of nature maximally *a priori*, this empirical concept must be the minimal empirical concept from which any determinate results will follow at all.[3] Kant thus proposes to begin from the minimal conception of matter as "the *moveable* in space" (4:480), a concept predicated on the single empirical assumption that it is only through motion that our senses can be affected by objects at all (4:476).[4] The metaphysical foundations of the natural science of body are then what we can systematically determine to be necessarily true of the moveable in space through an *a priori* investigation of the pure forms of intuition, the pure categories of the understanding, and the pure principles of judgment. Kant organizes this investigation under the four categorial headings of quantity, quality, relation, and modality.[5] The investigation of the quantitative principles of linear motion that can be determined *a priori* from the structure of space alone is entitled "phoronomy," i.e., the purely geometrical laws of motion, or what is now referred to as kinematics. Under the heading of quality, Kant investigates what can be determined *a priori* from the structure of space alone about the nature of the forces in virtue of which moveable matter fills space; this is what he refers to as "dynamics." Here he offers his famous theory that matter fills space in virtue of its repulsive and attractive forces, although he does not now, unlike thirty years earlier, assign these forces to indivisible "physical monads": they are themselves the most basic level of physical explanation. Under the heading of relation, Kant investigates how the transcendental principles of the conservation of substance, universal causation, and universal interaction are to be applied to matter as the moveable in space; this is the science of "mechanics." Finally, under the heading of "phenomenology," or the science of appearance,[6] Kant asks how the distinction between real and apparent motions in space can be made, and offers the Newtonian answer that linear motions are always relative and thus in a sense merely apparent – any sequence of positions that appears to be motion relative to one space can also be represented as rest relative to another space (inertial framework) that is supposed to be moving – and only rotational motions can be considered only as real changes of position in absolute space – although of course absolute space as understood in transcendental idealism, that is, as the framework of human intuition, not as the Newtonian *sensorium Dei*.

Kant's key claim in phoronomy is that all linear motion that is "an object of experience is merely relative," because while any such motion can be considered as a change of position within some particular space, "the space in which it is perceived is a relative space, which itself moves" – or can be regarded as moving – "in turn in an enlarged space, perhaps in an opposite direction" (4:481). That is, anything that can be regarded as motion in one space or inertial framework can also be regarded as at rest if the space in which it is located is envisioned as located in a surrounding space moving in the opposite direction; and since, in virtue of the very structure of space (here is where Kant appeals to a fundamental result of the "Transcendental Aesthetic"), any space can always be regarded as contained in a larger space, this process of relativization of motion and rest cannot come to a stop in any space that could be regarded as an absolute space (4:487). Kant also argues that the structure of space implies that there are only three ways in which the velocities of linear motions can be compounded: the velocities of two motions in the same direction must be added, the velocities of two motions in opposite directions must be subtracted; and two motions originating from the same point but proceeding from one another at any angle other than 0° or 180° must be combined in a straight line that intersects the angle formed by the original directions in a direction determined by the two velocities, i.e., if the two motions are at an angle of 90° but one is twice as fast as the other, then the resultant vector will not be at 45° but rather at 30° from the faster motion (4:489–95). All of this, Kant argues, follows systematically from the structure of space itself.

In "Dynamics," Kant derives *a priori* constraints on how matter can fill space from the structure of space itself. The property in virtue of which matter fills a space is impenetrability, or resistance to the motion of any other matter through that space (4:496).[7] Seventeenth-century atomists such as John Locke thought that matter filled space or was impenetrable in virtue of being composed of indivisible solid particles, but for Kant, impenetrability has to be conceived of as a force or the product of a force, because it offers resistance to motion (4:497); and in any case the infinite divisibility that is an essential characteristic of space – here again Kant appeals to a fundamental result of the "Aesthetic" – does not allow for any a priori conception of indivisible units of matter.[8] Kant further argues that there can only be two kinds of fundamental force, namely attractive and repulsive forces, because the three possibilities of linear motion that have been established in the "Phoronomy" can all be explained by two kinds of forces: if two objects are moving directly toward each other on a straight line, that would be explained by attractive force alone; if they are moving entirely away from each other on a straight line, that would be explained by repulsive force alone; and if they are moving toward or apart from each other at any other angle, that would be explained by some particular combination of attractive and repulsive forces (4:498). A body is impenetrable when it "fills its space through the repulsive forces of all of its parts" (4:499) and those repulsive forces are greater than any attractive forces that could attract another body through the surface of the first. Now there must be attractive as well as repulsive forces, because since space itself is infinitely extendible, insofar as the sphere of their action is determined a priori by the structure of space alone, repulsive forces could move bodies infinitely apart from one another, so if there were nothing to counteract them, bodies would be infinitely dispersed in space; and indeed since because of the infinite divisibility of space a body of any size can always be conceived of as consisting of smaller parts (4:503) between which there are also repulsive forces, if there were only repulsive forces alone the parts of bodies would also always be infinitely dispersed, and there would be no determinate bodies of matter as the moveable in space at all (4:508–9). At the same time, there is nothing in the nature of space itself to limit the reach of attractive forces either, so if there were only attractive forces then all matter would collapse to a single point and there would be no extended bodies either. Thus, Kant argues that there must be a universal force of attraction as well as repulsion throughout nature (4:517). So from the empirical assumption that we do have sensory experience of moveable bodies in space plus these a priori reflections on the structure of space itself, Kant derives the existence of these two fundamental forces, although he leaves it unclear whether the determination of the proportion between them that is necessary to explain why matter is neither infinitely dispersed nor collapsed into a single point is supposed to be an *a priori* or empirical matter. (Present-day cosmology seems to be uncertain about both whether the universe must contain a repulsive force as well as the attractive force of gravity and, if so, what its value or constant must be; Kant's argument suggests that there should be no uncertainty about the existence of the repulsive force, but the latter uncertainty suggests that the determination of the relative values of the attractive and repulsive forces should be empirical rather than *a priori*.)

Under the heading of "Mechanics," Kant next derives the three laws of Newtonian mechanics by applying the three principles of judgment derived in the first *Critique*'s "Analogies of Experience" to the conception of matter as the moveable in space that has been developed in the preceding phoronomy and dynamics.[9] Thus, the principle of "general metaphysics" that "in all changes of nature no substance either arises or perishes" becomes the "First Law of Mechanics" that "In all changes of *corporeal* nature the total quantity of matter remains the same, neither increased nor diminished" (4:541, emphasis added). Thus, what we naïvely regard as the increase or diminution of particular substances, or even their origination or cessation, can only be understood as changes in the number, location, and velocity of parts of objects in space and through time: "the quantity of matter, with respect to its substance, is nothing else but the aggregate of substances of which it consists" (4:541–2). The "Second Law of Mechanics," derived from the general principle that every alteration has some cause, is the law of inertia, namely, that "Every change in matter has an *external* cause," or that "Every body persists in its state of rest or motion, in the same direction, and with the same speed, if it is not compelled by an external cause to leave this state" (4:543, emphasis added).[10] This is derived from the recognition that the fundamental properties of bodies constituted by the action of attractive and repulsive forces of matter are simply their velocities, that is, their states of rest or motion (always relative to some inertial framework, of course), so that the only way bodies can affect each other is by changing their (relative) states of rest or motion. Finally, Kant transforms the third general principle of metaphysics, that "All substances, insofar as they can be perceived in space as simultaneous, are in thoroughgoing interaction" (CPuR, B 256), into the "Third Law of Mechanics" that "In all communication of motion, action and reaction are always equal to one another" (4:544). His argument for this law is more complicated than those for the first two laws, but his basic idea is that because of the relativity of motions in space established in phoronomy, any motion of one body toward another (through which the former could exercise action on the other) can always be redescribed as a motion of the latter toward the former that is equal in velocity but opposite in direction from the motion as originally described (4:545–7); thus an action is necessarily equal to the reaction to it. This argument may well equivocate on the concept of reaction, equating a *redescription* of one event from an alternative inertial framework with a *reaction* to that event. But in any case, the general structure of Kant's conception of the *a priori* foundations of systematic natural science of bodies remains clear: the laws of such a science are to be established by systematically determining the consequences of applying the *a priori* laws of nature established by the "Transcendental Analytic" to the empirical concept of matter as that which is moveable in space, the structure of which is in turn established *a priori* by the "Transcendental Aesthetic."

The final chapter of the *Metaphysical Foundations*, on "phenomenology," introduces only one new scientific principle, but also connects Kant's themes in the book with his more general theory of experience. The term "phenomenology" would later be put to very grand although very different uses by philosophers such as G.W.F. Hegel, who used it to characterize the process of the emergence of the self-awareness of reason,[11] and Edmund Husserl, who used it to name a purported general method for examining the structure of representations and concepts of objects independently of any assumptions about the existence of those objects;[12] and in his famous letter to Marcus Herz of February 21, 1772, Kant had also used the term in a very ambitious way to refer to what would subsequently become the entire contents of the "Transcendental Aesthetic" and "Analytic" of the *Critique of Pure Reason* (Corr, 10:129). However, he did not use the term at all when he published the *Critique* in 1781. But now he revives it to cover the principles by means of which the *appearance* of motion can be transformed into the *experience* of motion, that is, the principles in accordance with which apparent motions can – or cannot – be determinately assigned to particular *objects* (4:554). The principles of phenomenology in Kant's sense are actually very simple, and can readily be associated with the three categories under the final categorical heading, that of modality. The first principle is that linear motions are never more than *possible* motions of any particular object in a pair or larger group of objects, and any notion of *absolute* linear motion is *impossible*, because by a change in inertial framework any object that is regarded as moving relative to one or more other objects can always also be regarded as at rest while the others are reconceived as moving (4:555–6). Kant admits that this first principle of phenomenology does not add anything to the content of phoronomy (4:556), which is consistent with his general position that the categories of modality do not add any content to our concepts of objects, but only characterize our cognitive relation to those concepts (CPuR, A 74/B 100). The second principle of phenomenology, concerning the modal category of actuality, does make a genuinely new claim, however, for here Kant argues that circular motions are *actual* rather than merely possible predicates of particular objects (4:456–7). He gives an abstract argument for this claim, going back to Newton's argument for the existence of absolute space[13]: since because of inertia an object moving in a circular orbit would fly off on a tangent, that is, the straight line extending the direction of its motion at any instant, if not prevented from doing so by the force of another body, a circular motion that actually continues for any period of time provides sufficient evidence of real moving forces rather than merely apparent motions (4:557). He also illustrates this point by arguing that a stone dropped into a deep hole toward the center of the earth will seem to move west to east within the hole, due to its own inertial motion as acquired at the surface of the rotating earth, the rotation of which must therefore be real (4:561). Circular motions, unlike linear motions, must therefore be determinately ascribed to one particular rather than another. Finally, for a third principle, using the modal category of necessity, Kant reintroduces the content of the third law of mechanics, that "In every motion of a body, whereby it is moving relative to another, an opposite and equal motion of the latter is *necessary*" (4:558). This amplifies the first principle of phenomenology by reminding us that although it is arbitrary whether we ascribe motion to one object and rest to that in relation to which it moves, or conversely, in either case the amount of motion we ascribe to the moving object must be precisely the same.

The way in which Kant's phenomenology redescribes the results of the earlier chapters of the *Metaphysical Foundations* as well as introducing one new principle suggests that the project of the whole book can be conceived as that of determining on the strictly *a priori* grounds of the pure forms of intuition and thought which apparent motions – that is, motions that we detect empirically – can be determinately assigned to particular objects and which cannot be. The *Metaphysical Foundations* thus provide a systematic science of our experience of motion, where experience is understood as requiring the assignment of empirically intuited properties to objects. But this derivation of the foundations of a systematic science of body has proceeded entirely by applying the principles derived from the pure forms of sensibility and understanding to the empirical concept of matter as the moveable in space; it has not involved any new *a priori* principle derived from the faculty of *reason*. Does Kant think that *all* systematicity in science derives in this direct way from the most fundamental principles of sensibility and understanding? This cannot be, because, as we saw at the outset of this chapter, he claims in the appendix to the "Transcendental Dialectic" of the first *Critique* that reason makes an essential contribution to systematicity in human knowledge. We must now ask what that contribution could be.

THE SYSTEMATICITY OF COGNITION IN GENERAL

As was noted earlier, Kant follows his demolition of traditional metaphysics in the "Transcendental Dialectic" with an important appendix. The first part of this appendix is entitled "On the regulative use of the ideas of pure reason" (A 642/B 670) and the second "On the final aim of the natural dialectic of pure reason" (A 669/B 697). These titles suggest two points. The second title suggests that reason must have some legitimate aim, even in the cognitive rather than practical sphere, in spite of the dialectic to which it can give rise. This is also suggested by Kant's statement, partially quoted in the introduction to the present chapter, that "Everything grounded in the nature of our powers must be purposive and consistent with their correct use, if only we can guard against a certain misunderstanding and find out their proper direction" (A 642–3/B 670–1). It is also suggested by Kant's further remark that "all errors of subreption" – another of Kant's terms for dialectical inference – "are always to be ascribed to a defect in judgment, never to understanding or to reason" (A 643/B 671), that is, to our incorrect use or application of the ideas of reason, not to the ideas of reason themselves. The first title suggests that to avoid this defect in judgment and properly understand the final aim of reason we must see reason as regulative rather than constitutive, that is, not as giving us knowledge of any objects on its own but rather as functioning to regulate the use of our other cognitive powers. In that case, however, we must ask in what way reason regulates our other cognitive powers, but also how a merely regulative role for reason is consistent with Kant's assertion, also mentioned earlier, that "the law of reason to seek unity is necessary" because without it we would have "no coherent use of the understanding" and "no sufficient mark of empirical truth" (A 651/B 679), for this assertion certainly seems to say that reason is indispensable for the use of the understanding to discover any empirical truth at all, not merely that reason somehow regulates the use of the understanding without adding any constitutive principle to it.

It is relatively easy to describe Kant's ideas about how reason regulates the use of the understanding. Kant claims that it is a mistake to think that reason gives us knowledge about objects by itself. Instead, it serves to introduce unity into the results – judgments about the forms of empirical objects and laws in nature – obtained by the application of the understanding to sensibility. There are three ways in which reason contributes to the unification and systematization of the results of the understanding. First, Kant holds that reason, with its idea of its own purity, can contribute ideas of pure and fundamental explanatory concepts – such as "pure earth, pure water, pure air, etc." (A 646/B 674) – or simplest possible elements, to which our initially more complex explanatory concepts of nature ought to be, as far as is possible, reduced – although we cannot say a priori just how far it is possible to go in reducing our more complex concepts of natural elements to such simple forms. Second, Kant holds that reason provides the model of the form for systematizing the concepts of any science, whether that be a partial or comprehensive science of nature. It is at the behest of the faculty of reason that we seek to organize any body of empirical concepts and laws yielded by the use of the understanding in accordance with the principle of homogeneity, which dictates that we should always seek to subsume more specific concepts of natural forms or laws under more generic ones, in principle ultimately under some single concept of a fundamental substance or force (A 652–5/B 680–3); in accordance with the principle of specificity, which dictates that under whatever concepts of species of forms or forces we have formed we should seek to find further subspecies (A 655–7/B 683–5); and, finally, in accordance with the principle of the affinity or continuity of all concepts, which dictates that we should always seek to find a "graduated increase of varieties" among our conceptions of natural laws and forces (A 657–8/B 685–6). Finally, in the second part of the Appendix, Kant argues that reason's ideas of the unconditioned, that is, the ideas of the soul as the unconditioned subject of all thoughts, of the world-whole as the unconditioned completeness of all series of objects and events in space and time, and of God as the unconditioned condition of all existence in general, which played such a fatal role in traditional metaphysics, should be transformed into

> **regulative** principles for the systematic unity of the manifold of empirical cognition in general, through which this cognition, within its proper boundaries, is cultivated and corrected more than could happen without such ideas, through the mere use of the principles of understanding.
>
> (A 671/B 699)

What Kant means is this: we can have no sound theoretical argument that the soul actually is any sort of absolute unity, but in the scientific investigation of the powers of the mind we should nevertheless seek as far as possible to explain them in terms of a single underlying power (A 682–3/B 710–11); we can never succeed in making our synthesis of the series of objects and events in space and time unconditioned or actually infinite, but we should nevertheless be impelled by reason to seek to extend our knowledge of those series as far as possible (A 684–5/B 712–13); and we can never have theoretical proof of the existence of an intelligent author of all of nature, but we should nevertheless allow this idea to spur us to the search for "**purposive** unity" within nature (A 686/B 714), that is, for "utility and [a] good aim" for every sort of organ, organism, and ecology within nature (A 688/B 716). The presupposition that everything in nature *does* have a purpose, just like the presuppositions that the powers of the mind are ultimately unitary and that the world in space and time is actually infinite, Kant states, "if it is supposed to be constitutive, goes much further than previous observation can justify," so such a presupposition is instead

> nothing but a regulative principle of reason for attaining to the highest systematic unity by means of the idea of the purposive causality of the supreme cause of the world, **as if** this being, as the highest intelligence, were the cause of everything according to the wisest aim.
>
> (A 688/B 716)

Reason's unconditioned ideas of purity, systematicity, and unity can thus furnish open-ended ideals to regulate the use of our understanding in scientific inquiry into the objects of experience even if they cannot by themselves constitute metaphysical knowledge of any transcendent objects beyond the limits of understanding.

But *why* is it so important that reason regulate our use of the understanding in these ways? Kant gives one extended example of how the ideas of reason, in the first instance the ideas of the homogeneity, specificity, and affinity of a systematic body of empirical concepts but ultimately also the idea of a single underlying explanatory force and the idea of an unconditioned world-whole, can guide scientific practice:

> Reason presupposes those cognitions of the understanding which are first applied to experience, and seeks the unity of these cognitions in accordance with ideas that go much further than experience can reach. The

affinity of the manifold, without detriment to its variety, under a principle of unity, concerns not merely the things, but even more the mere properties and powers of things. Hence if, e.g., the course of the planets is given to us as circular through a (still not fully corrected) experience, and we find variations, then we suppose these variations to consist in an orbit that can deviate from the circle through each of an infinity of intermediate degrees according to constant laws; i.e., we suppose that the movements of the planet that are not a circle will more or less approximate to its properties, and then we come upon the ellipse. The comets show an even greater variety in their paths, since (as far as observation reaches) they do not ever return in a circle; yet we guess at a parabolic course for them, since it is still akin to the ellipse and, if the major axis of the latter is very long, it cannot be distinguished from it at all in our observations. Thus under the guidance of those principles we come to a unity of genera in the forms of these paths, but thereby also further to unity in the cause of all the laws of this motion (gravitation); from there we extend our conquests, seeking to explain all variations and apparent deviations from those rules on the basis of the same principle; finally we even add on more than experience can ever confirm, namely in accordance with the rules of affinity, even conceiving hyperbolical paths for comets in which those bodies leave our solar system entirely and, going from sun to sun, unite in their course the most remote parts of a world system, which for us is unbounded and yet connected through one and the same moving force.

(A 662–3 / B 690–1)

We have here a variety of ways in which ideals of reason can guide our conduct of scientific inquiry. First, we have the idea that in the face of the disconfirmation of an initial scientific hypothesis (that the orbits of heavenly bodies are all circular), we should not throw up our hands in despair, but investigate alternative hypotheses that are consistent with both our previous data and our new, refractory observations. Second, we have the suggestion that we should not formulate and test new hypotheses at random, but should seek such new hypotheses by means of a systematic extension of what we already have: thus, we should not be at a loss for hypotheses that are alternative to the discredited idea that all heavenly orbits are circles or invent them at random, but should instead systematically investigate the family of curves of which circles are a member, so that we can rise to as general a concept of curved lines as we need to comprehend all the celestial motions we can observe and then descend back down in that family as far as we need to in order to comprehend any particular orbit, such as the almost circular elliptical orbits of the planets in our solar system and the less circular elliptical orbits of comets. But further, if we have found a single higher-order concept under which to subsume a variety of initially disparate natural forms, such as the orbits of different types of celestial bodies, then we can also formulate the idea of a single underlying cause of all these motions, such as gravitation, and we can extend both the idea of motion along curved lines and its cause in gravitation throughout the regions of the observable universe and even beyond what we can observe – although of course in none of this can our strategy of seeking to systematize observable phenomena and to explain them by a single cause by itself confirm the correctness of our hypothesis for the observable part of the universe, let alone for what lies beyond the limits of our observation. (That the supposition that the comets follow a regular path when they are altogether out of the range of our observation does not count as genuine knowledge would be self-evident for Kant; his reasons for holding that the paths of observable bodies such as the planets are not strictly speaking known must be more subtle, depending perhaps upon the still-fresh remembrance that all of our observations of the positions of planets are compatible with at least two different mathematical models, the Ptolemaic and the Copernican, even if one of these is obviously preferable to the other for considerations of simplicity and the like – that is, on grounds of *reason*.)

But even with this last qualification, which must surely be at least part of what Kant has in mind in insisting that in order to avoid a "defect in judgment" we must use the ideas of reason only regulatively and not constitutively, Kant has described only a *heuristic* use of these ideas: that is, they can provide us with *strategies* for the discovery of hypotheses and explanations that we might nevertheless also hit upon through other methods, or even at random, even if not as reliably or efficiently. That is, Kant does not seem to have shown that the regulative use of the ideas of reason in the several ways he has described is *indispensable* for the formulation of hypotheses for the successful use of the understanding in scientific inquiry. And he certainly does not seem to have shown that anything other than empirical observation can *confirm* hypotheses, however formed. So what can he mean by saying, as we saw him say, that "the law of reason to seek unity" can contribute a "sufficient mark of empirical truth" (A 651 / B 679), when even in his most detailed example it seems to contribute at best one strategy, even if a maximally efficient one, for formulating hypotheses the empirical truth of which must be left up to subsequent observation?

Nothing in the appendix in the first *Critique* seems to offer an answer to this question. But Kant returns to the question of the systematicity of scientific knowledge of nature in the Introduction to the third *Critique*, the *Critique of the Power of Judgment*, and there he suggests at least part of an answer to this question.

Kant's renewed discussion of systematicity in the third *Critique* is complicated, and there is not room here to consider all of its intricacies. But one feature that requires comment is the very fact that in this discussion Kant reassigns the search for systematicity in scientific knowledge from the faculty of reason to the faculty of judgment, more precisely what he now calls "reflecting judgment," which is our capacity to search for a concept or universal when we are given a particular rather than the simple capacity to apply a given concept to a particular, the ordinary exercise of the faculty of judgment that he now renames "determining judgment" (CPJ, Introduction, section IV, 5:179). In fact, in this discussion Kant does not even mention his previous ascription of the search for unity and systematicity to the faculty of reason.[14] Does this represent a complete retraction of his view in the first *Critique*? Not necessarily: remember that in the earlier work Kant had claimed that the fallacies of traditional metaphysics were not due to the faculty of reason, that is, our ability to form ideas of the unconditioned, alone, but rather due to a "defect in judgment"; what Kant is now doing is making it explicit that the right way to use the ideal of systematicity that comes from the faculty of reason can only be the right way for the faculty of judgment to make use of this ideal of reason. Kant's position that we must use the ideal of systematicity only to regulate our search for universals to apply to the particular objects that we experience, that is, to regulate our exercise of the reflecting power of judgment, is a clarification of his previous exposition, which left it merely implicit that there must be a right way as well as a defective way for the power of judgment to use the ideas of reason, rather than a fundamental revision of his previous position.

But the question remains, why should reflecting judgment's regulative use of pure reason's idea of systematicity be not merely a useful heuristic for the conduct of scientific inquiry but an actual mark of "empirical truth"? Kant does not initially seem to advance an answer to this question in the third *Critique* any more than he did in the first, for in his first draft of its introduction he argues simply that even given the "general concepts of nature" furnished by the categories, there remains such a "great diversity of [nature's] empirical laws" that "we could not hope to find our way in a labyrinth of the multiplicity of possible empirical laws" unless we assume that these laws constitute a system in which we can search for the particular laws that apply to particular objects in an organized fashion rather than at random (FI, section V, 20:213–14). This still does not seem to mean anything more than that the assumption that the particular laws of nature constitute a system is a useful heuristic for *conceiving* of particular laws to be tested against our experience of objects; it does not show that their membership in a system is either a necessary or a sufficient condition of the *truth* of those laws. But in the final, published version of the introduction, Kant makes an argument that starts in the same way, but comes to a very different conclusion. Again Kant observes that the "universal transcendental concepts of nature" – that is, the categories of the understanding and the very general principles of judgment derived from them, such as the general principle that every event has a cause – leave the particular "manifold of forms in nature . . . undetermined, since these pertain only to the possibility of a nature (as object of the senses) in general." But what he now goes on to argue is "that there must nevertheless also be laws for it which, as empirical, may indeed be contingent in accordance with the insight of **our** understanding, but which, if they are to be called laws (as is also required by the concept of a nature), must be regarded as necessary on a principle of the unity of the manifold," and then that

> this principle can be nothing other than this: that since universal laws of nature have their ground in our understanding, which prescribes them to nature (although only in accordance with the universal concept of it as nature), the particular empirical laws, in regard to that which is left undetermined in them by the former, must be considered in terms of the sort of unity they would have if an understanding (even if not ours) had likewise given them for the sake of our faculty of cognition, in order to make possible a system of experience in accordance with particular laws of nature.
>
> (CPJ, Introduction, Section IV, 5:179–80)

There are two main elements to Kant's thought here. First, he is maintaining that even though the necessary truth of the most general principles of nature, such as that every event must be caused in accordance with some law, does not entail the necessary truth of any particular laws of nature, there must still be some way in which those particular laws can appear to be necessarily true to us; and it is precisely their membership in a hierarchical *system* of laws, in which higher-level laws do appear to entail the more concrete laws beneath them, that will lend particular laws their appearance of necessity. If we regard their claim to necessity as part of their claim to truth, then we can see why membership in a system should be a condition of the truth of empirical laws of nature after all, and not just a heuristic for discovering them. Second, Kant is maintaining that since we can only understand the necessary truth of the most general laws of nature that we derive from the pure forms of intuition and thought as a consequence of the fact that our minds impose these laws on our experience, we must also think of the systematicity of more particular laws which explains their appearance of necessary truth *as* if it were the product of an intelligence that imposes that system upon nature, although obviously this intelligence is not our own. But of course such an "as if" supposition does not amount to the kind of theoretical *cognition* of things that transcend the limits of experience which Kant has proscribed in the first *Critique*, a point that Kant emphasizes by continuing the last quotation thus: "Not as if in this way such an understanding must really be assumed (for it is only the reflecting power of judgment for which this idea serves as a principle, for reflecting, not for determining); rather this faculty thereby gives a law only to itself, and not to nature" (5:180). Thus, Kant's new emphasis on reflecting judgment rather than reason as the source reminds us not only that there must be a right way as well as a wrong way to use the ideas of reason; it is also a reminder that no matter how indispensable the ideas of reason may be in the pursuit of empirical truth, we still cannot claim to have theoretical cognition of transcendent objects defined by those ideas of reason on their own.

SUMMARY

Once we understand the full role of the ideal of systematicity in scientific inquiry, Kant's whole picture of knowledge becomes quite complex. On the one hand, he is committed to the view of the first *Critique* that we can have *a priori* knowledge of the most general principles of any knowledge, and in the *Metaphysical Foundations of Natural Science* he has also argued that given the simplest empirical assumption about matter we can use the *a priori* principles of the first *Critique* for a systematic derivation of the most general principles of a natural science of body as well. On the other hand, he has argued in the appendix to the "Transcendental Dialectic" that we should also always seek to arrange the more particular or concrete laws of natural science into a system, even though we know that if for no other reason than the sheer extent of space and time – the unobservable realms into which the comets disappear – such a system can never be conclusively completed; and in the third *Critique* he has also argued that even though we can only lend an appearance of necessity to particular laws of nature by conceiving of them as if they were part of a system conceived by an intelligent author of nature, we can never have actual knowledge of such authorship. Thus while we can have an authoritative deduction of the systematic foundations of natural science, a whole system of science must always remain an ideal, but only an ideal for us. Although we have the cognitive autonomy within our own resources to dictate the most fundamental laws of natural science, in the end we cannot conceive of the concrete laws of nature as reflecting *merely* the structure of our own minds. Kant expresses this restriction with a striking coinage:

> The power of judgment thus also has in itself an *a priori* principle for the possibility of nature, though only in a subjective respect, by means of which it prescribes a law, not to nature (as autonomy), but to itself (as heautonomy) for reflection on nature, which one could call the **law of the specification of nature** with regard to its empirical laws, which it does not cognize in nature *a priori* but rather assumes in behalf of an order of nature cognizable for our understanding.
>
> (CPJ, Introduction, Section V, 5:186)

By "heautonomy" Kant attempts to connote the complex attitude we must take toward the principles of judgment when we have to regard them as both laws for our own conduct of inquiry into nature but not as conclusively demonstrable cognitions of nature itself. We will eventually have to ask whether "heautonomy" would not in fact be a good model for much of what Kant initially calls "autonomy," perhaps even in moral conduct as well as the conduct of scientific inquiry. But before we can do that, we need to turn to our examination of Kant's moral philosophy itself. That will be our concern in the next part of this volume.

FURTHER READING

Buchdahl (1969) recounts the relations between its two title subjects throughout the early modern period, culminating in a study of Kant, while his (1992) work, in addition to the chapter on the *Metaphysical Foundations* mentioned in note 1, also includes in its Part III several important papers on the issue of systematicity, discussed in the second half of this chapter. Brittan evaluates Kant's philosophy of mathematics and physical science from a modern point of view. Kitcher (1986) is an important paper on systematicity in an important collection on Kant's philosophy of science; it is reprinted in Patricia Kitcher (ed.), *Kant's Critique of Pure Reason: Critical Essays* (Lanham, MD: Rowman and Littlefield, 1998), pp. 219–38. Friedman contains a general sketch of Kant's philosophy of science, the papers on philosophy of mathematics noted in Chapter 2, a detailed analysis of Kant's derivation of Newtonian physics in its Chapter 4, and, in its Part II, a detailed study of Kant's later philosophy of science, including chemistry, in the *Opus postumum*. Edwards discusses Kant's dynamics both prior and subsequent to the *Metaphysical Foundations*. Finally, Watkins contains several general papers on Kant's philosophy of science and papers on his philosophy of physics, psychology, chemistry, and biology; Westphal discusses Kant's dynamics and proof of Newton's laws in the context of a realist approach to Kant; and Guyer contains in its Part I five papers on Kant's conception of the systematicity of science, his ether proofs in the *Opus postumum*, and his philosophy of biology.

Gordon G. Brittan, Jr., *Kant's Theory of Science* (Princeton, NJ: Princeton University Press, 1978).

Gerd Buchdahl, *Metaphysics and the Philosophy of Science* (Oxford: Basil Blackwell, 1969).

——, *Kant and the Dynamics of Reason* (Oxford: Blackwell, 1992).

Jeffrey Edwards, *Substance, Force, and the Possibility of Knowledge: On Kant's Philosophy of Material Nature* (Berkeley, CA: University of California Press, 2000).

Michael Friedman, *Kant and the Exact Sciences* (Cambridge, MA: Harvard University Press, 1992).

Paul Guyer, *Kant's System of Nature and Freedom: Selected Essays* (Oxford: Clarendon Press, 2005).

Philip Kitcher, "Projecting the Order of Nature," in Robert E. Butts (ed.), *Kant's Philosophy of Physical Science* (Dordrecht: Reidel, 1986), pp. 201–35.

Eric Watkins (ed.), *Kant and the Sciences* (Oxford: Oxford University Press, 2001).

Kenneth R. Westphal, *Kant's Transcendental Proof of Realism* (Cambridge: Cambridge University Press, 2004).

Part Two

Freedom

Five

Laws of Freedom

The foundations of Kant's moral philosophy

We now turn from the abstraction of Kant's philosophy of science to his practical philosophy, which can seem equally remote from our everyday experience. Kant is famous for the derivation of an apparently formalistic fundamental moral law from the most abstract and austere premises. He begins his *Groundwork for the Metaphysics of Morals* (1785) with the claim that the only thing of unconditional value is a good will, argues that such a will manifests itself only in doing one's duty for its own sake, and then concludes that since doing duty for its own sake deprives the will of any object of desire as a reason for action, nothing is left as a possible principle of morality "but the conformity of actions as such with universal law" (G, 4:402). In the second section of the same work, he maintains that "moral laws are to hold for every rational being as such" and must therefore be derivable from the very "universal concept of a rational being as such" (4:412). In the *Critique of Practical Reason* (1788), he premises that a moral law must be completely necessary and universal and then concludes that only a moral principle that is entirely formal and makes no reference to any object of desire can satisfy that requirement. Specifically, he argues that genuine moral laws or "practical **principles**" must hold "for the will of every rational being as such" (CPracR, 5:19), that any "practical principles that presuppose an **object** (matter) of the faculty of desire as the determining ground of the will are, without exception, empirical and can furnish no practical laws" (5:21), and thus that "If a rational being is to think of his maxims as practical universal laws, he can think of them only as principles that contain the determining ground of the will not by their matter but only by their form" (5:27). We will give these arguments a hearing shortly, but it seems clear from the outset that they presuppose what might be a controversial assumption about what a moral law must be like, and it is by no means obvious how they could be expected to gain a grip on the moral sensibilities of ordinary human beings.

Elsewhere, however, Kant suggested a more intuitive foundation for his moral philosophy. In the classroom lectures on ethics that he gave during the decade before he began publishing the works just mentioned, he is reported to have argued that "Freedom . . . is the capacity which confers unlimited usefulness on all the others" and therefore is "the highest degree of life," the "inner worth of the world," but that "insofar as it is not restrained under certain rules of conditioned employment, it is the most terrible thing there could be"; in order to realize its potential value, therefore, freedom must be exercised in accordance with a rule "under which alone the greatest use of freedom is possible, and under which it can be self-consistent" (LEC, 27:344, 347). The rule is simply that freedom must be "consistent with itself," that is, that my use of freedom on one occasion be consistent with my continued use of it on all other possible occasions, and that my use of freedom be consistent with everyone else's use of their freedom. Of course, to state this rule at such a level of abstraction is easy; to say what it actually requires of us in the concrete circumstances of human life considerable thought will be required. That is why we must employ our reason to formulate the moral law in a variety of forms and then to derive a detailed system of duties from them. But on this approach, we do not have to begin with the completely abstract idea that rationality as such is of intrinsic value or that there is some inexplicable necessity for acting in accordance with a necessary and universal law. Instead, as Kant put it in lectures on "natural right" (political philosophy) that he gave during the very semester when he was composing the *Groundwork*, "If only rational beings can be an end in themselves, this is not because they have reason, but because they have freedom. Reason is merely a means" (NFey, 27:1321). That is, through reason we grasp the rules that we need to follow in order fully to realize our freedom as autonomy, or "the property that a will has of being a law to itself" (G, 4:447).

Of course, one might well think that the claim that freedom itself is our most fundamental value could use some support. Kant sometimes wrote as if this is an obvious truth about human psychology. In some notes that he made in his own copy of his early work *Observations on the Feeling of the Beautiful and Sublime*, Kant wrote:

> The human being has his own inclinations, and by means of his capacity of choice a clue from nature to conduct his actions in accordance with these. Nothing can be more appalling than that the action of a human stand

under the will of another. Hence no abhorrence can be more natural than that which a person has against servitude. On this account a child cries and becomes bitter if it has to do what another wants without having made an effort to make that pleasing to him. And it wishes only to become a man quickly and to operate in accordance with its own will.

(NF, pp. 10–11)

This makes it sound as if the love of freedom is a basic trait of human psychology, and thus that the moral force of laws for the realization of freedom ultimately comes from a fact about human nature. It is not clear that such a foundation for morality would be consistent with Kant's insistence that the moral law must be valid for every rational being, human or otherwise, thus that "a pure moral philosophy" must be "completely cleansed of everything that may be only empirical and that belongs to anthropology" (G, 4:389). But it is also not clear whether Kant really has an alternative but equally gripping account of the normative force of the moral law, so this psychological assumption may play an indispensable role in Kant's subsequent moral philosophy even if he does not acknowledge it.

In what follows, our first order of business will be to examine the arguments that Kant made for his formulation of the moral law in his mature published works, then to see how his earlier idea of the inner worth of freedom reappears in his mature works and how the various formulations of the fundamental principle of morality that he offers in those works can be understood as formulations of the rules necessary in order to realize the value of freedom. As autonomy in its practical sense is nothing other than freedom achieved and sustained through its adherence to law, this will constitute the next step in our study of Kant's overarching conception of autonomy. Then we can return to the question of how or even whether Kant can argue for his fundamental normative assumption or conception of value.

THE DERIVATION OF THE CATEGORICAL IMPERATIVE

The fundamental principle of morality, Kant has claimed, must be unconditionally valid for any rational being. If any being were perfectly rational, it would automatically act in accordance with this law, and the law would therefore not appear to be a constraint. But we human beings are not perfectly rational, and thus although we recognize the unconditional validity of the moral law, it also appears as a constraint to us, something that may be in conflict with our irrational side. The fundamental principle of morality thus presents itself to us in the form of a "categorical imperative": categorical, because we recognize that its demands are unconditional, but an imperative, because we recognize this law as something we *ought* to follow, thus as a constraint, that is, not something we always *want* to follow. The concept of the categorical imperative is thus not identical to the concept of the fundamental principle of morality, but is rather the way in which the fundamental principle of morality presents itself to us as beings who are rational but not purely rational.[1] But Kant takes it to be obvious and not in need of any special argument that we will often experience the stringent demands of morality as a constraint; thus, although his arguments are aimed at a derivation of the categorical imperative, all of his effort is aimed at demonstrating the content of the fundamental principle of morality and proving that it is valid or binding for us, not at reminding us that we often experience that validity as a constraint.

Kant discusses the derivation of the categorical imperative at length in the *Groundwork*, and then more briefly in the *Critique of Practical Reason*, which is devoted primarily to the problem of free will and then, under the topic of what Kant calls the "highest good," to reestablishing a relation between virtue and happiness that he seems to have severed completely in the *Groundwork*.[2] The *Groundwork* is divided into three sections, which Kant labels respectively the "Transition from common rational to philosophical moral cognition" (G, 4:393), the "Transition from popular moral philosophy to the metaphysics of morals" (4:406), and the "Transition from metaphysics of morals to the critique of pure practical reason" (4:446). He does not mean the same thing by "transition" in each case: while the argument of the second section is that "popular moral philosophy" must be *replaced* by a philosophically sound "metaphysics of morals," the first and third sections argue that this metaphysics of morals must be *grounded* in *both* genuine common sense *and* a philosophically sophisticated "critique of pure practical reason." However, this organization of his arguments is also in some tension with another claim that Kant makes, namely that in the first two sections he is just *analyzing* the content of the fundamental principle of morality for any rational beings, and that it is only in the third section that he will show that this principle *applies to us* as the categorical imperative (see 4:392, 425). The tension is that Kant at least tacitly supposes that sound common sense always knows both what the categorical imperative requires and that it requires that *of us*, not needing a subtle philosophical argument to prove that. In the *Critique of Practical Reason* Kant will resolve this tension in favor of common sense when he asserts that our consciousness of our obligation under the moral law is a "fact of reason" from which the freedom of our will may be inferred but which cannot itself be deduced from any more fundamental premise (CPracR, 5:29–31). We will return to this issue, but for now let us follow the opening arguments of the Groundwork.

Kant begins his analysis of "common rational moral cognition" by arguing that common sense recognizes that the only thing of unconditional value is a good will. He argues first that gifts of nature and fortune, such as strength, talent, and resources, are not unconditionally valuable, because whether they are good or evil depends on whether they are put to use by a good or evil will (G, 4:493–4). This is indeed a bit of common sense, but it does not imply, as Kant seems to think, that a good will is of any value by itself, entirely independently of "what it effects or accomplishes" (4:394). More importantly, it does not tell us anything about the content of the good will or the principle by which it is governed beyond the obvious fact that a good will cannot simply be the will to possess goods of nature or fortune. Kant's next argument, that the point of a good will cannot be to produce *happiness* because it is not particularly good at doing that (4:395), is more important, but it rests on the teleological premise that each of our faculties is naturally intended for one purpose and that it must be good at that purpose; as we saw in Chapter 4, Kant relies on this principle in his general theory of the function of reason, but it could certainly be questioned. Kant will provide a much better account of why the principle of morality cannot simply be to seek (or maximize) happiness in the *Critique of Practical Reason*. Having made these opening sallies, Kant then offers a more careful analysis of the common conception of what it is to have a good will. He argues first that a person demonstrates possession of a good will not just by performing an action that is in conformity with duty, but by performing such an action from duty (4:397–8). In other words, a person with good will does not just do what duty requires but is also motivated by the recognition that the action is her duty or by the general principle to perform an action if and only if it is her duty.[3] We are supposed to recognize this from such common examples as the honest shopkeeper: if a shopkeeper refrains from cheating even his most inexperienced customers because he thinks that a reputation for honesty will be good for his business in the long run, that is just action out of self-interest, for which to be sure he cannot be criticized, but for which he also does not earn our esteem, because he does not demonstrate a good will (4:397). Second, Kant claims that it follows from this that the moral value of an action cannot lie in the end or state of affairs to be attained by it, because that end can be produced by the action regardless of its motivation; so if the moral value of an action is to be connected to its motivation rather than its outcome, then it must lie **"in the principle of the will** without regard for the ends that can be brought about by such an action" (4:400), that is, in a moral principle that has nothing directly to do with the ends or consequences of the actions it commands. From this, Kant next infers, **"duty is the necessity of an action from respect for law"** rather than from any "inclination" – that is, naturally occurring desire – for an object or state of affairs (4:400). And from this – which is still supposed to be part of the common sense conception of a good will – the categorical imperative can be directly inferred: "Since I have deprived the will of every impulse that could arise for it from obeying some law," that is, every inclination for an object or state of affairs,

> nothing is left but the conformity of actions as such with universal law, which alone is to serve the will as its principle, that is, **I ought never to act except in such a way that I could also will that my maxim should become a universal law**.
>
> (4:402)

A "maxim" is the principle on which one actually acts, such as "I will enrich myself at all costs" or "I will never break a promise for reasons of self-interest," so this categorical imperative requires that *each* of us act only on principles on which *everyone* could act without contradiction: it requires that our "subjective principles of volition" also be "objectively valid" or universal laws (4:401n.).[4] In my examples, the maxim " I will enrich myself at all costs" could *not* be acted upon by everyone, because something that I might do under that maxim is bound to conflict with something somebody else would do; but there would be no contradiction in all of us never breaking a promise for reasons of self-interest, so that could be a universal law and should be one. (I formulate this maxim as "I will never break a promise for reasons of self-interest" because there might be *other* reasons, such as saving an innocent life, that could make it permissible or even obligatory to break some promise. As can be seen from this, a maxim does not merely specify a general type of action to be performed or avoided, but also a specific reason for performing or avoiding that type of action.)

Kant's assumption that the fundamental principle of morality cannot be based on any mere desire for some end or object seems sound, but does his conclusion that this principle can therefore concern no end at all but only the universally valid form of our maxim in acting, that is, his purely formalistic conception of the categorical imperative, follow from this assumption? It does not seem to, since even if it is obvious that no object of merely *contingent* inclination could serve as the basis for morality, there still might be some sort of *necessary* object, perhaps of pure reason rather than inclination, which is the basis of the moral law, and if so then the fundamental principle of morality could be the substantive requirement to act only on maxims that would bring about that necessary object rather than just the formal requirement to act only on maxims that should also be universal laws. Let us look at Kant's further derivations of the categorical imperative to see whether he excludes this alternative or rather ends up exploiting it.[5]

In the second section of the *Groundwork*, Kant first argues against "popular moral philosophy" that the fundamental principle of morality can never be derived from examples of actual human conduct (as opposed to the imaginary examples or thought-experiments that he used in the first section, such as the case of the shopkeeper), because in real life people's innermost motivations are never certain, and are all too likely to turn out to be self-love, the "dear self" (G, 4:407). However, he claims that we can proceed by means of a philosophical analysis of the concept of a rational being instead of trying to extract our moral principle from examples of actual human behavior. In the first place, a rational being is one that acts, not just in accordance with laws (everything in nature acts according to some law, even stones falling in accordance with the law of gravity), but in accordance with its own *consciousness* or "representation" of laws (4:412). But to an imperfectly rational being, that is, one who has temptations to do otherwise than what its reason tells it to do, the laws in accordance with which it should act will present themselves as *constraints*, that is, "imperatives" (4:413). These imperatives can be of several different types. The major distinction between them is between those that are *hypothetical* and those that are *categorical*, that is, those that tell you what you must do if you want to attain some end – these are hypothetical – and those that tell you what you must do regardless of any such "reference to another end" – categorical imperatives (4:414).[6] Hypothetical imperatives, in turn, can be divided into two further types: "problematic" ones, which tell you what you must do in order to attain some particular end you *might* have, and "assertoric" ones, which tell you what you need to do in order to attain an end you *do* have (4:415). Problematic hypothetical imperatives are obviously unfit to serve as principles of morality, since they clearly

depend upon merely contingent ends. But assertoric hypothetical imperatives are also unfit to be moral principles, since the only end that everyone
obviously does have is that of happiness, and that has already been
excluded as a possible foundation for morality. Thus the only possible
candidate for a fundamental principle of morality is a categorical imperative, one that tells you what you *must* do independent of any end you
might have. Kant then argues that:

> When I think of a **categorical** imperative I know at once what it contains.
> For, since the imperative contains, beyond the law, only the necessity that
> the maxim be in conformity with this law, while the law contains no condi-
> tion to which it would be limited, nothing is left with which the maxim of
> action is to conform but the universality of a law as such . . . There is,
> therefore, only a single categorical imperative and it is this: **act only in
> accordance with that maxim through which you can at the same
> time will that it become a universal law**.
>
> (4:420−1)

Thus from the analysis of the concept of a rational being Kant ends up
with the same imperative that he previously derived from the common-
sense notions of good will and duty (with the possibly significant
difference that the earlier formulation told us to act only on maxims that
we *should* will to be universal laws while this one tells us to act only on
maxims that we *could* will to be universal laws).[7]

Is this argument any better than the earlier one? Actually, it looks worse,
for not only does it again apparently simply overlook the possibility that in
addition to the contingent ends that give rise to conditional, hypothetical
imperatives, there might be a necessary end that could give rise to an
unconditional, categorical imperative; it also simply assumes from the
outset that a rational being must aim to act in accordance with a categorical imperative rather than merely hypothetical ones, and does not even
attempt to derive this premise from anything like the commonly accepted
conceptions of good will and duty appealed to in Section I.

The same apparently has to be said about Kant's derivation of the categorical imperative in the *Critique of Practical Reason*. Here Kant offers his most
detailed account of why happiness cannot be the basis of a moral law: our
conceptions of happiness are simply too indeterminate, for often what we
think would make us happy at one moment conflicts with what we think
would make us happy at another, or what one person thinks will make her
happy conflicts with what would make another happy. (Kant relishes the

irony in the story of Francis I of France and Charles V of the Holy Roman Empire, each of whom would have been made happy by the same thing, namely, possessing Milan. But obviously they could not both have Milan, so they could not both be happy in spite of agreeing on what would make them happy. See CPracR, 5:25–8.) So no genuine practical principle can be "material," or specify a particular object (5:21–2); instead, "If a rational being is to think of his maxims as practical universal laws, he can think of them only as principles that contain the determining ground of the will not by their matter but by their form," namely, that they have that form "by which **they are fit for a giving of universal law**" (5:27). But again, Kant simply assumes without argument that a rational being must will to act only in accordance with a truly universal law, and likewise that there are only contingent ends, no necessary end, so that the moral law must be strictly "formal" rather than "material."

When we return to the main line of Kant's argument in the second section of the *Groundwork*, however, we can see that the next thing that Kant does is precisely to fill the gap he has thus far left in his argument by over-looking the possibility of a necessary end by now introducing one. Kant does not, of course, acknowledge that there is a gap in his arguments to this point, but he seems to recognize that the purely negative arguments that he has offered thus far – arguments that arrive at the categorical imperative by the elimination of possible alternatives – would be more compelling if the principle were positively grounded in something of unconditional value. He acknowledges that "the principle of action being free from all influences of contingent grounds" needs to be connected "with the concept of the will of a rational being as such" (G, 4:426); in other words, precisely insofar as it is rational, a rational being needs a reason to adhere to a law, an end that can be advanced by and only by adherence to that law. And if the law is to be unconditionally valid, as the moral law is supposed to be, then that end must be unconditionally valuable. As Kant puts it, he must find "something the **existence of which in itself** has an absolute worth, something which as **an end in itself** could be . . . the ground of a possible categorical imperative." And then he goes on:

> Now I say that the human being and in general every rational being *exists* as an end in itself, ***not merely as a means*** to be used by this or that will at his discretion; instead he must in all his actions, whether directed to himself or also to other rational beings, always be regarded **at the same time as an end**.
>
> (4:428)

From this Kant derives the second main formulation of the categorical imperative: "**So act that you use humanity, whether in your own person or in the person of any other, always at the same time as an end, never merely as a means**" (4:429).

Now if this imperative expresses the unconditional value of an end that can be the ground of any possible categorical imperative, then Kant's other formulations of that imperative, both the one commanding that we act only on universally valid maxims and any others to follow, ought to be derivable from it. So one question we need to ask is whether that is so. But before we can answer that question, we need to know just what this impressive-sounding statement means, and whether it can be proven any more convincingly than the original formulation of the categorical imperative. To determine what the statement means, we have to figure out what is meant by the concept of humanity as well as by the idea of an end in itself. One might think that by "humanity" Kant just means humankind, the biological species *homo sapiens*, or the defining character-istics of this species. In fact, Kant seems to mean something more like biological human beings insofar as they are also rational beings, and it is the embodiment of rational being rather than human life as such that he is declaring to be an end in itself. (In his *Lectures on Ethics*, Kant states that by engaging in various vices one can "throw away his humanity" without throwing away his life as such, and that "It is not life that is to be so highly treasured, but rather that one should live it throughout as a human being" [LEC, 27:341−2]. Kant did not believe in the sanctity of life as such.) Since human beings are the only rational beings we know, however, Kant often uses "rational being" and "humanity" interchange-ably, and so we can glean what he means from statements about both. In the *Groundwork*, he says that "Rational nature is distinguished from the rest of nature by this, that it sets itself an end" (G, 4:437). A dozen years later, in the *Metaphysics of Morals*, he says that "what characterizes humanity (as distinguished from animality)" is the "capacity to set oneself an end − any end whatsoever" (MM, Doctrine of Virtue, Introduction, section VIII, 6:392), but also goes on say that "bound up with the end of humanity in our own person" there is that

> rational will, and so the duty, to make ourselves worthy of humanity by culture in general, by procuring or promoting the **capacity** to realize all sort of possible ends . . . In other words, the human being has a duty to cultivate the crude predispositions of his nature, by which the animal is first raised into the human being.

The term "humanity" in Kant's formula thus seems to mean our capacity freely to set ourselves ends – form intentions and adopt aims – and to entail a duty to develop the various abilities that as rational beings we can see will be necessary in order to pursue effectively and thus realize the ends that we have set for ourselves.[8]

Now what can it mean to treat this capacity as an "end in itself," something that has "unconditional" or "absolute worth"? At the very least, something of unconditional value must not be destroyed or damaged for the sake of something of merely conditional value: thus our capacity to freely set and rationally pursue particular ends is not to be sacrificed for the sake of any particular contingent end. Sometimes that seems to be all that Kant means, as when he says in the *Groundwork* that rational nature "must here be thought not as an end to be effected," that is, produced, "but as an **independently existing** end, and hence thought only negatively, that is, as that which must never be acted against" (G, 4:437). But it is clear from Kant's remarks in the *Metaphysics of Morals* that there is more to making humanity our end than merely not acting against it; humanity includes capacities that must be *developed* in order to raise ourselves from the level of mere animality. Our humanity is both a predisposition and a potential, something that we must both preserve and promote. Further, although our humanity is something that is never to be sacrificed for any particular ends, it is nothing other than the capacity to freely set and rationally pursue particular ends. Our humanity and our particular ends cannot simply be contrasted to each other, the latter simply being sacrificed for the former. Rather, the requirement that we make humanity our end and never merely a means requires that we set and pursue our particular ends in a way that is consistent with the preservation and promotion of our general capacity to set and pursue ends.

The capacity to set ends for ourselves and pursue them in effective ways sounds very much like the freedom that Kant talks about in his lectures on ethics: the capacity to set our own ends is freedom of choice, and the capacity to pursue them effectively requires freedom of action. In the lectures, as we saw earlier, Kant also says that freedom must be made "consistent with itself." What does that mean? One thing it seems to mean is that I must make free choices on particular occasions in a way that preserves and promotes my ability to make and carry out further free choices on other occasions. To use some of Kant's characteristic examples, particular decisions to commit suicide or get drunk considered by themselves would certainly be free choices – instances of setting myself "any end whatsoever" – but they would not be consistent with preserving and promoting my capacity to make and carry out further free choices: committing suicide, even if it is one free act, would obviously destroy me and therefore my ability to make any further free choices; choosing to get drunk, even if it is itself a free choice, would deprive me of the ability to make or successfully carry out free choices for some number of hours, and, were I to drive while drunk, could even end up killing me, thus directly destroying my freedom.

Or I could kill someone else, and thus destroy his or her freedom – remember that Kant's requirement is that we treat humanity as an end and never merely as a means in my own person or in that of any other person. This means that my use of my own freedom on particular occasions must be consistent not only with my own future use of freedom but also with the preservation and promotion of the freedom of others. I could obviously make all sorts of choices that would be perfectly free choices, considered in isolation, and might even be consistent with my continued freedom, but which would be inconsistent with the preservation and promotion of the freedom of others. My decision to kidnap you might be a free choice, but would not be consistent with the preservation of your freedom; my decision not to pay my school taxes might be a free choice, but would not be consistent with the education of the children in my school district, thus with the promotion of their capacities to pursue their own freely chosen ends now or as they grow up. (Of course, we might expect or even hope that my violation of the freedom of others in such cases would lead to my punishment, and thereby a subsequent restriction or even destruction of my own freedom as well.) Consistently treating humanity as an end and never merely as a means requires the consistency of one's own free choices over time and consistency between one's own free choices and those of others both at one time and over time. The fundamental principle of morality commands that we seek such consistency in our use of freedom, and the concrete laws of morality are the more particular rules our reason tells us we must follow in order to achieve this general goal.

Interpreted along these lines, Kant's principle that we must always treat humanity as an end and never merely as a means not only sounds uplifting, but is also informative. But does it rest on anything more than mere assertion ("Now I say . . . ")? Does Kant have any argument for it?

At the outset of this chapter, I quoted Kant's early observation that even children are bitter at being constrained, and long to be able to make their own decisions. This might explain why one loves one's own freedom or humanity. But even if reflection on this fact about themselves were somehow to lead people to value *everyone's* freedom, the initial fact that even as children we love freedom seems to be only an anthropological or psychological fact, thus an empirical, contingent fact, not suitable for the foundation of a fundamental principle of morality, at least given Kant's expectation that such a principle must be valid for any possible rational being. In any case, in his mature publications on the foundations of morality Kant does not appeal to this psychological fact about us in order to justify the categorical imperative.

Kant says that his second formulation of the categorical imperative results from a step into metaphysics (G, 4:426), and some commentators have found in Kant a metaphysical argument, according to which the "conditional worth" or value that we assign to any particular end needs a foundation, indeed that it cannot simply be "relative" to some other conditional value but must ultimately be grounded in something of unconditional value, and that there is no other candidate for the unconditionally valuable source of conditionally valuable ends than our own capacity to choose those ends, so our capacity of choice must be the very thing that has unconditional value.[9] But why shouldn't there be nothing but things of conditional or merely relative value, that is, things that are valuable only if something else is valued, but nothing that is of unconditional value? In fact, Kant does not suggest that the possibility of conditional value presupposes the existence of something with unconditional value; rather, he *assumes* that morality requires the existence of something of unconditional value, and *infers* from this that conditional or relative value cannot be the whole story about value. He does not try to infer the existence of unconditional value from the existence of conditional values (G, 4:428).

Are we in the end then just supposed to recognize the fundamental principle of morality as a basic norm that we all accept and which philosophy can clarify and confirm by deriving from it more concrete moral principles and duties that we all acknowledge, but which it cannot deduce from anything more basic? There is ample evidence to suggest exactly this. In the essay on metaphysical method written two decades before the *Groundwork*, Kant had said that the fundamental "material" principles of morality are "indemonstrable" (PNTM, 2:299). In the Preface to the *Groundwork* he had written that we "proceed analytically from common cognition to the determination of its supreme principle, and in turn synthetically from the examination of this principle and its sources back to the common cognition in which we find it used" (G, 4:392), which might be taken to mean that the only thing we can substantively add to the clarification of the supreme principle of morality is the confirmation of the correctness of our analysis of that principle by examples of its use. And in the *Critique of Practical Reason* he says that "consciousness of this fundamental law" is a "fact of reason" that just "forces itself upon us" (CPracR, 5:31). Maybe there can be no argument from some even more basic premise that there must be a fundamental principle of morality, although at least in the third section of the *Groundwork*, which we have not yet discussed, Kant tries to avoid this conclusion. But even if this is so, one could still argue that if there is a fundamental principle of morality, then it must have a certain character. Kant's second formulation of the categorical imperative might then be preferred to the first not because it has a better metaphysical foundation, but because it makes better sense of our common conception of our duties and it therefore better illuminates what the normative character of any moral law must be.

Perhaps in the end that is right. But there is one more thing that Kant says that we should think about. Back in his analysis of our common conception of the value of acting from duty as a motive, Kant had written that

> I cannot have respect for inclination as such, whether it is mine or that of another; I can at most in the first case approve it and in the second sometimes even love it, that is, regard it as favorable to my own advantage. Only what is connected with my will merely as ground and never as effect . . . can be an object of respect and so a command. Now an action from duty is to put aside entirely the influence of inclination.
>
> (G, 4:400)

This suggests that we can have no esteem or respect for what merely *happens* to us, but only for what we *do*, and if what we ultimately *do* is *choose* our ends and choose to develop and use various means to pursue them, but not in fact *realize* them, since that always depends at least in part on factors beyond our own action, then perhaps the only thing we can really respect is our choice of ends and the capacities on which that choice rests (just as the only thing we can really disrespect is a bad choice of ends, not the bad inclinations that people just happen to have or the bad things that just happen to them). This might suggest that humanity as the capacity to freely choose and rationally pursue ends is the only candidate for something of *unconditional* value because it is the only genuine object of *respect* or the only real object of value at all.

Now it seems undeniable that the premise that we can have respect only for genuine actions is itself a normative assumption that is not derived from anything more fundamental, whether descriptive or normative. But perhaps some will find such a basic claim about moral *judgment* or *evaluation* more intuitively compelling than the more abstract and possibly unfamiliar theory of moral *value* that Kant enunciates in his principle that humanity should always be an end and never merely a means, and therefore find the former a possible premise for an argument to the latter. If not, well, then, Kant's argument is no worse off than before: it recognizes that concrete claims about moral norms can only be derived from something we acknowledge as a more fundamental moral norm, but that there can be no deduction of that fundamental norm from any metaphysical fact that is somehow more certain. We simply have to find what is presented as the most fundamental moral norm compelling, and certainly many people do find Kant's second formulation of the fundamental principle of morality immediately compelling.

Let us leave the problem of the derivability of Kant's second fundamental principle of morality there for now, and instead turn next to the question of whether Kant's other formulations of the categorical imperative can be derived from this one. After that, we can see whether even more concrete principles of duty can be derived from the categorical imperative, thereby lending it additional confirmation.

UNIVERSAL LAW AND HUMANITY AS AN END IN ITSELF

Kant actually formulates the categorical imperative in at least five different ways, although he himself usually refers to only three (see *G*, 4:432, 436–7). Commentators have argued for every conceivable relationship among these formulations,[10] but I will here develop the view that all the others may be derived from the formula of humanity as an end in itself (abbreviated "FHE"), in accordance with Kant's own suggestion that this formulation reveals the "ground of a possible categorical imperative."

What I have been referring to as Kant's second formulation of the categorical imperative is not in fact the first variant that follows his initial formulation, the formula of universal law ("FUL") requiring us to act only on maxims that we could also will to be universal laws (*G*, 4:421). Kant's first variant on that initial formulation is actually the formula of the universal law *of nature* ("FLN"), "**act as if the maxim of your action were to become by your will** a universal law of nature" (*G*, 4:421). Some commentators have claimed that this introduces something new into Kant's theory, namely a teleological conception according to which *nature* itself has certain purposes in giving us capacities and that we must act only in ways consistent with those purposes of nature.[11] Kant's first illustration of this formulation is consistent with this interpretation: he argues that we should not commit suicide from self-love (that is, out of a desire to avoid further pain) because nature has given us the tendency to self-love to preserve our lives, not to end them (G, 4:422). But this teleological interpretation is not required by Kant's general conception of a law of nature, for all that Kant officially means by a law of nature is an unexceptionable uniformity in the behavior of some specified domain of objects: nature is just "the **existence** of things, insofar as that existence is determined according to universal laws" (PFM, §14, 4:294). So when Kant asks us by means of FUL to consider whether we could will a maxim on which we are considering acting to also be a universal law, or asks us to consider whether we could will to act upon our maxim if everyone else were also to do so, he is already asking us to consider whether we could will to act upon our maxim if that maxim were (somehow) to become one of the laws of nature in accordance with which everyone actually behaves, thus already implying FLN. Kant puts the same point in the *Critique of Practical Reason* when he says that

> The rule of judgment under laws of pure practical reason is this: ask yourself whether, if the action you propose were to take place by a law of the nature of which you were yourself a part, you could indeed regard it as possible through your will.
>
> (5:69)

Our actions take place in the natural world, so the question we are asking when we ask whether we could will our maxim as a universal law (FUL) is the same question as whether we could will it to be a law of nature (FLN).

Now as Kant points out, there are actually two questions I must ask when I ask whether I could will my proposed maxim to be a universal law of nature: first, whether it would even be logically possible for me to act on my maxim if everyone else were to do so too; and second, even if it would be logically possible for me to will the universalization of my maxim, whether that is something I could rationally will, that is, something that would be consistent with my willing things in a rational way (G, 4:424). What Kant means by the first of these tests is clear enough: if it would be impossible for me to act on my maxim if everyone did, then acting on my proposed maxim while willing it to be universal is logically impossible. For example, if everyone were to make false promises whenever they thought they could gain something by so doing, the very practice of promising – in which people act on promises made by others because they expect those promises will be kept – would quickly collapse, and once that happened it would be logically impossible for me to make even a false promise – the words "I promise" would be meaningless if there were no practice of promising based on the expectation that people generally keep their promises.[12] The meaning of the second test is not quite so clear, but what Kant seems to have in mind is that the universalization of certain maxims would be inconsistent with a fundamental canon of rationality even if not logically impossible, namely the fundamental principle that if I am rationally to will an end then I must always be able to will an adequate means for it. As he puts it, "Whoever wills the end also wills (insofar as reason has decisive influence on his actions) the indispensably necessary means to it that are within his power" (G, 4:417). His idea would then be that while as a rational being you must will that there be suitable means available for your ends, whatever they might be, but that if you were to will the universalization of such maxims as "I will not cultivate my talents" or "I will not help others in need," that is, if you were to will that no one cultivates talents or helps anyone in need, then you would in fact be willing that adequate means for the realization of your ends not be available – the height of irrationality.[13] Now Kant explicitly says only that the rule that if you will the end you must will some adequate means is the only principle of rationality needed to explain the force of hypothetical imperatives, e.g., such "rules of skill" as "If you want to assemble this furniture you must use a Phillips screwdriver," or such "rules of prudence" as "If you want to be healthy you must control your weight." This might make it seem as if this principle figures only in matters of prudence, not morality. But that does not follow, for Kant does not explain the moral, categorical imperative by this principle *alone*: the *moral* question is whether I would have adequate means for my ends *if I were to will the universalization of my proposed maxim* – as morality and only morality requires me to do. In other words, as the highest form of practical reason, morality comprises *both* the principle of universalization and the principle of instrumental rationality.

Kant associates his version of an important traditional distinction, that between perfect and imperfect duties, with the distinction between the two tests for universalizability.[14] On Kant's account, perfect duties are those that prescribe a specific type of action, or more typically the omission of a specific type of action, while imperfect duties prescribe only a general goal or policy, but not the specific types of action by which that policy needs to be implemented.[15] To use Kant's examples, suicide, or more precisely, in light of our previous discussion, suicide committed solely from the motivation of avoiding pain, is a specific type of action that is always prohibited, so the duty not to commit such suicide is a perfect duty; but, since you cannot possibly help everybody else in every way they might need, the general policy to help other people does not tell you what specific acts of beneficence to perform, and so is an imperfect duty. Kant's claim is that the proposed rejection of any perfect duty would fail the first test of universalizability, while the proposed rejection of any imperfect duty could pass the first test but would fail the second (G, 4:424). It is not clear whether this correlation holds in every case, but it is also not clear whether anything rides on that: as long as any duty that we are sure we have can be derived either from one or from both of the two parts of FUL/FLN, that would seem to confirm the adequacy of this version of the categorical imperative.

Of course, questions have been raised about whether FUL and/or FLN really do yield all our duties and only our duties. Many commentators have formulated immoral maxims that apparently pass the test of univer-salizability and clearly harmless ones that fail it,[16] while several have argued that the universalizability test gives rise only to negative and not positive duties.[17] The latter objection seems incorrect: if I must reject the maxims of letting all my talents rust or never helping anyone else, then I must accept their logical contraries, namely, maxims of cultivating at least some of my talents and helping at least some other people some of the time. To be sure, the latter maxims do not tell me specifically *which* talents I should develop or *which* people I should help *when, how,* and *how much* – but that is precisely the point that Kant himself makes by calling these maxims of imperfect duty, and if it is an objection at all then it would be an objection to the very idea of imperfect duty no matter how it was derived. But I do not want to go into these details here. For what I want to argue is that the force of the general idea of universalizability as a test of morality arises from the idea that humanity must always be treated as an end in itself (FHE), rather than FHE adding something to FUL/FLN, and if *that* is an adequate basis for all our actual duties then surely there must be a way to formulate FUL and/or FLN so that they are adequate as well.

The basic idea here is simply that FHE, the requirement that humanity whether in oneself or in anyone else must always be treated as an end and never merely as a means, requires that each one of us always respect the free choice and action of *everyone* else, and therefore act only on *maxims* that *could be accepted by everyone else* as preserving their capacity for free choice as well. In the first instance, that means that everyone else ought to be able to accept *my acting* on my proposed maxim, but full respect for their freedom also means that *they should be able to adopt any maxim on which I propose to act*, although they need not actually adopt every maxim on which I permissibly act. This is because to treat everyone equally as an end requires adopting only maxims on which everyone *could* act, if they were to so choose: there will be an unfair distribution of freedom, one on which not everyone is treated as an end in himself or some are treated as more of an end than others, if maxims are allowed on which some could act only if others cannot. Others will not be treating my humanity as equal in value to their own if they act on maxims that I could not also act on, and I will not be treating others as ends in themselves equal in value to myself if I act on maxims that they could not at the same time act upon. Kant puts the point in terms of ends – he says that to value others as ends and not merely as means requires that they "must also be able to contain in them-selves the end of the very same action" I propose to do (G, 4:430) – but the same point goes for maxims: to treat others as ends equal in value to myself means that they must be free to adopt any maxim on which I propose to act. If they could not, then neither may I act upon such a maxim.

Of course, this means that treating everyone as equally free to exercise humanity or freedom of choice and action cannot be the same as anarchy: there will be many maxims we will all have to choose to forgo if we are all to treat each other as equally free. I obviously cannot adopt the maxim of committing homicide for any reason whatever if I value my own continued life and freedom, for that would mean allowing you to be free to act on the same maxim, and thus to kill me if you so choose.[18] I cannot adopt the maxim of making false promises while allowing you the freedom of adopting the same maxim, for then I will not be able to accomplish anything at all by going through what would have become merely the motions of making a promise – again, in a world in which people routinely broke promises without good reason, no rational person would accept any promises, and thus the words "I promise . . . " would turn into meaningless noise. I cannot adopt the maxim of letting my talents rust if I am to allow you the same freedom, for then none of us might have the means necessary to realize any of our ends. And so on. Treating us all as equally free to adopt any maxim that any one of us is free to act upon means that we must all forgo certain maxims altogether and must all commit ourselves to adopting their contraries. That is why FHE implies FUL / FLN.

CONFIRMATION OF THE CATEGORICAL IMPERATIVE
FROM COMMONLY RECOGNIZED DUTIES

Before we see how the imperative always to treat humanity as an end and
never merely as a means also implies Kant's remaining formulations of the
categorical imperative, let us stop to consider whether this formulation
seems to be an adequate foundation for all the kinds of duties that we
commonly recognize. This is not merely a natural question to ask, but also
seems to be one that Kant himself promises to answer when he says, as we
already noted, that we must be able to proceed "synthetically from the
examination of this principle . . . to the common cognition in which we
find it used" (G, 4:392). He illustrates both FUL/FLN and FHE with four
examples, one each of a perfect duty to self, a perfect duty to others,
imperfect duty to self, and imperfect duty to others, precisely because such
a scheme is commonly recognized (G, 4:421–2n.). This classification is
obviously exhaustive – leaving aside duties to God, which Kant rejects
(see for example MM, Doctrine of Virtue, §18, 6:443–4) – so if Kant's
formulations of the categorical imperative offer a way of grounding characteristic examples of duties in each of these four classes, that will be a
strong argument from "common moral cognition" in their favor. As earlier
noted, Kant's example of a perfect or strict duty to oneself is the prohibition of suicide. His argument is that one cannot "dispose of a human
being in [one's] own person by maiming, damaging, or killing him"
because one's humanity – not one's merely biological existence, but one's
existence as a free and rational being capable of choosing and pursuing
ends – is an end in itself; while to commit suicide, *at least for such a reason* as
just to avoid further pain or disappointment, is to make "use of a person
merely as a means to maintain a tolerable condition up to the end of life"
(G, 4:429). The notion of making use of one's own existence merely as a
means to achieving a certain condition in one's existence seems strange,
but the general idea that one simply should not destroy something,
namely, one's own humanity, that should always be treated as an end and
never merely as a means, is clear enough. Presumably precisely the same
argument applies in the case of homicide as well.

The permissibility of suicide was a standard topic in the ethical discussions of classical Stoicism and Epicureanism with which Kant was well
acquainted, and had also become a fashionable topic in eighteenth-century
Germany after the publication of Johann Goethe's bestseller *The Sorrows of
Young Werther* (1774). For these reasons it greatly interested Kant – at least
nothing that we know about him suggests that he ever struggled with any

suicidal inclinations of his own – and he frequently discussed it. Two points that he raises elsewhere can help clarify his present argument. First, in the lectures on ethics that he gave in the years before publishing the *Groundwork*, he said that what is "inherently abominable" about suicide is "the fact that a man uses his freedom to destroy himself, when he ought to use it solely to live as a man"; a man is free "to dispose over everything pertaining to his person, but not over that person itself, nor can he use his freedom against himself" (*LEC*, 27:343). What this implies is, as I suggested earlier, that an act of suicide is itself a use of freedom, that is, a freely chosen act, but a free act against one's continued existence as a free agent, that is, one free act that would destroy the possibility of any further free acts. For that reason suicide cannot be endorsed but must be rejected in the name of humanity as freedom: what treating humanity as an end in itself requires is not that any free act considered in isolation, but that freedom as an on-going condition, be preserved.

That we cannot allow any free act in isolation but must think instead of the preservation of freedom over a lifetime suggests that there is a certain quantitative aspect built into the requirement of treating humanity as an end and never merely a means, even though many people assume that quantitative considerations are relevant only to consequentialist theories such as utilitarianism. The second point that Kant makes about suicide in his lectures bears that out. Kant is generally inclined to treat the prohibition of suicide as absolute, but in pursuing the topic with his students he allows that certain exceptions may at least be possible. In particular, he discusses the case of the Roman leader Cato (Marcus Porcius Cato Uticensis, 95–46 BCE), who killed himself not to escape the tyranny of Julius Caesar personally but rather to encourage the Romans to "dedicate their final efforts to the defense of their freedom"(*LEC*, 27:370).[19] Although Kant does not himself draw such a conclusion unequivocally, we can take this example to suggest that the (freely chosen) destruction of one free being in order to save many more free beings may be permissible, or even mandatory, because making humanity in both our own person and that of all others an end and never merely a means might well require preserving as many instances of humanity as possible; and in cases in which all instances cannot be preserved, then more rather than fewer instances should be preserved, even if it is our own instance of humanity that may have to be sacrificed in order to preserve others. Humanity is not just an abstraction, but something that exists in its instances, and so in making humanity our end numbers not only can but in fact must count.[20] (However, Kant never suggests that making humanity our end requires *producing* more instances of humanity; he typically treats humanity, recall, as an end not to be acted against. Just why this should be so might not be easy to explain: it readily fits the ethical intuitions of those who believe the earth should not be overpopulated, for example, but not the religious views of those who believe they have a duty to procreate without limit.)

The same reasoning may apply in the case of homicide as well (which Kant does not actually discuss). Again, we may initially regard the prohibition of homicide as absolute, but in fact we do recognize exceptions to this prohibition. Thus, we acknowledge that the right to self-defense may sometimes license killing an attacker, and that means that we cannot think of the inviolability of each human life as if it were independent of all others, but rather recognize that sometimes one life can be preserved only at the cost of another, and that in certain circumstances one may have the right to preserve his or her own life rather than that of another. In this case, the reason for that right may be that one is innocent of any crime while one's attacker is not. But there will be other cases in which all the parties involved are equally innocent of any crime and yet they still cannot all be saved. To take one well-worn example, imagine that an out-of-control train is racing toward a switch where you just happen to be standing, and that a van with a family of six is stuck on the track to which the train will switch if you do nothing while a car with just one occupant is stuck on the other track. You might well think that it is not merely permissible but even obligatory for you to throw the switch so that only one person is killed by the train rather than six – your intervention will cause the death of the one, to be sure, but your decision to leave the switch as it is will cause the death of six, and that decision not to throw the switch would be just as much of an action on your part as your physical act of throwing the switch. If you accept this reasoning, you will be reasoning that if humanity is always an end, your duty is to preserve as many instances of humanity as possible, and that in unfortunate cases where for reasons beyond your own control not everyone can possibly be saved, then your duty is always to show your respect for humanity as an end in itself by saving more rather than fewer humans.[21]

Thus, Kant's principle that humanity should always be an end and never merely a means can give a plausible derivation of our obligations in the prohibition of suicide as a perfect duty to self and the prohibition of homicide as a perfect duty to others. As I noted, Kant does not explicitly refer to the case of homicide; his example of a perfect duty to others is the prohibition of false promises, that is, promises made with no intention of being kept. (Not every *broken* promise is a *false* promise, since you may sometimes have morally permissible or even mandatory reasons for breaking a promise; a false promise is one that you *never meant* to keep.) In illustration of FUL/FLN, Kant had argued that making a false promise in order to accomplish some goal is impermissible because universalizing the practice of making false promises would undermine the practice of making promises altogether, and in that case you could not achieve your goal by making a false promise after all (G, 4:422). In illustrating FHE, Kant argues that in making a promise that you have no intention of keeping in order to accomplish a certain goal you are keeping your real intention and end hidden from the promisee, and thereby deceiving him into performing an action and adopting an end that he would not freely choose if he were properly informed about your real aim. False promises are impermissible, Kant concludes, because they "use the person of others merely as a means" to the hidden ends of the false promiser, "without taking into consideration that, as rational beings," the promisees "are always to be valued at the same time as ends, that is, only as beings who must also be able to contain in themselves the end of the very same action" (G, 4:430). That is, to treat others as ends and not merely as means is to treat them as entitled to *choose their own particular ends*, and thus to treat people as ends in themselves requires not merely preserving their *existence* as free beings but also preserving their capacity *to exercise their freedom* by choosing their own ends. Of course, this does not prohibit ever using another as a means at all, for even when you make an *honest* promise, say through a fair contract freely accepted by both parties, you are still using the other or the performance that the contract requires of him as a means for your own end in making the contract. But as long as the other party is agreeing to the contact *freely*, because he sees it as being in his own interest as well as in yours, then you are treating him as an end *as well as* a means, and this is what FHE requires.

So Kant's examples of perfect duties to self and others can plausibly be analyzed as duties to *preserve* the existence and the possibility of the *exercise* of humanity, as the capacity to set and pursue ends freely.[22] What about his examples of imperfect duties to self and others, which are prescriptions of certain general policies or goals rather than proscriptions of very specific types of actions. How can they be understood? Kant suggests that these should be understood as duties to *further* or *promote* humanity rather than to just *preserve* it. Now even though, as we have already seen, the duty to preserve humanity is in the first place a duty to preserve instances of humanity, by the duty to promote humanity Kant does not seem to mean a duty to *produce more instances* of humanity – he never asserted a duty to procreate. Rather, he has in mind duties to facilitate the realization of the particular ends that are freely chosen in the exercise of humanity both indirectly by the provision of general capabilities for successfully realizing such ends and directly by actually assisting in the realization of particular ends. The first of these cases is illustrated by Kant's example of an imperfect duty to oneself, namely, the duty to cultivate "predispositions to greater perfection," that is, skills and talents, in oneself (G, 4:430), because it is only by that means that one can develop the capacities that will be necessary to serve "all sorts of possible purposes" (4:423) that one may freely adopt over the course of one's life. We exercise our humanity precisely by freely choosing and pursuing ends, and one part of treating humanity as an end is therefore to take steps to promote the effectiveness of those choices. This is not a prudential or utilitarian argument that we will be *happier* if we take steps to enable ourselves to realize more rather than fewer of our chosen ends – though no doubt we usually will be – but is rather an argument that because our free choice of ends is an intrinsically valuable exercise of our humanity and cultivating our talents in order to realize these ends is also an expression of our rationality, cultivating those talents is also part of what is required to treat humanity in our own person as an end in itself.

Before turning to Kant's example of imperfect duty to others, one observation about this imperfect duty to oneself is in order. At one point, Kant says that "as a rational being [one] necessarily wills that all the capacities in him be developed" (G, 4:423). This cannot be true, because in many cases it simply will not be possible to develop all of one's potential skills or talents. One might have equal potential to become a great violinist or a great linebacker, but it is extremely unlikely that one could actually become both, because of the amount of practice time each would require, the incompatible developments in physique they would require, and so on. Usually one will have to make a choice of which talents to cultivate, and factors other than the completely general obligation to cultivate some talents will be necessary to make that choice. Again one such factor might be quantitative – one might ask which skill will ultimately allow one to realize more of one's possible ends, or even more of one's own ends as well as the ends of others whom one might help through one's own talents and their fruits. Happiness too might be a factor – faced with two equally good ways of facilitating your successful pursuit of "all sorts of possible purposes," you might simply ask yourself which one would make you happier. Of course, as Kant likes to stress, we are not particularly good at answering that question for ourselves.[23]

Finally, Kant's explanation of the duty to assist others in the realization of their ends also turns on the assumption that to treat humanity as an end and never merely as a means requires treating the ends that people choose in the exercise of their humanity as worthy of promotion precisely because of the value of the humanity that is exercised in their choice. Merely preserving the existence of others and allowing them to choose their ends but then leaving them entirely on their own in their attempts to realize those ends is not enough; as Kant says:

> there is still only a negative and not a positive agreement with **humanity as an end in itself** unless everyone also tries, as far as he can, to further the ends of others. For the ends of a subject who is an end in itself must as far as possible be also **my ends**, if that representation is to have its **full** effect in me.
>
> (G, 4:430)

Again, the argument is not a utilitarian argument: the claim is not that I should assist others in the realization of their goals because that will make them happier, though no doubt it usually will. The claim is rather that their ends are valuable and worthy of being made my ends as well because of the intrinsic value of the humanity – capacity for setting ends – that they exercise in choosing those ends.

Now, of course, we will want to recognize at most a duty to promote the morally permissible ends of others. But this is readily explained on Kant's analysis: morally impermissible ends would be those that would in some way destroy or violate humanity, whether in the person whose ends they are or in others, and we obviously have no duty to assist in that. On the contrary, since our duty to assist in the realization of the particular ends of others derives from our general duty to preserve and promote humanity, we can have such a duty only when those particular ends are themselves consistent with that general duty. Kant also observes later that "it is open to me to refuse" to help others with "many things that **they** think will make them happy but that I do not, as long as they have no right to demand them from me as what is theirs" (MM, Doctrine of Virtue, Introduction, Section V, 6:387) (that is, as long as I do not already owe them what they want because of some prior contract, promise, etc.). This reservation could easily be explained if our duty were simply to promote the happiness of others – of course we all have to exercise our own judgment in figuring out how to fulfill our duties. The explanation will have to be more subtle given that Kant's underlying theory is not that happiness is intrinsically valuable and that we have a duty toward the happiness of others for that reason. His thought must rather be that even though we have a general duty to assist in the realization of the ends of others, it is of course impossible for us to assist with the realization of *all* the ends of *all* other people; so we must again appeal to further factors in deciding where to address our necessarily limited assistance. At this point it certainly seems appropriate to appeal such considerations of number, reliability, and efficiency: how can we help the *most* other people? How can we *most reliably* help others? How can we *most effectively* help other people? In trying to answer these questions, we will certainly have to make our own judgments about what is actually in the best interest of those whom we would try to help.

Kant's derivation of specific examples of duties from the general requirement that we treat humanity as an end and never merely as a means thus seems plausible. I will just add one remark before returning to the remaining formulations of the categorical imperative. Kant offers the duty of perfecting one's own natural predispositions and assisting in the realization of the ends of others merely as examples of imperfect duties to oneself and to others respectively. But in the later *Metaphysics of Morals*, he will argue that one's only duty to oneself is to promote one's perfection and that one's only duty to others is to promote their happiness, thus that one has no duty to promote one's own happiness or the perfection of others (MM, Doctrine of Virtue, Introduction, Sections IV–V, 6:385–8). His reasons for these claims are, first, that one can have a duty only to do something to which one is not naturally inclined, but everyone is naturally inclined to pursue their own happiness, so one cannot have a duty toward that, and, second, that the perfection of humans consists precisely in their setting their ends in accordance with their own concepts of duty, and obviously no one can do that for someone else (6:386). Both these arguments are weak. First, while one may not need to constrain oneself to pursue some immediate inclination, one's long-term happiness often conflicts with immediate inclination, and one may well need to constrain oneself to pursue it. So one's long-term happiness may often seem more like a duty than an inclination; and if we have a duty to promote the long-term happiness of *others* because of the value of their humanity, then we could well have a duty to promote *our own* long-term happiness because of the value of our own humanity. Second, while we certainly cannot make each other's choices, Kant's discussion of self-perfection ultimately makes it clear that this involves far more than simply making choices in accordance with duty: it involves the perfection of a whole variety of natural as well as moral capacities that we need in order to make wise choices, whether moral or just prudential, as well as to realize them successfully. In other words, self-perfection requires the education of our natural and moral capacities, and we can certainly assist others with that. For example, we can have a duty to assist in the education of children, both our own and those of others. Such a duty may be in part a perfect duty – our obligations to pay our school taxes and make sure our own children go to school until they are 16 may be specific and unremitting – but it may at least in part be imperfect – there may be all sorts of ways in which we should promote the education of children, whether our own or others', that cannot be specified in such precise ways.

AUTONOMY AND THE REALM OF ENDS

Let us now return to Kant's further formulations of the categorical imperative. He twice speaks of a third formulation, after FUL/FLN and FHE, but each time he mentions a different formulation. So there seem to be two further formulations, not identical but presumably related. Kant's first derives the "third practical principle of the will" from the preceding formulations of the categorical imperative thus:

> The ground of all practical lawgiving lies (in accordance with the first principle) **objectively in the rule** and the form of universality which makes it fit to be a *law* (indeed a law of nature); **subjectively**, however, it lies in the **end**; but the subject of all ends is every rational being as an end in itself (in accordance with the second principle); from this there follows now the third practical principle of the will, as supreme condition of its harmony with universal practical principle, the idea **of the will of every rational being as a will giving universal law**.
>
> (G, 4:431)

A page later he gives a slightly different formulation when he says that "the principle of every human will as **a will giving universal law through all its maxims**" (G, 4:432). Together, these two statements suggest that the third formulation of the categorical imperative is something like "Act only on maxims that could be given by *all* human wills as part of a *complete system* of maxims."[24] Kant calls this third formulation "the principle of the **autonomy** of the will in contrast with every other, which I accordingly count as **heteronomy**" (G, 4:433), so this version is often called the formula of autonomy (FA). His reason for this name is his definition of "autonomy" as "the property of the will by which it is a law to itself (independently of any property of the objects of volition)" (G, 4:440). His idea is that for your will to be determined simply by inclination toward some object is for your will as it were to allow itself to be pushed around by those inclinations, or to be "heteronomous," rather than to be freely self-determined, or "autonomous," and that the only way for your will to be free or autonomous is for it to be governed by a law that it gives itself rather than to allow itself to act on whatever mere inclination happens to be alluring at the moment. And because your will would be determined heteronomously rather than autonomously whether it let itself be pushed around by one of your own inclinations or by someone else's inclination (perhaps the latter would be the everyday sense of heteronomy), the only rule that can truly free you (along with everyone else) from heteronomy and truly realize your potential for autonomy is the rule that *no one* should act on any maxim determined by mere inclination, but rather that *all* should act only on a *set* of rational principles consistent with the freedom of each, thus a *system* of maxims that each could freely will. It may seem strange that the freedom of anyone can be realized – preserved and promoted – only if all act on a common system of universalizable maxims, but Kant's idea is that if that is not the case, then someone will always be pushed around by some mere inclination, whether his own or someone else's.[25]

Kant's claim, then, is that the formula of autonomy (FA) follows from FUL/FLN and FHE because treating *every* human being as an *end in itself* requires that *all* of the maxims on which you act could be freely willed by *all* human beings, and that only if all act on such a set of maxims will the freedom of all be preserved and promoted in the way commensurate with the value of each person as an end in itself. As we earlier observed, however, FUL/FLN itself follows from FHE: the requirement to treat humanity whether in yourself or in *anyone* else as an end in itself already requires that each of us act only on maxims that could be freely accepted by everyone else; so we can also see FA as following from FHE alone.

Kant next says that "the concept of every rational being as one who must regard himself as giving universal law through all the maxims of his will . . . leads to a very fruitful concept dependent upon it, namely that of a **realm of ends**," where by such a realm he understands "a systematic union of various rational beings through common laws," or more fully "a whole of all ends in systematic connection (a whole both of rational beings as ends in themselves and of the ends of his own that each may set himself)" (G, 4:433).[26] He then represents the principle "that all maxims from one's own lawgiving are to harmonize with a possible realm of ends, as with a kingdom of nature" (the formula of the realm of ends, or FRE) as the third formulation of the categorical imperative, instead of FA, when he derives it, just like FA, as the "**complete determination** of all maxims" following from the prior requirements that all maxims have "a **form**, which consists in universality," stated in the formula that "maxims must be chosen as if they were to hold as universal laws of nature," and "a **matter**, namely an end," stated in the formula "that a rational being, as an end by its nature and hence as an end in itself, must in every maxim serve as the limiting condition of all merely relative and arbitrary ends" (G, 4:436). The idea behind the derivation of FRE from FUL/FLN and FHE should be immediately clear from our original analysis of what Kant means by treating humanity as an end in itself: it is just that since to treat any human being as an end in itself is both to preserve that person's existence as a being capable of freely setting ends and to promote the realization of those ends both indirectly and directly, to treat all human beings as ends in themselves is both to preserve the existence and freedom of all such beings (or as many as possible) "as a whole" in "systematic connection" and to promote the realization of as many as possible of their freely chosen ends as a "whole" in "systematic connection" – thus, to act only on maxims consistent with a realm of ends and indeed to work toward the realization of such a realm. Once again, of course, since FHE itself already implies FUL/FLN, FRE can be seen as really following from FHE alone.

Kant's moral theory is often described as "non-consequentialist," as if it took no account of the consequences of our actions, but that is clearly misleading. To be sure, his theory gives no intrinsic value to states of affairs or consequences merely because they are desired as objects of inclination, but it greatly values the realization of our freely chosen ends as an expression of our respect for the value of our capacity of free choice itself. The realm of ends as the systematic union both of human beings as ends in themselves and of their freely chosen particular ends would be nothing other than the consequence of everyone's acting on the categorical imperative; and while the idea of humanity as an end in itself may best express the ultimate *source* of value in Kant's moral theory, the idea of all humanity as a kingdom of ends may best express the ultimate *consequences* of acknowledging this value, and thus give us our clearest idea of the *goal* of morality. Similarly, the full force of Kant's idea of the realm of ends is often understated when it is described, for example by John Rawls, simply as the idea of a "moral commonwealth" in which we are all co-equal "legislators . . . of the public moral law."[27] This brings out the first half of Kant's idea – that morality requires us to think of every person as equally free and thus as an equal legislator of the maxims on which we must all act – but does not bring out the second half of Kant's idea – that morality requires us to promote the systematic realization of freely chosen particular ends.[28] Allen Wood recognizes that "Rational beings constitute a *realm* to the extent that their ends form a *system*" in which "these ends are not only mutually consistent, but also harmonious and reciprocally supportive," thus that "the laws of a realm are such that universally following them would result in the agreement and mutual furthering of the ends of all rational beings in a single unified teleological system."[29] In spite of this, he also holds that "FA and FRE are merely general characterizations of the entire system of moral laws, which resist direct application to individual cases,"[30] and that we can only decide individual cases by applying all of FUL/FLN, FHE, FA and FRE to particular cases. The view I have presented here is that FHE tells us in the most basic terms how we must treat people in order to be moral; that FUL/FLN and FA successively bring out the universalistic implications of FHE, FUL/FLN telling us first that we must treat each of our maxims as universally acceptable and FA then telling us that we must treat the system of all of them as such; but that only FRE fully brings out FHE's implication that we must act so that not just human beings but also their freely chosen ends can become a systematic union. It, therefore, provides Kant's most concrete and fullest account of the goals of moral conduct.

Having completed his formulations of the categorical imperative, Kant tells us that he has only analyzed or explicated "the generally received concept of autonomy" and not yet "affirmed its truth" (G, 4:444). In other words, Kant has not in fact given up on the idea of proving that we are subject to the moral law by more than just an appeal to common sense. To do that, however, or to show that "morality is no phantom," he says, "requires a possible **synthetic use of pure practical reason**" (G, 4:445), which he will provide in the final section of the *Groundwork*. This section introduces Kant's theory of the freedom of the will into his moral philosophy, because he holds that we can only realize our freedom by acting in accordance with the moral law but can only act in accordance with the moral law if we are free, thus we must prove that we have freedom of the will if we are to prove both that we ought to obey the moral law and that we can. But Kant's views on the freedom of the will are complex, even paradoxical, and underwent considerable evolution over his career. They deserve a chapter of their own. Before we see how Kant more fully developed his idea of a realm of ends into the form of the system of political and ethical duties that he finally published, a dozen years after the *Groundwork* and at the very end of his career, in the *Metaphysics of Morals*, we must therefore pause to discuss Kant's views on the freedom of the will and two other "postulates of pure practical reason" that he often links to that topic, namely the postulates of immortality and the existence of God.

SUMMARY

Kant begins his presentation of his normative ethics in both the *Groundwork* and the *Critique of Practical Reason*, and thus his account of autonomy in its practical sense, with the formulation of the categorical imperative that we must act only on maxims that we could also will to be acted upon by everyone else. In the *Groundwork*, he then goes on to formulate the principles that we should act only on maxims that treat humanity in both ourselves and others as an end in itself of unconditional value, never merely as a means, that we should act only on maxims that could be universally legislated within a consistent system of maxims, and that we should act so as to bring about a realm of ends, in which each human being is treated as an end in him- or herself and his or her freely chosen ends are promoted to the extent that so doing is consistent with treating each as an end in him- or herself. I have argued here that Kant's most fundamental normative notion is the idea of treating humanity as an end in itself, that is, treating each human being as an autonomous agent capable of setting his or her ends both freely and yet in harmony with others, and that the other formulations of the categorical imperative as well as Kant's examples of the chief classes of moral duties can all be derived from this basic idea. Now we are to see how Kant attempts to prove that this conception of the requirements of morality is binding on us.

FURTHER READING

Not surprisingly, the literature on Kant's moral philosophy is very extensive. I begin with four translations of the *Groundwork* that include valuable supplementary material:

Groundwork for the Metaphysics of Morals, trans. Thomas K. Abbott, edited by Lara Denis (Peterborough, ONT: Broadview, 2005) (updates an 1873 translation and includes supplementary texts as well as responses from Fichte, Schiller, Hegel, and Henry Sidgwick).

Groundwork of the Metaphysic of Morals, ed. Lawrence Pasternack (London and New York: Routledge, 2002) (presents the classical translation by H.J. Paton (1948) and papers, several cited in this chapter, by Thomas E. Hill, Jr., Christine Korsgaard, Onora O'Neill, Henry Allison, Andrews Reath, and Hud Hudson).

Groundwork for the Metaphysics of Morals, trans. Arnulf Zweig, ed. Thomas E. Hill, Jr., and
    Arnulf Zweig (Oxford: Oxford University Press, 2002) (contains a detailed
    commentary and analysis).
Groundwork for the Metaphysics of Morals, ed. and trans. Allen W. Wood (New Haven, CT:
    Yale University Press, 2002) (adds essays by Marcia Baron, Shelly Kagan, J.B.
    Schneewind, and Wood).

Commentaries on the *Groundwork* include the following. Paton offers a sympathetic
commentary which originated contemporary discussions of the formulations of
the categorical imperative, while Williams is a briefer study building upon Paton's
work. Wolff presents a more critical commentary. Beck is the only work devoted to
Kant's second *Critique* but discusses it with reference to the whole range of Kant's
writings. Schönecker and Wood is the most incisive commentary of all, but unfortunately has not been translated into English.

Lewis White Beck, *A Commentary on Kant's Critique of Practical Reason* (Chicago: Univer-
    sity of Chicago Press, 1960).
H.J. Paton, *The Categorical Imperative: A Study in Kant's Moral Philosophy* (London:
    Hutchinson, 1947).
Dieter Schönecker and Allen W. Wood, *Kants "Grundlegung zur Metaphysik der Sitten": Ein
    einführender Kommentar* (Paderborn: Schöningh, 2002).
T.C. Williams, *The Concept of the Categorical Imperative: A Study of the Place of the Categorical
    Imperative in Kant's Ethical Theory* (Oxford: Clarendon Press, 1968).
Robert Paul Wolff, *The Autonomy of Reason: A Commentary on Kant's Groundwork of the Meta-
    physic of Morals* (New York: Harper & Row, 1973).
Other crucial works on Kant's ethics that include significant analyses of the topics of
    this chapter, the categorical imperative and its formulations and applications,
    include the following.

Aune contains detailed discussion of Kant's formulations of the categorical
imperative in the *Groundwork* and then briefer discussions of Kant's applications of the
categorical imperative in the later *Metaphysics of Morals*. Baron defends Kant's conception of duty from objections that it is too demanding or not sufficiently demanding.
Guyer (2000) contains articles on the strategy and contents of the *Groundwork* with
articles on the development of Kant's moral philosophy and its applications in Kant's
political philosophy and philosophies of history and religion, while his (2005) adds
articles on Kant's concept of autonomy, the place of ends in Kant's moral philosophy,
and the place of Kant's practical philosophy in his whole philosophical system.
Herman discusses issues in the application of the categorical imperative. The three
works by Hill (1992, 2000, 2002) collect the author's seminal articles on many
issues in Kant's moral and political philosophy from three decades. Korsgaard
(1996a) contains the author's important articles on the formulae of universal law
and of humanity, as well as others; it can be read in conjunction with her (1996b)
text, a development of her own Kant-inspired moral theory, with comments by
O'Neill, G.A. Cohen, Raymond Geuss, Thomas Nagel, and Bernard Williams. Rawls
combines an extended and lucid study of Kant's ethics, naturally reflecting some of

the methodological and substantive assumptions of the renowned author of *A Theory of Justice*, with shorter treatments of Hume, Leibniz, and Hegel, while Moore builds an interpretation of Kant's moral and religious philosophy on the basis of a conception of rationality rather than of autonomy. Finally, Wood combines a detailed analysis of the formulations of the categorical imperative with a discussion of the anthropological aspect of Kant's ethics.

Bruce Aune, *Kant's Theory of Morals* (Princeton, NJ: Princeton University Press, 1979).

Marcia W. Baron, *Kantian Ethics Almost without Apology* (Ithaca, NY: Cornell University Press, 1995).

Paul Guyer, *Kant on Freedom, Law, and Happiness* (Cambridge: Cambridge University Press, 2000).

——*Kant's System of Nature and Freedom* (Oxford: Clarendon Press, 2005).

Barbara Herman, *The Practice of Moral Judgment* (Cambridge, MA: Harvard University Press, 1993).

Thomas E. Hill, Jr., *Dignity and Practical Reason in Kant's Moral Theory* (Ithaca, NY: Cornell University Press, 1992).

——*Respect, Pluralism, and Justice: Kantian Perspectives* (Oxford: Oxford University Press, 2000).

——*Human Welfare and Moral Worth: Kantian Perspectives* (Oxford: Clarendon Press, 2002).

Samuel J. Kerstein, *Kant's Search for the Supreme Principle of Morality* (Cambridge: Cambridge University Press, 2002) (a study of the derivation of the categorical imperative).

Christine M. Korsgaard, *Creating the Kingdom of Ends* (Cambridge: Cambridge University Press, 1996a).

——*The Sources of Normativity*, ed. Onora O'Neill (Cambridge: Cambridge University Press, 1996b).

A.W. Moore, *Noble in Reason, Infinite in Faculty: Themes and Variations in Kant's Moral and Political Philosophy* (New York and London: Routledge, 2003).

Onora O'Neill (Nell), *Acting on Principle: An Essay on Kantian Ethics* (New York: Columbia University Press, 1975) (a path-breaking analysis of the categorical imperative).

——*Constructions of Reason: Explorations of Kant's Practical Philosophy* (Cambridge: Cambridge University Press, 1989) (containing articles continuing O'Neill's analysis of the categorical imperative).

——*Bounds of Justice* (Cambridge: Cambridge University Press, 2000) (arguing for the relevance of Kant's ethics to contemporary moral debates).

John Rawls, *Lectures on the History of Moral Philosophy*, ed. Barbara Herman (Cambridge, MA: Harvard University Press, 2000).

Philip Stratton-Lake, *Kant, Duty, and Moral Worth* (London and New York: Routledge, 2000) (a detailed study of Kant's idea of acting from and not merely in conformity to duty).

Allen W. Wood, *Kant's Ethical Thought* (Cambridge: Cambridge University Press, 1999).

Six

Freedom, Immortality, and God
The presuppositions of morality

In 1788, just three years after the *Groundwork of the Metaphysics of Morals* and one year after the publication of a substantially revised second edition of the *Critique of Pure Reason*, Kant published a second major work on the foundations of morality, the *Critique of Practical Reason*. He had apparently not foreseen the need for a second critique when he first wrote the *Critique of Pure Reason* – after all, he had not restricted it to a "Critique of Pure Theoretical Reason" – nor when he wrote the *Groundwork* – for its third and final section was already supposed to include a "critique of pure practical reason." But two things may have made a second critique seem necessary. First, a major debate over the rationality of faith that erupted in 1783 between F. H. Jacobi and Moses Mendelssohn, the so-called "Pantheism controversy," may have pushed Kant toward a restatement of his own theory of the "postulates of pure practical reason" as the solution to this issue, first in the 1786 essay "What does it mean to orient oneself in thought?" and then in the "Dialectic" of a new *Critique of Practical Reason*.[1] Second, Kant may have become dissatisfied with his treatment of freedom of the will in the *Groundwork*, thought about revising his treatment of that subject in the new edition of the *Critique of Pure Reason*, but realized that he had so much more to say on free will and its relation to the moral law that he needed to write an altogether new book. Many commentators have stressed the first of these motivations, but the fact that so much of the first part of the new *Critique* is devoted to the proof of the existence of freedom of the will from our consciousness of our obligation under the moral law and then to the reconciliation of freedom of the will with determinism through transcendental idealism suggests that the latter motivation may have been more important for Kant.

Kant begins the Preface to the new work by explaining why, unlike the third section of the *Groundwork*, it is not called a critique of *pure* practical reason, but a critique of practical reason in general. The reason is that this book is meant to establish that there is such a thing as pure practical reason, governed by an "apodictic law of practical reason" which is nothing other than the moral law analyzed in the *Groundwork*, but that to do this the new book must "criticize reason's entire **practical faculty**" in order to show that practical reason, that is, our ability to determine our actions by our reason, is not limited to *empirical* practical reason (CPracR, 5:3) even though the *theoretical* use of reason is limited by the limits of our empirical sensibility.[2] In particular, the possibility of pure practical reason means that we are not confined to the merely instrumental use of reason, that is, to using practical reason only in order to figure out the most effective way to satisfy our desires, which are not themselves given by reason. David Hume had famously insisted that the role of our reason is restricted in just this way when he wrote that "Reason is, and ought only to be the slave of the passions, and can never pretend to any other office than to serve and obey them."[3] So just as a central argument of Kant's *Critique of Pure Reason* was that Hume had seriously underestimated theoretical reason's basis for its commitment to the principle that every event has a cause, so the *Critique of Practical Reason* is meant to argue that his instrumental conception of practical reason seriously underestimates our freedom to choose to act in accordance with the moral law given by pure reason rather than being determined by mere inclination or "passion."

The first task for the second *Critique*, then, is to show that the "reality" of the "concept of freedom" is proved by an "apodictic law of practical reason," that is, the moral law itself. But Kant also says that this concept of freedom

> constitutes the **keystone** of the whole structure of a system of pure reason, even of speculative reason; and all other concepts (those of God and immortality), which as mere ideas remain without support in the latter, now attach themselves to this concept and with it and by means of it get stability and objective reality, that is, their **possibility** is **proved** by this: that freedom is real, for this idea reveals itself through the moral law.
>
> (CPracR, 5:3–4)

Kant calls our beliefs in the existence of freedom, immortality, and God the "postulates of pure practical reason," "not theoretical dogmas but **presuppositions** having a necessarily practical reference," which "do not extend speculative cognition" but "give objective reality to the ideas of speculative reason in **general** (by means of their reference to what is practical)" (5:132). But he also differentiates among these postulates, saying that "among all the ideas of speculative reason freedom is . . . the only one the possibility of which we **know** *a priori* . . . because it is the condition of the moral law, which we do know," while the "ideas of **God** and **immortality** . . . are not conditions of the moral law but only conditions of the necessary object of a will determined by this law" (5:4). What he means by this is that in order for us to believe that we are bound by the moral law at all, we must believe that we are free to act in accordance with it, but that once we fully understand what the moral law commands us to achieve – what Kant calls the "highest good," a "whole in which the greatest happiness is represented as connected in the most exact proportion with the greatest degree of moral perfection (possible in creatures)" (5:129–30) – then we will also see that we must believe in the existence of personal immortality and God.

The latter claim is certainly surprising. As we saw in the last chapter, in the *Groundwork* Kant argued that morality ultimately commands us to realize a *realm of ends*, in which all people are treated as ends in themselves and in which therefore a consistent system of their particular ends is also promoted, and this seemed to be a result that could at least in principle be achieved by ordinary human beings, within ordinary human life spans, without any need for God or immortality. So we will certainly have to ask why Kant believes that the "object" of morality requires the presuppositions of God and immortality. But before we can consider that question, we must examine Kant's position on the freedom of the will. For there seems to be a major reversal of position between the *Groundwork* and the *Critique of Practical Reason*: in the first work, Kant seemed to think that after analyzing its content he still needed to prove that the moral law really applies to us, and that he could prove that by proving that we have free will, while in the later work Kant seems to think that he can prove the reality of free will as a presupposition of the "apodictic" or incontrovertible fact that we are obligated by the moral law, which itself is not capable of any proof. And in addition to this issue about just what he is trying to prove, there is also a problem created by Kant's close connection of freedom with action in accordance with the moral law in both the *Groundwork* and the second *Critique*: namely, if truly free action is action performed in accordance with the moral law, how can anyone be free and yet perform *evil* actions, thus how can anyone be responsible for evil deeds? Only in yet another work, namely *Religion within the Boundaries of Mere*

Reason (1793), does Kant tackle this problem and thus develop his final position on the relation between freedom and the moral law.

The agenda for this chapter is therefore twofold. First, we must review the complex development of Kant's position on the freedom of the will, considering his attempts both to prove our obligation under the moral law and to explain the possibility of evil. Then we must examine Kant's further postulates of practical reason, seeing why he thinks that the rationality of attempting to realize the object of morality requires belief in God and immortality, and just what he means by such belief.

THE MORAL LAW AND FREEDOM OF THE WILL

The problem of freedom of the will and moral responsibility fascinated Kant throughout his life, although only in his central works on moral philosophy did he tie this traditional problem to the problem of validating the moral law itself. For our purposes here, we can divide Kant's thought on freedom of the will into five phases: (1) his earliest position, in which he rejects any alternative to determinism and interprets free human actions simply as those that have internal rather than external causes; (2) the position of the 1781 *Critique of Pure Reason*, in which he makes metaphysical room for the possibility of free human actions not dictated by deterministic laws of nature, but also argues that we cannot prove the existence of such free actions; (3) the position of the 1785 *Groundwork*, in which Kant argues that we can after all prove the existence of human freedom and thereby also prove that the moral law applies to us, neither just assuming the latter as a matter of common sense nor merely proving it analytically from the concept of a rational being while leaving it open whether it binds us as actual human beings; (4) the position of the 1788 *Critique of Practical Reason*, which argues that we cannot prove the validity of the moral law from a prior proof of the freedom of our will, but rather that we can prove the freedom of our will from the indisputable fact of our obligation under the moral law; and, finally, (5) the position of the 1793 *Religion*, in which Kant is no longer concerned with proving the existence of free will but rather with showing that its existence implies the inescapable possibility of human evil but equally the concomitantly indestructible possibility of human conversion to goodness.

Kant's earliest position on freedom of the will

Kant's earliest publication in philosophy, the 1755 dissertation *A New Elucidation of the First Principles of Metaphysical Cognition*, was devoted to improving upon the Leibnizian and Wolffian proofs of the principle of sufficient reason or as Kant called it "determining ground," but to then defending the Leibnizian reconciliation of the principle of sufficient reason with a conception of the freedom of the will. Kant's refinement of the proof of the principle of sufficient reason need not concern us here; our concern is only with Kant's defense of the principle itself from the attack that this principle undermines human freedom and moral responsibility because if

> whatever happens can only happen if it has an antecedently determining ground, it follows that **whatever does not happen could not happen either** . . . And thus, by tracing one's way along the inexorable change of events which, as Chrysippus says, once and for all snakes its way along and weaves its path through the eternal series of consequences, one eventually arrives at the first state of the world.
>
> (NE, 1:399)[4]

This must place responsibility for any human deed there rather than in a free choice of the merely apparent agent of that deed. As Kant indicates, this objection to determinism goes back to antiquity, but Kant takes up his cudgel against the Pietist philosopher Christian August Crusius, who had brought this traditional objection against Leibniz and especially against Leibniz's rationalist heir Christian Wolff.[5] Kant presents Crusius as endorsing the "indifference of equilibrium," or the view more standardly known as the "liberty of indifference," that is, the idea that a person is truly free only when all the antecedent determinants of his character and circumstances nevertheless "leave him in a state of indifference relative to both alternatives" in some particular action, so that his action will not be determined by any of those antecedent conditions which are now no longer in his control. Kant objects that this means that a person has no control of his actions at all, so that even if you had previously made the strongest possible commitment to do what is right, you could still "immediately slide in the direction of what is less good, for the grounds which solicit you do not determine you" (NE, 1:402). Indeterminism leaves no room for a conception of responsibility at all, Kant argues, so any basis for responsibility must be compatible with determinism.[6] Like Leibniz,[7] Kant then proposes that "those things which happen through the will of beings endowed with understanding and the spontaneous power itself of self-determination," thus those actions for which people are properly held responsible, "obviously issue from an inner principle, from conscious desires and from a choice of one of the alternatives according to the freedom of the power of choice" (NE, 1:404). On this account, freedom exists simply when the power of choice **"is determined in conformity with the representation of what is best"** rather than by any external factor (NE, 1:402). What makes people free is simply that they act in accordance with their own conceptions of what is best rather than being pushed around by any forces outside of themselves. Those who act in accordance with such a representation are free even if their actions are in fact determined by antecedent conditions and thus they could not have chosen to act otherwise than they did at the time of their actions.

Freedom in the first *Critique*

By the time he wrote the *Critique of Pure Reason*, however, Kant had clearly become dissatisfied with this position, and used the metaphysics of transcendental idealism, itself derived from assumptions about space and time having nothing to do with the problem of free will, to show that the opposition between indeterminism and determinism assumed in the *New Elucidation* and in every other contemporary treatment of free will is too simple.

Kant's argument in the first *Critique* that space and time are characteristic of the appearances of things to us but not of those things as they are in themselves, that our intuitions of those appearances yield knowledge only when they are subsumed under concepts structured in accordance with the pure concepts of the understanding, and that those categories in turn yield knowledge only when they are applied to our intuitions, culminated in the justification but also the restriction of the principle of sufficient reason or universal law of causation to appearances: "Thus the principle of sufficient reason is the ground of possible experience, namely the objective cognition of appearances with regard to their relation in the successive series of time" (A 201 / B 246). This does not mean that the logical relation of ground and consequence applies only to objects as they appear in time (and space), because that logical relation structures any hypothetical judgment about any subject-matter we can even consider; but the schematization of that logical relation into the relation of cause and effect has an essential reference to things in time – the "schema of the cause and of the causality of a thing in general . . . consists in the succession of the manifold insofar as it is subject to a rule" (A 144 / B 183) – and the principle that every event has a cause has been proven to apply to all but only appearances of objects in time. Thus Kant's transcendental idealism opened the possibility that we do not have to and indeed cannot think of causation in its usual sense as applying to things as they are in themselves, although we can still think of such things as grounds and consequences in some other, unspecified sense.

This possibility of conceiving even if not of knowing some alternative to the ordinary conception of thinking of all consequences as the subsequent effects of antecedent causes is what Kant exploited in order to resolve the third antinomy of pure reason.[8] This was the conflict between the thesis that "Causality in accordance with laws of nature is not the only one from which all the appearances of the world can be derived," for it "is also necessary to assume another causality through freedom in order to explain them," and the antithesis that "There is no freedom, but everything in the world happens solely in accordance with laws of nature" (A 444–5/B 472–3). While such contradictory theses as that the world is both finite and infinite in extent could not both be true, because both refer to the spatial extent of the world but make incompatible claims about it, the theses that there is a causality through freedom that is not in accordance with the laws of nature yet that everything in the world happens in accordance with laws of nature could both be true, because while the latter clearly refers to the world of appearances, the former need not be so understood, but can instead be taken to refer to the world of things in themselves. Transcendental idealism's distinction between appearance and the in-itself thus opens up at least the possibility of a causality through freedom that is an exception to the deterministic causal laws of nature.

In the first instance, Kant supposes, we need to be able to conceive of an act of freedom that is not itself determined by a temporally antecedent cause only in order "to make comprehensible an origin of the world," in other words, a first act of creation from which all further consequences would then flow as "a result of merely natural laws." But once we have opened up the logical possibility of a kind of action that is not determined by causal laws of nature, then

> we are permitted also to allow that in the course of the world different series may begin on their own as far as their causality is concerned, and to ascribe to the substances in those series the faculty of acting from freedom
>
> (A 448–50/B 476–8)

In other words, Kant argues that once we have made conceptual space for God's free creation of the world, we also have conceptual space for the free initiation of series of events by human beings (while sidestepping all of the traditional arguments that God's freedom itself might preclude human freedom, against which Leibniz, for example, had so mightily struggled).[9] Of course, we cannot think of acts of freedom, whether divine or human, as breaches or gaps in the causal order of appearances, for that would be inconsistent with the universal validity of the principle of causation for appearances, which has already been proven. We must instead suppose that at the level of appearances events succeed one another smoothly in accordance with deterministic causal laws, but yet that the phenomenal world itself is also the expression of noumenally free choices, and would have been different if those noumenal choices had been different. Kant puts this point by saying that we must think of willed actions as reflecting both the "empirical character" of their agents, "through which ... actions, as appearances, would stand through and through in connection with other appearances in accordance with constant natural laws, from which, as their conditions, they could be derived," but also the "intelligible character" of their agents, through which they are indeed "the cause of those actions as appearances, but which does not stand under any conditions of sensibility and is not itself appearance" (A 539 / B 567).[10] Thus Kant writes:

> Now even if one believes the action to be determined by [natural] causes, one nonetheless blames the agent, and not on account of his unhappy natural temper, not on account of the circumstances influencing him, not even on account of the life he has led previously; for one presupposes that it can be entirely set aside how that life was constituted, and that the series of conditions that transpired might not have been, but rather that this deed could be regarded as entirely unconditioned in regard to the previous state, as though with that act the agent had started a series of consequences entirely from himself. ... the action is ascribed to the agent's intelligible character.
>
> (CPuR, A 555 / B 583)

Because of the distinction between noumena and phenomena, things in themselves and their temporal, causally determined appearances, we can think that even though the temporal world of appearances including our own actions is fully determined by causal laws, if we had chosen differently at the noumenal level that phenomenal world would also have been different, indeed even if that means that some of its laws would have been different.

With this analysis, Kant has ended up combining the Leibnizian[11] and Crusian conceptions of freedom that he had opposed in 1755: while our actions must transpire in accordance with exceptionless causal laws that may be traced back long before our individual existences, that is true only at the phenomenal level; at the noumenal level there may be free choices that cannot be explained in terms of any antecedent conditions, because the very idea of explanation by means of antecedent conditions is itself a temporal notion that does not apply to the noumenal realm. To be sure, this means that noumenal choices are ultimately inexplicable, the very result that Kant had so strongly objected to in Crusius; but now Kant is willing to accept that result as the price of the possibility of genuine freedom, and even to argue that this makes noumenal freedom no worse off than phenomenal determinism, because although we can prove *that* we must conceive of the phenomenal world in causal terms we really cannot explain *why* we are so constituted as to have to experience objects in this way. "How such a faculty" of noumenal or as he also calls it transcendental freedom "is possible is not so necessary to answer," Kant insists, "since with causality in accordance with natural laws we likewise have to be satis-fied with the *a priori* cognition that such a thing must be presupposed, even though we do not in any way comprehend how it is possible for one exis-tence to be posited through another existence" (A 448 / B 476). The idea that we must posit noumenal or transcendental freedom but can never explain why we have chosen to exercise our noumenal freedom in one way rather than another because all explanation takes place at the phenom-enal level will remain a central theme in Kant's continuing treatment of freedom of the will, although he will not fully understand its implications until *Religion within the Boundaries of Mere Reason.*

Of course, all that Kant has said thus far is that transcendental idealism makes freedom of the will *possible*; nothing that has been said thus far proves it to be *actual*. Kant insists upon this; indeed, he insists that transcen-dental idealism by itself does not even establish the *real* possibility of genuine freedom of the will, but only its *logical* possibility, that is, the possibility of forming a non-contradictory conception of it, because "from mere concepts *a priori* we cannot cognize anything about the possibility of any real ground or any causality." He claims that all that he has thus far established is that "nature at least **does not conflict with** causality through freedom" (A 558 / B 586). Since the existence of freedom of the will obvi-ously cannot be proven empirically, because the empirical realm is essentially deterministic, nor can it be proven *a priori* from theoretical concepts, apparently any proof of the reality of the freedom of the will must take place outside of the theoretical realm altogether.

This would seem to imply that the freedom of the will can be proven only from practical grounds, as a necessary presupposition of morality. This is the position that Kant will adopt in the second edition of the Critique of Pure Reason (see B xxviii–xxxi), in the Critique of Practical Reason which grew out of his revisions for the second edition of the first Critique, and in all of his subsequent writings. But it is not so clear that he confined himself to this position in the third section of the Groundwork, written between the two editions of the first Critique, where he ultimately seems to argue that we can prove that we are obligated under the moral law only by first proving, apparently on purely theoretical grounds, that we have freedom of the will.

Freedom in *Groundwork* III

Remember that Kant's stance at the end of the second section of the Groundwork is that he has derived the form and content of the moral law from analysis of both the "generally received concept of morality" and the philosophical concepts of a categorical imperative and the will of a rational being, but that he has yet to show that it is valid for us, thus that we are actually bound by the categorical imperative (G, 4:445). The natural next step for him to take should therefore be to prove that we are rational beings for whom the moral law necessarily holds.[12] That is essentially what he attempts to do, but through an argument that is meant to show, first, that the moral law is necessarily the law of a free will and only then that we are rational beings, next, that our rationality implies the freedom of our will, and therefore, finally, that our rationality implies our subjection to the moral law. This argument creates a famous problem: if our freedom implies that we not merely should but do act in accordance with the moral law, then the only explanation for our immoral acts is that in performing them we were not really free after all – and thus should not be held responsible for them. Kant would not address the problem until the Religion within the Boundaries of Mere Reason in 1793,[13] although other problems with the argument of the Groundwork would already force Kant radically to reconceive the relation between the moral law and freedom of the will in the Critique of Practical Reason in 1788.

The argument of Groundwork III is notoriously controversial, and our brief treatment of it here will have to overlook some details.[14] Kant begins by stating that we may form a *negative* conception of the freedom of the will as its freedom from determination by "alien causes" operating in accordance with mere "natural necessity," but that we must also form a *positive* conception of the law *by means of which* the will frees itself from such alien causes – for freedom, "although it is not a property of the will in accordance with natural laws, is not for that reason lawless, but must instead be a causality in accordance with immutable laws but of a special kind" (G, 4:446). He then argues that since "Natural necessity was a heteronomy of efficient causes," or a determination of the will by something external to itself, freedom of the will can be positively understood only as "autonomy, that is, the will's being a law to itself." But of course the only way that the will can be a law to itself is "to act on no other maxim than that which can also have as object itself as a universal law" – to act on any other maxim will be to subject the will to some alien, heteronomous cause, and thus to deprive it of its freedom. But that is just the categorical imperative, "hence a free will and a will under moral laws are one and the same" (G, 4:447).

This means that the will is free and autonomous if and only if it is governed by the moral law: autonomy is neither lawlessness nor subjection to mere laws of nature, but is achieved only by adherence to the moral law, which as we saw in the previous chapter is what preserves freedom beyond a single instance of choice. Given that freedom of the will (in any sustained sense) and the moral law thus imply each other,[15] we could attempt to prove that either one applies to us by proving that the other one does: we could in principle prove that we have a free will by proving that we are subject to the moral law, or prove that we are subject to the moral law by proving that we have free will. But since Kant takes his task at this point in the *Groundwork* to be to prove that the moral law really does apply to us, he obviously chooses the second option: he will now attempt to prove that freedom of the will is not just a conceptual possibility, as had already been established in the *Critique of Pure Reason* with the assistance of transcendental idealism, but a reality. Thereby the moral law, which has thus far been proven only to apply to any rational will, will be shown to apply to us.

Here is where things become tricky. Kant first says that:

> every being that cannot act otherwise than **under the idea of freedom** is just because of that really free in a practical respect, that is, all laws that are inseparably bound up with freedom hold for him just as if his will had been validly pronounced free.
>
> (G, 4:448)

This has often been taken to mean that if you think of yourself as acting freely then you must also attempt to guide your action by a conception of what is best or right to do rather than merely predicting what you might do in accordance with some natural law, which would not be to act at all. Thus if you even think of yourself as free, you will attempt to make your action comply with the moral law.[16] This may be true, but clearly it is not enough for Kant: he wants us to be able to prove to ourselves that we really *are* free, because he fears that if we cannot do this then our resolve to do what is right could be undermined by the thought that our actions are already determined by factors other than the moral law, so that there is no use in trying very hard to conform to the moral law. So Kant offers the following argument. First, he says that it takes "no subtle reflection" to distinguish between appearances and things in themselves, or the "world of sense" and the "world of understanding" (G, 4:451) – even though this might come as a surprise to anyone who has struggled through the first *Critique*! Further, Kant claims that we apply this inescapable distinction to ourselves as well as other objects: "Even as to himself, the human being cannot claim to cognize what he is in himself through the cognizance he has by inner sensation." So beyond his mere representations of appearance, every human being "must necessarily assume something else lying at their basis, namely his I as it may be constituted in itself." But, Kant assumes, one must have *some* way of conceiving of himself as he really is. And then he asserts, "Now, a human being really finds in himself a capacity by which he distinguishes himself from all other things, even from himself insofar as he is affected by objects, and that is **reason**" (G, 4:452). This means that "as belonging to the intelligible world," every human being stands under "laws which, being independent of nature, are not empirical but grounded in reason." But what law is grounded only in reason? Clearly, only the moral law, which says that the law for the autonomous will should not include anything empirical but instead requires only conformity of maxims with the form of universal law. Thus Kant argues that we must recognize the difference between our phenomenal and our noumenal selves, that our noumenal selves must be governed by a law different from any laws of empirical nature, and that such a law can only be the moral law: our noumenal selves must therefore be both free and governed by the moral law.

Even before we worry about the substantive issue of the possibility of free but immoral actions, there are clearly procedural difficulties with this argument. For not only does the argument presuppose the transcendental idealist distinction between phenomena and noumena in order to explain the possibility of freedom of the will, which the *Critique of Pure Reason* had already done; it now supposes that the fact of our freedom and thus our subjection to the moral law can be proven merely from this distinction, which the first *Critique* had clearly not supposed. How does transcendental idealism suddenly yield this positive result? Apparently only by taking what distinguishes us from other things *in the phenomenal world*, namely our rationality, and assuming that *we can know* that this is *more than a mere appearance*, but something that is true of us in the noumenal world. But that simply seems to assume what the first *Critique* had denied, namely that we can have genuine *knowledge* and not just a mere *conception* of how something really is rather than how it appears. Kant offers no justification for this sudden departure from the epistemological constraint that is central to the entire argument of the first *Critique* (although he may also have violated this constraint there too, when he suggests that pure apperception can give us positive insight into our intelligible character; see CPuR, A 546–7/B 574–5).[17]

Freedom in the *Critique of Practical Reason*

Kant's attempt to prove that we have freedom of the will and then to derive our obligation under the categorical imperative clearly violates the most fundamental rule of his own epistemology. Kant must quickly have realized this, for without acknowledging that he is doing so, he reverses the direction of his argument in the second *Critique*, and argues precisely that because we cannot give any theoretical proof of the freedom of our will at all, we can only take our awareness of our obligation under the moral law *as a given* and infer the freedom of our will from that. He thus gives up entirely on the project of proving that the moral law is valid, returning to the presumption of the first section of the *Groundwork* that this is a matter of common sense, and instead uses the validity of the moral law to prove the freedom of our will.[18]

As in the *Groundwork*, in the *Critique of Practical Reason* Kant argues from the premise that "freedom and unconditional practical law reciprocally imply each other." The basis for this claim is that if the moral law requires the determination of the will by "the mere form of a law" independent of any inclinations toward the object of an action, then only a will that can be determined independently of the "natural law for appearances" (5:28) could act on such a law, while conversely if a free will is one that must be "independent of empirical conditions" but "must nevertheless be determinable" by some law, then "the lawgiving form, insofar as this is contained in the maxim, is therefore the only thing that can constitute a determining ground of the will" (5:29). Note that Kant makes two assumptions here, both of which can be questioned: first, he assumes that the only kind of "natural" determination of the will is determination by mere inclinations, so that determination of the will by anything other than mere inclinations requires that the will is determined in a manner beyond the reach of nature altogether; and second, he assumes that even a will that is beyond the reach of determination by merely natural laws of inclination must still be determined by some law, which by an argument from elimination can only be the moral law. This second assumption is of course consistent with Kant's original rejection of the liberty of indifference, that is, the idea that the free will is a will not determined in any lawlike fashion whatever, but will continue to cause a problem about the very possibility of immoral actions. Kant's first assumption here precludes any naturalistic interpretation of freedom and responsibility, and that is to say the least a debatable move.

Nevertheless, himself satisfied that the will can be free if and only if it is determined by the moral law, Kant now reverses his argument from the *Groundwork*. He argues that we cannot directly prove the freedom of our will, because we cannot have empirical or indeed any theoretical evidence for that: as he has argued in the first *Critique*, the unity of our experience and our theoretical view of the world is predicated on the principle that every event has its antecedent cause. "It is therefore the **moral law**, of which we become immediately conscious (as soon as we draw up maxims of the will for ourselves) that first offers itself to us and . . . leads directly to the concept of freedom" (5:29–30). This claim again rests on two assumptions. First, Kant assumes that whenever we reflect on what we should do in some circumstance – what maxim we should adopt – we in fact, whether we do so consciously or not, test our maxim against the standard of rationality and therefore of morality: he is confident that

> One need only analyze the judgment that people pass on the lawfulness of their actions in order to find that, whatever inclination may say to the contrary, their reason, incorruptible and self-constrained, always holds the maxim of the will in an action up to the pure will, that is, to itself inasmuch as it regards itself as *a priori* practical.
>
> (5:32)

Here Kant essentially reverts to the assertion of the first section of the *Groundwork* that knowledge of the moral law is common even if tacit: we may not consciously vocalize the categorical imperative every time we consider acting (let alone run through all three or five of its formulations!), but in fact we always test our proposed maxims by this standard

or, more plausibly, at least know that we *can* and *should* do so. Our immediate awareness of the moral law and its obligatory status is what Kant calls
the "fact of reason":

> Consciousness of this fundamental law may be called a fact of reason
> because one cannot reason it out from antecedent data of reason . . . and
> because it instead forces itself upon us of itself as a synthetic *a priori*
> proposition that is not based on any intuition.
>
> (5:31)

In the end, Kant supposes that the very existence of our most fundamental
norm is simply indemonstrable – it cannot be derived from any more
fundamental theoretical proposition, because then it would not be normative, but neither can it be derived from any more fundamental normative
proposition, because then it would not be fundamental – but is nevertheless indubitable.[19]

Kant's second assumption in the argument from our consciousness of
the moral law to the freedom of our will is the premise that we can only
be obligated to do something that it is possible for us to do, or that a
genuine *ought* implies *can*. Kant does not attempt to derive this premise by
means of any argument from further antecedent premises either, but rather
tries to persuade us of it by a striking argument from examples:

> Suppose someone asserts of his lustful inclinations that, when the desired
> object and the opportunity are present, it is quite irresistible to him; ask
> him whether, if . . . he would be hanged . . . immediately after gratifying
> his lust, he would not then control his inclination. One need not conjecture
> very long what he would reply. But ask him whether, if his prince
> demanded, on pain of the same immediate execution, that he give false
> testimony against an honorable man . . . , he would consider it possible to
> overcome his love of life, however great it may be. He would perhaps not
> venture to assert whether he would do it or not, but he must admit without
> hesitation that it would be possible for him. He judges, therefore, that he
> can do something because he is aware that he ought to do it, and
> cognizes freedom within him, which, without the moral law, would have
> remained unknown to him.
>
> (5:30)

We often make excuses for our behavior by claiming that our inclinations
are irresistible, but, Kant is claiming, we do not really believe this. We

know that we could resist a momentary gratification, no matter how desirable, if our life were at stake, and in fact we know that we can always choose to do what is right, even at the greatest cost to ourselves. But while the first case is one in which we can in fact pit a greater inclination against a lesser one – the love of life versus some lesser desire – the second case is one in which we must be able to overcome all possible inclinations, even the love of life itself. The only way this could happen is if we can determine our will independently of inclination altogether, thus if we have freedom of the will. Our awareness of our moral obligation combined with our belief that we can only be obligated to do what we can do – which may also be a fundamental yet indemonstrable normative premise, an expression of our basic view that it is only fair to hold people responsible for what they freely do – together imply that we are always free to do what the moral law requires.[20]

Kant's remark that the man threatened with death if he will not bear false witness does not know whether he will resist even though he knows that he *could* might well suggest that he now clearly recognizes that the moral law cannot be the *causal* law of our free will, that is, that the moral law cannot *necessarily* determine the will, thereby making free but immoral choices impossible. But while Kant could have come to this recognition in the *Critique of Practical Reason* – his new method of argument would certainly allow it, for it depends on the premise that ought implies *can*, not that ought implies *does* – he does not seem to have done so. On the contrary, there are numerous passages in the second *Critique* that suggest that, as in the *Groundwork*, Kant still conceives of the moral law as the causal law of the noumenal will. His continued acceptance of this conception is evident even in his original statement that freedom of the will implies the moral law, for what he says there is that the "lawgiving form" required by the moral law is the "only thing that can constitute a determining ground of the will" (5:29). Subsequently he says that once the determination of the will by inclinations which is characteristic of the sensible world has been excluded from the noumenal world, "Pure practical reason now fills this vacant place with a determinate law of causality in an intelligible world (with freedom), namely the moral law" (5:49). And later on he also says that

> if one had insight into the possibility of freedom as an efficient cause, one would also have insight into not merely the possibility but even the necessity of the moral law as the supreme practical law of rational beings, to whom one attributes freedom of the causality of their will.
>
> (5:93)

But if the moral law is the necessary, *causal* law of the noumenal will, then there is no possibility that the free will should ever choose to oppose or violate the moral law. The possibility of freely chosen immoral action remains inconceivable.

Even though Kant spends many pages in the second *Critique* expanding upon the first *Critique*'s reconciliation of phenomenal determinism with noumenal freedom (see 5:89–106), he never addresses this problem. But this is precisely what he does five years later in *Religion within the Boundaries of Mere Reason*.

Radical freedom and radical evil

Religion within the Boundaries of Mere Reason is a remarkable book, revealing Kant's profound familiarity with the biblical basis and theological traditions of Christianity and with many other religions as well. Indeed, the book can seem like a philosophical defense of the Christian idea of original sin, which would be a shock after Kant's previous insistence on the freedom of human beings to do what is morally right or even on the inevitability of their doing what is right; thus Kant seems to state "The human being is by nature evil" in one heading, accompanying it by the quotation "Nobody is born without vice" (although he draws this from the Roman poet Horace rather than from any Christian source) (*Religion*, 6:32). But Kant's aim in this book is not to defend the doctrine of original sin, but rather precisely to exclude that from the portion of Christianity that can survive the scrutiny of pure reason – as was well understood by the court of the Prussian king Friedrich Wilhelm II, the conservative successor to his irreligious uncle Frederick the Great, which banned Kant from any further publication on religion after the appearance of this book.[21] Kant's argument in this work is that although we have natural predispositions or tendencies to both good and evil, we are not in fact good or evil by nature, but only as a result of our free choice to base our conduct on one tendency or the other by adopting either the maxim of morality or that of self-love. And that means that even if virtually all human beings have chosen to give in to their tendencies to evil, as history and anthropology all too sadly suggest, nevertheless we always retain the freedom to choose to do what is right, or to undergo a radical conversion from evil to good. The figure of Jesus Christ may give us a model of the moral life and the idea of divine grace may give us encouragement to make the hard choice of good or evil, but Kant's message is that conversion from evil to good is always in our own power and only in our own power – no one else can do it for us. And this entire argument makes sense, of course, only on the assumption that our will is not automatically determined by the moral law, but that we are truly free to choose between the moral law and its opposite.[22]

Kant begins the argument of the *Religion* with the observation that we have natural tendencies that can lead to good – such as the animal tendency to self-preservation, reproduction, and congregation with others of our kind, as well as the specifically human tendency to compare ourselves to others and strive for equality with them – but which can also lead to vice, as when our tendency to reproduction degenerates into mere lust or our desire for equality with others becomes jealousy and rivalry (6:26–7). We also have a "predisposition to personality," in the form of "the susceptibility to respect for the moral law **as of itself a sufficient incentive to the power of choice**" (6:27). But now Kant assumes that neither of these works automatically: the natural tendencies to good do not produce good conduct on their own, nor do they automatically degenerate into vice; and the predisposition to make the moral law a sufficient incentive for our will does not automatically make it into our incentive. We must freely choose whether to let our native tendencies to the good degenerate into vice or whether, out of respect for the moral law, to prevent them from doing so. And this, of course, makes sense only if it is within our own power either to commit ourselves to the moral law or to oppose it. That is why, as previously noted, Kant repeatedly insists that "if the moral law commands that we **ought** to be better human beings now, it inescapably follows that we must be **capable** of being better human beings" (6:50), but now does not even once say that the moral law is the *causal* law of the human will.

Perhaps Kant's earlier doctrine does not disappear without a trace. One thing that is striking about his analysis in the *Religion* is that he models the choice between good and evil as a choice of *priorities*, the choice whether to make the moral law the condition of self-love or to make self-love the condition of morality: that is, to choose to be good is to choose to act on self-love only when that is permitted by the moral law, while to choose to be evil is to choose to act as morality requires only when that is compatible with one's self-love (6:36). Kant conceives of the choice to be evil in this way because he does not think that anyone is ever simply ignorant of the moral law or simply repudiates it for no reason whatever.[23]

> The law rather imposes itself on him irresistibly, because of his moral predisposition, and if no other incentive were at work against it, he would also incorporate it into his supreme maxim as the sufficient determination of his power of choice, i.e., he would be morally good.
>
> (6:36)

But sometimes, alas, people do place self-love above the moral law. Kant's confidence that no one is simply unaware of the moral law or repudiates it for no reason whatever seems to be the heir to his earlier doctrine that the moral law is the causal law of the noumenal will: even if we do not all necessarily act upon the moral law, apparently as creatures who are intelligible as well as sensible we all do know it, and can be evil only by subordinating it to self-love but not by suppressing it altogether.

Because evil is always the product of a free choice to subordinate morality to self-love, Kant calls it "a **radical** innate **evil** in human nature (not any the less brought upon us by ourselves)" (6:32). Evil is radical in two senses: it consists in a fundamental choice to give self-love priority over morality, not merely an occasional exception to a commitment to morality; and it goes hand in hand with the very possibility of freely choosing to be good. Meaningful freedom is itself radical, nothing less than the possibility of choosing whether to be good or evil; and both our freedom and our evil are radical, reflecting our most fundamental free choice rather than any merely natural predisposition or accident. And if our evil is radical in the sense of being the result of our own free choice, then we are also free to reject evil, even our own past evil, and to choose to be good.

Because this is his real point, Kant can afford to be casual in his demonstration that people *are* generally evil. He says that "We can spare ourselves the formal proof that there must be . . . a corrupt propensity rooted in the human being, in view of the multitude of woeful examples that the experience of human **deeds** parades before us" – whether those are the deeds of so-called savages or so-called civilized people (6:32–3). If Kant's point were to prove that people are evil, this dismissal of the need for a proof would be remarkable. But Kant takes it to be *obvious* that people generally have been and are evil; his philosophical point is that we do not have to *remain* evil, but have the power to change from evil to good. Thus Kant sums up the key points of the whole book in the following paragraph:

> Now if a propensity to this [subordination of morality to self-love] does lie in human nature, then there is in the human being a natural propensity to evil; and this propensity itself is morally evil, since it must ultimately be sought in a free power of choice, and hence is imputable. This evil is **radical**, since it corrupts the ground of all maxims; as natural propensity, it is also not to be **extirpated** through human forces . . . Yet it must equally be possible to **overcome** this evil, for it is found in the human being as acting freely.
>
> (6:37)

Because we blame people for their evil deeds, we cannot think their evil is necessitated by merely natural predispositions, but must think of it as their free choice to give in to certain natural predispositions.[24] At the same time, it would be foolish to think that people can ever simply eliminate their natural predispositions to evil, or become "holy" wills who simply have no temptations to do evil. That is a completely unrealistic picture of human nature. Human beings are creatures who always have to choose between morality and self-love. But just because when they are evil it is because they have freely chosen to give in to self-love, so it must also be at least possible for them to choose to overcome this evil by subordinating their ineliminable tendency to self-love to their equally ineliminable predisposition to morality.

This then seems to be Kant's ultimate position on the moral law and freedom as well as his striking reinterpretation of Christianity: we all have immediate knowledge of the moral law, we can infer our freedom from it, and that freedom is the freedom to choose good or evil entirely on our own, with no guarantee from within or without that we will choose good but likewise no condemnation from within or without to remain evil. Before turning to Kant's further postulates of immortality and God, perhaps we should step back a moment to evaluate this position. I think we will find it difficult to accept without qualification Kant's confidence that we all know the moral law, with need perhaps for philosophical clarification but without need for philosophical demonstration, and are all always free to act in accordance with it. Of course there are some human beings who are too mentally defective or disabled to conceive of the moral law or to control their actions. But even among normally functioning adults, there seem to be many who hold the dictates of their particular religion or creed to be moral absolutes, no matter how different those may be from Kant's conception of the moral law, and who also think of themselves as bound by forces beyond themselves to act in accordance with those dictates. Perhaps we could show such people that they really accept Kant's categorical imperative at the most fundamental level – that is, they assume that what is right for themselves must be right for others as well – and are only confused about what particular dictates of conduct can actually pass that test. Let us suppose that this is right. Even so, we are unlikely to be convinced that even the normal among us are really always free, at all times and in all circumstances, to do what is right. Yet we might also think that if we cannot know that we are really free to do what is right in any imaginable circumstance, then we also cannot know that we really are not free to do what is right in any particular circumstance. In that case, we

may well think that even if we cannot believe that the categorical imperative is the causal law of our wills, we can still adopt it as the *ideal* for our
wills, that is, the principle to which we strive to conform, without any
guarantee that we always can but equally without any guarantee that we
cannot. After all, if morality is as important as Kant thinks – and no doubt
most of us agree – then we do not need a guarantee that we can live up to
its demands in order to make it rational for us to try to do so; we only
need the *absence* of a guarantee that we *cannot* live up to it.

This conclusion will ultimately be crucial to an evaluation of Kant's
theory of the postulates of immortality and the existence of God. So let us
turn to those next.

IMMORTALITY AND THE EXISTENCE OF GOD

As we saw at the outset of this chapter, Kant began the *Critique of Practical
Reason* by arguing that the postulate of freedom is the presupposition of the
very possibility of morality, while the existence of God and immortality
are the presuppositions of the *object* of morality. What does he mean by
the object of morality? We might have thought from our discussion of the
formulations of the categorical imperative in the previous chapter that the
realm of ends, as the state of affairs that would be brought about if
everyone were to follow the moral law, would be the object of morality.
But in his discussions of the postulates of pure practical reason – which
culminate each of Kant's three critiques – he always uses a different term;
as he puts it in the "Canon of Pure Reason" in the *Critique of Pure Reason*, his
first discussion of the postulates, "the ideal of the highest good" is the
"ultimate end of pure reason" (A 804/B 832). In what follows we must
therefore ask what Kant means by the highest good, how this idea relates
to that of the realm of ends, and why it necessitates the postulates of God
and immortality.

Kant takes happiness to be the natural goal of human beings. But also he
takes our rational commitment to morality to mean that we would wish to
be happy only insofar as we have proven ourselves to be *worthy of happiness*
because of our respect for the moral law (A 806/B 834). He thus
conceives of the highest good – or more precisely, for reasons we shall see
shortly, the "highest derived good" – as "all happiness in the world,
insofar as it stands in exact relation with morality (as the worthiness to be
happy)" (A 810/B 838). Sometimes Kant makes it seem as if this highest
good is the conjunction of two separate goals, a merely natural goal of
happiness, which has no basis in morality at all, and the purely moral goal

of acting only in accordance with the moral law, which subjects our pursuit of any non-moral goal, including that of happiness itself, to its compatibility with our observation of the moral law (see CPracR, 5:110–11). But that this cannot be what he really means by the highest good should already be evident from the earlier discussion of happiness in the second Critique, because "*all* happiness," that is, the happiness of all, is not anyone's merely *natural* goal, which is at best one's own happiness or even just one's happiness in the present and the near future, and the happiness of those to whom one currently has some personal connection. The happiness of all can itself be only a moral goal, although not a *direct* moral goal: we do not approve of the happiness of all for its own sake, but rather because it is what would *result* under ideal circumstances from treating everyone as an end and therefore promoting a maximally consistent set of their particular ends. The highest good, in other words, is the state of affairs that would at least under ideal circumstances result from the establishment of the realm of ends: it would be the state in which all were happy because their ends were fulfilled in the name of morality.[25] Without using the expression "realm of ends," which he did not introduce until the *Groundwork*, Kant puts this point in the first *Critique* in terms of the idea of a "moral world":

> I call the world as it would be if it were in conformity with all moral laws (as it **can** be in accordance with the **freedom** of rational beings and **should** be in accordance with the necessary laws of **morality**) a **moral world** . . . Now in an intelligible world, i.e., in the moral world, in the concept of which we have abstracted from all hindrances to morality (of the inclinations), such a system of happiness proportionately combined with morality can also be thought as necessary, since freedom, partly moved and partly restricted by moral laws, would itself be the cause of the general happiness, and rational beings, under the guidance of such principles, would themselves be the author of their own enduring welfare and at the same time that of others.
>
> (A 808–9 / B 836–7)

This passage makes it clear that the ideal of the highest good is not the idea of the combination of the merely natural goal of one's own happiness with the moral requirement that one pursue that natural goal only in a virtuous and worthy way; it is a thoroughly moral ideal, the idea of the system of happiness that would necessarily result in a world in which there were no hindrances to the complete observation of morality. And why that would be so can be understood only through the idea of a realm of ends: it is because morality requires the systematic union of both persons as ends in themselves and the ends that they set for themselves that morality would produce the happiness of all, which consists in nothing but the satisfaction of the ends that people set for themselves.[26]

But now why should this conception of the goal of morality lead to the postulation of God and immortality? For the simple reason that Kant states immediately following the lines just quoted: "this system of self-rewarding morality is only an idea, the realization of which rests on the condition that **everyone** do what he should" (A 810/B 838); yet clearly everyone does not always do what he should, but this does not free anyone from the obligation to be moral. Kant's argument is then, first, that it is rational to pursue a goal only if we have good reason to believe that this goal can be realized; that the goal imposed by morality obviously is not always realizable in the natural world, which has no place for God or immortality, because of the wayward inclinations of others or even ourselves; so we must therefore postulate an as it were unnatural world, beyond the temporal frame of ordinary existence and ruled by a wise, benevolent, and powerful God, in which the ideal result of morality will become actual. In particular, God turns out to be the "highest **original** good" from whom the "highest derived good," the happiness of all as a result of the morality of all, is derived:

> I call the idea of such an intelligence, in which the morally most perfect will, combined with the highest blessedness, is the cause of all happiness in the world, insofar as it stands in exact proportion with morality (as the worthiness to be happy), **the ideal of the highest good**. Thus only in the ideal of the highest **original** good can pure reason find the ground of the practically necessary connection of both elements of the highest derived good, namely of an intelligible, i.e., **moral** world. Now since we must necessarily represent ourselves through reason as belonging to such a world, although the senses do not present us with anything except a world of appearances, we must assume the moral world to be a consequence of our conduct in the sensible world; and since the latter does not offer such a connection to us, we must assume the former to be a future world. Thus God and a future life are two presuppositions that are not to be separated from the obligation that pure reason imposes on us in accordance with principles of that very same reason.
>
> (A 810–11/B 838–9)

Since we do not find that morality inevitably produces the happiness of all in this world, but since morality even if only indirectly commands the happiness of all, and, as we have seen, even morality cannot tell us that we *ought* to strive for a goal that *cannot* be brought about, we must believe that morality will produce happiness in another world; and since the existence of this other world as well as the conjunction of happiness and morality is surely something that exceeds our own powers, we must believe that it has its ground in an intelligence that combines "the morally most perfect will" with the "highest blessedness."

At least in his published works, Kant never wavers from his thought that we must postulate the existence of a God with all *and only* the properties necessary to ensure that the ideal of morality can become real.[27] He stresses that we can assign the properties of omnipotence, omniscience, and omnipresence to God only because those properties are necessary for God to play his moral role of guaranteeing the possibility of the highest good and that we have no basis for assigning any other properties to God in each of the three critiques (CPuR, A 814–15/B 842–3; CPracR, 5:138–9; CPJ, §86, 5:444). This is why Kant holds that the only rational theology is what he calls "moral theology," the determination of the nature of God only from moral considerations. Kant also always stresses that although the postulation of the existence of God has the same logical and grammatical, that is, theoretical form as the assertion of the existence of any object, he has not offered a theoretical *argument* for the existence of God based on either empirical or *a priori* grounds (the very possibility of which he has already denied in the "Transcendental Dialectic" of the first *Critique*): a postulate of pure practical reason, he says, is "a **theoretical** proposition, although not one demonstrable as such," but demonstrable only "insofar as it is attached inseparably to an *a priori* unconditionally valid **practical** law" (CPracR, 5:122). Kant goes to great lengths to try to characterize the practical rather than theoretical basis for the assertion of the postulates. In the first *Critique*, he distinguishes between theoretical *opinion*, which is on the same scale as knowledge but with incomplete evidence, and practical *belief* or *faith* (Glaube), which has no theoretical basis at all but must be adopted on completely different grounds (A 820–31/B 848–59), and concludes his argument by saying that "I must not even say '**It is** morally certain that there is a God' but rather '**I am** morally certain'" (A 829/B 857). In the second *Critique* Kant explains that although the postulates of practical reason cannot contradict theoretical reason, neither are they "its insights, but are yet extensions of its use from another, namely a practical perspective" (5:121). In the third *Critique*, as if to emphasize the difference between theoretical cognition and practical postulation for readers who still have not gotten the message, Kant restates the doctrine of practical postulates within the framework of a theory of merely "reflecting" rather than "determining" judgment, which yields only regulative ideals rather than constitutive principles of knowledge. He also makes this plain statement:

> This moral argument is not meant to provide any **objectively** valid proof of the existence of God, nor meant to prove to the doubter that there is a God; rather, it is meant to prove that if his moral thinking is to be consistent, he **must include** the assumption of this proposition among the maxims of his practical reason. – Thus it is also not meant to say that it is necessary to assume the happiness of all rational beings in the world in accordance with their morality **for** morals, but rather that it is necessary **through** their morality. Hence it is a **subjective** argument, sufficient for moral beings.
>
> (CPJ, §87, 4:450–1n)

In drafts for an essay on the Berlin Academy question "What Real Progress has Metaphysics made since the Time of Leibniz and Wolff?" that he wrote a few years after the third *Critique* (but never submitted or published), Kant introduced the idea of the "practico-dogmatic" rather than the "theoretico-dogmatic" to try to capture the status of the postulates (20:273, 293). Finally, in the so-called *Opus postumum*, that is, his unfinished notes for a last restatement of his transcendental philosophy, Kant repeatedly says things like God is "not a world-soul in nature but . . . a personal principle of human reason" (21:19) and that "The concept of such a being is not that of substance – that is, of a being which exists independent of my thought – but the idea (one's own creation, thought-object, *ens rationis*)" (21:37). But however he describes it, Kant's message remains the same: somehow we have to combine the recognition that there can be no theoretical proof of the existence of God with a faith in God that is sufficient to assure us of the realizability of the goal that morality imposes upon us.[28]

Kant's commitment to the postulate of immortality, however, is not so unwavering. There is an immediate problem with his argument about immortality in the first *Critique*: if morality commands happiness because it commands the promotion of the ends that we actually set for ourselves, those will be the kinds of ends that we set for ourselves within our natural lives, not some unknown ends that could be realized only in an unknown world. So while some unknown happiness to be granted in a future life might be some sort of external compensation for the failure to achieve happiness within our natural lives, it could not possibly be the happiness promised by what Kant called "self-rewarding" morality.[29] Perhaps for this reason, Kant gives a very different account of the postulate of immortality in the second *Critique*: here he argues that we need immortality not to achieve happiness at all but rather in order to make **"endless progress"** toward "the **complete conformity** of dispositions with the moral law," that is, toward *virtue* or *worthiness* to be happy (5:122). (And in fact he also adjusts his account of the role of God, who is no longer seen as the ground of a *future* world but rather as an author *of nature* who makes sure that the laws of nature are consistent with the moral law, so that happiness can after all be realized *in nature*; 5:124−5). But even this argument subsequently becomes problematic, because as we have already seen Kant argues in the *Religion* that the radical freedom of human beings implies the possibility of a complete moral conversion − although not the extirpation of all natural temptations to evil − *at any time*. So there is no need to postulate an afterlife to guarantee the possibility of moral conversion after all.[30] Thus there seems to be no good basis for the postulate of immortality, and in fact apart from occasional formulaic references to it as part of the triad "freedom, God, and immortality," this postulate tends to disappear from Kant's expositions of the theory of the practical postulates after the second *Critique*. What he emphasizes in the third *Critique*, for example, is solely that we must postulate "a **moral** being as author of the world" so that it will be rational for us to "strive after" that which morality "makes obligatory for us," namely "the **highest good in the world** possible through freedom" (CPJ, §88, 5:455; §87, 5:450). The object of morality, Kant here makes clear, is something that we must believe can be achieved "in the world," not somewhere else.

It was immediately objected to Kant's account of the highest good and the practical postulates that by insisting that virtue must be rewarded with happiness he was thereby making the promise of happiness into the motivation for being virtuous, and thus undermining the purity of moral motivation on which he had so strongly insisted in the *Groundwork*. In an important essay of 1793, "On the Common Saying: That May Be Correct in Theory but It Is of No Use in Practice," Kant rejected this criticism by insisting on the difference between the *motive* or "incentive" and the *object* of morality. He argues there that he is in no way departing from "the concept of duty in its complete purity" (TP, 8:286), that is, his rigorous claim that the motive for morality has nothing to do with one's own desire for happiness; rather, his argument is that morality itself commands one "to work to the best of one's ability toward . . . universal happiness combined with and in conformity with the purest morality throughout the world" (8:279), and that if one does not have reason to believe that this goal is possible, then it will be irrational to try to achieve it. So even though one's motivation to be moral is not the desire for one's own happiness, that motivation would be weakened or undermined by the idea that what morality commands cannot be brought about. On this point, Kant seems entirely right.

However, his argument is still open to the same sort of question that we raised at the end of the previous section, namely does rationality require a guarantee of the possibility of achieving a goal that we would rationally pursue, or only the *absence* of any reason to believe that it is *impossible* to achieve that goal? Kant's argument that we must believe in the actual existence of God in order to be sure of the possibility of the highest good (CPracR, 5:126) is clearly predicated on the first conception of rationality. But again, it might be perfectly rational to pursue a goal as long as we have good reason to believe that achieving it is *not impossible*, especially if it is important – and what could be more important than trying to achieve the object or final end of morality as a whole? And if all that the rationality of attempting to be moral requires is that we not know it to be impossible to realize the object it commands, it would seem that our empirical knowledge of nature should suffice: for even if our observation of nature suggests that widespread virtue has not yet been accompanied by equally widespread happiness, that cannot imply that it is *impossible* that virtue should be accompanied with happiness. For if no amount of empirical evidence can entail necessity, neither can it entail impossibility (which is logically equivalent to necessary non-existence). Indeed, even if one wanted to bring God into the picture, and assume like Kant that only the existence of God could be an adequate explanation of the realization of the highest good, it does not seem as if a special practical postulation of his existence should be necessary. For if Kant has successfully shown that there can be no theoretical proof of the existence of God, then he has also shown, as he himself often stresses, that there can be no theoretical *disproof* of the existence of God. So from the theoretical point of view, the existence of God always remains *possible*, and then so too should the realizability – that is, the *possibility* of the realization – of the highest good.

Kant's thesis that the moral command to establish a realm of ends also entails that we attempt to realize the highest good possible in this world seems entirely reasonable. But his claim that we must postulate our own immortality in order rationally to attempt to realize this goal collapses into incoherence, and his argument that we must believe in the existence of God in order to pursue this goal depends on an overly strong interpretation of the conditions of rationality. Indeed, as we shall see in the final chapter of this book, in his reflections on history Kant supposes that we can see human history as the locus of moral progress without any appeal to theology at all. It thus looks as if we could accept the normative content of Kantian moral philosophy without accepting Kant's moral theology. So let us now resume our discussion of that normative content by examining Kant's system of ethical and political duties a little more closely than we have thus far done, and seeing precisely how they contribute to the realization of human autonomy.

SUMMARY

Kant's goal of establishing the validity of the moral law became intertwined with his lifelong interest in the problem of the freedom of the will. In both the *Groundwork* and the *Critique of Practical Reason*, he held that a being with free will would necessarily be bound by the moral law (the "Reciprocity Thesis"), but he changed his mind about what to do with this thesis: in the *Groundwork*, he attempted to give a theoretical proof of the reality of our freedom, from which he could then deduce the binding force of the moral law for us, while in the second *Critique* he held that we are simply conscious of the binding obligation of the moral law as a "fact of reason," thus giving up any attempt to prove the validity of the moral law, but held that we could infer the reality of our freedom from this consciousness by means of the principle that "ought implies can." However, as long as Kant held that a free being necessarily acts in accordance with the moral law, it was impossible for him to explain the all too evident possibility, indeed reality, of human evil. To escape this predicament, Kant reconceived human freedom in the *Religion within the Boundaries of Mere Reason* as the possibility of choosing to make self-love subordinate to the moral law or the moral law subordinate to self-love, thus making the possibility of radical evil part and parcel of radical freedom, but at the same time securing the possibility of moral conversion as well. Once having established the possibility of human freedom attempting to realize the highest good as the object of morality, Kant could then argue for the rationality of belief in the existence of immortality and God as further conditions for the possibility of the highest good, although these arguments suffer from a number of problems, most deeply that the mere *possibility* of the "highest derived good" may not require the *actuality* of the "highest original good" or God.

FURTHER READING

To the general sources on Kant's moral philosophy suggested in the previous chapter, the following may be added. Allison is a detailed study of Kant's theory of freedom in both Critiques and other moral writings. Hudson discusses Kant's theory of freedom in contemporary terms, while di Giovanni places Kant's theory of freedom and the postulates of pure practical reason in the context of contemporaneous philosophical and theological debates.

Henry E. Allison, Kant's Theory of Freedom (Cambridge: Cambridge University Press, 1990).

George Di Giovanni, Freedom and Religion in Kant and His Immediate Successors: The Vocation of Humankind, 1774–1800 (Cambridge: Cambridge University Press, 2005).

Hud Hudson, Kant's Compatibilism (Ithaca, NY: Cornell University Press, 1994).

On the highest good and the postulates of pure practical reason, see, in addition to John Silber's introduction to the Greene and Hudson translation of Religion within the Limits of Reason Alone, his important journal articles (1959, 1962–3). Wood contains an important analysis of the conception of practical rationality underlying Kant's arguments for the postulates; and Yovel argues for an historical rather than a transhistorical, theological conception of the highest good.

John Silber, "Kant's Conception of the Highest Good as Immanent and Transcendent," Philosophical Review 68 (1959): 469–92.

———, "The Importance of the Highest Good in Kant's Ethics," Ethics 73 (1962–3): 179–97.

Allen W. Wood, Kant's Moral Religion (Ithaca, NY: Cornell University Press, 1970).

Yirmiahu Yovel, Kant and the Philosophy of History (Princeton, NJ: Princeton University Press, 1981).

Seven

Kant's System of Duties I
The duties of virtue

KANT'S DIVISION OF DUTIES

A dozen years after he published the *Groundwork for the Metaphysics of Morals*, and more than thirty years after he had written that he would shortly publish a "little essay" on the "Metaphysical Foundations of Practical Philosophy,"[1] Kant finally published a book entitled *Metaphysics of Morals*, which appeared during 1797 in two parts, entitled "Metaphysical Foundations of the Doctrine of Right" and "Metaphysical Foundations of the Doctrine of Virtue." The first of these parts, for which Kant had prepared the way with the 1793 essay "On the common saying: That may be correct in theory but it is of no use in practice" and the 1795 pamphlet *Toward Perpetual Peace*, presents Kant's legal and political philosophy. The gist of Kant's argument in this part of the work is that personal freedom and private property can be *secure* only within the framework of a state and ultimately an international league of states, but that they can be *rightfully* exercised and acquired only within a just national and international order. Kant borrows much of the trappings of his account from the modern traditions of natural law and social contract theory beginning with Thomas Hobbes and Samuel Pufendorf, but differs fundamentally from his predecessors in arguing that not just prudence but also morality must constrain our freedom of action and the acquisition of property, and that we therefore have a duty to enter into a social contract and thereby establish a just national and international order. The second part of the work concerns ethical duties toward ourselves and others that should constrain our individual pursuits of happiness, but that should not be enforced through the juridical mechanisms of the state. Kant calls these duties "duties of virtue" (*Tugendpflichten*) because the only way they can be enforced is through the strength of our own virtue or respect for the moral law; he also calls them "ethical" (*ethisch*) duties or duties of "ethics" (*Ethik*) (see MM, Introduction, 6:220–1), thereby confusing some readers into thinking that Kant intends only these duties and not political obligations to be part of morality.[2] But Kant clearly intends "ethics" to be only a part of "morality" (*Sitten, Moralität*) as a whole, with the legal and political duties of "right" comprising the other part of morality. The most straightforward proof of this is that while Kant defines duties of right as those that permit of coercive enforcement through the legal system of the state, he begins the "Doctrine of Right" with a *moral* justification of such coercion itself. There would be no need for him to do so if these obligations were not themselves part of morality.

The reader will immediately ask what place for coercion there can be in a moral philosophy that is supposed to value the preservation and promotion of freedom or autonomy above all else. The answer to this question lies precisely in the distinction between mere freedom of the will and the achievement of autonomy that Kant finally clarified by the time of the *Religion*, that is, the difference between mere freedom of choice in isolated acts, on the one hand, and, on the other, the choice to preserve and promote the continued exercise of freedom, throughout a lifetime and throughout a community, ultimately the realm of ends, in accordance with laws of reason. As Kant's discussion of radical evil assumed, people do not always use their freedom to preserve and promote their own autonomy or that of others. But preserving and promoting autonomy is what morality requires, and sometimes the untrammeled exercise of freedom by some agent or agents on some particular occasion or occasions will have to be constrained to protect the continued autonomy of all agents on all occasions. In Kant's terms, lawless acts that would be hindrances to freedom must themselves be hindered (MM, Doctrine of Right, Introduction §D, 6:231). Determining when such coercion for the sake of freedom is possible and even necessary is the essential task of the doctrine of right and the key to discriminating between duties of right and duties of virtue.

This suggests that the basic difference between duties of right and duties of virtue is that the former are ways of preserving and promoting freedom that can be coercively enforced and the latter are ways of preserving and promoting freedom that cannot be enforced by anything other than respect for the moral law itself. This suggestion fits with Kant's account in the general introduction to the *Metaphysics of Morals*, where he writes that "Ethical legislation (even if the duties might be external) is that which **cannot** be external," that is, enforced by incentives external to respect for the moral law, while "juridical legislation is that which can also be external" (MM Introduction, 6:220), that is, enforced by "aversions" or the desire to avoid punishment (6:219). But it does not obviously match the definition of duties of virtue that Kant offers in the later introduction to the "Doctrine of Virtue." Here Kant states that while

> the doctrine of right dealt only with the **formal** condition of outer freedom (the consistency of outer freedom with itself if its maxim were made universal law) . . . ethics goes beyond this and provides a **matter** (an object of free choice), an **end** of pure reason which it represents as an end that is also objectively necessary, that is, an end that, as far as human beings are concerned, it is a duty to have.
>
> (MM, Doctrine of Virtue, Introduction, 6:380)

That is, duties of right are duties to preserve the possibility of the consistent use of external freedom, or freedom of action, regardless of the aims and motives of the actors involved, while duties of virtue are duties to promote certain ends endorsed by reason, or are duties that are also ends. As Kant goes on to explain, the ends that are also duties that are to be promoted under the category of duties of virtue are one's own perfection and the happiness of others (6:385): only one's own perfection and not one's own happiness, because one desires that naturally, not as a matter of duty; and only the happiness and not the perfection of others, because the perfection of others consists in the perfection of their morality, and that is something that each must perfect on his or her own. There are obvious problems with Kant's identification of the ends that are also duties. First, one may well naturally desire one's own short-term pleasure, but that is certainly not the same as one's long-term happiness, and one may well need to constrain oneself to pursue the latter. Second, although one may not be able to make moral choices for others, one can certainly assist with their education and the perfection of their capacities, including even their capacity to make moral choices.[3] But there is also a larger problem with this account, namely that it is congruent neither with Kant's previous distinction between duties of right and duties of virtue nor with the list of the duties of virtue that Kant subsequently provides in the body of his work. That enumeration of the duties of virtue includes all those duties either to preserve the existence of freedom in oneself and others or to promote its successful exercise in oneself and others that cannot properly be coercively enforced. For example, the first duty of virtue to oneself is the duty not to commit suicide, but this is not a duty to perfect oneself, only a duty not to destroy oneself as a free being; and the duties of virtue toward others include the duty not to defame or ridicule them, even though this is not a duty to promote or even merely preserve their happiness, but only a duty not to show disrespect to them as persons who are free in their own right. The only thing that all these duties of virtue have in common is that for either practical or moral reasons they cannot be coercively enforced through a legal system of justice. The duties of virtue turn out to be simply all of our moral duties that are not properly subject to coercive enforcement – just as Kant originally suggested.[4]

Does this mean that there is no systematic basis for the inclusion of duties on Kant's list of ethical duties or duties of virtue? Not at all. If we recall the classification of duties that Kant used to illustrate the first two formulations of the categorical imperative, which we discussed in Chapter 5, we will see that Kant's list of both the duties of right and the duties of virtue has a deep foundation in his fundamental principle of morality, and that the justification but also the restriction of the permissibility of coercion that he uses to distinguish between the two classes of duties is also deeply based on that fundamental principle.

Kant appealed to these examples in the *Groundwork* in order to confirm his analysis of the categorical imperative by showing that it gives rise to all the main kinds of commonly recognized moral duties. To do this, he chose his examples from "the usual division of [duties] into duties to ourselves and to other human beings and into perfect and imperfect duties" (G, 4:422n.) (thereby omitting without comment the traditional category of duties toward God, although he has much to say against that category elsewhere).[5] He then offered one example from each of the four classes that arise from these two divisions: as an example of a perfect duty toward oneself, he adduced the proscription of suicide; as an example of a perfect duty toward others, he used the duty not to make false promises, that is, promises that one has no intention of keeping; as the example of imperfect duty toward oneself, he offered the duty to cultivate one's natural predispositions for skills and talents; and for imperfect duty toward others he instanced the duty of beneficence or mutual aid (G, 4:422–4, 429–30). If we recall Kant's definition of humanity as the capacity to both freely set and attempt to realize ends, we can derive these examples of duties from the general requirement always to treat humanity as an end and never merely as a means in the following way. The duty to refrain from suicide is obviously a case of the more general duty not to destroy a being capable of free choice, a duty that would obviously proscribe homicide as well as suicide, that is, the destruction of a free agent other than oneself.

Since Kant analyzes a false promise as one that compromises the free choice of another by inducing him to adopt as his own an end that he would not endorse if he were properly informed of the promiser's real intention (G, 4:429–30), the proscription of such promises is an example of the general duty not to compromise the exercise of free agency or destroy the possibility of its exercise on a particular occasion, rather than the duty not to destroy a free agent altogether. There will of course be other examples of this general class of duty, including cases of such a duty toward oneself rather than toward others; one example that Kant will give is the duty to avoid drunkenness (MM, Doctrine of Virtue, §8, 4:427), which can be understood as a duty not to compromise one's ability to exercise one's own freedom of choice during a period of intoxication. Third, Kant's example of the duty to cultivate one's talents, "fortunate natural predispositions" which if developed can serve one "for all sorts of possible aims" (G, 4:423), can be understood as a duty to develop general conditions that will facilitate the realization of the particular ends that one may freely set for oneself in the exercise of one's humanity. One might have such a duty with regard to others as well, for example, the duty to educate one's children or to contribute to the education of the children of others by paying one's local property taxes. Finally, the duty of beneficence can be understood as the duty to assist others in the realization of particular ends they have freely set for themselves: as Kant puts it, "there is still only a negative and not a positive agreement with **humanity as an end in itself** unless everyone also tries, as far as he can, to further the ends of others" (G, 4:430). We might also think that treating one's own humanity as an end in itself would entail a duty to further the particular ends that one freely sets for oneself, although this could begin to sound like a duty to promote one's own happiness, an idea toward which, as already mentioned, Kant is hostile.[6]

Summing up, we can take Kant's analyses of his examples of the four commonly accepted classes of duty to imply the following comprehensive interpretation of the duty always to treat humanity as an end and never merely as a means: this consists of the duties not to destroy human beings qua agents capable of free choice, not to compromise the possibility of their exercise of their freedom of choice and action, to cultivate general capacities that will facilitate the successful pursuit of the ends that they freely set for themselves, and, as circumstances warrant and allow, to take particular actions in order to facilitate the realization of the particular ends that they freely set for themselves. We can add one further consideration that we can derive from Kant's discussion of "private right," that is, the right to property, from the "Doctrine of Right" (to which we will return in the next chapter). The underlying empirical assumption of Kant's theory of property rights is that we are embodied creatures who can function only by means of the movement of our bodies – this gives rise to what Kant calls the "innate rights to freedom" (MM, Doctrine of Right, Introduction, 6:237–8) – and the use of bodies other than our own, including the use of non-human bodies, such as land, minerals, vegetables, and non-human animals, and also other human beings, such as those of spouses, servants, other employees, contractors, and so on – this is what gives rise to the various categories of what Kant calls "acquired right." The preservation of our own humanity and that of others as well as the pursuit of the freely chosen ends of ourselves and others will require us to be able to move our own bodies freely and to control and use various other bodies as well. Of course, the free movements of our own bodies as well as the free use of other bodies, whether non-human or human, can come into conflict with the free use of their own bodies and other bodies by other persons, and thus the general duty to treat humanity, that is, the capacity for freedom of choice and action, as an end and not merely as a means in both ourselves and others means that we will have to find ways to regulate the movements of our own bodies and the use of other bodies in order to preserve freedom not only in ourselves but also in others. The general duties to preserve free beings and the possibility of their exercise of their freedom as well as to promote the success of such exercise and the realization of particular freely chosen ends will all require the regulation of the use of both our own bodies and other bodies in ways designed to respect the humanity of all.

Against this background, we can now enumerate the classes of juridical and ethical duties that Kant deploys in the *Metaphysics of Morals*. Juridical duties are those that, as stated at the outset, permit of coercive enforcement. There are three classes of them, although the first is only mentioned in the Introduction and only the latter two receive extended discussion in the two main sections of the "Doctrine of Right." The class of duties mentioned in the Introduction is that arising from the innate right to freedom, by which presumably Kant means freedom of the person to perform actions that do not involve the control or use of external objects or other persons. This innate right would therefore include freedom from restriction of or violence against the person, giving rise to prohibitions against kidnapping, assault, homicide, and other obvious attacks upon bodily existence, integrity, and motion, but also to rights such as freedom of speech.[7] The second main class of juridical duties, discussed under the rubric of "Private

Right," includes the rights to acquire property in things, rights toward specific performances by other persons through contracts, and rights toward other persons as if they were things, that is, long-term rights against others such as the rights of spouses regarding each other; the juridical duties, of course, are the duties to respect these rights. The overall purpose of Kant's discussion is to explain how such rights can be acquired consistently with the general moral obligation to treat each person as an end and never merely as a means – to explain, for example, how one person can claim an exclusive right to control a piece of property that others might also use in a way that is consistent with the freedom of others, or how a husband can claim rights over a wife consistent with her own status as an end in herself. Kant then argues that a state is necessary in order to make all these rights both determinate and secure, and that our moral freedom to claim these rights therefore creates a moral obligation to institute and preserve a state (see MM, Doctrine of Right, §§8–9, 41–2). The third main class of rights and duties, expounded under the rubric of "Public Right," are then those that are necessary to ensure that the state can perform its allotted role. The gist of Kant's argument here is that only a republican government, characterized by the division of powers and the denial to rulers of proprietary rights in the land and offices of the nation, can fulfill the morally rightful purpose for which the state exists, and therefore that all, but especially the rulers of a state, however they have come to power, have an obligation to institute and maintain republican government.[8]

Now on this scheme there is a fairly clear distinction between duties to *preserve* the existence of free agents and the possibility of the exercise of their freedom and duties to *promote* the successful exercise of their freedom – Kant's original distinction between perfect and imperfect duties. The duties to refrain from suicide and deceitful promises are perfect duties to preserve free beings and the possibility of their exercise of their freedom, while the duties to develop one's own talents (part of one's own perfection) and to assist others in the pursuit of their ends (and thus contribute to their happiness) are imperfect duties to promote the successful exercise of freedom in either general or specific ways. So this scheme includes both duties to treat human beings as ends in themselves and duties to promote the realization of the particular ends that they set for themselves. The problem is just that Kant does not restrict his complete list of duties of virtue to the latter, as his characterization of such duties as duties that are also ends might have suggested he should. Rather, Kant's complete list of the duties of virtue simply includes all those duties derivable from the general scheme we have just described that cannot be coercively enforced.

To be sure, Kant does not spell out a general theory of why none of the duties of virtue are coercively enforceable; and it seems as if there would be a variety of reasons why specific duties of virtue would not be so enforceable. In some cases, there is clearly a physical or even a logical barrier to the coercive enforcement of a duty of virtue. One duty of virtue that Kant will discuss, for example, is the duty to develop and hearken to one's conscience, and this could not be coercively enforced simply because coercive enforcement can modify one's outer actions through fear of consequences, but not change one's moral character. In other cases, it might be the case that while a duty could be coercively enforced, no one has the moral or legal standing necessary to do so: there are sanctions that might deter suicide, for example, such as the threat of the confiscation of a suicide's estate or his burial outside of hallowed ground, but if the would-be suicide is a competent adult whose action would injure no one but himself (which is of course not always the case), then no one else may have the right to threaten or enforce these sanctions against him. Kant's predecessors spelled out these considerations by maintaining that the coercive enforcement of any obligation requires both a logical and / or physical possibility of successful coercive enforcement as well as a moral possibility, capacity, or title for such enforcement.[9] Kant does not explicitly mention these conditions, perhaps because he could take them for granted. But he in fact assumes them. Thus, for example, in explaining why even though there is not a moral right to self-preservation at the cost of the life of an innocent there cannot be a legal prohibition of it – he refers to the alleged "right of necessity," such as the right to push another off a floating piece of shipwreck in order to save oneself – he argues simply that there could not be an effective sanction to enforce such a prohibition: the threat of drowning is more immediate and certain than the mere threat of a later legal sanction (MM, Doctrine of Right, Introduction, Appendix II, 6:235–6). In this case Kant thus assumes that a coercive sanction requires a physical possibility of efficacy. His general argument in behalf of the coercive enforcement of juridical duties, however, turns, as has already been mentioned, on the claim that hindrances to hindrances of freedom are "consistent with freedom in accordance with universal laws" (MM, Doctrine of Right, Introduction, §D, 6:231). This is clearly an attempt to provide the *moral* title for coercive sanctions.

On this account, then, juridical duties would simply be those of our obligations arising from the fundamental principle of morality that satisfy the criteria for coercive enforcement, and ethical duties would be those that fail to satisfy these criteria. On such an account there would thus be a systematic derivation of all duties as well as a systematic basis for their division. And indeed, the basis for the division of duties would ultimately be the same as the basis for their derivation, namely the fundamental principle of morality itself. The requirement that there be a moral basis for the exercise of any coercive sanction, specifically the requirement that such a sanction actually preserve freedom itself, obviously derives directly from the principle that the freedom of every person is to be an end in itself. But the further requirement that there can be a coercive sanction only when there can be an effective sanction can also be regarded as part of morality itself, at least if the principle that "ought implies can" is regarded as part of the foundation of morality – as Kant clearly regards it.[10] In other words, the division between coercively enforceable duties and duties that cannot be coercively enforced but can only be motivated by respect for duty is itself required by morality.

In the text of the *Metaphysics of Morals*, Kant expounds the duties of right before the duties of virtue, because the former are a subset of perfect duties, which come before imperfect duties in his original classification – in fact, the duties of right are just a subset of our perfect duties to others. But just because Kant's discussion of the duties of right is more extensive and in some ways more difficult to understand than his discussion of the duties of virtue, we will discuss the duties of virtue in the remainder of this chapter and then give Kant's duties of right, his medium for the exposition of his legal and political philosophy, a chapter of their own. First, however, we must distinguish from the specific duties of virtue a more general conception of virtue that Kant also proposes.

THE GENERAL OBLIGATION OF VIRTUE

Ethical duties are duties to preserve and promote the freedom to set and pursue ends that cannot be coercively enforced.[11] This means that they are duties of freedom in a double sense: they are aimed at preserving and promoting freedom in action, but since they cannot be coercively enforced, they must also be freely willed, or motivated by nothing other than respect for the moral law or its ground, the value of humanity. Kant expresses this by including under ethical duties both the specific *duties of virtue* (*Tugendpflichten*) and the general *obligation of virtue* (*Tugendverpflichtung*), "respect for law as such" (MM, Doctrine of Virtue, Introduction, 6:410). The latter reflects our common usage of the word "virtuous," where in calling a person "virtuous" we assert the purity of her motivation. Kant makes a number of important points about virtue in this sense. First, consistent with his earlier claim that a good will is the only thing that merits esteem, he emphasizes that it is being motivated by "respect for right" that is truly meritorious (6:390). Next, he stresses that in the actual circumstances of human existence, where we are always subject to temptations to stray from what morality requires, virtue in this sense will express itself in the form of resistance to temptation and thus as a form of self-constraint: "Virtue is, therefore, the moral strength of a **human being's** will in fulfilling his **duty**, a moral **constraint** through his own law-giving reason, insofar as this constitutes itself an authority **executing** the law" (6:405). He also emphasizes that human beings cannot really be expected to resist temptation on every possible occasion, or at least cannot be expected always to do so out of completely pure motivation, so that the general duty of virtue is in one regard an imperfect duty, a duty to strive for a purity of motivation that is always greater than whatever one has thus far actually achieved. As he puts it, a "human being's duty to himself to increase his **moral** perfection" is "a **narrow** and perfect one in terms of its quality" – there is only one specific way to be morally perfect, namely to act out of respect for the moral law as such – "but it is wide and imperfect in terms of its degree, because of the **frailty** (*fragilitas*) of human nature" (MM, Doctrine of Virtue, §§21–2, 6:446). Although Kant's insistence on the purity of moral motivation may seem to hold human beings up to a harsh standard for judgment, the present points suggest a more generous approach to human virtue: we earn esteem for the purity of our motivation, but no demerit, let alone punishment, merely for the typical impurity of our motivation; we earn demerit only for evil deeds, not impure motives. Moreover, since virtue is always only something we strive for, not something we ever fully achieve, we earn this esteem for the strength of our efforts, not for the completeness of our achievement. This is not an inhumane standard, but rather one that praises us for the vigor of our moral efforts while reminding us that we can always do better.[12]

Finally, Kant makes it clear from the outset of the *Metaphysics of Morals* that all specific duties, thus duties of right as well as specific duties of virtue, can be fulfilled on the basis of respect for the moral law alone. We can be motivated to fulfill our juridical duties by external, coercive incentives, but we do not have to be. The legal system does not care why people fulfill their juridical duties. It is in the business only of threatening and enforcing sanctions against those who violate their duties, not praising those who fulfill them, and no one has a legal right to demand that anyone else fulfill their legal duties out of respect for the moral alone. So from the legal point of view, "it is an external duty," for example, "to keep a promise made in a contract." But from a more general moral point of view, we praise people for the purity of their motivation, yet cannot of course force them to be pure; "so the command" to keep a promise made in a contract or to fulfill any other legal duty "merely because it is a duty, without regard for any other incentive, belongs to **internal** lawgiving alone" (MM, Introduction, 6:220). In principle, people could fulfill all of their duties from the motive of respect for the moral law alone, and they earn esteem only for fulfilling their duties from this motive. In practice, it would be unrealistic to expect human beings always to fulfill all of their duties only from this motive, and that is why we add external incentives for the fulfillment of those duties where it is both physically and morally possible to do so. Indeed, we might say that the importance of preserving freedom wherever we can impose a duty upon us to preserve it where we can do so by external incentives without destroying freedom itself. We could think of this as a *general* obligation of justice analogous to the general obligation of virtue.

THE SPECIFIC DUTIES OF VIRTUE

Now we can turn from the general obligation of virtue to the specific duties of virtue. These are the non-coercively enforceable ways to preserve and promote the freedom to set and pursue ends that are necessary in the *actual circumstances of human existence* – as Kant puts it, ends that are necessary "as far as human beings are concerned" (MM, Doctrine of Virtue, Introduction, 6:380). That is, while the fundamental principle of morality is the same for all rational beings, and no peculiarities of human nature should figure in the analysis and confirmation of that principle, that general principle must be applied to human beings, and thus the specific duties of virtue to which it gives rise do depend upon basic empirical facts about human nature and existence. As Kant says in the Introduction to the whole *Metaphysics of Morals*:

> just as there must be principles in a metaphysics of nature for applying [the] highest universal principles of a nature in general to objects of experience, a metaphysics of morals cannot dispense with principles of application, and we shall often have to take as our object the particular **nature** of human beings, which is cognized only by experience, in order to **show** in it what can be inferred from universal moral principles.
>
> (MM, 6:216–17)

In other words, Kant continues, "a metaphysics of morals cannot be based upon anthropology but can still be applied to it" (6:217).[13]

What are the most basic facts about human nature and existence that determine what sorts of ethical duties we human beings actually have? In the most general terms, they are that we are both animal and rational, or that we are free and rational beings who are embodied. This means two things: that our reason has to be exercised in and through our bodies, and thus that we must maintain and develop our bodies in order to exercise our freedom; but also that our reason has to be exercised on our bodies, in the dual sense that we have to choose particular ends from among those suggested by the nature of our bodies but also exercise control over the inclinations arising from our bodies. As rational animals, we are both like and unlike other animals. We are like them in having bodily needs and abilities, but unlike them in also having a capacity for reason that must be realized in but can also be subverted by our bodily conduct, and thus in having temptations we may need to overcome – we could not have temptations unless we had both bodies and reason. But our bodies themselves are also different from those of most other animals, for we are not born with nor do we quickly develop all the bodily instincts and capabilities that we need to survive and flourish, but must use our reason to develop both our bodily as well as our mental capacities. Specifically, we have bodies that must be preserved, cared for, and developed if we are to be able to exercise our choice freely and effectively, and we also have general mental as well as specifically moral dispositions that must be maintained and cultivated to the same end. These are the general facts about the human condition that give rise to our specific duties of virtue regarding both ourselves and others.

Duties to ourselves

Kant begins the "Doctrine of Virtue" with the exposition of our duties to ourselves. He admits at the outset that the very idea of a duty to oneself may seem incoherent, because, it might be thought, if one imposes such a duty on oneself one could also release oneself from it, and then it would not really be a duty after all (MM, Doctrine of Virtue, §1, 6:417). His reply to this question reveals the premise of his entire theory of duties of virtue: we are both "sensible" and "intelligible" or animal and rational creatures, and our "personality" or capacity for both reason and freedom can put our merely physical being under obligation (§3, 6:418). He then divides our duties to ourselves into perfect and imperfect duties, the former being duties not to destroy, permanently or temporarily, the bodily and mental faculties on which the exercise of our freedom depends, and the latter being duties to cultivate and improve the bodily and mental faculties on which that exercise depends. The mental faculties that we must both preserve and promote include both general intellectual and specifically moral capacities.

Our first duty to ourselves, straightforwardly enough, is the duty not to commit suicide, for the simple reason that while the act of suicide considered by itself may be a perfectly free act, it is an act that destroys one's further existence and therefore the possibility for one's further freedom (MM, Doctrine of Virtue, §6, 422–3). However, as with all duties of virtue, or perhaps even all specific duties whether of right or of virtue (see MM, Preface, 6:205), some judgment must be used to interpret this duty. While Kant assumes that maiming oneself for monetary gain is forbidden under the general prohibition of self-destruction, obviously undergoing an operation, even an amputation, in order to save one's life is not; and while committing suicide merely to escape one's own pain is forbidden, intentionally sacrificing one's life in order to save one's country (6:423) may not be. In the first case, one may have to sacrifice part of one's body, and thus even some of one's future freedom of action, in order to save one's life and therefore one's freedom, even if somewhat impaired, for the future; in the second case, one might properly give up one's own existence, and therefore one's own freedom, in order to save the freedom of many others. Next, Kant claims that our perfect duties to ourselves also include the prohibition of "self-defilement" (masturbation) (§7, 6:424–6) as well as "self-stupefaction" by the "excessive use of food or drink" (§8, 6:427–8). The first of these duties depends on a dubious argument that anyone engaging in the prohibited activity would "surrender his personality" by using "himself merely as a means to satisfy an animal impulse." But the latter duty depends on the entirely plausible premise that "Brutish excess in the use of food and drink is a misuse of the means of nourishment that restricts or exhausts our capacity to use them intelligently." In other words, as embodied rational beings, we have bodies that need nourishment, and cannot act or even survive without such nourishment; but we need to take such nourishment in a way that preserves and promotes our ability to act freely and rationally, not in a way that undermines that capacity. While moderate amounts of alcohol may have health benefits and some amount and variety of food is an indisputable necessity of life and thus of our continued ability to act freely and rationally, too much of either, thus drunkenness and gluttony, can destroy that ability, whether temporarily, while one is in a drunken or gluttonous stupor, or permanently, if one kills oneself by driving while drunk or permanently incapacitates or prematurely kills oneself through alcohol poisoning or obesity.

Next, Kant lists perfect duties to oneself as a moral rather than merely physical being. These include the prohibitions of lying, avarice, and servility. Here Kant's idea is that by lying, quite apart from the deception of others that may involve, one undermines one's own ability to communicate one's thoughts with others, and thus destroys a natural capacity – the capacity for communication – that one could use in the successful exercise of one's freedom (§9, 6:429–30).[14] By "miserly avarice," one turns what ought to be mere "means to good living" into ends in themselves that "leave one's own true needs unsatisfied" (§10, 6:432). Here the basic idea is that by turning what should be a mere means for the pursuit of one's freely chosen ends into something that is to be accumulated but never used – the riches that the miser hoards – one actually undermines one's ability to act freely in all sorts of ways. Of course, this would not be true if our ability for free action were not dependent upon bodily needs that can themselves be served with the assistance of wealth. Finally, by servility or "false humility" you give up the respect as a free being that one has a right to expect from others (§11, 6:434–5), and by so doing invite others to "tread with impunity on your rights" and to make you their "lackey," thus literally surrendering your freedom to them (6:436). Of course, false humility should be distinguished from true humility, the "consciousness and feeling of the insignificance of one's moral worth **in comparison with the law**" (6:435). As part of the general duty always to seek greater moral perfection, every human being should recognize that he has not achieved it yet; therefore while we have a duty to avoid false humility, we also have a duty to exercise true humility.

Kant calls the duties just mentioned perfect duties to ourselves as "moral beings." They are certainly duties to preserve our character and dignity rather than simply our bodily existence and well-being from self-inflicted wounds. But next Kant expounds duties to preserve our specific capacities for moral judgment and feeling. First, he describes "the human being's duty to himself as his own innate judge." Here what Kant supposes is that in addition to inescapable knowledge of the moral law, as a standard by which to evaluate possible maxims for action, every human being also has a conscience, a disposition to judge how well he has done in actually conforming his action to the demands of morality. Our duty in connection with conscience is to "know, scrutinize, or fathom" ourselves, that is, to be "impartial" and "sincere" in recognizing what our motivations really have been and are – indeed, to descend "into the hell of self-cognition" – so that we can then "remove the obstacle within (an evil will actually present in [ourselves])," in order "to develop the original predisposition to a good will within [ourselves], which can never be lost" (MM, Doctrine of Virtue, §§14–15, 6:441). The task of honestly scrutinizing our own motives might seem to be an open-ended one, a lifelong process in which we can always make progress but which we can never complete, and thus this duty might seem more like an imperfect duty than a perfect one. Perhaps Kant includes it among the perfect duties because he thinks conscience is always there – it is something one cannot but "help hearing" even when one cannot bring oneself to "heed it" (§13, 6:438) – so he first conceives of our duty in negative terms, as simply that of not shutting out its voice. Finally, in the "Episodic Section" that completes Kant's list of perfect duties to ourselves as moral beings, he describes what seem to be duties to things other than ourselves and other human beings altogether, namely duties concerning non-human nature and God (§16, 6:442). Here Kant argues that we do not actually have any duties directly to such things, but that we have duties to ourselves but *regarding* such things. His view is that we cannot have duties directly to such things because they are not rational beings whom we can affect by our actions, but that we have a "natural predisposition" to be respectful of both nature and God "that greatly promotes morality or at least prepares the way for it," a "predisposition that is very serviceable to morality in one's relation with other people" (§17, 6:443). Our duty is then not to destroy or uproot this morally beneficial disposition by "wanton destruction" of nature or (presumably) indifference to (the idea of) God, and instead to cultivate this natural predisposition. The duty to do nothing that would destroy this natural predisposition could be considered a perfect duty, although again the task of cultivating and strengthening it seems more like an open-ended one, therefore a candidate for imperfect duty.

Kant's discussion of this last duty is very brief, but also very revealing. It makes clear that although he thinks that the only morally estimable motivation is the pure respect for the moral law characteristic of a good will, he also recognizes that in real life we are moved to act by various sorts of feelings and predispositions, and thus that our overarching respect for the moral law requires us to mold the feelings that actually affect our actions, strengthening those that can move us in the direction of actions required by the moral law and constraining those that would lead us astray. In spite of his theoretical commitment to the utter freedom of choice of the noumenal will, here again Kant clearly recognizes that human beings are embodied wills, rational animals and not pure rational beings, who must exercise their freedom and reason through their nature and not independently of it.[15] We will see this realism about the nature and limits of human action at work in Kant's account of our duties to others as well.

Before we turn to those duties, however, we need to comment on Kant's brief treatment of our imperfect duties to ourselves. In the *Groundwork*, Kant gave the duty to develop one's natural predispositions for skills and talents useful as means to the various ends we might choose in the exercise of our freedom as the example of imperfect duty to ourselves. It now turns out to be not just an example of this category, but rather as it were one whole side of our twofold duty to perfect both our natural and our moral capacities for effectively exercising our freedom. On the natural side, Kant observes that we have purely bodily powers, powers of mind (*Geist*), which are powers to reason *a priori* from principles as in mathematics and logic, and powers of soul (*Seele*), by which he means more empirical mental capacities such as "memory, imagination, and the like, on which can be built learning, taste . . . and so forth, which furnish instruments for a variety of purposes" (§19, 6:445). Our duty with regard to these sorts of natural capacities is simply to develop all of them as much as we can, consistent with our other obligations to both ourselves and others, so that we can be as effective as possible both in pursuing our own freely chosen ends and in assisting others in their pursuit of their ends as well. (Kant implies the last point when he describes this duty also as a human being's "duty to himself to be a useful member of the world"; §20, 6:446.) This is clearly an open-ended rather than well-defined task in several senses. First, "a human being's duty to himself regarding his **natural** perfection is only a **wide** and imperfect duty" which allows a "latitude for free choice." We cannot appeal to a rule of duty in order to decide, for example, whether "a trade, commerce, or a learned profession" will best suit us to realize our freely chosen goals in life and to help others in the realization of theirs; here only experience and judgment can help us, and we must have the latitude to gain experience and sharpen our judgment. Second, of course, a talent or skill is never completely perfected, but can always be improved – although there may be both prudential and moral reasons for sometimes concluding that one has developed some talent sufficiently and should now devote time and energy to other tasks, such as putting that talent to work to help oneself or others directly.

To this account of our duty to ourselves to increase our natural perfection, Kant finally adds "a human being's duty to himself to increase his

moral perfection," which is simply the duty to perfect the moral purity of one's motivation or "disposition to duty" (§21, 6:446). Although, as we saw in the previous chapter, Kant's final theory of the radical freedom of the will in the *Religion* implies that we always have the possibility of a self-generated conversion from an evil disposition to a good one, the "anthropological" realism characteristic of the *Metaphysics of Morals* naturally suggests that even the best of us is always subject to temptation, and that maintaining a morally good disposition will be a never-ending struggle which might gradually become easier for us but will never become automatic. So it can only be our duty "to **strive** for this perfection," and this duty will thus be "wide and imperfect in terms of its degree" even though it is "a **narrow** and perfect one in terms of its quality" (§22, 6:446) – that is, a duty that it is by no means optional for us to recognize.

Duties to others

Having analyzed our duties to ourselves, Kant finally turns to our duties to others. Contemporary ethical theories would treat duties to others before duties to self if they recognize the latter kind of duties at all.[16] One might think that Kant's treatment of duties to others only after duties to self is a merely accidental effect of the scheme he has used to classify duties, but it really reflects his deep-seated conviction that since we can only serve others if we have preserved and developed our own natural as well as moral capacities, we can fulfill our duties to others only if we have striven to overcome the internal struggle between physical and moral self-indulgence on the one hand and physical and moral self-development on the other to which each of us is always subject.

Kant does not confine our ethical duties to others to the imperfect duty of beneficence that he used as an example in the *Groundwork*. Rather, he now divides our duties to others "as human beings" into two categories, the duties of *love* and the duties of *respect*. Both of these categories need some comment. First, while we might have thought that *all* of our duties to others arise from our fundamental obligation to respect their humanity as an end in itself and never merely a means, by the "duties of respect toward other human beings arising from the **respect** due them" Kant means something more specific, namely the obligations not to be arrogant to others, not to defame them, and not to ridicule them (MM, Doctrine of Virtue, §§42–4, 6:465–8), but instead to be modest, dignified, and humane in relation to others (§37, 6:462) – even to those who have themselves dishonored humanity through an actual crime and are subject to punishment

(§38, 6:463). Kant's explanation for the necessity of these duties is that being arrogant, defamatory, and mocking and fault-finding do not just coarsen one's own moral sensibilities, but also, by "diminish[ing] respect for humanity as such, . . . finally cast[s] a shadow of worthlessness over our race as such, making misanthropy . . . or contempt the prevalent cast of mind," thereby dulling *everyone's* "moral feeling by repeatedly exposing" everyone "to the sight of such things and accustoming" all to them (§53, 6:466). One's own misuse of one's otherwise rightful entitlement toward the free expression of one's views can thereby contribute to everyone's tendency to use their own freedom in ways that undermine rather than preserve and promote freedom in general.

Now Kant stresses that the "failure to fulfill the duty arising from the **respect** owed to every human being as such is a **vice**," a real demerit rather than a mere absence of merit (MM, Doctrine of Virtue, §41, 6:464). Thus in this case we have a negative duty, a prohibition: expressions of arrogance, contempt, and the ridicule of others are simply to be avoided, and there is no room for judgment or "latitude" here. The duties of respect are therefore perfect rather than imperfect duties to others. Yet Kant includes them among the duties of virtue rather than the duties of right, presumably because they cannot be judicially enforced. Kant implies this point when he contrasts defamation or "backbiting" to "**slander**, a **false** defamation to be taken before a court" (§43, 6:466), but he does not explain *why* violations of the duties of respect should not be judicially enforced. One might suggest that the deleterious effects of these vices on the general use of freedom are too diffuse and too difficult to quantify for them to be met with specific sanctions. Indeed, one cannot always be sure who the injured party in a case of defamation or mockery is: it might seem obvious that it is the specific person defamed or mocked, but maybe that person is not only morally upright but also has a thick skin and thus ignores such insults, while it is really the moral character of some indeterminate group of onlookers or peers which is weakened. Perhaps it would also be hard to see how we could collectively punish these offenses through a judicial system without ourselves seeming arrogant and contemptuous of others. Here Kant's thought clearly needs some further development.

We can now turn back to the "duties of love" toward others, which include not only the duty of beneficence mentioned in the *Groundwork* but also the duties of "gratitude and sympathy" (MM, Doctrine of Virtue, §§29–35, 6:452–8). These are clearly general obligations, both because no one can possibly be beneficent or even sympathetic to everyone else in

the world, and there is no determinate way to specify to whom in particular one must be beneficent and sympathetic (the case of gratitude may be
different), and also because there is no mechanical way to determine how
much beneficence, sympathy, and in this case gratitude too is enough,
especially given all of anyone's other obligations. So these are clearly
imperfect duties, and there is no question that they should be included
among the non-enforceable duties of virtue rather than among the coercively enforceable duties of right – a point we might put by saying that
while I have an obligation to be beneficent to others, for example, no
particular person has a specific claim or right to my beneficence.

But there are a number of other points about these duties. First, while
Kant calls them "duties of love," he also explains that he does not mean
that they are duties to have specific *feelings* toward others, what he calls
"pathological" love, but rather duties to *act* toward them in certain ways
(MM, Doctrine of Virtue, §§25–6, 6:449–50); and although Kant thinks
that actual feelings of love toward others will tend to follow from the
practice of beneficence toward them (MM, Introduction, 6:402), this is
clearly an empirical generalization to which there will no doubt be exceptions. But the basic point remains, that one has a general duty to practice
beneficence toward others regardless of how one feels about them. Kant
argues for this general duty, in the same way that he did in the first discussion of it in the *Groundwork*, by arguing that even someone who is not
inclined to help others can find himself in situations of need where he
will wish to be helped by others, but that if his own policy of not helping
others were to be a "universal permissive law," then others would not be
prepared to help him in his time of need. This might seem like a merely
prudential argument, but it is more than that for two reasons: first, one's
interest in having the help of others available as a means to the realization
of one's own particular ends is not a mere matter of desire for one's own
happiness, but also a matter of respect for one's status as a human being
who freely chooses ends and attempts to realize them in a rational way;
and second, one's recognition that one can expect help from others only if
one is prepared to help them is not merely prudential,[17] but also an
expression of respect for them – one has a *right* to ask others for help only
if one recognizes their own status as free and rational beings who may also
need assistance in the successful pursuit of their freely chosen ends.

Next, however, a qualification of Kant's claim that the duties of love
command only maxims of action and not actual feelings is needed in the
case of the duty of sympathy, for here Kant explicitly claims that we do
have a duty to cultivate certain feelings toward others. He says that we have

a duty not to avoid the places where the poor who lack the most basic necessities are to be found but rather to seek them out, and not to shun sickrooms or debtors' prisons and so forth in order to avoid sharing painful feelings.

(§35, 6:457)

We must instead expose ourselves to such situations in order to develop such feelings. But the point of cultivating such feelings is not just to "share the sufferings" of others, which of itself does no one any good; it is rather "a duty to sympathize *actively* in their fate" (emphasis added). That is, we are "to cultivate the natural (aesthetic)[18] feelings in us" in order "to make use of them as so many means to sympathy based on moral principles" (6:457), or to use these feelings as a "means to promoting active and rational benevolence" (§34, 6:456). Kant stresses that the duty to cultivate our "receptivity to these feelings" is a "particular, though only a conditional duty," by which he means that we have a duty to cultivate these feelings only because they are means to an end derivable from the moral law, not for their own sake, and also that we must not act blindly on these feelings, but must subject our tendency to act on them to review by the moral law. For example, one should not let one's natural inclination to help anyone struggling to move a large and heavy object cause one to help someone who is actually attempting to move stolen goods;[19] but to know when one should and when one should not act upon even a sympathetic feeling one needs to know the moral law. The important point here is that we not only often have to constrain our natural tendencies to act on feelings and inclinations, but also often have to implement our general commitment to morality by acting upon our natural tendencies when those are consistent with morality. Once again, we are not disembodied rational beings, but real human beings with feelings as well as reason, and because our rationality requires that we cultivate effective means for realizing our ends, we must learn how to use our natural dispositions to action arising from those feelings as means to morally mandatory and permissible ends, both of which express our autonomy, but also only as means to those ends. Here again we have evidence of the realism of Kant's moral anthropology.

One last expression of the realism of Kant's moral anthropology can also be found in Kant's discussion of the duty of beneficence. This comes when Kant finally realizes that one can and does have a duty to promote one's own happiness as a free and rational being as part of one's duty to promote the freely chosen ends of human beings generally. Initially, as we earlier saw, Kant was extremely hostile toward the idea that one could have a duty to promote one's own happiness, on the ground that although a duty always involves an element of constraint, one is naturally inclined toward one's own happiness and therefore does not have to constrain oneself to promote it (MM, Doctrine of Virtue, Introduction, 6:386). Kant then grudgingly admitted that one might have a duty to provide oneself with some sort of minimal level of happiness, but that this would be only an indirect duty, namely, a duty to eliminate temptations to crimes one might otherwise commit for the sake of one's own happiness. Kant's assumption that one always naturally desires one's own happiness is patently false, at least if one understands happiness in a long-term rather than short-term sense, as his own example of a gouty man who might take another drink now without worrying about his health tomorrow shows (G, 4:399). We could argue that in order to promote the efficacy of his own pursuit of freely chosen ends and his ability to assist others in the pursuit of theirs, such a man does indeed have an obligation to place his long-term happiness over his short-term gratification. But finally Kant does recognize that if one's duty to promote the happiness of others arises from one's duty to promote the realization of the freely chosen ends of rational beings, then that applies to oneself as much as to anyone else: "since all **others** with the exception of myself would not be **all**," the maxim to help only others "would not have within it the universality of a law, which is still necessary for imposing obligation," and therefore "the law making benevolence a duty will include myself, as an object of benevolence" (MM, Doctrine of Virtue, §27, 6:451). No doubt part of Kant's reason for initially denying that we can have a duty to promote our own happiness is his completely realistic fear of our tendency to self-love, our tendency to put our own interests ahead of anyone else's, which, as we have seen from the *Religion*, is the fundamental enemy of morality. And even in the present context he still wants to emphasize that I am not "under an obligation to love myself," which I am all too inclined to do anyway, but rather only that

> lawgiving reason, which includes the whole species (and so myself as well) in its idea of humanity as such, includes me as giving universal law along with all others in the duty of mutual benevolence, in accordance with the principle of equality, and **permits** [me] to be benevolent to [myself] on the condition of [my] being benevolent to every other as well.
>
> (6:451)

As this statement makes clear, the reason we all have a duty to promote the happiness of others is not because we or they merely desire it, but because respect for humanity as such entails respect for and promotion of the freely chosen ends of human beings, and the realization of such ends is what brings happiness. But respect for humanity as such entails self-respect as much as respect for others – as Kant originally said, the most fundamental moral obligation is to treat humanity as an end and never merely a means "in your own person or that of any other" (G, 4:429). Indeed, it would be incoherent to hold the maxim of benevolence to be valid for *everyone* without also considering one's own happiness as morally worthy of promotion, for that maxim certainly imposes on others the duty to promote one's own happiness, and what would be the point of that if one's own happiness had no moral worth in one's own eyes?

Although some of the details of Kant's duties of virtue can seem anti-quated or alienating, in general his doctrine reflects the application of his demanding general conception of morality to a realistic assessment of human nature. Let us now see if the same holds true for his duties of right.

SUMMARY

In the *Metaphysics of Morals*, Kant analyzes the specific duties that arise from the requirements that we treat human beings always as ends, never merely as means, and act toward them only on universalizable maxims – though he gives more emphasis to the first of these formulations of the categorical imperative than to the second. His most basic distinction is between those of our duties to others that can be enforced through the coercive mechanisms of the state, that is, duties of right or juridical duties, and the duties of virtue, those of our duties toward ourselves and others that cannot be enforced through coercion but only through our own respect for the moral law. All of our duties arise from the requirements that we preserve the existence of free beings, preserve as far as possible the possibility of their exercise of their freedom, promote the development of the skills and talents they will need to pursue their freely set ends effectively, and where both necessary and possible promote the realization of their specific ends, thus contributing to their happiness. The duties of virtue specifically include the duties to preserve our own existence and our own physical, mental, and moral capacities and to develop our own skills and talents, and our duties to others include the duties of respect and of love, that is, the duties to preserve their dignity and promote their happiness, consistently, of course, with the lawfulness of their desires and our other obligations and own needs and preferences.

FURTHER READING

Gregor remains the indispensable text on the *Metaphysics of Morals* and the duties of virtue in particular. O'Neill is a recent discussion of the virtues by this important writer, in a volume that represents a wide range of contemporary approaches to the virtues. Baron *et al.* offer contrasts between Kant's conception of the virtues and those of utilitarianism and contemporary virtue ethics. Sherman offers a sustained analysis of Kant's conception of virtue and demonstrates that it is not so remote from Aristotle's conception as is often supposed. Guyer (2000) contains an extended study of Kant's conception of virtue in the chapter "Moral Worth, Virtue, and Merit," pp. 287–329, while his (2005) develops the distinction between duties of right and virtue and the approach to the latter taken in this chapter in more detail in "Kant's System of Duties," pp. 243–74. Louden stresses the anthropological context of Kant's application of moral principles. And Denis is the only book-length study of Kant's distinctive theory of duties to oneself. Finally, Grenberg interprets the virtue of humility as the foundation of Kant's theory of duties by equating it with the basic duty of respect for the moral law itself under the actual conditions of human nature.

Marcia W. Baron, Philip Pettit, and Michael Slote, *Three Methods of Ethics* (Oxford: Blackwell Publishers, 1997).

Lara Denis, *Moral Self-Regard: Duties to Oneself in Kant's Moral Theory* (New York: Routledge, 2001).

Mary J. Gregor, *Laws of Freedom: A Study of Kant's Method Applying the Categorical Imperative in the* Metaphysik der Sitten (Oxford: Basil Blackwell, 1963).

Jeanine Grenberg, *Kant and the Ethics of Humility* (Cambridge: Cambridge University Press, 2005).

Paul Guyer, *Kant on Freedom, Law, and Happiness* (Cambridge: Cambridge University Press, 2000).

——*Kant's System of Nature and Freedom* (Oxford: Clarendon Press, 2005).

Robert B. Louden, *Kant's Impure Ethics: From Rational Beings to Human Beings* (New York: Oxford University Press, 2000).

Onora O'Neill, "Kant's Virtues," in Roger Crisp (ed.), *How Should One Live? Essays on the Virtues* (Oxford: Clarendon Press, 1996), pp. 77–98.

Nancy Sherman, *Making a Necessity of Virtue: Aristotle and Kant on Virtue* (Cambridge: Cambridge University Press, 1997).

Eight

Kant's System of Duties II

Duties of right

THE UNIVERSAL PRINCIPLE OF RIGHT, COERCION, AND INNATE RIGHT

Kant's legal and political philosophy is presented as a "doctrine of right" (*Rechtslehre*). The very name of this doctrine creates problems for readers of English. The noun *Recht* (Latin *ius*) does not mean a specific moral or legal claim against one or more other persons who have an obligation to satisfy that claim, like the English noun "a right," but refers to the entire body of legal obligations with corresponding legal rights that people ought to have. But note the "ought": *Recht* also does not refer to the body of rights and obligations that some particular population actually has under some particular legal and political system, or does so only as part of the expression "positive right"; it refers to the rights and obligations that everyone ought to have under an ideal legal and political system, what Kant's predecessors called "natural right" (*Naturrecht*). So *Recht* cannot be translated as "law," because that term is too closely connected with actual rather than ideal legislation. Nor can it comfortably be translated as "justice," as is sometimes done[1]: in English, that term is too broad, subsuming not only criminal justice but also distributive justice, and suggesting at least in part considerations of fairness and equity that may go beyond what we are willing to enforce through the legal and political system. For Kant, as we saw in the previous chapter, *Recht* denotes only that part of morality and justice that can and should be coercively enforced. In the face of these difficulties, it seems best just to translate *Recht* as "right," although using that term as a mass-noun rather than a count-noun (like "a right"). But we can also translate some of its derivatives by latinate words with the "iur-" stem, deriving from *ius*, such as "juridical." Thus we can speak of "duties of right" or "juridical duties." I will use both expressions in this chapter.

So much for style. Now for substance. With little ado, Kant begins the "Doctrine of Right" with the statements that "Right is the sum of the conditions under which the choice of one can be united with the choice of another in accordance with a universal law of freedom" (MM, Doctrine of Right, Introduction §B, 6:230). Since the *choices* of different agents can be incompatible with each other only when they are acted upon, the compatibility of choices to which this definition refers is actually the compatibility of freely chosen *actions* with each other. So Kant next states the "universal principle of right" thus: "Any action is **right** if it can coexist with everyone's freedom in accordance with a universal law, or if on its maxim the freedom of choice of each can coexist with everyone's freedom in accordance with a universal law" (§C, 6:230). The derivation of this principle from the universal value of humanity as such is obvious if humanity is understood as the freedom to both choose and pursue ends: the principle says that each person must be allowed as much freedom to pursue her own ends as is compatible with everyone else having as much freedom as they can to pursue their ends.[2] The actions that are prohibited by the universal principle of right are free actions by one person that would deprive others of a similar degree of freedom. For example, taking control of an external object can be consistent with this principle if so doing leaves others equally free to take control of relevantly similar objects as well; committing homicide is typically not consistent with this principle because it is a free action on the part of one person that deprives another of his freedom. (Homicide in self-defense may be the atypical exception to this rule precisely because the freedom of the agent who commits such an act has already been threatened by the attack of the other.) The principle of right can also be understood as the principle that each person must have the *maximal* sphere of freedom consistent with the similarly *maximal* freedom of everyone else. It is not a maximizing principle like the classical utilitarian principle "greatest happiness for the greatest number," however, for that principle is indifferent to equality in the distribution of happiness among persons, while Kant's principle calls for equally maximal spheres of freedom for all.

As we saw in the previous chapter, Kant distinguishes duties of right from duties of virtue by the fact that the former are consistent with external incentives, and can thus be coercively enforced. A necessary condition for this is that duties of right concern only the external use of choice, or freedom of action. My intentions or maxims as such do not restrict the freedom of others; only my actions, or my maxims carried out as patterns of action rather than considered as mere patterns of intention, can. So insofar as law is to enforce right in Kant's sense, it is not concerned with the purity or impurity of motives, but only with the effects of actions.[3] For the same reason, justice could at least possibly employ external sanctions, inducing people to conform to the law by the threat of sanction or punishment rather than just appealing to their respect for duty, a motivation that by its very nature could not be induced by any threat or inducement, since these could produce only the desire to avoid or obtain them. But we may still ask whether right's concern with the effects of actions rather than with motives is a *sufficient* condition for coercive enforcement; indeed, since a coercive sanction is as it were by definition a restriction of freedom – incarcerating or fining someone, let alone executing them, obviously deprives them of freedom of action and freedom in the use of their means – we might ask how the use of coercion can even be *consistent* with the preservation of equally maximal spheres of freedom that is demanded by the universal principle of right.

Kant addresses this question immediately with the following brief argument:

> Resistance that counteracts the hindering of an effect promotes this effect and is consistent with it. Now whatever is wrong is a hindrance to freedom in accordance with universal laws. But coercion is a hindrance or resistance to freedom. Therefore, if a certain use of freedom is itself a hindrance to freedom in accordance with universal laws (i.e., wrong), coercion that is opposed to this (as a **hindering of a hindrance to freedom**) is consistent with freedom in accordance with universal laws, that is, it is right.
>
> (§D, 6:231)

In the abstract, it sounds right that blocking something that would block freedom will preserve freedom, so coercion to prevent an attack upon freedom will preserve freedom and must be right. But what about the freedom of the one who would hinder the freedom of others and for that reason is liable to have his own freedom hindered – does that count for nothing?[4] On one analysis of Kant's argument, it does not, because the freedom that is to be preserved in accordance with the universal principle of right is precisely "freedom in accordance with a universal law," and the freedom of one who would attack the freedom of others is precisely not freedom in accordance with a universal law, and therefore has no claim to protection.[5] But one could also argue that freedom in accordance with universal law should be freedom for *everybody*, and that it must therefore preserve at least the opportunity for free action for everyone. However, one could then save Kant's argument by observing that while a criminal act such as theft, kidnapping, or homicide is a free act on the part of the *perpetrator* that completely deprives the *victim* of his freedom of choice about what is to happen – the victim of one of these crimes is not given the opportunity to decide whether he wants to be robbed or kidnapped[6] – a publicly known system of threatened sanctions does not deprive *anyone, even the criminal*, of his freedom of choice. The criminal has the choice whether to commit a crime and suffer the sanction or to refrain from the crime and avoid the sanction, precisely the kind of freedom of choice of which he would deprive his victim if he commits the crime. So the commission of a crime is not consistent with freedom in accordance with a universal law, that is, universal freedom, but the existence of a legal system with publicly known sanctions is in fact consistent with the freedom of all. Of course, once someone does choose to go ahead and commit a crime and then suffers the sanction for it, that sanction will deprive him of his *future* freedom in whole or part; but he will have brought that upon his own head, that is, he will in effect have freely chosen to risk giving up his future freedom for the sake of some act that he wanted to perform now.[7]

Thus Kant could defend his claim that the use of coercion to punish crimes against freedom is consistent with freedom. Further, although it would certainly be nice if everyone were always motivated by respect for duty alone and never broke any morally justifiable law, we know human nature all too well to think that will ever happen. So we could argue that the threat and use of coercion is the only way even to approximate a guarantee that the universal principle of right will always be observed. Further, since that principle is itself a consequence of the fundamental principle of morality, it can be argued we are actually under a moral *obligation* to institute and maintain a system for the coercive enforcement of the principle of right. The coercive enforcement of right is then not merely permissible but mandatory. The central idea of Kant's legal and political philosophy is thus that we must not only define the rights and obligations that we have to one another in virtue of the universal principle of right, but must also institute a system for the coercive enforcement of those rights – a state – and define the rights and obligations that its citizens and officeholders must have in order for it to enforce the first sort of rights and obligations. This is the basis for Kant's twofold division of the "Doctrine of Right" into what he calls, following European tradition, "Private Right" and "Public Right": the first concerns the rights and duties people must observe in their interactions with each other in order to preserve equally maximal spheres of freedom, and the second concerns the mechanism by which people can and must collectively enforce those rights and duties, and the further rights and duties which the institution of such a mechanism, that is, the state, creates.

Kant's division of the main body of the "Doctrine of Right" into these two parts is a little misleading, because there are actually two kinds of rights against each other that people must have if freedom of action is to be preserved, both of which must in turn be collectively enforced by the medium of a polity. Kant distinguishes between "innate right" and "acquired right," dealing with the first only in the Introduction to the "Doctrine of Right" and with only the latter under the rubric of "Private Right"; both of these in turn are to be enforced through the political mechanisms described under "Public Right" (basically, by means of criminal and civil law respectively, although Kant does not spell this out). The distinction between innate and acquired right is basically that between rights that everyone ought to have without the antecedent consent of others and rights that people can acquire only through the consent of others, for example the right to freedom from unprovoked assault on one's body, on the one hand, and the right to enjoyment of a piece of property acquired from someone else, on the other.[8]

In the Introduction, Kant says that

> **Freedom** (independence from being constrained by another's choice), insofar as it can coexist with the freedom of every other in accordance with a universal law, is the only original right belonging to every human being by virtue of his humanity.
>
> (6:237)

This definition sounds just like what everyone would enjoy if the universal principle of right were fully observed, so it is hard to see what is specific about it. But a definition that Kant gave in his classroom lectures a few years before publishing the *Metaphysics of Morals* as well as the illustration with which he follows this initial statement clarify his meaning. In the lectures on the metaphysics of morals that he gave in 1793–94, Kant stated that:

> As to the object of innate right, viz. mine and thine, it can consist in nothing more than the possession of one's own person, in the totality of all those rights that constitute a part of me, and thus cannot be separated from me without violating the laws that comport with the freedom of everyone according to universal laws.
>
> (MMV, 27:588)

Thus, freedom of the person, that is, freedom from assaults upon one's body and motion, is a right that everyone has independently of any antecedent consent from anyone else, simply because everyone has an obligation to respect such freedoms as part of treating everyone as an end and not merely as a means. In the Introduction to the "Doctrine of Virtue," Kant offers another statement of what such freedom of the person involves: "being authorized to do to others anything that does not in itself diminish what is theirs, so long as they do not want to accept it," in other words, any free act that does not by itself diminish the freedom of anyone else. Thus, one has the right to use one's own body in any way that does not by itself injure the freedom of others. Kant understands this broadly rather than narrowly, and gives as a striking example the right of "merely communicating [one's] thoughts to others, telling or promising them something, whether what [one] says is true and sincere or untrue and insincere; for it is entirely up to them whether they want to believe him or not" (6:238). Here Kant argues for complete freedom of expression on the ground that merely expressing something, even making a promise, does not by itself force anyone else to do anything, but leaves their freedom of choice intact. This is why Kant, as we have already seen, must treat the duty to tell the truth as an ethical duty to oneself rather than a duty of right to others.[9] But Kant also includes under the category of innate right "innate **equality**, that is, independence from being bound by others to more than one can in turn bind them: hence a human being's quality of being **his own master**, as well as being a human being **beyond reproach**, since before he performs any act affecting rights he has done no wrong to anyone" (6:237–8). Behind this abstract language there stands the radical principle that no one can have any rights over others that they cannot have over him at the same time, so there can be no rightful slavery or feudal servitude, as well as the principle that no one can lose any of his rights except by his own misdeed.

The main part of Kant's discussion, however, concerns "acquired right," that is, rights that one can acquire only with the consent of others – in other words, property rights in the broadest sense, i.e., rights to objects other than oneself or even to the actions of others beside oneself which one can gain only with the consent of those who, other things being equal, could also use those objects or who will have to perform those actions. Kant's section on "Private Right" expounds property rights in this broad sense, and "Public Right" then describes the kind of state that is necessary to collectively enforce both these property rights and the rights implied under the innate right to freedom.

THE RIGHT TO PROPERTY

Kant's account of property rights is densely argued, detailed, and couched in the language of European legal traditions, which can make it difficult for the modern reader, especially the Anglo-American reader, to follow. But the basic idea is simple: property can be rightfully acquired only in ways that are consistent with the innate right of all who will be affected by such claims, that is to say, *only on terms to which they could rationally consent*. Kant expresses this basic premise for his discussion of property in what sounds like a legal principle for the adjudication of disputes about property:

> The aim in introducing such a division within the system of natural right (insofar as it is concerned with innate right) is that when a dispute arises about an acquired right and the question comes, on whom does the burden of proof (*onus probandi*) fall, either about a controversial fact or, if this is settled, about a controversial right, someone who refuses to accept this obligation can appeal methodically to his innate right to freedom . . . as if he were appealing to various bases for rights.
>
> (6:238)

But the reason why any party can appeal to his innate right to freedom in a dispute about an acquired right is precisely that such rights must be acquired in a way that is consistent with the innate right to freedom of all affected by them. Claims to property rights do restrict the outward exercise of freedom in all sorts of ways: if I acquire a piece of land and put up "No Trespassing" signs, then you no longer have the freedom to enter my land at will, even though from one point of view your doing so involves nothing more than freely moving your body in a way that does not obviously interfere with my freedom to do the same with my body. Kant's point is that just because the acquisition of property rights does have such effects, they can rightfully be acquired only in ways consistent with the innate right to freedom of all, including, as we saw, the "independence from being bound by others to more than one can in turn bind them." The implications of this principle are profound.

Kant divides property rights into three kinds: property in things, beginning with land, as the location for all things and the source of most wealth (natural enough assumptions for Kant to make in a country that was still largely agrarian and in a city that made its living primarily from trade in agricultural and forestry products); contract rights, or rights to specific acts by other persons acquired by making a contract; and rights to persons akin to rights to things, which are long-term rights regarding other persons, such as spouses or parents or children, which may be acquired by an explicit contract, as in the case of marriage or employment, or without such a contract, as in relations between parents and children. Kant's point in his discussion of all these rights is that they must be acquired and defined in ways consistent with the universal principle of right, that is, the preservation of equal spheres of freedom, and thus that there are constraints on these rights that are both moral and enforceable. The general structure of Kant's argument is perhaps clearest in the case of property rights in things and land, property in the most ordinary sense of the word, so I will discuss that case in some detail and then briefly comment on the other two.

The fundamental factual premise of Kant's analysis of property in things is that an individual's right to a particular piece of property – or at least any property beyond what he can physically grasp or occupy at a particular moment, interference with which would already violate his innate right to freedom of the person – does not consist in some sort of unilateral bond between the individual and the object of his right, but can only consist in a multilateral agreement among all those individuals who could otherwise control and use the object that one of them and not the others shall have that right.[10] A legitimate claim to property puts "all others under an obligation, which they would not otherwise have, to refrain from using certain objects of our choice" (MM, *Doctrine of Right*, §6, 6:247), and therefore depends upon an agreement among persons that one has the right to control and use such objects and others have the obligation to refrain from any use of the object not authorized by the owner. Since inanimate objects such as land as well as many animate objects such as cattle do not have wills, no agreement between them and their would-be owner is even possible, let alone necessary (6:250). A would-be owner of any such object therefore cannot create a property right in it simply by some transaction between himself and that object. Contrary to Locke's famous image, an individual cannot create a right to the object simply by "mixing his labour" with it.[11] Further, as Kant states under the grand name of the "postulate of practical reason with regard to rights" (6:250), it would be irrational to deny ourselves the right to control and use such objects – in the actual circumstances of human existence, in which we depend on external objects of all sorts, that would be to deny ourselves necessary means to freely chosen ends, and would thus contradict our own status as ends. But since in the actual circumstances of human existence we are always in contact and potential conflict with others, we must also find ways to control and use such objects to which others who could also use them would agree.[12] Thus, even though the objects that we would own have no rights against us, we can acquire property rights in particular objects only by gaining the consent of others who could also control and use them that they will refrain from claims to do so while allowing our claims, or at least that they will consent to the general system of property rights within which our claims are made.[13]

This factual analysis, however, is combined in Kant's thought with an equally fundamental moral premise. This is simply the idea that the recognition of particular property claims and the general practice of restraint from encroachment on the possessions of others could be secured in two ways, either by fear of brute force, typically wielded by a few who are in a position to determine and enforce the system of boundaries to their own advantage against the many, or by the free consent of all involved, but that for a system of property-rights to be morally acceptable, it must be possible for it to receive the *freely given consent* of all involved. That Kant's intention is to prescribe the principles of the possibility of property under the condition of the moral requirement of free consent rather than mere force is implied when he says that his concept of property "is concerned with the practical determination of choice in accordance with laws of **freedom** . . . and **right** is a pure practical **rational concept** of choice under laws of freedom" (MM, *Doctrine of Right*, §5, 6:249), and that the omnilateral rather than unilateral determination of wills with regard to the control of particular objects in which property consists is to be "united not contingently" – as any union of wills based on mere force would be –

> but *a priori* and therefore necessarily, and because of this is the only will that is lawgiving. For only in accordance with this principle of the will is it possible for the free choice of each to accord with the freedom of all, and therefore possible for there to be any right, and so too possible for any external object to be mine or yours.
>
> (MM, *Doctrine of Right*, §14, 6:263)

This means that for any system of property rights to be morally acceptable, all affected by that system must be able to freely consent to it. And if those who must be able to give their consent freely are to be reasonable agents making their choices in a situation free of constraints arising from the immoral exercise of force, then each agent must be able to see the whole system as working reasonably well for his own benefit, or at least as working better than any realistic alternative, so it must satisfy at least this much of a constraint of fairness.[14]

This starting-point has profound consequences. Kant's political philosophy is often included in the social contract tradition of Hobbes and Locke, but there are crucial differences between Kant's view and the traditional conception of the social contract. On the traditional theory, people are conceived of as establishing property rights in the state of nature and then instituting a state out of a purely prudential concern to increase the security of their property through the collective rather than individual use of force. The only constraints on how much property they can acquire are prudential – how much can they take yet still be able to enlist the support of others in defending it – or theological – how much can they take without violating God's concern for their neighbors.[15] But on Kant's view, property cannot exist at all except by means of agreement, so a social contract or proviso of distributive justice cannot be merely added to already existing property rights; it is inherent in the very idea of rightful or morally acceptable property. To be sure, as we have already seen, it is an underlying assumption of Kant's entire doctrine of right that in real life people are not always motivated by respect for the moral law alone, and we do have to make provision for the coercive enforcement of rights and obligations where that is physically and morally possible. So Kant does agree with the social contract tradition that the concentration of power in the hands of the collectivity will be necessary to defend even the most equitable system of property rights, and thus he concedes, or rather insists, that a state is necessary to sustain such rights. But he then goes beyond this tradition in insisting that in the actual circumstances of human life, where we do not live in isolation from one another and thus where no individual can control and use any object without in fact preventing others from claiming it, individuals have not merely a right but a moral responsibility to institute and maintain a state. But since any *morally defensible* claim to property must be claimed on terms of civil association that others can *freely* accept, those who enjoy property in a state have a moral responsibility to create and maintain some form of fairness – that is, what can be perceived as making adequate provision for their own ability to claim property by those who must agree to their civil association – in the distribution of property rights in their state. And, as Kant will subsequently make clear, those who hold offices and therefore power in a state have a special responsibility to ensure that the system of property rights in the state does not work for their own benefit, but for the benefit of all. Thus all citizens but especially all members of the government must govern in accord with the idea of a social contract that is fair to all. For an employee of the eighteenth-century Prussian monarchy whose appointment was made and salary fixed by the king, this was a radical position to take.

Kant's argument that a system of property rights needs an omnilateral agreement among wills expressed in the concrete form of a state actually rests on two empirical assumptions about the human condition. First, as already suggested, Kant assumes that the control of land is the necessary condition for the control of their objects, whether structures placed on that land, means of production placed on it, or produce from it: "Land (understood as all habitable ground) is to be regarded as the **substance** with respect to whatever is moveable upon it, while the existence of the latter is to be regarded only as **inherence**" (MM, Doctrine of Right, §12, 6:261). However, there are no natural divisions of land beyond the boundaries determined by the footprint or outline of particular human bodies, which are both much less than we need to control in order to sustain ourselves and are also always moving rather than fixed and so would not give us any predictable control over objects. Thus, in the state of nature we would all live together on a single, undivided territory, "because the spherical surface of the earth unites all the places on its surface" (§13, 6:262). And that has two implications. For one, it places a moral constraint on the distribution of land: for such a distribution to be fair, we have to be able to think of it as consistent with a way in which people who originally held land in common could have agreed to divide it up into individual plots – indeed, the ultimate test for the fairness of a system of property is whether all the people of the earth could have divided up all the land of the earth as that system does. As Kant puts this point, "Original possession in common is a practical rational concept that contains *a priori* the principle in accordance with which alone people can use a place on the earth in accordance with principles of right" (§13, 6:262). By this Kant does not mean to endorse regional or world-wide communism, for he is not prohibiting the division of the land into private property; he is rather proposing a test for the fairness of division. The further implication of Kant's empirical premise that the surface of the earth is not naturally divided is that for the land to be divided into determinate portions that could be held as individual properties, an artificial but publicly recognizable scheme of division has to be introduced. A factual condition for the existence of sustainable property rights in the actual circumstances of human existence is therefore a publicly recognized survey of the land and a publicly accessible record of that survey and of the assignment of claims on the basis of it. This is a function that can be carried out only by a state – in American terms, at the county level by the recorder of deeds.

Kant's second empirical assumption, which we have also already mentioned, is that human beings are not in fact always motivated by moral considerations alone, and therefore even a fair system of property rights also needs enforcement through the collective power of a state. In this Kant certainly agrees with the social contract tradition. So in addition to insisting as a matter of fairness that one has no right to claim property unless one is willing to grant comparable rights to others, Kant also recognizes that as a matter of prudence one will have no reason to recognize the property rights of others unless he can be sure that at least for the most part others will restrain themselves or be restrained from encroaching on his property – and of course these others may see no reason to refrain from encroaching on the property of the first unless they have some assurance that he will refrain from encroaching on theirs. This means that some general assurance that all property-holders will respect the boundaries of their properties is required for anyone's property rights to be more than a mere idea: "No one is bound to refrain from encroaching on what another possesses if the other gives him no equal assurance that he will observe the same restraint toward him" (MM, Doctrine of Right, §42, 6:307). Thus, some state force sufficient to provide assurance that all will respect the boundaries of their claims is also a necessary condition for the existence of property – again in American terms, the office of a sheriff who will enforce the rights of owners is also a condition of the possibility of property.

There is another aspect of traditional social contract theory that has to find a place in Kant's theory of property. The traditional theory was based on the assumption that individuals could and would establish property rights in the state of nature, and would need to enter into a civil condition only to make those rights more *secure*. Thus property rights temporally precede the civil condition, and the latter at best perfects them. Kant concedes the empirical fact that people must already have some pretensions to property rights in order to be motivated to enter into the civil condition, even though on his own analysis property rights cannot really exist apart from the agencies of a state. His way of avoiding paradox is by then arguing that claims to property rights are only "provisional" prior to the institution of the state, and that they cannot become "conclusive" except by the institution of the state – and then adding that all who would claim even provisional property rights in the state of nature are under the *moral* duty to enter the civil condition and thereby make those rights conclusive. "**Provisionally rightful** possession" is:

> possession in anticipation of and preparation for the civil condition, which can be based only on a law of common will . . . the way to have something

> external as one's own **in a state of nature** is physical possession which
> has in its favor the rightful **presumption** that it will be made into rightful
> possession through being united with the will of all in a public lawgiving.
>
> (§9, 6:257)

Thus "From private right in the state of nature there proceeds the postulate
of public right: when you cannot avoid living side by side with all others,
you ought to leave the state of nature and proceed with them into a
rightful condition, that is, a condition of distributive justice" (§42,
6:307). Since as far as we are concerned we can never avoid living side by
side with others, however, we are *always* under the duty to "proceed with
them into a rightful condition."

In fact, Kant argues that our duty to enter into the civil condition with
others gives us the right to *coerce* them into entering that condition with
us, since their refusal to do so would be equivalent to a threat against our
property claims – "No one . . . need wait until he has learned by bitter
experience of the other's contrary disposition" (6:307) – and is therefore
itself wrongful and indefensible (see also §9, 6:257). But just as he will
argue in *Toward Perpetual Peace* that even when nations are forced to make war
in an international state of nature, prior to the establishment of the world-
wide federation of republics that will someday ensure peace, they still have
a duty to wage that war in a way that will allow and facilitate the subsequent establishment of peace (see PP, Preliminary Article 6, 8:346), so we
can assume that our provisional possession "in anticipation and preparation for the civil condition" means that we have the responsibility even
prior to or in the absence of a well-functioning state to make only property claims that could be fairly enforced against others and to coerce them
only into a state that would maintain a fair system of property rights. The
duty to institute a state based on a fair distribution of property rights is
thus for Kant our primary political responsibility.

It would seem to follow directly from this that we also have a constant
responsibility to ensure that our state once instituted not only endures but
also maintains a system of property rights that all involved can continue to
judge to be fair enough to deserve their free consent. Kant does not state
this as explicitly as one might like, but given his general argument from
property to the state it may be fairly inferred from what he does say about
taxation:

> To the supreme commander there belongs **indirectly**, that is, insofar as he
> has taken over the duty of the people, the right to impose taxes on the

people for its own preservation, such as taxes to support organizations providing for the **poor**, **foundling homes** and **church organizations**, usually called charitable or pious organizations.

> The general will of the people has united itself into a society which is to maintain itself perpetually; and for this end it has submitted itself to the internal authority of the state in order to maintain those members of the society who are unable to maintain themselves.
>
> (MM, Doctrine of Right, General Remark C, 6:325−6)

Since in Kant's analysis the people have not united themselves into a state through their general will merely from prudence or love of life, however, but in order to institute a rightful system of property, the duty to maintain the state that is delegated to their executive must therefore include the duty to maintain such a rightful system of property − and since the executive can maintain such a system in good part only through taxation, this is a duty that is incumbent not just on the executive but on all of those who are put into a position to pay taxes through the prevailing system of property. Now it is of course a sign of Kant's times that he thinks of the rightfulness of the system of property as being maintained through poorhouses, foundling homes, and charitable hospitals, rather than through fair labor laws, the regulation of large businesses, and the redistribution of income through estate taxes, welfare schemes, and the like; but that should not obscure the general principle that if we are under an obligation to institute a state to secure a rightful but only a rightful system of property then we must also have the responsibility of maintaining that state and its rightful system of property. This puts the officials of the state under an indirect obligation to impose taxes, but puts all the citizens of the state able to do so under an even more direct obligation to pay their taxes,[16] as well as to maintain compliance with whatever other laws and institutions turn out in changing historical circumstances to be necessary to sustain a rightful system of property.[17]

But before we get deeper into Kant's theory of the state, the second half of the "Doctrine of Right," let's take a brief look at the two remaining parts of the first half, that is, the discussion of contract rights and rights to persons akin to things. In his discussion of contracts, Kant makes the obvious point that from a moral point of view "A right against a person can never be acquired originally and on one's own initiative," but requires the free consent of that other person as someone who has the right to set his own ends freely in virtue of his own humanity. But Kant also makes the less obvious point that any contract must "conform to the principle of the consistency of my choice with the freedom of everyone" (MM, Doctrine of Right, §18, 6:271). Although Kant does not draw out the implications of this requirement, it means that even contracts to which both parties agree are not morally acceptable – and therefore also should not be enforced by the state – if they violate the freedom and legitimate interest of people who are not parties to the contract. Freely entered contracts between thieves are not to be enforced through the universal will because they are contracts to violate the rights of others. And a contract to enter into slavery cannot be enforced because it violates the future freedom of the person who would freely enter into it.

We can turn now to Kant's discussion of rights to persons akin to things, which he also calls domestic rights. He recognize three such rights, with their correlative duties: marriage rights, parental rights, and the rights of the head of a household. Kant's discussion of marriage rights is both perverse and profound. Kant's views about sex are, to put it mildly, bizarre, in part at least either the views of a bachelor or the views that made him a bachelor. In his discussion of "self-defilement" in the "Doctrine of Virtue," Kant held that solitary sex turns one into a mere means for one's own enjoyment, thereby dishonoring one's own humanity as an end in itself; and now he argues that in sex between two persons – although he has only heterosexual persons in mind – each partner "makes use of the other's sexual organs" for mere "**enjoyment**, for which each one gives itself up to the other," each thereby making "himself [or herself] into a thing, which conflicts with the right of humanity in his [or her] own person" (MM, Doctrine of Right, §25, 6:278). However, Kant is not about to outlaw heterosexual sex; rather, his point is that "if the sexual inclination is to be recognized as allowed by morality, then it must be able to co-exist with the freedom sanctified by humanity"(MMV, 27:638). And this is possible, Kant argues, if sex takes place within marriage, where "while one person is acquired by the other **as if it were a thing**, the one who is acquired acquires the other in turn; for in this way each reclaims itself and restores its personality." Further, Kant says, "acquiring a member of a human being is at the same time acquiring the whole person, since a person is an absolute unity." Kant's idea seems to be that sex can be raised from an animal into a human act only in a situation where each person fully recognizes the humanity of the other, and where each is thus committed to treating the other not just as a sexual partner but as another human being all of whose rights are to be respected and whose ends are to be promoted as of equal value to his or her own. By respecting each other as a whole person and not just a sex object, each partner raises both herself and the other from the level of mere animality to the level of humanity, each thereby "recouping" him- or herself as a person. Harsh and repressive as the starting point of this argument may seem, Kant draws from it the progressive conclusion that "the relation of the partners in a marriage is a relation of **equality** of possession, equality both in their possession of each other as persons . . . and also equality in their possession of material goods." Kant certainly does not treat wives as equal to husbands in every respect; in a discussion of voting rights elsewhere, he argues that women cannot have the right to vote because they are dependent upon men (husbands, fathers, etc.), which he takes to mean that they would always cast their vote as their man decides, thereby unfairly multiplying his vote (see TP, 8:292). But he does reject the view that the possessions a wife brings to a marriage as well as everything earned during a marriage automatically belong to the husband, and he also rejects concubinage as well as morganatic marriage, "which takes advantage of the inequality of estate of the two parties to give one of them domination over the other" (§26, 6:279).[18] Finally, in recognition of the both animal and rational nature of human beings, Kant argues that a marriage can be consummated only with actual intercourse as well as a contract that both legitimizes that intercourse and prohibits intercourse between either member of the couple and anyone else.

In the lengthier discussion of marriage that he offered in his classroom lectures – to students most of whom, unlike himself, would actually marry – Kant distinguishes his position from a teleological interpretation of sex. His point is not that sex is naturally intended only for procreation, and therefore should take place only within marriage for the sake of procreation. That itself would be inhumane, "attending not at all to the worth of our humanity," because it would for example deny to infertile couples or those past child-bearing age the right to have sex or even the right to stay married (MMV, 27:639). His point is rather the moral point that sex should take place only in a relationship in which each partner fully recognizes the worth of the humanity of both partners. Of course, more than two hundred years after Kant wrote, many readers will feel that this moral obligation can be satisfied in heterosexual or homosexual relationships without the blessing of the law or the legal enforcement of the partner's rights to each other against outsiders. But even those who do not think that morally acceptable sexual relations need a blessing from the law or protection by enforcement of laws against adultery will recognize that marriage creates a variety of other rights, such as rights to medical and retirement benefits, rights to inheritance, rights to participate in vital health decisions, which should be enforced by the law, and for that reason some argue for the extension of the institution of marriage to include homosexual marriage.

But where there is procreative sex, of course, there will often be children, so Kant next turns to parental rights, which turn out to concern duties parents have to their children and rights regarding their children that they have against others, but not duties children have to parents – if children, who did not ask to be born, have any duty to parents, it is only the duty of gratitude, which is a duty of virtue, not a determinate nor legally enforceable duty of right. In Kant's view, parents rather mysteriously use their own freedom to create other free beings, which cannot, because of their freedom, really be explained in mechanical terms (MM, Doctrine of Right, §28, 6:280n.) However, children are not only free beings; they are also dependent beings. This gives parents a twofold obligation toward their children: since children are free beings, not mere mechanisms, parents "cannot destroy their child as if he were something they had **made**"; and since children are dependent beings who have been created by the free choice of their parents, they thereby have "an original innate (not acquired) right to the care of their parents until they are able to look after themselves" (6:280). This right is not acquired by a voluntary act of the child, that is, but the obligation toward the child is acquired by the parents through their voluntary act of procreation, so it can be treated under the general category of acquired right. The duty of the parents includes their obligation "not only to feed and care for him" but also that "to educate him, to develop him both **pragmatically**, so that in the future he can look after himself and make his way in life, and **morally**, since otherwise the fault of having neglected him would fall on the parents" (§29, 6:281) – indeed, if they have neglected the moral education of their child, the blame for the child's misdeed would fall upon the parents.

Now what Kant actually stresses is the *rights* that parents have with regard to their obligations to their children: their rights to manage and educate their children as they see fit, and their rights against both their children and others to recover the children if they run away (6:282). These we may presume are intended to be legally enforceable rights. But Kant does not explicitly discuss legal enforcement of the direct *duties* that parents have toward their children, thus the right and even the duty of the state to intervene in cases where parents themselves are not fulfilling their duties toward their children. Presumably all of the rights and duties that Kant discusses in the "Doctrine of Right" are intended to be duties that are legally enforceable, therefore enforceable by the state, and thus the parents' duties toward their children and the children's rights against their parents are legally enforceable. But perhaps in a society where the only provision for children outside of their own homes was foundling homes and orphanages, and where much education took place within the home and there was very little public education, let alone compulsory education, Kant could hardly have envisioned how a broad set of children's rights to both nourishment and education could have been publicly enforced. However, we do not depart from the spirit of Kant's thought when we enforce the right of children to an education through the provision of public schools and enforce parents' duty to provide education for their children through compulsory education laws. Indeed, through such institutions as school taxes we institutionalize the obligation of all adults to provide education for all children, not just their own.

Finally, under the rubric of the "right of a head of the household," Kant discusses the rights of employers with regard to their servants (as opposed to independent contractors). Here Kant's point is to stress the limits on the rights of heads of households, or their duties as well as their rights: his central claim is that the employer of servants "can never behave as if he owned them; for it is only by a contract that he has brought them under his control, and a contract by which one party would completely renounce its freedom for the other's advantage would be self-contradictory, that is, null and void, since by it one party would cease to be a person and so would have no duty to keep the contract but would recognize only force" (MM, Doctrine of Right, §30, 6:283). In other words, if you treat another person as subhuman, then you cannot expect him to recognize any obligations toward you either, and you have no right to control him, although maybe you can do so by sheer force. By this argument Kant rejected all forms of serfdom and slavery long before almost all of the supposedly enlightened governments of Europe and the Americas had done so.

All of the rights we have discussed are rights that need to be and can be enforced by the collective power of human beings united in a state. The existence of states in turn creates further rights and obligations. Let us now turn to those.

POLITICAL RIGHTS AND OBLIGATIONS

In Kant's view, the state exists in order to make determinate and collectively enforce each of its subjects' innate right to freedom of the person and the rights that they can legitimately acquire in their interactions with others, and is itself legitimate only to the extent that it does this and only this. In Kant's view (like that of all political theorists after Locke), a state is not created by a historical act in one generation and by the express or tacit consent of members of subsequent generations to that original compact. Rather, the *idea* of a social contract is a normative test of the justice of actual states, however they actually came into being and by whatever structure they are actually governed. As he succinctly says in the "Doctrine of Right," "The act by which a people constitutes itself into a state is the **original contract**. Properly speaking, the original contract is only the idea of this act, in terms of which alone we can think of the legitimacy of a state" (MM, Doctrine of Right, §47, 6:315). Or as he puts it more fully in the essay on "Theory and Practice":

> Now this is an **original contract**, on which alone a civil and hence thoroughly rightful constitution among human beings can be based and a commonwealth established. But it is by no means necessary that this contract . . . as a coalition of every particular and private will within a people into a common and public will (for the sake of a merely rightful legislation), be presupposed as a **fact** (as a fact it is indeed not possible) – as if it would first have to be proved from history that a people, into whose rights and obligations we have entered as descendants, once actually carried out such an act, and that it must have left some sure record or instrument of it, orally or in writing, if one is to hold oneself bound to an already existing civil constitution. It is instead only an **idea of reason**, which, however, has its undoubtedly practical reality, namely, to bind every legislator to give his laws in such a way that they **could** have arisen from the united will of a whole people and to regard each subject, insofar as he wants to be a citizen, as if he has joined in voting for such a will. For this is the touchstone of any public law's conformity with right. In other words, if a public law is so constituted that a whole people **could not possibly** give its consent to it . . . it is unjust; but if it is **only possible** that a people could agree to it, it is a duty to consider the law just.
>
> (TP, 8:297)

In Kant's view, all governments have the obligation to govern in accordance with the ideal of a social contract, or of legislation to which all citizens of a state could freely agree. But there is one form of government that in real life most naturally tends to realize the ideal of the social contract, and which should not only provide the model for the laws in other forms of governments but also the goal into which other forms of government have a duty to transform themselves, namely, a republic. Kant's view is that the innate right to freedom and the acquired rights he has expounded can and must be enforced by a republic or a republican government, one that legislates as if it were a republic and is on the way to becoming a republic. So let us see what he means by a republic.

In his most general moral terms, Kant defines a republican constitution as one

> established, first, on principles of the **freedom** of the members of a society (as individuals), second on principles of the **dependence** of all upon a single common legislation (as subjects), and third on the law of their **equality (as citizens of a state)**.

He declares this to be "sole constitution that issues from the idea of the original contract, on which all rightful legislation of a people must be based" (PP, 8:349–50). These abstractions have radical implications, remarkable for an elderly philosopher who was in fact an employee of an absolute monarchy that had already censured him for his writings on religion. For what these principles mean is that the state exists only to protect external freedom in accordance with universal law for each of its members. It does not exist to advance the happiness of its citizens, which might be accomplished by a paternalistic government treating its subjects like "minor children" who do not know their own best interest – what Kant calls the "greatest despotism thinkable" (TP, 8:290–1) – let alone to promote the interests of one or some small number of its members who may happen to currently hold the reins of power. The state exists to secure the freedom of each of its members to use their innate and acquired rights as each sees best, consistent of course with the innate and acquired rights of every other member of the state. Second, Kant's principle that every member of the state *depends* upon and is *equal* before a "single common legislation" means that no one stands *above* the law, again not even those who happen to rule the state, whether by historical accident or by the free election of the rest of the citizens. Locke had argued against the divine right of kings, but Kant goes further and implies that there is *no* source of rights other than the innate and acquired rights of all subjects and what is necessary to enforce those rights.

This does not mean that Kant advocates democracy in its purest form, that is, simple decision by the majority of all citizens on any question that might come before them. In Kant's view, this would also be "a **despotism** because it establishes an executive power in which all decide for and, if need be, against one (who thus does not agree), so that all, who are never-theless not all, decide" (PP, 8:352). In other words, in a pure democracy the rights of any minority can always be trampled if the majority so decides. What Kant instead advocates is a division of legislative and execu-tive power, in which of course actual laws will be legislated by a group of legislators who are a subset of the whole citizenry, but who will be estab-lishing laws not in their own personal interest but will instead be doing their best to pass laws in accordance with the ideal of freedom in accor-dance with universal law expressed by the idea of a social contract. Like other eighteenth-century theorists, especially Montesquieu, Kant often argues that there must be a threefold division of powers, although he goes beyond other writers in suggesting that this is actually a matter of logic:

> Every state contains three **authorities** within it, that is, the general united will consists of three persons: the **sovereign authority** [*Herrschergewalt*] (sovereignty) in the person of the legislator; the **executive authority** in the person of the ruler [*Regierer*] (in conformity to law); and the **judicial authority** (to award to each what is his in accordance with the law) in the person of the judge (*potestas legislatoria, rectoria et iudiciaria*). These are like the three propositions in a practical syllogism: the major premise, which contains the **law** of the will; the minor premise, which contains the **command** to behave in accordance with the law, that is, the principle of subsumption under the law; and the conclusion, which contains the **verdict** (sentence), what is laid down as right in the case in hand.
>
> (MM, Doctrine of Right, §45, 6:313)

Kant might more simply have said that the legislature makes the laws for a state (in conformity with the idea of an original contract), that the judi-ciary determines how that law applies to individual cases, and that the role of the executive is basically just to enforce the decisions of the judiciary. But the essential points are, first, that there be a firm division between making law and enforcing law and, second, that the legislature, as the representative of the citizenry as a whole, is the ultimate source of sovereignty. Kant makes the first point when he states in *Perpetual Peace* that "**Republicanism** is the principle of the separation of the executive power (the government [*Regierung*]) from the legislative power": the fundamental point is that those who write the laws should not be distracted from their aspiration to justice by the possibilities of personal benefit inherent in the power to apply the laws, while those who will have the power to apply the laws – and thereby will already have ample opportunity for personal benefit – should not have the additional opportunity to benefit by writing the laws that they will then apply. Whether the powers of adjudication and enforcement should be further separated is less important, as long as enforcement is firmly separated from legislation itself.[19] Kant emphasizes the second point when he declares that "The legislative authority can belong only to the united will of the people": his argument here is that by writing laws the legislative authority will decide what is enforceably right or wrong in a society; that one "can never do wrong in what he decides upon with regard to himself"; and thus that "only the concurring and united will of all . . . can be legislative" in determining correctly what is right or wrong (§46, 6:313–14).

Kant emphasizes that the ruler or executive power of a state exists to enforce the laws passed by the legislature and not to serve its own interest by insisting that in a genuinely republican constitution the ruler cannot be regarded as the proprietor of the land, granting tenure of his own land to other subjects only as he sees fit (MM, Doctrine of Right, General Remark B, 6:323), and that the ruler cannot have a hereditary right to office, for such a right would in principle block the freedom of "everyone to be able to rise from lower to higher offices" (and in practice, as the example of many European dynasties in Kant's own time had amply shown, would increase the probability that offices "would otherwise fall into the hands of sheer incompetents") (General Remark D, 6:329). These positions were radical and risky for Kant to take, for they utterly deny the justice of both feudalism and absolute monarchy. Yet, as we already noted in our discussion of Kant's views about marriage, his view of the right to vote for legislators is restrictive and conservative by our own standards. Kant assumes, of course, that the legislature of a large modern state will not consist of all the citizens sitting in assembly, but of their elected representatives or deputies. But he is prepared to allow the right to vote for these representatives only to those who are financially and otherwise independent, thereby excluding all women (whom he apparently assumes will be dependent either on a father or a husband or maybe a brother) as well as all servants or other employees who do not own the products of their labor but can merely sell their labor to others – although even these "passive" rather than "active" citizens are to enjoy the full benefit of the law, especially that of losing none of the other rights to freedom except by their own commission of a punishable crime (TP, 8:291–2). Kant's reason for this restriction of the right to vote is, as was earlier noted, his concern that if they could vote, dependents would just multiply the vote of their masters, so that large householders or employers would end up with an unfair advantage over small ones, and that would not have been a completely unreasonable concern in a society where, for example, laborers had no right to unionize or protection through fair labor laws. But the exclusion of whole classes such as women and laborers from the electorate places great responsibility on the part of the active citizens to vote not merely in their own interest but in the interest of all citizens, active and passive, a responsibility which many of us would now think unlikely to be fulfilled by legislators elected by such a restricted segment of the citizenry. While immensely important in practice, however, who gets to vote is a question of the application of the most fundamental principles of political justice, and there can be no question that Kant's general principles were radical for his time.

Another area where Kant's practice seems more conservative than his principles is in his notorious discussion of the right to rebellion. In his *Second Treatise of Government*, Locke had famously argued that a people contract with each other to appoint a ruler to execute laws in their common interest and enter into a contract with a ruler to do so, but retain the right to overthrow him when he is in their judgment not in fact carrying out the task for which they have contracted with him.[20] The recognition of a right to rebellion then became a hallmark of radicalism for eighteenth-century thinkers. Kant, however, seems to reject such a right completely, and thus in spite of his insistence on republicanism to end up in the camp of absolute monarchy after all.

As usual with Kant, however, his position is more nuanced than that: what Kant really rejects is the possibility of a constitutional right to rebellion against the legislature, but not the possibility of a legislative rebellion against the executive. This is the real meaning of his insistence that it is the legislature and not the ruler who is the real expression of the sovereignty of the people. To see this, let us look at his discussion of rebellion in a little detail.

REBELLION AND REFORM

Kant prominently argued against the possibility of a right to rebellion in the essay on "Theory and Practice" in 1793, as the French revolution was taking a disastrous turn for the worse, and again in the "Doctrine of Right" in 1797, after the horrors of the Terror in France were long well-known. In "Theory and Practice," Kant starts his discussion by rejecting any right on the part of "the people" to rebel against "a certain actual legislation" on the ground of "the happiness that a subject may expect from the institution or administration of a commonwealth." Such a right is rejected for the reason that Kant always criticizes the use of happiness as a fundamental moral principle, namely, that happiness is such an indeterminate goal that it makes "any fixed principle impossible and [is] in itself unfit to be a principle of legislation." Instead, he claims, any laws that are "directed chiefly to happiness (the prosperity of the citizens, increased population and the like)" by the "supreme power" in a state are in fact concerned with happiness only indirectly, as "means for *securing a rightful condition*" – and "A head of state must be authorized to judge for himself and alone whether such laws pertain to the commonwealth's flourishing" (TP, 8:298). Two things are striking about this opening argument. First, Kant's term "supreme power" (*die oberste Macht*) leaves it unclear whether he is referring to the executive or legislative power. He seems to be referring to the former, thus reserving to the executive the right to determine what measures aimed at happiness are necessary means to the end of right or justice; but it is not clear why this power should be assigned to the executive rather than the legislature. More importantly, Kant seems to put any defender of a right to rebellion in an unfairly weak position by assuming that it is always for the sake of greater *happiness* that citizens claim such a right: even if we were to concede his general claim that unhappiness is not an adequate ground for rebellion, this leaves open the question whether *injustice* might not be an adequate or even mandatory reason for it. Why should a people be denied the right or even the duty to rise up against their ruler if the latter, whether through the laws or the administration of them, is maintaining a condition of injustice rather than the condition of justice for which claimants to property need a state in the first place?

Kant's subsequent arguments circumvent this problem by offering general objections against the possibility of a right to rebellion that have nothing to do with the *grounds* for any claim to such a right. In the "Doctrine of Right," he begins with the claim that

> since a people must be regarded as already united under a general legislative will in order to judge with rightful force about the supreme authority [*die oberste Staatsgewalt*] (*summum imperium*), it cannot and may not judge otherwise than as the present head of state [*das gegenwärtige Staatsoberhaupt*] (*summus imperans*) wills it to.
>
> (Doctrine of Right, General Remark A, 6:318)

This tries to make it sound as if it is some sort of ontological impossibility for a people to rebel, because it is constituted as a people only through being united under a supreme authority or head of state, and thus for it to rebel against the latter would be for it to rebel against itself. But any such argument seems to depend upon a none too subtle slide from the union of a people under a general *legislative* will to their union under a general *executive* will: even if the union of the people into a legislature is necessary to constitute them a people at all, and it would thus be impossible for a people, *as a people*, to rebel against their own legislature, it does not follow that their identity as a people depends upon their current executive, so it does not seem impossible for a people, through their legislature, to rebel against their executive – which is precisely what happened, at least initially, in the English civil war of the 1640s and the French revolution of 1789, Kant's chief historical models of revolutions.

In both "Theory and Practice" and the "Doctrine of Right," however, Kant offers a third argument against a constitutional right to rebellion which does not turn upon a conflation of the legislative and executive powers in a state, but simply upon the need for a single executive power – although it should also be noted that Kant does not separate the executive from the judicial authority in this argument, perhaps thereby tacitly acknowledging that the judiciary is dependent on the executive for the enforcement of its decisions. This is Kant's argument that if the people were to be allowed a right to judge the actions of the actual head of the state, then the latter would not be the actual head of state after all, although he would have just as much of a claim to be so as the people, and thus "another head above the head of state" would be needed to adjudicate the matter. In "Theory and Practice" Kant puts the point in terms of adjudication, thereby emphasizing the judicial aspect of executive power:

> in an already existing civil constitution the people's judgment to determine how the constitution should be administered is no longer valid. For suppose that the people can so judge, and indeed contrary to the judgment of the actual head of state; who is to decide on which side the right is? Neither can make the decision as judge in its own suit. Hence there would have to be another head above the head of state, that would decide between him and the people; and this is self-contradictory.
>
> (TP, 8:300)

In the "Doctrine of Right" he emphasizes the enforcement power of the executive:

> Indeed, even the constitution cannot contain any article that would make it possible for there to be some authority in a state to resist the supreme

commander in case he should violate the law of the constitution, and so to limit him. For, someone who is to limit the authority in a state must have even more power than he whom he limits, or at least as much power as he has . . . In that case, however, the supreme commander in a state is not the supreme commander; instead it is the one who can resist him, and this is self-contradictory.

(MM, Doctrine of Right, General Remark A, 6:319; see also 6:320)

Either way, the general point seems clear enough: a constitution that reserves to the people a right to overthrow the authorities it establishes in their name, whether on grounds of unhappiness or grounds of injustice, does not really establish any secure authority at all. But "There exists no rightful commonwealth that can hold its own without a force of this kind that puts down all internal resistance, since each resistance would take place in conformity with a maxim that, made universal, would annihilate any civil constitution and eradicate the condition in which alone people can be in possession of rights generally" (TP, 8:299).

Yet even if we accept Kant's argument that there cannot be a constitutional right to rebellion, because any constitution that allowed such a right would be a self-destructive document, does that mean there can be no moral right or even duty to rebel under some circumstances?[21] Cannot some regimes be so unjustly constituted or administered that it is right or even mandatory for its subjects to overthrow them in spite of the fact that this cannot be done through their own constitutions? – in other words, even if it cannot be done by a people as a people, in accordance with their positive laws? Kant's deepest objection to a right to rebellion denies precisely this; it is not an argument within constitutional law at all, but a moral objection based on the premise that the overthrow of an existing state, even if in the hope of greater justice and not merely greater happiness, can never be an immediate transition to a better-constituted state, but is always a reversion to a condition of lawlessness. From such anarchy a better state might arise, but then again it might not, and since in Kant's view we are always imputable for all the consequences of our actions, whether foreseen or not, when we depart from the law, any rebels who risk anarchy would be fully responsible for it and thus in violation of the fundamental duty to enter into and remain in a state in any condition in which contact with other human beings cannot be avoided. As Kant writes in "Theory and Practice,"

even if it is granted that by such an uprising no wrong is done to a ruler (perhaps one who had violated a *joyeuse entrée*, an actual basic contract with the people), nevertheless the people did wrong in the highest degree by seeking their rights in this way; for this way of doing it (adopted as a maxim) would make every rightful constitution insecure and introduce a condition of complete lawlessness (*status naturalis*) in which all rights cease, at least to have effect . . . Even if the actual contract of the people with the ruler has been violated, the people cannot react at once **as a commonwealth**, but only as a mob. For the previously existing constitution has been torn up by the people, while their organization into a new commonwealth has not yet taken place. It is here that the condition of anarchy arises with all the horrors that are at least possible by means of it.

(TP, 8:301–302n.)

In Kant's view, rebellion is both an unlawful but also an immoral act, from which a condition of civil right and moral law may or may not emerge. So if there is no state, then our first duty in the actual circumstances of human life is to institute one; but if there is a state, then our responsibility, even in the face of its injustice, is to maintain it rather than to return to the state of nature – which, because of the threat of theft and war that is inherent to it, is guaranteed to be a condition of injustice.

This argument is open to question.[22] Kant conceives of any condition of anarchy as a condition of injustice, because in anarchy there is no power to prevent anyone from violently infringing the rights of others, and even the mere threat of such violence is already a form of injustice: it can force others to modify their own behavior in ways they would not freely choose to do so if the threat did not exist (see MM, Doctrine of Right, §42, 6:307). That is what leads to arms races, after all. But sometimes, of course, new regimes are very quickly accepted, and anarchy does not really result from a revolution. This point aside, we might also suppose that while in a state of anarchy it is entirely accidental whether justice obtains or not, that the probability of injustice is always more or less 50 percent, in a truly *malicious* regime, intentionally aimed at doing injustice to some or many of its citizens – such as Nazi Germany or the Stalinist Soviet Union – the probability of such injustice is much higher, let's say 99 or 100 percent. In that case we might well think that the subjects of such a regime have a moral right or even a moral duty to overthrow it even at the risk of anarchy, although of course they cannot legally do that through the regime's own constitution.

Although Kant himself does not acknowledge this objection, he does reserve to citizens a remedy for injustice, perhaps the strongest remedy he could prudently propose in the political circumstances in which he wrote.

For in addition to his insistence upon a rightful system of property and the impermissibility of rebellion, the third great theme of Kant's political philosophy is the necessity of reform to compensate for the moral as well as constitutional impossibility of rebellion. After his several arguments against the right to rebellion in the "Doctrine of Right," which as we have seen at least sometimes blur the difference between the legislative and executive authorities within the state, Kant suddenly states his position with complete clarity:

> A change in a (defective) constitution, which may certainly be necessary at times, can therefore be carried out only through **reform** by the sovereign itself, but not by the people, and therefore not by **revolution**; and when such a change takes place this reform can affect only the **executive authority**, not the legislative. – In what is called a limited constitution, the constitution contains a provision that the people can legally **resist** the executive authority and its representatives (the minister) by means of its representatives (in parliament). Nevertheless, no active resistance (by the people combining at will, to coerce the government to take a certain course of action, and so itself performing an act of executive authority) is permitted, but only **negative** resistance, that is, a **refusal** of the people (in parliament) to accede to every demand the government puts forth as necessary for administering the state.
>
> (MM, Doctrine of Right, General Remark A, 6:321–2)

Here is Kant's assignment of rights. The sovereign in a constitutional state is ultimately the legislature, the representative of the people, not the executive. The people cannot indeed rightfully rebel against their legislature, because apart from the legislature they are only an anarchic mob, and a rebellion by such a mob would violate the fundamental duty of right by destroying government and returning to the anarchic state of nature. But the executive authority has no fundamental right against the true sovereign, that is, the people in parliament. The people "combining at will" or "arbitrarily" (in willkürlichen Verbindung) have no right to take active steps against the executive authority or the parliament, but the people in parliament have every right to reform the executive authority. Thus the fundamental political responsibility to institute and maintain a civil condition must be transformed into the responsibility of citizens to institute and maintain a parliament, and through that parliament to reform their executive power as needed.

Kant advocated the non-anarchic reform of governments from the relatively early essay "What is Enlightenment?" of 1784 to the Conflict of the

Faculties, one of his two last works of 1798.[23] Throughout these writings he makes it clear that citizens have the right to inform their governments of unjust practices that need to be reformed, thus that governments have a correlative duty to allow this right. He also comes very close to asserting that governments have the duty to *undertake* the reforms that are called for, and in light of the argument just considered this will ultimately mean that parliaments have not only the right but also the duty to reform the executive authorities of the state if the latter are neither moral nor even prudent enough to do it for themselves. Kant never explicitly argues that the citizenry of a state has the duty to exercise its right to inform its government of injustice and petition for redress and reform; but maybe this does not need to be said, because it is both implicit – in theory – in the fundamental duty to enter into and maintain a civil condition, which is a rule of law and not merely of force, and because it is typically the rulers who would deprive the citizenry of their rights rather than the citizenry that would exercise their rights who most need to be reminded – in practice – of their duty.

In "Theory and Practice," Kant maintains that citizens must have the right to inform their government of injustices – failures to live up to the ideal of a commonwealth – and that they must be able to assume that their rulers at least *want* to rule a just commonwealth:

> A nonrecalcitrant subject must be able to assume that his ruler does not **want** to do him any wrong. Accordingly, since every human being still has his inalienable rights, which he can never give up even if he wanted to and about which he is authorized to judge for himself, while, on that assumption, the wrong that in his opinion is done to him occurs only from the supreme power's error or ignorance of certain consequences of his laws, a citizen must have, with the approval of the ruler himself, the authorization to make known publicly his opinions about what it is in the ruler's arrangements that seems to him to be a wrong against the commonwealth . . . For . . . to withhold from the [supreme commander] – whose will gives order to the subjects as citizens only by representing the general will of the people – all knowledge of matters that he himself would change if he knew about them [is] to put him in contradiction with himself.
>
> (TP, 8:304)

In "What is Enlightenment?" Kant makes it clear that this right cannot be denied to any citizen on the basis of any special status, even that of office within the state itself. For the state to function at all, its officers must certainly follow orders in the conduct of their office, that is, in what Kant calls the "private use" of their reason. But being an officer of the state does not deprive the officeholders of their humanity and thus of their inalienable rights, so even officeholders in their "public use of reason" – that is, the use of reason "which someone makes of it **as a scholar** before the entire public of the world of readers" – retain the right to publicize their views about errors in the state – for example, "errors in the military service" or the "inappropriateness or even injustice" of taxation decrees – simply as citizens rather than as "passive members" of the machinery of the state (*WE?*, 8:37). The freedom of the pen is among the "inalienable rights" of human beings, and human beings do not lose their inalienable rights merely because they hold offices in the state.

This is not to say that all citizens have the *duty* as well as the right to express their opinions about the errors and imperfections of the state. But even if all citizens merely have the right to free expression of their views, then the state, conversely, must not merely *want* to hear their views, but has a *duty* to allow them to be heard – that follows from the concept of a right, and it is what Kant signals, by the use of his deepest term of moral criticism, by saying that the ruler would be "in contradiction with himself" if he were to deny this right. This leaves open two questions. First, does *any* citizen have the duty as well as the right to call for reform? And second, beyond the duty to allow itself to *hear* about the need for reform, does the state, whether in the person of both executive and legislative authorities or if need be in the person of the latter alone, have the duty to *undertake the reforms* that are called for? Let's start with the second question. Kant is not explicit that governments have a duty to reform themselves in either "Theory and Practice" or the "Doctrine of Right," although in the former text he implies that they have the duty to listen to calls for reform, asking "how else, again, could the government get the knowledge it requires for its own essential purpose than by letting the spirit of freedom, so worthy of respect in its origin and in its effects, express itself?" (*TP*, 8:305). However, by stating that it is an "essential purpose" of government to redress injustices and therefore reform itself in the direction of a more ideal commonwealth, Kant at least suggests that the government has a duty to undertake the reforms that the people call for in the exercise of their right to free expression.

A further suggestion that governments have a duty actually to undertake reform may be found in the remarkable text in which Kant also suggests that at least some citizens in the state have a duty and not merely the right to call for reform. This text is one of Kant's two final published works, *The*

Conflict of the Faculties – published only a year later than the *Metaphysics of Morals*, but after the death of King Friedrich Wilhelm II, when Kant felt himself to be liberated from the censorship which that king had imposed in his anger over Kant's publication of *Religion within the Boundaries of Mere Reason* in 1793.24 The *Conflict of the Faculties* is Kant's paean to academic freedom – the conflict it describes is not the abstract conflict between faculties of the mind such as sensibility and reason that structures the *Critique of Pure Reason* but a concrete conflict between university faculties. More precisely, it is an argument for the freedom of the "lower" faculty of philosophy (what we would now call the faculty of arts and sciences, whose highest degree is still the "Doctor of Philosophy") and the "higher" faculties of theology, law, and medicine, especially the first of these. Kant conceives of the higher faculties as training students to hold offices within the state or to practice professions licensed and regulated by the state, and thus as training students in the "private use" of reason. To that end, the teachers in these faculties must also exercise the private use of reason, teaching their students the state-mandated doctrines and regulations, compliance with which will allow them to practice their intended professions, regardless of their own feelings about the wisdom of those regulations. But the faculty of philosophy, even though in Kant's time all its teachers were themselves employees of the state (as they remain in almost all German and European universities to this day), is in the business of exercising and training its students in the "public use" of reason – and thus, precisely since many of those students will go on to the higher faculties, in training those who will have to exercise the private use of reason in their professions how to exercise the public use of reason as well, like every other human being and citizen. In Kant's view, the members of the philosophy faculty clearly have not only the right but also the duty to seek the truth on any matter they choose or are charged by their acceptance of their position to investigate, even at the cost of conflict with the other faculties, and the duty to ensure that whatever they publish they freely believe to be true – "the lower faculty has not only the title but also the duty, if not to state the *whole* truth in public, at least to see to it that *everything* put forward in public as a principle is true" (CF, First part, 7:32). That is, it is the duty of the philosophy faculty to do what it can to ensure not only that what it says (on philosophy itself, for example) is true, but also that what all the higher faculties say is true: "The philosophy faculty can, therefore, lay claim to any teaching, in order to test its truth" (7:28). But further, Kant also suggests that the government itself has a duty to ensure that there is a faculty of philosophy and that it can fulfill its duty to seek the truth, even the truth about the government itself: he signals this, with language similar to what he used in "Theory and Practice," by saying that "The government cannot forbid" the faculty of philosophy to test any claim to truth "without acting against its own proper and essential purpose" (7:28). The philosophy faculty "must enjoy" its freedom of inquiry "unimpaired" (7:29), so the government that maintains this faculty must allow it this freedom.

Yet while this analysis of the duties and rights of the philosophy faculty may well institutionalize the government's obligation to allow freedom of inquiry and expression and perhaps to listen to such expression, it does not yet seem to impose upon the government a duty actually to reform itself. In the Second Part of *The Conflict*, however, which is ostensibly concerned with the conflict between the faculties of philosophy and law – it is actually an essay on the "old question . . . Is the human race constantly progressing?" that Kant had written, perhaps as early as 1795, in response to the French revolution – he addresses this question briefly but bluntly. Here he straightforwardly asserts the general thesis that citizens have the duty to enter into civil societies striving to realize the ideal of justice but that rulers likewise have the duty to govern in accordance with that ideal:

> The idea of a constitution in harmony with the natural right of human beings, one namely in which citizens obedient to the law, besides being united, ought also to be legislative, lies at the basis of all political forms; and the body politic . . . conceived in conformity to it by virtue of pure concepts of reason . . . is not an empty figment of the brain, but rather the eternal norm for all civil organization in general . . . Consequently, it is a duty to enter into such a system of government, but it is provisionally the duty of the monarchs, if they rule **as autocrats**, to govern in a **republican** (not democratic) way, that is, to treat people according to principles which are commensurate with the spirit of laws of freedom (as a nation with mature understanding would prescribe them for itself).
>
> (CF, Second Part, 7:90–1)

Here Kant assumes that actual states typically fall short of the republican ideal, but that while the citizens have both the duty to remain within them and the right merely to petition for improvement, their rulers have the obligation to rule as republicans, that is, to rule in spirit as if their states were already republics and ultimately to transform their states from autocracies to republic in the letter.[25] In other words, kings and dictators have the duty to put themselves out of business. Not exactly Locke's right to rebellion, but a radical opinion for eighteenth-century Prussia, perhaps one so risky that it could have been ventured only by an elderly and retired professor in what he knew would be one of his final publications!

TOWARD PERPETUAL PEACE

We cannot leave Kant's political philosophy without discussing his 1795 pamphlet *Toward Perpetual Peace*, which immediately became one of his most widely read writings. After the wars that tore Europe apart in the mid-seventeenth century, such as the English civil war and the Thirty Years War that ravaged much of central Europe, the essay on how to achieve perpetual peace became a well-established genre, with famous examples from writers as diverse as William Penn, Jean-Jacques Rousseau, and Jeremy Bentham.[26] But it was especially important for Kant to address the problem of a stable foundation for world peace because of what we have already seen to be the fundamental empirical premise of his entire legal and political philosophy: that we live on the naturally undivided surface of a sphere any point of which can be reached by human beings from any other point. This means that no claim to property within one state is ultimately secure unless that state is at peace with all other states, and that no claim to property within a state is ultimately just unless that state coexists with all other states in a peace that is founded on some sort of international justice rather than mere force.

Now history might seem to suggest that the idea of permanent international justice and peace is a pipe dream, but Kant thought that there is a means to such a peace, namely an international league of the very same sort of republican governments that, as we have just seen, he argued must be the moral ideal for any particular state. Kant writes first that even in a condition of warfare among any kinds of states there are certain "preliminary articles" that can eliminate causes of future wars, such as the prohibition of dynastic acquisition of states, standing armies, national debts for making war, "forcible interference in the constitution and government of another state," and "acts of hostility as would have to make mutual trust impossible during a future peace," such as assassinations, encouragement of treason within another state, and so on (PP, 8:344–6). But in the long run, Kant holds that there can only be perpetual peace if all states become republics governed by the will of the whole people rather than by the whims of autocrats, especially, as is already implicit in the first preliminary article, autocrats who regard whole states as their personal property, which can be enlarged or put at risk entirely at their own choice.

The three "definitive articles" for perpetual peace are thus that "The civil constitution in every state shall be republican" (PP, 8:349), that "The right of nations shall be based on a **federalism** of free states" (8:354), and that there shall be "Cosmopolitan right" consisting in "conditions of universal **hospitality**" (8:358). Under the last of these articles Kant launches a powerful attack upon the rampant European colonialism of his own time, arguing that no matter what the cultural and political conditions of another region are, foreigners have no more than the right to visit in order to offer their goods and ideas, never a right to establish themselves forcibly in another people's territory no matter how exalted or crass their aims may be. Kant's second article has been the source of debate, scholars arguing over whether he meant the federation of states to have any centralized powers of enforcement or not, thus to be a mere league or a superstate.[27] But here I want to focus on Kant's first article, namely his claim that the world-wide spread of republican constitutions promises perpetual peace.

Kant begins *Toward Perpetual Peace* with what sounds like a *guarantee* of perpetual peace[28]:

> What affords this **guarantee** (surety) is nothing less than the great artist **nature** . . . from whose mechanical course purposiveness shines forth visibly, letting concord arise by means of the discord between human beings even against their will; and for this reason nature, regarded as necessitation by a cause the laws of whose operation are unknown to us, is called **fate**, but if we consider its purposiveness in the course of the world as the profound wisdom of a higher cause directed to the objective final end of the human race and predetermining the course of this world, it is called **providence**.
>
> (PP, 8:362)

Kant then proposes "to examine the condition that nature has prepared for the persons acting on its great stage, which finally makes its assurance of peace necessary" (8:362–3), and to examine how nature "affords the guarantee that what man **ought** to do in accordance with laws of freedom but does not do, it is assured he **will** do, without prejudice to [his] freedom, even by a constraint of nature" (8:365). Kant seems to suggest that nature will guarantee perpetual peace by means of the following scenario: war drives human beings to all corners of the earth, seeking safety from one another; but no part of the earth is completely inaccessible to any other, so even once people have been driven to all corners of the earth they will still be in fear of one another and thus make war upon one another. But the burdens of war upon the populations that must carry them will be so great that over time people will transform their governments into republics more fully expressing their own interests than any other form of regime can, and once people have transformed their own governments into republics they will not have any internal cause to make war on other nations. So once all nations have become republics, thereby removing any external cause for one nation to make war upon another, all cause for war will be removed and there will henceforth be no war (8:363–8). But by the conclusion of *Toward Perpetual Peace*, Kant uses more modest language:

> If it is a duty to realize the condition of public right, even if only in approximation by unending progress, and if there is also a well-founded hope of this, then the **perpetual peace** that follows upon what have till now been falsely called peace treaties (strictly speaking, truces) is no empty idea but a task that, gradually solved, comes steadily closer to its goal (since the times during which equal progress takes place will, we hope, become always shorter).
>
> (PP, 8:386)

And in his brief discussion of the "Right of Nations" in the *Metaphysics of Morals*, two years after *Toward Perpetual Peace*, Kant again writes more cautiously:

> So **perpetual peace**, the ultimate goal of the whole right of nations, is indeed an unachievable idea. Still, the political principles directed toward perpetual peace, of entering into . . . alliances of states, which serve for continual **approximation** to it, are not unachievable. Instead, since continual approximation to it is a task based on duty and therefore on the right of human beings and of states, this can certainly be achieved.
>
> (MM, Doctrine of Right, §61, 6:350)

That the definitive articles of perpetual peace offer something less than an iron-clad guarantee is also evident in Kant's exposition of the first definitive article, the requirement of republican government itself. What Kant writes here is this:

> The republican constitution does offer the prospect of the result wished for, namely perpetual peace; the ground of this is as follows. When the consent of the citizens of a state is required in order to decide whether

there shall be war or not (and it cannot be otherwise in this constitution), nothing is more natural than that they will be very hesitant to begin such a bad game, since they would have to decide to take upon themselves all the hardships of war (such as themselves doing the fighting and paying the costs of the war from their own belongings . . .); on the other hand, under a constitution in which subjects are not citizens of the state, which is therefore not republican, [deciding upon war] is the easiest thing in the world; because the head of state is not a member of the state but its proprietor and gives up nothing at all of his feasts, hunts, pleasure palaces, court festivals, and so forth, he can decide upon war, as upon a kind of pleasure party, for insignificant cause.

(PP, 8:350)

This is not the language of guarantee, but of probabilities. That citizens who are collectively the sovereign of a republic may be highly averse to risking their own lives or livelihoods in order to make war and that sovereigns who are proprietors of absolutistic regimes may not be especially averse to risking the lives and goods of their subjects in order to aggrandize their own wealth or status does not guarantee that the former will never make war or that the latter will always do so.

Indeed, the problem here is not just an empirical one, namely that while voters in a republic will usually not be willing to endorse a war that puts their own lives and goods at risk, they might occasionally be willing to do so if the promise of gain seems great enough and if the fighting can be done by hired hands. For Kant, there must be a deeper problem here, namely that his own analysis of radical evil, published just two years before *Toward Perpetual Peace* in his book on *Religion*, implies that human beings can subvert *any* natural means toward a beneficial outcome if that is how they choose to use their freedom. While Kant's idea in the essay on peace is clearly that citizens of a republic will generally vote against war out of *self-interest* or *self-love*, the point of the *Religion* is that our perceptions of what is in our self-interest do not always coincide with what morality requires, and in that case we are inescapably free to put self-love above morality. Further, of course, there is always the possibility that what we currently think is in our self-interest is not really so, especially over the long term, yet we are frequently tempted to prefer our short-term self-interest over our real, long-term self-interest. So there can be no guarantee that even republics will always prefer peace over war.

However, Kant does not argue for the radical nature of human evil as a counsel of despair, but precisely in order to demonstrate that the possibility

of conversion from evil to good is always within our grasp. His point in
the *Religion* is that if evil is always a product of our own choice, then we are
also always free to choose what is right. In fact, he illustrates this point in
that book by nothing other than a reference to perpetual peace:

> **Philosophical chiliasm** which hopes for a state of perpetual peace based
> on a federation of nations united in a world-republic, is universally derided
> as a sheer fantasy as much as **theological chiliasm**, which awaits for the
> complete moral improvement of the human race.
>
> (RBMR, Part One, 6:34)

Kant's point is clearly that perpetual peace is *not* a complete fantasy, for if
the widespread evil of constant war is a product of free choice then we are
also free to choose the alternative, thus the state of perpetual peace. And
this, I suggest, is the point of *Toward Perpetual Peace* as well: Kant's aim is not
to provide a natural guarantee of the *actuality* or even the *probability*
of perpetual peace, but rather a philosophical guarantee of the *possibility* of
perpetual peace, by which it can be proven that such peace, no matter how
remote it may seem, is in fact within our grasp, and therefore that it is
rational as well as morally requisite for us to work toward it.

That this is Kant's real concern in *Toward Perpetual Peace* becomes apparent
in its crucial first appendix, "On the Disagreement between Morals and
Politics with a View to Perpetual Peace." This section begins with nothing
less than a statement of Kant's general premise that a moral "ought"
presupposes a "can":

> Morality is of itself practical in the objective sense, as the sum of laws
> commanding unconditionally, in accordance with which we **ought** to act,
> and it is patently absurd, having granted this concept of duty its authority,
> to want to say that one nevertheless **cannot** do it.
>
> (PP, 8:370)

Kant reiterates the point a few pages later when he writes:

> If there were no freedom and no moral law based upon it and everything
> that happens or can happen is instead the mere mechanism of nature,
> then politics (as the art of making use of this mechanism for governing
> human beings) would be the whole of practical wisdom, and the concept
> of right would be an empty thought. But if one finds it indispensably
> necessary to join the concept of right with politics, and even to raise it to

the limiting condition of politics, it must be granted that the two can be united.

(PP, 8:372)

The central task of Kant's critique of practical reason is to show that it is always *possible* for us to act as morality demands, no matter what the prior history of our conduct might seem to predict;[29] and the chief point of *Toward Perpetual Peace* is then to show not that there are natural mechanisms that make perpetual peace necessary, but rather that there are natural mechanisms that will make peace possible if they are freely used with the intention to bring it about.

Kant makes the point that the articles of perpetual peace describe only natural means to a morally necessary goal when he writes:

It is just the general will given *a priori* (within a nation or in the relation of various nations to one another) that alone determines what is laid down as right among human beings; but this union of the will of all, if only it is acted upon consistently in practice, can also, in accordance with the mechanism of nature, be the cause bringing about the effect aimed at and providing the concept of right with efficacy.

(PP, 8:378)

This suggests that the achievement of "what is laid down as right among human beings," namely in the final analysis perpetual peace, is both consistent with the mechanisms of nature, that is, "in accordance" with them, but also to be achieved *through* the use of these mechanisms, which can, if used with the morally right intention, provide "the concept of right with efficacy." But, Kant argues, the mechanisms of nature that *can* drive us toward peace will do so only if they are employed by "a **moral politician**, that is, one who takes the principles of political prudence in such a way that they can coexist with morals," rather than by "a **political moralist**, who frames a morals to suit the statesman's advantage" (PP, 8:372). Kant's position is therefore not a "fantasy" that nature will produce perpetual peace, but a realistic recognition that nature does provide the means for perpetual peace, but only the means.[30]

Indeed, Kant's thesis that the mechanisms of nature that *can* produce perpetual peace will do so only if used by a *moral politician* rather than merely a *moralist* or entirely moral person reflects a further important element of realism in Kant's political theory. This is his recognition that actual states do not arise in conditions of moral purity, in some convention where real people freely choose to form a republic, but in conditions of violence and injustice, typically as the outcome of war or revolution. So the politicians who hold power in a state have not always gained it in a pretty way. As Kant puts it, "the only beginning of the rightful condition to be counted upon is that by **power**, on the coercion of which public right is afterward based" (PP, 8:371). But a *moral* politician is precisely one who, however he has come to power, will "take to heart the maxim that . . . an alteration is necessary, in order to keep constantly approaching the end (of the best constitution in accordance with laws of right)" (8:372). Continuing his insistence on the responsibility of rulers to reform their own states, Kant concludes that however they have come to power, if and only if politicians will freely choose to use the mechanisms afforded them by nature for achieving the end of perpetual peace will that end be achieved.

Through the image of the moral politician, Kant makes his point that nature can at least but also at most provide us with the means to justice, which can actually yield justice only if we freely choose to use them toward that end rather than to subvert them. If this is Kant's conclusion, however, why does he begin *Toward Perpetual Peace* by suggesting that there could be a *guarantee* of perpetual peace? More generally, if Kant could really prove at the most general level of his philosophy that we are always free to choose good instead of evil, which would entail that we are always free to choose perpetual peace rather than constant war, then why should he need to argue that there are specific natural mechanisms such as the spread of republican government that can be used to bring about progress toward perpetual peace? Why should he not rest with the general assurance that *whatever* our present conception of the laws of nature inherent in human action might seem to predict we will do, we are at the transcendental level always free to do what is right, and can be assured that if we do choose what is right then empirical nature will reflect our noumenal choice of what is right after all?

The answer to this question is complex, and its complexity ultimately reflects the complex view of human beings as creatures who are both rational and sensible which as we have seen underlies Kant's entire metaphysics of morals. Even as purely rational creatures, we must be assured that what we *ought* to do we also *can* do; and since the goal of perpetual peace, although required by pure practical reason, is clearly a goal that must be achieved within nature, we must be assured that there are means available within nature by means of which we could bring about this goal. But as sensible as well as rational creatures, we may need more than an abstract argument that peace is possible within nature and that nature affords us means by which we can bring it about; our moral motivation to seek perpetual peace may also need the concrete encouragement of a view of history that can make the achievement of peace seem inevitable as long as we cooperate with rather than undermine the natural forces that make it so. In writing as if nature could guarantee perpetual peace, Kant is not appealing to our purely rational nature, which requires only that it be demonstrable that what we ought to do is also something we can do if our motivation to attempt to do it is not to be undermined, but is rather appealing to our sensible nature, where our wavering motivation to do what is right, which can always be tempted by deluded conceptions of self-love, may need to be buttressed by a sense that what we ought to do is in fact the aim of nature itself. As rational creatures, we need only the thought that nature makes it possible for us to do what we know we ought to do; but as sensible creatures, we may need the thought that nature will push us towards that which we ought to do even if we ourselves are tempted not to do that.

The idea that we are sensible as well as rational creatures who need both palpable encouragement to be moral as well as the abstract knowledge that we can do so is in fact an underlying theme of all of Kant's works in the 1790s, not only those we have discussed in this part of the book but also of Kant's first work of the decade, the *Critique of the Power of Judgment*, about which we have thus far said very little. So here is the place to turn to that work, and to examine the unification of the realm of nature with the realm of freedom that it proposes.

SUMMARY

Kant's philosophy of right concerns those of our obligations not to restrict the freedom of others that can be coercively enforced by the power of a state, and which indeed, in view of the moral necessity of those obligations on the one hand and the unquenchable human tendency to violate them on the other, morally must be enforced through the state. We thus have a moral duty to enter into and maintain a state. The state exists in order to protect the innate right of every human being to personal freedom as well as acquired property rights in physical objects, contracts, and the services of other people; but all claims to such rights must themselves be rightful, or restricted by the general demands of morality. Thus our moral duty to enter into and maintain a state is also a duty to maintain an equitable system of property rights. The kind of state that can do this,

Kant argues, is a republic, which separates legislative and executive power and also separates political office from ownership of the state, or at least a regime that governs in a republican spirit. Because entering into and maintaining a state is a moral obligation, Kant rejects the possibility of a right to rebellion that was popularized by other Enlightenment liberals, but at the same time he argues that the state has a duty to listen to calls for reform and even to maintain a group of public employees – the faculty of philosophy – whose duty is to search after truth, even truth about misgovernment. Kant concludes his political philosophy by arguing that justice can truly exist anywhere only if it exists everywhere, and that the ultimate duty of justice is therefore the establishment of perpetual peace. He argues that perpetual peace will be promoted by the spread of republican government, and that nature creates certain pressures toward the formation of such governments, but ultimately genuine republics and therefore world peace can be instituted and maintained only by the free choice of rulers who are moral politicians. And only such a conclusion is compatible with Kant's insistence upon the radical character of human freedom.

FURTHER READING

Williams (1983) remains the broadest treatment of Kant's political philosophy and its historical context, although it has a somewhat Hegelian and Marxist bent, while his (2003) work emphasizes the differences between Kant's ideal contractarianism and the prudential contractarianism of Hobbes. Kersting (1993), with a new Introduction, is the most detailed commentary on the subject, while his (2004) work presents the author's main points more briefly and accessibly. Mulholland offers the most rigorous analysis of Kant's theory of right available in English. Beiser, while treating Kant's political philosophy briefly, is the most extensive survey of its immediate influence, while Baynes, Flikschuh, and Höffe discuss Kant's influence on the most important political philosophies and philosophers of our own period, especially John Rawls and Jürgen Habermas.

Kenneth Baynes, *The Normative Grounds of Social Criticism: Kant, Rawls, and Habermas* (Albany, NY: State University of New York Press, 1992).

Frederick C. Beiser, *Enlightenment, Revolution, and Romanticism: The Genesis of Modern German Political Thought, 1790–1800* (Cambridge, MA: Harvard University Press, 1992).

Katrin Flikschuh, *Kant and Modern Political Philosophy* (Cambridge: Cambridge University Press, 2000).

Otfried Höffe, *Categorical Principles of Law: A Counterpoint to Modernity*, trans. Mark Migotti (University Park, PA: Pennsylvania State University Press, 2002).

Wolfgang Kersting, *Wohlgeordnete Freiheit: Immanuel Kants Rechts- und Staatsphilosophie* (Frankfurt am Main: Suhrkamp, 1993).

——*Kant über Recht* (Paderborn: Mentis, 2004).

Leslie A. Mulholland, *Kant's System of Rights* (New York: Columbia University Press, 1990).

Howard Williams, *Kant's Political Philosophy* (New York: St. Martin's Press, 1983).

——*Kant's Critique of Hobbes* (Cardiff: University of Wales Press, 2003).

Three important collections of essays on Kant's political philosophy are:

Ronald Beiner and William James Booth (eds), *Kant and Political Philosophy: The Contemporary Legacy* (New Haven, CT: Yale University Press, 1993).

Mark Timmons (ed.), *Kant's Metaphysics of Morals: Interpretative Essays* (Oxford; Oxford University Press, 2002) (includes essays on the duties of virtue, the topic of our previous chapter).

Howard Williams (ed.), *Essays on Kant's Political Philosophy* (Chicago: University of Chicago Press, 1992).

A few important items from the vast literature on *Perpetual Peace*, many published in the year of its bicentenary, include the following. Bohman and Lutz-Bachman which contains essays by Jürgen Habermas and Martha Nussbaum among others; Cavallar both places Kant's work in historical context and evaluates its treatment by contemporary political scientists.

James Bohman and Matthias Lutz-Bachman (eds), *Perpetual Peace: Essays on Kant's Cosmopolitan Ideal* (Cambridge, MA: MIT Press, 1995).

Georg Cavallar, *Kant and the Theory and Practice of International Right* (Cardiff: University of Wales Press, 1999).

Volker Gerhardt, *Immanuel Kants Entwurf "Zum Ewigen Frieden"* (Darmstadt: Wissenschaftliche Buchgesellschaft, 1995).

Otfried Höffe, *"Königliche Völker": Zu Kants kosmopolitischer Rechts- und Friedenstheorie* (Frankfurt am Main: Surhkamp Verlag, 2001).

Finally, O'Neill is not a discussion of Kant's political philosophy *per se*, but is an application of Kant's basic moral principles to the most pressing problems of international justice.

Onora O'Neill, *Faces of Hunger: An Essay on Poverty, Justice and Development* (London: Allen and Unwin, 1986).

Part Three

Nature and Freedom

Nine

The Beautiful, the Sublime, and the Morally Good

BRIDGING THE GULF

In 1790, just three years after publishing the second edition of the *Critique of Pure Reason* and two years after the *Critique of Practical Reason* which had grown out of his work on that revision, Kant published the *Critique of the Power of Judgment*, a third critique that had not been promised in either of the first two. This third critique comprises two main parts, the "Critique of the Aesthetic Power of Judgment" and the "Critique of the Teleological Power of Judgment." The first of these discusses our judgments about beauty and sublimity in both nature and art, judgments we now call "aesthetic" (although the philosophical specialty of aesthetics has concentrated almost exclusively on art since Hegel's famous lectures three decades after Kant's book).[1] The second part discusses our judgments about the systematic organization of specific things within nature, namely organisms, as well as our tendency to think of nature as a whole as if it were a single and well-designed system and to that extent like one big organism itself. Kant had discussed both the nature of aesthetic judgment and the system of the arts in his lectures on anthropology, logic, and metaphysics, and had published an early book entitled *Observations on the Feeling of the Beautiful and the Sublime* (1764), although that had not contained much analysis of these two central concepts of aesthetics themselves, offering instead what we would now consider sociological observations on differences in taste between men and women, different nations and races, and the like. He had touched upon the teleological conception of nature as a goal-directed system in both an early work like the *Only Possible Basis for a Demonstration of the Existence of God* (1763) as well as in the Appendix to the "Transcendental Dialectic" of the *Critique of Pure Reason*. But he had never connected the two subjects of aesthetics and teleology. Why did he suddenly bring them together in a third critique?

Kant suggests several explanations of this new connection. One is that aesthetic judgments about the beautiful and the sublime and teleological judgments about the goals of natural systems and of nature as a whole are both instances of what he calls "reflecting judgment," a use of judgment that seeks to discover a concept for a particular object that is given to it rather than to find a particular object to which to apply a concept that it already has (Kant now calls the latter "determining judgment"; FI, Section V, 20:211; CPJ, Introduction, Section IV, 5:179). Kant's contrast between determining and reflecting judgments cannot simply be equated with a distinction between cognitive and non-cognitive judgments, for one use of reflecting judgment is to find empirical concepts to mediate between the abstract categories of the understanding and the concrete objects that are given in actual experience, and that is definitely a cognitive use of this power of judgment (we have already discussed this use of reflecting judgment in chapter 4). But Kant will argue that both aesthetic and teleological judgment are strictly speaking non-cognitive: they may discover concepts or something like concepts and use them for various purposes, but they do not themselves yield knowledge. A second connection between aesthetic and teleological judgment is that both involve perceptions of what Kant calls "purposiveness" (Zweckmäßigkeit; since Zweck can mean "goal" as well as "purpose," we might also translate this term as "goal-directedness"): in finding an object beautiful or sublime, our *experience* of the object is purposive or satisfies a goal of our own even though we do not think of the object itself as having been designed for a purpose (Kant calls this "purposiveness without a purpose"); in teleological judgment, we think of an organism or even the whole of nature *as* if it were designed for a purpose, a conception of nature which is supposed to have heuristic value for us even though we do not and cannot *know* that anything in nature has been designed for a purpose.[2]

Kant's deepest reason for connecting aesthetics and teleology in a single book, however, is that both aesthetic and teleological judgment lead us to look at products of *nature* and indeed all of nature itself – and in his theory of genius Kant will imply that even works of fine art must be considered to be gifts of nature – as if they also have *moral* significance, and thus both aesthetic and teleological experience give us crucial encouragement in our fundamental task of literally transforming the *natural world* into a *moral world* (see again CPuR, A 808–9 / B 836–7). Kant signals this underlying aim of the third critique when he concludes its introduction by calling for "the connection of the legislations of understanding and reason through the power of judgment":

> The understanding legislates *a priori* for nature, as object of the senses, for a theoretical cognition of it in a possible experience. Reason legislates *a priori* for freedom and its own causality, as the supersensible in the subject, for an unconditioned practical cognition. The domain of the concept of nature under the one legislation and that of the concept of freedom under the other are entirely barred from any mutual influence that they could have on each other by themselves (each in accordance with its fundamental laws) by the great chasm that separates the supersensible from the appearances. The concept of freedom determines nothing in regard to the theoretical cognition of nature; the concept of nature likewise determines nothing in regard to practical laws of freedom; and it is to this extent not possible to throw a bridge from one domain to the other . . . [N]evertheless . . . [the] **effect** [of a causality of freedom] in accordance with its formal laws is to take place in the world . . . The effect in accordance with the concept of freedom is the final end, which (or its appearance in the sensible world) should exist, for which the condition of its possibility in nature (in the nature of the subject as a sensible being, that is, as a human being) is presupposed. That which presupposes this *a priori* and without regard to the practical, namely, the power of judgment, provides the mediating concept between the concepts of nature and the concept of freedom, which makes possible the transition from the purely theoretical to the purely practical, from lawfulness in accordance with the former to the final end in accordance with the latter, in the concept of a **purposiveness** of nature.
>
> (CPJ, Introduction, Section IX, 5:195–6)

I have quoted this passage at length because it reveals the deepest implications of Kant's conception of human beings as rational animals, enjoying both sense and reason. We can give theoretical laws to nature through our pure intuition and understanding, and we can give the moral laws for our own conduct through pure reason, but it is not enough for us merely to know both sets of laws or even merely to choose to act morally in some noumenal realm, behind or above the natural realm of appearances; we must act on the commands of morality in the natural world and thereby transform the natural world into a moral world. We must make our own autonomy effective in the natural world, and both aesthetic and teleological judgment support us in our belief that we can do that.

In the last two chapters, we saw in some detail what duties actually arise when we apply the moral law and the ideal of autonomy given by pure practical reason to the specifics of the human condition. Now Kant is telling us that it is not enough to know *what* our duties are, but we must also make this knowledge *causally efficacious* in the natural world, or use our *noumenal* freedom in the *phenomenal* world we actually inhabit; and somehow our experience of purposiveness in aesthetic and teleological judgment will help us. But before we can even ask *how* this help is supposed to come, we must stop to ask *why* we need any help in this task at all. Hasn't Kant already addressed this question in his moral theory?

In a way, of course, he has. Throughout his exposition of his practical philosophy, Kant has clearly recognized that in order to act morally, we need to (1) understand the moral law and what it requires of us; (2) believe that we are in fact free to choose to do what it requires of us rather than to do what all our other motives, which can be subsumed under the rubric of self-love, might suggest to us; (3) believe that the objectives or ends that morality imposes upon us can actually be achieved, and (4) have an adequate motivation for our attempt to do what morality requires of us in lieu of the mere desirability of particular goals it might happen to license or even impose in particular circumstances. And, especially in the *Critique of Practical Reason*, Kant has argued that at one level all these conditions are satisfied by pure practical reason itself: (1) the very form of pure practical reason gives us the moral law (CPracR, Theorem III, 5:27); (2) this first "fact" of pure practical reason implies the reality of our freedom to be moral by means of the principle that we must be able to do what we know we ought to do (CPracR, Problem II, Remark, 5:30); (3) we can postulate by pure practical reason alone that the laws of nature are compatible with the demands of morality because both laws ultimately have a common author (CPracR, 5:124−32); and, finally, (4) pure respect for the moral law itself can be a sufficient motivation for us to attempt to carry it out (and attempts to do so have "moral worth" only when that is our motivation) (G, Section I, especially 4:400−1). But in the third critique, and indeed throughout his works of the 1790s, Kant now emphasizes that we are sensuous as well as rational creatures, and therefore need sensuous as well as rational presentation and confirmation of the conditions of the possibility of morality. He explicitly acknowledges this three years after the *Critique of the Power of Judgment*, when in *Religion within the Boundaries of Mere Reason* he asserts "the natural need of all human beings to demand for even the highest concepts and grounds of reason something that **the senses can hold on to**, some confirmation from experience or the like" (RBMR, 6:109). In

Kant's mind, the deepest connection between aesthetic and teleological experience and judgment is that both give us sensuous images of morality and a feeling of its achievability that can supplement and strengthen our purely – but also merely – rational insight into its demands and the possibility of our fulfilling them.

This sounds grand, but could it possibly be right? In particular, isn't Kant renowned in the history of aesthetics in particular precisely for having introduced the ideas of the "disinterestedness of aesthetic judgment" and the "autonomy of art" – in other words, the idea that our aesthetic judgment in general and of art in particular is completely independent of the demands of morality, as it were our only respite from them? Doesn't Kant begin the "Critique of the Aesthetic Power of Judgment" by asserting that the "satisfaction that determines the judgment of taste is without any interest" (*CPJ*, §2, 5:204), and for that reason completely independent from both our gratification in the physiologically agreeable (§3) and our approval of the morally good (§4)? Doesn't Kant write that "The agreeable, the beautiful, and the good therefore designate three different relations of representations to the feeling of pleasure and displeasure," and that "among all these three kinds of satisfaction only that of the taste for the beautiful is a disinterested and **free** satisfaction," where "no interest, neither that of the senses nor that of reason, extorts approval" (§5, 5:209–10)?

Indeed, Kant does say this, and it is central to his analysis of the judgment of beauty that it is not merely a veiled approval of an object for prudential or moral reasons, but rather an expression of the imagination's *free play* with an object, whether with the mere form of the object, as in judgments of natural beauty, or with both the form of and the concepts expressed by the object, as is typically the case with works of art. But what I will suggest is that the real basis for Kant's interest in aesthetic phenomena is precisely his view that the freedom of the imagination that we *experience* in our encounter with beautiful objects can give us a feeling of the reality of the freedom of the will that we can only *postulate* within purely moral reasoning, and the natural *existence* of beauty can give us a feeling that nature is hospitable to the achievement of our moral goals as well, again something we can only *postulate* in the moral theory of the highest good – aesthetic feelings with an emotional impact that can support the effect of pure reason upon our sensible side. Similarly, Kant will argue that our teleological judgment of nature, although inspired by our attempt to comprehend the functioning of organisms, a task for natural science independent of any explicit moral concerns, gently but firmly leads us to a vision – though not knowledge – of nature as a system with our own moral development as its ultimate goal, again giving sensible support for what is merely postulated in the theory of the highest good. In the present chapter, I will review Kant's analysis of aesthetic judgment and his description of the varieties of aesthetic experience with an eye to their moral consequences. In the next chapter, I will offer a parallel account of Kant's teleology.

VARIETIES OF AESTHETIC JUDGMENT

Kant begins his aesthetic theory, in the "Analytic of the Beautiful," with an analysis of what he calls "pure" judgments of beauty, that is, judgments that a particular, natural object such as a flower or a bird is beautiful. But in spite of what Kant's term "pure" might seem to suggest, it would be a mistake to think that such judgments should be the norm for all aesthetic judgments; rather, Kant begins with them because they are the *simplest* cases of aesthetic judgment. They will reveal central features that are also present in more complex cases, but they do not reveal all the important features of aesthetic experience and judgment, nor does Kant suggest that they are the most important form of the aesthetic.[3] In fact, Kant analyzes three main forms of aesthetic experience: the experience of beauty, beginning with pure cases of natural beauty but also including cases of both natural objects and artifacts whose beauty is connected to their purpose as well as the special case of the beauty of the human form; the experience of the sublime, which does seem to be exclusively an experience of nature rather than of art, but which is subdivided into two cases, the sublimity of vast size and that of vast power, or what Kant calls the "mathematical" and the "dynamical" sublime; and finally the experience of fine art, which is now usually assumed to be the sole subject of aesthetics.[4] Each of these forms of aesthetic experience has distinctive connections to morality, so we can only appreciate the full range of the links that Kant draws between aesthetics and morality once we have recognized that Kant does not reduce all aesthetic experience to a single model.

As we already saw, Kant begins his analysis of the pure judgment of taste from the premise that our pleasure in a beautiful object occurs independently of any interest in the existence of the object as physiologically agreeable (CPJ, §3, 5:205–7) or as good for some purpose expressed by a determinate concept of utility or morality (§4, 5:207–9). This was a point that had been suggested by a number of earlier eighteenth-century theorists, most notably Francis Hutcheson, the professor of moral philosophy at Glasgow who was the teacher and predecessor of Adam Smith.[5] But Kant does not base the point on an appeal to academic authority; instead, he here appeals to the common sense of the reader (just as he had done at the outset of the exposition of his moral theory in the *Groundwork for the Metaphysics of Morals*): we are supposed to agree immediately that if someone who is asked whether he finds a Parisian palace beautiful says he likes the restaurants better or complains that the money and labor could have been better spent in some other way, he is simply sidestepping the question of its beauty. When it comes to beauty, all that matters is "whether the mere representation of the object is accompanied with satisfaction in me, however indifferent I might be with regard to the existence of the object" (§2, 5:205), that is, to the physical and moral costs and benefits of the object. To dislike an object merely because of its cost is not to make an aesthetic judgment about it, any more than to admire it solely because of its costliness is to do so.

But Kant does not mean it to follow from this emphasis on representation rather than existence that a judgment of taste is entirely subjective in the sense of being personal or idiosyncratic. On the contrary, he insists that to call an object beautiful is to speak with a "universal voice," that is, to assert that the pleasure one takes in the object oneself is a pleasure that should be felt by *anyone* who responds to the object, *at least under ideal or optimal circumstances*, even though "there can also be no rule in accordance with which someone could be compelled to acknowledge something as beautiful" (CPJ, §8, 5:216). "The **beautiful**," Kant claims, "is that which pleases universally without a concept" (§9, 5:219). Here too Kant appeals to common sense to anchor his analysis: no one will object "if, when he says that sparkling wine from the Canaries is agreeable," someone who does not like that kind of wine corrects him and reminds "him that he should say 'It is agreeable **to me**'"; but we would find it "ridiculous if someone who prided himself on his taste thought to justify himself by saying 'This object (the building we are looking at, the clothing someone is wearing, the concert that we are hearing, the poem that is presented for judging) is beautiful **for me**'" (§7, 5:212). When I make a genuine judgment of taste, I do so on the basis of my own feeling of pleasure in the experience of an object, but also claim that everyone else should feel the same pleasure. Kant subsequently reiterates this point by claiming that a proper judgment of taste possesses an "exemplary" necessity, the "necessity of the assent of **all** to a judgment that is regarded as an example of a universal rule that one cannot produce" (§18, 5:237), although this may also suggest that in making what I regard as a valid judgment of beauty I do not just predict the assent of others but also mean to set an example for how they should respond. In any case, that I must make a judgment of taste on the basis of my own feeling, and yet that I can regard my own feeling as if it were a law for the response of others as well, is the special autonomy of judgments of taste (see also §32, 5:282–3).

These claims immediately raise two questions. On the one hand, why must our pleasure in a beautiful object be independent from any concept of that object? On the other hand, how can a judgment about an object that is based on something as subjective as one's own feeling of pleasure in it apart from any concept of the object also claim universal validity? To answer these questions, Kant shifts from the level of common sense and ordinary language to the level of philosophical theory, and offers his central thesis that our pleasure in a beautiful object comes from the harmonious free play between our imagination and our understanding that such an object induces. As he puts it in the Introduction to the third critique,

> If pleasure is connected with the mere apprehension of the form of an object without a relation of this to a concept for a determinate cognition, then the representation is thereby related not to the object, but solely to the subject, and the pleasure can express nothing but its suitability to the cognitive faculties that are in play in the reflecting power of judgment, insofar as they are in play.
>
> (CPJ, Introduction, Section VII, 5:189–90)

In the section that he entitles the "key to the critique of taste" he says that "The state of mind in this representation must be that of a feeling of the free play of the powers of representation in a given representation for a cognition in general" (§9, 5:217) and that our pleasure in a beautiful object is our "sensation of the effect that consists in the facilitated play of both powers of the mind (imagination and understanding), enlivened through mutual agreement" (219). Or as he puts it in summing up the "Analytic of the Beautiful," we experience a beautiful object as having a form "that contains precisely such a composition of the manifold" of its perceived properties and aspects "as the imagination would design in harmony with the **lawfulness of the understanding** in general if it were left free by itself" (General Remark following §22, 5:240–1). In all of these formulations, Kant suggests that we experience a beautiful object as having the kind of unity that we ordinarily find in objects by subsuming the manifold of impressions or empirical intuitions they present to the imagination under a determinate concept of the understanding, but we find that unity in a free play between imagination and understanding – our faculty for receiving and retaining impressions on the one hand and our faculty for unifying the data of our intuition on the other – rather than in any constraint of the imagination by its subsumption under a particular concept. Finding unity in the materials of our sensibility and imagination is our ultimate cognitive aim, but we take an especially noticeable pleasure in this discovery of unity when it appears to be contingent, as it were unexpected, which is exactly what happens if it is not linked to any determinate concept (see *CPJ*, Introduction, Section VI, 5:186–7). So, Kant thinks, our pleasure in a beautiful object must come from a free play of imagination and understanding rather than from the application of a determinate concept to the object, and that is why there can be no precise rules for our judgments of taste: rules presuppose determinate concepts. But since this pleasure does arise from our most fundamental cognitive powers, rather than from merely idiosyncratic associations, we can safely assert that others should find the same pleasure in a beautiful object that we do – at least if we have actually set aside our own idiosyncratic associations with the object and they do so too, which is, as Kant stresses, not always the case (see §8, 5:216, and §19, 237).

There are many questions about this theory.[6] The first, of course, is just what does this idea of the free play of imagination and understanding mean? Many readers have taken Kant to be claiming that in experiencing an object as beautiful we go through all the steps of normal cognition but are so struck by the unity of our experience of the object we simply stop short of applying any determinate concept to it.[7] Others have taken Kant to mean that in experiencing an object as beautiful the mind plays back and forth between a number of different conceptualizations for it without being forced to settle on any one of them.[8] But neither of these approaches can be quite right, for the simple reason that in both common sense and Kant's own epistemology, as we saw in chapter 2, any judgment about an object already applies some determinate concept to it. We never simply say "*That* is beautiful" but, to use Kant's examples, "*That rose* is beautiful" or "*That palace* is beautiful," in each case identifying the object of our judgment by means of a determinate concept. Thus the free play of our imagination and understanding cannot be an experience of unity in an object that *precedes* any application of a determinate concept to it, but must be an experience of unity that seems to us to *go beyond* whatever sort of unity or organization is entailed by the concept or concepts that we have to apply to the object in order to think or talk about it at all. Of course, this "something more" could take various forms: it might be an unforced and indeterminate play among further concepts of the object beyond those we use to recognize it in the first place, or a play with aspects of the representation of the object that has nothing to do with concepts at all, or maybe something else.

Once we have settled the question of what Kant means by his idea, another obvious question is why we should assume that everyone's mind works the same way, so that any object that truly induces this free play of imagination and understanding in one person should do the same for everyone else who experiences it without distraction or preconception. This is a question on which Kant lays great weight, and which he tries to answer in what he calls the "Deduction of judgments of taste" (CPJ, §38). I want to defer this question, however, until we have seen the full range of aesthetic experiences that Kant attempts to explain with his concept of the free play of cognitive powers.

Kant first asserts that in "pure" judgments of taste our pleasure in beauty is a response only to the perceptible form of an object, not to any matter or content it may have – for example, in pictorial arts, "the **drawing** is what is essential," while the "colors that illuminate the outline . . . can . . . enliven the object in itself for sensation, but cannot make it . . . beautiful" (CPJ, §14, 5:225). Kant gets to this claim by means of a fallacy. Using his general term "purposiveness," he describes the experience of the harmony of imagination and understanding induced by a beautiful object as an experience of "purposiveness without purpose," because it is an experience in which our entirely *general* cognitive purpose of finding unity in our manifolds of intuition seems to be satisfied independently of the subsumption of the object under any *particular* concept, and therefore of course under any concept of its *particular* purpose. "Purposiveness without a purpose" can also be called the mere "form of purposiveness" (§11, 5:221). But Kant then simply equates the *form of purposiveness* with *purposiveness of form* (§13, 5:223), in the narrow sense of form in which the spatial or temporal structure of something (a drawing, a melody) can be contrasted to everything else about it, such as the material of which it is made, the colors of that material, the intellectual content it might have, emotions it might arouse, and so on. There is no question that sometimes the form of an object alone might stimulate a free play of the imagination and understanding, but there is also no reason why we should suppose that only form in that narrow sense can do so – presumably we can also experience a free play between the form and matter of an object, between its form and its content, and so on.[9]

In fact, Kant implicitly recognizes although he does not explicitly acknowledge this fact, and the remainder of his theory of beauty and of fine art is devoted to analyzing such more complex experiences of beauty. Immediately after having restricted pure judgments of taste to beautiful form alone, he draws a contrast between pure or "free" and "self-subsisting" beauty, which "presupposes no concept of what the object ought to be," and "adherent" or "conditioned beauty," which is "ascribed to objects that stand under a definite end" – such as "the beauty of a human being (and in this species that of a man, a woman, or a child), the beauty of a horse, of a building (such as a church, a palace, an arsenal, or a garden house)," all of which "presuppose a concept of the end that determines what the thing should be" (CPJ, §16, 5:229–30). Now Kant rejects the theory of some of his predecessors that a judgment of beauty is always and only a veiled judgment about the perfection of an object or its suitability to some purpose (see §15), so we might expect him to deny that judgments that presuppose a concept of what their object is supposed to be are judgments of beauty at all. But he does not: adherent beauty is still a species of beauty. So what Kant must mean is that in these cases the free play of our imagination and understanding in response to the object is both constrained by our concept of the purpose of an object but also in some way goes beyond that concept. For example, the concept of a church or an arsenal obviously determines certain features of a building: a traditional Christian cathedral had to have a cruciform floor plan, for example, and an arsenal has to have stout walls. But obviously not every church or arsenal that satisfies these conditions is beautiful. The beauty of one that is beautiful must lie in some way that it gives the imagination and understanding room to play with features beyond what are necessary just for the object to satisfy its concept. In fact, there are a number of ways this might happen: in some cases, the object might simply satisfy the criteria for being an object of the kind it is and then have other aspects with which the mind can independently play; in others, the mind may freely play with the relation *between* the functional features of the object and other aspects of its form and matter.[10] But whatever the details, an object with adherent beauty can still be genuinely beautiful because *all* beautiful objects somehow give the mind room for play in some aspect that goes beyond the mere application of determinate concepts to them.

A similar analysis applies in Kant's next case, what he calls the "ideal of beauty." An ideal of beauty would be something that is uniquely and maximally beautiful. Now it does not follow from Kant's general analysis of judgments of taste that there should be an ideal of beauty in this sense: that everyone should be able to take pleasure in *any* genuinely beautiful object does not imply that there must be some *one* object that everyone finds *maximally* beautiful. Kant admits as much when he says that the idea of an "archetype of taste" rests on "reason's indeterminate idea of a maximum" (CPJ, §17, 5:232), which implies that it does not derive from the logic of taste itself. Kant then appeals to his moral principle that the only thing of unconditional value is "the **human being** who determines his ends through reason" (5:233), and infers from this that the only possible ideal of beauty is the expression of the unique moral dignity of human beings through beautiful human form (5:235). But what can make this a genuine ideal of *beauty*, that is, the object of a genuine aesthetic judgment, as opposed to something that is entirely moral? It can only be that there can be no fixed rule for how a beautiful human being must look nor any fixed rule for how the outward appearance of a human being should express the inner property of moral worth, but that we can nevertheless experience a free play *between* a human form and the idea of human dignity. It is in that free play between form and concept or idea, not in the mere exemplification of the concept, that the aesthetic element of the experience must lie – but that is not a problem, because as we have seen beauty always consists in the possibility of a free play beyond the mere satisfaction of the terms of some determinate concept.

Since Kant's analysis of our experience of artistic beauty exploits the same idea, we can turn to that now, deferring for a moment his intervening discussion of the sublime.[11] Kant begins with the claim that all art is intentional human production that requires skill or talent, not "that which one **can** do as soon as one **knows** what should be done" (CPJ, §43, 5:303). This contrasts art to science, but it yields only a broad concept of art that includes crafts as well as the fine arts proper, or what Kant, following German practice, calls "beautiful art" (*schöne Kunst*). He somewhat ungenerously characterizes a craft as "an occupation that is disagreeable (burdensome) in itself and is attractive only because of its effect (e.g., the remuneration)," although he admits that some crafts may require as much talent as fine arts proper. He also acknowledges that all fine arts presuppose mastery of a body of techniques without which "the **spirit**, which must be **free** in the art and which alone animates the work, would have no body at all" (5:304). But the key difference between mere craft and fine art is that the latter is produced with the specific intention of producing pleasure by promoting the free play of the cognitive powers in its audience: "its end is that pleasure accompany the representations . . . as **kinds of cognitions**" (§44, 5:305), Kant says, and "Beautiful art is . . . a kind of representation that is purposive in itself and, though without an end, nevertheless promotes the cultivation of the mental powers for sociable communication" (5:306).

This definition seems paradoxical: a work of fine art must be the product of an intention to produce a free play of cognitive powers, a state which is defined precisely by the fact that it *cannot* follow from any specific concept and thus, one would think, any specific intention. Kant initially tries to avoid this paradox by saying:

> In a product of art one must be aware that it is art, and not nature; yet the purposiveness in its form must still seem to be as free from all constraint by arbitrary rules as if it were a mere product of nature [so that] the purposiveness in the product of beautiful art, although it is certainly intentional, must nevertheless not seem intentional.
>
> (CPJ, §45, 5:306–7)

This makes it sound as if in order to enjoy a work of art we must somehow both recognize and yet suppress the fact that it is the product of human intentionality. But perhaps this suggestion is just meant as an introduction to Kant's theory of genius, which gives a far more satisfactory resolution of the threatened paradox.[12] The key idea of this theory is that "**Genius** is the talent . . . **through which** nature gives the rule to art" (§46, 5:307) because the beauty of a work of genius lies precisely in the way that it goes *beyond* anything that could be mechanically derived from any conscious intention of the artist. Kant expands upon this:

> Genius is 1) a **talent** for producing that for which no determinate rule can be given, not a predisposition of skill for that which can be learned in accordance with some rule, consequently . . . **originality** must be its primary characteristic. 2) . . . since there can also be original nonsense, its products must at the same time be models, i.e., **exemplary**, hence, while not themselves the result of imitation, they must yet serve others in that way, i.e., as a standard or a rule for judging. 3) . . . it cannot itself describe or indicate scientifically how it brings its product into being, but rather . . . it gives the rule as **nature**, and hence the author of a product that he owes to his genius does not know himself how the idea for it came to him, and also does not have it in his power to think up such things at will or according to a plan, and to communicate to others precepts that would put them in a position to produce similar products.
>
> (§46, 5:307–8)

And this passage suggests the resolution for another paradox about fine art as well: even if a beautiful object is the product of a free play of imagination and understanding in the *artist* who creates it, how can it produce a free play and therefore an experience of beauty in a member of the *audience* who simply observes what the artist has done? Kant's answer is that a work of genius is a model of *originality* precisely because it can stimulate the free play of imagination and understanding in others: a work of artistic genius and beauty is not one that *dictates* the response of its audience, but one that *stimulates* a free play of imagination and understanding in its audience that is similar to but not identical to that which the artist experienced in producing the work.

Kant illustrates his conception of genius in his theory of "aesthetic ideas." Kant assumes that all works of fine art are mimetic, that is, that they have a representational content or theme. As he puts it, "A beauty of nature is a **beautiful thing**; the beauty of art is a **beautiful representation** of a thing" (CPJ, §48, 5:311) (although not necessarily of a beautiful thing). For those who have grown up after the advent of abstract art – or as the founder of New York's Guggenheim Museum originally called it, "non-objective art" – such an assumption might seem to need a justification, but to Kant it must have seemed self-evident. He further assumes that art concerns "concepts of reason," by which he here seems to mean primarily moral concepts or concepts related to morality, such as "death, envy, and all sorts of vices, as well as love, fame, etc.," although perhaps his model could apply to ideas of theoretical reason as well (we cannot really represent the infinite, but perhaps an artist of genius can intimate it). But if it is to be beautiful, art cannot be *didactic*, that is, merely mechanical illustration of its themes. Instead, in beautiful art a genius adds

> to a concept a representation of the imagination that . . . stimulates so much thinking that it can never be grasped in a determinate concept, hence which aesthetically enlarges the concept itself in an unbounded way . . . in this case the imagination is creative, and sets the faculty of intellectual ideas (reason) into motion.
>
> (§49, 5:314)

In other words, a beautiful work of art is one that leaves room for the play of the imagination *beyond* its purely intellectual content, or even one that creates a play *between* its content on the one hand and its form and materials on the other – its surface features and visual imagery in the case of painting, its diction and imagery in the case of lyric poetry, its language and its episodes in the case of an epic or a novel, and so on. Thus, genius "displays itself not so much in the . . . presentation of a determinate **concept** as in the exposition or the expression of **aesthetic ideas**, which contain rich material for that aim," and in the "unsought and unintentional purposiveness in the free correspondence of the imagination to the lawfulness of the understanding" from which it results in the artist and produces in its audience (5:317).

When it comes to art, therefore, Kant is not the pure formalist he might initially have seemed to be. Thus, building upon this theory of aesthetic ideas, he proposes a system of the fine arts that classifies them according to their use of word, gesture, and tone or "articulation, gesticulation, and modulation" as means of expression (CPJ, §51, 5:320). But instead of exploring the details of this classification,[13] we must now turn to Kant's treatment of the sublime. Kant gives a distinctive twist to his treatment of this standard topic in eighteenth-century aesthetics[14]: the experience of the sublime involves a free play among cognitive powers, but in this case between imagination and reason rather than imagination and understanding.

Kant recognizes two forms of the sublime, the "mathematical" and the "dynamical," thus making it explicit that ideas of theoretical as well as practical reason can enter into aesthetic experience in a way that he does not do in his account of aesthetic ideas in art. In both cases, he holds that our experience is a mixture of pain and pleasure, an initial moment of pain due to a feeling of the inadequacy of the imagination which is followed by a feeling of pleasure in response to an ultimate harmony between imagination and reason. The mathematical sublime involves a relationship between imagination and theoretical reason's idea of infinite magnitude. Ordinarily, we use both imagination and understanding to reach a "logical comprehension" of the magnitude of any object or distance by reiterating a determinate unity of measurement a determinate number of times; and in principle, we could measure a magnitude of any size by this means. But sometimes we experience vistas so vast that we try to take them in by a single "aesthetic comprehension" rather than by measuring them; we cannot actually do this, so our attempt to do so is initially painful, but then we somehow realize that our very effort to do so has been stimulated by the effect of our faculty of reason upon our imagination, and this recognition of the demand of reason is deeply pleasurable (CPJ, §26, 5:254–5). Kant holds that in this experience we do not just infer that we have such a faculty, but actually *experience* "a feeling that we have pure self-sufficient reason" (§27, 5:258) – somehow, in seeing a vast mountain range or the "starry skies above" it *feels* to us as if we are directly grasping the infinite, even though in the cool light of the understanding we know that we are not. In this case, we feel as if there is a free play between the imagination and theoretical reason.

In the case of the dynamical sublime, what we experience is ultimately a harmony between our imagination and practical reason. This experience is induced by natural objects that seem not just vast, but overwhelmingly powerful and threatening – volcanoes, raging seas, and the like (CPJ, §28, 5:261). Here we experience an element of fear and pain at the thought of our own physical injury or destruction, which is however accompanied by the satisfying feeling that we have "within ourselves a capacity for resistance of quite another kind, which gives us the courage to measure ourselves against the apparent all-powerfulness of nature," namely,

> our power (which is not part of nature) to regard those things about which we are concerned (goods, health and life) as trivial, and hence to regard its power (to which, to be sure, we are subjected in regard to these things) as not the sort of dominion over ourselves and our authority to which we would have to bow if it came down to our highest principles and their affirmation or abandonment.
>
> (§28, 5:262)

In other words, the experience of the dynamical sublime is a *feeling* of our freedom to adhere to our fundamental moral principles no matter what threats or for that matter blandishments nature puts in our way. This feeling is not a determinate *judgment* that we have the freedom of will necessary to be able to choose to fulfill the demands of the moral law; a determinate judgment of that sort would not be aesthetic. It must rather be a feeling that suggests a certain interpretation that we can only spell out by means of concepts, but at the same time gives us a certain palpable sense of the validity of those concepts before we have even spelled them out. In this way the experience of the dynamic sublime can be understood as a free play between imagination and practical reason rather than as a determinate, strictly cognitive relation between them.

With the dynamical sublime, we obviously have already arrived at a connection between aesthetics and morality. But before we can turn to that subject directly, we must return to a topic that was previously deferred, namely the plausibility of Kant's claim that if aesthetic judgments are genuinely grounded in the free play of imagination and understanding then they are universally valid. Kant attempts to justify this claim in the

"Deduction of judgments of taste." Kant's basic idea in the section of this name (§38) as well as in an earlier anticipation of it (§21) is simply that since aesthetic experience involves powers of the mind that are also necessary for ordinary cognition, and all normal human beings are certainly capable of ordinary cognition, then they also have the powers necessary for aesthetic experience, and indeed must all be capable of having any genuine aesthetic experience that any one of them has. In Kant's words, in any case in which one person's judgment is genuinely "pure, i.e., mixed with neither concepts of the object nor with sensations as determining grounds," then

> the power of judgment . . . can be directed only to the subjective conditions of the use of the power of judgment in general . . . and thus to that subjective element that one can presuppose in all human beings (as requisite for possible cognitions in general.

Therefore, "the correspondence of a representation with these conditions of the power of judgment must be able to be assumed to be valid for everyone *a priori*." Thus, if someone making a judgment of taste has in fact correctly ascribed his own pleasure to the occurrence of the harmony of the imagination and understanding – something that cannot be guaranteed in practice, because we can all too easily be deceived about the sources of our own feelings – then "the pleasure or subjective purposiveness of the representation . . . can rightly be expected of everyone" (CPJ, §38, 5:290).

This argument is not completely convincing. Using Kant's own language, we might say that even if the cognitive faculties *work* the same way in everyone, they need not *play* in the same way for everyone. Indeed, we might say that just as there are some people who seem to know only how to work and not how to relax in the ordinary sense of those terms, so there might be some people whose cognitive faculties work but do not play at all. Or even if that objection seems extreme, surely we might hold that everybody's cognitive powers work in the same way in some general sense but not in every specific detail: perhaps everyone is capable of applying some concept or another to any given group of data or observations, but they do not all necessarily apply the *same* concept to any such manifold. Anthropology and linguistics since the nineteenth century have established that different cultures often carve up the same domain of objects with quite different concepts. Further, even if everyone is capable of experiencing the free play of the cognitive powers in response to *some* object or other, it does not follow that everyone will experience the pleasurable free play of those powers in response to the *same* objects as everyone else.[15]

Does this objection undermine the value of Kant's entire aesthetic theory? I do not think it does, for two reasons. First, even if Kant cannot provide a guarantee that we can reach agreement in our aesthetic judgments, by giving us an interpretation of our aesthetic experience in terms of the play of our cognitive powers, he has lifted that experience out of the realm of the completely inarticulate and ineffable, and at least suggested a way to talk about it so that we can rationally try to communicate our judgments to each other. He has shown us how we can do more than simply stand in front of an object and say "It's beautiful": we can talk about how its various parts fit together to give us a sense of unity, even though they don't fit together like the steps of a proof; and we can talk about how they enliven a theme, even though there is no rule that says this is the only way that theme can be enlivened.

Second, once we see why Kant thinks that it is *important* that we be able to agree about judgments of taste, we may see that it is indeed important that everyone be capable of having aesthetic experience but not necessarily so important that they have the same aesthetic experiences in response to the same objects as everyone else. Almost at the end of the "Critique of the Aesthetic Power of Judgment," Kant says that "the beautiful is the symbol of the morally good, and also that only in this respect (that of a relation that is natural to everyone, and that is also expected of everyone else as a duty) does it please with a claim to the assent of everyone else" (CPJ, §59, 5:353). It is because aesthetic experience ultimately has moral significance that we have a right to demand that others have it. But unless others can get the moral benefit of aesthetic experience only from the very same objects from which any one of us gets it, we may not need to demand agreement about particular judgments of taste. So let us now turn at last to Kant's account of the connections between aesthetic and morality, and see if those connections can hold even if people do not necessarily agree in their particular judgments of taste.

AESTHETICS AND MORALITY

Kant draws at least six specific connections between aesthetics and ethics. First, as we have seen from the theory of aesthetic ideas, he evidently holds that objects of aesthetic experience can present morally significant ideas to us in an imaginative and pleasing way. In fact, in one place Kant goes so far as to maintain that *all* forms of beauty, natural as well as artistic, can be regarded as expressions of aesthetic ideas: natural objects can suggest moral ideas to us even if such suggestion is not the product of any intentional human activity (CPJ, §51, 5:319). In "The Ideal of Beauty," Kant, as we saw, also maintained that the beauty of the human form can be taken as "the visible expression of moral ideas, which inwardly govern human beings"; here he argued that only human beauty can be taken as a unique archetype or standard for beauty, because it is the only form of beauty that expresses something absolutely and unconditionally valuable, namely the moral autonomy of which humans alone are capable, but at the same time that there is no determinate way in which this unique value can be expressed in the human form, thus that there is always something free and therefore aesthetic in the outward expression in the human figure of the inner moral value of the human character (§17, 5:235−6).

We have also already touched upon the second connection Kant makes, in his claim that the experience of the dynamical sublime is nothing other than a feeling of the power of our own practical reason to accept the pure principle of morality and to act in accordance with it in spite of all the threats or inducements to do otherwise that nature might place in our way. Indeed, because the experience of the dynamical sublime so centrally involves an intimation of our own capacity to be moral, Kant actually insists that "the sublime in nature is only improperly so called, and should properly be ascribed only to the manner of thinking, or rather its foundation in human nature" (CPJ, §30, 5:280). And while he obviously does not want to claim that this experience is identical to explicit moral reasoning, but only a "disposition of the mind that is similar to the moral disposition" (General Remark following §29, 5:268), he does in at least one place argue that the complex character of the experience of the sublime makes it the best representation in our experience of our moral situation itself:

> The object of a pure and unconditioned intellectual satisfaction is the moral law in all its power . . . and, since this power actually makes itself aesthetically knowable only through sacrifices (which is a deprivation, although in behalf of inner freedom . . .), the satisfaction on the aesthetic side (in relation to sensibility) is negative . . . but considered from the intellectual side it is positive . . . From this it follows that the intellectual, intrinsically purposive (moral good), judged aesthetically, must not be represented so much as beautiful but rather as sublime, so that it arouses more the feeling of respect (which scorns charm) than that of love and intimate affection, since human nature does not agree with that good of its

own accord, but only through the dominion that reason exercises over sensibility.

(General Remark following §29, 5:271)

In spite of this emphatic statement, however, Kant elsewhere argues thirdly that there are crucial aspects of our moral condition that are symbolized by the beautiful rather than the sublime. Here I refer to his claim, alluded to at the end of the last section, that the beautiful is the symbol of the morally good because there are significant parallels between our experience of beauty and the structure of morality, and indeed that it is only insofar as the beautiful is the symbol of the morally good that we have any right not merely to *predict* that under ideal circumstances others should agree with our appraisals of beauty but actually to *demand* that they do so (§59, 5:353). Kant adduces "several aspects of this analogy, while not leaving unnoticed its differences":

> 1) The beautiful pleases **immediately** (but only in reflecting intuition, not, like morality, in the concept). 2) It pleases **without any interest** (the morally good is of course necessarily connected with an interest, but not with one that precedes the judgment on the satisfaction, but rather with one that is thereby first produced). 3) The **freedom** of the imagination (thus of the sensibility of our faculty) is represented in the judging of the beautiful as in accord with the lawfulness of the understanding (in the moral judgment the freedom of the will is conceived as the agreement of the latter with itself in accordance with universal laws of reason). 4) The subjective principle of the judging of the beautiful is represented as **universal**, i.e., valid for everyone . . . (the objective principle of morality is also declared to be universal).
>
> (5:354)

The most striking of Kant's claims here is that because the experience of beauty is an experience of the freedom of the imagination in its play with the understanding, it can be taken as a palpable symbol of the freedom of the will to determine itself by moral laws that is necessary for morality but not itself something that can be directly experienced (see CPracR, 5:29). In other words, it is the very independence of aesthetic response from direct determination by concepts, including moral concepts, thus its disinterestedness, that makes the experience of beauty an experience of freedom that can in turn symbolize moral freedom.[16]

Presumably this thesis can be reconciled with Kant's earlier claim that the sublime is the most appropriate symbol of morality by observing that while the experience of beauty makes the freedom of the will palpable to us, it is only the mixed experience of the sublime that brings home to feeling that this freedom must often be exercised in the face of resistance offered by our own merely natural inclinations.[17] But however this tension is to be handled, we can now see that Kant's claim that the experience of beauty is a feeling of freedom can be separated from his claim that particular judgments of beauty are universally valid: the experience of beauty could symbolize the freedom of our wills even if we do not all derive this experience from the same particular objects; and if it is important to us that we have this feeling, it might suffice that we each get this experience from some object or other that strikes us as beautiful, and be unnecessary that we all get this experience from the very same objects.

Kant's fourth connection between the aesthetic and the ethical lies in his theory of the "intellectual interest" in the beautiful. Here Kant argues that although our basic pleasure in a beautiful object must be independent of any antecedent interest in its existence, we may add a further layer of pleasure to that basic experience if the existence of beautiful objects suggests some more generally pleasing fact about our situation in the world. What Kant then argues is that since in the case of morality

> it also interests reason that the ideas (for which it produces an immediate interest in the moral feeling) also have objective reality, i.e., that nature should at least show some trace or give a sign that it contains in itself some sort of ground for assuming a lawful correspondence of its products with our satisfaction . . . reason must take an interest in every manifestation in nature of a correspondence similar to this; consequently the mind cannot reflect on the beauty of **nature** without finding itself at the same time to be interested in it.
>
> (CPJ, §42, 5:300)

Kant's claim is that it is of interest to practical reason that nature be hospitable to its objectives, so we take pleasure in *any* evidence that nature is amenable to our objectives, even when those are not specifically moral; and the natural existence of beauty is such evidence, because the experience of beauty is itself an unexpected fulfillment of our most basic cognitive objective. In his moral philosophy, recall, Kant said that we can *postulate* that nature has an author who has made its laws consistent with the realization of the ultimate object of morality, the highest good; but now he says that in the experience of beauty we can actually *feel* that the world is consistent with our aims, including our ultimate moral aim.

Kant's fifth claim is that aesthetic experience is conducive to proper moral conduct itself. In the third *Critique* he states that "The beautiful prepares us to love something, even nature, without interest; the sublime, to esteem it, even contrary to our (sensible) interest" (CPJ, General Remark following §29, 5:267), where being able to love without any personal interest and to esteem even contrary to our own interest are necessary preconditions of proper moral conduct. We saw in Chapter 7 that Kant later makes a similar point in the *Metaphysics of Morals* when he argues that "a propensity to wanton destruction of what is *beautiful* in inanimate nature," even though we do not owe any moral duties directly to anything other than ourselves and other human beings, nevertheless "weakens or uproots that feeling in [us] which, though not of itself moral, is still a disposition of sensibility that greatly promotes morality or at least prepares the way for it: the disposition, namely, to love something (e.g., beautiful crystal formations, the indescribable beauty of plants) even apart from any intention to use it" (MM, Doctrine of Virtue §17, 6:643).

Finally, in the very last section of the "Critique of the Aesthetic Power of Judgment," its brief "Appendix on the methodology of taste," Kant suggests that the cultivation or realization of common standards of taste in a society can be conducive to the discovery of the more general "art of the reciprocal communication of the ideas of the most educated part" of a society "with the cruder, the coordination of the breadth and refinement of the former with the natural simplicity and originality of the latter" (CPJ, §60, 5:356), where this art is apparently necessary to the realization of the goal of "**lawful** sociability," or the establishment of a stable polity on the basis of principles of justice rather than sheer force. Thus, Kant suggests that aesthetic experience can be conducive to the development of sound politics as well as personal ethics, although the two are of course not unconnected, since, as we saw in Chapter 8, Kant holds a moral politics on which we have a moral duty to establish a just state, not merely a prudential interest in doing so.

So in spite of the disinterestedness of aesthetic response, indeed on the basis of it, Kant recognized a variety of ways in which aesthetic experience is conducive to moral conduct. Looking back to the four conditions for the possibility of morality that were enumerated at the end of the first section of this chapter, we can now see how these links can support our fulfillment of this possibility.

First, the sensuous presentation of moral ideas, above all through aesthetic ideas in the case of works of artistic genius, but perhaps also through the image of a maximally coherent moral character that is expressed by the beautiful human figure as the "ideal of beauty," offers us a sensuous presentation of the moral law itself as well as of other thoughts connected with the very idea of morality, such as the blessedness that comes from fulfilling the demands of morality, the contempt that is deserved by their rejection, and the like – for so might we interpret the specific examples of rational ideas expressed through aesthetic ideas that Kant gives.

Second, the feeling of our freedom to choose to live up to the demands of morality in spite of all the threats of nature that we experience in the dynamical sublime as well as the tendency to interpret the beautiful as a symbol of the morally good are ways in which the freedom of will that we can intellectually infer from our consciousness of the moral law becomes palpable to us as sensory creatures. In the latter case, Kant explicitly argues that "to demonstrate the reality of our concepts, intuitions are always required," and that even ideas of pure reason that go beyond the limits of our sensibility need at least a symbolic "hypotyposis" or presentation that can make them sensible (CPJ, §59, 5:351). It is our nature, in other words, to seek sensible symbols even of that which is too abstract to be fully grasped by the senses, and just as we may use the image of a handmill to represent the despotism of absolute monarchy, so we may use the sensuous experience of the freedom of the imagination to represent the indubitable but intangible fact of the freedom of our will (5:354).

Third, the hint from the experience of beauty that nature is amenable to the realization of our objectives is a sensible suggestion of that which is otherwise only a postulate of pure practical reason, namely the consistency of the laws of nature and the law of freedom. Kant calls the pleasure that we take in such sensory suggestion the basis of an "intellectual interest" in beauty, presumably because the fact that beauty confirms for us is of interest to us as agents with pure practical reason, and does not interest us in the merely empirical way that the possibility for self-aggrandizement or harmless socializing through the possession of valuable works of art does. Nevertheless, the suggestion of the amenability of nature to our objectives that the existence of beauty offers us has an impact upon our emotions, and thus supplements the postulate of pure practical reason (just as the historical story about the emergence of peace that Kant told in *Perpetual Peace* can supplement our purely rational conviction that what morality demands must be possible in a way that satisfies the sensuous aspect of our nature).

Finally, when Kant suggests that the experience of beauty prepares us to love disinterestedly and that of the sublime to esteem even contrary to our own interest, and that aesthetic experience may help bridge the gaps between the different classes and interest-groups that inevitably arise in any complex polity, he is suggesting that aesthetic experience can actually help us to act as morality requires.

But now there may be a problem: all these claims that aesthetic experience can be conducive to proper moral conduct could seem to undermine Kant's famous claim that only pure respect for the moral law can be a truly estimable motivation to be moral. If Kant is to be consistent, he needs to argue that aesthetic experiences can prepare us for successful moral conduct without substituting for pure moral motivation. How might he do this?

There are two approaches to this problem. First, we could argue that Kant adduces the purity of motivation from all mere inclination that is required for moral worth just in order to determine the character of the moral law – it must be a law that someone actually free of all inclination could act upon, thus a merely formal law (see G, 4:402). But once that law and the particular obligations that follow from it have been identified, it is surely our duty always to comply with it, thereby avoiding moral condemnation, *out of whatever motivation to do so is actually available to us*, even if the kind of motivation that is available to us will not win us any special moral praise. Thus, we would have a duty to develop morally useful feelings from aesthetic experience even if fulfilling our moral obligations by using those feelings as motivations will only spare us moral contempt but not earn us moral esteem. This must be at least partly right, since it is certainly our duty always to observe the moral law, even when the pure motivation of respect for the law is not available to us and we cannot earn any special esteem by doing so.

But instead of looking at aesthetically-induced feelings just as second-best motives for fulfilling our duty, we can also look at the motivation of respect for duty as a *higher-order* motivation, which grounds our commitment to do what the moral law requires of us in any and all particular circumstances and therefore gives us a motive to develop whatever *particular* feelings and dispositions will enable us to perform the morally requisite actions in those particular circumstances, including aesthetically-induced feelings if they turn out to be effective for this purpose. As we saw, Kant suggests such a model when he discusses feelings of benevolence and sympathy in the "Doctrine of Virtue" of the *Metaphysics of Morals*. There he suggests that nature has "implanted in human beings receptivity" to "sympathetic" feelings as *means* by which we can accomplish the moral end of beneficence to others, and thus that we have a "particular, although only conditional, duty" to use such feelings "as a means to promote active and rational benevolence" (MM, Doctrine of Virtue, §34, 6:456), or to use them "as so many means to sympathy based on moral principles" (MM, Doctrine of Virtue, §35, 6:457). There are two thoughts here. First, although the general motivation of respect for duty is what must lead us to make the fulfillment of the moral law our overarching objective and commits us to particular duties such as beneficence, we are moved to act in particular circumstances by more concrete feelings, and thus, precisely because of that general motivation, must develop feelings, and especially develop dispositions to feeling that are natural to us – dispositions to sympathy, but also dispositions to admire natural beauty – that can serve as such means. But second, this duty is always "conditional" – that is, our sympathy must be "based on moral principles" – for it always remains for reason to check whether what our feelings, even our most benevolent and beneficial feelings, prompt us to do in any particular situation is in fact morally appropriate. The idea would be that we cannot act without feelings, but that we cannot act on feelings alone, because feelings, no matter how well-cultivated, may not always be fully responsive to the moral situation at hand, and need the guidance of moral principles for their proper exercise. We should not act on our benevolent feelings, whether developed through aesthetic experience or otherwise, in cases where our so doing might, for example, help another to violate his own moral duty. Natural feelings, including those prompted by or developed out of aesthetic experience, may be necessary conditions for performing particular actions required by morality, but can never be sufficient conditions – they always require the guidance of moral principles.

But Kant never argues that any feelings stimulated by aesthetic experience are a *necessary* condition for the fulfillment of our moral obligations. And although he does insist that we always need some form of sensible presentation for even the most abstract ideas of reason, and that our feeling of the freedom of the imagination in the experience of beauty can serve as such a symbol for the intangible freedom of the will postulated by morality, he never says that it is the only possible sensible symbol of that freedom – his reinterpretation of the central symbols of Christianity in the *Religion* precludes this (RBMR, 6:60–2, 82), and the later discussion of sympathetic feeling to which we have just appealed to show how feelings might be morally appropriate means to the accomplishment of ends enjoined upon us by the pure motivation of respect for duty itself assumes that there are sympathetic feelings that are directly "implanted" in us by nature rather than produced through aesthetic experience and education. Thus, although Kant clearly supposes that dispositions flowing from aesthetic experience *can* be morally beneficial and should be preserved and cultivated for that reason, he could not mean to argue that such feelings are the *only* morally beneficial feelings, or even necessary, let alone sufficient conditions for the fulfillment of our moral obligations. And if this is so, then perhaps we should conclude that the cultivation of taste should be *encouraged* because of the support for morality that it may afford, but we do not have the right to *demand* that others cultivate their aesthetic sensibilities if they have found other ways in which to support their own morality.

SUMMARY

Kant interprets aesthetic experience as both its own unique form of autonomy and as a support for our efforts as creatures who are both rational and sensuous to achieve autonomy in the moral sense. Kant analyzes aesthetic judgment as based on feelings of pleasure produced by the free play of the imagination and the higher cognitive powers: in the case of pure beauty, a free play between imagination and understanding induced by the form of an object; in the case of adherent beauty, a free play between imagination and understanding with features of the form of an object going beyond the concept of its purpose that we apply to it, or a free play between the concept and the form; in the case of artistic beauty, a free play between imagination and the ideas of reason expressed by works of art; and in the case of the sublime, an initially painful but ultimately pleasurable play between imagination and reason induced by either the magnitude or the might of nature. Kant then analyzes a variety of ways in which aesthetic experience can support our realization of moral autonomy without undermining its own distinctive form of autonomy. The key to his solution to this potential paradox is that it is precisely in virtue of its own freedom that the imagination and its works can symbolize and support the exercise of the freedom of the will that is essential to moral autonomy.

FURTHER READING

The arguments in this chapter have drawn heavily from my own works on Kant's aesthetics, including Guyer (1979), which is a commentary on the central themes of the "Analytic of the Beautiful" and the "Deduction of Pure Judgments of Taste"; (1993), containing essays on the historical context of Kant's aesthetics and on the links between aesthetics and morality; and (2005) which includes essays on the harmony of the faculties, adherent beauty, ugliness, genius, and aesthetics and morality, as well as essays on figures in aesthetics other than Kant.

Paul Guyer, *Kant and the Claims of Taste* (Cambridge, MA: Harvard University Press, 1979; revised edition, Cambridge: Cambridge University Press, 1997).

——*Kant and the Experience of Freedom* (Cambridge: Cambridge University Press, 1993)

——*Values of Beauty: Historical Essays on Aesthetics* (Cambridge: Cambridge University Press, 2005).

Other important works on Kant's aesthetics include the following. Crawford is the first rigorous analysis of Kant's central arguments in English. Schaper presents stimulating essays on Kant from the point of view of British analytical philosophy. Savile (1987) is a challenging analysis of some of Kant's central ideas, and his (1993) work presents discussions of Kant's views on particular arts. Ginsborg offers a radically different account of aesthetic judgment than the one presented here, seeing aesthetic judgment as a precondition of all cognition; while Allison is a sympathetic defense of many of Kant's ideas that have been challenged by commentators such as myself; and Budd, the heart of which is a series of three critical essays on Kant's approach to natural beauty, sublimity, and the connection between beauty and morality.

Henry E. Allison, *Kant's Theory of Taste: A Reading of the Critique of Aesthetic Judgment* (Cambridge: Cambridge University Press, 2001).

Malcolm Budd, *The Aesthetic Appreciation of Nature: Essays on the Aesthetics of Nature* (Oxford: Clarendon Press, 2002).

Donald W. Crawford, *Kant's Aesthetic Theory* (Madison, WI: University of Wisconsin Press, 1974).

Hannah Ginsborg, *The Role of Taste in Kant's Theory of Cognition* (New York: Garland, 1990).

Anthony Savile, *Aesthetic Reconstructions: The Seminal Writings of Lessing, Kant, and Schiller* (Oxford: Basil Blackwell, 1987).

——*Kantian Aesthetics Pursued* (Edinburgh: Edinburgh University Press, 1993).

Eva Schaper, *Studies in Kant's Aesthetics* (Edinburgh: Edinburgh University Press, 1979).

Representative European approaches to Kant's aesthetics are Derrida, who applies Derrida's method of deconstruction to Kant's central distinctions; and Lyotard, who exploits Kant's analysis of the complex relationship between imagination and reason as an illustration of Lyotard's general model of the antinomial nature of human thought. Schaeffer defends Kant's aesthetics from the "speculative" philosophy of art that dominated European thought afterwards; while Recki is a full-length discussion of the connections between aesthetics and morality in Kant.

Jacques Derrida, *The Truth in Painting*, translated by Geoff Bennington and Ian McLeod (Chicago: University of Chicago Press, 1987).

Jean-François Lyotard, *Lessons on the Analytic of the Sublime*, translated by Elizabeth Rottenberg (Stanford, CA: Stanford University Press, 1994).

Jean-Marie Schaeffer, *Art of the Modern Age: Philosophy of Art from Kant to Heidegger*, translated by Steven Rendell (Princeton, NJ: Princeton University Press, 2000).

Birgit Recki, *Ästhetik der Sitten: Die Affinität von ästhetischem Gefühl und praktischer Vernunft bei Kant* (Frankfurt am Main: Vittorio Klostermann, 2001).

Four collections of essays on Kant's aesthetics are:

Ted Cohen and Paul Guyer (eds), *Essays in Kant's Aesthetics* (Chicago: University of Chicago Press, 1992) (with an extensive bibliography of literature on Kant through 1980).

Paul Guyer (ed.), *Kant's Critique of the Power of Judgment: Critical Essays* (Lanham, MD: Rowman and Littlefield, 2003) (with further bibliography).

Ralf Meerbote and Hud Hudson (eds), *Kant's Aesthetics* (Atascadero, CA: Ridgeview Publishing Company, 1991) (which extends the Cohen and Guyer bibliography up to 1990).

Herman Parret (ed.), *Kants Ästhetik – Kant's Aesthetics – L'esthétique de Kant* (Berlin and New York: Walter de Gruyter, 1998) (a collection of forty-seven papers by scholars from Germany, France, Britain, the US, and elsewhere, presented at two conferences in 1993).

Ten

THE REJECTION OF TRADITIONAL TELEOLOGY

Traditional teleology is the view that everything in nature has a purpose, and indeed has been created for a purpose. One example of traditional teleology with which Kant was well acquainted was that presented by Christian Wolff in his *Rational Thoughts on the Intentions of Natural Things*, first published in 1723. Wolff confidently argued that we know two definite things about the purpose of the world and everything in it: first, that the world was created by God in order to reveal his greatness to us, and, second, that beyond being created to teach us this lesson, everything else in the world was created for our own use and happiness. Thus, Wolff first asserted that

> The chief aim of the world is that we should know God's perfection from it. Now if this is what God wanted to achieve, then he had to arrange the world in such a way that a rational being could draw from consideration of these grounds his attributes and infer with certainty everything else that one can know of him.[1]

Wolff then proceeded to explain how various aspects of the created world are a mirror in which we can come to see the perfections of God. Thus, for example, the sheer number of things in the world is "a mirror of the infinite cognition of God";[2] "the connection of the things in the world to each other" by the most direct possible routes is a "mirror of his wisdom";[3] and even the contingency of the existence of the particular things in the world is a mirror of God's freedom: "If the world were necessary, then we could no longer know from it that there is a God, that is, a being distinct from it in which the ground of its reality is to be found,"[4] for it is precisely "the contingency of the world" that "makes it into a mirror of the freedom of the divine will."[5] Wolff expresses the second main thesis of his teleology, that the world is created for the purposes of man, in language like this:

> One cannot say otherwise than that God made the earth so that it would be occupied, and on that account arranged everything in it so that it would be fit as a dwelling for men and animals. Man finds here everything that may be suitable to him for his nourishment, dress, dwelling, attainment of science and art, and whatever is necessary for the fulfillment of his duties.[6]

Human happiness is not only man's end, as Wolff had argued in his moral philosophy, but also God's end for man.

David Hume subjected traditional teleology to corruscating criticism in his *Dialogues Concerning Natural Religion*, first written in 1751, not published until 1779, three years after Hume's death, but then almost immediately translated into German (1781). In these dialogues, Hume's spokesman "Philo" argues that we can have no basis for inferring that the world as a whole had a cause at all, since it is a unique rather than a repeated phenomenon, and that even if we could, we certainly could not infer that the cause of the world was an intelligent and beneficent designer, since the world seems to be a pretty messy place with little concern for human happiness. Hume seems to reject the possibility of teleological speculation altogether when he has Philo say:

> But when we look beyond human Affairs and the Properties of the surrounding Bodies: When we carry our speculations into the two Eternities, before and after the present State of things; into the Creation and Formation of the Universe; the Existence and Properties of Spirits; the Powers and Operations of one universal Spirit, existing without Beginning and without End; omnipotent, omniscient, immutable, infinite, and incomprehensible: We must be far removed from the smallest Tendency to Scepticism not to be apprehensive, that we have here got quite beyond the Reach of our Faculties.[7]

Kant's rejection of theoretical arguments for the existence of God was even more thorough than Hume's: while Hume's primary target in the *Dialogues* was the argument for design, or what Kant called the "physico-theological proof," which attempts to infer the existence of God from empirical observation of order in the world, Kant had also rejected all *a priori* proofs of the existence of God, summed up for him in the form of the ontological and cosmological arguments. So Kant, who clearly knew Hume's *Dialogues*,[8] had even more reason than Hume to reject the kind of teleology in which Wolff and so many others indulged. So why did he include a teleology in his own system of philosophy? Did he really think there was anything to traditional teleology that could be salvaged from Hume's critique?

There are two parts to the answer to this question. Hume's rejection of teleology was not as complete as it might initially seem, for just as he did in the case of other metaphysical conceptions such as causation, Hume held that even though our belief in an intelligent designer of the world has no rational justification, it is still natural and unavoidable for us. Thus Philo also says:

> A Purpose, an Intention, a Design strikes every where the most careless, the most stupid Thinker; and no man can be so harden'd in absurd Systems, as at all times to reject it. *That Nature does nothing in vain*, is a Maxim establish'd in all the Schools, merely from the Contemplation of the Works of Nature, without any religious Purpose: and, from a firm Conviction of its Truth, an Anatomist, who had observ'd a new Organ or Canal, wou'd never be satisfy'd, till he had also discover'd its Use and Intention. One great Foundation of the *Copernican* System is the Maxim, that *Nature acts by the simplest Methods, and chooses the most proper Means to any End*; and Astronomers often, without thinking of it, lay this strong Foundation of Piety and Religion. The same thing is observable in other Parts of Philosophy: And thus all the Sciences almost lead us insensibly to acknowledge a first intelligent Author.[9]

Kant agrees with Hume that it is natural for human beings to think of certain things in nature and then of nature as a whole as if they were the product of intelligent design. The first step in his revision of traditional teleology is to pick up on Hume's reference to "maxims" here in order to develop the view that we can put our natural tendency to think of nature as designed to *heuristic* work in the guidance of our scientific investigation of nature, directing our search for ever more *naturalistic* rather than *supernatural* explanations of natural phenomena. But Kant also takes a major step beyond Hume, without relapsing into traditional teleology of the Wolffian sort. Kant accepts Hume's argument that we have no basis for a theoretical determination of the character and purposes of an author of nature, accepts Hume's supposition that it is nevertheless natural for us to believe in an intelligent author of nature, and then adds that it is incoherent for us to conceive of an intelligent yet purposeless author of nature. We cannot conceive of nature as having a design without also conceive of it as having a point or "final end." To fill this gap, Kant then holds that the only thing that we must represent as having unconditional value, namely the development of our own freedom, is also the only thing that we can conceive of as the final end of the creation of nature. In a word, Kant accepts Hume's rejection of theoretical cognition of an anthropomorphic God, but argues that we must replace that with an anthropocentric, but morally anthropocentric, conception of nature. Since this conception does not amount to theoretical cognition, yet unlike a postulate of pure practical reason it characterizes not just the author of nature but nature itself, the same thing that is the object of our theoretical cognition, Kant attributes this conception to the power of judgment, but to the reflecting rather than determining power of judgment.

Kant's revised teleology thus comprises several stages. First, Kant shows why we naturally introduce the concept of purposiveness into our thought about nature, beginning with our experience of organisms but then extending this conception to the whole of nature. The thought of purposiveness has heuristic value in the investigation of particular natural phenomena, but also leads us to think about the purpose of nature as a whole. And that leads us to the view that we must think of nature as if it were meant to be an arena hospitable to the realization of the goals of human morality. This is a conception of nature that in our earlier discussion of the highest good we saw is necessitated by morality itself, but now we see that we must also arrive at it beginning from our experience of nature as well. And this parallels one of Kant's thoughts about the moral significance of aesthetic experience, thus explaining Kant's connection of aesthetics and teleology in a single book: just as we must initially experience beauty free of any moral concerns but subsequently realize with pleasure that its very existence is a sign of nature's hospitality to our objectives, including our moral goals, so we are lead from our attempt to comprehend nature scientifically to the recognition that the only possible point of nature is our own moral development. Of course, since the goal of our moral development is our own use of our freedom for the full realization of our autonomy, we cannot think of nature as if it were designed to achieve this goal for us, but can think of it at most as if it were designed to facilitate our realization of this goal. We will see that Kant signals this point subtly.

FROM ORGANISMS TO NATURE AS A WHOLE

Kant begins the "Critique of the Teleological Power of Judgment" with an argument about our experience of organisms, which he calls both "organized beings" and "natural ends." He claims that we cannot comprehend organisms by our ordinary mechanical model of causality, where the existence and properties of a whole are always explained simply by the aggregation of previously existing parts, but can instead comprehend them only as systems where whole and parts are each cause and effect of the other; and then he claims that we can only conceive of such systems as the products of intelligent design, although precisely since our theoretical cognition is limited to mechanical causality, we can have no theoretically adequate grounds for asserting the existence of the necessary designer. Nevertheless, once we have introduced the idea of an intelligent design and hence a designer for organisms within nature, two further steps are inevitable for us: first, we will think of such a design and designer as manifest not only in parts of nature, namely organisms, but in the whole of nature as a single system; second, we will also think of such a design and designer not only as intelligent but purposive, and thus seek a purpose for the system of nature as a whole. Here is where Kant then assumes that only something of unconditional value could count as the purpose of such a system, that only the realization of our own freedom in the form of the highest good is of unconditional value, and thus that we can conceive of nature as a system only if we conceive of it as a system compatible with and indeed intended for the realization of the highest good as the final end of morality. The conception of nature that begins with our experience of organisms is thus supposed to lead to the same conclusion to which we are also reach in the postulates of pure practical reason, namely that nature must be conceived of as an arena for the realization of our moral ends – although since our virtue is an essential component of the highest good, and virtue can be achieved only through our own free choice, nature can supply necessary but never sufficient conditions for the realization of our virtue and therefore of the highest good.

At this level, Kant's argument is straightforward. But its details are complex and sometimes confusing. In fact, Kant suggests several different reasons why we cannot comprehend organisms on the model that is otherwise adequate for our conduct of scientific inquiry. Further, Kant's attempt to reconcile our ordinary mechanical model of causation with our conception of both organisms and nature as a whole as purposive systems in the "Dialectic of the Teleological Power of Judgment" is not as simple as it may first seem, and will need some discussion.

Kant begins his discussion of teleology with a critical argument that we have no apparent justification for seeing some things in nature as mere means to others as ends or, in his terms, for introducing the concept of "relative purposiveness" into our conception of nature. For example, we have no *prima facie* justification for seeing the sandy plains of northern Europe, left behind by ancient seas, as intended to be means to extensive pine forests that are in turn intended to be useful as means to our own ends, or for thinking that herbivores are meant to exist in order to nourish humans when we could just as well think that humans exist merely to care for herbivores (CPJ, §63, 5:366–9). Instead, any application of the idea of purposiveness to nature can begin only with the "internal purposiveness" of organisms as "natural ends" (§64, 5:369). Kant "provisionally" defines a natural end as a thing that "**is cause and effect of itself**" (5:370), and then gives three examples of what he has in mind. In the case of reproduction, one organism is the cause of another as an individual, but "generates itself as far as the **species** is concerned," and in this (somewhat tenuous) sense the organism as a whole is the cause of itself. In the case of growth, an organism "generates itself as an **individual**" by transforming bits of external matter into parts of itself, thus by the whole being the cause of its own parts and through them of its own subsequent condition. And in the case of ordinary self-maintenance, the parts of an organism are the cause of the whole, as when the leaves of a tree keep it nourished, but the whole is also the cause of the parts, since the leaves cannot function without the rest of the tree (5:371–2). Kant's claim is that we cannot understand such organic processes on our ordinary, mechanical model of causation, where the character of a whole is determined entirely and only by the character of its parts, and that in these cases we must also see the character of the parts as dependent on the character of the whole.[10] He then argues that we can partially model such an alternative conception of causation by analogy with our own intentional production, where the whole determines the parts in the sense that our antecedent conception and plan of a whole lead to the production of the parts that are then assembled into the actual whole. But this analogy is not really adequate for comprehending organisms, because in organisms "each part is conceived as if exists only **through** all the others, thus as if existing **for the sake of the others** and **on account of** the whole," but also "as an organ that **produces** the other parts," and "only then and on that account can" something, "as an **organized** and **self-organizing** being, be called a natural end" (§65, 5:373–4). Our own works of art (in the broad sense, not restricted to fine art) are organized but not *self*-organizing; for example, in a watch, "one part is the instrument for the motion of another, but one wheel is not the efficient cause for the production of the other: one part is certainly present for the sake of the other but not because of it" (5:374). So we can only conceive of organisms by means of "a remote analogy with our own causality in accordance with ends" (5:375); we have to think of organisms as if they were the product of a designer *more* intelligent than ourselves, whose conception of the whole of such organisms can produce parts capable of producing each other as well as the whole, and of yielding a whole that can then maintain, produce, and reproduce its own parts.

Kant emphasizes his distance from traditional teleology here by adding:

> The concept of a thing as in itself a natural end is . . . not a constitutive concept of the understanding or of reason, but it can still be a regulative concept for the reflecting power of judgment, for guiding research into objects of this kind and thinking over their highest ground . . . not, of course, for the sake of knowledge of nature or its original ground, but rather for the sake of the very same practical faculty of reason in us in analogy with which we consider the cause of that purposiveness.
>
> (CPJ, §65, 5:375)

This dense statement makes three important points. First, the concept of organisms as natural ends with the special kind of internal systematicity that Kant has attempted to characterize, as well as the concept of the ground or cause of such natural ends and their internal systematicity, is regulative rather than constitutive. Second, the concept of the organism as a natural end can guide research into it, which in the next section Kant will in fact suggest to be research into the *mechanical* causality by means of which an organism effects the various purposes that can be ascribed to it as a system and to its organs as subsystems. And third, the further point of such a conception of organisms will be for the sake of our "practical faculty of reason." That is the point that Kant will develop in the "Methodology of the Teleological Power of Judgment," but only after the intervening claim that the concept of matter as a natural end "necessarily leads to the idea of the whole of nature as a system in accordance with the rule of ends" (§67, 5:378–9).

Kant is insistent that the idea of nature as a product of intelligent design is not itself a scientific theory in competition with any other scientific theory about the origination and function of nature, but that it has a merely heuristic use to help us in the formation of scientific theories and the conduct of scientific research, as well as the practical use which is his ultimate concern. Thus he would hardly have agreed with the position in the contemporary American "culture wars" that intelligent design should be taught as a scientific alternative to the modern theory of evolution. Even so, contemporary scientists could certainly object that the later stages of Kant's teleology stand on a rotten foundation, because the organic processes that he has invoked can in fact be understood by means of our ordinary mechanical model of causation. The ability of organisms to reproduce themselves is now well understood as a process in which parts of one or two organisms, namely their genetic material, combine to initiate and direct the growth of the next generation of such organisms. The ability of organisms to grow is now well explained by the function of specific parts, such as enzymes, to extract nutrients from their intake that can be transformed by ordinary chemical processes into fuel and materials for other parts of the organism, such as voluntary and involuntary muscles. The ability of organisms to maintain their existence is also explained by the powers of their parts, such as the ability of immune system cells to destroy foreign pathogens. Of course, not every element of mechanical explanations of reproduction, growth, and self-maintenance is available yet: for example, it remains to be discovered how the approximately 20,000 genes in the human genome express themselves in the 120,000 different proteins of the human proteome, or how infant stem cells differentiate themselves at the right times into a variety of different adult tissues. But contemporary scientists proceed in the confidence that "mechanical" answers to these questions will be found. Moreover, contemporary scientists also proceed in the confidence that further mechanical, in this case evolutionary explanations for the existence of the mechanical bases of organic processes will likewise be found. Further, although one might be tempted to say that contemporary scientists surely accept Kant's view that every part of an organism serves some function in the systematic life of the whole, although unlike Kant they are confident that a mechanical explanation of both the origination and the activity of every part of an organism can at least in principle be found, even that assumption may be indefensible: Stephen Jay Gould long argued that the mechanism of natural selection can carry along all sorts of non-functional by-products or "spandrels" that are mechanically connected with functional and selected traits, as long as those spandrels are not dysfunctional, that is, as long as they do not compromise the reproductive success of the organism; or traits can be carried along that were adaptive for an organism in an old environment but are no longer adaptive in a new or changed environment, as long as they are not too dysfunctional. These possibilities are reflected in contemporary genomics in the idea of stretches of "junk DNA" in chromosomes, by-products of past evolution, that can be carried along with the currently vital stretches of DNA as long as they do not harm the organism, that is, again, reduce the probability of its reproductive success. So even as a regulative principle the idea that every part of an organism is a vital and valuable part of it as an internally purposive system seems doubtful.

Thus, Kant's argument that the experience of organisms necessarily introduces a conception of purposiveness that we must extend to nature as a whole and then connect to our moral objectives may seem dubious from the start. But before we can conclude that, we must observe that Kant may suggest one or two alternative accounts of how this experience leads us to a reflective judgment that applies the idea of purposiveness to nature. The argument considered thus far turns on the claim that paradigmatic sorts of organic processes cannot be explained mechanically, and thereby lead us to the idea, although not to theoretical knowledge, of an alternative sort of causation through intelligent and purposive design. But at a later point in his exposition – in the "Dialectic of the Teleological Power of Judgment," to which we shall subsequently return – Kant suggests that it is not specific organic processes but the general "possibility of a living matter" that "cannot even be conceived" on the basis of our ordinary conception of matter, because while "lifelessness, *inertia*, constitutes [the] essential characteristic" of matter, living organisms apparently violate the law of inertia (CPJ, §73, 5:394).[11] Kant does not actually explain the "contradiction" in the concept of a "living matter," but presumably his thought is that living organisms violate the law of inertia whenever they initiate a change in their own condition without being acted upon by an external agent. If this is what he means, then his argument would be that the mere possibility of self-generated change or motion, surely the most elementary characteristic of any organism, defies comprehension by our ordinary model of causation and requires at least the conception of an alternative model of causation for organisms.

However, contemporary scientists are hardly more likely to be moved by this argument than by Kant's first. Indeed, one would presumably appeal precisely to a mechanical model of organisms to refute this argument: that is, one would appeal to the motions of specific parts of an organism to explain any changes in the rest or motion of the whole, and then explain the motions of those specific parts as the effects either of antecedent motions of other specific parts of the organism or of the influence of external objects on the motion of the internal parts. Kant would have to do a lot more than to appeal to a "contradiction" between life and inertia to find a starting point for his teleology here.

Kant returns to the "special character of the human understanding, by means of which the concept of a natural end is possible" – indeed, necessary – "for us" in three sections of the "Dialectic of the Teleological Power of Judgment," culminating in §77, the title of which has just been quoted (5:405). The general thesis of these sections is that the "discursive" nature of the human intellect is what stands in the way of our complete understanding of organisms and requires us to "base the possibility of those natural ends on . . . an intelligent being . . . in accord with the maxims of our reflecting power of judgment" (CPJ, §75, 5:400). However, Kant suggests two different accounts of what he means by the discursive character of the human intellect. In §76, he suggests that the human intellect is discursive because it can form only general concepts, which can never fully determine all the properties of a particular object, and which therefore can never fully explain the necessity of all those properties; but since reason requires us to think of those properties as necessary, we must at least form the idea of an intelligent design for nature that would fully determine "the purposiveness of nature in its products," although to be sure as a "regulative (not constitutive)" principle of reason (5:404). In §77, however, although he again says that it is characteristic of our understanding "that in its cognition, e.g., of the cause of a product, it must go from the **analytical universal** (of concepts) to the particular (of the given empirical intuition)," so that there is much that always remains contingent in the particular relative to the general concept under which we subsume it, he contrasts our understanding with one that would be "intuitive" and therefore go "from the **synthetically universal** (of the intuition of a whole as such) to the particular, i.e., from the whole to the parts, in which, therefore, and in whose representation of the whole, there is no **contingency** in the combination of the parts" (5:407). Here Kant suggests that the discursivity of our intellect is what limits us to inferring the properties of wholes from the properties of their parts and prevents us from seeing the necessity with which the whole also determines the parts. In order to accommodate our experience of organisms as wholes that do determine the character of their own parts, we then "represent products of nature as possible only in accordance with another kind of causality than that of the natural laws of matter, namely only in accordance with that of ends and final causes," where "the **representation** of a whole containing the ground of the possibility of its form and of the connection of parts that belongs to that" is considered as the cause of the object, although once again "this principle does not pertain to the possibility of such things themselves (even considered as phenomena) . . . but pertains only to the judging of them that is possible for our understanding" (5:408).[12]

Kant's appeal to the discursivity of our understanding in §77 seems then just to provide a new name for the argument already made in §§64–5, the argument that since in our experience of organisms the whole seems to determine the character of the parts in a way that we cannot explain by the power of our own intellect, we conceive of organisms as if they were products of an intellect more powerful than our own. The argument then seems open to the criticism of that argument that has been afforded by the progress of modern biology, namely that such progress consists in the increasing ability to explain how organisms function to preserve and reproduce themselves by means of the specific actions of their parts, and that there is no obvious end in sight for such explanatory progress. If, however, Kant's argument is rather that our general concepts of organisms necessarily leave some of their particular properties unexplained and therefore at least apparently contingent, as §76 seems to suggest, then Kant's present argument seems to collapse into the argument of the introduction to the third *Critique*: while the inability of our general concepts to explain every property of a particular may be especially salient in our experience of organisms, surely this general principle is true for every phenomenon in nature. Indeed, at the end of §76, Kant explicitly returns to the language of the introduction, suggesting that we need the concept of the purposiveness of nature to compensate for "what is contingent" in "the derivation of the particular laws of nature from the general" (4:404). And in that case not only does our experience of organisms seem to lose its special place in Kant's teleology, but the argument is also again exposed to the objection that we may not need to be able to see the particular laws of nature as necessary truths in any strong sense anyway.

So it is by no means clear that Kant has a sound argument that the experience of organisms in nature requires us to introduce even a regulative idea of the purposive design of nature. Thus, his claim that, "It is in fact indispensable for us to subject nature to the concept of an intention if we would even merely conduct research among its organized products by means of continued observation" and his key inference that "once we have adopted such a guidelines for studying nature and found it to be reliable we must also at least attempt to apply this maxim of the power of judgment to the whole of nature" (CPJ, §75, 5:398) both seem to be ill-founded. It is nevertheless possible that there may be an important lesson in Kant's attempt to connect the view of nature as a purposive systematic whole with the demands of morality. I will shortly argue that this is indeed the case, but before doing so I want to discuss briefly another issue about the "Dialectic of the Teleological Power of Judgment."

Kant begins the Dialectic by contrasting two "maxims" of the power of judgment, the maxim that "All generation of material things and their forms must be judged as possible in accordance with merely mechanical laws" and the maxim that "Some products of material nature cannot be judged as possible according to merely mechanical laws (judging them requires an entirely different law of causality, namely that of final causes)." He contrasts this pair of maxims to a pair of "constitutive principles of the possibility of the objects themselves," namely the "Thesis" that "All generation of material things is possible in accordance with merely mechanical laws" and the "Antithesis" that "Some generation of such things is not possible in accordance with merely mechanical laws" (CPJ, §70, 5:387). Many commentators have assumed that the resolution to the antinomy of the teleological power of judgment is simply to note this contrast, that is, to note that the first pair of maxims are just regulative principles of judgment and not constitutive claims about the nature of reality itself.[13] Indeed, Kant himself insists in the next section that

> All appearance of an antinomy between the maxims of that kind of explanation which is genuinely physical (mechanical) and that which is teleological (technical) therefore rests on confusing a fundamental principle of the reflecting with that of the determining power of judgment.
>
> (§71, 5:389)

However, Kant also entitles this section merely a "preparation" for the solution of the antinomy, and as others have noted, talking about judgments rather than objects does not avoid an antinomy: that some objects in nature can only be judged teleologically is still inconsistent with the claim that all objects in nature can be judged mechanically.[14] So Kant's resolution of the antinomy of teleological judgment must be more complex than it initially appears.

The key to Kant's real solution to the antinomy emerges in the next two sections. In §72, Kant canvasses "various systems concerning the purposiveness of nature" (5:389). There are two main possibilities, he says, namely the "**idealism** or . . . the **realism** of natural ends" (5:391), the former of which basically attempts to explain away the appearance of purposiveness or design in nature, while the latter accepts it and attempts to account for it. Kant further distinguishes two forms of each of these main possibilities. The idealism of purposiveness can take the form of "casuality" or perhaps better "accidentality," as in ancient atomism, according to which the appearance of any design is a product of pure chance in the collision of atoms, or of "fatality," the view that Kant ascribes to Spinoza, according to which the appearance of design is a necessary product of an original being, but not of the intellect and therefore not of any intention of this being, thus not a form of purposiveness (5:391–2). The two forms of realism of purposiveness are then "hylozoism," according to which there is life in matter, in the form of "an animating inner principle, a world-soul" that accounts for its design and purposiveness, and "theism," which posits an "intentionally productive" "original ground of the world-whole" which is not, however, itself a part of the world-whole (5:392). In the next section, Kant then argues that "None of the above systems accomplishes what it pretends to" (CPJ, §73, 5:392). The two forms of idealism do not explain how we even form the idea of the purposiveness of nature (5:393–4); hylozoism falls victim to the alleged contradiction, previously mentioned, between something essential to life and the principle of inertia that is essential to matter (5:394); and, finally, theism is "incapable of dogmatically establishing the possibility of natural ends as a key to teleology" (5:395), for reasons that Kant does not pause to explain but that presumably lie in the demonstration of the impossibility of any theoretical proof for the existence of God provided in the first Critique.

However, Kant also says that theism "has the advantage that by means of the understanding that it ascribes to the original being it can best rid the purposiveness of nature of idealism and introduce an intentional causality for its generation," and concludes that "for us there remains no other way of judging the generation of [nature's] products as natural ends than through a supreme understanding as the cause of the world" (although, as usual, "that is only a ground for the reflecting, not for the determining power of judgment, and absolutely cannot justify any objective assertion") (CPJ, §73, 5:395). Even after the complexities of §§75–7, it becomes clear that this is the basis for Kant's solution to the antinomy of judgment: "the principle which is to make possible the unifiability of both" the maxim of mechanical explanation and the maxim of teleological judgment "must be placed in what lies outside of both (hence outside of the possible empirical representation of nature) but which still contains the ground of both, i.e., in the supersensible . . . on which we must base nature as phenomenon" (although of course "from a theoretical point of view, we cannot form the least affirmative determinate concept of this") (CPJ, §78, 5:412). In other words, the only way that we can reconcile mechanical and teleological explanation is by a conception of the world as a whole that is a product of its intelligent and purposive cause. Mechanical explanation can then be allowed full rein in phenomenal nature – even if we cannot always see how it is to work, and even if we have some reason to think we will never be able to see completely how it works – while purposiveness can be attributed to the extramundane ground of the world, which can be thought of as achieving its ends through the mechanical laws of phenomenal nature for which it is responsible. Only through the idea of such a ground, Kant argues, can we even conceive how "the principle of the mechanism of nature and that of its causality according to ends in one and the same product of nature [can] cohere in a single higher principle and flow from it in common" (5:412). Only by means of such a model can we maintain both that "It is of infinite importance to reason that it not allow the mechanism of nature in its productions to drop out of sight and be bypassed in its explanations; for without this no insight into nature can be attained" (5:410) and yet that "it is an equally necessary maxim of reason not to bypass the principle of ends in the products of nature" (5:411). The two maxims of judgment originally contrasted do conflict if we attempt to apply them to the same objects without the benefit of transcendental idealism, but if we conceive of nature as a whole as governed by mechanical laws through which the ground of nature can nevertheless effect its purposes, then we do have a way of applying the concepts of both mechanism and purpose to objects without contradiction.[15]

I will close this section with two comments on this solution to Kant's antinomy. First, Kant now assumes that we should always at least strive for a mechanical explanation of everything in nature, and his continuing insistence that there is a special limit on our ability to provide mechanical explanations of organic processes beyond the general limit of incompleteness in all of our knowledge of nature seems arbitrary. Once we have recognized that we can only conceive of an intelligent ground of nature as standing outside of it and as responsible for its laws, then we can conceive of the purposes of this ground as being effected through any and all of the laws it has prescribed to nature. We could thus think of the inorganic as well as of the organic as expressive of purposiveness, and we have no reason to insist upon any special limits to our comprehension of organisms. We might still want to hold that there is something psychologically or phenomenologically striking about our experience of organisms, some way in which they make the idea of purposiveness especially salient for us that can then turn our thoughts to the idea of a purpose for nature. But we would not have to argue that there is some *a priori* limit to our ability to understand and explain them. Kant himself does not concede this point: he claims that although "we do not know how far the mechanical mode of explanation that is possible for us will extend," we are "certain of this much, namely, that no matter how far we ever get with that, it will still always be inadequate for things that we once acknowledge as natural ends" (CPJ, §78, 5:415) – but it is not clear why. Second, we may also note that Kant's resolution of the antinomy of judgment suggests the only possible model for a reconciliation of science and religious belief: if science is to permit a rational belief in the existence of a purposive creator of the cosmos, it can only conceive of such a creator as creating the natural laws of the world and of achieving his purposes through those laws rather than through any other interventions or miracles. In other words, Kant has firmly placed himself in the camp of both empiricists and rationalists who would accept only a watchmaker God, although he has added his critical insistence that the concept of such a God yields only a regulative principle for judgment and not a constitutive principle of knowledge.

FREEDOM, HAPPINESS, AND THE END OF NATURE

The culmination of the "Critique of the Teleological Power of Judgment," thus of the whole third *Critique*, and indeed of the whole philosophy developed in Kant's three critiques, is the "Methodology" of teleological judgment. Here Kant argues that if we are to view nature as a whole as a system, then we must find a point – a "final end" (*Endzweck*) – for that system, but that the only thing that could possibly play that role is the one thing of unconditional value, namely human freedom, and its full effect, the highest good. Thus, we must see nature as a system that is not merely compatible with the achievement of the object of human morality but that even leads up to it, although of course in a way that does not undermine the fact that the object of morality, comprising virtue as well as happiness, can only be the product of human autonomy.

The key steps in the argument are these. First, as we have already noted, Kant regards it as necessary and inevitable that once we have been compelled to see individual organisms in nature as internally purposive systems that are the apparent products of intelligent design, we will also see nature as a whole as a purposive system (CPJ, §67, 5:379; §75, 5:398). This is to say that although there initially seemed to be no justification for ascribing "relative purposiveness" to relations among creatures and environments in nature (§63), once we have experienced "internal purposiveness" in nature then we will also seek to find relative purposiveness in it. Kant never really explains what makes this transition inevitable, but at least suggests a premise for it when he says that "all of the mechanism of nature" must "be subordinated" to the idea of "a system in accordance with the rule of ends" "in accordance with principles of reason" (§67, 5:379). His thought is presumably that since the concepts of a system and of an intelligent designer of organisms are ideas of reason – although of course ones that can be employed only in the reflecting use of judgment – and reason always seeks unity, it will be inevitable for reason to seek to use judgment to apply these ideas in a unified way to the whole of nature. As he concludes §67, "the unity of the supersensible principle must then be considered as valid in the same way not merely for certain species of natural beings but for the whole of nature as a system" (5:381). Once again, this suggests that although Kant may suppose that there is something distinctive in our experience of organisms that leads us to the thought of purposive systematicity, once he has argued that this idea can be reconciled with mechanism only by applying it to a supersensible ground of nature that effects its purposes through mechanical laws, he really has no need to insist that organisms must forever remain beyond the explanatory scope of mechanism at the phenomenal level.

Assuming thus that reason requires us to look at all of nature as a system if we must look at anything within it as a system, Kant then infers that we must conceive of the system of nature as a whole as a product of intelligent design just as we conceive of any particular organisms within it. The next step in the argument is then Kant's assumption that once we conceive of the ground of nature as intelligent we will also conceive of it as purposive, that is, as having a goal in its creation of nature. He does not argue extensively for this premise either, but at least suggests it when he equates the (reflective idea of the) *intelligent* production of individual systems in nature or of nature as a system with the *intentional* production of such systems (CPJ, §75, 5:399, and §78, 5:414), and holds that to think of the mechanism of nature itself as a product of intentional design is to think of it "as if it were the tool of an intentionally acting cause to whose ends nature is subordinated, even in its mechanical laws" (§81, 5:422). Then he assumes that if we must conceive of the ground of nature as an intelligent and intentional agent similar to but even more powerful than ourselves, surely we cannot conceive of it as acting without an adequate reason for its action, indeed an ultimately satisfying or "final" end. This seems to be the Kant's point in the following:

> Once we have had to base [the] internal possibility [of an organized being] in a causality of final causes and an idea that underlies this, we also

cannot conceive of the existence of this product otherwise than as an end. For the represented effect, the representation of which is at the same time the determining ground of its production in an intelligently acting cause, is called an **end**. In this case, therefore, one can either say that the end of the existence of such a natural being is in itself, i.e., it is not merely an end, but also a **final end**; or it is outside of it in another natural being, i.e., it exists purposively not as a final end, but necessarily at the same time as a means.

(§82, 5:426)

Kant also clearly assumes that we cannot think that the end of the creation of everything in the system of nature can always lie in something other than itself, for then there would be an unsatisfyingly infinite regress of reasons; we can conceive of a reason for the creation of nature only if we can conceive of something that is an end in itself or a final rather than merely relative end. Thus, Kant argues that our mind naturally moves from the systematicity of particular organisms to the systematicity of nature as a whole, from there to the idea of an intelligent cause of nature as a whole, and from there to the idea of a purposive cause of nature that must create nature in order to realize a final end of unconditional value.

The next stage of Kant's argument begins with another version of what he told us in §63, namely that nothing in nature as such is evidently a final end of unconditional value for which anything or everything else in nature is merely a means (CPJ, §82, 426–8). He now explicitly applies this stricture to human beings as well, at least as far as humans aim directly at happiness and at the "culture of **skill**," that is, at the development of talents or aptitudes for the achievement of happiness as such (§83, 5:430–1). Instead, the only candidate for a final end for nature even in human beings is "the formal, subjective condition, namely the aptitude for setting [ourselves] ends at all and (independent from nature in [our] determination of ends) using nature as a means appropriate to the maxims of [our] free ends in general" (5:431). As Kant argues in the next section:

Now we have in the world only a single sort of beings whose causality is teleological, i.e., aimed at ends and yet at the same time so constituted that the law in accordance with which they have to determine ends is represented by themselves as unconditioned and independent of natural conditions but yet as necessary in itself. The being of this sort is the human being, though considered as noumenon: the only natural being in which we can nevertheless cognize, on the basis of its own constitution, a supersensible faculty (**freedom**) and even the law of the causality together with the object that it can set for itself as the highest end (the highest good in the world).

(§84, 5:435)

Thus, Kant concludes that if we are to see nature as a whole as a systematic product of purposive design, as our experience of organisms makes inevitable, and if we are to see such a purposive design as having a final end, as our own conception of rational agency requires, then the only thing we can possibly conceive of as the final end for nature is our own freedom or autonomy and then the object that it sets for us, the highest good.

The two key questions now to be considered are: (1) why Kant thinks that the unconditional value of our own freedom makes the highest good our ultimate object; and (2) what follows from the fact that we must conceive of the highest good as something that is to be realized in nature, or as Kant says "in the world." But a preliminary yet crucial point is that Kant is careful about just how much of this we can coherently see as the end of nature. Thus far, I have ignored the distinction that Kant draws between the final end of nature and its *ultimate* end, as well as the contrast that he makes between the "culture of skill" and the "culture of training" or "discipline" (CPJ, §83, 5:432). The distinction between the "ultimate" and the "final" end of nature is the distinction between that *within* nature to which we can take everything else to be a means and that *outside* of nature or that which is not merely natural which we can take to give a point to the creation of the whole system of nature. As the quotation from §84 makes clear, Kant understands human freedom as something non-natural or beyond nature that is of unconditional value and can thus give its point to the creation of nature. But precisely because it is non-natural, we cannot conceive it to be realized by natural processes alone. Rather, there must be an *ultimate* end *within* nature that is connected with but not identical to human freedom as the *final* end of nature, and which we can conceive of as being brought about by natural processes but also as providing the point of connection between nature and the unconditional value of freedom. This is the role that the culture of *discipline* rather than skill is supposed to play: the culture of discipline must be an ability to control our own inclinations that we can see as developing within nature and by natural means but as allowing us to make our noumenal freedom of choice effective in the natural world. Kant's idea must be that the choice to use our freedom in the name of the moral law rather than self-love is a noumenal choice, but that to make it effective in nature we need to gain discipline and control over our inclinations by natural processes of education and maturation. We can see these processes as the ultimate end of nature, achievable within nature, because they are necessary conditions within nature for the realization of the unconditional value that can lie in freedom as a non-natural property of human beings. But they are only necessary conditions, not sufficient conditions, and thus nature cannot realize our freedom for us, which would be to rob us of our freedom, but can only facilitate our effective use of our freedom to realize our moral goal.[16]

To answer question (1). So much for why the ultimate end of nature can only be the culture of discipline, not freedom itself. But when he comes to the final end of nature, why does Kant make this not just human discipline but also the highest good in the world? That is, why does Kant so directly connect the value of freedom to the highest good? It is by no means always clear in Kant's writings that the highest good should be considered the necessary object of morality. In the Critique of Practical Reason, for example, Kant characterizes "virtue and happiness together" as the "whole and complete good as the object of the faculty of desire" (5:110), but also seems to suggest that virtue is the sole object of morality proper, which then, through the moral law, both constrains what ends we may pursue in the name of happiness and also, as the "worthiness to be happy," adds a condition of desert to the pursuit of happiness, which is not itself, however, of any direct moral significance. In other words, the highest good seems to be a conjunction of virtue as the object of morality and happiness as the object of the sum of our merely natural desires. However, as I argued in Chapter 6, the most fundamental premises of Kant's moral philosophy imply a more intimate connection between virtue and happiness, which is what Kant presupposes in the third Critique. If the moral law's requirement to act only on universalizable maxims is equivalent to the requirement to make "humanity, whether in your own person or that of another," the necessary "end in itself" in all our willing (G, 4:428–9), and if humanity is in turn conceived of as the "ability to set oneself an end – any end whatsoever" (MM, Doctrine of Virtue, Introduction, Section VIII, 6:392), then the requirement always to treat humanity as an end implies not merely the negative duty to refrain from destroying or unnecessarily restricting the ability to set ends in ourselves and others, but also the positive duty to promote the realization of the particular, freely chosen ends of others and even ourselves, as long, of course, as so doing is consistent with satisfying the negative part of duty. Kant made this clear in the Groundwork when he argued for the duty of beneficence by means of the premise that "there is still only a negative and not a positive agreement with humanity as *an end in itself* unless everyone also tries, as far as he can, to further the ends of others" (G, 4:430). This requirement to promote the particular ends of others – as far as we can do so consistently with our resources, with our own legitimate ends, and with our other duties – is then incorporated into Kant's characterization of the realm of ends as the ultimate object of morality. The realm of ends is defined as "a whole of all ends in systematic connection (a whole both of rational beings as ends in themselves and of the ends of his own that each may set himself)" (G, 4:433). This formula makes it clear that morality requires us not just to allow others to set their own ends but also to work toward the systematic satisfaction of the ends that they set, that is, toward the satisfaction of a system of particular ends that is consistent with the free choice of each agent as an end in itself and, presumably, with the laws of nature that constrain the realization of particular ends and combinations thereof. But if happiness just consists in the satisfaction of ends, then a systematic promotion of ends as is required by the idea of a realm of ends would, to be sure under ideal circumstances, yield systematic, collective happiness. Of course, Kant also insists, the desire for happiness, whether selfish or systematic, can never be part of the motivation or "incentive" for the pursuit of virtue, but it is nevertheless the necessary "object" of the "purest morality" (TP, 8:279–80). Thus, the concept of the highest good is not a mere conjunction of the aim of morality with our merely natural desires; rather, through the recognition that the freely chosen particular ends of ends in themselves are also necessary ends for us, it incorporates unselfish happiness into morality as the necessary object of virtue.[17] Virtue is in turn our sustained effort to realize autonomy in spite of the other temptations that can appeal to our freedom, so the highest good is ultimately the object of our autonomy.

To answer question (2). Thus, if we can conceive only of the moral use of human freedom to realize autonomy as the final end of the system of nature, we must also conceive of the highest good possible in the world as the final end of nature, as Kant assumes not only in the passage from §84 (5:435) already cited but also in his recapitulation of his "moral proof of the existence of God" in §87 (5:450) of the "Methodology of the Teleological Power of Judgment." From this result, two points of enduring importance follow. First, we cannot satisfy the demands of morality simply by considering what some specific maxim of duty requires of us on some isolated occasion, as philosophical examples, including Kant's own,[18] may so easily suggest; rather, we must always think about our duties systematically, and thus attempt to determine what the idea of a systematic whole of persons as ends in themselves and of their particular ends requires of us on any particular occasion of action. Kant himself does not say explicitly what this would actually require of us, but two thoughts seem obvious.

First, we must seek a systematic organization among the kinds of duty that flow from the general requirement to seek a realm of ends, for example, a lexical ordering of the classes of our duties.[19] We might think that the examples of types of duties that Kant enumerates in the *Groundwork* (4:422−3 and 429−30), and which we discussed in Chapter 7, do imply such a lexical ordering: our most fundamental obligation would be not to destroy rational agents (e.g., by suicide); our next obligation, not to destroy the conditions for the free exercise of rational agency (e.g., by lying or making deceitful promises), would be binding only when we can satisfy this duty without violating the first;[20] our further duty to cultivate our talents for all sorts of possible ends would be restricted by the condition that in so doing we do not violate either of the first two classes of duty; and finally we could only satisfy our duty to further the particular ends of others through beneficence in ways compatible with the satisfaction of the three prior sorts of duties. In addition, in attempting to satisfy the requirements of duty, perhaps especially although not exclusively the positive and "imperfect" duties of self-development and beneficence, we must think systematically about the *domain* of our duties, that is, the effects of our maxims and actions on *all* of those persons who might be affected by them, not just on the immediate and most obvious victims or beneficiaries of our actions. And of course that group of persons will always be open-ended and indeterminate. It will certainly include more living persons than one to whom we are considering making a deceitful promise, for example, but it may not reasonably include all of living mankind, some of whom we cannot possibly affect in either a positive or negative way by our present action or by any of our actions. It will certainly include some members of future generations of mankind, for example the next few generations of people who will live near a factory we are considering building, but cannot possibly include all future human beings, and so on. In other words, if the final end of nature must be a realm of ends to be realized among real human beings really living in the natural world, then the system of our duties will be open-ended and indeterminate in a variety of ways, and responsible moral reasoning will always have to take this fact into account, although we will never be able to formulate any simple rules by means of which to do so.[21]

The second result that follows from Kant's idea that we must think of the highest good of humankind as the final end of the system of nature is that we must always think of the system of humans as ends in themselves and of their particular ends as being realized *in a nature that is itself a system*, where our knowledge of *that* system is also always incomplete and open-ended. We must thus try to think systematically about the natural conditions for our actions and their effects on the system of nature as well as about the system of human beings, while at the same time realizing that our knowledge of nature and thus of the conditions for and consequences of our actions will always be indeterminate and incomplete, just as is our knowledge of the system of persons as ends who will be affected by our choices and actions. Kant makes clear in the introduction to the third *Critique* that the idea of a system of the particular laws of nature is always only a regulative ideal for us (see especially CPJ, Introduction, Section V, 5:185–6), and in the "Critique of the Teleological Power of Judgment" he makes it equally clear that the idea of a system of the organisms and other entities comprising nature materially rather than formally is also only a regulative ideal for us: the "idea of the whole of nature as a system," the principle that "everything in the world is good for something, that nothing in it is in vain," is "not a principle for the determining but only for the reflecting power of judgment, that . . . is regulative and not constitutive" (CPJ, §67, 5:379). But if we must think of the systematic realization of our duties as taking place within nature, and the ideal of systematic knowledge of nature is itself only a regulative principle, then our reasoning about our duties will always be subject to the inescapable limitations of our knowledge of nature as well as to the indeterminacies inherent in the ideal of a systematic whole of human beings as ends in themselves and of their particular ends.

There is no way to spell out the consequences of these points in a short compass; indeed, what follows from them is that there can be no determinate way to spell out the conditions for fulfilling our obligations within actual nature at all. What we can say is only that we stand under an obligation always to reflect systematically upon the consequences of our choices for humankind and for nature as a whole, because we cannot specify more determinately than that where our obligations to humankind must be fulfilled. Sometimes it will be clear that our obligations to current and future generations combined with the laws of nature must prohibit certain courses of action, such as careless disposal of nuclear waste. Sometimes it may be clear that our obligations to current and future generations of our fellow humans require a destructive intervention in nature, as when there is no option for securing water supplies for a large metropolitan area that can avoid the destruction of the habitat for some population of organisms that is zoologically unique but in our best judgment not indispensable to any larger ecology.[22] The idea that the systematic union of human ends must be achieved within the system of nature no more implies that we must treat every component of the system of nature as inviolable than it can require that every single human desire or even every single human life can be treated as inviolable in all conceivable circumstances, even though every human life and desire is when considered in itself as worthy of respect as every other. All we can say is that sometimes it may seem obvious what our duty to realize the highest good for mankind within the world of nature requires, and sometimes it may not seem obvious, but in neither case will we be able to find determinate rules that can make such decisions mechanical. That is what follows from the premises that our duties must comprise a system, that they must be fulfilled in a nature that we must conceive of as a system, but that our knowledge of a system is always incomplete and always a problem of the reflecting rather than determining use of judgment. Surely one of the deepest lessons of Kant's connection between teleology and morality is that the latter as well as the former requires not just a parallel but a conjoint use of reflecting judgment.

SUMMARY

As we saw at the beginning of this chapter, after Hume's *Dialogues Concerning Natural Religion* Kant could only ask whether anything could be salvaged from traditional teleology. We can now conclude the chapter by asking what is living and what is dead in Kant's own revised teleology after more than two hundred years of scientific progress.

The idea that the laws of nature should constitute a system certainly motivates every scientist, and the idea that both particular organisms and larger ecologies are systems in which every part has a particular role to play is also a natural presumption of scientific research, although one that is always subject to limitations by what is actually discovered, as in the case of evolutionary spandrels and junk DNA. To this extent Kant has no doubt correctly described the maxims of practicing scientists. It is far less clear that he has succeeded in showing that we can rationally seek to satisfy such maxims only if we think of nature as the product of some sort of intelligent design. Such an assumption might be necessary if rationality required us to have some sort of guarantee of the possibility of reaching our goals, whether cognitive or practical; but if the rationality of a line of inquiry or conduct requires only the absence of evidence for the impossibility of success, then the rationality of our inquiry into nature guided by such maxims does not require any speculation about the source of whatever order we might find in nature at all. It is also by no means clear that Kant has successfully argued that there is anything in our experience of organisms in particular that requires us to posit an intelligent design for nature; indeed, it is not even obvious that he has come up with a coherent argument for the inexplicability of organisms on a mechanical model of causation, for once he has argued that the only solution to the antinomy of teleological judgment is the idea of an intelligent ground of nature that lies outside of nature and achieves its purposes through the mechanical laws of nature, he has no reason for holding that our comprehension of organisms must forever remain separated from our comprehension of the rest of nature. The most he might argue, it seems, is that there is something about our experience of organisms that psychologically leads us to thoughts of intelligence and purposiveness in nature, and that we should treasure and cultivate such thoughts for their moral value as we treasure other forms of experience, such as the experience of the beauty of nature, that are not logically necessary but are nevertheless psychologically favorable for the promotion of morality (see MM, Doctrine of Virtue, §17, 6:443).

If Kant has not successfully argued that we must conceive of nature as the product of purposive intelligence, then he has also not successfully argued on this ground that we must conceive of a final end for nature. However, he has given us important hints about the implications of the fact that the final end of morality must be a systematic union of humans and their purposes that can only be realized within nature. By linking the system of nature and the highest good, he teaches us that we must think about our duties systematically and that we must think about their realization in nature systematically. That insight, combined with the recognition that completeness in our knowledge of both the system of duties and the system of nature can never be more than a regulative ideal, means that our conclusions about our duties and their effects on nature will always be, literally, a matter of judgment. That in turn means that among our duties will be the duty of recognizing and cultivating our power of judgment itself. In this regard Kant's critique of teleology offers a lesson of continuing and vital importance.

FURTHER READING

My arguments in this chapter have relied heavily on:
Paul Guyer, *Kant's System of Nature and Freedom* (Oxford: Clarendon Press, 2005), Part III.

Most commentaries on the *Critique of the Power of Judgment* in English have focused exclusively on Kant's aesthetics, but two that include extensive discussion of his teleology are shown below. Macmillan is the oldest and Banham is one of the most recent, which, however, interprets Kant's teleology as aimed at a political community rather than the highest good, and thus does not raise the issue about the relation between natural and moral progress that I have raised.

Gary Banham, *Kant and the Ends of Aesthetics* (Basingstoke and London: Macmillan Press, 2000).

R.A.C. Macmillan, *The Crowning Phase of the Critical Philosophy: A Study in Kant's Critique of Judgment* (London: Macmillan, 1912).

Two works below are devoted exclusively to Kant's teleology. Neither of these, however, discusses the "Methodology" of the "Critique of the Teleological Power of Judgment," so neither reaches the issues discussed in the second half of the present chapter.

J.D. McFarland, *Kant's Concept of Teleology* (Edinburgh: Edinburgh University Press, 1970).

Peter McLaughlin, *Kant's Critique of Teleology in Biological Explanation: Antinomy and Teleology* (Lewiston: Edwin Mellen Press, 1990).

For that reason, two more comprehensive German treatments of Kant's teleology must be mentioned:

Klaus Düsing, *Die Teleologie in Kants Weltbegriff*, 2nd edn (Bonn: Bouvier Verlag, 1986).

Reinhard Löw, *Philosophie des Lebendigen: Der Begriff der Organischen bei Kant, sein Grund und seine Aktualität* (Frankfurt am Main: Suhrkamp Verlag, 1980).

Finally, there is one collection of articles on Kant's teleology in English, which includes important articles by Henry Allison, Michael Friedman, Robert Butts, Gordon Brittan, and others:

System and Teleology in Kant's Critique of Judgment, Southern Journal of Philosophy XXX, Supplement (1991), ed. Hoke Robinson.

Eleven

A History of Freedom?

Kant's moral philosophy, his aesthetics, and his teleology have all culminated in the claim that we must be able to conceive of our moral goals, the preservation and promotion of freedom in accordance with a universal law and universal happiness achieved through freedom, as being realizable in the world of nature. That means that these goals must be realized in time, the most fundamental form of nature, and therefore in history. And that in turn means that we must conceive of these goals as being realizable in the history of the human species as a whole, rather than in the natural life or supernatural afterlife of individual human beings. Kant had already made this point clear in his 1784 essay on "The Idea for a Universal History with a Cosmopolitan Aim" (UH) thus at the outset rather than at the end of his publications in moral philosophy:

> **In the human being** (as the only rational creature on earth) **those natural dispositions that are aimed at the use of his reason are to be completely developed only in the species, not in the individual.** Reason in a creature is a faculty for extending the rules and aims of the use of all of its powers far beyond natural instinct, and it knows no boundaries to its projects. But it does not itself work instinctively, rather it requires experiments, practice, and instruction in order to progress gradually from one stage of insight to others. Hence each human would have to live immeasurably long in order to learn how he should make a complete use of all his natural dispositions; or if nature has fixed only a short term for his life (as is in fact the case), then it will require a perhaps incalculable series of generations, each of which passes its enlightenment on to the next, before nature's germs in our species can be brought to that stage of development which completely corresponds to nature's aim. And this point

in time must at least in his idea be the goal of the efforts of the human being.

(UH, Second Proposition, 8:18−19)[1]

This passage suggests that we must be able to see the complete moral development of humankind not merely as realizable in its natural history but as the goal of its natural history. But this immediately raises an obvious question, parallel to one raised in the previous chapter: if mankind's ultimate goal is universal or "cosmopolitan" freedom, how can that possibly be achieved by nature? Isn't Kant's idea of freedom that of a supersensible and therefore non-natural power, which might itself determine the laws of nature but cannot be determined by the laws of nature? Is there an outright contradiction between his philosophy of human history and his vision of human freedom and autonomy?

There is not, because what Kant really argues, entirely consistently with what we have seen to be a central idea of his moral philosophy, is that we must be able to see nature, that is, our own nature, as offering us the means that we can use for the universal preservation and promotion of freedom if we freely choose to do so, and perhaps beyond this grounds for the hope that we can do so; but he never argues that nature itself can realize our freedom for us. A concluding look at Kant's writings on history and the promise of perpetual peace should make this clear.

Kant describes mechanisms in the natural history of human kind that can bring about its moral development in the essay on "Universal History," in an essay on the "Conjectural Beginning of Human History" published two years later (1786), and then again a decade later in the pamphlet Toward Perpetual Peace (1795), which we discussed in Chapter 8. The essay on the "Conjectural Beginning" describes a natural mechanism for the emergence of individual morality, while the other two essays describe a natural mechanism for the emergence of national and then international justice, so let's begin with the former.[2] Kant wrote the essay as a riposte to his former student Johann Gottfried Herder, who had given an interpretation of the story of the creation of Adam and Eve in Ideas for a Philosophy of the History of Humankind (1784−91), the first two volumes of which Kant had previously reviewed in the Berlinische Monatsschrift, the leading journal of the German Enlightenment. Kant imagines Adam and Eve having been created as adults who have been guided solely by instinct to choose wholesome food from the riches around them. But with the first stirrings of reason, they went beyond mere instinct, and began comparing foodstuffs to which they were not naturally inclined with those to which they were, thereby generating new inclinations that might or might not be good for them. They would then have "discovered in [themselves] a capacity for choosing [their] own way of life and not being bound to a single one like other animals"; and since "once having tasted freedom it was now impossible for [them] to return to servitude (under the domination of instinct)" (CB, 8:112), they would now have been forced to learn how to use their reason to choose between healthy and unhealthy foods. Likewise, once Adam and Eve had discovered that sexual desire could be prolonged and heightened by hiding its object behind a fig leaf, they again would have attained "consciousness of a certain degree of mastery of reason over instinct" (8:113), and would have begun to learn the difference between mere animal desire and a "taste for beauty," even receiving a "first hint at the development of the human being as a moral creature." The ability to form a "conscious **expectation of the future**" would have necessitated further development of the capacity to control impulses by reason. Finally, Kant suggests, the first time early man took the skin of an animal for his own use, he would have become conscious of his rights over other animals, but conscious at the same time "that what he may say to an animal he may not say to a fellow human; that he must rather consider the latter as an equal participant in the gifts of nature" (8:114). And thus Adam and Eve would have been naturally led toward the use of their reason to regulate their own freedom in a way compatible with the freedom of other human beings – the aim of morality.

In the essay on "Universal History," however, Kant had also argued that human beings have an "**unsocial sociability**," both a natural "inclination to **live in society**" and a "great tendency to **live as an individual**," that is, both a need and a desire for the company of others but also an "unsocial characteristic of wanting to have everything his own way" that can only drive him apart from others, each of whom naturally wants no interference with having things his own way as well.[3] These natural inclinations set for human beings a challenge that they are forced to use their reason to solve, namely how each can live freely with others while allowing the others to live freely as well, and thus "all talents are gradually developed, taste is formed, and by continued enlightenment a start is made toward the foundation of a cast of mind that can with time transform the crude natural disposition toward moral discrimination into determinate practical principles and thus a **pathologically** enforced congregation in a society into a **moral** whole." Thus, Kant proposes, "**The means that nature employs to bring about all of the predispositions** [of humankind] **is their** antagonism in society, insofar as this finally becomes the cause of a **lawful order**" (UH, Fourth Proposition, 8:20–1).

Thus human beings are forced to use their reason in order to figure out how to accommodate their unsocial sociability in a society that satisfies some conception of justice. Kant presents this as a goal of nature itself:

> Since only in society and indeed in a society that has the greatest freedom and hence a thoroughgoing antagonism among its members but also the most precise determination and assurance of the boundaries of this freedom so that it can subsist with the freedom of others – since only in it can the highest aim of nature, namely the development of all of the predispositions of the human species, be attained, nature also wills that this species should accomplish this like all the ends of its vocation for itself.
>
> (UH, Fifth Proposition, 8:22)

In the essay on "Universal History" and in *Toward Perpetual Peace*, Kant then describes further mechanisms of nature that will drive individual societies toward perfecting their justice by becoming genuine republics and then drive all societies toward perfecting justice world-wide by establishing the league of republics that is necessary for perpetual peace. In *Perpetual Peace*, Kant describes how groups are driven toward the most inhospitable regions of the earth to escape others who threaten them and their livelihood, but since the earth literally has no end – it is a finite sphere, any point of which can eventually be reached from any other – there is no escape from others. Thus human societies live in a constant state of war or the threat of war (PP, 8:363–4). But the very pressures of war will force peoples to perfect their individual states into republics in which the power of decision for war or peace is widely shared (8:366), and then, Kant argues, as more and more nations are transformed into republics, they will lose their interest in making war upon one another. As Kant famously writes (in a passage already discussed in Chapter 8):

> When the consent of the citizens of a state is required in order to decide whether there shall be war or not (and it cannot be otherwise in [the republican] constitution), nothing is more natural than that they will be very hesitant to begin such a bad game, since they would have to take upon themselves all the hardships of war (such as themselves doing the fighting and paying the costs of the war from their own belongings . . .); on the other hand, under a constitution in which subjects are not citizens of the state, which is therefore not republican, [deciding upon war] is the easiest thing in the world; because the head of state is not a member of the state but its proprietor and gives up nothing at all of his feasts, hunts,

pleasure palaces, court festivals, and so forth he can decide upon war, as upon a kind of pleasure party, for insignificant cause.

(PP, 8:350)

But precisely through such wars rational human beings will learn to reform their own states and then to live in peace with one another. As Kant puts it in the essay on "Universal History":

Nature has thus again employed the quarrelsomeness of human beings, even of the larger societies and states of this sort of creature, as a means of arriving at a condition of calm and security through their inevitable **antagonism**; i.e., through wars, tense and unremitting armament for wars, through the necessity for all of that which every state must itself feel even in peace, nature drives them to initially imperfect attempts, but finally, after many devastations, upheavals, and even complete internal exhaustion of their forces toward that which reason could have suggested to them even without so much tragic experience: namely to depart from the lawless condition of savages and to enter into a federation of nations in which every state, even the smallest, could expect its security and rights not from its own power or its own judicial judgment but only from this great federation of nations . . . from a united power and from the decision in accordance with laws of the united will.

(UH, Seventh Proposition, 8:24)

Thus, it seems, the natural history of mankind must result in the preservation and promotion of freedom in accordance with universal law.

But can Kant really mean by either his interpretation of the story of Adam and Eve or his interpretations of subsequent human history that natural processes can *guarantee* universal justice? He may certainly seem to; in *Perpetual Peace*, he entitles its "First Supplement" nothing less than "On the guarantee of perpetual peace," and writes: "What affords this **guarantee** (surety) is nothing less than the great artist **nature** . . . from whose mechanical course purposiveness shines forth visibly, letting concord arise by means of the discord between human beings even against their will" (PP, 8:360). But there are a number of reasons why this cannot be what Kant really means. For one thing, as we saw earlier, the natural mechanisms that Kant describes yield only empirical *probabilities*, not metaphysical *necessities*. Kant's own language makes this clear when he says that "nothing is more natural" than that citizens will be *very hesitant* to begin such a bad game as war, or that making war is "the easiest thing" for the proprietor of an autocratic rather than republican state: for citizens to be very hesitant to start a war does not mean they will never do it, and for starting wars to be easy for autocrats does not mean that they always will. Second, Kant's own theory of the freedom of the will means there can be no *metaphysical* guarantee that human beings will ever do what is right no matter how well they understand either prudential or purely moral reasons why they should. Kant writes in the essay on "Universal History" that "from such crooked wood as the human being is made, nothing entirely straight can be made"; "only the approximation toward this idea is demanded of us by nature" (Sixth Proposition, 8:23). Again, as we earlier saw, he made the reason for this clear in *Religion within the Boundaries of Mere Reason*: our genuine freedom to choose what is right is necessarily accompanied with an equal freedom to choose what is wrong, so we cannot be free without being free to do evil no matter what inducements either nature or reason gives us to be good. As Kant explains in the *Religion*, although we have within us an "original predisposition to good," that is, natural predispositions to animality, humanity and personality that can lead to morally desirable outcomes (RBMR, 6:26), as well as a natural "propensity to evil" that manifests itself in the superficially different but perhaps not morally distinguishable forms of frailty, impurity, and depravity (6:29–30), whether any particular human being is ultimately either good or evil cannot be explained by either of these natural tendencies, but only by the free choice of that human being to realize his predisposition toward the good or to pervert that predisposition by giving in to the propensity toward evil. In Kant's words:

> The human being must make or have made **himself** into whatever he is or should become in a moral sense, good or evil. These two [characters] must be an effect of his free choice, for otherwise they could not be imputed to him and, consequently, he could be neither **morally** good nor evil. If it is said: The human being is created good, this can only mean nothing more than: He has been created for the **good** and the original **predisposition** in him is good; the human being is not thereby good as such, but he brings it about that he becomes either good or evil, according as he either incorporates or does not incorporate into his maxims the incentives contained in that predisposition (and thus must be left entirely to his free choice).
>
> (RBMR, 6:43)

Kant's argument here is simply that if a person is to be given moral credit for doing or being good, then his so doing or being cannot be the result of any merely natural predisposition, but must be the result of his own free choice to incorporate that predisposition into his own principles or, in Kant's term, maxims; but if that choice is truly free, then the person is in fact also free to choose to do evil by perverting that predisposition, thus to be evil by his own choice or radically evil. The possibility of radical evil is inseparable from the possibility of imputable goodness. Kant could hardly have forgotten this central doctrine in the mere two years between the *Religion* and *Perpetual Peace*, so surely his position in the latter must be that nature – in the form of both human nature and elementary empirical facts about our environment, the globe – can create predispositions to peace and global justice, but that it must ultimately be up to the free choice of human beings whether to use those predispositions for good or for evil.

Yet Kant did not write the *Religion* as a counsel of despair. On the contrary, the central point of the work is that if whether we are good or evil is up to us, not determined by nature, then even if we have been evil we are still free to become good – nature can no more force us to remain evil than it can force us to become good. In Kant's words, "This evil is **radical**, since it corrupts the ground of all maxims . . . Yet it must equally be possible to **overcome** this evil, for it is found in the human being as acting freely" (RBMR, 6:37). In fact, recall, Kant illustrated this point in the *Religion* with an explicit allusion to perpetual peace:

> **Philosophical chiliasm**, which hopes for a state of perpetual peace based on a federation of nations united in a world-republic, is universally derided as a sheer fantasy as much as **theological chiliasm**, which awaits for the complete moral improvement of the human race.
>
> (6:34)

But, he replies, it is *not* a complete fantasy, for the very fact that evil is a product of our own free choice implies that goodness, and thus perpetual peace, can also be a product of our free choice.

The *Religion*'s emphasis upon the fact that just because evil is radical moral conversion is always within our own power – the ultimate expression of the power of autonomy, one could say – might seem to rest uneasily with Kant's attempt in that work to rescue the Christian conception of God's grace and of Jesus as the savior of humankind: these ideas would seem to put the power of conversion beyond rather than within human beings. However, Kant clearly wants to reinterpret these ideas in a way that is consistent with his basic point. So what he argues is that human beings always *start* from a condition of evil (RBMR, 6:72) – his concession to original sin – and that their subsequent self-chosen conversion to good, should that occur, cannot change that fact; thus human beings have a debt that cannot be repaid even by their subsequent conversion to the good. By his grace, however, God allows this debt to be remitted through his son, who "bears as **vicarious substitute** the debt of sin" for the human being (6:74). We do not need divine assistance in order to become good, but only to repay the debt for our original evil.

I leave to the reader the question whether this is a satisfying interpretation of the concept of grace, and return to Kant's conception of the possibility of moral progress within the natural history of humankind. As we saw earlier, Kant argues that both domestic and international justice can be brought about not by nature, but only by "moral politicians." The intellectual problem of devising a just constitution, he famously maintains, "is **soluble** even for a nation of devils (if only they have understanding)" (PP, 8:366), but such a constitution can actually be instituted and maintained only by politicians who choose to make it "indispensably necessary to join the concept of right with politics, and even to raise it to the limiting condition of politics." Kant assumes that in fact these moral politicians will find themselves in less than perfectly just states – they may well have come to office by autocratic rather than republican means – and that they both cannot and should not transform their states instantaneously – for that risks a lapse into anarchy, where no state exists at all – but can do so only by a gradual process of internal reform. But as moral politicians they will "take to heart the maxim that such an alteration is necessary, in order to keep constantly approaching the end (of the best constitution in accordance with laws of right)" (6:372). Kant's claim that a just constitution can be instituted and maintained only by moral politicians might seem to contradict his thesis in the "Doctrine of Right" that duties of right can be enforced by external sanctions regardless of the motivation of those who must fulfill such duties. But it does not. For what Kant recognizes is that even a system that would *enforce* just laws by practically effective and morally appropriate sanctions must itself *be created and maintained* by human beings; so even if we can suppose that the actions of those who must be governed by such a system once it is in place can be motivated by mere prudence, we must still suppose that a just system of laws can be initiated only by politicians who choose to exercise their power in accordance with what is right and that its justice can be maintained only if those who exercise power within it choose to exercise their power rightfully. Even once a true system of justice has been instituted, which should ensure externally lawful behavior by those who are subject to it through its system of threats and sanctions, it can always be corrupted by those who are responsible for maintaining it if they are not committed to preserving justice.

In light of this analysis of our radically free choice between good and evil and of the consequent need for moral politicians, what could Kant have then meant by writing in *Perpetual Peace* of nature as *guaranteeing* the eventual arrival of peace, or by his claim in the essay on "Universal History" that nature has itself *willed* that humankind "should go beyond the mechanical ordering of his animal existence" on his own initiative (*UH*, Third Proposition, 8:19)? In fact, Kant can only mean that nature has made peace *possible* both by providing us with the *means* that we can use to achieve peace and by putting no obstacle in our way that would make our achievement of peace by those means *impossible*. Kant makes the first of these points clear in "Universal History" when he says that "Nature gave the human being reason and freedom of will based upon that, and this was already a clear indication of its aim regarding his endowment" (8:19). This does not say that nature has forced or will force humankind to perfect its freedom and to achieve its happiness through its own freedom, but only that nature has given us the equipment necessary to achieve those ends if we so choose. The opportunities for the development of individual rationality in the Garden of Eden that Kant describes in "The Conjectural Beginning of Human History" and the opportunities for the development of collective, national and international rationality that he describes in "Universal History" and *Perpetual Peace* are opportunities that nature affords us, means it puts at our disposal, but not decisions it can make for us. The pattern of Kant's thought here is thus precisely the same as he displays in his discussion of the virtue of beneficence in the "Doctrine of Virtue," when he proposes that sympathetic feelings that nature offers us are means to the performance of beneficent actions, but means that we will use only if we have freely chosen to make beneficence our end and that we must use only in light of that end (see Chapter 7).

Kant makes the second point explicit in another discussion of international justice, in the 1793 essay "On the common saying: That may be correct in theory but it is of no use in practice," when he says simply that "a moral purpose" becomes a duty "if only it is not demonstrably impossible to effect" or accomplish it (*TP*, 8:310). Because, as Kant assumes, a genuine "ought" implies "can," we can have a duty only to do what is in our power; but then all it takes to show that an end commanded by morality is a duty is that it is in our power. Of course, we cannot responsibly determine that a goal is not impossible just by seeing that its *concept* is free of internal contradiction; we must make a sustained attempt to determine whether it is consistent with everything we know about reality. In the terminology of Kant's first critique, the rationality of our attempting to do as morality demands requires our justified conviction of the "real possibility" of its goals, not the mere fact of their "logical possibility" (see CPuR, A 220−1/B 267−8). But this is precisely what Kant accomplishes through his analysis of the means to and opportunities for the achievement of the final goal of morality that nature affords us and by providing an account of history that shows how in the fullness of time that goal could be achieved. The moral and political history of mankind that Kant outlines is conjectural but consistent with everything we know about human nature and nature in general. Kant says: "**A philosophical attempt to work out a universal world-history in accordance with a plan of nature that aims at the perfect civil union of the human species must be regarded as possible and even as promoting this natural aim**" (UH, Ninth Proposition, 18:29). Such a history must be possible if the achievement of perfect civil union is to be a duty, and working out how our natural endowments and opportunities could result in such a history shows it to be possible. But again, nothing could ever show that such a history for mankind is *necessary*; that will always depend upon our free choice.

Still, Kant does not just say that nature guarantees the *means* to and the *possibility* of perpetual peace; as we saw earlier, at least sometimes he says that nature guarantees *peace* itself (PP, 8:360).[4] Why does he talk like this? I think that the answer to this question is a fundamental insight that has been mentioned numerous times in the course of this book, namely, Kant's recognition that we are sensuous as well as rational creatures, and that although as purely rational beings we may require only a guarantee that achieving the final goal of morality is not impossible, as sensuous creatures we may need more positive grounds for *hope* that this end will be achieved in order to be motivated to strive for it as hard as we can. As he puts it in the conclusion of the essay on "Universal History":

> a comforting prospect of the future . . . in which the human species . . . finally works its way up to the condition in which all of the germs that nature has planted in it can be fully developed and its vocation can be fulfilled here on earth.

This gives us "grounds for hope" and is "no unimportant motivating ground for choosing a particular point of view in considering the world" (Ninth Proposition, 8:30) but even more so for attempting to change it.

Indeed, as sensible as well as rational creatures we may well need not just strong talk about a guarantee of progress in some distant future of the species, but concrete evidence that progress will soon occur or even has recently occurred. With the liberty afforded by his retirement from the university and the security for his old age afforded by a lifetime of saving, Kant was willing to announce publicly that he found such evidence in the French revolution. In an essay on the "old question: Is the human race constantly progressing?" which he apparently wrote in 1795, before he retired, but which he included in one of his last works, the *Conflict of the Faculties* of 1798, published after his retirement, Kant wrote that there was an occurrence in his own time that demonstrated the "moral tendency of the human race":

> The revolution of a gifted people which we have seen unfolding in our day may succeed or miscarry, it may be filled with misery and atrocities to the point that a right-thinking person, if he could hope to execute it success-fully the second time, would nonetheless never resolve to make the experiment at such cost – this revolution, I say, nonetheless finds in the minds of all spectators (who are not involved in this game itself) a wishful **participation** that borders closely on enthusiasm, the very expression of which is fraught with danger, and which therefore can have nothing other than a moral predisposition in the human race as its cause.
>
> (CF, 7:85)[5]

Kant says that the evidence we need in order to confirm our hope for the moral progress of the human race is to be found in the response of the *spectators* of the French revolution rather than in the actions of the *revolution-aries* themselves for two reasons: specifically, because when he wrote and published this essay he knew that the revolution of 1789 had already degenerated into the Terror of 1793; and more generally because (as we saw in Chapter 8) he thought that the act of rebellion itself is not only constitutionally but also morally impermissible, although it is also often inevitable, so those who have initiated the rebellion cannot themselves be thought to have acted morally – rather, the politicians who have come into power through rebellion have the opportunity to become moral politicians and make their new state a genuine republic. So even though the motives of the initial participants in the French revolution could not have been morally pure, the approbation of the progress of the revolution on the part of spectators who had nothing to gain directly from that revolution except perhaps encouragement to bring about the peaceful reform of their own governments, Kant holds, was genuine evidence of the real possibility of moral progress.

As rational creatures, we can find in our natural endowments the means for achieving the final goal of morality in this world, and in a philosophical view of our own history we can find an argument for the possibility of achieving this goal. As sensuous creatures we can go beyond this and take hope from actual moments in our history, and thus be encouraged to work even harder toward our moral goal. But nothing outside our own choice can guarantee the realization of our goal, and we would delude ourselves and undermine our efforts to be moral if we thought otherwise. Perhaps that should stand as the deepest of all of Kant's insights.

SUMMARY

In his political, historical, and theological writings Kant frequently spoke of natural tendencies pushing human beings toward a condition of justice and even virtue. But he could not have meant that nature could itself ever produce human virtue, and thus the highest good, of which virtue is the primary component, because virtue can only be produced by an act of human freedom. Nor can he even have meant that natural processes themselves can guarantee justice among human beings, because even though justice can employ external incentives that work on our self-interest rather than our virtue, even a merely just society must be initiated and maintained by moral politicians, that is, politicians who have freely chosen to govern justly, or more precisely such a just society must be transformed by moral politicians from the violence by which an unjust society has been maintained and the violence by which it has been brought down by rebellion. So nature, through history, can only offer means for us to use for the realization of justice and beyond that virtue and the highest good, and indeed we must be able to conceive of it as offering us such means. But it remains up to us to choose to use them freely and thereby realize our autonomy in all of its dimensions.

FURTHER READING

Many of the works on Kant's political philosophy and teleology recommended in Chapters 8 and 10 are relevant here too. On Kant's philosophy of history, in particular, see:

William A. Galston, *Kant and the Problem of History* (Chicago: University of Chicago Press, 1975).

Pauline Kleingeld, *Fortschritt und Vernunft: Zur Geschichtsphilosophie Kants* (Würzburg: Königshausen & Neumann, 1995).

Yirmiahu Yovel, *Kant and the Philosophy of History* (Princeton, NJ: Princeton University Press, 1980).

For a treatment with the methods of comparative literature rather than philosophy, see also:

Peter D. Fenves, *A Peculiar Fate: Metaphysics and World-History in Kant* (Ithaca, NY: Cornell University Press, 1991).

This glossary lists only terms that Kant uses in a distinctive sense. The German equivalent of the English term is noted only where it is not a direct cognate.

aesthetic (1) Pertaining to the contribution of sensibility to knowledge; (2) a form of judgment or experience based on the feeling of pleasure.

aesthetic judgment A judgment based on a feeling of pleasure.

analytic (1) An analytic judgment is true because its predicate is contained in its subject-concept; (2) an analytic method employs a regress from a conclusion to its presupposition.

antinomy A pair of contradictory theses each of which rests on an apparently sound argument.

a posteriori Known or formed on the basis of experience; empirical.

appearance (Erscheinung) (1) The undetermined object of an empirical intuition; (2) how such an object appears to us rather than how it is in itself.

apperception Unity of consciousness; often, unity of self-consciousness.

a priori Known or formed independently of particular experience; non-empirical.

autonomy Freedom of the will exercised in accordance with a self-given law.

capacity of choice (Willkür) The ability to choose an action, the elective will.

categorical imperative The moral law insofar as it presents itself to us as an unconditional and universal constraint.

categories The twelve pure and most basic concepts of the understanding, by means of which judgments can apply to objects, and in accordance with which empirical concepts are structured.

cognition (Erkenntnis) A representation of an object or state of affairs, often but not always used in the sense of a true judgment about an actual object or state of affairs.

concept (Begriff) A general representation of an attribute or mark of a class of objects; can be either empirical or pure.

constitutive principle A principle that is necessarily true of objects because it determines how we must represent them.

cosmological (1) Pertaining to the representation of the world as a whole; (2) a proof of the existence of God as the necessary condition of the existence of anything contingent.

deduction A derivation of a concept, judgment, or principle; it may be empirical, metaphysical (showing that its conclusion is given a priori), or transcendental (showing why its conclusion is a priori).

determining judgment The application of a given concept to a particular.

dialectic The critique of metaphysical illusions and/or resolution of metaphysical contradictions.

duty (Pflicht) A moral or legal obligation, valid either directly from the moral law, and thus valid for all rational beings, or from the application of the basic principles of morality and justice to the empirical conditions of human existence.

empirical Based on actual experience, a posteriori.

empiricism The philosophical view that all knowledge and principles derive from actual experience.

end (Zweck) The goal or purpose of an action or object; may be instrumentally or intrinsically valuable.

ethics Properly, the duties of virtue, or those moral obligations that cannot be coercively enforced.

experience (Erfahrung) (1) The sensory inputs that are the raw material of cognition; (2) the cognition of objects or the self resulting from the application of concepts to such sensory inputs.

faculty (1) A mental capacity (Vermögen); (2) that part of a university teaching staff training students for a particular degree (Fakultät).

faith (Glaube) A belief or conviction that cannot be supported by theoretically sufficient grounds but which may be justified and required by practical considerations.

good will A will motivated by respect for the moral law and thus by the necessity of duty alone.

ground A basis or reason for a belief or judgment, or a cause of an event or state of affairs.

happiness (Glückseligkeit) Awareness of the satisfaction of a desire or set of desires.

heautonomy The legislation of a regulative principle to ourselves rather than to nature.

heteronomy The determination of the will by a principle other than pure reason, thus by mere desire whether from oneself or another.

highest good The complete object of the moral will, comprising maximal virtue, which is the strength of moral motivation and establishes the worthiness to be happy, with the happiness that would result from virtue under ideal conditions.

humanity (1) The capacity of human beings to set themselves ends; (2) in RBMR Kant contrasts humanity as the capacity to be determined by comparison between oneself and others with personality as the capacity to be determined by consciousness of the moral law, but elsewhere he often equates humanity with the latter.

hypothetical imperative The representation of an action as a necessary means to an end that is not itself necessary.

idea Not any content of thought, as in Locke, but a representation of something unconditioned, such as the self, the world, or God, originating from pure reason.

ideal The representation of an individual thing as the object of an idea of pure reason.

idealism Doubt (problematic idealism) or denial (dogmatic idealism) that there are any objects other than minds and their representations.

imagination (Einbildungskraft) The capacity to have a sense-like representation of an object not currently present to the sensed, either by reproducing the representation of an object previously present to the sensed (reproductive imagination) or by producing the representation of an enduring object out of momentary representations in the first place (productive imagination).

intelligible Represented or representable by pure reason.

intuition (Anschauung) An immediate and singular representation of an object; may be either empirical or pure and *a priori*.

judgment (1) A representation of a state of affairs through a combination of concepts ultimately referring to one or more intuitions (Urteil); (2) the ability to make judgments by applying concepts to intuitions (Urteilskraft), either applying a given concept to a particular (determining judgment) or seeking a concept for a given particular (reflecting judgment).

justice (Recht) The body of laws expressing interpersonal obligations that may be coercively enforced, or the state of affairs in which such laws are observed. May also be translated as "right" in the singular.

knowledge (Wissen) Holding something to be true on the basis of subjectively and objectively sufficient evidence, or the body of what is thus held to be true.

law (Gesetz) A universally and necessarily true generalization, whether theoretical (a law of nature) or practical (a moral or juridical law).

legislation (Gesetzgebung) Giving or promulgating law, whether to nature in a theoretical capacity or to oneself or others in a moral or juridical capacity.

manifold A body of data, typically the multiplicity of sensory data out of which the mind synthesizes its representations of both the objective world and its own experience.

maxim The principle of volition on which a person acts, specifying a type of action to be performed in certain circumstances for a certain end; it may or may not also be objectively valid, that is, consistent with or necessitated by moral law.

metaphysics (1) Traditionally, a body of entirely *a priori* knowledge about objects transcending experience, the possibility of which Kant denies; (2) for Kant, the body of our *a priori* knowledge about objects of experience deriving from the structure of our own minds; and (3) in a special sense, the body of synthetic *a priori* knowledge that arises from the application of our most basic principles to certain fundamental empirical facts about our perception of nature (the metaphysics of nature) or the circumstances of human action (the metaphysics of morals).

noumenal Pertaining to a noumenon

noumenon An object supposedly known by pure reason alone, thus an intelligible object, or a thing in itself in a positive sense.

object (Objekt, Gegenstand) That which we take some representations to represent, in virtue of a necessary connection among them.

objective reality (objecktive Realität) A representation's having an actual object.

objective validity (objektive Gültigkeit) A representation's being universally and necessarily applicable to objects of a relevant class.

ontological argument The argument purporting to derive the existence of God from the mere concept of God.

paralogism An invalid inference turning on an ambiguous middle term.

perception (Wahrnehmung) Empirical consciousness of an object involving sensation of it.

personality (1) In CPuR, the identity of a conscious self over time; (2) in RBMR, the capacity of a human being to be motivated by consciousness of the moral law.

phenomenal Pertaining to the appearance of things.

phenomenon A thing as it appears to us, contrasted to how it may be in itself.

physicotheological argument The argument purporting to derive the existence of God from the appearance of design in the world, the argument from design.

postulate (1) In mathematics, a procedural rule for the construction of an object; (2) in theoretical philosophy, a rule specifying the conditions for the empirical use of modal concepts; (3) in practical philosophy, an assertion of the existence of freedom, immortality, or God that cannot be theoretically justified but which must be presupposed as the condition of the possibility of a morally necessary mode of conduct.

practical Pertaining to action.

practical reason Reason applied to action, whether in the service of mere desire (empirical practical reason) or the moral law (pure practical reason).

pure (rein) Not dependent upon actual experience, although possibly applicable to it; opposed to empirical.

purposiveness (Zweckmäßigkeit) (1) Serving a purpose (Zweck); (2) being actually or apparently designed to serve a purpose.

rationalism The philosophical view that pure reason can yield knowledge and principles that are not derived from or justifiable by actual experience.

realm of ends (Reich der Zwecke) The morally ideal condition in which each person is treated as an end in him- or herself and in which the lawful particular ends of each are ends for all; also translated as "kingdom of ends."

reason The faculty for inference and unconditional generalization, which yields ideas and ideals.

receptivity The capacity to be acted upon by an external object, typically to receive representations of objects through stimulation of the senses.

reflecting judgment The capacity to seek a concept for a given particular.

regulative principle A principle that does not constitute our representation of an object but that should regulate our conduct of inquiry into objects.

representation (*Vorstellung*) Any mental content, typically any kind of consciousness of an object, whether actual or not; includes sensations, intuitions, concepts, and ideas.

respect (*Achtung*) (1) Recognition of duty or the moral law as a sufficient reason for action; (2) the distinctive effect of such recognition upon our feelings, containing both displeasure at the necessity of constraining our desires and pleasure at our power to do so.

right (*Recht*) (1) Used as a mass-term, the body of coercively enforceable interpersonal obligations; (2) used as a count-term, an enforceable obligation of one person to a specific other person or persons.

schema A spatio-temporal structure or relation through which a category is applied to empirical intuition.

schematism The provision of schemata for the categories.

sensation (*Empfindung*) The immediate effect of an external object or one's own bodily or psychological condition upon the senses, which furnishes the matter of empirical intuition.

sensibility (*Sinnlichkeit*) The faculty for having both empirical and pure intuitions.

spontaneity The ability to originate a representation or an action.

synthesis The combination of any representations into a more complex representation.

synthetic (1) Applied to a judgment, it means that the predicate is not contained in the subject-concept but must be asserted on the basis of some "third thing"; (2) applied to a method, it means inferring conclusions from a premise rather than presuppositions from a conclusion.

teleological judgment A judgment asserting the existence of a purpose for an object.

thing in itself (*Ding or Sache an sich*) A thing as it is in itself, independently of our representation of it; properly, a noumenon in the negative sense, for we can know that there must exist some thing in itself corresponding to any appearance but cannot know anything more about it by means of pure reason.

transcendent Surpassing the limits of experience.

transcendental Properly, that which can be known as a condition of the possibility of experience generally or of synthetic *a priori* knowledge in particular; but sometimes Kant uses it when he means "transcendent."

transcendental deduction Proof of the objective validity of synthetic *a priori* cognition.

transcendental unity of apperception The synthetic unity of the self in its manifold of representations, known to obtain *a priori*.

understanding The faculty of concepts; pure understanding is the source of the categories (pure concepts of the understanding).

virtue (Tugend) The strength of the morally motivated will in the face of contrary inclination; duties of virtue (*Tugendpflichten*) are moral obligations that cannot be coercively enforced.

will (Wille) (1) Used generally, the ability to initiate an action through a representation of it as either desirable or required by a law, thus including *Willkür* (capacity for choice); (2) used specifically, the ability to give oneself a law for action as contrasted with the capacity to choose to act in accordance with *Willkür*.

INTRODUCTION

1 Or at least, this is how "transcendental idealism" will be understood in this book. For an alternative approach to transcendental idealism, see Henry E. Allison, *Kant's Transcendental Idealism: An Interpretation and Defense*, rev. edn (New Haven, CT: Yale University Press, 2004).
2 I have discussed the "bridging" role of the third *Critique* in detail in the essays in Part III of my *Kant's System of Nature and Freedom* (Oxford: Clarendon Press, 2005).
3 I have outlined my approach to Kant's attitude toward skepticism in "Kant on Common Sense and Skepticism," *Kantian Review* 7 (2003): 1–37. For another recent discussion, see Gary Hatfield, "What Were Kant's Aims in the Deduction?" *Philosophical Topics* 31 (2003): 165–98.
4 Kant's word here, *Erinnerung*, usually just means "recollection" or "remembrance," but in a legal context can also mean "objection." I have chosen "reminder" because it can mean both "recollection" and "warning."

ONE A LIFE IN WORK

1 In the following, I rely on Manfred Kuehn, *Kant: A Biography* (Cambridge: Cambridge University Press, 2001).
2 The character of Pietism is well described by Kuehn in *Kant*, pp. 34–5. See also Lewis White Beck, *Early German Philosophy: Kant and his Predecessors* (Cambridge, MA: Harvard University Press, 1969), pp. 156–9.
3 A contemporary description by Christian Schiffert of the curriculum of this remarkable school is reprinted in Heiner F. Klemme (ed.), *Die Schule Immanuel Kants*, Kant-Forschungen Band 6 (Hamburg: Felix Meiner Verlag, 1994), pp. 61–114.
4 On Knutzen, see Kuehn, *Kant*, pp. 78–84, and Martin Schönfeld, *The Philosophy of the Young Kant: The Precritical Project* (Oxford: Oxford University Press, 2000), p. 13.
5 See Kuehn, *Kant*, pp. 73–8.
6 See Kuehn, *Kant*, pp. 93–4, as well as Martin Schönfeld, "Kant's Intellectual Development," *Stanford Encyclopedia of Philosophy* (on-line resource).
7 On pre-established harmony and physical influx, see also Eric Watkins, *Kant and the Metaphysics of Causality* (Cambridge: Cambridge University Press, 2005), pp. 23–100. For a discussion of the *True Estimation*, see Schönfeld, *The Philosophy of the Young Kant*, pp. 17–55.

8 On the *Universal Natural History*, see Schönfeld, *The Philosophy of the Young Kant*, pp. 96–127.

9 For a detailed account of the *Physical Monadology*, see ibid., pp. 161–79; for a succinct contrast between the early and later versions of Kant's dynamical theory of matter, see Michael Friedman's introduction to his translation of Kant's *Metaphysical Foundations of Natural Science*.

10 See Descartes, *Meditations on First Philosophy* (1641), Fifth Meditation. Leibniz criticized Descartes by arguing that the ontological argument should be preceded by a proof that all the properties assigned to God by the concept of the most perfect being are compatible – he raised this objection in letters to Henry Oldenburg in 1675 and Arnold Eckhard in 1677, and first published it in a famous paper "Meditations on Knowledge, Truth, and Ideas," in the *Acta Eruditorum* in November, 1684, with which Kant could easily have been familiar – but then accepted the argument once this defect was remedied.

11 See, for example, Leibniz's famous 1686 paper "Primary Truths."

12 Baumgarten introduced the term "aesthetics" in his 1735 master's thesis, translated as *Reflections on Poetry* by Karl Aschenbrenner and William B. Holther (Berkeley, CA: University of California Press, 1954).

13 On the *New Elucidation*, see Alison Laywine, *Kant's Early Metaphysics and the Origins of the Critical Philosophy* (Atascadero, CA: Ridgeview Publishing Company, 1993), pp. 25–42; Schönfeld, *The Philosophy of the Young Kant*, pp. 128–60; and Watkins, *Kant and the Metaphysics of Causality*, pp. 112–60.

14 On Crusius, see Beck, *Early German Philosophy*, pp. 394–402; on Crusius's position on freedom of the will, see J.B. Schneewind, *The Invention of Autonomy: A History of Modern Moral Philosophy* (Cambridge: Cambridge University Press, 1998), pp. 445–56.

15 At virtually the same time, in far off New England, Jonathan Edwards was making a similar objection to the liberty of indifference; see his 1754 treatise on *The Freedom of the Will*, in which he attacks, far more thoroughly than Kant here attacks Crusius, the version of liberty of indifference or spontaneity defended by the Arminians, a Dutch reform sect not entirely dissimilar from the Pietists.

16 This was a central question for much of the eighteenth century; see Ernst Cassirer, *The Philosophy of the Enlightenment*, translated by Fritz C.A. Koelln and James P. Pettegrove (Princeton, NJ: Princeton University Press, 1951), pp. 7–15.

17 Kant's critique of the ontological argument in *The Only Possible Basis* is discussed in Dieter Henrich, *Der ontologische Gottesbeweis*, 2nd edn (Tübingen: J.C.B. Mohr, 1960), pp. 178–88.

18 On *The Only Possible Basis*, see Schönfeld, *The Philosophy of the Young Kant*, pp. 183–208.

19 A translation of the Academy's official French abridgment of Mendelssohn's essay is included in Immanuel Kant, *Theoretical Philosophy, 1755–1770*, edited by David Walford with the collaboration of Ralf Meerbote (Cambridge: Cambridge University Press, 1992), pp. 276–86; the full German text, "On Evidence in Metaphysical Sciences," is translated in Moses Mendelssohn, *Philosophical Writings*, edited by Daniel O. Dahlstrom (Cambridge: Cambridge University Press, 1997), pp. 251–306.

20 I provide a detailed comparison between the essays of Mendelssohn and Kant in "Mendelssohn and Kant: One Source of the Critical Philosophy," *Philosophical Topics* 19 (1991): 119–52, reprinted in my *Kant on Freedom, Law, and Happiness* (Cambridge: Cambridge University Press, 2000), pp. 17–59. For a brief discussion of Mendelssohn's essay alone, see Alexander Altmann, *Moses Mendelssohn: A Biographical Study* (University, AL: University of Alabama Press, 1973), pp. 112–30, and for a detailed discussion, see the same author's *Moses Mendelssohns Frühschriften zur Metaphysik* (Tübingen: J.C.B. Mohr, 1969), pp. 252–391.

21 The title of Kant's work would have reminded any reader of the time of Edmund Burke's *Philosophical Enquiry into the Origin of our Ideas of the Sublime and the Beautiful* (first edition 1757, expanded edition with an introductory essay on taste, 1759), which was such a work.

22 For discussion of this work, see Susan Meld Shell, The Embodiment of Reason: Kant on Spirit, Generation, and Community (Chicago: University of Chicago Press, 1996), pp. 81–105.

23 A selection from these important notes is now available in Kant, Notes and Fragments, edited by Paul Guyer, translated by Curtis Bowman, Paul Guyer, and Frederick Rauscher (Cambridge: Cambridge University Press, 2005), pp. 1–24.

24 See Laywine, Kant's Early Metaphysics, Chapters I, IV, and V.

25 2:303–313; translated in Theoretical Philosophy, 1755–1770, pp. 289–300.

26 In this passage Kant uses the gendered term Mann rather than the gender-neutral Mensch ("human being"). Since at this time in history only young men were admitted to universities in Germany, as elsewhere, the use of the gendered term is natural.

27 This is equally clear in the late lectures on pedagogy, edited from Kant's notes by his student Rink; the old translation by Annette Churton will soon be superseded by Robert Louden's translation in the Cambridge edition volume on Anthropology, History, and Education (forthcoming).

28 2:377–83; in Theoretical Philosophy, 1755–1770, pp. 363–72.

29 Translated by H.G. Alexander (Manchester: Manchester University Press, 1956); for discussion, see Ezio Vailati, Leibniz and Clarke: A Study of their Correspondence (New York: Oxford University Press, 1997).

30 On "incongruent counterparts" and this essay and the subsequent inaugural dissertation, see Jill Vance Buroker, Space and Incongruence: The Origin of Kant's Idealism (Dordrecht: D. Reidel, 1981); James van Cleve and Robert E. Frederick, The Philosophy of Left and Right (Dordrecht: Kluwer, 1991); and James van Cleve, Problems from Kant (New York and Oxford: Oxford University Press, 1999), pp. 44–51.

31 See Kuehn, Kant, pp. 188–9.

32 The inaugural dissertation is translated in Theoretical Philosophy, 1755–1770, pp. 375–416. An earlier English translation may be found in Kant: Selected Pre-Critical Writings and Correspondence with Beck, translated by G.B. Kerferd and D.E. Walford (Manchester: Manchester University Press, 1968). Kant's "respondent" or spokesman at the defense was Marcus Herz, a Jewish medical student at Königsberg (the medical faculty was the only one that admitted Jews), who would become a prominent physician and man of letters in Berlin over the next several decades, and who would be the recipient of the most important progress reports on Kant's work on the eventual Critique of Pure Reason during the "silent decade" of 1771–1780 that was about to ensue. See Kant's Correspondence, translated by Arnulf Zweig (Cambridge: Cambridge University Press, 1999), pp. 107–81 passim.

33 On the inaugural dissertation, see Laywine, Kant's Early Metaphysics, Chapter VI.

34 See R 5037, 18:69; in Notes and Fragments, p. 207.

35 A work that argues that the "great light" of 1769 was indeed the discovery of the "Antinomies of Pure Reason" is Lothar Kreimendahl, Kant: Der Durchbruch von 1769 ("The Breakthrough of 1769") (Köln: Jürgen Dinter Verlag, 1990), especially Chapters VII – VIII.

36 Letter of October 13, 1770; in Corr, p. 117; see also the letter from Mendelssohn, December 25, 1770; Corr, p. 124.

37 Letter of February 21, 1772; Corr, pp. 132, 135. In another letter to Herz, toward the end of 1773, Kant promised the work no later than the following Easter (the date of the annual Leipzig book fair at which most new books in Germany were released).

38 Letter to Herz of November 4, 1776; in Corr, p. 160.

39 For attempts to reconstruct Kant's progress on the Critique during the "silent decade," see W.H. Werkmeister, Kant's Silent Decade: A Decade of Philosophical Development (Tallahassee, FL: University Presses of Florida, 1979); my Kant and the Claims of Knowledge (Cambridge: Cambridge University Press, 1987), pp. 25–70; and Wolfgang Carl, Der schweigende Kant:

Die Entwürfe zu einer Deduktion der Kategorien vor 1781 (Göttingen: Vandenhoeck & Ruprecht, 1989).

40 Letter from Moses Mendelssohn, April 10, 1783; in Corr, p. 190.

41 Letter to Moses Mendelssohn, August 16, 1783; in Corr, p. 202.

42 This statement has been adduced in behalf of the famous "patchwork thesis," according to which Kant could have completed the book in four or five months only by piecing it together from manuscripts written at various times over the preceding years; alleged inconsistencies in Kant's views could then be explained as reflecting differences in the views he had held at these different times. For the foremost presentation of the patchwork thesis in English, see Norman Kemp Smith, *A Commentary to Kant's 'Critique of Pure Reason'*, 2nd edn (London: Macmillan, 1923), especially pp. 202–34. The "patchwork thesis" was rejected by H.J. Paton, in *Kant's Metaphysic of Experience*, two vols (London: George Allen & Unwin, 1936), vol. I, pp. 38–43, and by Lewis White Beck, who trenchantly argued that if a man was inconsistent enough to put together inconsistent texts written at different times, he would also have been capable of writing an inconsistent text in one go. That's how Beck once put it in a lecture; for his published rejection of the thesis, see his *Early German Philosophy*, p. 469. Of course, even if the patchwork thesis is false, there might still be inconsistencies in Kant's work!

43 The story of the Göttingen review is a complicated one. It had been written by Christian Garve, a house philosopher to the Prussian court whom Kant respected, but was harshly revised by the editor of the Göttingen journal, Johann Feder, a staunch empiricist in the British-influenced university of Göttingen (which had been founded in 1737, after the Hannoverian rulers had also become the kings of Great Britain). Garve told Kant that his review had been doctored by Feder, and Kant remained friendly with Garve. But Garve's original review, which was subsequently published in another journal, was not really much friendlier to the *Critique* than Feder's redaction of it. For translations of both reviews, see Brigitte Sassen (ed.), *Kant's Early Critics: The Empiricist Critique of the Theoretical Philosophy* (Cambridge: Cambridge University Press, 2000), pp. 53–77. Translations may also be found in the edition of the *Prolegomena* by Gary Hatfield (rev. edn, Cambridge: Cambridge University Press, 2004), pp. 201–11.

44 See especially Henry Allison, *The Kant–Eberhard Controversy* (Baltimore, MD: Johns Hopkins University Press, 1973); Allison has revised his translation of Kant's contribution to this controversy, the 1790 essay "On a discovery whereby any new critique of pure reason is to be rendered superfluous by an older one," in Kant, *Theoretical Philosophy after 1781*, ed. Henry Allison and Peter Heath (Cambridge: Cambridge University Press, 2002), pp. 283–336. Kant continued his self-defense in drafts for another Berlin Academy competition, on the "Real Progress of Metaphysics since the Time of Leibniz and Wolff," but didn't finish or submit his essay. The drafts were published by his student Rink after Kant's death in 1804.

45 See his letter to Marcus Herz of June 7, 1771, in Corr, p. 127, as well as the letter of February 21, 1772, p. 132.

46 For details of this infamous episode, see the translator's introduction to the *Religion* in Kant, *Religion and Rational Theology*, ed. Allen Wood and George Di Giovanni (Cambridge: Cambridge University Press, 1996), pp. 41–50.

47 I discuss these argument's in "Kant's Ether Proofs," Chapter 4 of *Kant's System of Nature and Freedom*.

48 The publication of these manuscripts, known as the *Opus postumum*, which finally occurred in 1936–38, was doubly disrupted by death: first by Kant's own, and then by that of the editor of much of Kant's notes and fragments, Erich Adickes, in 1928. Adickes had planned a chronological edition of the material, but his successor,

Gerhard Lehmann, published the manuscripts in the largely accidental order in which they had been found after his death (although he did include a chart of the chronological sequence that Adickes had established). The English translation of a selection from this material, Immanuel Kant, *Opus postumum*, edited by Eckhart Förster, translated by Förster and Michael Rosen (Cambridge: Cambridge University Press, 1993), presents its selection in the sequence that Adickes had established. See also Förster's monograph on the *Opus postumum*, *Kant's Final Synthesis* (Cambridge, MA: Harvard University Press, 2000). Förster is preparing a new edition of the *Opus postumum* for the *Akademie* edition.

TWO KANT'S COPERNICAN REVOLUTION

1 See, for example, Antoine Arnauld and Pierre Nicole, *Logic or the Art of Thinking* ("Port-Royal Logic," 1662), edited by Jill Vance Buroker (Cambridge: Cambridge University Press, 1992), Fourth Part, Chapter 2, p. 233; for a general discussion, see John Herman Randall, Jr., *The Career of Philosophy* (New York: Columbia University Press, 1962), vol. 1, pp. 284–307.

2 The Latin phrases "*a priori*" and "*a posteriori*" – which Kant regarded as borrowed terms and always had printed in Roman rather than German type – are adverbial phrases tacitly modifying some form of the verb "to know"; they literally mean what is known prior to experience and what is known only subsequent to experience. But Kant typically used them as adjectives, sometimes modifying "knowledge" or "cognition," but also, in due course, as modifying components of knowledge such as intuitions and concepts as well.

3 In recent years, Saul A. Kripke controversially argued that there could be *a posteriori* knowledge of necessary truths; see his *Naming and Necessity* (Cambridge, MA: Harvard University Press, 1980). For a brief defense of Kant's position on this matter, see Georges Dicker, *Kant's Theory of Knowledge: An Analytical Introduction* (Oxford: Oxford University Press, 2004), p. 10.

4 For an important discussion of Kant's concept of the *a priori*, see Philip Kitcher, "A Priori Knowledge," *Philosophical Review* 89 (1980): 3–23, and "Kant's *A Priori* Framework," in Patricia Kitcher (ed.), *Kant's Critique of Pure Reason: Critical Essays* (Lanham, MD: Rowman & Littlefield, 1998), pp. 1–20.

5 We may think of the word "bachelor" as having two very different senses, that of an unmarried male and that of the recipient of a first degree from a university; taken in the second of these senses, the proposition "All bachelors are unmarried" is not only not analytic, it's not even true. But as late as the eighteenth century, only unmarried males could go to university and receive the first degree, so "All bachelors are unmarried" would have been analytically true in both of its senses.

6 Contemporary logic also treats propositions that are true in virtue of their form alone, independently of their content, as analytically true, e.g., any sentence satisfying a schema like "Not (p and not-p)" or "If (p and q) then p." Willard V.O. Quine famously argued that we do not have a well-defined conception of the meaning of a concept and therefore of precisely what it contains, so for him only this last sort of proposition could count as analytical; see "Two Dogmas of Empiricism" in his *From a Logical Point of View* (Cambridge, MA: Harvard University Press, 1953). Lewis White Beck famously argued that Kant actually anticipated Quine in certain ways in his argument that all analysis presupposes synthesis; see "Can Kant's Synthetic Judgments Be Made Analytic?", in his *Studies in the Philosophy of Kant* (Indianapolis and New York: Bobbs-Merrill Company, 1965), pp. 74–91. For further discussion of types of analyticity, see Dicker, *Kant's Theory of Knowledge*, pp. 10–14.

7 David Hume, *An Enquiry Concerning Human Understanding*, Section 4, Part 1; in the critical edition by Tom L. Beauchamp (Oxford: Clarendon Press, 2000), p. 24.

8 Like any discipline, philosophy will of course also include analytic propositions, making explicit containment relations among well-defined concepts at various points in arguments or proofs.

9 The literature on Kant's response to Hume, or even whether Kant was responding to Hume, is vast. For further discussion, see my "Kant on Common Sense and Skepticism," *Kantian Review* 7 (2003): 1–37, and Gary Hatfield, "The *Prolegomena* and the *Critiques of Pure Reason*," in Volker Gerhardt, Rolf-Peter Horstmann, and Ralph Schumacher (eds), *Kant und die Berliner Aufklärung: Akten des IX. Internationalen Kant-Kongresses* (Berlin and New York: Walter de Gruyter, 2001), vol. 1, pp. 185–208.

10 In *Kant's Theory of Knowledge*, Dicker proposes that Kant uses the analytical method in his arguments about space and time in the "Transcendental Aesthetic" and the synthetic method in his discussion of concepts and principles in the "Transcendental Analytic" (pp. 24–5). I will suggest later that this simplifies what goes in both of those parts of the work, each of which in fact uses both methods of argument.

11 As is well known, Copernicus could not actually get rid of the numerous epicycles that were necessary to reconcile the apparent motions of the planets to the perfectly circular orbits he continued to suppose, and it was not until Johannes Kepler proposed that the orbits are actually elliptical that the desired mathematical simplification was achieved. So Copernicus's switch from a geocentric to a heliocentric model of the solar system was only a first step toward mathematical simplification.

12 For brief discussions of Kant's Copernican revolution, see Norman Kemp Smith, *A Commentary to Kant's 'Critique of Pure Reason*,' 2nd edn (London: Macmillan, 1923), pp. 18–25); H.J. Paton, *Kant's Metaphysic of Experience* (London: George Allen and Unwin, 1936), vol. 1, pp. 75–6; and Anthony Savile, *Kant's Critique of Pure Reason: An Orientation to the Central Theme* (Oxford: Blackwell Publishing, 2005), pp. 1–13. For a more extended discussion, see Robert Hahn, *Kant's Newtonian Revolution in Philosophy* (Carbondale and Edwardsville, IL: Southern Illinois University Press, 1988), Chapters 6–8.

13 Of course, Kant's inference from the necessity of the conformity of objects to our conditions of cognition to the application of those conditions only to the appearances of objects has been very controversial. Peter Strawson has argued that the former does not imply the latter at all; see *The Bounds of Sense: An Essay on Kant's Critique of Pure Reason* (London: Methuen, 1966), pp. 40–2. Dicker has argued that Kant's premise implies only that we cannot answer questions about the nature of things in themselves one way or the other; see *Kant's Theory of Knowledge*, pp. 46–8.

14 See Giorgio Tonelli, *Kant's Critique of Pure Reason within the Tradition of Modern Logic*, ed. David H. Chandler (Hildesheim: Georg Olms Verlag, 1994).

15 While philosophers have of course been arguing over issues about taste and art since the time of Plato, the *name* "aesthetics" for this part of philosophy was first coined by Alexander Gottlieb Baumgarten in his 1735 *Meditationes philosophicae de nonnullis ad poema pertinentibus* ("Philosophical mediations on Some Matters Concerning Poetry"), and used as the title for his much larger (although incomplete) treatise *Aesthetica* in 1750–58. Although the *subject* of aesthetics in this sense was very lively in eighteenth-century Britain, the *name* "aesthetics" did not come into common usage in English until the nineteenth century.

16 There has been extensive discussion of Kant's concept of intuition and his use of two different criteria for it. See especially Charles D. Parsons, "Kant's Philosophy of Arithmetic" (1969), reprinted with a postscript in his *Mathematics and Philosophy: Selected Essays* (Ithaca, NY: Cornell University Press, 1983), pp. 110–49; Manley Thompson, "Singular Terms and Intuitions in Kant's Epistemology," *Review of Metaphysics* 26 (1972–73): 314–43; Michael Friedman, "Kant on Concepts and Intuitions in the

Mathematical Sciences," *Synthese* 84 (1990), revised as Chapter 2 of his *Kant and the Exact Sciences* (Cambridge, MA: Harvard University Press, 1992), pp. 96–135, 213–57; and Lorne Falkenstein, *Kant's Intuitionism: A Commentary on the Transcendental Aesthetic* (Toronto: University of Toronto Press, 1995), pp. 28–71.

17 Among the many treatments of these arguments, see Paton, *Kant's Metaphysic of Experience*, vol. 1, pp. 107–26; Strawson, *The Bounds of Sense*, pp. 57–68; my *Kant and the Claims of Knowledge* (Cambridge: Cambridge University Press, 1987), pp. 345–50; Falkenstein, *Kant's Intuitionism*, pp. 186–252; Henry E. Allison, *Kant's Transcendental Idealism: An Interpretation and Defense*, revised edition (New Haven, CT: Yale University Press, 2004), pp. 99–116; Dicker, *Kant's Theory of Knowledge*, pp. 36–43; and Savile, *Kant's Critique of Pure Reason*, pp. 14–22.

18 Savile suggests that Kant's argument is not that the representation of space cannot be *abstracted* from particular experiences that would already have to be spatial, for an argument about abstraction would apply to general concepts rather than intuitions; he instead interprets Kant to mean that the form of space as a whole, which is essentially relational, cannot be given by the experience of particular objects, which are not essentially relational. See *Kant's Critique of Pure Reason*, pp. 17–18.

19 This contrast makes it confusing that Kant labels all of these arguments as metaphysical and transcendental expositions of the *concepts* of space: how can he say this when he is arguing precisely that our representations of space and time are intuitions and *not* concepts? Presumably in his titles he is using "concept" (*Begriff*) in the ordinary sense of any *conception*, rather than in his technical sense in which a concept is contrasted to an intuition. Then what he would be arguing is that our conceptions of space and time are in fact particular and therefore intuitions rather than general and therefore concepts. He could also say that he is discussing our conceptions of our intuitions of space and time. See also Dicker, *Kant's Theory of Knowledge*, p. 37.

20 OP, 21:13; in Kant, *Opus postumum*, ed. Eckart Förster, trans. Förster and Michael Rosen (Cambridge: Cambridge University Press, 1993), p. 171.

21 This problem was raised many years ago in Anthony Quinton, "Spaces and Times," *Philosophy* 37 (1962): 130–47.

22 See Strawson, *The Bounds of Sense*, pp. 58–9.

23 See Savile, *Kant's Critique of Pure Reason*, pp. 22–3.

24 Lisa A. Shabel, in "Kant's 'Argument from Geometry'," *Journal of the History of Philosophy* 42 (2004): 195–215, defends Kant's transcendental geometry by arguing that it builds upon the previous metaphysical exposition, which had established that we have a pure intuition of space, inferring from this fact that the propositions of geometry are synthetic *a priori*. But this interpretation is not consistent with Kant's present account of what a transcendental exposition is, nor does it fit Kant's procedure in the *Prolegomena*, from which this paragraph is lifted.

25 Michael Friedman defends Kant's position as required by the logic of his own time, but as superseded by these later developments in logic and the foundations of mathematics. See "Kant's Theory of Geometry," *Philosophical Review* 94 (1985): 455–506, revised as Chapter 1 of his *Kant and the Exact Sciences*, pp. 55–95.

26 In fact, precisely such a view was defended in Kant's own time by Moses Mendelssohn, in his 1762 prize essay "On evidence in metaphysical sciences," translated in Moses Mendelssohn, *Philosophical Writings*, ed., Daniel O. Dahlstrom (Cambridge: Cambridge University Press, 1997), pp. 251–306. Since this was the essay that beat Kant's own "Inquiry into the Distinctness of the Principles of Natural Theology and Ethics" and which was published together with it, Kant had to be aware of this standard view. Of course, Mendelssohn thought that the empirical evidence *confirmed* the truth of Euclidean geometry rather than *disconfirming* it, as we now believe. For further discussion, see "Kant and Mendelssohn: One Source of the Critical

Philosophy," in my *Kant on Freedom, Law, and Happiness* (Cambridge: Cambridge University Press, 2000).

27 Kant was so far from imagining that anyone could question the necessity and strict universality of mathematical propositions that he even believed that if only David Hume had thought about mathematics, he would have been saved from his skeptical empiricism (see PFM, §2, 4:272−3). Because Kant did not read English, and thus had read only the German translation of Hume's 1748 *Enquiry Concerning Human Understanding*, which does not discuss mathematics, but not the 1739−40 *Treatise of Human Nature*, he did not realize that in the earlier work Hume had explicitly asserted an empiricist account of the basic principles of geometry (see *Treatise*, Book I, Part 2, "Of the ideas of space and time").

28 This was the substance of the famous charge that Kant simply neglected to consider a "missing alternative," first raised by Adolf Trendelenberg in the nineteenth century. For discussion, see Norman Kemp Smith, *A Commentary to Kant's 'Critique of Pure Reason,'* pp. 113−14. Kemp Smith refers to the detailed discussion of this issue in Hans Vaihinger, *Commentar zu Kants Kritik der reinen Vernunft*, vol. 2 (Stuttgart, Berlin, Leipzig: Union deutsche Verlagsgesellschaft, 1892), pp. 290−313. See also Allison, *Kant's Transcendental Idealism*, pp. 128−32.

29 A similar question is formulated by Dicker, *Kant's Theory of Knowledge*, pp. 30−1, with reference back to an example from Paton, *Kant's Metaphysic of Experience*, vol. 1, pp. 143n., 166.

30 I have presented this analysis in detail in *Kant and the Claims of Knowledge*, pp. 354−69. It was anticipated by Strawson in *The Bounds of Sense*, p. 60, and has been endorsed by James van Cleve, *Problems from Kant* (New York and Oxford: Oxford University Press, 1999), pp. 34−43, and Savile, *Kant's Critique of Pure Reason*, pp. 30−1. Henry Allison has criticized this interpretation in *Kant's Transcendental Idealism*, p. 123, and in "Transcendental Idealism: A Retrospective," in his *Idealism and Freedom: Essays on Kant's Theoretical and Practical Philosophy* (Cambridge: Cambridge University Press, 1990), pp. 3−26.

31 See Allison, *Kant's Transcendental Idealism*, pp. 35−8. Allison's interpretation was influenced by Gerold Prauss, *Kant und das Problem der Dinge an sich* (Bonn: Bouvier Verlag, 1974), and in turn influenced Sebastian Gardner, *Kant and the Critique of Pure Reason* (London: Routledge, 1999), Chapter 5.

32 See Karl Ameriks, "Recent Work on Kant's Theoretical Philosophy," *American Philosophical Quarterly* 19 (1982): 1−24, reprinted in his *Interpreting Kant's Critiques* (Oxford: Clarendon Press, 2003), pp. 67−97, especially pp. 69−78. Although Ameriks's article does not survey additional work on the question of transcendental idealism from the past twenty years, it remains an invaluable analysis of the issues that are involved.

33 It should be noted here, though, that Allison clearly recognized that Kant's treatment of freedom of the will could be an objection to his "two-aspect" interpretation, and devoted an important second book to the attempt to defuse such an objection. See Allison, *Kant's Theory of Freedom* (Cambridge: Cambridge University Press, 1990).

34 Such an objection to Kant goes back at least to Hegel, who lampooned the idea of a "supersensible" world of things in themselves as an "inverted world" in the *Phenomenology of the Spirit* (1807), §157; in the translation by A.V. Miller (Oxford: Clarendon Press, 1977), pp. 96−7. For commentary on this passage, see Terry Pinkard, *Hegel's Phenomenology: The Sociality of Reason* (Cambridge: Cambridge University Press, 1994).

35 This interpretation has been argued in Rae Langton, *Kantian Humility: Our Ignorance of Things in Themselves* (Oxford: Clarendon Press, 1998).

36 Kant's term *Leitfaden* may refer to the thread that Ariadne gave Theseus to allow him to retrace his steps out of the labyrinth after he had slain the Minotaur (see Savile, *Kant's Critique of Pure Reason*, p. 134, n.7). If there is any philosophically interesting difference between the translations "clue" and "guiding-thread," it may be that a clue, once used,

is left behind, while one holds on to a guiding-thread until one's passage through a labyrinth of argument is complete.

37 Of course, Descartes himself was not a Cartesian skeptic. He thought he had adequately answered the skeptical doubts about our knowledge of external objects that he raised in the first of his *Meditations on First Philosophy* (1641) with the proofs of the existence of an omniscient and benevolent, therefore non-deceiving God, that he offered in the third and fifth meditations. As we will see in the next chapter, Kant rejected Descartes' "theoretical" proofs of the existence of God and therefore any appeal to the existence of God in epistemology; so for him, Descartes was a Cartesian skeptic even if he did not want to be one. As we will also see, however, Kant also argued that we have adequate "practical" grounds for belief in the existence of God – but a God characterized only by moral predicates, which do not bear on our epistemological needs.

38 For a slightly different account of Kant's distinction between "negative" and "infinite" judgments, see Dicker, *Kant's Theory of Knowledge*, p. 55.

39 So Kant's conception of modality is an epistemic or subjective one: whether we call a judgment problematic, assertoric, or apodictic depends upon whether we may think it to be true, do think it to be true, or must think it to be true. Kant's view is thus opposed to contemporary "possible-world semantics," which attempt to give an extensional interpretation of the modality of a judgment – for example, a judgment that is necessarily true is one that is true in all possible worlds – thereby turning modality into a kind of quantity, and thus part of the contents of judgments rather than our attitude toward them after all. Of course, the very fact that one cannot give the definition of one modal term ("necessity") without relying on another one ("possible") may indicate a flaw in this entire approach to modality.

40 For an extended account of the table of functions of judgment along these lines, see Reinhard Brandt, *The Table of Judgments: Critique of Pure Reason A 67–76, B 92–101*, North American Kant Society Studies in Philosophy, vol. 4, trans. Eric Watkins (Atascadero, CA: Ridgeview Publishing Co., 1995). Brandt's book is a response to the earlier work by Klaus Reich, *The Completeness of Kant's Table of Judgments* (originally 1932), translated by Jane Kneller and Michael Losonsky (Stanford, CA: Stanford University Press, 1981). The most detailed discussion of the subject is Michael Wolff, *Die Vollständigkeit der kantischen Urteilstafel* (Frankfurt am Main: Vittorio Klostermann, 1995).

41 There have certainly been multi-valued logics that allow some truth-value in addition to "true" or "false." But it is not clear whether the extra truth-value is ever more than epistemic, that is, not *known* or *proven* to be either true or false (like the verdict "not proven" in Scottish law, which means not proven guilty beyond a reasonable doubt, but then again not proven innocent either).

42 It is thus misleading to characterize the categories as *summa genera* of things, as Wilfrid Sellars sometimes does ("Some Remarks on Kant's Theory of Experience," in his *Kant's Transcendental Metaphysics*, ed. Jeffrey F. Sicha (Atasacadero, CA: Ridgeview Press, 2002), p. 277); it is informative to say that *metal* or *mineral* is the *summum genus* of *gold*, but not that *substance* is. It is better to say that the categories are "*summa genera* of conceptual items" rather than of "entities" themselves, as Sellars does in "Toward a Theory of the Categories" (*Kant's Transcendental Metaphysics*, p. 329).

43 See Dicker, *Kant's Theory of Knowledge*, pp. 76–7.

44 I have discussed this strategy in "Space, Time, and the Categories: The Project of the Transcendental Deduction," in Ralph Schumacher (ed.), *Idealismus als Theorie der Repräsentation?* (Paderborn: Mentis, 2001), pp. 313–38.

45 The distinction between two different senses of "experience" (*Erfahrung*) is already present at B 1, although Kant does not acknowledge it. For discussion of the two

senses, see *Kant and the Claims of Knowledge*, pp. 79–87, and Dicker, *Kant's Theory of Knowledge*, pp. 88–90.

46 It should be noted, however, that some commentators do defend the position that the Transcendental Deduction is only meant to establish that all empirical knowledge of objects ("experience" in the second sense) requires the categories. See Karl Ameriks, "Kant's Transcendental Deduction as a Regressive Argument" (1978), reprinted in his *Interpreting Kant's Critiques* (Oxford: Clarendon Press, 2003), pp. 51–66, and Gary Hatfield, "What Were Kant's Aims in the Deduction?", *Philosophical Topics* 31 (2003): 165–98.

47 See *Kant and the Claims of Knowledge*, pp. 83–4.

48 I originally analyzed it in "Kant on Apperception and *A priori* Synthesis," *American Philosophical Quarterly* 17 (1980): 205–12, and discussed it again in *Kant and the Claims of Knowledge*, pp. 133–49.

49 Dicker alludes to this problem in *Kant's Theory of Knowledge*, pp. 105, 111.

50 See also ibid., pp. 97–105.

51 Kant actually continues the last quotation by equating "the relation of representations to an object" with "their objective validity"; that is actually a weaker sense of "objective validity" than the one defined at A 93/B 126, because it says nothing about the *necessary* application of concepts to *all* objects.

52 See *Kant and the Claims of Knowledge*, pp. 117–18, and my "The Failure of the B-Deduction," in *Southern Journal of Philosophy* XXV, Supplement (1987): 67–84. See also Dicker, *Kant's Theory of Knowledge*, p. 135.

53 A famous article on this dilemma is Lewis White Beck, "Did the Sage of Königsberg Have No Dreams?" in his *Essays on Kant and Hume* (New Haven, CT: Yale University Press, 1978), pp. 38–60; Beck is responding to a problem raised by C.I. Lewis in *Mind and the World Order* (New York: Charles Scribner's Sons, 1929), p. 221.

54 Dieter Henrich drew attention to the fact that a second major step starts at §21, in a famous article, "The Proof-Structure of Kant's Transcendental Deduction," *Review of Metaphysics* 22 (1969): 640–59, reprinted in Ralph C.S. Walker (ed.), *Kant on Pure Reason* (Oxford: Oxford University Press, 1982), pp. 66–81. This article has spawned a large literature; for those who read German, a valuable discussion between Henrich and a number of critics can be found in Burkhard Tuschling (ed.), *Probleme der "Kritik der reinen Vernunft"* (Berlin: Walter de Gruyter, 1984), pp. 34–96.

55 See also Kant's remark in the Preface to the *Metaphysical Foundations of Natural Science*:

> if we can prove **that** the categories which reason must use in all its cognition can have no other use at all, except solely in relation to objects of possible experience (insofar as they simply make possible the form of thought in such experience), then, although the answer to the question **how** the categories make such experience possible is important enough for **completing** the deduction where possible, with respect to the principle end of the system, namely, the determination of the limits of pure reason, it is in no way **compulsory**, but merely **meritorious**.
>
> (4:474n.)

The limiting role of the deduction is emphasized by Hatfield in "What Were Kant's Aims in the Deduction?"

56 The idea that ultimately the deduction just adumbrates the strategy of the Analogies was earlier advanced by Robert Paul Wolff, *Kant's Theory of Mental Activity* (Cambridge, MA: Harvard University Press, 1962), and has recently been adopted by Dicker in *Kant's Theory of Knowledge*, Chapters 5–7.

57 In using the term "preformation-system," Kant obviously is referring to and criticizing Leibniz's theory of the pre-established harmony, that is, the theory that there is no direct connection between one subject's representation of the rest of the unverse and what is actually true of the rest of the universe, but only a parallel between the two established by a benevolent God. But Kant may also be using a metaphor from eighteenth-century embryological theory, which was divided between "preformationists," who believed that the embryos of all succeeding generations were already contained, nested like Russian dolls, in the first generation of creatures created by God, and "epigenesists," who believed (as we now all believe) that in each generation the combination of maternal and paternal material creates embryos that did not previously exist. See CPJ, §81, 5:422–4.

58 Thus the fact that requires schemata for the categories is not simply their purity, as Lauchlan Chipman suggests ("Kant's Categories and their Schematism," Kant-Studien 63 (1972): 36–50, reprinted in Ralph C.S. Walker (ed.), Kant on Pure Reason (Oxford: Oxford University Press, 1982), pp. 100–16, at pp. 104–6), or their generality, as Jonathan Bennett suggests (Kant's Analytic, p. 148), but the fact that they have only logical content yet must be applied to spatio-temporal objects.

59 Kant did not know of the modern kinetic theory of heat, but still thought in terms of phlogiston. But even on that theory, a change in temperature (an intensive magnitude) would be caused by a change in the amount of phlogiston present (an extensive magnitude).

60 It is also open to the objection that a series of only moderately enduring but not permanent objects would be sufficient to represent – or measure, as he is often taken to mean – the permanence of time itself, for example, a series of clocks each of which is replaced by the next after, say, a few years in service. See Strawson, The Bounds of Sense, p. 129, and Dicker, Kant's Theory of Knowledge, p. 149.

61 An interpretation of Kant's thought along these lines was first suggested by Arthur Melnick in his Kant's Analogies of Experience (Chicago: University of Chicago Press, 1973), pp. 71–7, and further developed in my Kant and the Claims of Knowledge, pp. 224–30.

62 This objection was made to Kant by Strawson in The Bounds of Sense, p. 130.

63 A famous example from Jonathan Bennett, Kant's Analytic (Cambridge: Cambridge University Press, 1966), pp. 187–9.

64 What about the "Big Bang"? Isn't that a case of something literally coming out of nothing? Kant's view would be that cosmologists cannot literally mean that; they can only mean that everything about the currently observable universe seems to come from a single very drastic change in some previously existing substance. The latest theory that perhaps the existing universe tracing back to the "Big Bang" is just one "bubble" in an infinite series of bubbles suggests that at least some cosmologists have realized that the idea that something comes from nothing is just not admissible within empirical knowledge.

65 As Kemp Smith (Commentary, p. 375), Paton (Kant's Metaphysics of Experience vol. II, pp. 253–7), and Wolff (Kant's Theory of Mental Activity, pp. 272–3) do. Each of these authors treat as six separate "proofs" what are clearly Kant's repeated attempts to clarify a single basic idea, but apart from this their analyses of the "Analogy" remain valuable (Kemp Smith, pp. 369–77; Paton, vol. II, pp. 224–61; Wolff, pp. 260–80).

66 The following account is based on Kant and the Claims of Knowledge, pp. 241–9. It has recently been adopted by Dicker, Kant's Theory of Knowledge, pp. 166–78.

67 Strawson (and long before him Arthur Lovejoy) accused Kant of committing a "non sequitur of numbing grossness," roughly, inferring from "If state of affairs A precedes state of affairs B, then necessarily my representation of A precedes that of B (other things being equal)" to "If my representation of A precedes that of B, then A necessarily precedes B" (The Bounds of Sense, p. 137; Arthur O. Lovejoy, "On Kant's Reply to Hume" (1906), reprinted in Moltke S. Gram, Kant: Disputed Questions (Chicago: Quadrangle Books,

1967), pp. 284–308, at pp. 302–3; see also Dicker, *Kant's Theory of Knowledge*, pp. 166–70). But Kant does not make such a move; rather, he argues that we cannot know that the order of our representations is necessary unless we know that the order of the objective states of affairs is necessary, and we can only infer *that* from a causal law. See also Paton, *Kant's Metaphysic of Experience*, vol. II, pp. 269–71.

68 For a related assessment of the possible accomplishment of Kant's argument, see Strawson's later book *Skepticism and Naturalism: Some Varieties* (New York: Columbia University Press, 1985).

69 "Transcendental arguments" were first revived by Peter Strawson in *Individuals: An Essay in Descriptive Metaphysics* (London: Methuen, 1959), before *The Bounds of Sense*. The probative force of this supposedly unique style of argument was doubted in a famous paper by Barry Stroud, "Transcendental Arguments," *Journal of Philosophy* 65 (1968): 241–56, reprinted in numerous places, including Ralph C.S. Walker (ed.), *Kant on Pure Reason* (Oxford: Oxford University Press, 1982), pp. 117–31, and Stroud's *Understanding Human Knowledge* (Oxford: Oxford University Press, 2000), pp. 9–25. The bottom line to which I refer was essentially drawn by Richard Rorty in several of his earlier papers, including "Strawson's Objectivity Argument," *Review of Metaphysics* 24 (1970): 207–44, and "Verificationism and Transcendental Arguments," *Nous* 5 (1971): 3–14. The ensuing literature is vast, but for several surveys see Anthony Brueckner, "Transcendental Arguments I," *Nous* 17 (1983): 551–75, and "Transcendental Arguments II," *Nous* 18 (1984): 197–224; my *Kant and the Claims of Knowledge*, pp. 417–28; and Robert Stern (ed.), *Transcendental Arguments: Problems and Prospects* (Oxford: Clarendon Press, 1999).

70 David Hume, *A Treatise of Human Nature*, Book I, Part III, Section ii.

71 See also Michael Friedman, "Causal Laws and the Foundations of Natural Science," in Paul Guyer (ed.), *The Cambridge Companion to Kant* (Cambridge: Cambridge University Press, 1992), pp. 161–99.

72 Kant actually says that "All substances, insofar as they are **simultaneous**, stand in thoroughgoing community (i.e., interaction with one another)." But if all genuine substances are permanent, neither coming into nor going out of existence, then they necessarily also all exist at the same time as each other, namely through all time. (This point was made by Paton, *Kant's Metaphysic of Experience*, vol. II, p. 298; see also Dicker, *Kant's Theory of Knowledge*, pp. 181–2.) So Kant can only be talking about simultaneous states of substances.

73 These are the criteria for representation that Descartes lays down in the third of his *Meditations on First Philosophy*, paragraph eight.

74 The charge of Berkeleian idealism was made in the first review of the *Critique of Pure Reason* to appear, the notorious review in the journal *Göttingsche Anzeigen von gelehrten Sachen* in January, 1782. For a translation of this review and the fuller review by Christian Garve which the editor of the Göttingen journal, J.H. Feder had adapted (or mangled), see Brigitte Sassen (ed.), *Kant's Early Critics: The Empiricist Critique of the Theoretical Philosophy* (Cambridge: Cambridge University Press, 2000). For Kant's initial response, see the *Prolegomena*, §13, Note III, 4:290–4.

75 Reflections 5653–4, 6311–17, 6319, and 6323 in Kant's *Handschriftliche Nachlaß* ("Handwritten Remains"), in vol. 18 of the *Akademie* edition, translated in Kant's *Notes and Fragments*, edited by Paul Guyer, translated by Curtis Bowman, Paul Guyer, and Frederick Rauscher (Cambridge: Cambridge University Press, 2005), pp. 281–6, 355–71, and 374–7. And these of course are only the notes that survived – who knows how many other drafts Kant attempted either before or after he published the version of 1787? I drew upon these notes in my original interpretation of the "Refutation" in "Kant's Intentions of the Refutation of Idealism," *Philosophical Review* 92 (1983): 329–83; they have also been discussed by Allison in *Kant's Transcendental Idealism*, pp. 298–303,

and Eckart Förster, "Kant's Refutation of Idealism," in A.J. Holland (ed.), *Philosophy and its History* (Dordrecht: Reidel, 1985), pp. 295–311.

76 See *Meditation* VI.

77 See *Meditation* I, paragraph four.

THREE THE CRITIQUE OF METAPHYSICS

1 See *Republic*, Books VI – VII.

2 It may be observed here that the word "noumenon" does not *mean* the same as the expression "thing in itself," although Kant *uses* "thing in itself" and "noumenon in the negative sense" coextensively, and also assumes that if we *could* have knowledge of a "noumenon in a positive sense" then we would also have knowledge of things as they are in themselves.

3 The idea that reason always leads us to form the idea of something unconditioned is central to the interpretation of the "Dialectic" offered by Michelle Grier, *Kant's Doctrine of Transcendental Illusion* (Cambridge: Cambridge University Press, 2001).

4 In *Kant's Dialectic* (Cambridge: Cambridge University Press, 1974), Jonathan Bennett interpreted paralogisms as *valid* arguments, the conclusions of which however are "inflated" beyond what is allowed by the premises (p. 72). This contradicts Kant's own statement that paralogisms are formally *invalid*, but was meant to capture Kant's thought that there is *something* true in each paralogism. However, as we will see, what is true in each paralogism is each of the premises, *properly understood*, but not the conclusion that is drawn from them.

5 G.W. Leibniz, "Principles of Nature and Grace, Based on Reason," §1, in G.W. Leibniz, *Philosophical Essays*, ed. and trans. Roger Ariew and Daniel Garber (Indianapolis: Hackett Publishing Co., 1989), p. 207.

6 Of course, Leibniz was not ignorant of this fact, but instead used it precisely to argue that the ultimate simple substances underlying all reality are not spatial at all, but the indivisible centers of consciousness that he called "monads." See, e.g., "Principles of Nature and Grace Based on Reason" (1714), §2, and "Monadology" (1714), §§1–14; in G.W. Leibniz, *Philosophical Essays*, trans. Roger Ariew and Daniel Garber, pp. 207, 213–14.

7 This was always a problem for Leibniz, whose explanations of human freedom typically turned into explanations of divine freedom that do not entail human freedom. See, for example, "On Freedom and Possibility" (1680–82), in *Philosophical Essays*, p. 19, and *Theodicy*, §8, in the abridgment of the E.M. Huggard translation by Diogenes Allen (Indianapolis: Bobbs-Merrill, 1966), p. 35.

8 I have worked out this alternative to Kant's solution of the antinomies in more detail in my *Kant and the Claims of Knowledge* (Cambridge: Cambridge University Press, 1987), pp. 404–15.

9 Hume's *Dialogues Concerning Natural Religion* were published only in 1779, three years after his death, and were first translated into German in 1781, the same year that Kant published the *Critique of Pure Reason*; so Kant could not have known them when he was writing the *Critique*. But Hume had already presented the essence of his argument in Section 11 of his 1748 *Enquiry Concerning Human Understanding*, which had been translated into German in 1755, and Kant was intimately familiar with that book.

10 While most philosophers since Kant have accepted his contrast between the presupposition of existence and predication and thus his critique of the ontological argument, Allen Wood points out there has been remarkably little argument for the modern conception of existence and predication; see his *Kant's Rational Theology* (Ithaca, NY: Cornell University Press, 1978), pp. 110–12. Some contemporary philosophers have attempted to reconstruct the ontological argument, e.g., Alvin Plantinga, *The Nature of*

Necessity (Oxford: Clarendon Press, 1974), which attempts to do so using realism about possible worlds. But it is hard to see how anyone working within Kant's framework could accept realism about possible worlds or anything that follows from it.

11 The classic statement of the argument from design was provided by William Paley, in *Natural Theology, or Evidences of the Existence and Attributes of the Deity Collected from the Appearances of Nature* (London, 1802), published several decades after Hume had devastated the argument in his posthumous *Dialogues Concerning Natural Religion* (1779) and Kant had criticized it in the *Critique of Pure Reason*. But there were numerous presentations of the argument from the end of the seventeenth century to which Hume was responding, including John Ray, *Wisdom of God Manifested in the Works of the Creation* (1691) and *Three Physico-Theological Discourses* (1721); William Derham, *Physico-Theology, or a Demonstration of the Being and Attributes of God from his Works of Creation* (1713); George Cheyne, *Philosophical Principles of Religion, Natural and Revealed* (1725); William Wollaston, *The Religion of Nature Delineated* (1726); Richard Bentley, *A Defence of Natural and Revealed Religion* (1739); and many more. An extensive catalogue of works on "physico-theology" and "teleology" from both Britain and Germany that would have been known to Kant is provided in a textbook on philosophy of religion on which he lectured several times during the 1780s, Johann August Eberhard's *Vorbereitung zur natürlichen Theologie* ("Preparation for natural theology") (Halle, 1781), §§30, 39, reprinted at 18:571–2, 577–8. A brief discussion of representative versions of the argument from design can be found in Basil Willey, *The Eighteenth-Century Background: Studies on the Idea of Nature in the Thought of the Period* (London: Chatto & Windus, 1940), Chapter 2, "The Wisdom of God in the Creation."

12 In the *Critique of the Power of Judgment*, he will argue that we do experience design in nature that we can comprehend only *as if* it were the product of an intelligence *greater than our own* (CPJ, Introduction, Section IV, 5:180), but this is not meant as a theoretical proof of the existence of such an intelligence, nor is there any claim here that we must conceive of such an intelligence as perfect or maximal.

13 Kant returns to and clarifies this point in the *Critique of the Power of Judgment*, §§76–7, 5:401–10.

FOUR BUILDING UPON THE FOUNDATIONS OF KNOWLEDGE

1 For this general characterization of Kant's project, see Gerd Buchdahl, *Metaphysics and the Philosophy of Science* (Oxford: Basil Blackwell, 1969), pp. 672–4, and "Kant's 'Special Metaphysics' and the *Metaphysical Foundations of Natural Science*," in his *Kant and the Dynamics of Reason* (Oxford: Blackwell, 1992), pp. 288–314.

2 For detailed discussion of this issue, see Michael Friedman, *Kant and the Exact Sciences* (Cambridge, MA: Harvard University Press, 1992), Part II.

3 See Peter Plaass, *Kant's Theory of Natural Science*, trans. Alfred E. and Maria G. Miller (Dordrecht: Kluwer, 1994), Chapters 4 and 5.

4 This assumption goes back to Aristotle's equation of physics with the science of motion; see *Physics* Book I, Chapter 2, 185a12–20, and Book III, Chapter 1, 200b12–201b15.

5 For a brief account of the organization of the *Metaphysical Foundations*, see Friedman, *Kant and the Exact Sciences*, pp. 43–7 and 167–70.

6 This term, which would come to name some very diverse movements in twentieth-century philosophy, was previously defined in this sense by Johann Heinrich Lambert in his *Neues Organon oder Gedanken über die Erforschung und Bezeichnung des Wahren und dessen Unterscheidung vom Irrtum und Schein* ("New Organon, or Thoughts on the Investigation and

Designation of the True and its Distinction from Error and Illusion") (Leipzig: Johann Wendler, 1764), vol. II, part two.

7 For a detailed discussion of Kant's view of impenetrability, see Daniel Warren, *Reality and Impenetrability in Kant's Philosophy of Nature* (London and New York: Routledge, 2001).

8 This is the precise point at which Kant revises his original conception of attractive and repulsive forces, which were properties of indivisible physical monads. For an account of the change in Kant's views, see Michael Friedman's introduction to his edition of the *Metaphysical Foundations* (Cambridge: Cambridge University Press, 2004), pp. vii-xxx.

9 See Martin Carrier, "Kant's Mechanical Determination of Matter in the *Metaphysical Foundations of Natural Science*," and Eric Watkins, "Kant's Justification of the Laws of Mechanics," in E. Watkins (ed.), *Kant and the Sciences* (Oxford: Oxford University Press, 2001), pp. 117–35, 136–59.

10 See Kenneth R. Westphal, *Kant's Transcendental Proof of Realism* (Cambridge: Cambridge University Press, 2004), pp. 205–27.

11 Georg Wilhelm Friedrich Hegel, *The Phenomenology of Spirit* (1807), trans. A.V. Miller (Oxford: Clarendon Press, 1977).

12 See, for example, Edmund Husserl, *Ideas toward a Pure Phenomenology and Phenomenological Philosophy* (1913, 1950), trans. F. Kersten, R. Rojcewicz, A. Schuwer, T.E. Klein, and W.E. Pohl, three vols (The Hague: Martinus Nijhoff, and Dordrecht: Kluwer, 1980–89).

13 Isaac Newton, *Philosophiae Naturalis Principia Mathematica*, Definition 8, Scholium; in Newton, *Philosophical Writings*, ed. Andrew Janiak (Cambridge: Cambridge University Press, 2004), pp. 67–70.

14 I first discussed this reassignment in "Reason and Reflective Judgment: Kant on the Significance of Systematicity," *Noûs* 24 (1990): 17–43, reprinted in my *Kant's System of Nature and Freedom: Selected Essays* (Oxford: Clarendon Press, 2005), pp. 11–37.

FIVE LAWS OF FREEDOM

1 This distinction has been made by many authors, even if they themselves sometimes causally identify the categorical imperative and the fundamental principle of morality. For a clear statement of the difference, see John Rawls, *Lectures on the History of Moral Philosophy*, edited by Barbara Herman (Cambridge, MA: Harvard University Press, 2000), p. 167. Bruce Aune interestingly argues that each of the different formulations of the categorical imperative that Kant will provide allows for the distinction between a pure form applicable to all rational beings and a distinctive form in which the pure principle applies to human beings; see his *Kant's Theory of Morals* (Princeton, NJ: Princeton University Press, 1979), pp. 111–20.

2 Kant's moral philosophy is often described as paying no attention to the consequences of our actions for our happiness at all. We will see in due course that this is a gross exaggeration of Kant's point that happiness cannot be the *principle* and *motive* of morally worthy action, although under ideal circumstances it would be its *consequence* and in a sense its ultimate "object." As Lewis White Beck pointed out, in Kant's theory "every one of the heteronomous principles . . . banished from the foundations of moral volition, re-enters the moral scheme of things, once the purity of the sources of morals has been secured"; *A Commentary on Kant's Critique of Practical Reason* (Chicago: University of Chicago Press, 1960), p. 107.

3 Allen Wood has recently argued that a person need not always demonstrate her good will by acting from duty in the absence of or in opposition to any other inclinations, but often does; see "The Good Will," *Philosophical Topics* 31 (2003): 457–84, at 464–5. But this is enough of a premise for Kant's real point, which is that the principle of a good will cannot rest on any mere inclination or desire for a particular object, because

it must be such that persons can still act upon it in the absence of any such inclination or desire (cp. Wood, p. 466).

4 The literature on maxims is vast. For the conception used here, see Onora Nell (O'Neill), *Acting on Principle: An Essay on Kantian Ethics* (New York: Columbia University Press, 1975), pp. 34–42, and Christine M. Korsgaard, "Kant's Analysis of Obligation: The Argument of *Groundwork* I" (1989), reprinted in her *Creating the Kingdom of Ends* (Cambridge: Cambridge University Press, 1996), pp. 43–76, at pp. 57–8. All maxims are subjective in the sense of being the principle on which an agent actually acts, and clearly some are subjective in the second sense of *not* being universally valid. But there is a question whether any maxim is also an objective law, since a maxim always retains a reference to the agent ("I will *A* in B in order to C"). Henry E. Allison argues that it would be most precise to say that maxims are personal principles of action that pass the test of universally valid laws, or conversely that "objective practical principles are more properly viewed as second-order principles that specify the norms for maxim selection and action"; see *Kant's Theory of Freedom* (Cambridge: Cambridge University Press, 1990), p. 88.

5 I have discussed this issue in "The Derivation of the Categorical Imperative: Kant's Correction for a Fatal Flaw," *Harvard Review of Philosophy* X (2002): 64–80.

6 Most discussion of Kant's moral philosophy focuses on categorical imperatives. For discussion of hypothetical imperatives, see Thomas E. Hill, Jr., "The Hypothetical Imperative" (1973), reprinted in his *Dignity and Practical Reason in Kant's Moral Philosophy* (Ithaca, NY: Cornell University Press, 1992), pp. 17–37, and Onora O'Neill, "Consistency in Action" (1985), reprinted in her *Constructions of Reason: Explorations in Kant's Moral Philosophy* (Cambridge: Cambridge University Press, 1989), pp. 81–104, at pp. 90–2, 98–101.

7 In line with our earlier distinction between the fundamental principle of morality and the categorical imperative, what Kant is actually doing here is deriving the content of the fundamental principle of morality for all rational beings from the only possible content of a categorical imperative for human beings, rather than vice versa. The attempt to derive the content of the moral law directly from constraints such as its universality rather than necessity is what has recently come to be called a "criteriological" derivation; see Samuel J. Kerstein, *Kant's Search for the Supreme Principle of Morality* (Cambridge: Cambridge University Press, 2002).

8 Here I differ from the account of humanity adopted by Rawls, who equates it with "those of our powers and capacities that characterize us as reasonable and rational persons who belong to the natural world," specifically the powers, first, "of moral personality, which makes it possible for us to have a good will and a good moral character, and second, those capacities and skills to be developed by culture: by the arts and sciences and so forth" (*Lectures on the History of Moral Philosophy*, Cambridge, MA: Harvard University Press, 2000, p. 188), thus specifically omitting the power to set ends that Kant makes central to his (at least later) definition. This omission has a number of significant consequences for Rawls's interpretation of Kant, requiring him to introduce an entirely empirical notion of basic human needs to generate positive duties and making it more difficult for him to explain the relation between happiness and morality than it needs to be.

9 See Christine Korsgaard, *Creating the Kingdom of Ends* (Cambridge: Cambridge University Press, 1996), pp. 119–24, and Allen W. Wood, *Kant's Ethical Thought* (Cambridge: Cambridge University Press, 1999), pp. 116, 124–7.

10 The modern discussion of this issue begins with H.J. Paton, *The Categorical Imperative: A Study in Kant's Moral Philosophy* (London: Hutchinson, 1947), Book III, pp. 129–98. Among many other useful discussions, see also Aune, *Kant's Theory of Morals*, Chapters II–IV, pp. 35–130; Onora O'Neill, "Universal laws and ends-in-themselves," reprinted in her

Constructions of Reason, pp. 126–44; Philip Stratton-Lake, "Formulating Categorical Imperatives," *Kant-Studien* 83 (1993): 317–40; Wood, *Kant's Ethical Thought*, Chapters 3–5, pp. 76–190; and Rawls, *Lectures*, pp. 162–216. I have given a detailed account of my own position on this issue in "The Possibility of the Categorical Imperative," *Philosophical Review* 104 (1995): 353–85, reprinted in my *Kant on Freedom, Law, and Happiness* (Cambridge: Cambridge University Press, 2000), pp. 172–206.

11 See Paton, *The Categorical Imperative*, pp. 149–50. Paton has been followed in this regard by Beck, *Commentary*, pp. 160–1, and Aune, *Kant's Theory of Morals*, p. 59. Because of his teleological interpretation of FLN, Aune in this passage regards it as "obsolete," though his larger interpretation of the relation between pure laws of morality and their "typics," the forms in which they apply to human beings (see again his pp. 111–20), would suggest that there must be some interpretation of FLN as the typic of FUL on which it is not "obsolete."

12 This interpretation of the first version of the FUL/FLN test, namely the consistency of my acting on a certain maxim with everyone acting on that maxim, has been clearly stated by Nell (O'Neill), *Acting on Principle*, pp. 61–3, 69–73; Christine Korsgaard, "Kant's Formula of Universal Law" (1986), in her *Creating the Kingdom of Ends*, pp. 77–105, at pp. 92–4; and Rawls, *Lectures on the History of Moral Philosophy*, pp. 167–70. Rawls makes it clear that we may need to figure out empirically what would result from the generalization of the maxim on which we propose to act to everyone else (p. 169). However, this should not be taken to mean that we must figure out empirically whether our acting on that maxim would in fact lead everyone else to act upon it. As both Rawls and Nell (O'Neill) make clear, the test is whether we could both *intend* to act upon the maxim and *intend* that everyone else do so as well, with whatever consequences that would have.

13 See O'Neill, "Consistency in Action," *Constructions of Reason*, pp. 98–103.

14 The precise interpretation of this distinction is complicated. See Nell (O'Neill), *Acting on Principle*, pp. 43–58; Rawls, *Lectures*, pp, 185–7; and Mary J. Gregor, *Laws of Freedom: A Study of Kant's Method of Applying the Categorical Imperative in the Metaphysik der Sitten* (Oxford: Basil Blackwell, 1963), pp. 95–112.

15 On more traditional accounts, perfect duties are those that can be enforced and imperfect duties those that cannot be enforced; but the possibility of enforcing a duty presupposes that the duty entails specific performances owed to specific persons, which is the case for Kant's perfect but not imperfect duties. See for example, Samuel Pufendorf, *The Whole Duty of Man, According to the Law of Nature* (1673), Book I, Chapter II, Section XIV and note; in the translation by Samuel Tooke (1691), edited by Ian Hunter and David Saunders (Indianapolis: Liberty Fund, 2003), p. 50.

16 For a detailed discussion of such cases, see Nell (O'Neill), *Acting on Principle*, especially Chapters 2 and 3, pp. 12–42.

17 See Aune, *Kant's Moral Theory*, pp. 31, 78, and Wood, *Kant's Ethical Thought*, pp. 97–107.

18 See Nell (O'Neill), *Acting on Principle*, pp. 79–80.

19 The English writer Joseph Addison's *Cato, A Tragedy*, which debuted in April, 1713, was wildly popular throughout the eighteenth century, not just in Britain and North America but throughout Europe as well. It could well have been the source of Kant's interest in this tragedy. See Joseph Addison, *Cato: A Tragedy, and Selected Essays*, edited by Christine Dunn Henderson and Mark E. Yellin (Bloomington, IN: Indianapolis Liberty Fund, 2004). Johann Christoph Gottsched based his play *Der Sterbende Cato* (1721) in part on Addison's play.

20 See also the discussion in Rawls, *Lectures on the History of Moral Philosophy*, pp. 192–93, where he interprets Kant not as "saying that suicide is always wrong" but rather that "a moral title for it is always needed." I have suggested a particular "moral title" for it here based on my interpretation of the underlying value of instances of freedom.

21 Some philosophers seems to think these sorts of cases are very difficult, arguing that since you were not the one who set the switch and sent the train careening down the track in the first place, you will not be responsible for any deaths if the train follows its predetermined course and kills the six, but if you intervene and reset the switch, then you will be responsible for one death and will therefore be blameworthy. That seems crazy. Life is surely unfair, for otherwise nobody would be stuck on the tracks and you would not be the one who has to decide between saving one and saving six; but given those circumstances, surely you must save six rather than one, and any plausible moral theory must justify and require that choice. I have suggested an intepretation of Kant's theory on which it does.

22 Nell (O'Neill) asks, "What exactly should we understand by the preservation and cultivation of (human) rational nature?", and answers thus:

> In his examples of what must be done to treat men as ends and never as mere means, Kant interprets the maintenance of human nature as avoiding the destruction of its animal substratum and not impeding rational natures in their pursuit of ends, and the cultivation and promotion of rational nature as the development of human talents and providing positive help to rational natures in their pursuit of ends.
>
> *(Acting on Principle*, p. 107)

This is basically the same account of the preservation of humanity as I have just given and of promoting it that I am about to give, although I do not think that her phrase "not impeding rational natures in their pursuit of ends" makes the necessity of preserving the possibility of others' exercising their free choice in the setting of their own ends sufficiently explicit. For an account which makes this aspect of Kant's conception more explicit, see Hill, "Humanity as an End in Itself" (1980), in *Dignity and Practical Reason in Kant's Moral Theory*, pp. 38–57, at pp. 50–1. Allen Wood offers an interesting account of treating humanity as an end in itself in *Kant's Ethical Thought*, Chapter 4, but his interpretation of the application of the general requirement to Kant's four examples (see pp. 147–50) places too much emphasis on expressing one's own respectful attitude toward the humanity of others and not enough on actually preserving and promoting their humanity by one's actions.

23 Aune objects that Kant should not have held us to an obligation to develop talents sufficient for the realization of all possible ends, since that will include ones we will not actually have, and indeed which talents we choose to develop will affect what ends we can subsequently adopt (*Kant's Moral Theory*, p. 56). This is a different point from the one I am making here, which is that one might not be able to develop talents sufficient even for all the ends one actually does have or would at least like to have.

24 Thus the key difference between FA and FUL/FLN is that the latter requires you to consider the universalizability or acceptability of a particular maxim to others, while the former requires you to consider the consistency of your whole set of maxims as well as its acceptability to all others, just as legislators must consider the consistency of any proposed laws with their whole body of legislation as well as the acceptability of that law to all (or at least a majority). For a similar interpretation of FA, see Wood, *Kant's Ethical Thought*, pp. 164–5, and Rawls, *Lectures on the History of Moral Philosophy*, pp. 205–6.

25 I have developed this analysis more fully in "Kant on the Theory and Practice of Autonomy," in *Social Philosophy and Policy* 20 (2003): 70–98, and in Ellen Frankel Paul, Fred D. Miller, and Jeffrey Paul (eds), *Autonomy* (Cambridge: Cambridge University Press, 2003), pp. 70–98, reprinted in my *Kant's System of Nature and Freedom* (Oxford: Clarendon Press, 2005), pp. 115–45.

26 Kant's phrase *Reich der Zwecken* has usually been translated as "kingdom of ends." But the idea of a kingdom might suggest subjects under a single ruler and lawgiver, whereas Kant's claim is that *all* human beings on a par with one another must be both the legislators and the subjects of moral laws in something more like an empire of equal moral agents than a kingdom under a single moral agent (although in the Holy Roman Empire, at least, the several electors, who were in any case hardly the whole population, got to vote for the next emperor, but not for the laws). Perhaps the term "realm" brings this out better, or at least avoids the potentially misleading implication of "kingdom."

27 Rawls, *Lectures on the History of Moral Philosophy*, p. 204.

28 In some later passages (e.g., pp. 311–12), Rawls comes closer to acknowledging this requirement, but still seems to underplay the significance of particular, freely chosen ends in the concept of the realm of ends, thus leading to a sharper distinction between the realm of ends and the highest good, which explicitly includes happiness as a component, than is warranted. I will return to this in a subsequent chapter.

29 Wood, *Kant's Ethical Thought*, p. 166.

30 Ibid., p. 186.

SIX FREEDOM, IMMORTALITY, AND GOD

1 On the "Pantheism controversy," see Frederick C. Beiser, *The Fate of Reason: German Philosophy from Kant to Fichte* (Cambridge, MA: Harvard University Press, 1987), chapters 2–4, and George di Giovanni, *Freedom and Religion in Kant and His Immediate Successors: The Vocation of Humankind, 1774–1800* (Cambridge: Cambridge University Press, 2005), chapters 4–5. Some of the relevant texts can be found in Gérard Vallée, editor, *The Spinoza Conversations Between Lessing and Jacobi* (Albany, NY: State University of New York Press, 1988).

2 For a similar interpretation, see Lewis White Beck, *A Commentary on Kant's Critique of Practical Judgment* (Chicago: University of Chicago Press, 1960), pp. 42–7, and John Rawls, *Lectures on the History of Moral Philosophy* (Cambridge, MA: Harvard University Press, 2000), pp. 147–8.

3 David Hume, *A Treatise of Human Nature*, Book II, Part 3, Chapter 3; in the edition by David Fate Norton and Mary J. Norton (Oxford: Oxford University Press, 2000), p. 266.

4 By "Chrysippos" Kant means Chrysippus (c. 280–207 BCE), successor of Cleanthes as head of the Stoa in Athens. His many works, not even a complete catalogue of which has survived, formalized early Stoic orthodoxy, which included determinism.

5 In 1723, Wolff had been driven from his post at the Prussian university in Halle and indeed from all Prussian territory – on pain of death – by a cabal of Pietist professors, led by Joachim Lange, who convinced king Friedrich Wilhelm I that Wolff's version of determinism implied that deserters were not responsible for their actions. The Landgrave of Hesse gave Wolff refuge at the University of Marburg, in spite of the fact that its statutes required its professors to be Calvinists, and Wolff was only persuaded to return to Halle in 1740, after the accession of the more liberal Frederick the Great to the Prussian throne. After that Crusius resumed the Pietist attack against Wolff, but to little effect, as Wolff completed his career at Halle with great renown. For these events, see Lewis White Beck, *Early German Philosophy: Kant and His Predecessors* (Cambridge, MA: Harvard University Press, 1969), pp. 258–61.

6 One year before Kant's work, although certainly unknown to him, the American theologian and philosopher Jonathan Edwards had made virtually the same objection to the liberty of indifference in his treatise *Freedom of the Will* (Boston: S. Kneeland, 1754).

7 See, for example, *Discourse on Metaphysics* (1686), §30, in Leibniz, *Philosophical Essays*, edited by Roger Ariew and Daniel Garber (Indianapolis and Cambridge: Hackett Publishing Company, 1989), pp. 60–1; "A New System of Nature" (*Journal des Savants*, 1695), in *Philosophical Essays*, pp. 143–5; Letter to Coste, "On Human Freedom" (1707), in *Philosophical Essays*, pp. 194–5; *New Essays on Human Understanding*, Book II, chapter xxi, §15; in the edition by Peter Remnant and Jonathan Bennett (Cambridge: Cambridge University Press, 1981), p. 180. Of these, the last was known to Kant, but only after its posthumous publication in 1765; the second would likely have been known to Kant in 1755.

8 For discussion of the third antinomy, see Beck, *Commentary*, pp. 181–8, and Henry E. Allison, *Kant's Theory of Freedom* (Cambridge: Cambridge University Press, 1990), Chapter 1, pp. 11–28; for comments on Allison's approach, Daniel Guevara, *Kant's Theory of Moral Motivation* (Boulder, CO: Westview Press, 2000), pp. 71–4.

9 This was the central issue in the only book that Leibniz published during his lifetime, the *Theodicy* of 1710; an abridgement of the E.M. Huggard translation of this voluminous work was done by Diogenes Allen (Don Mills, ON: J.M. Dent and Indianapolis: Bobbs-Merrill, 1966).

10 On empirical and intelligible character, see Allison, *Kant's Theory of Freedom*, Chapter 2, pp. 29–53.

11 For a discussion of Kant's later position that emphasizes his objections to Leibniz's account of freedom, see Rawls, *Lectures on the History of Moral Philosophy*, pp. 277–82.

12 As Bruce Aune puts it, the moral law would be descriptively and analytically true for a rational being as such; what needs to be proved therefore is that we are in fact rational beings for whom this description in fact holds, and then turns out to have normative implications. See Aune, *Kant's Theory of Morals*, p. 37.

13 This problem was famously formulated by the British moral philosopher Henry Sidgwick in an article originally published in *Mind* in 1888, reprinted as an appendix to the seventh edition of Sidgwick's *The Methods of Ethics* (London: Macmillan, 1907), pp. 511–16. In fact, it had been noticed as early as 1792 by Kant's earlier advocate Karl Leonhard Reinhold, in the second volume of the second edition of his *Letters on the Kantian Philosophy* (Leipzig: Göschen, 1792). It may well have been Reinhold's insistence on this problem that caused Kant to clarify his position in the *Religion*. For discussion of Reinhold's version of the objection, see Allison, *Kant's Theory of Freedom*, pp. 133–6.

14 One scholar has written a 400 page commentary just on the 17 pages of *Groundwork III*; see Dieter Schönecker, *Kant: Grundlegung III, Die Deduktion des kategorischen Imperativs* (Freiburg and Munich: Verlag Karl Alber, 1999). For a briefer version of Schönecker's discussion, although one still in German, see Schönecker and Wood, *Kants "Grundlegung zur Metaphyysik der Sitten,"* pp. 170–206; Paton, *The Categorical Imperative*, Book IV, pp. 207–53; and Onora O'Neill, "Reason and Autonomy in *Grundlegung III*," in her *Constructions of Reason*, pp. 51–65.

15 This is what Allison has dubbed the "Reciprocity Thesis"; see *Kant's Theory of Freedom*, Chapter 11, pp. 201–13.

16 There is a particularly clear presentation of this idea in Rawls, *Lectures on the History of Moral Philosophy*, pp. 285–9.

17 For a related but not identical criticism of the argument of *Groundwork III*, see Allison, *Kant's Theory of Freedom*, pp. 227–8. The gist of Allison's objection is that in this argument Kant confuses the mere possibility of a world different from the phenomenal world with its actuality, thus violating, we might add, his own distinction between "noumenon in the negative sense" and "noumenon in the positive sense."

18 There has been considerable discussion of the relation between Kant's argument in *Groundwork III* and the *Critique of Practical Reason*. Karl Ameriks argued that Kant changed the direction of his argument, from attempting to prove our freedom and from that our subjection to morality to attempting to prove our freedom from the fact of our subjec-

tion to morality, between the Groundwork and the Critique of Practical Reason in "Kant's Deduction of Freedom and Morality," Journal of the History of Philosophy 19 (1981), which subsequently became Chapter VI of his Kant's Theory of Mind: An Analysis of the Paralogisms of Pure Reason, new edition (Oxford: Clarendon Press, 2000). Ameriks's account has largely been followed by Allison, Kant's Theory of Freedom, p. 201, and Rawls, Lectures in the History of Moral Philosophy, pp. 261–2. Dieter Henrich argued that even in the Groundwork Kant had not intended to give a formal deduction of the fact of our freedom, thus that there is no great reversal between the Groundwork and the Critique of Practical Reason, in "Kants Deduktion des Sittengesetzes," in Alexander Schwan (ed.), Denken im Schatten des Nihilismus (Darmstadt: Wissenschaftliche Buchgesellschaft, 1975), pp. 55–112, translated in Paul Guyer (ed.), Kant's Groundwork of the Metaphysics of Morals: Critical Essays (Lanham, MD: Rowman and Littlefield, 1998), pp. 303–41.

19 On this interpretation, the "fact of reason" argument of the second Critique does not represent a complete departure from the reasoning of the Groundwork as a whole, but only a rejection of the argument of Groundwork III. For detailed discussions of the "fact of reason," see Beck, Commentary, pp. 166–70, and especially Rawls, Lectures on the History of Moral Philosophy, pp. 253–72.

20 I have heard it said that Kant never actually asserted "ought implies can." But he certainly does say that in the final sentence of our last quotation, and also no fewer than six times in Religion within the Boundaries of Mere Reason (6:45, 47, 49n, 50, 62, and 66). What is true is that Kant never argues for this claim, but treats it as self-evident. Because it is hard to know how one would actually go about arguing for this claim, I suggest we regard it as a second indemonstrable moral norm, alongside the moral law itself, reflecting our basic sense of when it is fair to assign responsibility. We do not think it is fair to hold people legally or morally responsible for failing to do things that it is physically impossible for them to do, nor would we hold people responsible for failing to do things that are psychologically impossible for them to do. But we do think it is fair to hold people responsible for behaving morally, so we must believe that is in their power.

21 See Lewis White Beck, Early German Philosophy: Kant and his Predecessors (Cambridge, MA: Harvard University Press, 1969), p. 435, and Manfred Kuehn, Kant: A Biography (Cambridge: Cambridge University Press, 2001), pp. 361–82, 404–9.

22 The indispensable discussion of Religion remains John Silber's introduction to the translation Religion within the Limits of Reason Alone by Theodore M. Greene and Hoyt H. Hudson (New York: Harper & Row, 1960), pp. lxxiii – cxxxiv.

23 Rawls stresses this point in Lectures on the History of Moral Philosophy, pp. 294–303.

24 There has been a tendency in recent commentary on Religion within the Boundaries of Mere Reason to interpret Kant as holding that the origin of evil is always social in character – social pressures, competition, and so on – and that evil can therefore be overcome only socially, through what Kant calls an "ethical commonwealth"; see Allen Wood, Kant's Ethical Thought, pp. 283–320; Sharon Anderson-Gold, Unnecessary Evil: History and Moral Progress in the Philosophy of Immanuel Kant (Albany, NY: State University Press of New York, 2001), pp. 25–52; and Philip J. Rossi, S.J., The Social Authority of Reason: Kant's Critique, Radical Evil, and the Destiny of Humankind (Albany, NY: State University of New York Press, 2005), pp. 67–112. But while it may be obvious that society provides both the opportunity and the temptation to choose evil, and that social institutions can provide education and encouragement for choosing good over evil, for Kant both the choice to give in to temptations to do evil and the choice to overcome such temptations must always be the free act of the individual.

25 Kant's statement that the highest good exists when an "exact relation" between happiness and morality obtains has often been understood as the claim that virtue should be rewarded with happiness and vice punished with unhappiness, and the postulation of

the existence of God is then interpreted to be necessary to make sure that both of these things happen. But there is in fact no mention of the need for divine punishment of vice in any of Kant's inferences from the need for the highest good to the existence of God. As we will see, his argument is simply that it would be irrational to pursue the happiness of all as what morality indirectly requires if we did not have a reason to believe that the achievement of that goal is possible.

26 Rawls argues that the concepts of the realm of ends and of the highest good are entirely distinct, the former being that of a moral ideal to be achieved, insofar as it can be, entirely by our own action, while the latter is the idea of a conjunction of worthiness (or unworthiness) to be happy with the happiness (or unhappiness) that is deserved, a conjunction which is not required by the moral law itself, and which can be secured only by God, not by our own actions. See *Lectures on the History of Moral Philosophy*, pp. 309– 17. There can be no doubt that Kant sometimes speaks of the highest good as if it is based on the notion of merit, requiring proportionality between worthiness (or unworthiness) and reward (or punishment). But Kant does not always speak of the highest good this way, and sometimes speaks of the highest good as that which would automatically result from morally correct action, and thus from the establishment of a realm of ends, under ideal circumstances; see especially RBMR, 6:4–6, and TP, 8:279–80. This makes sense if the realm of ends is seen to include the requirement of promoting the realization of particular ends as far as that is possible and consistent with treating all as ends in themselves, and if happiness is simply what results from the realization of ends. Rawls may not have seen this because he did not give adequate weight to the promotion of particular ends as part of what is required by the realm of ends. It is thus better to distinguish between two conceptions of the highest good, one a "secular" conception on which the highest good is what would result from the realization of the realm of ends, and the other a "religious" conception of divine reward or retribution in response to worthiness or unworthiness to be happy. For a similar distinction, see Andrews Reath, "Two Conceptions of the Highest Good in Kant," *Journal of the History of Philosophy* 26 (1988): 593–619. Beck makes a related distinction between the "maximal" conception of the highest good, which requires the realization of maximal happiness to complement the maximization of virtue, and the "juridical" conception, which requires the proportionality of happiness to worthiness to be happy, and thus may not require the maximization of happiness at all if virtue has not been maximized; see *Commentary*, pp. 268–9.

27 See Beck, *Commentary*, p. 277. As we shall shortly see, however, in his last manuscripts Kant often insists that while we must form the *idea* of God, we have no ground to think that God is a *substance* that exists outside our own idea of Him. See my *Kant's System of Nature and Freedom*, Chapter 11.

28 For further discussion of the meaning of a "postulate" of pure practical reason, see Beck, *Commentary*, pp. 245–58, 260–65; Paul Guyer, "From a Practical Point of View," in *Kant on Freedom, Law, and Happiness*, pp. 333–71; and Paul Guyer, "Kant's Deductions of the Principles of Right," in Mark Timmons, editor, *Kant's Metaphysics of Morals: Interpretative Essays* (Oxford: Oxford University Press, 2002), pp. 24–64, reprinted in Guyer, *Kant's System of Nature and Freedom* (Oxford: Clarendon Press, 2005), pp. 198–242, at pp. 208–17.

29 See also Beck, *Commentary*, p. 271.

30 See ibid., pp. 269–70. It should be noted that in the *Religion*, Kant accompanies his claim that the *noumenal* complete conversion of the will from evil to good is always possible with the claim that the *phenomenal* effects of such a conversion will always be gradual, and thus that the completeness of the conversion can in fact be known only to God, not to any mortal, even oneself (6:74–5). But this cannot yield an argument for immortality, since there is no moral necessity that any mortal know about anyone's moral

conversion or complete achievement of the worthiness to be happy, and, in any case, Kant never suggests elsewhere that he means to argue for *phenomenal* immortality.

SEVEN KANT'S SYSTEM OF DUTIES I

1 Corr, letter to Johann Heinrich Lambert, December 31, 1765, 10:55–7.
2 Among those who have recently argued that Kant's principle of political right or justice is not founded on the fundamental principle of morality itself are Allen Wood, Marcus Willaschek, and Thomas Pogge; their articles appear in Mark Timmons (ed.), *Kant's Metaphysics of Morals: Interpretative Essays* (Oxford: Oxford University Press, 2002), along with my argument against that approach, "Kant's Deductions of the Principles of Right," also reprinted in my *Kant's System of Nature and Freedom* (Oxford: Clarendon Press, 2005), pp. 198–242. A discussion of this debate by Robert Pippin appears in Paul Guyer (ed.), *The Cambridge Companion to Kant and Modern Philosophy* (Cambridge: Cambridge University Press, 2006).
3 As is briefly noted by Onora Nell (O'Neill), *Acting on Principle: An Essay on Kantian Ethics* (New York: Columbia University Press, 1975), p. 91n45.
4 For other discussions of the complexities of the distinction between juridical and ethical duties, see Nell (O'Neill), *Acting on Principle*, Chapter 4, pp. 43–58; Mary J. Gregor, *The Laws of Freedom: A Study of Kant's Method of Applying the Categorical Imperative in the Metaphysik der Sitten* (Oxford: Basil Blackwell, 1963), Chapter VII, pp. 95–112; and John Rawls, *Lectures on the History of Moral Philosophy* (Cambridge, MA: Harvard University Press, 2000), pp. 185–7.
5 See, for example, LEC, 27:327–34; MMV, 27:712–29; MM, Doctrine of Virtue, §18, 6:443–4 (in §17, Kant also gives an analysis of duties regarding but not directly to animals and other non-human parts of nature); and RBMR, especially Book Three, Section V, 6:102–9, and Book Four, Second Part, 6:167–202.
6 In the Introduction to the "Doctrine of Virtue," Kant argues that one cannot have a direct duty to make oneself happy, because duty requires overcoming an aversion but one has no aversion to one's own happiness, although he also concedes that one might have an indirect duty to make oneself sufficiently happy in order to avoid temptation to doing something immoral (section V, 6:387–8). But he eventually acknowledges that "all *others* with the exception of myself would not be *all*" (§27, 6:451), and that therefore the duty to promote the realization of the freely chosen ends of human beings and thereby their happiness must include the promotion of my own ends and therefore my own happiness. In practice, of course, taking the steps necessary for one's own long-term happiness requires considerable constraint of one's current inclinations in so many cases that examples are hardly necessary, so the premise of Kant's initial argument that one's own happiness cannot be a duty because one simply desires it naturally is obviously false.
7 Barbara Herman makes the location of the foundation of a prohibition of "murder and mayhem" in Kant's moral theory more problematic than it need be precisely because she sees the "Doctrine of Right" as concerning only "institutional rights of property and contract," thus omitting reference to Kant's category of the innate right to personal freedom. See *The Practice of Moral Judgment* (Cambridge, MA: Harvard University Press, 1993), p. 115.
8 See especially "On the Common Saying: That may be correct in theory but it is of no use in practice," part II, and "Toward Perpetual Peace," First Definitive Article, 8:349–53.
9 See for example the textbook that Kant used for his lectures on natural right, Gottfried Achenwall and Johann Stephan Putter, *Elementa Iuris Naturae*, §145 (modern Latin-German edition by Jan Schröder [Frankfurt am Main: Insel Verlag, 1995]).

10 See especially RBMR, e.g., 6:45, 47, 49n, 50, 62, and 66.

11 Allen Wood has stressed that Kant almost invariably derives the duties of virtue from the formula of humanity as an end in itself rather than from the formula of universal law; see *Kant's Ethical Thought*, pp. 139–50.

12 Thus Jeanine Grenberg has recently argued for the centrality of humility to Kant's account of virtue, where humility is interpreted neither as a self-demeaning comparison of oneself to other people nor abasement before an impossible standard of moral perfection, but as a realistic assessment of the limits of human nature, particularly of the need to be vigilant for the often hidden influence of self-love. See her *Kant and the Ethics of Humility* (Cambridge: Cambridge University Press, 2005).

13 Robert B. Louden usefully calls this the "species-specific" application of Kant's general moral principles; see *Kant's Impure Ethics: From Rational Beings to Human Beings* (New York and Oxford: Oxford University Press, 2000), Chapter 1 generally and pp. 12–13 particularly.

14 Kant's notorious argument that one must not lie even to a would-be murderer in order to protect the life of his innocent target thus does not turn on a claim that one owes the truth to the murderer, but on the claim that one owes it to oneself only to tell the truth. Of course this does not mean that one must always tell all of the truth; but if one cannot avoid answering a question, then one owes it to oneself to answer it truthfully. See "On a Supposed Right to Lie from Philanthropy" (1797); for further discussion, see Christine M. Korsgaard, "The Right to Lie: Kant on Dealing with Evil," in her *Creating the Kingdom of Ends* (Cambridge: Cambridge University Press, 1996), pp. 133–58.

15 I have stressed this point in "Duty and Inclination," in *Kant and the Experience of Freedom* (Cambridge: Cambridge University Press, 1993), pp. 335–93. Marcia Baron has made the point by describing respect for the moral law as a second-order, "general, overarching maxim" that can be used to regulate first-order motivations of feeling; *Kantian Ethics Almost without Apology*, p. 179. See also Nancy Sherman, *Making a Necessity of Virtue: Aristotle and Kant on Virtue* (Cambridge: Cambridge University Press, 1997), pp. 141–58.

16 See, for example, T.M. Scanlon's influential characterization of the subject matter of ethics as *What We Owe to Each Other* (Cambridge, MA: Harvard University Press, 1998).

17 See Barbara Herman, "Mutual Aid and Respect for Persons," in *The Practice of Moral Judgment*, Chapter 3, pp. 44–72.

18 Here Kant does not use "aesthetic" in its specific sense connoting a connection to natural or artistic beauty, but in its general sense of having to do with any sort of feelings.

19 This example comes from Herman, *The Practice of Moral Judgment*, pp. 4–5. Bruce Aune gives a general account of why acting on a beneficent feeling toward one person might not always be the right thing to do, since in some particular circumstances doing so may conflict with duties owed to others or oneself (*Kant's Theory of Morals*, pp. 22–3).

EIGHT KANT'S SYSTEM OF DUTIES II

1 For example, by John Ladd in his translation of the first half of the *Metaphysics of Morals* as "The Metaphysical Elements of Justice" (Indianapolis: Bobbs-Merrill, 1965), second edition (Indianapolis: Hackett Publishing Company, 1999).

2 While Kant's universal principle of right is often thought of as following from the universal law formulation of the categorical imperative, some writers do present it as following from the formula of humanity as an end in itself (as, so I argued in chapter 5, does the universal law formulation itself). See Mary J. Gregor, *Laws of Freedom: A Study of Kant's Method of Applying the Categorical Imperative in the Metaphysik der Sitten* (Oxford: Basil

Blackwell, 1963), pp. 39—40, and Bruce Aune, *Kant's Theory of Morals* (Princeton, NJ: Princeton University Press, 1979), p. 137.

3 Of course, criminal law often requires specific intent (*mens rea*), for example, prior intent in the case of murder rather than accidental homicide; but this is simply, as the latter term suggests, to exclude accidental harms which are regrettable but for which people should not be punished. But the law still may not care about the agent's deepest *motivation*, that is, *why* someone formed a criminal intent. The concern for "motive" in addition to "means" and "opportunity" in a criminal trial should be only epistemological, that is, showing that the accused had a motive for the crime increases the probability that it was that person and not someone else who committed the crime. The motive is not necessarily part of the crime itself.

4 This question goes unasked by almost all commentators on Kant's argument for the coercive enforceability of duties of right, who accept his argument that being a hindrance to a hindrance to freedom is a sufficient condition for coercion. See for example Gregor, *Laws of Freedom*, p. 43, and "Kant's Theory of Property," *Review of Metaphysics* 41 (1988): 757—97, at pp. 771—2. Leslie A. Mulholland, *Kant's System of Rights* (New York: Columbia University Press, 1990), pp. 186—7, recognizes that Kant's coercion proof needs a lemma to prove that a hindrance to a hindrance to freedom can actually preserve freedom as opposed to simply redoubling coercion.

5 This is the solution proposed by Bernd Ludwig in *Kants Rechtslehre*, Kant-Forschungen, vol. II (Hamburg: Felix Meiner Verlag, 1988), p. 97.

6 One might object that the armed robber who says "Your money or your life" leaves his victim with freedom of choice. But while he leaves his victim with *some* choice, he certainly puts him into a situation which the victim would not have freely chosen and in which his choices are severely and unlawfully restricted: thus, by no choice of his own, he can no longer choose to have both his money and his life.

7 Some discussions make it sound as if the *antecedent threat* of a coercive sanction is not a hindrance to the freedom of a would-be perpetrator, but that the *subsequent execution* of the sanction for deeds already done is; see Aune, *Kant's Theory of Morals*, p. 163. But of course a system of threats would not be an effective deterrent unless those threats were sufficiently often carried out; and as the present analysis has suggested, when the threat of the deterrent punishment is antecedently known, the criminal can be regarded as having freely chosen to risk suffering its execution (even of course if he does not like it). Aune goes some way toward conceding this point on p. 164. Mulholland stresses that the execution of a punishment should not be regarded as retribution for the deed done, but a condition for the efficacy of the deterrence of an unlawful hindrance of freedom; *Kant's System of Rights*, pp. 189—90. Kant himself suggests this point when he writes that "All punishments by authority are deterrent, either to deter the transgressor himself, or to warn others by his example"; *LEC*, 27:286.

8 For a clear discussion of Kant's concept of the innate right to freedom, see Gregor, *Laws of Freedom*, pp. 46—9. Katrin Flikschuh, *Kant and Modern Political Philosophy* (Cambridge: Cambridge University Press, 2000), p. 119, is misled by Kant's mention of innate right only in the introduction to the "Doctrine of Right" to argue that the work is concerned only with acquired rights. Kant's justification of the enforcement of rights by coercion clearly applies to both innate and acquired right; the latter takes up so much more space in Kant's exposition only because he thinks there is a philosophical puzzle about how we can acquire rights to anything other than our own person, while innate right flows so directly from the necessity of treating humanity as an end rather than a mere means that it needs no elaborate explanation.

9 Of course, once a judicial system has been established, it can create a duty not to state a falsehood or even to tell the truth in specific circumstances, e.g., the duty to tell "the

whole truth and nothing but the truth" when testifying under oath in a court proceeding.

10 Because a property right cannot be established by a unilateral relation between one person and an object but only by an agreement among persons, Kant calls it "intelligible" rather than "physical" or sometimes even "noumenal" rather than "phenomenal"; MM, Doctrine of Right, §§1, 5–6, 6:245, 249–50. For useful discussion of this distinction, see Gregor, *Laws of Freedom*, pp. 52–3, and Mulholland, *Kant's System of Rights*, pp. 241–2.

11 See John Locke, *Second Treatise of Government*, chapter V, §27. Discussions of the difference between Kant's and Locke's theories of property may be found in Wolfgang Kersting, *Kant über Recht* (Paderborn: Mentis, 2004), pp. 71–7, and Howard Williams, *Kant's Political Philosophy* (New York: St. Martin's Press, 1983), pp. 86–91.

12 In his own "deduction" of the "postulate," Kant makes explicit only that mere objects have no rights against us and that it would therefore be irrational to deny ourselves the possibility of their use and control (MM, Doctrine of Right, §6, 6:250). Several authors have recognized that the argument requires a second step, postulating the consent of others to our control of particular objects. See Gregor, *Laws of Freedom*, pp. 55–6, and "Kant's Theory of Property," pp. 775–6, and Mulholland, *Kant's System of Rights*, p. 253.

13 Of course even in a system of property-rights which enjoys general consent there can be dispute over particular property-claims; in a just system those disputes will be adjudicated within a judicial system that also enjoys the consent of all involved.

14 In her treatment of the "postulate," Gregor stresses that the possibility of property requires civil society or the state in order to give *assurance* to those who forgo claims to some property that their own claims to other property will be recognized, and that it is therefore rational for them to do so (*Laws of Freedom*, pp. 57–9, and "Kant's Theory of Property," p. 779). However, this omits the prior point that it is only *moral* to claim property rights to which others can agree, which claims then need to be guaranteed through the power of a state because of the imperfection of human nature and thus the tendency of people sometimes to take that to which they have no right unless forcibly prevented from doing so.

15 This is the source of Locke's famous "proviso" that even though one can create property unilaterally by mixing their labor with an object, they should also be sure to leave enough for others: God has created nature for the benefit of all human beings; see *Second Treatise of Government*, Chapter V, §34.

16 As Kant points out in "What is Enlightenment?": "the citizen cannot refuse to discharge the taxes imposed upon him" (7:37).

17 There has been debate about the place of "welfare legislation" or state support for the poor in the literature on Kant's political philosophy. Many authors have interpreted Kant to hold that the state, which has no concern with the happiness or welfare of its citizens but only with their rights, is justified in enforcing welfare legislation only insofar as that is necessary to preserve the state as a political entity, e.g., Aune, *Kant's Theory of Morals*, pp. 157–60, and Williams, *Kant's Political Philosophy*, 196–8, although as Aune points out the state does not need to preserve every one of its citizens in order to preserve itself as an entity. In response, Allen D. Rosen has defended the view that the ground for welfare legislation is the *ethical* duty of beneficence, transferred from the people to the government in a state; see *Kant's Theory of Justice* (Ithaca, NY: Cornell University Press, 1993), pp. 174–9, 183–5, 191. Alexander Kaufman has in turn objected to Rosen that this erases the boundary between duties of right and duties of justice, and instead argued that the state has the duty to provide whatever level of support is necessary to ensure that there is equality of the value of freedom for all; see *Welfare in the Kantian State* (Oxford: Clarendon Press, 1999), pp. 28–32. The approach taken here differs from all of these by arguing that a rightful system of property rights

that could rightfully be defended by a state must be one to which all affected could freely consent, which they would do only if guaranteed some acceptable minimal level of property rights themselves; thus the maintenance of at least some minimal property rights is a necessary condition of the rightful existence of the state itself.

18 A morganatic marriage is one between a person (typically the man) of a high estate and another (the woman) of a low estate, in which the latter agrees to forgo the privileges that might be inherited from the former not only for herself but for her children.

19 In real life, of course, the powers of the state are not really so neatly divided. In the U.S. Constitution, at least since *Marbury v. Madison*, the judiciary, in the person of the Supreme Court, has the last word against the executive when it comes to the interpretation of the law, but is dependent upon the executive for the enforcement of the law, and thus in fact dependent upon the good will of the executive for the application of Supreme Court decisions to itself. And since the Supreme Court can declare laws passed by Congress to be unconstitutional, the legislature does not in fact have undivided sovereignty – a fact decried by those who would replace "activist judges" with "strict constructionists" (or would do so when they think that is in their current economic or ideological interest).

20 Locke, *Second Treatise of Government*, Chapter XIX.

21 Christine M. Korsgaard argues for this position in "Taking the Law into our own Hands: Kant on the Right to Revolution," in Andrews Reath, Barbara Herman, and Christine M. Korsgaard (eds), *Reclaiming the History of Ethics: Essays for John Rawls* (Cambridge: Cambridge University Press, 1997), pp. 297–328, at 316–21.

22 Frederick C. Beiser criticizes it for confusing a *de facto* state with a *de jure* state, that is, confusing an actual regime whether just or not with a regime that satisfies the ideal of justice. See his *Enlightenment, Revolution, and Romanticism: The Genesis of Modern German Political Thought, 1790–1800* (Cambridge, MA: Harvard University Press, 1992), pp. 46–7. Rosen makes a converse objection to Kant's argument, objecting that destroying an existing *government* is not necessarily the same as destroying an existing *political society* (*Kant's Theory of Justice*, p. 165). In other words, he does not accept Kant's claim that a people can exist *as a people* only if they have an extant government. He also objects to Kant's argument that the people cannot be the ruler over their ruler that the *highest* power in a state need not have *unrestricted* power (p. 167). But even so, in case of a dispute between the people and their ruler over the limits of the latter's authority, there will still be need for an arbitrator, and thus Rosen does not show how to evade Kant's worry about the need for a (non-existent) third party to referee such a dispute.

23 Kant's consistency on this point is an objection to Beiser's claim that Kant's advocacy of reform rather than a right to rebellion in the 1790s represents a loss of courage and a relapse into conservatism; see *Enlightenment, Revolution, and Romanticism*, pp. 53–6. Kant's antipathy toward a right to rebellion was deeply seated in his premise that we have a duty to enter into the civil condition, and his insistence that the people have a right to ask for reform was equally deeply seated in his premise that the state has a duty to realize the ideal of justice.

24 See the editors' introductions to both the *Religion* and the *Conflict of the Faculties* in Immanuel Kant, *Religion and Rational Theology*, ed. Allen W. Wood and George Di Giovanni (Cambridge: Cambridge University Press, 1996), pp. 41–50 and 235–6, as well as the description of this episode in Kuehn, *Kant: A Biography*, pp. 361–82, 404–9.

25 The difference between the form of government and the form of sovereignty or better between the spirit of a regime and its mere structure or between how a state is ruled and who rules it, is discussed by Williams, *Kant's Political Philosophy*, p. 173.

26 William Penn, *An Essay Towards the Present and Future Peace of Europe by the Establishment of an European Dyet, Parliament, or Estates* (London, 1693), reprint edited by Peter van den Dungen (Hildesheim: Georg Olms Verlag, 1983); Jean-Jacques Rousseau, *Jugement sur la Paix*

Perpétuelle (1756/82), in Stanley Hoffmann and David P. Fidler (eds), *Rousseau on International Relations* (Oxford: Clarendon Press, 1991), a response to the "Plan for a Perpetual Peace in Europe" of 1712 by the Abbé Charles Irénée Castel de Saint-Pierre, translated in David Williams, (ed.), *The Enlightenment* (Cambridge: Cambridge University Press, 1999), pp. 355–63; Jeremy Bentham, *A Plan for a Universal and Perpetual Peace*, composed 1786–89 although published only in 1843 in *The Works of Jeremy Bentham*, ed. J. Bowring, vol. II (Edinburgh, 1843), pp. 546–60. For a detailed discussion of the historical context of Kant's essay, see Georg Cavallar, *Kant and the Theory and Practice of International Right* (Cardiff: University of Wales Press, 1999).

27 Among those who argue that Kant intends a federation of republics without powers of enforcement to be only a way-station on the way to the ideal of a true world-republic, see Williams, *Kant's Political Philosophy*, pp. 256–7, and Pauline Kleingeld, "Kants Argument für den Völkerbund," in Herta Nagl-Docerkal and Rudolph Langthaler (eds), *Recht – Geschichte – Religion: Die Bedeutung Kants für die Gegenwart* (Berlin: Akademie Verlag, 2004), pp. 99–112. However, since Kant argues that republics will have neither cause nor will to make war upon one another, it is not clear why he should have thought that a mere league of republics would need any enforcement powers once all its members had in fact become genuine republics.

28 And so he has been read by many commentators, who therefore treat the argument of *Perpetual Peace* as a teleological-historical argument that can only be parallel to Kant's moral theory of international justice rather than a part of it; see for example Kersting, *Kant über Recht*, pp. 163–8. I will suggest here that what Kant means to argue is that a guarantee of the *possibility* of perpetual peace is a necessary condition for the morally mandatory effort to bring it about.

29 In the *Critique of Practical Reason*, see especially the "Critical Elucidation of the Analytic of Pure Practical Reason," 5:89–106.

30 Howard Williams recognizes this point when he writes:

> The natural path of history may lead mankind gradually toward a more civilized and stable international order but, at the end of the day, justice and peace have to be instituted as a result of conscious moral choice ... at the international level Kant has unavoidably to look to the moral improvement of mankind as the only possible element that can ultimately ensure peace.
>
> (*Kant's Political Philosophy*, p. 260)

NINE THE BEAUTIFUL, SUBLIME, AND MORALLY GOOD

1 See T.M. Knox, translator, *Hegel's Aesthetics: Lectures on the Fine Arts*, 2 vols. (Oxford: Clarendon Press, 1975).

2 I have discussed Kant's concept of reflecting judgment and the relations among its several varieties at length in "Kant's Principles of Reflecting Judgment," in Paul Guyer (ed.), *Kant's Critique of the Power of Judgment: Critical Essays* (Lanham, MD: Rowman and Littlefield, 2003), pp. 1–61. See also Christel Fricke, *Kants Theorie des reinen Geschmacksurteils* (Berlin and New York: Walter de Gruyter, 1990).

3 For the claim that Kant does not intend the distinction between "pure" beauty and what will follow, namely "adherent" beauty, as a hierarchy of value, see Eva Schaper, *Studies in Kant's Aesthetics* (Edinburgh: Edinburgh University Press, 1979), pp. 78–98; my "Free and Adherent Beauty: A Modest Proposal," *British Journal of Aesthetics* 42 (October, 2002), 357–66, reprinted in my *Values of Beauty: Historical Essays in Aesthetics* (Cambridge: Cambridge University Press, 2005); and James Kirwan, *The Aesthetic in Kant* (London and New York: Continuum, 2004), pp. 32–3.

4 Only in the past few decades has the topic of natural beauty again become a topic for discussion in philosophical aesthetics. For a representative selection of papers, beginning with Ronald Hepburn's seminal "Contemporary Aesthetics and the Neglect of Natural Beauty" (1966), see Allen Carlson and Arnold Berleant (eds), The Aesthetics of the Natural Environment (Peterborough: Broadview Press, 2004).

5 Hutcheson's 1725 Inquiry into the Original of our Ideas of Beauty and Virtue (4th edn, London, 1738), might be considered the first treatise on aesthetics by a British academic, although the discipline would only receive its name ten years later from the German Alexander Gottlieb Baumgarten, who first used it in his dissertation Meditationes philosophicae de nonnullis ad poema pertinentibus ("Philosophical mediations on some matters pertaining to poetry") and then published a massive although incomplete Aesthetica in 1750–58, the first treatise to use the new name of the discipline as its title.

6 There is also an extensive literature about it. I presented my original interpretation of Kant's conception of the free play of the cognitive faculties in Kant and the Claims of Taste (1979, 2nd edn: Cambridge: Cambridge University Press, 1997), Chapter 3; I have categorized a wide variety of interpretative approaches and refined my own approach in "The Harmony of the Faculties Revisited," Chapter 3 of my Values of Beauty: Historical Essays in Aesthetics.

7 See, for example, Dieter Henrich, "Kant's Explanation of Aesthetic Judgment," in his Aesthetic Judgment and the Moral Image of the World: Studies in Kant (Stanford, CA: Stanford University Press, 1992), p. 38, and Donald W. Crawford, Kant's Aesthetic Theory (Madison, WI: University of Wisconsin Press, 1974), p. 90.

8 See Fred L. Rush, Jr., "The Harmony of the Faculties," Kant-Studien 92 (2001): 38–61, at p. 52, and Henry E. Allison, Kant's Theory of Taste: A Reading of the Critique of Aesthetic Judgment (Cambridge: Cambridge University Press, 2001), p. 171.

9 See Kant and the Claims of Taste, Chapter 5. For an extended discussion of Kant's concept of form, see Theodore E. Uehling, Jr., The Notion of Form in Kant's Critique of Aesthetic Judgment (The Hague: Mouton, 1971).

10 I have analyzed these possibilities more closely in "Free and Adherent Beauty: A Modest Proposal," cited above, n.3, and "Beauty and Utility in Eighteenth Century Aesthetics." Eighteenth Century Studies 35 (2002): 439–53, also reprinted in Values of Beauty. See also Eva Schaper, "Free and Dependent Beauty," in her Studies in Kant's Aesthetics, pp. 78–98, and Kirwan, The Aesthetic in Kant, Chapters 2 and 7.

11 See my "Kant's Conception of Fine Art," Journal of Aesthetics and Art Criticism 52 (1994): 175–85, reprinted as Chapter 12 of the second edition of Kant and the Claims of Taste. For further works on Kant's conception of fine art, see Salim Kemal, Kant and Fine Art: An Essay on the Philosophy of Fine Art and Culture (Oxford: Clarendon Press, 1986), and Kirk Pillow, Sublime Understanding: Aesthetic Reflection in Kant and Hegel (Cambridge, MA: MIT Press, 2000). Each of these works makes controversial claims, however: Kemal, that Kant regards beautiful art as morally more significant than beautiful nature; and Pillow, that Kant's conception of the experience of art should be understood through his analysis of the experience of the sublime rather than that of beauty.

12 Kant's theory of genius has not received the attention in philosophical commentaries on his aesthetic theory that might have been expected; this is certainly true of the first edition of Kant and the Claims of Taste. But for some attempt to remedy this deficiency, see my "Genius and the Canon of Art: A Second Dialectic of Aesthetic Judgment," Monist 66 (1983): 167–88, reprinted as Chapter 8 of my Kant and the Experience of Freedom (Cambridge: Cambridge University Press, 1993), pp. 275–303, and "Exemplary Originality: Genius, Universality, and Individuality," in Berys Gaut and Paisley Livingston (eds), The Creation of Art: New Essays in Philosophical Aesthetics (Cambridge: Cambridge University Press, 2003), pp. 116–37, reprinted in Values of Beauty. See also Donald W. Crawford, "Kant's Theory of Imagination," in Ted Cohen and Paul Guyer

(eds), *Essays in Kant's Aesthetics* (Chicago: University of Chicago Press, 1982), pp. 151–78, reprinted in *Kant's Critique of the Power of Judgment: Critical Essays*, pp. 143–70, and Timothy Gould, "The Audience of Originality: Kant and Wordsworth on the Reception of Genius," in *Essays in Kant's Aesthetics*, pp. 179–94. For a treatment of Kant's concept in the context of an extended history of German thought about genius, see Jochen Schmidt, *Die Geschichte des Genie-Gedankens in der deutschen Literatur, Philosophie und Politik* (Darmstadt: Wissenschaftliche Buchgesellschaft, 1985), vol. I, pp. 354–80.

13 Kant discussed the classification of the arts for many years in his lectures on anthropology, which he began in 1772–73. For some discussion, see my "Beauty, Freedom, and Morality: Kant's *Lectures on Anthropology* and the Development of his Aesthetic Theory," in Brian Jacobs and Patrick Kain (eds), *Essays on Kant's Anthropology* (Cambridge: Cambridge University Press, 2003), pp. 135–63, reprinted in *Values of Beauty*.

14 This topic was popularized in Britain, beginning with Edmund Burke's *Philosophical Enquiry into the Origin of Our Ideas of the Sublime and Beautiful* (1757), and then imported into Germany through Moses Mendelssohn's review of Burke in the following year, "Philosophische Untersuchung des Ursprungs unserer Ideen vom Erhabenen und Schönen," reprinted in Mendelssohn, *Ästhetische Schriften in Auswahl*, edited by Otto F. Best (Darmstadt: Wissenschaftliche Buchgesellschaft, 1974), pp. 247–65. For the classical history of the subject, see Samuel Monk, *The Sublime: A Study of Critical Theories in XVIII-Century England* (1935; reprinted Ann Arbor, MI: University of Michigan Press, 1960). For an extensive selection of pre-Kantian British texts, see Andrew Ashfield and Peter de Bolla, *The Sublime: A Reader in British Eighteenth-Century Aesthetic Theory* (Cambridge: Cambridge University Press, 1996). For a work drawing on the entire European discussion of the sublime, see Baldine Saint Girons, *Fiat lux: Une philosophie du sublime* (Paris: Quai Voltaire, 1993). For an extended interpretation of Kant's theory, see Paul Crowther, *The Kantian Sublime: From Morality to Art* (Oxford: Clarendon Press, 1989).

15 I have developed my criticism of Kant's deduction of judgments of taste in detail in *Kant and the Claims of Taste*, Chapters 7–9. Before my book, Donald W. Crawford, in *Kant's Aesthetic Theory* (Madison, WI: University of Wisconsin Press, 1974), and, after it, Kenneth F. Rogerson, *Kant's Aesthetics: The Roles of Form and Expression* (Lanham, MD: University Press of America, 1986), defended Kant's deduction by arguing that the ultimate connection of aesthetic judgment to morality provides the guarantee of agreement that our cognitive faculties alone cannot provide. I have responded that this defense is of no avail, because the moral significance of taste is meant to presuppose rather than prove the intersubjective validity of taste; see the Introduction to *Kant and the Experience of Freedom*, pp. 12–19. Anthony Savile has offered a variant of this defense, arguing that once aesthetic objects are laden with moral significance through the theory of aesthetic ideas, then it becomes imperative for individuals to agree in their assessment of particular objects because each object will express an important moral idea in a unique way; see his *Aesthetic Reconstructions: The Seminal Writings of Lessing, Kant, and Schiller* (Oxford: Basil Blackwell, 1987), pp. 168–73, 179–82. But it seems implausible to suppose that morality requires that each important idea be presented to each individual in every possible way. More recently, Henry E. Allison has held that our possession of common cognitive capacities is sufficient to guarantee agreement in response to particular objects under ideal circumstances, in *Kant's Theory of Taste: A Reading of the Critique of Aesthetic Judgment* (Cambridge: Cambridge University Press, 2001), pp. 179–82, while Kirwan has argued that the assumption that everyone should respond to objects of taste in the same way is so implausible that it can only be an inconsistent addition to Kant's basic phenomenology of taste, which holds only that every judgment *feels* to its subject *as if* it were necessarily and universally valid (*The Aesthetic in Kant*, pp. 22–8). Obviously, the success of Kant's deduction remains deeply controversial.

16 For further discussion of Kant's claim that the beautiful is the symbol of the morally good, see Ted Cohen, "Why Beauty is a Symbol of Morality," in Cohen and Guyer, *Essays in Kant's Aesthetics*, pp. 221–36; G. Felicitas Munzel, "The Beautiful is the Symbol of the Morally-Good: Kant's Philosophical Basis of Proof for the Idea of the Morally-Good," *Journal of the History of Philosophy* 33 (1995): 301–30; Allison, *Kant's Theory of Taste*, pp. 236–67; Mihaela Fistioc, *The Beautiful Shape of the Good: Platonic and Pythagorean Themes in Kant's Critique of the Power of Judgment* (London and New York: Routledge, 2002), which puts Kant's theory in the context of neo-Platonism, as is also suggested by Kirwan, *The Aesthetic in Kant*, pp. 172–3; and Heiner Bielefeldt, *Symbolic Representation in Kant's Practical Philosophy* (Cambridge: Cambridge University Press, 2003), pp. 121–5.

17 See my "The Symbols of Freedom in Kant's Aesthetics," in Hermann Parret (ed.), *Kant's Ästhetik – Kant's Aesthetics – L'esthétique de Kant* (Berlin and New York: Walter de Gruyter, 1998), pp. 338–55, reprinted in *Values of Beauty*.

TEN FREEDOM AND NATURE

1 Christian Wolff, *Vernünftige Gedanken von der Absichten der natürlichen Dinge*, 2nd edn (Leipzig and Frankfurt: Renger, 1726), Chapter II, §8, p. 6.

2 Ibid., Chapter II, §13, p. 16.

3 Ibid., Chapter II, §14, p. 19.

4 Ibid., Chapter II, §9, p. 7.

5 Ibid., Chapter II, §11, p. 12.

6 Ibid., Chapter VII, §66, p. 97.

7 *Dialogues Concerning Natural Religion*, Part I; in David Hume, *The Natural History of Religions and Dialogues Concerning Natural Religion*, ed. A. Wayne Colver and John Valdimir Price (Oxford: Clarendon Press, 1976), pp. 151–2.

8 That is, after they were translated into German and thus after Kant had published the first *Critique*. But since Hume had already presented the essence of the argument of the *Dialogues* in Chapter 11 of *An Enquiry Concerning Human Understanding*, first published in 1748 and translated into German by 1755, Kant had long been familiar with the essence of Hume's argument.

9 *Dialogues Concerning Natural Religion*, p. 245.

10 Peter McLaughlin in particular has argued that the aspect of our ordinary conception of causation that makes it unsuitable for the explanation of characteristic organic processes is not that we ordinarily assume that a cause must be temporally antecedent or at least not successive to its effect, but rather that the character of a whole is always the effect of the character of its parts and not vice versa; see his *Kant's Critique of Teleology in Biological Explanation: Antinomy and Teleology* (Lewiston: Edwin Mellen Press, 1990), pp. 152–6.

11 Kant made this argument more than once, also including it in his lectures on metaphysics (e.g., 28:275). For this extract and further discussion, see my "Organisms and the Unity of Science," originally in Eric Watkins (ed.), *Kant and the Sciences* (Oxford: Oxford University Press, 2001), pp. 259–81, reprinted as Chapter 5 of my *Kant's System of Nature and Freedom* (Oxford: Clarendon Press, 2005), pp. 86–111, at pp. 96–8.

12 In his article "Kant's Antinomy of Teleological Judgment" (*Southern Journal of Philosophy* XXX (Supplement, 1991): 25–42), Henry Allison bases his account of the antinomy of teleological judgment on the account of discursivity suggested in §76, while Peter McLaughlin, in *Kant's Critique of Teleology* (pp. 169–76), bases his interpretation of the antinomy on the account suggested in §77. As I have just suggested, each of these interpretations has a basis in Kant's text. As I will now suggest, each faces a philosophical problem of its own.

13 For examples of such commentators, see McLaughlin, *Kant's Critique of Teleology*, p. 138, n. 5, and Allison, "Kant's Antinomy," p. 29 n. 1. See also Lewis White Beck, *A Commentary to Kant's Critique of Practical Reason*, pp. 192–4.

14 See McFarland, *Kant's Concept of Teleology*, p. 121, Allison, "Kant's Antinomy," p. 29–30, and McLaughlin, *Kant's Critique of Teleology*, pp. 134. Indeed, McLaughlin argues that if Kant is to present a distinctive antinomy of judgment rather than reason, he must intend that the two maxims about judging and not merely the thesis and antithesis about the things themselves conflict (p. 135).

15 My suggestion that Kant's ultimate solution to the antinomy of teleological judgment depends upon the ascribing purposiveness to the supersensible ground of nature is hardly new; see McFarland, *Kant's Concept of Teleology*, pp. 121–2. However, McFarland does not emphasize Kant's view that to see nature in this way inevitably leads us to see its mechanical laws as themselves instruments for the realization of a final end, as I am about to do.

16 I do not think this point has been made as clear in the literature on Kant as it needs to be. Allen W. Wood has argued that we do not need to cooperate with the teleological tendency of history understood as a natural process unless we have moral reasons to endorse the "goals" of history (*Kant*, Oxford: Blackwell Publishing, 2005, pp. 119–21), but has not emphasized the converse point that history by itself can never achieve our moral goals of autonomy and virtue themselves, and thus also cannot achieve the kind of happiness demanded by the ideal of the highest good, which must be achieved through virtue. William A. Galston draws attention to the difference between historical processes that can compel outward compliance with moral requirements and genuine "morality," which "consists in the free choice of an intention that is the product or reflection of freedom" (*Kant and the Problem of History*, Chicago: University of Chicago Press, 1975, pp. 242–30), but does not connect this to the distinction between mere discipline and virtue. Yirmiahu Yovel does draw attention to Kant's distinction between the cultures of skill and of discipline while also pointing out that while the latter "cultivates . . . freedom of choice" it "is still a far cry from morality proper" (*Kant and the Philosophy of History*, Princeton, NJ: Princeton University Press, 1980, pp. 184–5), so he comes closest to anticipating my present point.

17 I have defended this interpretation of the highest good in a number of publications, especially "Ends of Reason and Ends of Nature: The Place of Teleology in Kant's Ethics," *Journal of Value Inquiry* 36 (2002): 161–86, reprinted as Chapter 8 of *Kant's System of Nature and Freedom*.

18 I have in mind especially Kant's notorious 1797 essay "On a supposed right to lie from philanthropy" (8:425–30). For further discussion, see Christine M. Korsgaard, "The Right to Lie: Kant on Dealing with Evil," in her *Creating the Kingdom of Ends* (Cambridge: Cambridge University Press, 1996), pp. 133–58, and my "Kant's System of Duties," in *Kant's System of Nature and Freedom*, pp. 243–74, at pp. 270–2.

19 I borrow the phrase "lexical ordering," of course, from John Rawls's lexical ordering of the principles of justice; see *A Theory of Justice*, rev. edn (Cambridge, MA: Harvard University Press, 1999), pp. 37–8, 53–4, 130–1.

20 Such a lexical ordering of the duty not to destroy rational agents as more fundamental than the duty not to restrict the free exercise of their agency is what would undermine Kant's argument in the essay on the right to lie that the duty not to lie is an absolute duty that must be satisfied even at the risk of costing the life of an innocent person.

21 I have developed the argument of this paragraph more fully in "Kant's System of Duties."

22 I am here suggesting that current U.S. legislation aimed at preserving endangered species may not always be rational or moral.

ELEVEN A HISTORY OF FREEDOM?

1 Kant's title *Idee zu einer allgemeinen Geschichte in weltbürgerlicher Absicht* is usually translated as "Idea for a universal history from a cosmopolitan point of view." But I have translated *Absicht* as "aim" rather than "point of view" because it brings out better the point of the essay, which is that we must be able to conceive of human history as if the achievement of universal rationality and justice which Kant connotes with the term "cosmopolitan" were its *goal*. The translation here is my own.

2 This essay is discussed by William Galston in *Kant and the Problem of History*, pp. 39–69; Allen Wood in *Kant's Ethical Thought* (Cambridge: Cambridge University Press, 1999), pp. 233–44; and Peter D. Fenves in *A Peculiar Fate: Metaphysics and World-History in Kant* (Ithaca, NY: Cornell University Press, 1991), pp. 180–4.

3 Allen Wood has stressed the importance of Kant's conception of "unsocial sociability" in "Unsocial Sociability: The Anthropological Basis of Kantian Ethics," *Philosophical Topics* 19 (1991): 325–51, as well as throughout Part II of *Kant's Ethical Thought*.

4 See also UH, Proposition Seven, where Kant writes that the evils of war "compel our species to discover a law of equilibrium to regulate the essentially healthy hostility which prevails among states and is produced by their freedom" and that we "are compelled to reinforce this law by introducing a system of united power, hence a cosmopolitan system of general political security" (8:26).

5 On this passage, see Williams, *Kant's Political Philosophy*, pp. 208–14, and Christine Korsgaard, "Taking the Law into Our Own Hands," in Reath *et al.* (eds), *Reclaiming the History of Ethics* (Cambridge: Cambridge University Press, 1997), pp. 298–300. On the *Conflict of the Faculties* as a whole, see Reinhard Brandt, "Zum 'Streit der Fakultäten'," in Reinhard Brandt and Werner Stark (eds), *Kant-Forschungen*, vol. I (Hamburg: Felix Meiner Verlag, 1987), pp. 31–78. On the "Old Question" section, see the extended discussion in Fenves, *A Peculiar Fate*, pp. 171–289.

Select Bibliography

PRIMARY SOURCES

The standard German edition of Kant's published works, correspondence, notes, and lectures, the volume and page numbers widely used for citing Kant, is:

Kant's gesammelte Schriften, edited by the Royal Prussian (later German, then Berlin-Brandenburg) Academy of Sciences. 29 vols. Berlin: Georg Reimer (later Walter de Gruyter), 1900 – .

However, more modern editions of Kant's published works (which include the Academy edition pagination) are available in the *Philosophische Bibliothek*. Hamburg: Felix Meiner Verlag.

The standard English edition of Kant's works, including all of his published works and extensive selections from his correspondence, notes, and lectures, is:

Guyer, Paul, and Wood, Allen W. (general co-editors), *The Cambridge Edition of the Works of Immanuel Kant in English Translation*. 16 vols. Cambridge: Cambridge University Press, 1992 – .

As of 2006, the following twelve of the sixteen volumes planned in this edition have been published:

Immanuel Kant. *Theoretical Philosophy, 1755–1770*. Ed. and trans. David Walford in collaboration with Ralf Meerbote. Cambridge: Cambridge University Press, 1992.

——*Lectures on Logic*. Ed. and trans. J. Michael Young. Cambridge: Cambridge University Press, 1992.

——*Opus postumum*. Ed. Eckart Förster, trans. Eckart Förster and Michael Rosen. Cambridge: Cambridge University Press, 1993

——*Practical Philosophy*. Ed. and trans. Mary J. Gregor. Cambridge: Cambridge University Press, 1996.

——*Religion and Rational Theology.* Ed. and trans. Allen W. Wood and George di Giovanni. Cambridge: Cambridge University Press, 1996

——*Lectures on Metaphysics.* Ed. and trans. Karl Ameriks and Steve Naragon. Cambridge: Cambridge University Press, 1997.

——*Lectures on Ethics.* Ed. Peter Heath and J.B. Schneewind, trans. Peter Heath. Cambridge: Cambridge University Press, 1997.

——*Critique of Pure Reason.* Ed. and trans. Paul Guyer and Allen W. Wood. Cambridge: Cambridge University Press, 1998.

——*Correspondence.* Ed. and trans. Arnulf Zweig. Cambridge: Cambridge University Press, 1999.

——*Critique of the Power of Judgment.* Ed. Paul Guyer, trans. Paul Guyer and Eric Matthews. Cambridge: Cambridge University Press, 2000.

——*Theoretical Philosophy after 1781.* Ed. Henry Allison and Peter Heath, trans. Gary Hatfield, Michael Friedman, Henry Allison, and Peter Heath. Cambridge: Cambridge University Press, 2002.

——*Notes and Fragments.* Ed. Paul Guyer, trans. Curtis Bowman, Paul Guyer, and Frederick Rauscher. Cambridge: Cambridge University Press, 2005.

The remaining volumes, currently in preparation, are Kant's published writings on *Anthropology, History, and Education*; his writings on *Natural Science*; *Lectures on Anthropology*; and *Notes and Drafts on Political Philosophy*. Older translations of some of the important works in these volumes include:

Immanuel Kant. *Universal Natural History and Theory of the Heavens.* Trans. W. Hastie, with a new Introduction by Milton K. Munitz. Ann Arbor, MI: University of Michigan Press, 1969.

——*Anthropology from a Pragmatic Point of View.* Trans. Mary J. Gregor. The Hague: Martinus Nijhoff, 1974.

And, for Kant's important historical essays, discussed in Chapter 11:

Immanuel Kant. *Political Writings.* Ed. Hans Reiss, trans. H.B. Nisbet. 2nd edn. Cambridge: Cambridge University Press, 1991.

Reference works and collections of essays

Caygill, Howard. *A Kant Dictionary.* Oxford: Blackwell Publishers, 1995.

Chadwick, Ruth F., and Cazeaux, Clive (eds) *Immanuel Kant: Critical Assessments.* 4 vols. London and New York: Routledge, 1992.

Guyer, Paul (ed.) *The Cambridge Companion to Kant.* Cambridge: Cambridge University Press, 1992.

——(ed.) *Kant's Groundwork of the Metaphysics of Morals: Critical Essays.* Lanham, MD: Rowman & Littlefield, 1998.

——(ed.) *Kant's Critique of the Power of Judgment: Critical Essays.* Lanham, MD: Rowman & Littlefield, 2003.

——(ed.) *The Cambridge Companion to Kant and Modern Philosophy.* Cambridge: Cambridge University Press, 2006.

Kitcher, Patricia (ed.) *Kant's Critique of Pure Reason: Critical Essays.* Lanham, MD: Rowman & Littlefield, 1998.

Klemme, Heiner F., and Kuehn Manfred (eds) *Immanuel Kant.* International Library of Critical Essays in the History of Philosophy. 2 vols. Aldershot: Ashgate / Dartmouth, 1999.

Schaper, Eva and Vossenkuhl, Wilhelm (eds) *Reading Kant: New Perspectives on Transcendental Arguments and Critical Philosophy.* Oxford: Basil Blackwell, 1989.

SECONDARY LITERATURE

Due to the sheer magnitude of the literature on Kant, only works cited or suggested in this volume and a very small number of other important works are listed here. Works by or about philosophers other than Kant that have been cited in the notes are omitted.

Al-Azm, Sadik. *The Origin of Kant's Argument in the Antinomies.* Oxford: Clarendon Press, 1972.

Allison, Henry E. *The Kant–Eberhard Controversy.* Baltimore, MD: Johns Hopkins University Press, 1973.

——*Kant's Theory of Freedom.* Cambridge: Cambridge University Press, 1990.

——"Kant's Antinomy of Teleological Judgment." *Southern Journal of Philosophy* XXX (Supplement, 1991): 25–42; reprinted in P. Guyer (ed.), *Kant's Critique of the Power of Judgment: Critical Essays,* pp. 219–36.

——*Idealism and Freedom: Essays on Kant's Theoretical and Practical Philosophy.* Cambridge: Cambridge University Press, 1996.

——*Kant's Theory of Taste: A Reading of the Critique of Aesthetic Judgment.* Cambridge: Cambridge University Press, 2001.

——*Kant's Transcendental Idealism: An Interpretation and Defense.* New Haven, CT: Yale University Press, rev. edn, 2004.

Ameriks, Karl. *Kant's Theory of Mind: An Analysis of the Paralogisms of Pure Reason.* Oxford: Clarendon Press, 1982; new edn, 2000.

——*Interpreting Kant's Critiques.* Oxford: Clarendon Press, 2003.

Anderson-Gold, Sharon. *Unnecessary Evil: History and Moral Progress in the Philosophy of Immanuel Kant.* Albany, NY: State University of New York Press, 2001.

Aune, Bruce. *Kant's Theory of Morals.* Princeton, NJ: Princeton University Press, 1979.

Banham, Gary. *Kant and the Ends of Aesthetics.* Basingstoke and London: Macmillan Press, 2000.

Baron, Marcia W. *Kantian Ethics Almost without Apology.* Ithaca, NY: Cornell University Press, 1995.

Baron, Marcia W., Pettit, Philip and Slote, Michael. *Three Methods of Ethics.* Oxford: Blackwell Publishers, 1997.

Bayne, Steven M. *Kant on Causation: On the Fivefold Routes to the Principle of Causation.* Albany, NY: State University of New York Press, 2004.

Baynes, Kenneth. *The Normative Grounds of Social Criticism: Kant, Rawls, and Habermas.* Albany, NY: State University of New York Press, 1992.

Beck, Lewis White. *A Commentary on Kant's Critique of Practical Judgment*. Chicago: University of Chicago Press, 1960.

—"Can Kant's Synthetic Judgments Be Made Analytic?" In *Studies in the Philosophy of Kant*. Indianapolis and New York: Bobbs-Merrill Company, 1965, pp. 74–91.

—*Early German Philosophy: Kant and his Predecessors*. Cambridge, MA: Harvard University Press, 1969.

—"Did the Sage of Königsberg Have No Dreams?" In *Essays on Kant and Hume*. New Haven, CT: Yale University Press, 1978, pp. 38–60.

Beiner, Ronald, and Booth, William James (eds) *Kant and Political Philosophy: The Contemporary Legacy*. New Haven, CT: Yale University Press, 1993.

Beiser, Frederick C. *The Fate of Reason: German Philosophy from Kant to Fichte*. Cambridge, MA: Harvard University Press, 1987.

—*Enlightenment, Revolution, and Romanticism: The Genesis of Modern German Political Thought, 1790–1800*. Cambridge, MA: Harvard University Press, 1992.

—*German Idealism: The Struggle Against Subjectivism, 1781–1801*. Cambridge, MA: Harvard University Press, 2002.

Bennett, Jonathan. *Kant's Analytic*. Cambridge: Cambridge University Press, 1966.

—*Kant's Dialectic*. Cambridge: Cambridge University Press, 1974.

Bielefeldt, Heiner. *Symbolic Representation in Kant's Practical Philosophy*. Cambridge: Cambridge University Press, 2003.

Bird, Graham. *Kant's Theory of Knowledge: An Outline of One Central Argument in the Critique of Pure Reason*. London: Routledge and Kegan Paul, 1962.

Bohman, James, and Lutz-Bachman, Matthias (eds) *Perpetual Peace: Essays on Kant's Cosmopolitan Ideal*. Cambridge, MA: MIT Press, 1995.

Brandt, Reinhard. *The Table of Judgments: Critique of Pure Reason A 67–76, B 92–101*. North American Kant Society Studies in Philosophy, vol. 4. Trans. Eric Watkins. Atascadero, CA: Ridgeview Publishing Co., 1995.

Brittan, Gordon G., Jr. *Kant's Theory of Science*. Princeton, NJ: Princeton University Press, 1978.

Brook, Andrew. *Kant and the Mind*. Cambridge: Cambridge University Press, 1994.

Brueckner, Anthony. "Transcendental Arguments I." *Nous* 17 (1983): 551–75.

—"Transcendental Arguments II." *Nous* 18 (1984): 197–224.

Buchdahl, Gerd. *Metaphysics and the Philosophy of Science*. Oxford: Basil Blackwell, 1969.

—*Kant and the Dynamics of Reason*. Oxford: Blackwell, 1992.

Budd, Malcolm. *The Aesthetic Appreciation of Nature: Essays on the Aesthetics of Nature*. Oxford: Clarendon Press, 2002.

Buroker, Jill Vance. *Space and Incongruence: The Origin of Kant's Idealism*. Dordrecht: D. Reidel, 1981.

Carl, Wolfgang. *Der schweigende Kant: Die Entwürfe zu einer Deduktion der Kategorien vor 1781*. Göttingen: Vandenhoeck & Ruprecht, 1989.

Carrier, Martin. "Kant's Mechanical Determination of Matter in the *Metaphysical Foundations of Natural Science*." In Eric Watkins (ed.), *Kant and the Sciences*. Oxford: Oxford University Press, 2001, pp. 117–35.

Cassirer, Ernst. *Kant's Life and Thought.* Trans. James Haden. New Haven, CT: Yale University Press, 1981.

Cavallar, Georg. *Kant and the Theory and Practice of International Right.* Cardiff: University of Wales Press, 1999.

Chipman, Lauchlan. "Kant's Categories and their Schematism." *Kant-Studien* 63 (1972): 36–50. Reprinted in Ralph C.S. Walker (ed.), *Kant on Pure Reason.* Oxford: Oxford University Press, 1982, pp. 100–16.

Cohen, Ted. "Why Beauty is a Symbol of Morality." In T. Cohen and P. Guyer (eds), *Essays in Kant's Aesthetics.* Chicago: University of Chicago Press, 1982, pp. 221–36.

Cohen, Ted and Paul Guyer (eds). *Essays in Kant's Aesthetics.* Chicago: University of Chicago Press, 1982.

Couturat, Louis. *La Philosophie des Mathématiques de Kant.* Paris: Éditions Manucius, [1905] 2004.

Crawford, Donald W. *Kant's Aesthetic Theory.* Madison, WI: University of Wisconsin Press, 1974.

——"Kant's Theory of Imagination." In T. Cohen and P. Guyer (eds), *Essays in Kant's Aesthetics.* Chicago: University of Chicago Press, 1982, pp. 151–78.

Crowther, Paul. *The Kantian Sublime: From Morality to Art.* Oxford: Clarendon Press, 1989.

Denis, Lara. *Moral Self-Regard: Duties to Oneself in Kant's Moral Theory.* New York: Routledge, 2001.

Derrida, Jacques. *The Truth in Painting.* Trans. Geoff Bennington and Ian McLeod. Chicago: University of Chicago Press, 1987.

Di Giovanni, George. *Freedom and Religion in Kant and His Immediate Successors: The Vocation of Humankind, 1774–1800.* Cambridge: Cambridge University Press, 2005.

Dicker, Georges. *Kant's Theory of Knowledge: An Analytical Introduction.* Oxford: Oxford University Press, 2004.

Dryer, Douglas P. *Kant's Solution for Verification in Metaphysics.* London: George Allen and Unwin, 1966.

Düsing, Klaus. *Die Teleologie in Kants Weltbegriff.* 2nd edn. Bonn: Bouvier Verlag, 1986.

Edwards, Jeffrey. *Substance, Force, and the Possibility of Knowledge: On Kant's Philosophy of Material Nature.* Berkeley, CA: University of California Press, 2000.

Ewing, A.C. *Kant's Treatment of Causality.* London: Routledge & Kegan Paul, 1924.

Falkenburg, Brigitte. *Kants Kosmologie: Die wissenschaftliche Revolution der Naturphilosophie im 18. Jahrhundert.* Frankfurt am Main: Vittorio Klostermann, 2000.

Falkenstein, Lorne. *Kant's Intuitionism: A Commentary on the Transcendental Aesthetic.* Toronto: University of Toronto Press, 1995.

Fenves, Peter D. *A Peculiar Fate: Metaphysics and World-History in Kant.* Ithaca, NY: Cornell University Press, 1991.

——*Late Kant: Towards Another Law of the Earth.* London and New York: Routledge, 2003.

Fistioc, Mihaela. *The Beautiful Shape of the Good: Platonic and Pythagorean Themes in Kant's Critique of the Power of Judgment.* London and New York: Routledge, 2002.

Flikschuh, Katrin. *Kant and Modern Political Philosophy.* Cambridge: Cambridge University Press, 2000.

Förster, Eckart. "Kant's Refutation of Idealism." In A.J. Holland (ed.), Philosophy and its History. Dordrecht: Reidel, 1985, pp. 295–311.

——Kant's Final Synthesis: An Essay on the Opus postumum. Cambridge, MA: Harvard University Press, 2000.

Forum für Philosophie Bad Homburg (eds) Übergang: Untersuchungen zum Spätwerk Immanuel Kants. Frankfurt am Main: Vittorio Klostermann, 1991.

Freydberg, Bernard. Imagination in Kant's Critique of Practical Reason. Bloomington, IN: Indiana University Press, 2005.

Fricke, Christel. Kants Theorie des reinen Geschmacksurteils. Berlin and New York: Walter de Gruyter, 1990.

Friedman, Michael. Kant and the Exact Sciences. Cambridge, MA: Harvard University Press, 1992.

——"Causal Laws and the Foundations of Natural Science." In Paul Guyer (ed.), The Cambridge Companion to Kant. Cambridge: Cambridge University Press, 1992, pp. 161–99.

Frierson, Patrick. Freedom and Anthropology in Kant's Moral Philosophy. Cambridge: Cambridge University Press, 2003.

Galston, William A. Kant and the Problem of History. Chicago: University of Chicago Press, 1975.

Gardner, Sebastian. Kant and the Critique of Pure Reason. London: Routledge, 1999.

Gerhardt, Volker. Immanuel Kants Entwurf "Zum Ewigen Frieden." Darmstadt: Wissenschaftliche Buchgesellschaft, 1995.

Ginsborg, Hannah. The Role of Taste in Kant's Theory of Cognition. New York: Garland, 1990.

Gould, Timothy. "The Audience of Originality: Kant and Wordsworth on the Reception of Genius." In T. Cohen and P. Guyer (eds), Essays in Kant's Aesthetics, Chicago: University of Chicago Press, 1982, pp. 179–94.

Gregor, Mary J. Laws of Freedom: A Study of Kant's Method of Applying the Categorical Imperative in the Metaphysik der Sitten. Oxford: Basil Blackwell, 1963.

Grenberg, Jeanine. Kant and the Ethics of Humility. Cambridge: Cambridge University Press, 2005.

Grier, Michelle. Kant's Doctrine of Transcendental Illusion. Cambridge: Cambridge University Press, 2001.

Guevara, Daniel. Kant's Theory of Moral Motivation. Boulder, CO: Westview Press, 2000.

Guyer, Paul. Kant and the Claims of Taste. Cambridge, MA: Harvard University Press, 1979; rev. edn. Cambridge: Cambridge University Press, 1997.

——"Kant on Apperception and A priori Synthesis." American Philosophical Quarterly 17 (1980): 205–12

——"Kant's Intentions of the Refutation of Idealism." Philosophical Review 92 (1983): 329–83.

——"The Failure of the B-Deduction." Southern Journal of Philosophy XXV, Supplement (1987a): 67–84.

——Kant and the Claims of Knowledge. Cambridge: Cambridge University Press, 1987b.

——*Kant and the Experience of Freedom*. Cambridge: Cambridge University Press, 1993.

——*Kant on Freedom, Law, and Happiness*. Cambridge: Cambridge University Press, 2000.

——"Space, Time, and the Categories: The Project of the Transcendental Deduction." In Ralph Schumacher (ed.), *Idealismus als Theorie der Repräsentation?* Paderborn: Mentis, 2001, pp. 313–38.

——"The Derivation of the Categorical Imperative: Kant's Correction for a Fatal Flaw." *Harvard Review of Philosophy* X (2002): 64–80.

——"Kant on Common Sense and Skepticism." *Kantian Review* 7 (2003): 1–37.

——*Kant's System of Nature and Freedom: Selected Essays*. Oxford: Clarendon Press, 2005a.

——*Values of Beauty: Historical Essays in Aesthetics*. Cambridge: Cambridge University Press, 2005b.

Hanna, Robert. *Kant and the Foundations of Analytic Philosophy*. Oxford: Clarendon Press, 2001.

Hatfield, Gary. *The Natural and the Normative: Theories of Spatial Perception from Kant to Helmholtz*. Cambridge, MA: MIT Press, 1990.

——"The *Prolegomena* and the *Critiques of Pure Reason*." In Volker Gerhardt, Rolf-Peter Horstmann, and Ralph Schumacher (eds), *Kant und die Berliner Aufklärung: Akten des IX. Internationalen Kant-Kongresses*. Berlin and New York: Walter de Gruyter, 2001. vol. 1, pp. 185–208.

——"What Were Kant's Aims in the Deduction?" *Philosophical Topics* 31 (2003): 165–98.

Hahn, Robert. *Kant's Newtonian Revolution in Philosophy*. Carbondale and Edwardsville, IL: Southern Illinois University Press, 1988.

Henrich, Dieter. *Der ontologische Gottesbeweis*. 2nd edn. Tübingen: J.C.B. Mohr (Paul Siebeck), 1960.

——"The Proof-Structure of Kant's Transcendental Deduction." *Review of Metaphysics* 22 (1969): 640–59.

——"Kants Deduktion des Sittengesetzes." In Alexander Schwan (ed.), *Denken im Schatten des Nihilismus*. Darmstadt: Wissenschaftliche Buchgesellschaft, 1975, pp. 55–112; trans. in Paul Guyer (ed.), *Kant's Groundwork of the Metaphysics of Morals: Critical Essays*, pp. 303–41.

——*Aesthetic Judgment and the Moral Image of the World: Studies in Kant*. Stanford, CA: Stanford University Press, 1992.

——"Identity and Objectivity: An Inquiry into Kant's Transcendental Deduction" (1976). Trans. in his *The Unity of Reason: Essays on Kant's Philosophy*, ed. Richard L. Velkley. Cambridge, MA: Harvard University Press, 1994, pp. 123–208.

Herman, Barbara. *The Practice of Moral Judgment*. Cambridge, MA: Harvard University Press, 1993.

Hill, Thomas E., Jr. *Dignity and Practical Reason in Kant's Moral Philosophy*. Ithaca, NY: Cornell University Press, 1992.

——*Respect, Pluralism, and Justice: Kantian Perspectives*. Oxford: Oxford University Press, 2000.

——Human Welfare and Moral Worth: Kantian Perspectives. Oxford: Clarendon Press, 2002.

Höffe, Otfried. "Königliche Völker": Zu Kants kosmopolitischer Rechts- und Friedenstheorie. Frankfurt am Main: Surhkamp Verlag, 2001.

——Categorical Principles of Law: A Counterpoint to Modernity. Trans. Mark Migotti. University Park, PA: Pennsylvania State University Press, 2002.

Hudson, Hud. Kant's Compatibilism. Ithaca, NY: Cornell University Press, 1994.

Kaufman, Alexander. Welfare in the Kantian State. Oxford: Clarendon Press, 1999.

Kemal, Salim. Kant and Fine Art: An Essay on the Philosophy of Fine Art and Culture. Oxford: Clarendon Press, 1986.

Kerstein, Samuel J. Kant's Search for the Supreme Principle of Morality. Cambridge: Cambridge University Press, 2002.

Kersting, Wolfgang. Wohlgeordnete Freiheit: Immanuel Kants Rechts- und Staatsphilosophie. Frankfurt am Main: Suhrkamp, 1993.

——Kant über Recht. Paderborn: Mentis, 2004.

Kirwan, James. The Aesthetic in Kant. London and New York: Continuum, 2004.

Kitcher, Patricia. Kant's Transcendental Psychology. New York and Oxford: Oxford University Press, 1990.

Kitcher, Philip. "A Priori Knowledge." Philosophical Review 89 (1980): 3–23.

——"Projecting the Order of Nature." In Robert E. Butts (ed.), Kant's Philosophy of Physical Science. Dordrecht: Reidel, 1986, pp. 201–35.

——"Kant's A Priori Framework." In Patricia Kitcher (ed.), Kant's Critique of Pure Reason: Critical Essays, 1998, pp. 1–20.

Kleingeld, Pauline. Fortschritt und Vernunft: Zur Geschichtsphilosophie Kants. Würzburg: Königshausen & Neumann, 1995.

——"Kants Argument für den Völkerbund." In Herta Nagl-Docerkal and Rudolph Langthaler (eds.), Recht – Geschichte – Religion: Die Bedeutung Kants für die Gegenwart. Berlin: Akademie Verlag, 2004, pp. 99–112.

Klemme, Heiner F. (ed.) Die Schule Immanuel Kants. Kant-Forschungen, vol. 6. Hamburg: Felix Meiner Verlag, 1994.

Korsgaard, Christine M. Creating the Kingdom of Ends. Cambridge: Cambridge University Press, 1996a.

——The Sources of Normativity. Ed. Onora O'Neill. Cambridge: Cambridge University Press, 1996b.

——"Taking the Law into our Own Hands: Kant on the Right to Revolution." In Andrews Reath, Barbara Herman, and Christine M. Korsgaard (eds), Reclaiming the History of Ethics: Essays for John Rawls. Cambridge: Cambridge University Press, 1997, pp. 297–328.

Kreimendahl, Lothar. Kant – Der Durchbruch von 1769. Köln: Jürgen Dinter Verlag, 1990.

Kuehn, Manfred. Kant: A Biography. Cambridge: Cambridge University Press, 2001.

Langton, Rae. Kantian Humility: Our Ignorance of Things in Themselves. Oxford: Clarendon Press, 1998.

Laywine, Alison. Kant's Early Metaphysics and the Origins of the Critical Philosophy. Atascadero, CA: Ridgeview Publishing Company, 1993.

Longuenesse, Béatrice. *Kant and the Capacity to Judge*. Princeton, NJ: Princeton University Press, 1998.

Louden, Robert B. *Kant's Impure Ethics: From Rational Beings to Human Beings*. New. York and Oxford: Oxford University Press, 2000.

Lovejoy, Arthur O. "On Kant's Reply to Hume" (1906). Reprinted in Moltke S. Gram (ed.), *Kant: Disputed Questions*. Chicago: Quadrangle Books, 1967, pp. 284–308.

Löw, Reinhard. *Philosophie des Lebendigen: Der Begriff der Organischen bei Kant, sein Grund und seine Aktualität*. Frankfurt am Main: Suhrkamp Verlag, 1980.

Ludwig, Bernd. *Kants Rechtslehre*. Kant-Forschungen, vol. II. Hamburg: Felix Meiner Verlag, 1988.

Lyotard, Jean-François. *Lessons on the Analytic of the Sublime*. Trans. Elizabeth Rottenberg. Stanford, CA: Stanford University Press, 1994.

Macmillan, R.A.C. *The Crowning Phase of the Critical Philosophy: A Study in Kant's Critique of Judgment*. London: Macmillan, 1912.

McFarland, J.D. *Kant's Concept of Teleology*. Edinburgh: Edinburgh University Press, 1970.

McLaughlin, Peter. *Kant's Critique of Teleology in Biological Explanation: Antinomy and Teleology*. Lewiston: Edwin Mellen Press, 1990.

Meerbote, Ralf, and Hudson, Hud (eds) *Kant's Aesthetics*. Atascadero, CA: Ridgeview Publishing Company, 1991.

Melnick, Arthur. *Kant's Analogies of Experience*. Chicago: University of Chicago Press, 1973.

——*Space, Time, and Thought in Kant*. Dordrecht: Kluwer, 1989.

Moore, A. W. *Noble in Reason, Infinite in Faculty: Themes and Variations in Kant's Moral and Political Philosophy*. New York and London: Routledge, 2003.

Mulholland, Leslie A. *Kant's System of Rights*. New York: Columbia University Press, 1990.

Munzel, G. Felicitas. "The Beautiful is the Symbol of the Morally-Good: Kant's Philosophical Basis of Proof for the Idea of the Morally-Good." *Journal of the History of Philosophy* 33 (1995): 301–30.

——*Kant's Conception of Moral Character: The "Critical" Link of Morality, Anthropology, and Reflective Judgment*. Chicago: University of Chicago Press, 1999.

Nell, Onora (O'Neill). *Acting on Principle: An Essay on Kantian Ethics*. New York: Columbia University Press, 1975.

Nuzzo, Angelica. *Kant and the Unity of Reason*. West Lafayette, IN: Purdue University Press, 2005.

O'Neill, Onora. *Faces of Hunger: An Essay on Poverty, Justice and Development*. London: Allen and Unwin, 1986.

——*Constructions of Reason: Explorations in Kant's Moral Philosophy*. Cambridge: Cambridge University Press, 1989.

——"Kant's Virtues." In Roger Crisp (ed.), *How Should One Live? Essays on the Virtues*. Oxford: Clarendon Press, 1996, pp. 77–98.

——*Bounds of Justice*. Cambridge: Cambridge University Press, 2000.

Parret, Hermann (ed.) *Kant's Ästhetik – Kant's Aesthetics – L'esthétique de Kant*. Berlin and New York: Walter de Gruyter, 1998.

Parsons, Charles D. "Kant's Philosophy of Arithmetic" (1969). Reprinted with a postscript in his *Mathematics and Philosophy: Selected Essays*. Ithaca, NY: Cornell University Press, 1983.

Paton, H.J. *Kant's Metaphysic of Experience*. 2 vols. London: George Allen & Unwin, 1936.

——*The Categorical Imperative: A Study in Kant's Moral Philosophy*. London: Hutchinson, 1947.

Pillow, Kirk. *Sublime Understanding: Aesthetic Reflection in Kant and Hegel*. Cambridge, MA: MIT Press, 2000.

Pippin, Robert. *Kant's Theory of Form*. New Haven, CT: Yale University Press, 1982.

Plaass, Peter. *Kant's Theory of Natural Science*. Trans. Alfred E. and Maria G. Miller. Dordrecht: Kluwer, 1994.

Powell, C. Thomas. *Kant's Theory of Self-Consciousness*. Oxford: Clarendon Press, 1990.

Prauss, Gerold. *Kant und das Problem der Dinge an sich*. Bonn: Bouvier Verlag, 1974.

Quinton, Anthony. "Spaces and Times." *Philosophy* 37 (1962): 130–47.

Rawls, John. *Lectures on the History of Moral Philosophy*. Ed. Barbara Herman. Cambridge, MA: Harvard University Press, 2000.

Reath, Andrews. "Two Conceptions of the Highest Good in Kant." *Journal of the History of Philosophy* 26 (1988): 593–619.

Recki, Birgit. *Ästhetik der Sitten: Die Affinität von ästhetischem Gefühl und praktischer Vernunft bei Kant*. Frankfurt am Main: Vittorio Klostermann, 2001.

Reich, Klaus. *The Completeness of Kant's Table of Judgments*. Trans. Jane Kneller and Michael Losonsky. Stanford, CA: Stanford University Press, 1981.

Rogerson, Kenneth F. *Kant's Aesthetics: The Roles of Form and Expression*. Lanham, MD: University Press of America, 1986.

Rorty, Richard. "Strawson's Objectivity Argument." *Review of Metaphysics* 24 (1970): 207–44.

——"Verificationism and Transcendental Arguments." *Nous* 5 (1971): 3–14.

Rosen, Allen D. *Kant's Theory of Justice*. Ithaca, NY: Cornell University Press, 1993.

Rosenberg, Jay F. *Accessing Kant: A Relaxed Introduction to the Critique of Pure Reason*. Oxford: Clarendon Press, 2005.

Rossi, Philip J. *The Social Authority of Reason: Kant's Critique, Radical Evil, and the Destiny of Humankind*. Albany, NY: State University of New York Press, 2005.

Rossi, Philip J. and Wreen, Michael (eds) *Kant's Philosophy of Religion Reconsidered*. Bloomington, IN: Indiana University Press, 1991.

Rush, Fred L., Jr. "The Harmony of the Faculties." *Kant-Studien* 92 (2001): 38–61.

Sassen, Brigitte (ed.) *Kant's Early Critics: The Empiricist Critique of the Theoretical Philosophy*. Cambridge: Cambridge University Press, 2000.

Savile, Anthony. *Aesthetic Reconstructions: The Seminal Writings of Lessing, Kant, and Schiller*. Oxford: Basil Blackwell, 1987.

——Kantian Aesthetics Pursued. Edinburgh: Edinburgh University Press, 1993.

——Kant's Critique of Pure Reason: An Orientation to the Central Theme. Oxford: Blackwell Publishing, 2005.

Schaeffer, Jean-Marie. Art of the Modern Age: Philosophy of Art from Kant to Heidegger. Trans. Steven Rendell. Princeton, NJ: Princeton University Press, 2000.

Schaper, Eva. Studies in Kant's Aesthetics. Edinburgh: Edinburgh University Press, 1979.

Schmücker, Josef. Die Ursprünge der Ethik Kants. Meinsenheim am Glan: Verlag Anton Hain, 1961.

Schneewind, J.B. The Invention of Autonomy: A History of Modern Moral Philosophy. Cambridge: Cambridge University Press, 1998.

Schönecker, Dieter. Kant: Grundlegung III, Die Deduktion des kategorischen Imperativs. Freiburg and Munich: Verlag Karl Alber, 1999.

Schönecker, Dieter, and Wood, Allen W. Kant's "Grundlegung zur Metaphysik der Sitten": Ein einführender Kommentar. Paderborn: Schöningh, 2002.

Schönfeld, Martin. The Philosophy of the Young Kant: The Precritical Project. Oxford: Oxford University Press, 2000.

Sellars, Wilfrid. Science and Metaphysics: Variations on Kantian Themes. London: Routledge and Kegan Paul, 1968.

——Kant's Transcendental Metaphysics. Ed. Jeffrey F. Sicha. Atascadero, CA: Ridgeview Press, 2002.

Shabel, Lisa A. Mathematics in Kant's Critical Philosophy: Reflections on Mathematical Practice. New York and London: Routledge, 2003.

——"Kant's 'Argument from Geometry'." Journal of the History of Philosophy 42 (2004): 195–215.

Shell, Susan Meld. The Rights of Reason: A Study of Kant's Philosophy and Politics. Toronto: University of Toronto Press, 1980.

——The Embodiment of Reason: Kant on Spirit, Generation, and Community. Chicago: University of Chicago Press, 1996.

Sherman, Nancy. Making a Necessity of Virtue: Aristotle and Kant on Virtue. Cambridge: Cambridge University Press, 1997.

Sidgwick, Henry. The Methods of Ethics. 7th edn. London: Macmillan, 1907. Appendix, pp. 511–16.

Silber, John. "Kant's Conception of the Highest Good as Immanent and Transcendent." Philosophical Review 68 (1959): 469–92.

——"Introduction." Religion within the Limits of Reason Alone. Trans. Theodore M. Greene and Hoyt H. Hudson. New York: Harper & Row, 1960, pp. lxxiii–cxxxiv.

——"The Importance of the Highest Good in Kant's Ethics." Ethics 73 (1962–3): 179–97.

Smith, A.H. Kantian Studies. Oxford: Clarendon Press, 1947.

Smith, Norman Kemp. A Commentary to Kant's 'Critique of Pure Reason.' 2nd edn. London: Macmillan, 1923.

Stern, Robert (ed.) Transcendental Arguments: Problems and Prospects. Oxford: Clarendon Press, 1999.

Stratton-Lake, Philip. "Formulating Categorical Imperatives." Kant-Studien 83 (1993): 317–40.

——Kant, Duty, and Moral Worth. London and New York: Routledge, 2000.

Strawson, Peter F. Individuals: An Essay in Descriptive Metaphysics. London: Methuen, 1959.

——The Bounds of Sense: An Essay on Kant's Critique of Pure Reason. London: Methuen, 1966.

——Skepticism and Naturalism: Some Varieties. New York: Columbia University Press, 1985.

Stroud, Barry. "Transcendental Arguments." Journal of Philosophy 65 (1968): 241–56.

——Understanding Human Knowledge. Oxford: Oxford University Press, 2000.

Thompson, Manley. "Singular Terms and Intuitions in Kant's Epistemology." Review of Metaphysics 26 (1972–73): 314–43.

Timmons, Mark (ed.) Kant's Metaphysics of Morals: Interpretative Essays. Oxford: Oxford University Press, 2002.

Tonelli, Giorgio. Kant's Critique of Pure Reason within the Tradition of Modern Logic. Ed. David H. Chandler. Hildesheim: Georg Olms Verlag, 1994.

Tuschling, Burkhard (ed.) Probleme der "Kritik der reinen Vernunft." Berlin: Walter de Gruyter, 1984.

Uehling, Theodore E. Jr. The Notion of Form in Kant's Critique of Aesthetic Judgment. The Hague: Mouton, 1971.

Vaihinger, Hans. Commentar zu Kants Kritik der reinen Vernunft. 2 vols. Stuttgart, Berlin, Leipzig: Union deutsche Verlagsgesellschaft, 1883–92.

van Cleve, James. Problems from Kant. New York and Oxford: Oxford University Press, 1999.

van Cleve, James, and Frederick, Robert E. (eds) The Philosophy of Left and Right. Dordrecht: Kluwer, 1991.

Vuillemin, Jules. Physique et Métaphysique Kantiennes. Paris: Presses Universitaires de France, 1955.

Walker, Ralph C.S. Kant. London: Routledge and Kegan Paul, 1978.

Warren, Daniel. Reality and Impenetrability in Kant's Philosophy of Nature. London and New York: Routledge, 2001.

Watkins, Eric (ed.) Kant and the Sciences. Oxford: Oxford University Press, 2001.

——Kant and the Metaphysics of Causality. Cambridge: Cambridge University Press, 2005.

Waxman, Wayne. Kant and the Empiricists: Understanding Understanding. Oxford: Oxford University Press, 2005.

Wenzel, Christian Helmut. An Introduction to Kant's Aesthetics: Core Concepts and Problems. Oxford: Blackwell Publishing, 2005.

Werkmeister, W.H. Kant's Silent Decade: A Decade of Philosophical Development. Tallahassee, FL: University Presses of Florida, 1979.

Westphal, Kenneth R. Kant's Transcendental Proof of Realism. Cambridge: Cambridge University Press, 2004.

Williams, Howard. Kant's Political Philosophy. New York: St. Martin's Press, 1983.

——(ed.) Essays on Kant's Political Philosophy. Chicago: University of Chicago Press, 1992.

——Kant's Critique of Hobbes. Cardiff: University of Wales Press, 2003.

Williams, T.C. The Concept of the Categorical Imperative: A Study of the Place of the Categorical Imperative in Kant's Ethical Theory. Oxford: Clarendon Press, 1968.

Wolff, Michael. Die Vollständigkeit der kantischen Urteilstafel. Frankfurt am Main: Vittorio Klostermann, 1995.

Wolff, Robert Paul. Kant's Theory of Mental Activity. Cambridge, MA: Harvard University Press, 1962.

——The Autonomy of Reason: A Commentary on Kant's Groundwork of the Metaphysic of Morals. New York: Harper & Row, 1973.

Wood, Allen W. Kant's Moral Religion. Ithaca, NY: Cornell University Press, 1970.

——Kant's Rational Theology. Ithaca, NY: Cornell University Press, 1978.

——Kant's Ethical Thought. Cambridge: Cambridge University Press, 1999.

——Unsettling Obligations: Essays on Reason, Reality and the Ethics of Belief. Stanford, CA: CSLI Publications, 2002.

——"The Good Will." Philosophical Topics 31 (2003): 457–84.

——Kant. Oxford: Blackwell Publishing, 2005.

Yovel, Yirmiahu. Kant and the Philosophy of History. Princeton, NJ: Princeton University Press, 1981.

Zammito, John H. The Genesis of Kant's Critique of Judgment. Chicago: University of Chicago Press, 1992.

——Kant, Herder, and the Birth of Anthropology. Chicago: University of Chicago Press, 2002.

Index

accidentality, system of, 347
Achenwall, Gottfried, 403
actuality, 115; *see also* modality
Adam and Eve, 361–62, 364
Adickes, Erich, 384
Addison, Joseph, 397
aesthetic ideas, 320–21
aesthetic judgment, 307; deduction
   of, 316, 322–24;
   disinterestedness of, 311, 312–
   13; and form, 316; universal
   validity of, 313–14, 316, 322–
   24; *see also* taste
aesthetics, 20, 36–37, 381, 385;
   and morality, 310–11, 324–32;
   connection to teleology, 308–9
affinity: principle of, 166–67;
   transcendental, 87–88
Al-Azm, Sadik, 154
Allison, Henry E., 67, 124, 238,
   333, 359, 380, 383, 386, 387,
   395, 399, 400, 408, 410
alteration, 107; *see also* causality
Altmann, Alexander, 381
Ameriks, Karl, 154, 387, 389, 400
Analogies of Experience, 57, 79,
   93, 105–15, 118, 119, 120,
   121, 155, 162; *see also* causality
analytic judgments, 20, 46–47,
   100, 383–84; in mathematics,
   61–62

analytical method, 48–49, 81, 385
anarchy, 287–88
Anderson-Gold, Sharon, 401
Anselm, St., 145
anthropology, 25, 179, 249–50, 258
Anticipations of Perception, 101–5,
   155
antinomies, in inaugural
   dissertation, 28, 31
Antinomy of Pure Reason, 128,
   133, 137, 138–44, 216–18
antinomy of teleological judgment,
   346–49, 411
appearances, 2–3, 29, 53, 63–70,
   103, 130, 221; of motion, 163–
   65; series of, 132–33, 138, 167;
   see also phenomena,
   transcendental idealism
apperception, transcendental unity
   of, 84–91
apprehension, synthesis of, 83
a posteriori cognition, 46
a priori, contrasted to *a posteriori*, 45–
   46
Aquinas, St. Thomas, 145
Aristotle, 394
arithmetic, 60–61
Arnauld, Antoine, 384
art, 307, 308, 312, 318–21, 340;
   autonomy of, 311
astronomy, 50, 168–69

atomism, 161
Aune, Bruce, 208–9, 394, 396, 397, 399, 404–5, 406
autonomy, 4–6, 7–8; of art, 311; in cognition, 50–51, 72, 88, 95, 129, 156, 173; formula of, 203–4, 398; practical, 156, 178, 220, 240, 354
avarice, 252
Axioms of Intuition, 101–5, 155

Banham, Gary, 358–59
Baron, Marcia, 208–9, 261, 403
Baumgarten, Alexander Gottlieb, 20, 126, 134, 381, 385, 408
Baynes, Kenneth, 302
beauty: adherent versus free, 317; analysis of, 313–14; and form, 316, 321; and free play, 314–17; ideal of, 317–18, 325, 329; and morality, 4, 308–9, 324–25, 326–30; natural, 37, 408
Beck, Lewis White, 41, 208, 380, 381, 383, 384, 389, 395, 396, 398, 399, 400, 401, 402
Beiner, Ronald, 303
Beiser, Frederick C., 41, 302, 398, 406, 407
beneficence, duty of, 193–94, 201–2, 243, 255, 257–60, 330–31
benevolence, 258–59, 330–31
Bennett, Jonathan F., 124, 154, 390, 392
Bentham, Jeremy, 407
Bentley, Richard, 393
Berkeley, George, 28, 33, 36, 69, 117, 391
Big Bang, 390
Bielefeldt, Heiner, 41, 410

Bird, Graham, 124
body, science of, 159–65
Bohman, James, 303
Booth, William James, 303
Brandt, Reinhard, 388, 413
Brittan, Gordon, 173–74, 359
Brook, Andrew, 154
Brueckner, Anthony, 391
Buchdahl, Gerd, 173–74, 393
Budd, Malcolm, 333
Burke, Edmund, 382, 409
Buroker, Jill Vance, 382, 384
Butts, Robert, 359

Canon of Pure Reason, 34, 152–53, 230–33
Carl, Wolfgang, 383
Carrier, Martin, 394
Cassirer, Ernst, 13–14, 381
categorical imperative: 24, 34–35; concept of, 179–80; derivation of, 179–91, 395; formulations of, 191–207; and duties, 242–47; and freedom of will, 219–26
categories, 33, 49–50; metaphysical deduction of, 71–80; schematism of, 96–100; transcendental deduction of, 80–95
Cato, Marcus Porcius, 197
causal laws, 112–13
causality, 12–13, 33; category of, 77, 79, 93, 98, 99, 112; Kant's argument for, 109–13; in mechanics, 160, 162–63; of will, 140–43, 215–19; see also Analogies of Experience
Cavallar, Georg, 303, 407

change: experience of, 110–13; reality of, 31

character, empirical and intelligible, 3, 217

Charles V, 185

chemistry, 159

Cheyne, George, 393

children, rights and duties regarding, 278–79

chiliasm, 298, 366

Chipman, Lauchlin, 390

Christianity, 38, 226, 229, 331

Chrysippus, 398

coercion, 240–42, 244–46, 263–66, 404

Cohen, Gerald A., 209

Cohen, Ted., 334, 410

communism, 272

community; *see* interaction

concepts, 53–54, 72–73, 84, 96–97, 386; in aesthetic judgment, 314–20; *see also* categories

conservation of substance, 107–8, 111, 160, 162

construction, in mathematics, 60–61

contingency, 143

contract, right of, 35, 38, 268, 275–76; *see also* social contract

conscience, 246, 252–53

constitutional power, 285–87

conversion, 226, 235, 402

Copernican Revolution, 49–51, 72, 385

cosmological argument, 145, 147–48, 151

cosmology: contemporary, 162; rational, 138–44

cosmopolitan right, 295

craft, 318

Crawford, Donald W., 333, 408, 409, 410

critique, 9

Crowther, Paul, 410

Crusius, Christian August 21, 214, 217–18, 381

D'Alembert, Jean Le Rond, 17–18

democracy, 281–82

Derham, William, 393

Derrida, Jacques, 333

Descartes, René, 9–10, 15, 19, 24, 117, 121, 134, 145, 147, 381, 388, 391

design: argument from, 145, 336–38, 393; in nature, 341–44, 350–51; *see also* physico-theological argument

desire, 177

despotism, 281–82

determinism, and free will, 1–3, 21, 140–43, 214–15; *see also* freedom, of will

di Giovanni, George, 238, 398

dialectic, 11, 126; *see also* Antinomy of Pure Reason, Ideal of Pure Reason, Paralogisms of Pure Reason, Transcendental Dialectic

Dicker, Georges, 124, 384, 385, 386, 387, 388, 389, 390

discipline, culture of, 351–53

discursivity, 344–45

disinterestedness, 311, 328

divisibility, infinite, 19

division of powers, 282–83

dogmatism, 9, 127

domestic rights, 276–79

dreams, 122

drunkenness, 187–88, 243, 251–52

Düsing, Klaus, 359
duty, duties: action from, 181–82; and categorical imperative, 196–203; to cultivate feeling, 253–54; regarding nature, 253, 356; to others, 255–60; perfect versus imperfect, 193–94, 242, 245, 355, 396; possibility of, 368–69; of right, 244–45, 247, 248–49, 262–302; to self, 250–55; of virtue, 239–60
dynamics, 159, 160–62

Eberhard, Johann August, 383, 393
education, duty of, 188, 278–79
Edwards, Jeffrey, 125, 174
Edwards, Jonathan, 381, 399
embodiment, 39, 250, 254
empiricism, 24, 54
ends: and duties, 241–42; and highest good, 6; humanity as, 35, 185–203, 242, 245, 259–60; of nature, 350–57; realm of, 25, 35, 205–7, 354, 398, 401; see also humanity, realm of ends
Epicureanism, 196
esteem, 190
ether, 40
ethics, 239–40
evil, radical, 38, 226–30, 240, 297–98, 365–67, 401
Ewing, A.C., 125
examples, in moral philosophy, 183, 242–44
executive power, 282–84, 285–87, 289
existence: and aesthetic judgment, 313; of God, 19–20, 24, 148–53; and synthetic judgments, 20;

not a predicate, 22, 393; see also ontological argument
experience: conditions of possibility of, 82–83; Hume on, 46; of motion, 163; two senses of, 389; see also time-determination

faculties, in university, 292–93
fairness, 270
faith, 9, 34, 127, 233
Falkenburg, Brigitte, 154
Falkenstein, Lorne, 124, 386
family, 35; see also children, marriage
fatality, system of, 347
Feder, Johann Heinrich, 383, 391
federalism, 295
Fenves, Peter, 41, 372, 412, 413
fine art, 318–21; see also art
Fistioc, Mihaela, 410
Flikschuh, Katrin, 302, 405
forces: attractive and repulsive, 103, 159, 160–62; measurement of, 17–18
form, and beauty, 316, 321
formalism: in mathematics, 62
forms, Platonic, 126
forms of judgment, 73–75
Förster, Eckart, 41, 384
frailty, 248
Francis I, 185
Frederick II (the Great), 37, 226, 399
Frederick William I, 399
Frederick William II, 37–38, 39, 226, 292
free play, 311, 314–17; see also imagination
freedom: academic, 292–94; external use of, 263–64, 266;

and coercion, 240–42, 263–64;
and duties of virtue, 241–47,
249–60; innate right to, 244,
266–67, 268, 405; Leibniz on,
392; and moral law, 6; and
nature, 3–4, 309, 349–57, 361,
365–66; and right to property,
269–70; of speech, 244, 267;
and the sublime, 322; and
universal principle of right, 263;
as value, 5, 178–79, 187–89,
194–95, 351–53; of will, 1–3,
21, 34, 36, 68–69, 140–43,
210–30

French revolution, 38, 284, 286,
370
Fricke, Christel, 408
Friedman, Michael, 41, 124, 174,
359, 381, 386, 391, 393, 394
functions of judgment, 73–75, 79

Galston, William A., 371, 412
Gardner, Sebastian, 387
Garve, Christian, 383, 391
gender, 25
genius, 4, 37, 308, 319–21, 328,
409
geometry, 55, 59–62, 64–66
Gerhardt, Volker, 303
Geuss, Raymond, 208
Ginsborg, Hannah, 333
gluttony, 251–52
God: and freedom, 216–17; and
grace, 366–67; in inaugural
dissertation, 28; as ground of
possibility, 20, 22, 132, 145–47,
152; moral argument for, 152–
53, 230–37; no duties to, 196,
253; theoretical arguments for
existence of, 19–20, 137, 145–

52; practical postulate of, 36,
211–13; and teleology, 335–38,
347–49; see also cosmological
argument, Ideal of Pure Reason,
ontological argument, physico-
theological argument, postulates
of pure practical reason
Goethe, Johann Wolfgang von, 196
good will, 34, 177, 181–82, 394;
see also freedom
Gottsched, Johann Christoph, 397
Gould, Stephen Jay, 342
Gould, Timothy, 409
grace, 366–67
gratitude, 256–57
Gregor, Mary J., 261, 396, 402,
404, 405
Grenberg, Jeanine, 261, 403
Grier, Michelle, 154, 392
Guevara, Daniel C., 399
Guyer, Paul, 14, 124, 174, 208–9,
261, 332–34, 358, 380, 381,
382, 383, 385, 386, 387, 389,
390, 391, 392, 394, 395, 396,
398, 402, 403, 408, 409, 410,
411, 412

Habermas, Jürgen, 302–3
Hahn, Robert, 385
happiness, 35, 39, 181–82, 184–
85, 202–3, 230–33, 235–37,
241, 258–60, 285, 335–36,
368, 402–3
Hatfield, Gary, 125, 380, 383, 385,
389, 390
heat, kinetic theory of, 390
Hegel, Georg Wilhelm Friedrich,
163, 307, 387–88, 394
Henrich, Dieter, 125, 154, 381,
389, 400, 408

Hepburn, Ronald, 408
Herder, Johann Gottfried, 35, 361
Herman, Barbara, 208–9, 403, 404
Herz, Marcus, 31, 32, 50, 163,
    382, 383
heteronomy, 203–4, 220
highest good, 6, 36, 180, 212,
    230–37, 339, 353–55, 401
Hilbert, David, 61
Hill, Thomas E., Jr., 208–9, 395,
    397
history, 360–71
Hobbes, Thomas, 15, 239, 271
Höffe, Otfried, 302–3
homicide, 198, 244
homogeneity: of intuition and
    concept, 96–97; principle of,
    166–69
hope, 6–7, 369
Horace (Horatius Flaccus Quintus),
    226
Hudson, Hud, 238, 334
humanity: as end in itself, 185–91,
    194–203, 242, 259–60, 353–
    54, 395–96, 397; and principle
    of right, 263
Hume, David, 12–13, 15, 46, 47,
    71, 98, 109, 111–13, 121, 145,
    211, 336–38, 357, 385, 387,
    391, 392, 393, 398, 411
humility, 252
Husserl, Edmund, 163, 394
Hutcheson, Francis, 312, 408
hylozoism, 347
hypothetical imperatives, 24, 183–
    84, 193
hypotheses, 168

Ideal of Pure Reason, 133, 145–53
idealism, see Berkeley,
purposiveness, Refutation of
    Idealism, transcendental idealism
ideas of pure reason, 34, 129–34;
    regulative use of, 165–73
illusions, in metaphysics, 126–27
imagination: and change, 110; free
    play of, 311, 314–17; in the
    sublime, 322; syntheses of, 86
immortality, 36, 136, 211–13,
    230, 232–33, 234–35
impenetrability, 161, 394
imperatives, categorical versus
    hypothetical, 183–84; see also
    categorical imperative,
    hypothetical imperative
inclination, 183, 202–4, 223
incongruent counterparts, 27, 382
indifference, liberty of, 214, 223,
    381
indifferentism, 9, 127–28
inertia, 160, 162, 343
infinitude, of space and time, 57–
    58
intellect, in inaugural dissertation,
    30–31
interaction, 17, 78, 99, 113–15,
    162–63, 391
interest, intellectual, 327–28
intuition, 33, 53–54, 386;
    empirical, 54, 56, 93; in
    judgments, 73; space and time as
    forms of, 49–50, 53, 55–58,
    164; see also sensibility
irreversibility, 110–11

Jacobi, Friedrich Heinrich, 35, 210
Jäsche, Benjamin Gottlob, 39
Jesus Christ, 226, 366
judgment: analytic and synthetic,
    45–50; and apperception, 90–

91; in metaphysical deduction, 72–80; power of, 5, 170–73; reflecting and determining, 170, 308; *see also* analytic judgments, synthetic *a priori* judgments
judicial power, 286
justice; *see* right

Kant, Immanuel: life of, 15–40; education, 16–17; parents, 15, professorship of, 27–28; works: "Announcement of Lectures for 1765–66," 26–27; *Anthropology from a Pragmatic Point of View*, 39; "Concept of a Human Race," 35; "Conjectural Beginning of Human History," 35, 361; *Conflict of the Faculties*, 39, 289–90, 291–93; *Critique of the Power of Judgment*, 3–5, 36–37, 157, 170–73, 234–35, 307–56; *Critique of Practical Reason*, 1–2, 3, 21, 36, 177, 180–81, 184–85, 190, 210–12, 213, 219, 222–26, 231, 233, 235, 236, 310, 353–54; *Critique of Pure Reason*, 3, 6–7, 9–11, 23, 31, 32–34, 36, 46–153, 155–57, 158, 165–69, 210, 213, 215–19, 221, 222, 231–33, 307, 308, 369; "Differentiation of Directions in Space," 27, 29; *Dreams of a Spirit-Seer*, 25–26; "False Subtlety," 22; *Groundwork for the Metaphysics of Morals*, 9, 11, 34–35, 36, 177, 180–96, 199–201, 203–6, 207–8, 210, 212, 213, 219–22, 223, 243, 254, 310, 353–54; inaugural dissertation, 28–31; *Lectures on Ethics*, 178, 186–87,

197, 277; *Lectures on Pedagogy*, 39; *Lectures on Physical Geography*, 39; *Logic*, 7, 12, 39, 54, 72; "Meditations on Fire," 18; *Metaphysical Foundations of Natural Science*, 9, 34, 39, 80, 157–65; *Metaphysics of Morals*, 9, 35, 38–39, 186–87, 201–2, 239–60, 263–70, 272–80, 282–83, 285–89, 296, 330, 353, 358; *Naturrecht Feyerabend*, 178; "Negative Quantities," 22, 23; *New Elucidation*, 19–21, 145, 213–15; *Observations on the Feeling of the Beautiful and Sublime*, 22, 24–25, 178–79, 307; *Only Possible Basis for a Demonstration of the Existence of God*, 22–23, 145, 307; *Opus postumum*, 8, 39–40, 234; *Perpetual Peace*, 38, 274, 281–82, 294–300, 329, 361, 363–64, 368; *Physical Monadology*, 18–19; *Prolegomena to any Future Metaphysics*, 12, 33, 34, 48, 64, 80, 94, 192; *Principles of Natural Theology and Morals*, 22, 23–24, 189; *Real Progress*, 234; *Religion within the Boundaries of Mere Reason*, 9, 38, 213, 218, 219, 226–30, 240, 297–98, 310, 331, 365–67; review of Herder, 35; "Teleological Principles in Philosophy," 37; "Theory and Practice," 38, 235–36, 239, 280, 281, 283, 285–88, 291, 354, 368; "Universal History from a Cosmopolitan Point of View," 35, 360–65, 368–69; *Universal Natural History*, 18; *True Estimation of Living Forces*, 17–18; "What Does it Mean to Orient oneself in Thought?" 35; "What is Enlightenment?" 35, 289–90

Kaufman, Alexander, 406

Kemal, Salim, 409

Kerstein, Samuel J., 209, 395

Kersting, Wolfgang, 302, 405, 407

kinematics, 159–60

Kirwan, James, 408, 409, 410

Kitcher, Patricia, 154, 384

Kitcher, Philip, 173–74, 384

Kleingeld, Pauline, 372, 407

Klemme, Heiner F., 380

Knutzen, Martin, 17, 380

Königsberg, 16

Körner, Stefan, 14

Korsgaard, Christine M., 208–9, 395, 396, 403, 406, 412, 413

Kreimendahl, Lothar, 382

Kripke, Saul A., 384

Kuehn, Manfred, 41, 380

Ladd, John, 404

Lambert, Johann Heinrich, 31, 394

land, right to, 272; see also property

Lange, Joachim, 399

Langton, Rae, 388

Laplace, Pierre Simon de, 18

law; see right

Laywine, Alison, 41, 381, 382

legislative power, 282–83, 285, 289

Lehmann, Gerhard, 384

Leibniz, Gottfried Wilhelm, 15, 17–18, 19–20, 28, 114, 126, 140, 154, 214, 217–18, 381, 390, 392, 399

Leibniz-Clarke Correspondence, 27, 154

Lewis, Clarence Irving, 389

limitation, category of, 104

limits of knowledge, 33–34

Lisbon earthquake, 18

Locke, John, 15, 81, 145, 161, 269, 271, 280, 284, 293, 405, 406

logic, 39, 388

Louden, Robert, 261, 382, 403

love: duties of, 255–60; feeling of, 257

Lovejoy, Arthur, 391

Löw, Reinhard, 359

Ludwig, Bernd, 404

Lutz-Bachmann, Matthias, 303

lying, 252, 403; see also promising

Lyotard, Jean-François, 333–34

Macmillan, R.A.C., 358–59

magnitude: extensive and intensive, 101–5; schema of, 98

materialism, 137–38

marriage, 269, 276–78, 406

mathematics: Kant's early view of, 24; Kant's mature view of, 33, 48–49, 53, 55, 59–62, 77–78, 101–5; in science, 158–59; see also arithmetic, construction, geometry

matter, 34, 159–65

maxims: in morality, 5, 35, 177, 182, 186, 191–95, 203–5, 263–64, 395; of power of judgment, 346

McFarland, John D., 359, 411

McLaughlin, Peter, 359, 411

mechanics, 160, 162–63

Meerbote, Ralf, 334

Melnick, Arthur, 125, 390

Mendelssohn, Moses, 22, 23–24, 31, 32, 35, 66, 210, 381, 382, 386–7, 409

mens rea, 404

metaphysical deduction of the
categories, 71–80
metaphysical expositions of space
and time, 55–58
metaphysics: method of, 20, 48–
49; in inaugural dissertation, 31;
Kant's critique of, 53, 96, 126–
53, 157–58; of morals, 180,
189; of nature, 157–65
method: analytic and synthetic, 48,
81; Doctrine of, 51–52, 126;
mathematical and philosophical,
60–61
Mill, John Stuart, 34
mind-body relation, 20, 25
missing alternative, 64–65, 387
modality: categories of, 78, 79–80,
100, 115–16; of judgments,
73–74; Kant's concept of, 388;
and motion, 159, 163–65
monads: Leibnizian, 392; physical,
18–19, 159
Monk, Samuel, 409
Montesquieu, Charles Louis de
Secondat, Baron de, 282
Moore, Adrian W., 209
moral law: application of, 39; and
autonomy, 4–6; as motive, 247–
49; and natural law, 1–3; proof
of, 219–26; see also categorical
imperative, morality
morality: and aesthetics, 310–11,
324–32; fundamental principle
of, 2, 25, 34, 37, 177, 179–80,
189–91, 242, 247, 395; and
nature, 349–57; and politics,
298–300, 367–68; and religion,
38; and right, 265; and self-love,
227–28; see also categorical
imperative

motion, 159–65
motives, 264, 404; purity of, 330–
32
Mulholland, Leslie A., 302, 404,
405
Munzel, G. Felicitas, 410

Nagel, Thomas, 208
nations, rights of, 296
nature: beauty in, 307, 312; and
freedom, 3–4, 349–57, 361,
365–66; Kant's concept of, 2, 8,
94, 192; and morality, 308–9,
349–57; and perpetual peace,
295–96, 299–301; as a system,
4, 165–73, 307; and teleology,
22–23, 156–57
nebular hypothesis, 18
necessity: and the *a priori*, 46; of
aesthetic judgments, 313–14;
category of, 115; and
contingency, 143; of first
principles, 13; of laws of nature,
171–73; right of, 246; see also
modality
Newton, Isaac, 30, 154, 164, 394;
see also mechanics, space
Nicole, Pierre, 384
nominalism, 54
non sequitur, 391
noumena, 29, 95, 129–30, 217–
18, 392, 400; see also things in
themselves, transcendental
idealism
number, 98
Nussbaum, Martha, 303

object, concept of, 89
objective validity, 49, 82, 389
obligation, and freedom, 224–25;
see also duty

occasionalism, 138
O'Neill, Onora (Nell), 208–9, 261, 303, 395, 396, 397, 400, 402
ontological argument, 19–20, 24, 145, 147–49, 151, 381
organisms, 4, 307, 339–45
organization, of *Critique of Pure Reason*, 51–52
original sin, 226

Paley, William, 393
Pantheism controversy, 210, 398
Paralogisms of Pure Reason, 116, 133, 134–38, 392
parliament, 289
Parret, Herman, 334
Parsons, Charles D., 386
patchwork thesis, 383
paternalism, 281
Paton, Herbert James, 124, 208, 383, 385, 386, 390, 391, 396
peace, perpetual, 38, 294–301
Peano, Gustav, 61
Penn, William, 407
perfection, of self, 39, 241, 254–55
permanence, 106–9
personality: moral, 227, 250; of soul, 136
Pettit, Philip, 261
phenomena, 29, 95, 129–30, 217–18; *see also* appearances, transcendental idealism
phenomenology, 160, 163–65
philosophy: faculty of, 39, 292–93; method of, 24; *see also* analytical method, synthetic method
phoronomy, 159–60
physical influx, 18, 138, 380
physico-theological argument, 145,

149–51; *see also* design, argument from
Pietism, 16, 214, 380
Pillow, Kirk, 409
Pinkard, Terry, 388
Plantinga, Alvin, 393
Plaass, Peter, 393
Plato, 34, 126
pleasure, in aesthetic judgment, 313–16
Pogge, Thomas, 402
possible worlds, 393
possibility: category of, 115; God as ground of, 20, 22, 132, 145–47, 152; *see also* modality
postulates: of empirical thinking, 80, 115–16; of pure practical reason, 16, 36, 211–13; *see also* God, immortality
Powell, C. Thomas, 154
Prauss, Gerold, 124, 387
pre-established harmony, 18, 20, 138, 380, 390
preformation, 94, 390
principles: of empirical judgment, 95–116; universality and necessity of, 13
progress, 368–71
promising, 192–93, 195, 198–99, 243
property, private, 35, 38, 239, 243–44, 267–79, 294, 405
psychology: and freedom, 178–79, 189; no science of, 158–59; rational, 134–38
Pufendorf, Samuel, 239, 396
purposiveness: in aesthetics, 308–9, 316; idealism and realism of, 346–47; of nature as a whole, 349–57; regulative principle of,

167; in teleology, 308–9, 340–43

Putter, Johann Stephan, 403

Pyrrho, 11–12

quality: categories of, 76–77, 99, 101; of judgments, 73–74; and motion, 160–62

quantity: categories of, 76, 93, 99, 101; of judgments, 73–74; of motion, 159–60

Quine, Willard V.O., 384–85

Quinton, Anthony, 386

race, 25, 37

rational being: concept of, 183–84; as end in itself, 185–89, 204–5; *see also* humanity

rationalism, 19–20, 24

Rawls, John, 205, 208–9, 394, 395–96, 397, 398, 399, 400, 401, 402, 412

Ray, John, 393

reaction, 163

realm of ends, 25, 35, 204–7, 354, 398, 401

reason: fact of, 3, 224–25; ideas of pure theoretical, 129–34; critique of practical, 211–12; and moral law, 221; public and private use of, 291; regulative rôle of, 156–57, 165–73; and skepticism, 10–11; and the sublime, 321–22

Reath, Andrews, 401

rebellion, Kant's arguments against, 38, 284–89, 370

receptivity, 54

reciprocity, 78

Recki, Birgit, 333–34

recognition, synthesis of, 83–84

reform, 289–94

Refutation of Idealism, 36, 71–72, 93–94, 116–22

regressive method, *see* analytical method

regulative principles, 165–73

Reich, Klaus, 388

Reinhold, Karl Leonhard, 37, 399

relation: categories of, 77–78, 99–100; judgments of, 73–74

relational properties, 69–70

religion, 38, 40

reproduction, synthesis of, 83

republicanism, 38, 245, 281–83, 293; and peace, 294–97

representation: contrasted to external existence, 118; species of, 53–54; *see also* appearances, concepts, intuition

respect, 240, 242, 247–49; duties of, 255–56

responsibility, 214

right: acquired, 244–45, 266, 267–69; and coercion, 240–42, 244–46, 263–66; definition of, 262; duties of, 262–302; distinguished from ethics or virtue, 240–42, 246–47, 263–66; innate, 244, 266–67; private and public, 265–66; public, 279–84; universal principle of, 263; *see also* property

Rink, Friedrich Theodor, 382, 383

Robinson, Hoke, 359

Rogerson, Kenneth F., 410

Rorty, Richard, 391

Rosen, Allen D., 406–7

Rossi, Philip J., 401

Rousseau, Jean-Jacques, 15, 407

Rush, Fred L., Jr., 408

Saint Giron, Baldine, 410
Saint-Pierre, Charles Irénée Castel
   de, 407
Sassen, Brigitte, 383, 391
Savile, Anthony, 124, 333, 385,
   386, 387, 410
Scanlon, T.M., 403
Schaeffer, Jean-Marie, 333–34
Schaper, Eva, 333, 408, 409
schema, 96
schematism, 95–100, 101
Schmidt, Jochen, 409
Schmucker, Josef, 41
Schneewind, J.B., 41, 381
Schönecker, Dieter, 208, 399
Schönfeld, Martin, 41, 380, 381
Schulz, Franz Albert, 16–17
science, Kant's concept of, 157–73
self-defilement, 251
self-knowledge, 93–95, 117–20;
   duty of, 252–53
self-love, 192, 227–28
self-stupefaction, 251
Sellars, Wilfrid, 388–89
sensation: and intensive magnitude,
   102–5
sensibility: forms of, 30; limits of,
   133, 139; as receptivity, 29; *see
   also* intuition, receptivity, space,
   time
servants, rights of, 279, 283–84
servility, 252
sex, 276–78
Shabel, Lisa A., 125, 386
Shell, Susan Meld, 14, 382
Sherman, Nancy, 261, 403
Sidgwick, Henry, 399
Silber, John, 238, 400
simplicity, of soul, 134, 136
simultaneity, 56, 113–15, 391

skepticism, 8–13, 127; Cartesian,
   9–10, 51, 71–72, 94, 95, 116–
   18, 120–21; Humean, 12–13,
   48–49, 51, 71–72, 78, 94, 95,
   116; Pyrrhonian, 11–12, 13, 95,
   116, 128, 133
skill, culture of, 351–52
Slote, Michael J., 261
Smith, A.H., 125
Smith, Adam, 313
Smith, Norman Kemp, 124, 383,
   385, 387, 390
social contract, 239, 271, 273,
   280–81
soul: immortality of, 136;
   metaphysics of, 134–38; as
   regulative idea, 167
space: absolute vs. relational views
   of, 27, 160, 164; divisibility of,
   140; empty, 56–57; and
   extensive magnitude, 102; finite
   or infinite, 139; as form of
   sensible intuition, 51–70; in
   inaugural dissertation, 28–30;
   and matter, 160–62; in *Physical
   Monadology*, 19; as pure intuition,
   57–58; in Refutation of
   Idealism, 117, 120–21; in
   schematism, 98; in
   transcendental deduction, 91–93
specificity, principle of, 166
speech, freedom of, 244, 267
Spinoza, Baruch or Benedictus de,
   15, 137, 347
spiritualism, 138
Stern, Robert, 391
Stoicism, 196
Stratton-Lake, Philip, 209, 396
Strawson, Peter F., 124, 385, 386,
   390, 391

Stroud, Barry, 391
subject, unconditioned, 132
subjectivism, 33
sublime, the, 37, 307, 312, 321–22, 325, 327–28
substance: category of, 77, 79, 97–98; Leibnizian view of, 19–20; and perception of time, 106–9; soul is not, 134–38; space and time not, 30; Kant's theory of, 33, 106–9, 162; see also conservation
succession: principle of, 20; representation of, 56
sufficient reason, principle of, 20–21, 111, 214, 215
suicide, 187–88, 192, 193–94, 196–97, 241–43, 246, 251
Sulzer, Johann Georg, 31
subreption, 165
Swedenborg, Emmanuel, 26
syllogisms: in Paralogisms, 135–36; and the unconditioned, 131–32
sympathy, 256–58, 330–31
synthesis: a priori, 85–88; infinite, 58; threefold, 83–84
synthetic a priori cognition, 30, 33, 45–51, 59; of appearances only, 53; in mathematics, 59–62
synthetic a priori judgments, 20, 33, 45–50, 100–101
synthetic method, 48–49, 51, 81
systematicity: in cognition in general, 156–57, 165–73; of nature, 307, 348–57; in organisms, 341; in science, 157–60

talents, duty to cultivate, 193, 200, 243, 254, 397
taste, 328; see also aesthetic judgment
taxation, 188, 203, 243, 274–75
teleological judgment, see teleology
teleology: and aesthetics, 308–9; Kant's early view of, 22–23; Kant's mature view of, 36–37, 156–57, 335–58; in Kant's conception of philosophy itself, 34, 127, 156, 181; in morality, 192, 311–12, 396; traditional conception of, 335–36
theism, 347–48
theology: moral, 152–53; rational, 144–52
things in themselves, 29, 53, 63–64, 67–70, 130, 221; see also noumena
Thompson, Manley, 386
time: divisibility of, 140; empty, 56–57; and extensive magnitude, 102; finite or infinite, 139; as form of intuition, 51–70; in inaugural dissertation, 28–30, 31; and intensive magnitude, 102–4; permanence of, 106–9; as pure intuition, 57–58; in schematism, 97–99; in transcendental deduction, 91–93
time-determination, 93, 97, 105–22
Timmons, Mark, 303
Tonelli, Giorgio, 385
Transcendental Aesthetic, 51–70, 79, 92–93, 94–95, 117, 121, 155, 160, 161, 163
Transcendental Analytic, 72–123, 155, 163

transcendental arguments, 112, 391
transcendental deduction of the
    categories, 33, 36, 48–49, 70–
    72, 85–90
Transcendental Dialectic, 52, 58,
    126, 127–54, 156–57; see also
    Antinomy of Pure Reason, Ideal
    of Pure Reason, ideas,
    Paralogisms of Pure Reason,
    unconditioned
transcendental expositions of space
    and time, 58–67
transcendental idealism, 2–3, 6,
    24, 28–29, 33, 36, 63–70, 94–
    95, 160; and freedom of will,
    214–19, 221–22; indirect proof
    of, 144; and Refutation of
    Idealism, 121–22; two-aspect
    interpretation of, 67–69; two-
    world interpretation of, 68
Transcendental Logic, 52, 70, 126
transcendental use, 129–30
Trendelenberg, Adolf, 387
truth, empirical, 156–57, 165

unconditioned, idea of the, 130–
    34, 139–40, 143, 147, 166, 392
understanding: free play with
    imagination, 314–17; as source
    of synthesis, 86–88; see also
    categories
Uehling, Theodore E., Jr., 409
universal law, formula of, 35, 185–
    86, 191–95, 396
universality: and the a priori, 46; of
    aesthetic judgments, 313–14,
    316, 322–24; of first principles,
    13; of maxims, 177, 186

unsocial sociability, 362–65

Vaihinger, Hans, 387
Vailati, Ezio, 382
van Cleve, James, 125, 154, 382,
    387
velocity, 160
virtue, 38–39; duties of, 239–60;
    general obligation of, 247–49
Vleeschauwer, Herman-Jean de, 14
voting rights, 283–84

war, 294–97, 363–64, 412–13
Warren, Daniel, 394
Watkins, Eric, 125, 174, 380
welfare, 406
Werkmeister, W.H., 383
Westphal, Kenneth R., 174, 394
will; see freedom, good will
Willaschek, Marcus, 402
Willey, Basil, 393
Williams, Bernard A.O., 208
Williams, Howard, 302–3, 405,
    406, 407, 408, 412
Williams, T.C., 208
Wolff, Christian Freiherr von, 16–
    17, 20, 126, 134, 145, 214,
    335–36, 398–99
Wolff, Robert Paul, 125, 208, 390
Wollaston, William, 393
Wöllner, Johann Christoph, 38
Wood, Allen W., 14, 154, 206,
    208–9, 238, 393, 395, 396,
    397, 398, 399, 401, 402, 403,
    411, 412
world-whole, 132

Yovel, Yirmiahu, 238, 372, 412